Gesundheitsmanagement und Gesundheitsökonomik

Reihe herausgegeben von
S. Fleßa, Greifswald, Germany

Die Gesundheitsökonomik ist die Lehre von der Beschreibung, Erklärung, Bewertung und Überwindung der Knappheit an Gesundheit durch Effizienz. Während sie sich traditionell eher den Strukturen und Prozessen des gesamten Gesundheitssystems widmet, intendiert das Gesundheitsmanagement eine Übertragung der Erkenntnisse der Allgemeinen Betriebswirtschaftslehre auf die Betriebe des Gesundheitswesens, wobei bislang noch von keiner vollständig etablierten Branchenbetriebslehre des Gesundheitswesens gesprochen werden kann. Ziel muss es sein, das Gesundheitsmanagement als „Spezielle Betriebswirtschaftslehre" zu etablieren, die dem Anspruch einer wissenschaftlichen Betriebsführung entspricht und sich konsistent aus den Erkenntnissen der stärker gesamtwirtschaftlich orientierten Gesundheitsökonomik ableitet. Die Schriftenreihe möchte einen Beitrag dazu leisten, Gesundheitsökonomik und Gesundheitsmanagement als interdependente Forschungsgebiete weiter zu entwickeln, die wissenschaftlich fundiert Handlungsanweisen für die Praxis entwickeln und von hoher Relevanz für Individuen und die Gesellschaft sind.

Weitere Bände in der Reihe http://www.springer.com/series/15970

Karin Bosshard

Law and Economics of Personalized Medicine

Institutional Levers to Foster the Translation of Personalized Medicine

Springer Gabler

Karin Bosshard
Küsnacht, Switzerland

Dissertation of the University of St. Gallen, 2017, under the title "Law and Economics of personalized medicine. Institutional levers to foster the translation of personalized medicine into Swiss clinical practice" written by Karin Bosshard.

ISSN 2523-7667 ISSN 2523-7675 (electronic)
Gesundheitsmanagement und Gesundheitsökonomik
ISBN 978-3-658-22073-0 ISBN 978-3-658-22074-7 (eBook)
https://doi.org/10.1007/978-3-658-22074-7

Library of Congress Control Number: 2018942634

Springer Gabler

Printed on acid-free paper

This Springer Gabler imprint is published by the registered company Springer Fachmedien Wiesbaden GmbH part of Springer Nature
The registered company address is: Abraham-Lincoln-Str. 46, 65189 Wiesbaden, Germany

Abstract

Clinical applications of personalized medicine are occurring at a slower pace than forecasted.[1] This thesis' argues that not only *science-related*, but also *institutional* barriers hinder the progression of personalized medicine. The purpose of this thesis is to identify and evaluate institutional policy levers to foster the translation of personalized medicine into Swiss clinical practice.

First, a literature analysis in the field of Public Health and Translational Medicine identifies institutional barriers hindering the clinical translation of personalized medicine for each link of the value chain. In a second step, a Law and Economic analysis is performed for each of the identified barriers with the aim of examining the incentives induced by the respective barrier separately for each stakeholder involved in the ecosystem of personalized medicine. The identified barriers are then assessed for their relevance in the Swiss context. On this basis, institutional policy levers to foster the translation of personalized medicine in the Swiss healthcare system are derived.

This thesis demonstrates that institutional barriers exist along every link of the value chain of personalized medicine. In Switzerland, institutional barriers predominantly concern the latter links of the value chain, namely the approval, provision, and reimbursement phase. As Switzerland has become active in addressing the barriers in the first part of the value chain, any strategy to foster the translation of personalized medicine in Switzerland should primarily target the latter links of the value chain. The most relevant institutional policy levers affect the provision and reimbursement phase. During the provision phase, the most relevant levers do not require any change of law. The identified levers predominantly concern the raising of healthcare providers', patients' and health professionals' awareness for personalized medicine. For the reimbursement phase several suggestions to change the Swiss law concerning the reimbursement scheme and the health technology assessment for personalized medicine diagnostics are made. The Swiss policy maker should consider putting them on the law making agenda.

1 References in RESEARCH CONCEPT, Chapter 1 Problem, *note* 12.

Kurzfassung

Die Personalisierte Medizin findet langsamer Eingang in die klinische Praxis als prophezeit.[2] Nicht nur fehlende *naturwissenschaftliche* Erkenntnisse, sondern auch Hemmfaktoren im *institutionellen* Umfeld stehen der klinischen Umsetzung der Personalisierten Medizin im Wege. Diese Arbeit identifiziert und evaluiert Massnahmen im institutionellen Umfeld, welche die klinische Umsetzung der Personalisierten Medizin in der Schweiz unterstützen.

In einem ersten Schritt identifiziert eine Literaturanalyse die institutionellen Hemmfaktoren für die klinische Umsetzung der personalisierten Medizin für jedes Glied der Wertschöpfungskette. In einem zweiten Schritt folgt eine rechtlich-ökonomische Analyse der einzelnen Faktoren, um deren Anreizsetzungen für die relevanten Anspruchsgruppen im Umfeld der Personalisierten Medizin zu identifizieren. Sodann folgt eine Untersuchung der institutionellen Hemmfaktoren im Hinblick auf ihre Relevanz in der Schweiz. Darauf aufbauend werden Handlungsempfehlungen abgeleitet, welche die klinische Umsetzung der Personalisierten Medizin in der Schweiz unterstützen.

Eine Grunderkenntnis der Arbeit ist die Existenz von institutionellen Hemmfaktoren entlang der gesamten Wertschöpfungskette der Personalisierten Medizin. In der Schweiz sind die Hemmfaktoren mehrheitlich in der zweiten Hälfte der Wertschöpfungskette zu finden. Die Schweiz hat Massnahmen für Erforschung und Entwicklung von Anwendungen in der Personalisierten Medizin ergriffen. Eine Strategie, die die klinische Umsetzung von Personalisierter Medizin bezweckt, sollte aus diesem Grunde vorwiegend auf die zweite Hälfte der Wertschöpfungskette fokussieren. Die bedeutendsten Massnahmen, um die Hemmfaktoren zu reduzieren, betreffen die Anwendungs- sowie die Rückerstattungsphase der Wertschöpfungskette. In der Anwendungsphase können die wichtigsten Massnahmen ohne Rechtsänderungen umgesetzt werden. Diese bezwecken vorwiegend eine Steigerung des Bewusstseins für Personalisierte Medizin unter Gesundheitsdienstleistenden, Patienten und übrigen Experten im Gesundheitsbereich. Im Gegensatz zur Anwendungsphase beinhalten die vorgeschlagenen Massnahmen für die Rückerstattungsphase Rechtsänderungen sowohl im Bereich des Rückerstattungsprozesses von Diagnostika, als auch im gegenwärtigen Ansatz für Gesundheitstechnologiefolgenabschätzung in der Schweiz. Diese sollte der Schweizer Gesetzgeber zur politischen Diskussion aufgreifen.

[2] Referenzen in RESEARCH CONCEPT, Kapitel 1 Problem, *note* 12.

Abrégé

La médecine personnalisée entre plus lentement que prévu dans la pratique clinique.[3] Non seulement des barrières liées *à la science*, mais aussi des barrières *institutionnelles* empêchent la progression de la médecine personnalisée. Cette thèse identifie et évalue des mesures politiques pour favoriser l'entrée en pratique clinique de la médecine personnalisée en Suisse.

Dans un premier temps, une revue de la littérature dans le domaine de la santé publique et de la médecine translationnelle identifie les actuelles barrières institutionnelles affectant adversement l'entrée en pratique clinique de la médecine personnalisée pour chaque maillon de la chaîne de valeur. Une analyse juridico-économique examine dans un deuxième temps les incitations créées par chacune de ces barrières pour les acteurs de l'écosystème de la médecine personnalisée. La pertinence de ces barrières est ensuite évaluée dans le contexte Suisse et des mesures politiques soutenant l'entrée en pratique clinique de la médecine personnalisée en sont finalement dérivées.

Cette thèse démontre que des barrières institutionnelles existent tout au long de la chaîne de valeur de la médecine personnalisée. En Suisse, les barrières institutionnelles concernent principalement les derniers maillons de la chaîne de valeur - les phases d'autorisation, d'application et de remboursement. La Suisse ayant déjà initiée des mesures pour surmonter les barrières dans la première partie de la chaîne de valeur, toute stratégie visant l'entrée en pratique clinique de la médecine personnalisée devrait se focaliser sur la deuxième partie de la chaîne de valeur. Les mesures les plus importantes pour réduire les barrières institutionnelles concernent les phases d'autorisation et de remboursement. Pour la phase d'application, les plus importantes mesures identifiées ne nécessitent aucun changement de loi. En effet, les mesures identifiées visent principalement la sensibilisation des professionnels de la santé et des patients pour la médicine personnalisée. Contrairement à la phase d'application, les mesures identifiées pour la phase de remboursement requièrent des changements de loi tant dans le domaine du processus de remboursement pour les diagnostics que dans l'approche actuelle de l'évaluation des technologies de la santé en Suisse. Il est par conséquent recommandé que le législateur suisse tienne compte de ces mesures dans la discussion politique.

[3] Références dans RESEARCH CONCEPT, Chapitre 1 Problem, *note* 12.

Preface

This thesis started with spitting into a little tube. I sent it to the US and some days later I started exploring my genetic data. I was fascinated. Suddenly, I was richer by more than a thousand relatives. I learned less relevant things like how much Neanderthal variants I have. Or that I am less likely to sneeze after eating dark chocolate. However, I also learned about my risks for diseases. I learned about what medicines in which doses I am able to metabolize. Additionally, I hopefully contributed to research by sharing my genetic data for research purposes.

A severe diagnosis and a pregnancy made my journey more serious and even more fascinating. I learned more about genetics and the limitations of genetic information. I also learned that my DNA family is suspected to have a rare mutation that is hypothesized to foster the progression of the disease I had. And I learned that I am able to metabolize the commercially available form of folic acid that is recommended during pregnancy in order to avoid spina bifida of the baby.

During this journey I wondered why my healthcare providers were not able to inform me about the relevant information that I have learned. I am convinced that "Personalized Medicine" – or "Precision Medicine" or whatever synonym is used for describing the relatively new sources of information taken into account for choosing a preventive measure, informing a diagnosis or a treatment decision – is able to significantly contribute to our health, one of the most valuable assets I know. Hopefully, this thesis brings personalized medicine one step closer to its clinical implementation.

Küsnacht, August 2017

Acknowledgements

First, I would like to thank PROF. DR. ANNE VAN AAKEN for supporting me in the adventure to apply a Law and Economics perspective to the translation of personalized medicine into clinical practice. She was a constant thought challenger and made sure that my thinking never stayed "in the box". She supported me with her excellent expertise and mentorship. I want to express my special, personal gratitude to her for supporting the adventure to have a baby during the PhD.

Equally, special thanks go to my co-referee DR. DR. RICHARD AMMER who has inspired and enriched this work with a professional perspective from the pharmaceutical industry, and who has supported me with his excellent expertise and – inter alia – several interesting case examples for personalized medicine.

I also thank Prof. Dr. THOMAS SZUCS and Prof. Dr. EFFY VAYENA for the inspiring conversations relating to this thesis. Likewise, I would like to express my gratitude to my employer MCKINSEY & COMPANY for enabling my PhD leave. I do also thank CAROLINE HENGGELER and PD Dr. GABOR MATYAS of the FOUNDATION FOR PEOPLE WITH RARE DISEASES as well as my family members MARTIN BOSSHARD and STEFANIE BOSSHARD for the careful perusal of this thesis and their helpful comments.

My very special and biggest thanks go to my husband DR. MIRO ZUZAK and my son David. I thank Miro for the careful perusal and his helpful comments, for his unconditional, constant, emotional, creative and intellectual support enabling this thesis, and for all the family time sacred to it. And I thank David for being such an even-tempered, positive, warm-hearted "beginners' baby" during the writing of this thesis.

Acknowledgements

Overview

Content Outline

FINAL CONCLUSION

List of Abbreviations

ADR	adverse drug reaction
AL	adaptive licensing - the approval of a pharmaceutical in a prospectively-planned, iterative process
Art.	article
B	barrier
CAGR	compound annual growth rate
CBA	cost-benefit analysis
CDS	clinical decision support – a system providing patient or population specific information to healthcare providers in order to facilitate fact-based, clinical decision making
CDx	companion diagnostic – a diagnostic determining the likelihood of a patient's responsiveness to a specific drug
CEA	cost-effectiveness analysis
Cf.	latin "confer" – compare with
CMS	US Centers for Medicare & Medicaid Services
CNS	central nervous system
CPIC	Clinical Pharmacogenetics Implementation Consortium
CUA	cost-utility analysis
DALYs	disability-adjusted life years
DCF	discounted cash flow
DNA	deoxyribonucleic acid

DRG	disease related group
DTC	direct to consumer - genetic tests offered to broad population without the involvement of a genetics specialist
Dx	diagnostics
e. g.	for example
EHR	electronic health record
EMA	European Medicines Agency
EPD	Swiss electronic patient file
EU	European Union
f.; ff.	and next page; and following pages
FDA	US Food and Drug Administration
FFS	fee-for-service
HGP	Human Genome Project
HTA	health technology assessment
i. c.	in casu
i. e.	in exemplo
IP	intellectual property
IT	information technology
IVD	in-vitro devices
L	policy lever
L&E	Law and Economics
LDT	laboratory developed test
Lit.	litera
NGS	next generation sequencing

NICE	UNITED KINGDOM'S NATIONAL INSTITUTE FOR HEALTH AND CLINICAL EXCELLENCE
NIE	New Institutional Economics
NIPT	non-invasive prenatal testing
NME	new molecular entity
NNT	number of needed treatments
Para., paras.	paragraph, paragraphs
PGt	pharmacogenetics
PGx	pharmacogenomic(s)
Pharma.	pharmaceutical
PM	personalized medicine
QALYs	quality-adjusted life years
R&D	research and development
RNA	ribonucleic acid
Rx	any drug requiring a medical prescription – Rx stemming from Latin "recipe"
SAMS	SWISS ACADEMY OF MEDICAL SCIENCES
SFOPH	SWISS FEDERAL OFFICE OF PUBLIC HEALTH
SMA	SWISS MEDICAL ASSOCIATION
SMB	SWISS MEDICAL BOARD
SNP	single nucleotid polimorphism – pronounced "snip" – represents a base variation in a nucleotide (part of DNA)
UK	United Kingdom
US	United States of America
VBP	value-based pricing

vs	versus

List of Tables

List of Figures

Research concept

"The most transformative technology of the next 10 years will be personalized medicine. Driverless cars will pale in comparison".

DR. ULF MARK SCHNEIDER[4]

1 Problem

2001 marked a milestone in the history of science: the HUMAN GENOME PROJECT published a working draft sequence of the human genome.[5] Two years later the WORLD HEALTH ORGANIZATION forecasted that *"The international Human Genome Project will rapidly make genetic information available on a worldwide scale previously impossible to imagine. All adults have a right, if they so choose, to know their genetic makeup and implications for the health of their potential offspring, to be educated about their own genetics, and to have the services available to act upon their knowledge".*[6]

In fact, since the decoding of the human genome, there have been significant advances in identifying the molecular basis behind diseases.[7] The potential of the developments in personalized medicine (PM) is being described as promising – not only in clinical, but also in economic terms.[8] Thus, personalized medicine is expected to revolutionize healthcare.[9]

4 Ex-CEO of FRESENIUS – current CEO of NESTLÉ – cited in FORBES' "Global 2000: Hall Of Fame CEOs" (2015), *Mark Schneider, Fresenius.*

5 HUMAN GENOME PROJECT (2015), *"Human Genome Project Information Archive".*

6 WERTZ, FLETCHER, & BERG (2003), *preface.*

7 For example, the number of medical phenotypes (an individual's observable characteristics or traits, cf. PWC & PMI (2015), p. 21) or disorders with known molecular bases has reached roughly 5000 and the number of genes with known phenotype or disease-causing mutations has reached roughly 3000 in 2014. An overview on the quantitative advances since the HUMAN GENOME PROJECT provides PERSONALIZED MEDICINE COALITION (2014), p. 5.

8 E. g., MOSER (2014), p. 570. For a detailed overview of the clinical as well as economic benefits of personalized medicine, cf. Part II, Chapter 2 Goals of personalized medicine, p. 65 and Chapter 3 Economic value of personalized medicine, p. 72 ff.

9 Cf. Part II, Chapter 1 Personalized medicine – a paradigm shift in healthcare, p. 54 ff.

K. Bosshard, *Law and Economics of Personalized Medicine*,
Gesundheitsmanagement und Gesundheitsökonomik,
https://doi.org/10.1007/978-3-658-22074-7_1

Despite voices claiming that personalized medicine is a "hype"[10] around an empty concept, personalized medicine has begun with concrete applications in clinical practice. Today, personalized medicine is tangible scientific reality in several medical areas.[11]

Despite its scientific progress, however, the translation of personalized medicine into clinical practice has been slower than expected.[12] Personalized medicine faces a *"last mile problem"*.[13] The numbers of personalized medicine applications have not reached the potential originally hoped for with the decipheration of the human genome.[14] The pace with which clinical applications of personalized medicine are occurring is being described as slow. Several studies share the view that there are gaps between published research and clinical application and that there remains a general sense of dissatisfaction about the progress of personalized medicine.[15] *"[...] the medical delivery model has largely been unchanged. It is as if the system has continually added more tools to its quiver, but continues to 'hunt' in the exact same manner"*.[16]

10 Cf. Part II, Chapter 4.1 Personalized medicine is a "hype", p. 92 ff., and discussion in K. SALARI, WATKINS, & ASHLEY (2012) about *"Personalized medicine: Hope or hype?"*.

11 E.g., FDA commissioner HAMBURG (2013) in her publication *"Personalized Medicine: The Future is now"*: *"The difference between science and fiction is a line that seems even harder to distinguish, thanks in part to a host of astonishing advances in medical science that are helping to create a new age of promise and possibility for patients"*. According to the FDA *„the era of personalized medicine has clearly arrived"*. Similarly the FDA (2013), p. 54, provides an analysis on the progress in the field of PM between 2011 and 2013, p. 54-56.
For further details and references, cf. Part II, Chapter 1.2 Status quo, p. 57 ff.

12 *All studies claiming a "slow" translation of PM into clinical practice:* J. COHEN (2011), 293 or J. COHEN (2012), p. 751. The slower than expected adoption of personalized medicine in practice is also described by e.g., ISSA (2008), p. 192; PRASAD & BRECKENRIDGE (2011), p. 869; CREWS, HICKS, PUI, RELLING, & EVANS (2012), p. 467; HAYES ET AL. (2013), p. 1 ff.; O'DONNELL (2013); p. 1-2; T. A MANOLIO ET AL. (2013), p. 258; THE ACADEMY OF MEDICAL SCIENCES (2013), p. 5; TOWSE & GARRISON (2013), p. 39; VOLLMANN (2013), p. 237; MOOSER (2014) mentions a *„discrepancy between the number of scientific publications and clinical applications in personalized medicine"*, p. 568; AKHMETOV ET AL. (2015), p. 223; JOHNSON (2016), p. 3; KICHKO, MARSCHALL, & FLESSA (2016), p. 2; PLUN-FAVREAU ET AL. (2016) specifically on molecular Dx, p. 145; RAVEGNINI & ANGELINI (2016), p. 1; PRITCHARD ET AL. (2017), p. 141; SCHELLEKENS ET AL. (2017), p. 2.

13 *"The last mile problem"* describes the *"failure to integrate newly developed technology, on which billions of dollars have been invested, into society in a way that improves human behavior and decision making"*, cf. BLUMENTHAL-BARBY, MCGUIRE, GREEN, & UBEL (2015), p. 1.

14 J. COHEN (2012), p. 751.

15 Cf. *note* 12.

16 JOHNSON (2016), p. 3.

Institutional environments can decisively influence the adoption speed of an innovation.[17] Multiple studies hypothesize that the institutional environment has failed to keep pace with the recent advances in science and the improved knowledge in the field of personalized medicine.[18] It is claimed that despite clinical and economic benefits of innovative treatments and diagnostics, *"institutional barriers"*[19] hinder market access and threaten patient access to personalized medicine. The current institutional environment was formed on a foundation of broadly applicable therapies ("one-size-fits-all approach") resulting in an "institutional lag" behind scientific progress.[20] An allegory for the description of the current situation is the following statement: *„So far, the way is a badly paved footpath and not the multi-lane superhighway we need in order to reach the potential of personalized medicine"*.[21] As various sectors of the healthcare industry are involved in PM, there are fears that their defined regulatory spaces are becoming *"diffuse, resulting in a risk of regulatory overlap omission and confusion: a 'regulatory soup' that could drown the promised advances in precision medicine"*.[22]

Scientific progress alone will not guarantee that patients receive the benefits of personalized medicine. Scholars stress that a successful translation of personalized medicine into clinical practice depends on the one hand upon the *scientific* discovery and the imagination of innovators in developing products,[23] but on the other hand as well upon the economic incentives set by the *institutional environment*.[24]

---

17 Cf. Chapter 6.2.3 Underlying assumption: Institutions influence innovation, p. 22 f.

18 *Exemplary studies mentioning institutional barriers:* MARCHANT (2011), p. 13; J. COHEN (2012), p. 751; KULKARNI, MA, FURSTENTHAL, & EVERS (2013), p. 9; TOWSE & GARRISON (2013), p. S40; TRUSHEIM (2013), p. 325 ff.; HAYES, MARKUS, LESLIE, & TOPOL (2014), p, 2; HORGAN ET AL. (2014), p. 287; PERSONALIZED MEDICINE COALITION (2014), p. 5; J. P. COHEN (2015), p. 6; TRUSHEIM, AUSTIN, RAUSCH, & BERNDT (2015), p. 325; DIETEL (2016), p. 152. More references in Part III Identification of institutional barriers to the translation of personalized medicine into clinical practice, p. 101 ff.

19 For the definition of *"institutional barriers"*, cf. Chapter 8.1 *In scope:* Non-science related institutional barriers to the translation of personalized medicine into clinical practice, p. 28 and *note* 155.

20 FERRARA (2007), p. 61; and O'DONNELL (2013), p. 2.

21 DOMDEY cited in "GoingPublic Spezialausgabe Personalisierte Medizin" (2015), p. 12, *translated by the author.*

22 NICOL ET AL. (2016), p. 1.

23 B. M. THOMPSON & BOIANI (2015), p. 1 ; and TRUSHEIM & BERNDT (2015)b, p. 12.

24 E.g., J. C. DAVIS ET AL. (2009), p. 279, state that the major barriers are increasingly related to economics: *"Overcoming the poor microeconomic alignment of incentives among key stakeholders is therefore crucial to catalysing the further development and adoption of personalized medicine"*.
E.g., TRUSHEIM & BERNDT (2012), p. 425, fear that the lack of adequate economic incentives risks scientific achievements not being translated into "bedside medicines", unless the regulatory environment is changed significantly. In an earlier article they talk about an *"economic knowledge*

Regulatory authorities are alleged that they have been too slow to adapt to the changing landscape.[25] EUROPABIO (2015) calls on European policymakers to *"remove the hurdles preventing European patients' access to personalised medicine".*[26] *"Systems will need to catch up with science".*[27] Similarly, others underline the importance of regulation in shaping the innovation system in the context of personalized medicine. Personalized medicine as a new paradigm[28] in medicine needs an adapted institutional environment.[29]

Switzerland has an outstanding reputation for being a hub for scientific research and innovation.[30] Its private and public institutions contribute significantly to the scientific progress of personalized medicine.[31] With this, Switzerland seems to comply well with its constitutional obligation to *"promote scientific research and innovation".*[32] At the same time, the SWISS CONSTITUTION anchors the social objective to ensure that *"every person has access to the healthcare that they require".*[33] Personalized medicine has certainly the potential to fulfill this constitutional objective.[34]

---

gap", TRUSHEIM ET AL. (2011), p. 279. Cf. also LANDER (2015), p. 1185; TRUSHEIM & BERNDT (2012), p. 425; and TRUSHEIM & BERNDT (2015)b, p. 12.

PERMED (2015), p. 29 and 36, claims that interdisciplinary research on regulatory and legal issues should be supported in order to update and adapt current regulations concerning PM.

B. M. THOMPSON & BOIANI (2015), p. 1, state that the progress of personalized medicine depends *"upon the creativity of regulators in adapting the legal environment to changing technologies".* They further elaborate on p. 4: *"The promise of precision medicine is becoming realized more and more each day, but to fully realize its potential we will need to improve the regulatory framework to ensure it promotes innovation of safe and effective products".*

STERN, ALEXANDER, & CHANDRA (2017), p. 1131 ff., about economic incentives shaping PM.

25 E.g., OLSEN & TRØST JØRGENSEN (2014), p. 4 and KAUFMANN (2015): *"Rapid technological developments in the field of personalized medicine have seemed to leave regulators lagging some distance behind"*, p. 390.

26 EUROPABIO (2015), *"press release"*; similarly KIEVITS ET AL. (2014) with recommendations and calls for action aimed at decision makers and other stakeholders in the area of personalized medicine.

27 EUROPEAN ALLIANCE FOR PERSONALISED MEDICINE (2013), p. 4.

28 Cf. Part II, Chapter 1 Personalized medicine – a paradigm shift in healthcare, p. 54 ff.

29 MITTRA & TAIT (2012), p. 711 and H. MÜLLER & SCHÄFER (2013), p. 17.

30 E.g., Switzerland ranking highest on the GLOBAL INNOVATION INDEX, cf. "Global innovation rankings: The innovation game" (2015) by THE ECONOMIST.

31 E.g., private companies like ROCHE and NOVARTIS or publicly funded research institutions like universities (e.g., ETH, EPFL), hospitals (e.g., CHUV) or other research institutions (e.g., PAUL SCHERRER INSTITUTE).

32 Art. 64 SWISS CONSTITUTION.

33 Art. 41 1b SWISS CONSTITUTION: *"The Confederation and the Cantons shall, as a complement to personal responsibility and private initiative, endeavor to ensure that... b) every person has access to the health care that they require".*

34 Cf. the Part II Chapter 2 Goals of personalized medicine, p. 67 ff.

However, the institutional environment of personalized medicine has been a neglected focus of research in Switzerland. Institutional barriers to the translation of personalized medicine have been limitedly discussed in a Swiss context.[35] This thesis aims to fill in this gap by identifying and assessing institutional policy levers to foster the translation of personalized medicine in the Swiss healthcare system.

35 Cf. the following Chapter 5 Research gap, p. 13 ff.

2 Research goal

From a *research theoretical perspective*, the results of this thesis aim to:

- shed light from a *social scientific perspective* on the challenge of the translation of personalized medicine into clinical practice in the Swiss context;
- contribute to Translational Medicine[36] by applying a *Law and Economics*[37] approach as a new perspective to it;
- and finally to perform an *interdisciplinary research approach*[38] by bringing together the disciplines Law and Economics and Translational Medicine.

The thesis' main addressee is the *Swiss policy maker*. The results of this thesis shall:

- demonstrate the available *scope of action* for the Swiss policy maker to foster the translation of personalized medicine into clinical practice;
- support the Swiss policy maker to choose and prioritize *strategic levers* to foster the translation of personalized medicine into clinical practice;
- and finally, help to fulfill the Swiss *constitutional objective* of every person having "access to the healthcare that they require".[39]

Also *pharmaceutical and diagnostics companies, payers* as well as *healthcare providers* and finally *patients* will profit from the results of this thesis as it aims to:

- increase the *knowledge* about personalized medicine in the public;
- raise awareness for the *non-science related hindering factors* to the progress of personalized medicine;
- and to foster the *discussion about the strategic approach towards personalized medicine* in Switzerland.

---

36 Cf. the following Chapter 6.3 Translational Medicine, p. 24 ff.

37 Cf. the following Chapter 6.1 Law and Economics, p. 18 ff.

38 As this is claimed by the current literature, cf. *note* 24.

39 Art. 41(1)b SWISS CONSTITUTION: *"The Confederation and the Cantons shall, as a complement to personal responsibility and private initiative, endeavour to ensure that [...] b) every person has access to the health care that they require"*.

3 Research question

This thesis states that there are not only science-related, but also non science-related, institutional barriers to the translation of personalized medicine.[40] Its *primary research subject* is to identify and evaluate institutional policy levers to foster the translation of personalized medicine – applied to the Swiss healthcare system.

In order to reach this thesis' research goals and to approach its main research subject, the following *sub-questions* are examined:

[40] The term *"translation"* refers to the "translation into clinical practice" in this thesis. Cf. Chapter 6.3 Translational Medicine, p. 24 ff.

PART I	– What is the definition for *personalized medicine*? – What are *common terminologies* used in the context of personalized medicine?
PART II	– How does personalized medicine *impact the healthcare landscape*? - What are *past, present and future developments* in the context of personalized medicine? - What are the *goals* of personalized medicine? - What is the *economic value* of personalized medicine? - What *criticism* does personalized medicine face? - What is the *ecosystem* of personalized medicine?
PART III	– What are *non-science related, institutional barriers* to the translation of personalized medicine into clinical practice? – How do the institutional barriers *incentivize* the stakeholders in the personalized medicine ecosystem?
PART IV	– How does the *current institutional setting* that governs the institutional barriers *incentivize* the stakeholders in the Swiss ecosystem for personalized medicine?
PART V	– What are available *policy levers* to reduce the institutional barriers to the translation of personalized medicine in the Swiss healthcare system?

Table 1: Research questions

4 Methodology

After providing the relevant *definitions* (I) and the *context* (II), this thesis follows a deductive approach and consists of a *theoretical* (III) and an *applied part* (IV). *Policy implications* are subsequently derived and evaluated in the final Part (V) of this thesis.

4.1 Theoretical part

Step 1: Literature analysis

First, based on a systematic literature analysis, the institutional barriers for the translation of personalized medicine into clinical practice are identified, synthesized and categorized. The categorization of the identified barriers is based on the value chain of personalized medicine:[41] A detailed description of the approach for the literature analysis follows at the beginning of Part III.[42]

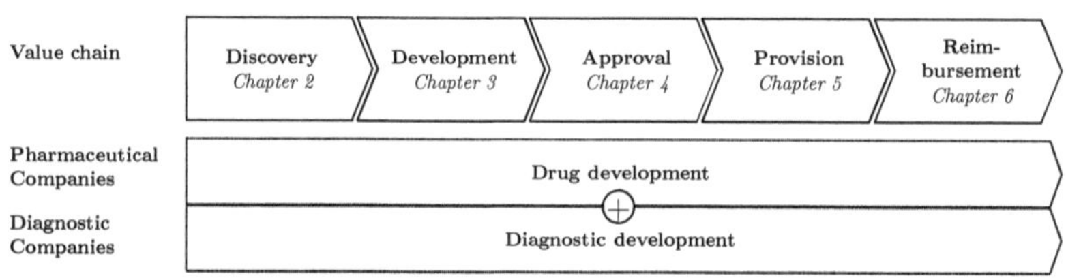

Figure 1: Value chain of personalized medicine

Step 2: Incentives analysis

In a second step, for each of the identified barriers an incentives analysis is performed – with the aim of examining the incentives induced by the respective barrier separately for each stakeholder involved in the PM ecosystem. The relevant stakeholders include: Research institutions, pharmaceutical companies, diagnostics companies, providers, patients, and payers.[43]

---

[41] The links of the value chain are separately described at the beginning of each respective chapter in Part III.

[42] Cf. Part III, Chapter 1.1 Literature analysis, p. 102 ff.

[43] Cf. Part II, Chapter 5.1 Framework for the personalized medicine ecosystem, p. 96 ff.

The incentives analysis is based on a theoretical, qualitative argumentation scheme following classic economic theory with the assumption of rationally behaving actors. A detailed description of the constitutive microeconomic assumptions and relevant interdependencies for the incentives analysis follows at the beginning of Part III.[44] Each chapter concludes with proposing a hypothesis about the respective barrier.

Part III concludes with an overview of the identified barriers, their induced incentives per stakeholder and an assessment of their relevance.[45]

Part III's theoretical framework and the resulting hypotheses are of general value and may be tested for in the context of different countries.

4.2 Applied part

Grounded on the findings of the theoretical Part III, the identified barriers to the translation of PM into clinical practice are consequentially evaluated for their relevance in Switzerland. The evaluation follows a Law and Economics approach: In a first step, the current institutional setting governing each barrier is identified. In a second step, the institutional setting is analyzed on the basis of rational choice in order to identify the resulting incentives for the relevant stakeholders in the context of PM in Switzerland:

Step 1: Analysis of the institutional setting in Switzerland

In a first step, the current institutional setting governing the barrier in Switzerland is examined. This includes the identification of the relevant institutions ranging from non-legal institutional mechanisms to hard law requirements concerning the respective barrier.[46]

Step 2: Incentives analysis

Based on analysis of the institutional setting in Switzerland, the incentives analysis tests the hypotheses proposed in Part III and assesses to what extend the incentives for the stakeholders in the Swiss PM ecosystem differ from the general analysis in Part III.

---

44 Cf. Part III Chapter 1.2 Analysis of incentives, p. 103 ff.

45 *"Relevance"* understood as illustrated in the following Chapter 4.3 Derivation and evaluation of policy levers, *Relevance*, p. 12.

46 Cf. following Chapter 6.2.1 Definition of institutions, p. 21 f.

The methodology is the same as applied in Part III – with the same constitutive assumptions and interdependencies.[47] Where possible and available, the incentives analysis is supplemented with empirical findings in the Swiss context.

Concluding Part IV, an overview of the resulting barriers for Switzerland, their induced incentives for each stakeholder and their "relevance"[48] is given and compared to the findings in the theoretical Part III.

4.3 Derivation and evaluation of policy levers

The Law and Economic analysis in Part IV forms the basis for the derivation of policy levers for each barrier to increase the incentives to foster the translation of PM in Switzerland. Subsequently, the policy levers are evaluated based on the two evaluation criteria *"relevance"* and *"ability to change"*:

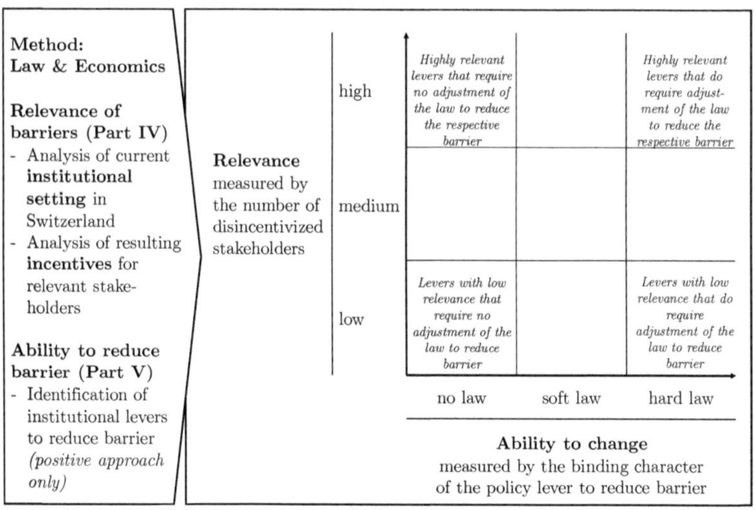

Figure 2: Evaluation matrix

47 Cf. detailed description of incentives analysis in Part III, Chapter 1.2 Analysis of incentives, p. 103 ff.

48 *"Relevance"* understood as illustrated in the following Chapter 4.3 Derivation and evaluation of policy levers, *Relevance*, p. 12.

Relevance:

The “relevance” of a barrier can be defined in various ways. This thesis measures a *barrier's relevance* by the number of stakeholders who are disincentivized to foster the translation of PM by the respective barrier.[49]

In the above definition of “relevance”, all stakeholders are weighted equally – despite the critique that the stakeholders' influence might vary. The definition is based on a simplified view of reality.[50]

Ability to change:

The “ability to change” is represented by three categories assessing the binding character of the suggested policy levers:

- Levers that do require *no legal changes* in the current institutional setting
- Levers that do require *soft law changes* in the current institutional setting
- Levers that do require *hard law changes* in the current institutional setting

Levers that reduce barriers which incentivize all stakeholders in the PM ecosystem are the most relevant. Levers requiring no legal changes in the current institutional setting represents relatively easy to implement and effective measures for a policy maker. Levers with a high relevance that do require a change in hard law should considered by the policy maker to be put on the law making agenda.

The evaluation presents an attempt to prioritize the suggested policy levers. Despite from the described relevance-based evaluation, this thesis does not take any further normative position on the prioritization of the policy levers. Neither does this part make a statement, if a policy lever should be triggered at all. This political decision is left to the Swiss policy maker.[51]

---

49 Limitations to this approach are described in the FINAL CONCLUSION, Chapter 4 Limitations & future research directions, Sub-chapter 4.3 Methodology, *Derivation and evaluation of the policy levers*, p. 346.

50 Limitations of the approach are described in the FINAL CONCLUSION, Chapter 4.3 Methodology, p. 345 f.

51 This thesis has a broad understanding of the *"Swiss policy maker"*: It includes regulators and public authorities on the federal, cantonal and communal level. In case, the implementation of a suggested lever should be considered, the concrete responsibilities would have to be further specified, and coordinated with involved professional organizations like e.g., the SAMS or the SMA. Cf. limitations of the approach described in the FINAL CONCLUSION, Chapter 4.3 Methodology, p. 345 f.

5 Research gap

This thesis adds from two new angles to existing research: *First*, its main research question has not been examined yet in Switzerland. Additionally, the categorization of the institutional barriers along the PM value chain as secondary research subject is new in the Swiss and global context. *Second*, the context of this thesis' research question is a relatively new field of research for social science. A Law and Economic approach has not been applied so far in Translational Medicine.[52] The two new perspectives are briefly elaborated in the following.

5.1 Degree of novelty of research question

New geographic focus

A growing body of literature is dealing with social scientific aspects of personalized medicine. Institutional barriers[53] to the translation of PM into clinical practice are a topic that is being discussed. However, most of the existing studies with a social scientific background have no specific geographic focus, some of them have a US or European focus, and only a few have a Swiss focus.

Studies of general nature: The relevant literature can be found in the literature analysis in Part III. The analyzed studies discuss the barriers to the translation of PM either as a central research subject or as secondary side topic.[54] In the following, only select studies are presented in order to illustrate the research gap.

Studies with a US focus: An organization at the forefront dealing with the translation of PM into clinical practice is the PERSONALIZED MEDICINE COALITION. It is active in nurturing the public debate around PM and publishing several reports related to the translation of PM into clinical practice.[55] Another active institution in the US discussion is the US FOOD AND DRUG ADMINISTRATION.[56] Furthermore, there are studies which focus on legal aspects around PM.[57] Other studies identify potential

[52] Cf. following Chapter 6.3 Translational Medicine, 24 ff.

[53] Or synonymously used terminologies, cf. *note* 155.

[54] E.g., KULKARNI ET AL. (2013), p. 9; HAYES ET AL. (2014), TOWSE & GARRISON (2013), p. S40, J. P. COHEN (2015), DIETEL (2016), p. 152 – not all studies are mentioned here. Additional literature is mentioned in Part III.

[55] E.g., PERSONALIZED MEDICINE COALITION (2013), PERSONALIZED MEDICINE COALITION (2014), PERSONALIZED MEDICINE COALITION (2015), PERSONALIZED MEDICINE COALITION (2016).

[56] E.g., FDA (2013); or FDA (2016)a.

[57] E.g., STERN ET AL. (2017), p. 1131 ff. focus on the US Orphan Act.

"catalysts" or "drivers" or "barriers" behind the translation of PM in the US.[58] The academic dialogue about the institutional barriers to the translation of PM seems to be more active in the US compared to Europe. Most of the studies with no specific geographic focus stem from US universities and associations.[59]

Studies with a European focus: In Europe, the EUROPEAN ALLIANCE FOR PERSONALISED MEDICINE is an active association in fostering the discussion about PM.[60] Also EUROPABIO published a white paper about *"realising the potential of personalised medicine"* and a conference report with calls for action.[61] Additionally, the EUROPEAN COMMISSION funded PERMED, a coordination and support action on PM. The main goals of the PERMED consortium are to complement existing activities in Europe by identifying and promoting promising research topics and bringing forward the implementation of PM for the benefit of society. Its main output is the development of a strategic research and innovation agenda.[62]

Like in the US, several studies focus on PM's translational barriers in Europe.[63] Further, there are a range of country-specific studies. For example, the edited book by EPPINGER, HALECKER, HÖLZLE, & KAMPRATH (2015) is a collection of analyses and concepts about service potentials and business models for PM in Germany. Specifically, the study by EPPINGER ET AL. (2015)[64] examined drivers and barriers behind PM and elaborated recommendations for action for Germany. Compared to the US, the academic dialogue of social scientific aspects related to PM is younger.

Studies with a Swiss focus: The number of studies related to social scientific aspects of PM in Switzerland is limited. However, there are a few studies which deal – amongst others – with social scientific aspects in the field of PM. An early technology assessment about pharmacogenetics and pharmacogenomics published RIPPE ET AL. (2004). The most notable and comprehensive study in the field of PM in Switzerland so far was published by ECKHARDT ET AL. (2014). Both studies were made under the authority of the SWISS CENTER FOR TECHNOLOGY ASSESSMENT (TA-SWISS) and contain a list of recommendations about how to better deal with the impacts of the new technologies. The *book "personalized medicine – hope or empty promise"*[65] edited by

58 E.g., J. C. DAVIS ET AL. (2009); and J. DAVIS, MA, & SUTARIA (2010).
59 Cf. Part III, Chapter 1.1 Literature analysis, p. 102 ff.
60 EUROPEAN ALLIANCE FOR PERSONALISED MEDICINE (2013).
61 KIEVITS ET AL. (2012) ; KIEVITS ET AL. (2014) ; and EUROPABIO (2015).
62 PERMED (2015), p. 36.
63 E.g., HORGAN ET AL. (2014).
64 EPPINGER, WIECK, ALMEIDA & SCHMID (2015) in EPPINGER ET AL. (2015), p. 156 ff.
65 *Title translated by the author.*

KLUSMAN & VAYENA (2016) contains a collection of articles ranging from biological to economic or ethical perspectives on PM.[66] Further, there are legal scholars in Switzerland focusing on the regulation of PM.[67]

None of the studies provide an overview of the institutional barriers in Switzerland, nor does one provide an attempt for evaluating the policy levers to reduce the institutional barriers in Switzerland. This thesis aims to close this research gap.

New categorization

The theoretical Part's categorization of the identified institutional barriers along the PM value chain is new.

The majority of existing studies does not contain a comprehensive picture of all institutional barriers and only a minority attempts to group the barriers into certain categories.[68] To the knowledge of the author this thesis is the first of its kind going one step further by examining which link of the PM value chain is hampered due to an institutional barrier.

5.2 Application of established methodology in new context

The medical concept of choosing a treatment or prevention measure based on somebody's genetic profile is a relatively young concept. The decipheration of the human genome in 2001 was a door-opener for PM.[69] Social scientific research dealing with research questions in the context of PM is even younger and gained relevance after the first commercial products became available.

Scholars stress the *"need for improvement in methods of translation from laboratory findings to clinical practice"*.[70] An interdisciplinary approach to the translation of PM is required: *"Personalized medicine can only fulfill the promise of optimizing our health care system by an interdisciplinary, translational, and transdiagnostic view"*.[71]

---

66 Among the most meaningful studies for this thesis of the edition are the health economic articles by BÜTLER (2016), FELDER (2016), and SZUCS & BLANK (2016); and the legal contribution by TAG & BAUR (2016).

67 E.g., GÄCHTER & VOKINGER (2012); and TAG (2012).

68 The majority of studies do not apply any categorization, a minority uses high-level categories. E.g., EASTMAN (2012) use reimbursement paradigm, collaborations and data sharing, regulatory paradigm, incentives for clinicians, privacy protection for patietns; T. A MANOLIO ET AL. (2013), p. 261-262 with several uncategorized challenges; ABPI (2014) use science & technology, regulation, reimbursement, IT, IP, privacy, physician & patient education, economics).

69 Cf. Part II Chapter 1.1 Historical background, p. 54 ff.

70 MALOTTKI ET AL. (2014), p. 1.

71 A. EVERS ET AL. (2012), p. 302.

Further, scholars stress the need for a more economic perspective on the translation of PM: "*The truly personalized approach in medicine faces two major problems: complex biology and complex economics. The greatest challenges are economic, not scientific*".[72] Others stress the importance of studying legal aspects to the translation of PM.[73]

Studies discussing institutional barriers behind the translation of PM are either *empirically* sourced results of expert discussions (e.g., workshops, Delphi-studies, expert panels, conference results)[74] or rely on *qualitative theoretical* argumentations by the authors.[75]

A number of *health economic* studies deal with the value of PM.[76] There are also studies with an *economic* approach that concern the translation of PM into clinical practice. One example is TRUSHEIM based at the MASSACHUSETTS INSTITUTE FOR TECHNOLOGY (MIT) who examines the interdependencies between the cut-off value of a companion diagnostic (CDx) and incentives to personalize a drug.[77] Several authors describe the *law* related to PM.[78] Studies with a *business* view focus on either technological aspects of PM[79] or on new business models in the context of PM.[80]

---

72 JAKKA & ROSSBACH (2013), p. 1, and similarly J. C. DAVIS ET AL. (2009), p. 279.

73 E.g., HOLLINGSWORTH (2015), p. 8, sees as the biggest challenge to the translation of PM the "*engagement and change from regulators, in policy and from policy makers, from governments, within reimbursement mechanisms, in education and adoption in clinical professionals...*".
E.g., TUTTON (2013), p. 192, calls to further study of the role of drug regulators.
E.g., CRAWFORD & ASPINALL (2012), p. 274 and p. 281 find "*absent substantive revision in the payment schemes for genomic medicine, the medical science of deploying this form of diagnostic testing will move far ahead of our health system's ability to recognize its direct economic value...*".
E.g., FAULKNER ET AL. (2012), p. 1162, argue that "*personalized medicine technologies are currently caught between expectations of improving health outcomes and uncertainty about navigating the rapidly changing regulatory and reimbursement environment*".

74 *Examples for empirical studies:* E.g., T. A MANOLIO ET AL. (2013), p. 258 ff.; and MESSNER ET AL. (2016), p. 12.

75 *Examples for qualitative studies:* E.g., BOMBARD (2015); DAVID PETTITT ET AL. (2016); and PLUN-FAVREAU ET AL. (2016).

76 Cf. Part II Chapter 3 Economic value of personalized medicine, p. 72 ff.

77 The biomarker-value with which a CDx separates the patient population that qualifies for treatment from those patients who are not treatable by the respective drug is called "cut-off" value. Cf. Part III Chapter 1.2.2 Interdependencies between the pharmaceutical and diagnostic component, p. 105 ff. with relevant citations of TRUSHEIM ET AL.

78 Cf. for Switzerland: GÄCHTER & VOKINGER (2012), TAG (2012) and NOVENTA (2014); for the US: B. M. THOMPSON & BOIANI (2015) and ELLIS (2016).

79 E.g., STELZER, MEYER-BRÖTZ, SCHIEBEL, & BRECHT (2015) combine scenario techniques and bibliometric analysis in order to produce a picture of future possible states of the fiel of PM, to identify emerging technologies in this field and to assess the future roles of these technologies in the different future states.

To the knowledge of the author, Translational Medicine[81] has not (yet) used methods from Law and Economics in order to understand the institutional barriers behind the translation of PM into clinical practice.

[80] HALECKER, KAMPRATH, BRAUN (2015), SMOLKA & KAMPRATH (2015), HALECKER & HOELZLE (2015), in EPPINGER ET AL. (2015), p. 156 ff.; and cf. *note* 543.

[81] Cf. following Chapter 6.3 Translational Medicine, p. 24 ff.

6 Epistemological foundations

Primarily, this thesis is epistemologically rooted in *Law and Economics*. An adjacent field of research is *New Institutional Economics*. Also, *Translational Medicine* belongs to some degree to this thesis' epistemological foundations as this thesis' primary research question examines the translation of PM into clinical practice. The following Chapter presents the three research streams, their basic assumptions and methodological approaches.

6.1 Law and Economics

Law and Economics (L&E) means the "economic analysis of law".[82]

The *"economic analysis"* comprises the theory of rational choice in a world with limited resources.[83] It provides the theory – based on how actors respond to incentives – to predict the effects of rules.[84]

"Law" is an instrument for achieving social goals or values[85] and can create positive or negative incentives for actors to choose certain actions.[86]

"Law and Economics" applies the instruments of economics to law in order to examine legal rules and their outcomes.[87] L&E provides a method of evaluating laws' effects on social values.[88] It has the aspiration to *"place the study of law on a scientific basis, with coherent theory, precise hypotheses deduced from the theory, and empirical tests of the hypotheses"*.[89]

The application of economics to law is an "uneasy marriage" and faces methodological differences as the Popperian positive science conflicts in many respects with the

[82] POSNER (1993), p. 83. About the history of L&E, cf. e.g., POSNER (2014), *chapter* 5.1 or COOTER & ULEN (2008), p. 2-3.

[83] POSNER (2014), *chapter* 5.1. Central to L&E is the assumption that persons are rational utility maximizers.

[84] COOTER & ULEN (2008), p. 4.

[85] *Ibidem.*

[86] KIRCHNER (1997), p. 7.

[87] KIRCHNER (1997), p. 6-8; PARISI (2004), p. 259; and POSNER (2014), *chapter* 1.1.

[88] COOTER & ULEN (2008), p. 4.

[89] POSNER (1989) cited in COOTER & ULEN (2008), p. 1.

existing paradigms in legal analysis.[90] The two different intellectual perspectives on this conflict are positive and normative L&E.[91]

The role of *positive* L&E is to examine legal rules and their outcomes based on an assumption about a behavior of economic actors (*rational choice theory*).[92] It restricts itself to the descriptive study of the incentives produced by legal rules and does not make any statement about the ultimate goal that rules should pursue.[93] In the focus of research are the description, explanation and prognosis of how humans react to law.[94]

The role of *normative* L&E is to formulate normative propositions on what the law ought to be like and to evaluate the law in accordance with the formulated criteria. Its aim is to *"make them [the rules] better"*.[95] "Better" often in the sense of maximizing efficiency in a society as outcomes of rules. Predominant evaluation criteria in normative L&E are the efficiency criteria from welfare economics like PARETO or KALDOR-HICKS efficiency.[96] However, also a consensus like a constitutional principle can act as evaluation criterion for an economic analysis of the law.[97]

In this sense, this thesis follows a normative L&E approach with the basic underlying assumption that the translation of PM into clinical practice is a goal to be pursued in line with the SWISS CONSTITUTION.[98]

6.2 New Institutional Economics

New Institutional Economics (NIE) is based on the belief that economic development cannot be understood without understanding the institutions in an economy.[99]

---

90 PARISI (2004), p. 259, or VAN AAKEN (2003), p. 13, talking about misunderstandings between legal and economic scholars.

91 PARISI (2004), p. 265, further distinguishes between *functional* L&E – a perspective which is neither fully positive nor fully normative. Functional L&E addresses the link between individual preferences and social outcomes. It integrates the findings of Public Choice theory into L&E and relies on methodological individualism, p. 265.

92 VAN AAKEN (2003), p. 81.

93 ZUZAK (2008), p. 24.

94 VAN AAKEN (2003), p. 45.

95 POSNER (2014), *chapter* 1.1. Positive L&E is also referred to as the *Chicago school* of L&E.

96 VAN AAKEN (2003), p. 183 and 210-222, PARISI (2004), p. 264, and SCHÄFER & OTT (2005), p. 24-38.

97 VAN AAKEN (2003), p. 183, argues that the *"formal concept of efficiency is capable to incorporate values and principles of the law"* (translated by the author), cf. also p. 235 f.

98 Cf. following Chapter 7 Underlying assumption, p. 27 *note* 33.

99 NIE has to be distinguished from the *New- or Neoinstitutionalism* -movements prominent in management science. Scholars of the *New- or Neoinstitutionalism* assume that an organizations strate-

NIE *"rejects or at least severely questions"* classical economic theory.[100] Classical economic theory rests upon often "unrealistic assumptions" that drive a wedge between economic theory and economic reality.[101] Classical economic theory assumes a system with "perfect competition" with the market as institution (*price theory*) and a world of costless transactions, perfect foresight and perfect rationality.[102] NIE challenges these assumptions and extends classical economic theory by examining institutions in a broader sense. Instead of studying the market, institutions *"that enable markets to work"* are studied.[103] NIE extends the classical economic theory's concepts with transaction costs economics, property rights analysis, economic theory of contracts and public choice.[104] COASE (1937) – as one of NIE's most prominent scholars – added the idea of transaction costs to classical economic theory.[105] Transaction costs are *"the costs of running the economic system"*, including the costs of using the market and the costs of using, maintaining, changing etc. of institutions or organizations in general.[106]

NIE places emphasis on the understanding of the incentives to different parties that engage in productive activities. Incentives arise through financial and non-

gic and economic activity is embedded in a social and normative context. The institutional environment can strongly influence the development of formal structures in an organization, often more profoundly than market pressures. The institutional context motivates economic actors to seek approval for their actions *("legitimacy")*, particularly from those constituents on whom the actors depend for physical, human, financial, or reputational capital, cf. eg., DACIN, OLIVER, & ROY (2007), p. 171. The "institutional pressure" exerts a constraining influence over organizations in the same population *("organizational field")*, forcing them to resemble other organizations *("isomorphism")* that face the same set of environmental conditions. The search of legitimacy can reduce efficiency and hinder the organization's competitive position in their technical environment. Thus, an organization is not only driven by competitive and efficiency criteria but also by rules, demands and expectations of the organization's institutional environment. C.f. e.g., seminal papers of J. W. MEYER & ROWAN (1977) or DIMAGGIO & POWELL (1983) revisiting WEBER's (1948) "iron cage" describing the rationalist order leading to bureaucratization due to competition amongst capitalist firms.

100 POSNER (1993), p. 74.

101 POSNER (1993), p. 74-75. E.g., the assumption *"that individuals and firms are rational maximizers, that information is costless, that demand curves facing firms are infinitely elastic, that inputs and outputs are infinitely divisible, that cost and revenue schedules are mathematically regular"*, etc.

102 DROBAK (2008), p. 2, the costs of measuring the multiple dimensions of the goods and legal rights being exchanged in an economic transaction and the costs of enforcing these rights.

103 POSNER (1993), p. 75.

104 FURUBOTN & RICHTER (2005), p. 37.

105 Although he does not explicitly name them "transaction costs".

106 ARROW (1969) cited in RICHTER (2008), p. 12.

financial benefits and costs associated with institutions. For a production and trade to occur, there must be incentives for both producers and traders.[107]

Also NIE's focus of research differs from classical economic theory. Whereas classical economic theory studies aggregated data using econometrics, NIE implies in turn an emphasis on the case study relying for example on cross country comparisons or the study of histories, judicial opinions, magazine accounts or interviews.[108]

6.2.1 Definition of institutions

NIE takes its name from the term *"institutions"*.[109] They are described as *"the rules of the game in a society"* or *"the humanly devised constraints that shape human interaction whether political, social, or economic"*.[110] Institutions are the constraints that reduce transaction costs and *"enable markets to work"*[111] and must be understood broadly. They can even include *"the engagement ring in a marriage market"*.[112]

NORTH (1990) distinguishes between *formal* (e.g., law, human-devised rules) and *informal* (e.g., social norms, conventions, codes of behavior).[113] Institutions are *"commonly known rules which help to structure repeated situations of interaction and which have an enforcement mechanism that implies a sanction or threat of a sanction in case of a rule violation"*.[114] VOIGT (2009) distinguishes between *internal* (e.g., conventions, ethical rules, customs, formal private rules) and *external institutions* (e.g., positive law).[115]

A further distinction is made between the *institutional environment* and *institutional arrangements*. The institutional environment represents the "rules of the game that guide individuals' behavior" and describes the set of institutions (formal or informal) within which particular parties or groups operate.[116] Institutional arrangements are *"specific guidelines designed by trading partners to facilitate a particular*

---

[107] DORWALD, KYDD, MORRISON, POULTON, & SMITH (2000), p. 98.

[108] POSNER (1993), p. 75; DROBAK (2008), p. 4.

[109] A more extensive definition of institutions than this chapter provides VOIGT (2009), *chapter* 1.2, p. 26 ff.

[110] NORTH (1990), p. 3.

[111] POSNER (1993), p. 75.

[112] POSNER (1993), p. 75. An essential part of the functioning of institutions is the costliness of violations. NORTH (1990), p. 4.

[113] NORTH (1990), p. 4; and DROBAK (2008), p. 1.

[114] VOIGT (2009), p. 27.

[115] *Ibidem.*

[116] KLEIN (1999), *"New institutional theory"*.

exchange" and describe specific mechanisms for exchange and for coordination (formal or informal) in an economy.[117]

6.2.2 Overlap of New Institutional Economics with Law and Economics

The two academic movements *Law and Economics* and *New Institutional Economics* are two sides of the same coin.[118] Law – in its various forms – is the *"most important and prevalent type"* of formal institution, so the focus on institutions is often a focus on the law.[119]

The main difference between NIE and L&E is that L&E *"has no, or at least very few, aspirations to change economic theory or economists' empirical methodology"*.[120] Other differences are mainly matters of emphasis and vocabulary and are described as being *"rather unimportant"* because both fields are part of applied economics.[121]

One of these differences is that NIE is more narrow in its theoretical concepts with a focus on transaction costs problems, whereas L&E has a broader subject matter.[122] Further, for long, informal institutions have been playing a secondary role in L&E. However, this changed and L&E experienced a broadening of the approach.[123]

Another difference is their origin. Whereas modern L&E is a *"product of American law schools"*, NIE is a product of economists who concentrate on institutions and among them the law.[124] L&E viewed as a movement in economics, it is *"subject matter"*, but viewed as a movement in law, it was described as *"methodologically radical"*.[125]

6.2.3 Underlying assumption: Institutions influence innovation

A main assumption of L&E and NIE – and consequently of this thesis –is that institutions influence the performance of countries. The assumption is *"hardly controversial"*.[126] In the early 1990s, institutions started gaining popularity as an explana-

117 DAVIS & NORTH (1971) cited in DORWALD ET AL. (2000), p. 98; and KLEIN (1999), *"New institutional theory"*.
118 E.g., POSNER (1993), p. 82; SCHÄFER & OTT (2005), p. 4; DROBAK (2008), p. 1.
119 DROBAK (2008), p. 1.
120 POSNER (1993), p. 82.
121 *Ibidem*, p. 73.
122 *Ibidem*, p. 83, with the examples of transaction cost theory, price theory, human-capital theory for the subject matter of L&E.
123 VOIGT (2009), p. 46.
124 DROBAK (2008), p. 6.
125 POSNER (1993), p. 83.
126 NORTH (1990), p. 3; also VOIGT (2009), p. 121-152.

tion of international differences in economic development. From the late 1990s, institutions have moved to *"the center stage in the debate on economic development"*.[127]

Similarly undebated in NIE and L&E is the assumption that institutions influence the degree of innovation.[128] Theoretical considerations from L&E suggest that an unregulated market undersupply creative works that embody ideas, such as science, inventions, etc.[129] There is the academic debate about how legal institutions, the different forms of law[130] and alternative institutional arrangements (e.g., reputation systems) can foster innovation. Law may have a potential function as a *leveler* (e.g., lowering market entry barriers), *protector* (e.g., property rights, limitation of liability), or *enforcer* (especially in case of contractual arrangements).[131]

The assumption that institutions influence innovation means in the context of this thesis, that the creation of value through PM and its allocation across the relevant stakeholders in the PM ecosystem depend among others on the institutional environment.[132] Which stakeholder "captures" this value influences how much investment in research and development is undertaken and therefore whether value is likely to be created in the first place.[133]

---

127 CHANG (2011), p. 473.

128 Literature discussing the Law and Economics of innovation includes for example SCOTCHMER (2004), BRONWYN & ROSENBERG (2010), LITAN (2011), SALZBERGER (2012); L&E literature specifically focusing on IP are e.g., LANDES & POSNER (2003) and MERGES (2014).
The assumption of institutions that influence innovation is congruent with movements in management science like *Neoinstitutionalism* (cf. *note* 99) or the *Industrial Organisation Theory (IOT)*. IOT acknowledges that the innovative capabilities of companies are not only influenced by its properties and resouces, but also by the innovation system constituting of the interactions between stakeholders and institutions through which new knowledge is generated. E.g., PORTER (1990), p. 73, cited in EPPINGER ET AL. (2015), p. 120.

129 *I. c.* Information Economics, cf. COOTER & ULEN (2008), p. 122. Remedies can be supply or subsidies, charitable contributions, trade secrets or intellectual property law, p. 124 ff. For Law and Economics of intellectual property law cf. *note* 128.

130 E.g., GASSER (2008) suggests the research on different types and forms of regulation, such as "direct vs. indirect regulation (e.g., regulation of capital markets); framework regulation, self-regulation, incentive-based regulation, command-and-control", etc. This thesis will distinguish between three categories of the binding character of the law, cf. Part V Chapter 1.3 Evaluation of policy levers, p. 296 f.

131 MAYER-SCHOENBERGER cited in GASSER (2008).

132 GARAU, TOWSE, GARRISON, HOUSMAN, & OSSA (2012), p. 16, with the same argument.

133 GARAU ET AL. (2012), p. 17.

6.3 Translational Medicine

Translational Medicine (TM) is a multidisciplinary form of science that bridges the translational gaps between basic science, applied science, and clinical practice.[134] It is colloquially described as the practice of transferring scientific knowledge *"from bench to bedside (and back)".*[135] TM's ultimate goals are better health outcomes at the individual and the population level through the incorporation of new products and therapies into clinical practice.[136]

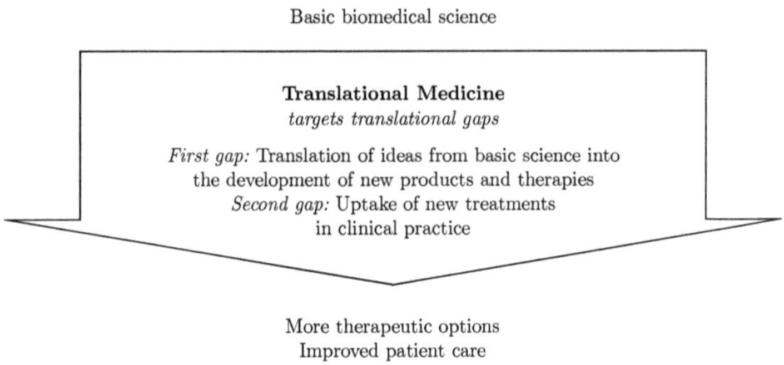

Figure 3: Goals of Translational Medicine

The term *"translation"* is used metaphorically and describes symbolically the two different languages between basic science and clinical research and practice.[137] The "translation" is driven by the development and use of new diagnostic tools and medicines, data analysis tools, procedures, education and policies. The role of TM is to support, accelerate and ease the translation by providing independent scientific reviews for reliability and accuracy.[138] The *"translation continuum"* is commonly categorized into four phases (*4T model*):[139]

---

134 Estape, Mays, & Sternke (2016), p. 12.
135 Solomon (2015), p. 1 and 4.
136 Estape et al. (2016), p. 12.
137 Solomon (2015), p. 11.
138 Estape et al. (2016), p. 12.
139 Khoury et al. (2008), p. 1603, Modell et al. (2014), p. 467, and European Patent Institute (2015), p. 3.

Translational phase	*End product*	*Focus of research*
T1	Basic scientific discovery (*basic knowledge*) to potential clinical application (*theoretical knowledge*)	Research is mainly concerned with gathering evidence on safety and analytical validity.
T2	Produces evidence-based guidelines (*efficacy knowledge*)	Research deals with tapping into the earliest available data at the point where an application enters the clinical setting, to produce a first assessment, particularly with respect to clinical validity, and when possible, effectiveness and clinical utility
T3	Produces clinical care or intervention knowledge (*applied knowledge*)	Research is mostly concerned with the aspects of dissemination, implementation and diffusion of a new application.
T4	Produces knowledge about how to influence the health of a community or population (*public health knowledge*)	Research aims to produce holistic assessments of the impacts of an application on the healthcare system as a whole.

Table 2: Translational research continuum

SOURCES: Illustrated by the author
based on MODELL, KARDIA, & CITRIN (2014), p. 467
and EUROPEAN PATENT INSTITUTE (2015), p. 3.

The T4 Model extends beyond the simple "bench to bedside" definition of translational research and includes *delivery research*[140] and *outcome research.*[141] Economic evaluation represents an integral part of translational research since it affects the process of translation in different phases.[142] This thesis primarily focuses on T3 of the translational continuum, but spills also into other phases.[143]

---

[140] Research on the best ways to deliver interventions in real-life settings.

[141] Evaluations of health outcomes and impact on population health.

[142] PACI (2009), p. 285.

[143] *Ibidem*, p. 285, *"This translational continuum can be seen, at first glance, as a linear process, as each phase is linked and based on the results of the previous one. However, the frontiers between each step are not clearly defined, and translation research that might be typically associated with one phase might spill in into other phases, or there might be cases of reverse translational research*

TM is a relatively new concept in biomedical sciences as well as in social sciences. It began to emerge in the broader academic and policy literature in the mid-1990. Concerns grew that the public investment in life science (e.g., the HUMAN GENOME PROJECT) might not deliver the promised economic and patient benefits. The gap between findings of basic science and the clinical applications is labeled as *"Valley of Death".*[144] This gap relates to a number of barriers that hinder the translation from "bench to bedside".[145]

There is a continuous debate about the exact *definition of TM.*[146] As different stakeholders use the term in diverse contexts, the expectations and goals of the field diverge and the term is described as *"ambiguous concept".*[147] At the beginning of TM, the term encompassed elements primarily related to gaps in natural scientific research (main focus on T1 and T2).[148] However, more recently, TM has broadened and refers now more broadly to *"the development and use of new scientific methods and technologies, interdisciplinary approaches, and collaborative institutional arrangements to bridge the gap between basic and clinical science, exploit new science and technology in healthcare, and facilitate better exchange of knowledge, information, and expertise from 'bench to bedside' and back again".*[149]

Methodologically, TM is an interdisciplinary field, but with the same focus as regards its ultimate research goal.[150] So far, a Law and Economic perspective has not been applied yet in TM and this thesis aims to close this research gap.[151]

---

when, for example, clinical observations lead to undertaking more fundamental research on earlier stages".

144 SOLOMON (2015), p. 8, about the *„Valey of Death".*

145 MITTRA (2013) and SOLOMON (2015) dedicate whole papers to the topic of finding a definition for TM.

146 MITTRA (2013), p. 103 and MITTRA & MILNE (2013), p. 3-5. For the history of TM cf. MITTRA & MILNE (2013), *chapter* 1.1; and KRAFT in MITTRA & MILNE (2013), *chapter* 2, p. 20 f.

147 MITTRA & MILNE (2013), p. 4; and similarly MITTRA (2013), p. 111. Cf. also MITTRA (2013), with an empirical approach demonstrating the different meanings of TM to different stakeholders; and EUROPEAN PATENT INSTITUTE (2015), p. 1; and SOLOMON (2015), p. 1.

148 SOLOMON (2015), p. 1. E.g., topics related to the application of new findings of basic science on humans, cf. SNOL – editor of the *Journal of Translational Medicine* - cited MITTRA & MILNE (2013), p. 5-6.

149 MITTRA & MILNE (2013), p. 6. Similarly the EUROPEAN PATENT INSTITUTE (2015), p. 3.

150 MITTRA & MILNE (2013), p. 6.

151 Cf. previous Chapter 5.2 Application of established methodology in new context, p. 15 ff.

7 Underlying assumption

This thesis is based on a central underlying assumption. It assumes that *the translation of PM into clinical practice is a normative goal.*

PM has the potential to save healthcare costs due to prevention, more accurate diagnoses, the elimination of unnecessary treatments, the reduction of adverse drug reactions and the higher effectiveness of personalized approaches.[152] However, PM is also regarded with skepticism and is claimed to raise healthcare costs and to set the wrong public health priorities.[153] This thesis assumes that PM's benefits outweigh its costs and that there are areas in PM that offer the opportunity to significantly contribute to the well-being of our society without compromising on the costs side.[154]

[152] Cf. Part II Chapter 2 Goals of personalized medicine, p. 67 ff.

[153] Cf. Part II Chapter 4 Criticism towards personalized medicine, p. 92 ff.

[154] For studies examining the economic value of PM, cf. Part II Chapter 3 Economic value of personalized medicine, p. 72 ff. For an overview of the empirical evidence cf. *Annex* 2.

8 Scope

8.1 *In scope:* Non-science related institutional barriers to the translation of personalized medicine into clinical practice

This thesis understands a *"barrier"* as a fact that provides a disincentive to foster the translation of PM for at least one of the stakeholders in the PM ecosystem. This scope implies that the identified incentives in this thesis' incentives analyses are negative per definition.

This thesis focuses solely on the identification and reduction of *non-science related, institutional barriers* to the translation of PM.[155] *"Institutional"* understood as related to institutions as previously described – including internal and external institutions.[156]

"*Institutional"* barriers are in contrast to *"science related"* barriers, meaning a lack of understanding in natural sciences about the fundamental basic science underlying the clinical applications in PM (e.g., understanding of genom-disease interactions).[157]

This thesis indends to provide a mutually exclusive, collectively exhaustive collection of *all* non-science related institutional barriers to the translation of PM, the incentives they provoke for the involved stakeholders and policy levers for their reduction.

8.2 *In scope:* Geographic focus on Switzerland in applied part

Although Part III's theoretical famework and the resulting hypotheses are of general value and may be tested for in the context of different countries, this thesis' applied Part IV focuses on the identification of barriers to the translation of PM and the respective policy levers to reduce them in Switzerland.

---

155 This thesis uses the expression *non-science related/institutional barriers* interchangeably. Other terminologies for "institutional barriers" are found in the relevant literature, e.g., *impediments, obstacles, hindering factors* to the adoption of PM; *societal* barriers, HOOD & AUFFRAY (2013), p. 1; or *institutional/social/political* boundaries in DIETEL (2016), p. 152; or *translational* hurdles, DAVID PETTITT ET AL. (2016), p. 2; or policy barriers in MESSNER ET AL. (2016), p. 1 ff.

156 Cf. previous Chapter 6.2.1 Definition of institutions, p. 21 f.

157 Cf. Part II Chapter 1.3.1 Tapping new scientific potential, p. 62.

8.3 *Out of scope:* Direct-to-consumer tests (DTCs)

This thesis focuses on PM applications consisting of a diagnostic and a pharmaceutical component involving the support of a healthcare provider.[158] Out of scope are *direct-to-consumer tests (DTCs)* which are accessible for everybody and which are directly distributed to consumers – predominantly via online channels – without a genetic consultation by a professional.[159]

Available DTCs vary in terms of offered services. Some tests are rather *lifestyle* products and offer personalized nutrition or wellness coaching (e.g., weight-loss, or fitness counseling) based on a person's genetic profile.[160] Some tests rather satisfy a consumer's *curiosity* (e.g., ancestry information).[161] Others do deliver *medically relevant data* (e.g., risk assessments for certain diseases).[162] More questionable may be DTC offerings which claim to be able to choose the "right" partner based on genetic information.[163]

The most prominent DTC test provider may be 23ANDME. The company was in the news in 2013 because the FDA halted their health-related DTC services by sending a warning letter. The warning letter explained that the company must obtain the agency's authorization for each of the tests health-related uses. The FDA expressed concerns about delivering health-related results directly to customers.[164] In 2017, the FDA has granted premarket authorization for ten genetic health-related reports from 23ANDME.[165]

DTC tests raise questions involving privacy protection, data security, the regulation of access to genomic information, the nature of what constitutes a medical test and patients' understanding of genetic information. Also the quality control of the

---

158 Cf. Part I Chapter 1.2 PM's underlying mechanism, p. 43.

159 ECKHARDT ET AL. (2014), p. 116; FELIX GUTZWILLER & BLANK (2014), p. 2 and dispatch for the D-GUMG, p. 10 f. HENGGELER & MATYAS (2017), *fig.* 1, p. 15, stressing and illustrating the differences between DTCs and genetic tests initiated by a medical doctor.

160 E.g., https://ubiome.com/, https://www.dnafit.com/, https://www.arivale.com/, https://www.daytwo.com/ (last visited July 17, 2017).

161 E.g., https://www.ancestry.com/dna/ or also https://www.23andme.com (last visited July 17, 2017).

162 E.g., https://www.veritasgenetics.com/, or https://www.23andme.com (last visited July 17, 2017). The offering differs between the US (only ancestry information available) and the UK (health relevant information still available).

163 E.g., http://www.genepartner.com/ (last visited July 17, 2017).

164 ZETTLER, SHERKOW, & GREELY (2014), p. 493.

165 FDA (2017), *na.*

DTC tests is questioned.[166] An example illustrating that certain criticism concerning the quality of DTC tests may be justified provides PEIKOFF (2013). She is a reporter for *The New York Times* and had her DNA analized (SNP genotyped) by three different DTC companies, with discordant risk predictions identified for several diseases.

Although DTC tests face criticism, consumers' demand is increasing. *"The digital and genomic eras ushered in an elevated public desire for health information"*.[167] The development are described as the start of a gradual transition towards more "user-centered" healthcare delivery[168] and as being part of a growing *"deprofessionalization"* of the medical doctor, in which the medical professional is no longer gatekeeper of services.[169]

The parallel developments of increasing criticism and at the same time increasing demand for DTC tests are described as "culture war": *"Accusations of paternalism on the one hand or recklessness on the other risk igniting a culture war"*.[170]

In *Switzerland*, DTCs tests providing medical information are banned. It is currently debated to what extend the GUMG should allow an excemption from the ban for lifestyle DTC tests with non-medically relevant information.[171] However, Swiss consumers can circumvent Swiss law by purchasing DTCs from foreign providers. National law has no means to set quality standards or to ban the test of foreign providers,[172] except from regulations about its marketing in Switzerland.[173]

8.4 *Out of scope:* Prenatal tests

Although personalized medicine has potential to be applied to unborn life, genetic prenatal tests testing for an unborn's genetic abnormalities, health risks or other genetic traits are not the primary focus of this thesis.

166 EVANS & GREEN (2009), p. 568; FELIX GUTZWILLER & BLANK (2014), p. 2.
167 OECD (2017), p. 170.
168 AKHMETOV & BUBNOV (2015), p. 3.
169 ROSE (2013), p. 347.
170 J. P. EVANS & GREEN (2009), p. 568.
171 Cf. dispatch for the D-GUMG, p. 11-12 and 34.
172 E.g., ECKHARDT ET AL. (2014), p. 118-119.
173 Cf. Art. 14 D-GUMG and dispatch for the D-GUMG, p. 78-79.

8.5 *Out of scope:* Ethical challenges in the context of personalized medicine

For the successful translation of personalized medicine into clinical practice, ethical challenges need to be discussed and tackled.[174] Any policy levers might be ineffective, if ethical concerns of the population are not taken into account. Ethical concerns might differ from country to country and from culture to culture. In the case of PM ethical questions can particularly involve the following themes:

Privacy, confidentiality and discrimination

Legal aspects around privacy, confidentiality and discrimination[175] give rise to ethical questions like *"What uses of a patient's genetic data are permissible? And, by whom?"* [176] Also the familial nature of genetic information must be discussed: Although the decision to choose a genetic test is the decision of the individual patient, the results necessarily affect family members who might be at risk for the same disease. Should these risks now be communicated to family members? Should the potential risks to other family members to be taken into consideration during genetic testing processes?[177]

Fairness and access to treatment

PM can identify patients who are likely to respond to a particular medicine. This offers the possibility to rule out patients for whom the medicine is not likely to be effective. Ethical questions that need to be addressed in this context are: *"What happens if there are no alternatives?", "Should the person still receive the only medicine available, even if that medicine is likely to cause severe side effects or even adverse reactions?"* or *"What happens if, conversely, the predictive information provided by the biomarker is perhaps not accurate enough and deprives the patient of access to life-saving treatments?"*[178]

---

174 *Sources stressing ethical issues' importance:* J. COHEN (2012), p. 752; HARVEY ET AL. (2012) p. 631; BOMBARD (2015), p. 58; HORGAN ET AL. (2014), p. 291; PERSONALIZED MEDICINE COALITION (2014), p. 40; ZIMMERMANN and PFLEIDERER in KLUSMAN & VAYENA (2016), p. 167 ff. and p. 179 ff.

175 Cf. Part III, Chapter 5.5 Privacy concerns regarding the use of personalized medicine, p. 178 ff.

176 N. COHEN & FRANGIOSA (2008), *Chapter* 6.4.2; and J. COHEN (2012), p. 752.

177 TUTTON (2013), p. 191.

178 FELIX GUTZWILLER & BLANK (2014), p. 2; and KIEVITS ET AL. (2014), p. 15.

Incidental findings

Additional ethical questions concern the "the incidentalome". In which cases should incidental or secondary findings from genetic tests be reported and communicated to patients?[179]

Patient autonomy & self-responsibility

PM changes the relationships between knowledge producers and knowledge recipients in healthcare. Patients are usually the owner of their genetic information. There need to be discussions on how to best accommodate these changes into existing institutional settings.

For example, questions about the need for new instruments for research ethics need to be adressed in instances where patients start organizing their own clinical studies, or contribute genetic and phenotypic information for research via commercial online testing services.[180]

The availability of genetic information to patients raises questions about the self-responsibility of patients. For example, has a person to take specific actions knowing the own genomic profile? Does a person or society have to bear the consequences for not having taken this specific action indicated by a patient's genomic profile?[181]

This thesis will not explicitly discuss ethical challenges arising in the context of PM. Reference is made to existing literature.[182] However, as boundaries between ethical and legal aspects are blurred, this thesis will discuss ethical challenges as far as they are captured by law.

---

179 RIPPE ET AL. (2004),p. 104, about *"Überschussinformation"*; MCCARTHY, MCLEOD, & GINSBURG (2013), p. 11; PASIC, SAMAAN, & YOUSEF (2013), p. 162-165; KIEVITS ET AL. (2014), p. 15; RELLING & EVANS (2015), p. 349; and DAVID PETTITT ET AL. (2016), p. 327.

180 For examples Cf. HARVEY ET AL. (2012) p. 631.

181 SCHLEIDGEN & MARCKMANN (2013), p. 228.

182 E.g., WERTZ ET AL. (2003); FLECK (2012); BRAUN, RIED, & DABROCK (2013); SCHLEIDGEN & MARCKMANN (2013); VOLLMANN (2013); CHADWICK (2014); DUSTER (2015); PRAINSACK (2015); BRALL & SCHRÖDER-BÄCK (2016) focusing on ethical issues surrounding scarce resources and rationalisation and their impact on PM taking an utilitarian, libertarian perspective and a capability approach.; GOTTWALD & HUSTER (2016); GRONOWICZ (2016), p. 151-164; and P. SALARI & LARIJANI (2017).

9 Structure

The following figure provides an overview of this thesis' structure and its corresponding results per Part:

Part	Results
PART I **Definitions & terminologies**	- Definition of personalized medicine - Explanation of common terminologies used in the context of PM
PART II **Context**	- Description of past, present and future developments in PM - Analysis of PM's economic value and criticism - Presentation of PM's ecosystem
PART III **Theoretical part**	- Identification of barriers to the translation of personalized medicine into clinical practice - Incentives per stakeholder per barrier - Hypotheses
PART IV **Applied part**	- Institutional setting governing each barrier in Switzerland - Incentives per stakeholder per barrier and comparison to theoretical Part III - Tested hypotheses
PART V **Policy implications**	- Policy levers in order to reduce the identified barriers to the translation of PM in Switzerland - Evaluation of policy levers
Conclusion	- Summary of the findings - Theoretical and practical contributions - Limitations and future research potential

Table 3: Structure of thesis

Part I: Definitions & terminologies

Overview of terminologies used in the context of personalized medicine

Part I defines the relevant terminologies used in this thesis in order to enable a reader with limited exposure to the concept of personalized medicine to understand the content of the thesis and to follow its line of argumentation.

First, the broad spectrum of definitions for "personalized medicine" and this thesis' definition for personalized medicine (PM) are presented *(Chapter 1)*. Second, the concept of PM involves not only a pharmaceutical but also always a diagnostic component. Several different categories of personalized medicine diagnostics (PM Dx) exist *(Chapter 2)*. Finally, some commonly used terminologies – namely biomarkers, biobanks and next generation sequencing – in the context of PM are explained *(Chapter 3)*.[183]

[183] An alternative glossary for the context of PM can also be found in FDA (2013), p. 58-59.

K. Bosshard, *Law and Economics of Personalized Medicine*,
Gesundheitsmanagement und Gesundheitsökonomik,
https://doi.org/10.1007/978-3-658-22074-7_2

1 Definition of personalized medicine

1.1 Different understandings of personalized medicine

A reader who is not familiar with the term "personalized medicine" may ask if any part of medicine is not personalized at all since the individual case has always been paramount in a patient-doctor relationship. This understanding is hopefully correct. However, the term "personalized medicine" is polysemous, and is frequently used without defining a theoretical and methodological background.[184] A whole continuum of understandings exists, in which three main positions can be identified:[185]

Figure 4: Spectrum of understanding of the term "personalized medicine"

SOURCE: Illustrated by the author with inputs from SCHLEIDGEN, KLINGLER, BERTRAM, ROGOWSKI, & MARCKMANN (2013), p. 1.

This thesis follows the understanding of the third category. PM does not literally mean the creation of drugs that are unique to each patient, but rather *"the ability to classify individuals into sub-populations that differ in their susceptibility to a particular disease or their response to a specific treatment"*.[186]

Technologically new sources of data[187] enable the transition away from the traditional "one-size-fits-all" type of therapeutic regimen to the type of regimen that enables healthcare providers to select a treatment that targets those patients that are

184 A. EVERS ET AL. (2012), p. 301.

185 For more information about the categories "Nothing new" and "holistic healthcare", cf. TUTTON (2012), p. 1721; and SCHLEIDGEN ET AL. (2013), p. 1.

186 J. COHEN (2012), p. 752.

187 MECKLEY & NEUMANN (2010) contains a framework for categorizing PM technologies.

most likely to respond.[188] PM does not refer to a specific technology. It is rather a group of technologies which make use of molecular techniques to detect, manage or predict diseases.[189]

Also within the latter category in the illustration above, the understanding of PM varies and there is no consensus about one definition.[190] REDEKOP & MLADSI (2013), SCHLEIDGEN ET AL. (2013), POKORSKA-BOCCI ET AL. (2014), GUCHET (2015) and PAOLO, SARKOZY, RYLL, & SIEBERT (2017) dedicated each a study to the term "personalized medicine" and examine the different aspects of the definitions for PM more extensively than this thesis in the following.

An often heard, simple but broad definition of PM is the delivery of *"the right treatment, for the right patient, at the right time"*.[191] More specific is the definition by the EU COUNCIL (2015): *"Personalised medicine refers to a medical model using characterisation of individuals' phenotypes and genotypes (e.g., molecular profiling, medical imaging, lifestyle data) for tailoring the right therapeutic strategy for the right person at the right time, and/or to determine the predisposition to disease and/or to deliver timely and targeted prevention"*.[192] The PERSONALIZED MEDICINE COALITION's understanding of PM is the following: *"Personalized medicine is an evolving field in which physicians use diagnostic tests to determine which medical treatments will work best for each patient. By combining the data from those tests with an individual's medical history, circumstances and values, health care providers can develop targeted treatment and prevention plans"*.[193]

188 TUTTON (2012), p. 1721; BRANZÉN (2013) p. 21; and DAVID PETTITT ET AL. (2016), p. 320.

189 MECKLEY & NEUMANN (2010), p. 91.

190 *Other discussions about the definition for PM:* EUROPEAN SCIENCE FOUNDATION (2012), p. 7; HARVEY ET AL. (2012), p. 626; FAULKNER ET AL. (2012), p. 1162; SAMS (2012), p. 10; BRANZÉN (2013) p. 21 f.; FDA (2013), p. 7; MÖLL in WIENKE, DIERKS, & JANKE (2013), p. 30; PERSONALIZED MEDICINE COALITION (2013), p. 3; SCHÄFER & MÜLLER in WIENKE ET AL. (2013), p. 13-15; SCHLEIDGEN ET AL. (2013), p. 225; VOLLMANN (2013), p. 235 f.; ECKHARDT ET AL. (2014), *chapter* 1.2; HORGAN ET AL. (2014), p. 287; EBERBACH (2014), p. 455 f.; JAMES (2014), p. 81, with a discussion of the term "personalized"; DUFFY (2015), p. 3, presents a number of concepts of PM; HALECKER, KAMPRATH & BRAUN in EPPINGER ET AL. (2015), p. 9 f.; JAMESON & LONGO (2015), p. 2229; KEIL (2015), p. 8 f.; MARSCHALL & FLESSA in EPPINGER ET AL. (2015), p. 303; MILNE & COHEN (2015)b, p. 1; NICHOLSON PRICE (2015), p. 9 ff.; ROGOWSKI ET AL. (2015), p. 2; DUFFY (2015), p. 1; DZAU ET AL. (2015), p. 2118; ESTAPE ET AL. (2016), p. 11; KICHKO ET AL. (2016), p. 1; SNYDER (2016), p. 1; and THOMAS, KIERMAIER, & CANNARILE (2016), p. 347.

191 FACKLER & MCGUIRE (2010), p. 1. Similarly the FDA (2013), p. 6, describing PM as providing *"the right patient with the right drug at the right dose at the right time"*.

192 COUNCIL OF THE EUROPEAN UNION (2015), C 421/03.

193 PMC (2015), p. 6.

The understandings of PM regarding the *type of patient data* that is used for a PM decision making range from the use of only genetic information and/or other "omics" information[194] to the inclusion of behavioral data. Some – including the definitions above – have a *broader* understanding of PM as the general possibility of taking new sources and quantities of health data into account for patient care and disease prevention (e.g., molecular data, "omics" data, disease phenotypes, behavioral health data).[195] More *narrow* definitions understand PM as choosing a medical treatment based on the use of only molecular[196] or genetic data (*genetic or genome-based medicine*).[197]

The understandings of PM do also differ regarding the *point of time* of a PM invervention. Some definitions emphasize the *preventive character* of PM as certain genetic biomarkers measure the suspectibility for a disease for a person, for which an individual can arrange the respective preventive measures. Others emphasize the *diagnostic character* of PM as some genetic biomarkers measure the likelihood of effectiveness of a drug in case of a disease.[198]

Several terms can be used interchangeably with this thesis' understanding of PM, others are closely related to PM but slightly different in their meaning:[199]

---

194 For an explanation of "omics", cf. Part I Chapter 3.1.3 „Omics"-based biomarkers, p. 50 f.

195 E.g., MEIER-ABT in MEIER-ABT & EGLI (2016); similarly is PM defined as *"[refining] our understanding of disease prediction and risk, onset and progression in patients, informing better selection and development of evidence-based targeted therapies and associated diagnostics. Disease treatment and other interventions are better targeted to take into account the patient's genomic and other biological characteristics, as well as health status, medications patients are already prescribed and environmental and lifestyle factors"*, cf. INNOVATE UK (2016) cited in OECD (2017), p. 22.

196 E.g., MOCH at the ETH LATSIS Forum on June 29th, 2016: *"Personalized Medicine is about using additional information compared to the information we see since 100 years in the microscope. It is about therapeutic decisions based on molecular data".*

197 E.g., RIPPE ET AL. (2004), p. 24; HANDSCHIN & MEYER (2012), p. 430, describing four stages of PM; K. SALARI ET AL. (2012), p. 1; MÖLL in WIENKE ET AL. (2013), p. 30; and MOOSER (2014), p. 567.
Similarly argued SZUCS and BEERENWINKEL at the ETH LATSIS Forum on June 29th, 2016: *"Personalized Medicine is about using and managing the data from genomic medicine".*

198 E.g., ABPI (2014), p. 1; and GRECH, SCERRI, SCERRI, & CESUROGLU (2015), p. 7. Critics argue that it is a mistake to equate PM with genetic medicine, because this diverts attention away from the broader application of personalized approaches to healthcare delivery, cf. SIMMONS, DINAN, ROBINSON, & SNYDERMAN (2012), p. 89. They claim that the lack of a common definition is hindering the translation of PM.

199 DUFFY (2015), p. 3, with an overview for the origins of the closely related terms (PGt/PGx, Systems Medicine, P4 Medicine, etc.).

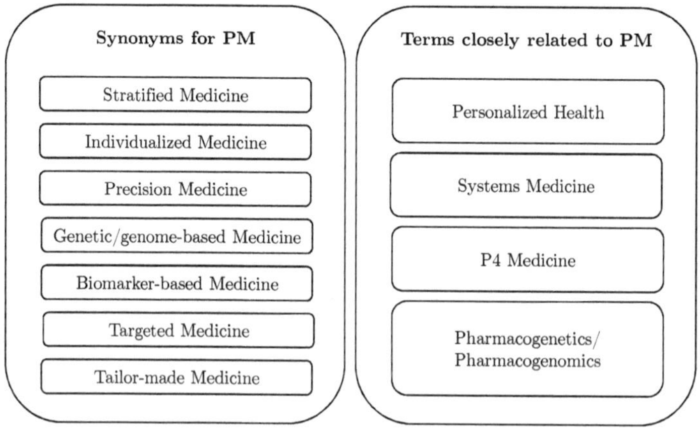

Figure 5: Synonyms for personalized medicine and closely related terms

1.1.1 Synonyms for personalized medicine

Synonymously used for PM is the term *"Stratified Medicine"*. A term which might be more precise in describing the ultimate meaning of PM.[200] "Stratification"[201] can be understood as the core element of PM. It refers to the molecular sub-classification of disease and disease susceptibility division of patients based on a shared biomarker. Patients within a sub-group respond better to a particular drug or are at decreased risk of side effects in response to a certain treatment.[202]

Often, also the terms *"Precision Medicine"* or *"Individualized Medicine"* are used synonymously with PM. However, some scholars define them even more narrowly than "Stratified Medicine", arguing that individualized medicine is tailored to one unique individual only instead of a stratified approach targeting a sub-group.[203]

A GOOGLE TRENDS analysis demonstrates that the term "precision medicine" overtook the use of the term "personalized medicine" at the beginning 2015, probably due

200 Cf. CHATAWAY, FRY, MARJANOVIC, & YAQUB (2012), p. 732.

201 Stemming from the latin words *"stratum"* (layer) and *"facere"* (to do).

202 E.g., FDA (2013), p. 8.

203 Cf. Part II Chapter 1.2.2 National and international personalized medicine initiatives, p. 59 ff.

to former US President BARACK OBAMA announcing the "Precision Medicine Initiative".[204]

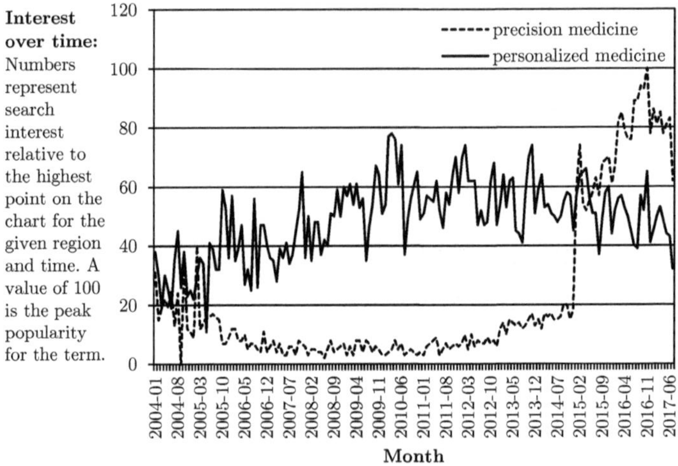

Figure 6: Comparison of terms "personalized medicine" vs "precision medicine" over time

SOURCE: Google trends analysis, performed on July 5, 2017.

1.1.2 Closely related terms

Personalized Health

The concept of *"Personalized Health"* includes PM, but goes beyond the concept of PM. Personalized Health aims to use scientific findings from personal data (e.g., genomics and other -omics data, clinical data from hospitals and primary care, data from biobanks or health data collected by individuals themselves) in order to achieve added value for the population at large and not only the individual. The data should

[204] However, BRALL & SCHRÖDER-BÄCK (2016), p. 179, make the same distinction between personalized and stratified medicine: *"While stratified medicine labels the approach that defines certain subpopulations at the cohort level according to shared biomarkers, personalised medicine aims to focus on the individual patient 'using omics and related tech- nologies (e.g., imaging) and based on computer models and simulations'. Combining omics and technologies such as imaging is expected to achieve the greatest potential for personalised medicine"*. Similarly make TRUSHEIM, BERNDT, & DOUGLAS (2007), p. 287, a difference between Stratified and Individualized Medicine. Similarly distinguish DAVID PETTITT ET AL. (2016), p. 320, between Stratified and Precision Medicine, but with Precision Medicine meaning an approach focusing on a unique individual.

make it possible to recognise health risks at an early stage and develop appropriate health strategies.[205]

Systems Medicine

The term *"Systems Medicine"* describes the application of Systems Biology approaches to medical research and drug development.[206] Thus, Systems Medicine describes rather the approach of how to make discoveries that are used in PM than PM itself. *Systems Biology* aims at the quantitative analysis and predictive mathematical modeling at all levels of biological organization. It *"targets networks, cells, organs and complete organisms by integrating experimental data with computational and theoretical approaches. It thus combines concepts from different scientific disciplines to obtain a quantitative understanding of complex biological systems in terms of their components and interactions".*[207] Systems biology departs from the „old" understanding of static one-dimensional cause-effect relationships between DNA leading to a incorrect expression of a gene. It understands cells as complex and dynamic interactions with a "social behavior" – explained by AEBERSOLD for non-scientists in an expert interview for this thesis.[208]

P4 Medicine

Often heard in the context of PM is the expression *"P4 Medicine"*. The term stands for *predictive, preventive, personalized and participatory medicine.*[209] Although the concept of P4 Medicine goes beyond the concept of PM, it is often misleadingly used as a synonym for PM.[210] The fourth "P" standing for *"participative"* reflects the increasing involvement of patients in their own health through social networks.[211] P4 Medicine describes the transformation of how medicine is already – or will be practiced in the near future – with the convergence of patient-activated social networks, technology providing "big data" and their analytics, and systems medicine. P4 Medicine rests upon the assumption of five fundamental megatrends inducing a change of how healthcare is being practiced: Big data, bigger cost effectiveness (from targeting symtoms to causes), biomedical innovation (systems medicine), a change in delivery

---

205 SAMS (2017)a, *personalized health.*

206 E.g., HOOD (2013), p. 4.

207 ETH (2017)c, *systems medicine.*

208 E.g., HOOD (2013), p. 4.

209 Exploratory interview with RUDOLPH AEBERSOLD on May 10, 2015.

210 E.g., GALLI (2016) using P4 Medicine as synonym to PM.

211 C.f. HOOD & AUFFRAY (2013), p. 1-4, about *"Participatory Medicine"*. An example for Participatory Medicine is www.patientslikeme.com (last visited August 11, 2017), more in HARVEY ET AL. (2012), p. 630.

of healthcare and the growth of the "wellness" industry.[212] P4 medicines main thesis is that the focus of medicine will be shifted from disease to wellness.[213]

Pharmacogenomics & Pharmacogenetics

Pharmacogenomics and pharmacogenetics are sub-areas of PM, and are part of predictive genetics.[214] In practical terms, they are the *"study of variations of DNA and RNA characteristics as related to drug response".*[215] In many publications the terms Pharmacogenomics and Pharmacogenetics are used interchangeably while others distinguish between the two concepts. The clear distinction is disputed.[216] This thesis primarily uses the broader term PGx following EMEA's definition:

Pharmacogenomics (PGx) is defined by the EMEA as *"the study of variability of the expression of individual genes relevant to disease susceptibility as well as drug response at cellular, tissue, individual or population level. The term is broadly applicable to drug design, discovery, and clinical development".*[217] PGx is the broader term than pharmacogenetics. It describes the examination of the whole genome and the different expressions of genes or their mutations, primarily with regards to the devel-

---

212 E.g., FLORES, GLUSMAN, BROGAARD, & HOOD (2013), p. 565 f.

213 *"The convergence of patient-activated social networks, big data and their analytics, and systems medicine has led to a P4 Medicine that is predictive, preventive, personalized, and participatory. Medicine will focus on each individual. It will become proactive in nature. It will increasingly focus on wellness rather than disease. For example, in 10 years each patient will be surrounded by a virtual cloud of billions of data points, and we will have the tools to reduce this enormous data dimensionality into simple hypotheses about how to optimize wellness and avoid disease for each individual. P4 medicine will be able to detect and treat perturbations in healthy individuals long before disease symptoms appear, thus optimizing the wellness of individuals and avoiding disease. P4 medicine will 1) improve health care, 2) reduce the cost of health care, and 3) stimulate innovation and newcompany creation"*, cf. HOOD (2013), for more details, see p. 11 f. Cf. also JAKKA & ROSSBACH (2013), p. 2 and 6.

214 GRECH, SCERRI, ET AL. (2015), p. 2.

215 FDA (2013), p. 8.

216 Two „schools" emerged – the academic and the public discussion: The academic school sees the distinction in the methods. The aim is always the optimization of the drug efficacy at an individual patient. PGt directly examines the role of the genetic variation in the drug efficacy, whereas PGx additionally studies gene expression patterns or RNA profiles closer to the protein- or enzyme level. The public school sees the distinction in the aim. PGt aims to treat patients, whereas PGx aims at the choice and development of drugs. Cf. RIPPE ET AL. (2004), p. 19-20. Further discussions about the distinction in SWEN ET AL. (2007), p. 1318, or THOMAS ET AL. (2016), p. 349.
Other authors defining PGx and/or PGt: HOPKINS ET AL. (2006), p. 403; FACKLER & MCGUIRE (2010) with a definition of PGx as one of three core elements of PM, p. 4 ff.; J. COHEN (2012), p. 751; K. SALARI ET AL. (2012), p. 1; HORGAN ET AL. (2014), p. 288; U. A. MEYER (2015); RELLING & EVANS (2015), p. 343 ff. including history and examples of PGx and other terminologies; ESTAPE ET AL. (2016), p. 11 with PGx examples; JOHAL & AMLANI (2016), p. 1; SNYDER (2016), p. 67; ALANAZI (2017), p. 18-19.

217 EMEA cited in RIPPE ET AL. (2004), p. 20.

opment of therapeutics.[218] PGx relates to three aspects: 1. The variability on the genome-level (i. e., PGt), 2. The effects of pharmaceuticals on gene expression and 3. the identification of new target structures for pharmaceuticals.[219] PGx is described as *"one of the first clinical applications of the postgenomic era"*[220] or as *"one of the leading and potentially most actionable areas of the personalized medicine paradigm"*[221] and as a historical starting point of PM.[222]

Pharmacogenetics (PGt) is defined by the EMEA as *"the study of interindividual variations in DNA sequence related to drug response"*.[223] It examines genetic factors which are responsible for individual differences in the response to drugs. It is limited to the examintation of the genetic profile and the efficacy and effectiveness of drugs. The aim of PGt is the optimization of a therapy through the choice and dosing based on an individual's genetic profile in order to increase ist efficacy and to reduce adverce events.[224] PGx can concern germline or somatic mutations.[225]

1.2 PM's underlying mechanism

Crucial for the understanding of PM's underlying mechanism and this thesis is the fact that PM generally involves the use of two medical products: A diagnostic device in order to measure a biomarker (PM Dx)[226] and the pharmaceutical component (Rx). The two components may or may not be developed, manufactured and distributed by the same provider.

---

218 THOMAS ET AL. (2016), p. 349.
219 RIPPE ET AL. (2004), p. 10.
220 SWEN ET AL. (2007), p. 1317.
221 SCOTT (2011), p. 2-3, with a whole chapter on the history of PGx, p.3-5.
222 GUCHET (2015), *note* 57 ff. and DIETER SCHNEIDER & BUBLAK (2015), p. 416.
223 EMEA cited in RIPPE ET AL. (2004), p. 20.
224 RIPPE ET AL. (2004), p. 19-20.
225 THOMAS ET AL. (2016), p. 349.
226 For definitions *cf.* following Chapters 2.1 Personalized medicine diagnostics, p. 45, and 2.2 Companion diagnostics, p. 45.

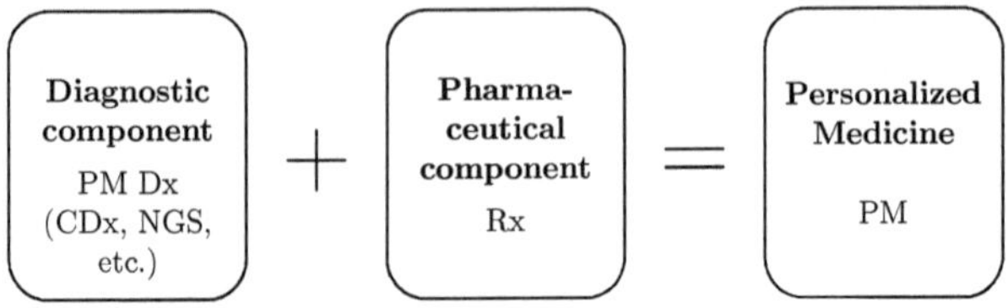

Figure 7: Components of personalized medicine

1.3 Working definition of personalized medicine

This thesis has the following understanding of PM: *Personalized medicine refers to a medical model using characterisation of individuals' phenotypes and genotypes for tailoring the right therapeutic strategy for the right person at the right time, and/or to determine the predisposition to disease and/or to deliver timely and targeted prevention. PM involves two components: a diagnostic test and a targeted treatment or prevention plan.*

Although other terms like "Precision Medicine" or "Stratified Medicine" might be more precise in the description of the concept, this thesis uses the term "Personalized Medicine" as is it seems to be the most established term.

This thesis' understanding of *"PM"* or a *"PM application"* refers to both components of the Rx-CDx combination, whereas the "*drug/pharmaceutical/Rx component*" and the "*CDx/PM DX/diagnostic component*" refer to the single components in a PM application.

This theses does neither understand PM as the production of any medical treatment from cells of a patient nor as the development of medical devices for individuals – both sometimes denoted as the "purest form" of PM.[227]

[227] Cf. DIETER SCHNEIDER & BUBLAK (2015), p. 416.

2 Terminologies used for personalized medicine diagnostics

2.1 Personalized medicine diagnostics

Diagnostic tests are central for PM. PM Dx can be developed as CDx or as stand-alone tests for diagnostic or prognostic purposes.[228] CDx (more details below) are a special sub-group of in vitro diagnostics among the different technologies shaping the PM spectrum as they are associated with a *specific* class of drugs. Besides CDx, other tests determine biomarkers (e.g., NGS, PGx or other molecular tests).

This thesis uses the broader term personalized medicine diagnostics (PM Dx) for all categories of tests related to PM.

2.2 Companion diagnostics

Simply stated, CDx are the diagnostic components in PM which determine the likelihood if a patient responds to a specific drug.[229] They create the difference in value between a traditional "one-size-fits-all" approach as they identify a patient sub-population having a differential expected clinical response PM.[230] CDx are the *"decisive stratification factor"* or the *"gatekeeper"* for PM.[231]

According to the definition in the revised EU IVD guideline, CDx are *"essential for defining patients' eligibility for specific treatment with a medicinal product through the quantitative or qualitative determination of specific markers identifying subjects at a higher risk of developing an adverse reaction to the medicinal product in question or identifying patients in the population for whom the therapeutic product has been adequately studied, and found safe and effective. Such biomarker or biomarkers can be present in healthy subjects and/or in patients".*[232]

The FDA defines CDx as a medical device, often an in vitro device, which provides information that is essential for the safe and effective use of a corresponding drug or biological product. The FDA describes four use cases for CDx:[233]

---

228 MILLER ET AL. (2011), p. 137.
229 Cf. previous Chapter 1.2 PM's underlying mechanism, p. 43.
230 TRUSHEIM & BERNDT (2015)b, p. 2 and 9.
231 OLSEN & TRØST JØRGENSEN (2014), p. 1, they also provide a historical background of CDx.
232 IVDR, p. 177. For the definition of „biomarkers" cf. the following Chapter 3.1 Biomarker, p. 49 ff.
233 FDA (2014)a, p. 7.

1. CDx can identify patients who are *most likely to benefit* from the therapeutic product;
2. CDx can identify patients likely to be at increased *risk for serious adverse reactions* as a result of treatment with the therapeutic product;
3. CDx can *monitor* response to treatment with the therapeutic product for the purpose of adjusting treatment (e.g., schedule, dose, discontinuation) to achieve improved safety or effectiveness;
4. CDx can identify patients in the population for whom the therapeutic product has been adequately studied, and found *safe and effective*, i.e., there is insufficient information about the safety and effectiveness of the therapeutic product in any other population.[234]

2.3 Categories of personalized medicine diagnostics

2.3.1 Diagnostic tests for somatic vs germline variations

Diagnostic tests for *somatic variations* refer to genetic variation (e.g., in a tumor). The variations are not inherited and may change over lifetime. Thus, multiple tests may be used in an individual's life time.[235]

Diagnostic tests for *germline variations* refer to inherited genetic variations, (e.g., SNPs affecting the function of proteins involved in drug metabolic pathways). These tests are PGx tests typically aimed at stratifying patient populations into sub-groups on the basis of clinical effectiveness or safety. It is sufficient to test only once in an individual's life time and can be viewed as an "asset" once done.[236] As soon as germline variations are not only used for diagnostic purposes, but also predictions are made based germline variations, the ethical, legal and social implications of the genetic testing increase.[237]

---

234 *More background about CDx:* MOORE, BABU, & COTTER (2012), p. 493; BYRON, CRABB, GEORGE, MARLOW, & NEWLAND (2014), p. 1469 on CDx (paper by NICE); OLSEN & TRØST JØRGENSEN (2014), p. 1 ff.; AGARWAL, SNYDER, & RESSLER (2015), p. 100 including a market overview; J. COHEN (2015), p. 5; TRUSHEIM & BERNDT (2015)b, p. 9.; HORGAN (2016), p. 130; PLUN-FAVREAU ET AL. (2016), p. 145; D. K. THOMPSON (2016), p. 1; and TERKOLA, ANTON, & POSTMA (2017), p. 1.

235 Explanation by SZUCS in an exploratory interview for this thesis on August 26th, 2015. Cf. also SHABARUDDIN, PAYNE, & FLEEMAN (2015), p. 115; and THOMAS ET AL. (2016), p. 349.

236 DAVID PETTITT ET AL. (2016). p. 324.

237 SZUCS (2015)b, p. 118.

2.3.2 Presymptomatic vs diagnostic tests

Generally, PM Dx tests can be separated into presymptomatic vs diagnostic tests.[238]

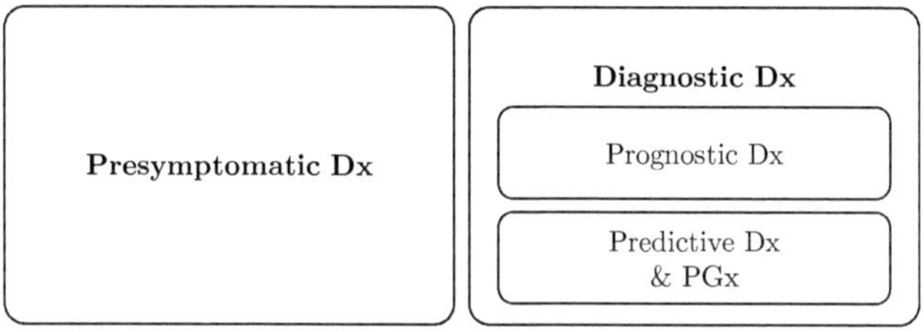

Figure 8: Categorization of personalized medicine diagnostics

Presymptomatic tests[239] aim to detect predispositions or risks for diseases. At the point of taking the test, there are no symptons yet and it is unclear if there may ever appear any symptoms. An example is the presymptomatic BRCA-test for breast cancer.[240]

Diagnostic genetic tests are used because of already existing symptoms. They can be further categorized into prognostic and predictive tests:

Prognostic tests assess the progression or aggressivess of a disease. They enable the natural course of an individual's cancer to be predicted, distinguishing good tumor outcome from poor tumor outcome.[241]

Predictive tests assess the probability that a patient will benefit from a particular treatment.[242] This thesis subsumes pharmacogenomic (PGx) tests also in this category as they assess the responses to medications and divide patients into those at risk of adverse events or those who respond differentially to medication doses. PGx tests are

238 E.g., ECKHARDT ET AL. (2014), p. 27.

239 Some authors do also call them "predisposition tests", e.g., MECKLEY & NEUMANN (2010), p. 92 or "predictive tests", e.g.,BRÄM & SZUCS (2016), p. 2.

240 E.g., MECKLEY & NEUMANN (2010), p. 92; FELIX GUTZWILLER & BLANK (2013), p. 630; and ECKHARDT ET AL. (2014), p. 27.

241 E.g., MECKLEY & NEUMANN (2010), p. 92; BRANZÉN (2013), p. 62; and FELIX GUTZWILLER & BLANK (2013), p. 630.

242 *Ibidem.*

not related to the underlying causes of disease and are only clinically relevant when patients are taking the specific drug in question.[243]

[243] Cf. Chapter 1.1.2 Closely related terms, *Pharmacogenomics & Pharmacogenetics*, p. 42 ff. *Other approaches to categorize PM Dx:* MECKLEY & NEUMANN (2010), p. 92; MCCARTHY ET AL. (2013), p. 3; PERSONALIZED MEDICINE COALITION (2013), p. 3; and SZUCS (2015)b, p. 93.

3 Other terminologies used in the context of personalized medicine

3.1 Biomarker

Simply stated, a biomarker can be any measurement values or procedures which support a diagnosis, a therapeutic decision or the therapeutic monitoring.[244] Diagnostic tests are used to identify and measure biomarkers.[245]

Often, the following, general definition of the US NATIONAL INSTITUTE OF HEALTH is used: *„A biomarker is a characteristic that is objectively measured and evaluated as an indicator of normal biologic process, pathogenic process or pharmacologic responses to a therapeutic intervention“.* [246]

The EUROPEAN COMMISSION (2013) defines a biomarker as *"an indicator of a biological state"*, subsequently follows the US NATIONAL INSTITUTE OF HEALTH*'s* definition and mentions that biomarkers can be used both in the medicine development process and for diagnostic, prognostic, monitoring and screening purposes.[247]

In a wider sense, a biomarker can be simple, like for example the blood glucose levels are a marker for diabetes or the blood cholesterol levels for heart disease. Even the size of a person can be a biomarker. In connection with PM, the term is predominantly used in more restrictive sense and molecular, biochemical or genetic ("omics"-)[248] biomarkers are meant.[249]

3.1.1 Categories

Biomarkers can be classified into the following sub-categories:[250]

- *Diagnostic biomarkers* assess or detect a specific disease as early as possible.
- *Susceptibility/risk biomarkers* assess or detect the risk of developing a disease.
- *Prognostic biomarkers* assess or detect the evolution of a disease.

244 U. A. MEYER (2015), p. 1.
245 J. COHEN (2015), p. 5.
246 US NATIONAL INSTITUTE OF HEALTH cited in EPPINGER ET AL. (2015), p. 320.
247 EUROPEAN COMMISSION (2013), p. 6.
248 Cf. following Subchapter 3.1.3 „Omics“-based biomarkers, p. 50 f.
249 MOOSER (2014), p. 570; J. COHEN (2015), p. 5; KEIL (2015), p. 9.
250 Classification scheme by the EUROPEAN COMMISSION (2013), p. 10.

- *Predictive biomarkers* assess or detect the response to and toxicity of a given treatment.
- *Surrogate biomarkers* substitute for a clinical endpoint (a trait that reflects a medical condition).[251]

3.1.2 Single Nucleotide Polymorphisms

Single Nucleotide Polymorphisms (SNPs)[252] are the most common type of genetic variation on germline DNA-building blocks among human beings. A "polymorphism" refers to a genetic variation which occurs in more than one percent of a healthy population.[253] SNPs may determine individual differences in drug responses.[254]

3.1.3 „Omics"-based biomarkers

PM is characterized through the use of biomarkers based on "omics" technologies.[255] The deciphering of the human genome sequence has contributed to the understanding of biological processes and several "omics" disciplines have emerged, like genomics, transcriptomics, epigenomics, proteomics, metabolomics, lipidomics, glycomics and others.[256]

"Omics" technologies measure data at the different levels of a living organism. It is a *"general term for a broad discipline in science and engineering for analysing the interactions of biological information objects in various 'omes' that include the genome, proteome, metabolome, transcriptome etc. Its main focus is on developing technologies and tools for gathering information on various classes of biomolecules and their ligands, and understanding relationships among them, including the related regulatory mechanisms".*[257]

Genomics is described as the most developed and closest to clinical application. But the information obtained from genomics needs to be considered in conjunction with the analysis of the functions of other classes of biomolecules. "Omics"

---

251 More about biomarkers: EUROPEAN COMMISSION (2013), p. 10 ff.; FRUEH (2013) with a historical background of biomarkers; MCCARTHY ET AL. (2013), p. 6, about "next generation biomarkers", e.g., multivariante index essays; MITTRA & MILNE (2013) (10), p. 131 ff.; KIEVITS ET AL. (2014), p. 6; CARRIGAN & KRAHN (2015) dedicate a book to biomarkers, their definition and technologies.

252 Pronounced "snips", see list of abbrevations.

253 HANDSCHIN & MEYER (2012), p. 428.

254 Many definitions in MICHEEL, NASS, & OMENN (2012), p. 285 ff.

255 ECKHARDT ET AL. (2014), p. XX.

256 For a more detailed explanation of the different "omics" technologies, cf. CRAWFORD & ASPINALL (2012), p. 265; MICHEEL ET AL. (2012), p. 1 ff; KEIL (2015), p. 8.

257 EUROPEAN COMMISSION (2013), p. 5.

technologies can *"provide that information in a high-throughput manner, providing a global view of molecular and cellular processes that have an impact on health and disease"*. The new disciplines contribute to the understanding of diseases at the molecular level and to the identification of new biomarkers as quantifiable parameters predictive of the development of a disease prognosis or medicine response or as targets for new treatments.[258]

3.2 Biobanks

Personalized medicine presumes an infrastructure allowing scientists to access health data from biobanks for conducting research. Biobanks *"collect biological samples and associated data for medical-scientic research and diagnostic purposes and organise these in a systematic way for use by others".* [259] Notwithstanding some shared features, the field of biobanking is heterogeneous.[260] There are several types of biobanks: private and public ones, population and disease related biobanks.[261]

Public biobanks are typically non-profit organications financed and managed by public institutions. Examples are the UK BIOBANK or the DANISH NATIONAL BIOBANK;[262] in Switzerland the BIOBANQUE INSTITUTIONELLE DE LAUSANNE (CHUV) or the tissue banks at the pathologic institutes at univerity hospitals (e.g., the LIQUID BIOBANK BERN, the TISSUE BANK BERN[263]).

Private biobanks are the collections of samples and data established by pharmaceutical companies and clinical research organizations, often stemming from clinical trials. Also comparably smaller biotech and life sciences companies or foundations may use private biobanks.[264] Although some private biobanks have commercial goals and sell their data for research purposes, most biobanks have a non-profit character. There are also *public-pivate-partnerships* operating biobanks.

In recent times, *patient-driven biobanks* emerged. People are starting to generate information on their biological status for themselves through "self tracking" of their

---

258 *Ibidem*, p. 6 and 8.

259 EUROPEAN COMMISSION (2012), p. 5.

260 *Ibidem*, p. 13.

261 The following descriptions stemm primarily from SWISS NATIONAL ADVISORY COMMISSION ON BIOMEDICAL ETHICS (2015), p. 12-13. The document contains more details on research-related biobanks – with a focus on Switzerland. Other documents discussing biobanks are KEIL (2015), p. 39; DANIEL SCHNEIDER ET AL. (2016), p. 163; THOMAS ET AL. (2016), p. 344.

262 Cf. also DANIEL SCHNEIDER ET AL. (2016), p. 163.

263 E.g., the SWISS SOCIETY FOR RHEUMATIC DISEASES manages a biobank with serum and DNA samples of rheumatic patients.

264 Cf. http://www.zlm.insel.ch/de/biobank-bern/ (last visited July 17, 2017)

physiological, environmental and lifestyle variables. Prominent examples are QUANTIFIED SELF[265] or 23ANDME.[266] The most prominent example in Switzerland is MYDATA.CH.[267]

A further distinction is made between *population* and *disease-related* biobanks. The former describes biobanks which collect samples of healthy and non-healthy subjects, whereas the latter do only collect samples of patients with a certain disease.

3.3 Next generation sequencing

Molecular diagnostic testing has undergone changes since the beginning of the twentyfirst century. Most in vitro diagnostics are typically intended to detect a limited number of predefined analytes to diagnose pre-specified diseases. *Next generation sequencing (NGS)* are faster and measure and sequence multiple fragments of the genome related to multiple conditions simultaneously. NGS-based tests often have broad intended uses. The types of variants and the nature of the clinical information that will be returned from these tests is often not known until after the test has been run.[268] The cost of generating a whole genome sequence have significantly decreased. Cost per genome sequencing are less than USD 1000.[269]

---

265 Cf. http://quantifiedself.com/ (last visited July 17, 2017)

266 Cf. https://www.23andme.com/ (last visited July 17, 2017)

267 Cf. https://midata.coop/ (last visited July 17, 2017)

268 STUDNEVA ET AL. (2015), p. 3, about the different methods in NGS; THE ACADEMY OF MEDICAL SCIENCES (2013), p. 20 ff. for a technological overview on NGS; FDA (2016)c, p. 2; and OECD (2017), p. 171.

269 E.g., VERITAS GENETICS offers a full genome sequencing for USD 999, cf. https://www.veritas-genetics.com/mygenome.(last visited July 5, 2017).

Part II: Context

Description of personalized medicine's impact on the healthcare landscape

Part II introduces the reader into the context of the emerging phenomenon of personalized medicine.

Chapter 1 sheds some light on PM's historical roots, its current applications and initiatives and provides an outlook of what future developments are expected to contribute the concept. The first chapter demonstrates that PM is not an empty "hype". Instead, it gives not only rise to "hope" to future applications, but is already concrete reality in certain areas of healthcare. *Chapter 2* provides an overview of how PM can add value to our current healthcare system. A separate *Chapter 3* is dedicated to the measurement of this value. It illustrates the existing approaches and challenges to assess the value of PM. *Chapter 4* gives attention to the manifold criticism towards the concept of PM. *Chapter 5* illustrates how this thesis understands the ecosystem of PM and its most relevant stakeholders. With PM, the pharmaceutical and the diagnostic business models come together in the co-development process, which is described as well in the last chapter.

K. Bosshard, *Law and Economics of Personalized Medicine*,
Gesundheitsmanagement und Gesundheitsökonomik,
https://doi.org/10.1007/978-3-658-22074-7_3

1 Personalized medicine – a paradigm shift in healthcare

"There are times in history when a new scientific idea becomes so powerful and compelling that it transforms the culture at large. This happened in the 17th century as the Copernican model of the universe gained traction and again in the 1940s as physicists emerged from their laboratories to usher in the atomic age. It may be happening now in genetics as genomic analysis promises to transform medical care. [...] nearly everyone agrees with the general prediction that genetics will ultimately revolutionize the practice of medicine".[270]

PM is claimed to "revolutionize" the healthcare landscape and is mentioned as classic example of a disruptive innovation.[271]. This thesis will neither judge this expectation nor will it discuss if PM is truly a "revolution". However, literature commonly agrees on the fact that there is a certain paradigm shift from a "one-size-fits-all" top-down approach towards a PM bottom-up approach in healthcare.[272] The following subchapters describe the paradigm shift by examining PM's historical roots, its status quo and its potential future developments.

1.1 Historical background

One can claim, that research in PM has started more than hundred years ago. A Scottish physician and surgeon, Sir GEORGE BEATSON, pioneered the hypothesis that there might be some connection between the ovaries and the breasts. He removed the ovaries from three women with breast cancer and reported that two of them had a response. It took about 70 years to understand the molecular biology behind. What BEATSON did not know yet, is that he was removing the growth factor estrogen from the organisms. BEATSON's observation has allowed to focus endocrine therapy on people who are likely to benefit from it, namely women whose cancer is estrogen receptor-positive.[273] Also the findings of REUBEN OTTENBERG in 1907 about the blood

270 EVANS & GREEN (2009), p. 568.

271 JAMESON & LONGO (2015), p. 2231.

272 DOWNING (2009), p. 272; PRASAD & BRECKENRIDGE (2011), p. 869 ff.; JAMES (2014), p. 383; MOOSER (2014), p. 571; DUFFY (2015), p. 8; VAN HEERTUM, SCARIMBOLO, FORD, BERDOUGO, & O'NEAL (2015), p. 5215; BLOBEL, LOPEZ, & GONZALEZ (2016), p. 1; BRALL & SCHRÖDER-BÄCK (2016), p. 179; EUROPEAN COMMISSION (2016)b, p. 5; and *"PM holds the potential to radically transform medicine, with a change of paradigm from 'a medicine of organs (heart, liver)' to a medicine targeting cells, molecules, genes, etc."* in OECD (2017), p. 22.

273 Example of BEATSON cited in HAYES ET AL. (2014), p. 1.

compatibility for transfusion using blood typing techniques and cross-matching between donors and patients to prevent hemolytic transfusion reactions belongs to the first examples of PM.[274] Since then, advancements in science and technology have allowed healthcare decisions to become increasingly "granular" over time.

In 1931, ARCHIBALD GARROD proposed the concept of genetic influence on individualized drug responses and anticipated the use of genetic tests to optimize treatment decisions.[275] Mid 20th century, observations of individual differences in response to drugs contributed to research focusing on identifying enzymes which play a role in variation in drug metabolism and response and which served as the foundation for *pharmacogenetics*.[276] Beginning in the 1980s, a series of important breakthroughs in the molecular characterization of disease provided the basis for new possibilities in PM.[277]

In 1997, *Nature Biotechnology* reported on how advances in genomics were laying the foundation for *"a new generation of personalized medicines"* describing drugs aimed at the individual as opposed to the "average person".[278] Since that time, the term *"personalized medicine"* has become the common term to describe the change in medicine from the "one-size-fits-all" model adapted to an individual's characteristics.[279]

The full decoding of the human genome at the beginning of the 21st century was the main driver for the transformation of PM from an idea to a practice. PM is also labeled as a *"direct descendant of the HUMAN GENOME PROJECT"*.[280] Since the completion of the HUMAN GENOME PROJECT advances in genome technology have led to an exponential decrease in sequencing costs. The sequencing costs for the human genome have fallen from one billion USD in 2001 to below USD 1000.[281]

Already around the turn of the millennium, the first PM applications came to market. For example in 1998, *Herceptin*, a monoclonal antibody used to treat HER2 receptor positive breast cancer, and *HerceptTest*™, the corresponding CDx, gained

---

274 Example of OTTENBERG cited in FDA (2013), p. 6.

275 GARROD cited in FLOCKHART, SKAAR, BERLIN, KLEIN, & NGUYEN (2009), p 109.

276 FDA (2013), p. 6-7. Cf. Part I, Chapter 1.1.2 Closely related terms, *Pharmacogenomics & Pharmacogenetics*, p. 42.

277 FDA (2013), p. 14.

278 A. MARSHALL (1997), p. 954.

279 TUTTON (2012), p. 1721.

280 DUFFY (2015), p. 9; similarly ROSE (2013), p, 343; and FLOCKHART ET AL. (2009), p 109.

281 NIH (2016), *How much does it cost to sequence a human genome in 2016*. E.g., VERITAS GENETICS offers a full genome sequencing for USD 999, cf. https://www.verytasgenetics.com/mygenome.(last visited July 5, 2017).

FDA approval.[282] Later, in 2001, *Gleevec*, a targeted anti-cancer drug, was FDA approved.[283] In 2004, the FDA approved ROCHE's microarray-based genotyping *AmpliChip CYP450* test as the first pharmacogenetic test.[284]

Although PGx remains central in several PM applications, in the last years, the concept of PM has broadened beyond strictly pharmacogenetic biomarkers to other "omics"-based biomarkers.[285]

In the roughly past 20 years, multiple PM applications entered the market and the importance of the topic has exponentially increased – as an analysis of the number of PUBMED[286] hits demonstrates:

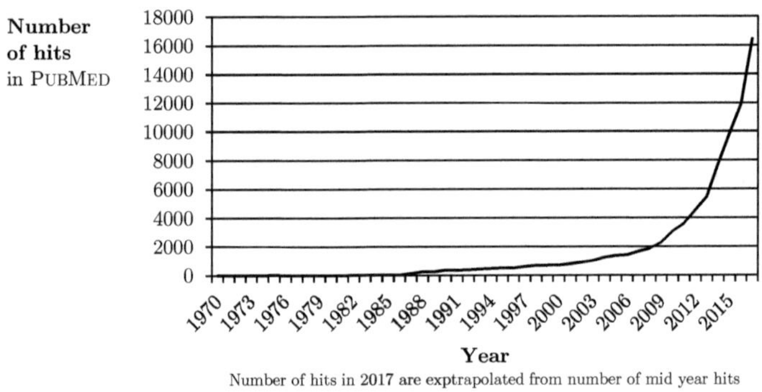

Figure 9: Number of PubMed hits for personalized medicine over time

SOURCE: PubMed Search performed on July 5, 2017
with search terms "personalized medicine" and "personalised medicine" and
"precision medicine" and "stratified medicine" and "individualized medicine"

282 Cf. https://www.accessdata.fda.gov/drugsatfda_docs/appletter/1998/trasgen092598L.pdf and https://www.accessdata.fda.gov/cdrh_docs/pdf/P980018S010b.pdf (last visited July 5, 2017). For more background on *Herceptin*, cf. FDA (2013), p. 15.

283 Cf. https://www.accessdata.fda.gov/drugsatfda_docs/nda/2001/21-335_Gleevec_Approv.pdf (last visited July 5, 2017). Gleevec increases the survival rates of leukaemia patients with a chromosomal abnormality in the tumours called the Philadelphia translocation.

284 Cf. https://www.accessdata.fda.gov/cdrh_docs/pdf4/k042259.pdf (last visited July 5, 2017). Based on the SNIPs CYP2D6 and CYP2D19, the AmpliChip aims to identify how patients metabolized drugs and thus guides the prescription of medicines.

285 GARRISON (2016), p. 211. Cf. also the call in *Nature Biotechnology*, "What happened to personalized medicine?" (2012), to *"broaden the concept of personalized medicine from the genetically reductionist version to one that includes other types of markers"*, p. 1.

286 PUBMED by the US NATIONAL LIBRARY OF MEDICINE is a online database which comprises more than 27 million citations for biomedical literature from MEDLINE, life science journals, and online books. Cf. www.pubmed.gov (last visited August 2017).

SIDE NOTE: In the late 1990s, a stream of literature understood "personalized medicine" to describe a patient-centered care. For these authors, "personalized medicine" was a practice endangered by continued technologization and reductionism of biomedicine, cf. TUTTON (2012), p. 1721 or Part I , Chapter 1.1 Different understandings of personalized medicine, p. 36. This literature was not filtered out in the above figure.

1.2 Status quo

1.2.1 Number of personalized medicine applications

Since the approval of the first therapeutic associated with a companion diagnostic, an increasing number of CDx technologies and personalized drugs have been developed. More than 90% of pharmaceutical companies utilize at least some genomic-derived targets in their drug discovery program – estimates range from 12-50% of the pipelines.[287]

Currently, 51'672 genetic diagnostic tests are available, covering over 5'152 genes. PM Dx have grown from 2012 to 2016 with a CAGR of 172%.

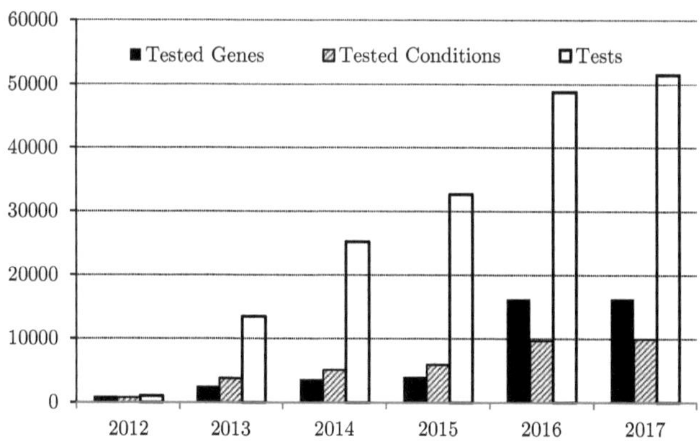

Figure 10: Number of tested genes, tested conditions and tests per year

SOURCE: https://www.ncbi.nlm.nih.gov/gtr/ (accessed July 6, 2017)
The source provides more details about the type of tests, conditions and genes tested for. 2017 represents the numbers in July 2017 and is not extrapolated.

287 TUFTS CENTER FOR THE STUDY OF DRUG DEVELOPMENT cited in FDA (2013), p. 56; AKHMETOV & BUBNOV (2015), p. 2; and FAULKNER ET AL. (2012), p. 1164, with an older estimate of 50%.

The US NATIONAL CENTER FOR BIOTECHNOLOGY INFORMATION offers a publicly accessible GENETIC TESTING REGISTRY. The source provides an overview of the status quo and details about the available types of tests, conditions and genes tested for.[288] In 2016, 27% of the NMEs approved by the FDA were personalized pharmaceuticals.[289]

A source of the current PGx applications is the knowledgebase PHARMGKB.[290] Further, the US FDA publishes a list of 238 drugs or drug pairs which contain pharmacogenomic information in their label.[291] Similarly EHMANN ET AL. (2015) reviewed the PGx drug labels of all 517 medicinal products centrally approved in the EU and found that 15% of the EMA evaluated medicines contain PGx information in their label, a number that is steadily increasing. For Switzerland, a comparable study was not found.

This thesis took another perspective and estimated the share of Swiss taking a medicine for which genetic testing is recommended.[292] Based on data provided by HELSANA, this thesis estimates that in Switzerland, 6% of the people are taking a medicine for which the CLINICAL PHARMACOGENETICS IMPLEMENTATION CONSORTIUM CPIC strongly recommends previous testing.[293]

Today, PM has multiple areas of applications in oncology,[294] but there are also other areas like psychiatry, immunology, inflammation, pneumology, endocrinology,

---

288 List accessible under https://www.fda.gov/drugs/scienceresearch/researchareas/pharmacogenetics/ucm083378.htm (last visited July 7, 2017).

289 6 out of 22 NMEs. This continues the trend reported by the PMC of roughly one quarter of the drugs being PMs (21% in 2014, 28% in 2015). Cf. PERSONALIZED MEDICINE COALITION (2017), p. 1.

290 Cf. www.pharmGKB.org (last visited July 7, 2017). The database encompasses clinical information including dosing guidelines and drug labels, potentially clinically actionable gene-drug associations and genotype-phenotype relationships.

291 https://www.fda.gov/drugs/scienceresearch/researchareas/pharmacogeneticsucm083378.htm (visited July 7, 2017). This statistic does not necessarily mean that these drugs are "personalized", but that pharmacogenomic biomarkers for these drugs have been identified which can be critical in the prescribing process. C.f., D. K. THOMPSON (2016), p. 1.

292 *CPIC recommendation level A: "Genetic information should be used to change prescribing of affected drug"* as the *"preponderance of evidence is high or moderate in favor of changing prescribing".*

293 Details behind this estimate in *Annex 1*: Share of patients in Switzerland taking a medicine for which pharmacogenetic testing is strongly recommended.

294 E.g., PERSONALIZED MEDICINE COALITION (2014), p. 10, mentioning several oncology examples, but also examples outside of oncology, p. 12; DUFFY (2015), p. 7; HOLDER & MERIC-BERNSTAM (2016), p. 3 ff. for examples in oncology; RAVEGNINI & ANGELINI (2016), p. 1; RYBAKOWSKI &

rheumatology or the study of allergies, etc. where patients could benefit from PM. Apart from the above illustrations – which should speak for themselves in demonstrating the significant increase of PM applications –this thesis does not explicitly state a list of examples for PM applications as there is sufficient literature doing this.[295]

As illustrated in the introduction of this thesis – one challenge today is that PM applications are clinically insufficiently adopted and do not reach the patients in the same extent as they grew - despite the significant increase of available PM applications.[296]

1.2.2 National and international personalized medicine initiatives

On the national as well as on the international level multiple initiatives have been started to support PM. In the following, some selected examples are mentioned.

National personalized medicine initiatives

"Tonight, I'm launching a new Precision Medicine Initiative to bring us closer to curing diseases like cancer and diabetes and to give all of us access to the personalized information we need to keep ourselves and our families healthier".[297] In his State of the Union Address in January 2015, the former President of the US BARACK OBAMA launched the PRECISION MEDICINE INITIATIVE. Personalized medicine *"gives us one of the greatest opportunities for new medical breakthroughs that we have ever*

SERRETTI (2016) for applications in major psychiatric disorders; and DAVID PETTITT ET AL. (2016), p. 319.

295 *Examples for PM applications:* FLOCKHART ET AL. (2009), p. 109; HANDSCHIN & MEYER (2012), p. 430-431; DORSCHNER ET AL. (2013), p. 632; MCCARTHY ET AL. (2013), p. 2; THE ACADEMY OF MEDICAL SCIENCES (2013), p. 15 ff., describes current techniques; J. COHEN & FELIX (2014), p. 166-168; HAYES ET AL. (2014), p. 1 ff.; PERSONALIZED MEDICINE COALITION (2014), p. 42 ff. with an overview; AGARWAL ET AL. (2015), p. 100; BÜRKI (2015) for gynecological predictive examples; GHOSH (2015) with case studies on MYRIAD, NITROMED, GENETIC TECHNOLOGIES LIMITED, and 23ANDME; HERMANN & SEITZ (2015), p. 18-19 for Germany-specific examples; JAMESON & LONGO (2015), p. 2230; MEADOWS ET AL. (2015), p. 6 ff., with a series of case studies of PM and their CDx; KAUFMANN, KEPPENS, & BLAIR (2015), p. 389; VAN HEERTUM ET AL. (2015), p. 5216; DIETEL (2016), p. 146-149; GALLI (2016) on PM's potential in allergic diseases; GARRISON (2016), p. 211, 216-217; DAVID PETTITT ET AL. (2016), p. 323; WURCEL ET AL. (2016), p. 141, etc. For an overview and specific examples in *Switzerland*, cf. ECKHARDT ET AL. (2014), p. 53-75.
Further, there are some databases on drug-gene/gene-disease interactions, cf. Part III, Chapter 5.3.2 Overview of existing guideline sources, p. 169 ff.

296 This challenge is more extensively discussed in the introduction of this thesis, cf. RESEARCH CONCEPT, Chapter 1 Problem, p. 1, especially *note* 12.

297 OBAMA cited in COLLINS & VARMUS (2015), p. 793.

seen".[298] The initiative aims to support research related to PM with USD 215 million in 2016 with the purpose to *"pioneer a new model of patient-powered research that promises to accelerate biomedical discoveries and provide clinicians with new tools, knowledge, and therapies to select which treatments will work best for which patients".*[299] The initiative plans to build a comprehensive scientific knowledge base to implement precision medicine on a larger scale by launching a national cohort study of a million or more Americans.[300]

Also in *Germany,* PM has gained attention. By the end of 2010, the GERMAN FEDERAL MINISTRY OF EDUCATION AND RESEARCH named PM to be one of six priorities and introduced the action plan called "Individualized Medicine: A new way in research and healthcare".[301] Since then the German BMBF supported the validation of biomarkers and implementation of personalized therapies into the clinical trials with over EUR 40 million.[302] The largest PM project in Germany was the GERMAN NATIONAL COHORT, launched in 2013. This project is a nationwide, long-term study.[303]

Similar efforts can be found in *Canada,*[304] the *UK,*[305] *France,*[306] *Norway,*[307] *Denmark,*[308] *Iceland, Estonia,*[309] *Saudi Arabia* and *Qatar,*[310] *Japan,*[311] *China.*[312]

---

298 OBAMA cited in ABE (2016), p. 1.

299 WHITE HOUSE cited in KHOZIN & BLUMETHAL (2015), p. 1.

300 For details about the US Precision Medicine Initiative: COLLINS & VARMUS (2015), p. 793 ff.; DUFFY (2015), p. 9; KAUFMAN, BAKER, MILNER, DEVANEY, & HUDSON (2016), p. 1 ff; KICHKO ET AL. (2016), p. 2; and KHOZIN & BLUMETHAL (2015), p. 1 ff.

301 BMBF (2013), *na.*

302 KICHKO ET AL. (2016), p. 2.

303 PERMED (2015), p. 21; and KICHKO ET AL. (2016), p. 2.

304 In 2013, the government granted $165 million to *Genome Canada*, the majority of which was applied to large-scale projects in the division of applied human health to develop personalized medicine, cf. JOHAL & AMLANI (2016), p. 1.

305 A *Stratified Medicine Initiative* was launched in 2011 with a £60 million budget. In 2012 GENOMICS ENGLAND launched the *100'000 Genomes Project* with the goal is to collect genome sequencing of 100'000 patients by 2017, cf. PERMED (2015), p. 21; KICHKO ET AL. (2016), p. 2 and DAVID PETTITT ET AL. (2016), p. 319. DZAU ET AL. (2015), p. 2118, mention the UK's NATIONAL PHENOME CENTER funded in 2015.

306 In France there are the *Integrated Cancer Research Centers* projects and the *French National Alliance for Life Sciences and Health* projects, cf. KICHKO ET AL. (2016), p. 2.

307 In Norway, the HUNT study combines genetic data with clinical records, cancer, stroke and death registries, cf. KICHKO ET AL. (2016), p. 2.

308 PRECISION MEDICINE FORUM (2017); and DANIEL SCHNEIDER ET AL. (2016), p. 163.

309 For the examples *Iceland, Estonia,* cf. OECD (2017), p. 160-161.

310 EL SHANTI, CHOUCHANE, BADII, GALLOUZI, & GASPARINI (2015), p. 1.

311 ABE (2016), p. 1 ff.

312 CYRANOSKI (2016), p. 9-10.

Switzerland mentions in the report about the FEDERAL COUNCIL'S HEALTH-POLICY PRIORITIES "HEALTH 2020" personalized medicine in one footnote as an exemplary new cost driver.[313] The number of genetic tests performed before a medical treatment in Switzerland is described as "still limited".[314] Nevertheless –besides the activities of Switzerland's pharmaceutical and diagnostic industry participants – there are some initiatives concerning PM, primarily in the research context of PM.[315] For example, there are several private and public biobanks.[316] In 2017, the government has initiated the research initiative SWISS PERSONALIZED HEALTH NETWORK (SPHN) granted with CHF 70 million over four years with the aim to promote nationwide interoperability of health-related data.[317]

International personalized medicine initiatives

PM has triggered discussions from the national to the global level. Cross-border collaborations and global partnerships are important elements in order to accelerate the adoption of PM. There are call for increased global collaboration.[318] For example, *Finland*, *Sweden* and *Norway* cooperate in the "Nordic Biobank Network" in order to link national biobanks and to enable international research projects.[319] Also the *EU* started its initiative EUROPEAN ALLIANCE FOR PERSONALIZED MEDICINE with the aim to accelerate the development, delivery, and uptake of PM.[320] Another European initiative which has been started in 2014 is the INNOVATIVE MEDICINE INITIATIVE, a joint undertaking between the EU and the pharmaceutical industry association EFPIA.[321] PERMED (2015) or EUROPABIO (2015) provide overviews of the activities in the EU.[322] As well on the *global* level, there started several public and private initi-

---

313 EDI (2013), *footnote* 10, p. 24.

314 MOOSER (2014), p. 570.

315 LUTERBACHER & HUNT (2015) with some examples.

316 For examples for biobanks in Switzerland, cf. Part I, Chapter 3.2 Biobanks, p. 51 ff.

317 Cf. MEIER-ABT (2016), p. 1.

318 E.g., T. A. MANOLIO, WARD, & GINSBURG (2016), p. 1 ff.; and ABE (2016), p. 1.

319 Cited in MEIER-ABT & EGLI (2016), p. 5.

320 Cf. http://euapm.eu/ (last visited July 17, 2017).

321 Cf. https://www.imi.europa.eu/ (last visited July 17, 2017). Other European initiatives like the EUROPEAN PROSPECTIVE INVESTIGATION INTO CANCER AND NUTRITION or the E-Rare-3 are described in KICHKO ET AL. (2016), p. 2.

322 EUROPABIO (2015), p. 16 ff.; or PERMED (2015), p. 14-15. The PERMED consortium is a coordination and support action financed by the European Commission in order to deliver a strategic research and innovation agenda with the aim is to develop recommendations to foster the implementation of PM in relation to research funding, the present and future potential of health systems, and the benefit that can accrue to the citizen. PERMED (2015), p. 5.

atives primarily aiming to foster the collaboration in the context of PM. PWC & PMI (2015) provide an overview of selected examples.[323]

1.3 Future developments

This thesis will not extensively speculate on future developments in the field of PM. Nevertheless, some potential future developments shall roughly be mentioned.[324]

1.3.1 Tapping new scientific potential

Alltough PM created innovative treatments that are used today; there remain multiple scientific challenges to the discovery and development of additional PM applications. Despite the ability to sequence the human genome, there is limited evidence on how most genomic variants are actually related to specific phenotypic characteristics or their associations with disease.

Especially in therapeutic areas outside of oncology, the current scientific understanding are not yet sufficient to realize the PM's full potential.[325] The FDA (2013) mentions the "*limited understanding of the intrinsic biology of disease*" as the most important limiting factor behind the progress PM.[326] Linked to this limited understanding of the underlying pathways and molecular networks in diseases is the scientific challenge of biomarker identification and the diagnostic test development as such.[327] A clinically useful PM Dx must predict the outcome of a drug treatment, but the pathways involved in the action and metabolism of drugs are complex.[328] "Traditional" association studies have been successful in revealing genes underlying *monogenic disorders.*[329] In the case of monogenic disorders, PM can provide medically useful forecasts.[330] However, disorders are seldom monogenic[331] and science needs to examine and identify more complex biological interactions in order to further realize the

323 PWC & PMI (2015), *appendix* iii.

324 *Others discussing future developments in PM:* JORDAN (2015) from ROCHE with some forecasts for products; KAUFMANN ET AL. (2015), p. 395 ff.; MIETZNER ET AL. in EPPINGER ET AL. (2015), p. 362-412, with an expert based Delphi study about future trends in PM; TOPOL (2015) with a book about increased patient involvement in healthcare; AUFFRAY ET AL. (2016); SNYDER (2016), p. 115; DAVID PETTITT ET AL. (2016), p. 320; and OECD (2017), p. 170 ff.

325 KULKARNI ET AL. (2013), p. 4-5, for the discussion on how to move PM beyond oncology.

326 FDA (2013), p. 56.

327 JAKKA & ROSSBACH (2013), p. 2; MILNE & COHEN (2015)a, p. 1.

328 SWEN ET AL. (2007), p. 1321.

329 HENGGELER (2017, e-mail to author). Monogenic disorders are caused by a single-gene (also Mendelian) germline modification, for detailed description including examples Cf. GRECH, SCERRI, ET AL. (2015), p. 11-21.

330 SAMS (2012), p. 5

331 CONSTANCE (2010), p. 43.

potential of PM.[332] Today, treatment decisions are most based on a univariate decision rule, which fails to account for interactions between the biomarkers. Additional factors that can regulate the functioning of the biomarkers (e.g., additional omics or environmental data) are seldom incorporated. It is expected that future applications will move away from relying solely on static mutational data and towards dynamic omic-profiling. Patients will be segregated into treatment groups by not only determining their genetic mutations, but also by using "omic" data as an output of disease network activation status.[333]

Additionally patient heterogeneity, ethnic variations and non-genetic influences also add to the complexity.[334] A challenge to somatic applications of PM is the presence of intratumoral heterogeneity.[335]

1.3.2 New nosology through personalized medicine

For years, scientific disciplines taught that patients with the same symptoms suffer from the same disease. PM is changing this view.

Clinical experience shows that patients diagnosed with the same disease based on the same diagnostic criteria may respond differently to the same treatment as the underlying mechanisms are different.[336] Also the other way round is it possible that diseases displaying rather different symptoms and characteristics might turn out to have a common molecular cause.[337] The transition from the conventional classification of diseases to stratification using biomarkers will increase the number of distinct "diseases". This trend is already visible in the field of oncology.[338] An ideal example to illustrate this trend is lung cancer. Today it is known, that there does not exist the "one" lung cancer, rather lung cancer can be characterized by several different mutations or chromosomal translocations.[339] Drugs, which are effective in targeting certain

332 Systems biology is one important discipline aiming to address this complexity, cf. also Part I, Chapter 1.1.2 Closely related terms, *Systems Medicine*, p. 41.

333 DUFFY (2015), p. 4, about *"network based precision medicine approaches"*. Cf. also Part I, Chapter 1.1.2 Closely related terms, *Systems Medicine*, p. 41.

334 PASIC ET AL. (2013), p. 164.

335 SWEN ET AL. (2007), p. 1321; KULKARNI ET AL. (2013), p. 7-8; PASIC ET AL. (2013), p. 165; and BOMBARD (2015), p. 1.

336 E.g., KIEVITS ET AL. (2014), p. 3.

337 PERMED (2015), p. 8.

338 KHOURY, GWINN, GLASGOW, & KRAMER (2012), p. 642.

339 KAUFMANN ET AL. (2015), p. 392, with the detailed split of existing non-small cell lung cancers.

lung cancers, are also effective against other types of tumors containing the same genetic alterations.[340]

Through PM, the trend is moving towards a *"molecular taxonomy of disease"*. SZUCS is speaking of a *"mutation nosology"*.[341] JAMESON & LONGO (2015) express it with the following words: *"Perhaps the most daunting challenge for precision medicine is to manage the complexity associated with the progressively refined nosology (classification) of disease. Medicine has a long history of being divided into "lumpers and splitters'; lumpers tend to group related entities together, and splitters tend to apply more precise definitions and thereby define more discrete entities. The advances in genetics and biomarkers will shift this balance in favor of the splitters"*.[342]

Diseases will increasingly be defined at the molecular level in terms of their molecular pathology rather than their symptoms, their gross pathology or the part of the body in which they appear. The nosology will move away from a *"symptom-, phenotype- and organ-based approach towards a network- and sys- tems-based classification"*.[343] Treatment will therefore be more specified in terms of this new nosology. Regulation and clinical practice need to take this into account and adapt to the new reality.[344]

1.3.3 Increased use of multi-target personalized medicine diagnostics

Advances in science and information capacities combined with falling costs for genetic sequencing are pushing for an increased use of NGS and other multi-target techniques.[345]

The current model of a single CDx tied to a single Rx is not expected to persist for long because of pressure for greater efficiency and cost-effectiveness. The move towards multiplex- and multiparameter PM Dx has already occurred in other Dx categories (e.g, blood work panels, metabolic panels). It is hypothesized that this move away from the "one test-one drug" scenario will happen in PM Dx and that NGS or other multi-target Dx will replace the recent increase of PM Dx.[346]

---

340 E.g., PERSONALIZED MEDICINE COALITION (2014), p. 40.

341 SZUCS in an exploratory interview for this thesis on August 26th, 2015.

342 JAMESON & LONGO (2015), p. 2231.

343 PERMED (2015), p. 24.

344 Similarly about a new taxomony: EUROPEAN SCIENCE FOUNDATION (2012), p. 48-49; MCCARTHY ET AL. (2013), p. 12; PRAINSACK (2015), p. 30; and DAVID PETTITT ET AL. (2016), p. 327.

345 Cf. *note* 816.

346 E.g., KULKARNI ET AL. (2013), p. 5-6; AGARWAL ET AL. (2015), p. 107; KAUFMANN ET AL. (2015), p. 389; and OECD (2017), p. 170 f.

This trend will diminish part of the disincentive that a new PM Dx may not need to be developed.[347] However, the trend will raise new questions, such as "how to calculate the value of a diagnostic that directs the use of multiple drugs", and "how to incentivize diagnostic development effectively for business models based on multiparameter platforms rather than single-use tests". A system will need to be developed to evaluate the value of these new forms of PM diagnostics.[348]

Connected to the increased future use of multi-target panel is the expectation that the major costs will not be the sequencing anymore, but the data handling and downstream analysis.[349]

1.3.4 Shift from reaction to prevention

With additional scientific insights (from e.g., Systems Biology[350]), the PM's possibilities to predict a person's risk of disease will increase. With this development, medicine is expected to move from a reactive mode to a preventive mode.[351]

1.3.5 Impact on hospitals' organization

According to the survey, from OXFORD ECONOMICS and SAP, which polled 120 healthcare professionals in Europe and North America, PM will bring a change on how hospitals are organized as they will no longer be focused on traditional approaches to care.[352]

1.3.6 Increase in patient involvement

Further, it is forecasted that patients – or consumers – become more involved in health or wellness decisions. Already now, there is an increase in DTC services.[353] There is also a move towards near-patient PM Dx or point-of-care testing. It is expected that PM Dx, which are today usually at a different location than the patient, will become smaller and closer to the patient setting (smart-phone compatible PM Dx). In the future, the availability of PM may increase people's being health literacy

---

[347] For the explanation of the disincentive, cf. Part III, Chapter 7.2 Resulting incentives, *Incentives for diagnostics companies*, p. 211 ff.

[348] Cf. THE ACADEMY OF MEDICAL SCIENCES (2013), p. 59.

[349] BEERENWINKEL (2015), *slide* 24.

[350] Cf. also Part I, Chapter 1.1.2 Closely related terms, *Systems Medicine*, p. 41.

[351] E.g., HARVEY ET AL. (2012), p. 629; or ROSE (2013), p, 343; PERSONALIZED MEDICINE COALITION (2014), p. 8; and SZUCS in ESCHER CLAUSS (2016), p. 8.

[352] AUFFRAY ET AL. (2016), p. 4.

[353] Cf. RESEARCH CONCEPT, Chapter 8.3 *Out of scope:* Direct-to-consumer tests (DTCs), p. 29 ff.

and patients will start using tools to monitor and manage their health status as part of their everyday life.[354]

There are predictions that people will have an *„integrative personal omices profile" (iPOP)* which contains longitudinal data on the personal genome, transcriptome, proteome, metabolome, etc., on which medical, preventive and personal decisions can be based on.[355]

1.3.7 Prospect of human gene editing

With the increased understanding of genes' role in diseases, also possibilities for new treatments will grow. The prospect of being able to edit the human genome with for example the CRISPR-Cas9 technology will foster this development. The cure of monogenic diseases via human gene editing and its ethical acceptability will have to be discussed.[356]

354 Cf. HARVEY ET AL. (2012), p. 630, mention the handheld device example of the "SNIP doctor" for analyzing SNIPs which has been reported as successful in pilot studies; TOPOL (2015) dedicates a book to this trend.

355 HANDSCHIN & MEYER (2012), p. 430; and PASIC ET AL. (2013), p. 160.

356 OXFORD ECONOMICS (2016), p. 1.

2 Goals of personalized medicine

2.1 Risk assessment & prevention

Already today it is possible to better assess the risks for some – primarily monogenic – diseases. A prediction of polygenetic diseases is still too complex due to an interaction of multiple genetic and epigenetic influences.[357]

PM allows people to assess their risks for certain diseases and to take pre-emptive measures, such as lifestyle changes or preventive surgery in order to avoid development of disease.[358]

One prominent example ("Angelina Jolie example") is the significantly increased probability for breast or ovarian cancer in case a person is carrier of mutation in the BRCA1 or BRCA2 gene.[359]

2.2 Accurate diagnosis

Today, most medical practitioners have been practicing "intuitive" medicine[360] whereby they use clinical judgment to select a treatment based on a patient's symptoms. The traditional approach does not take into account person's genetic characteristics and other personal dispositions. In the traditional approaches to medicine, *"effective therapies were educated guesses"*.[361] PM helps to more accurately diagnose diseases and to increase the certainty about a diagnosis and its mechanism of disease.

Again, the mentioned example of lung cancer[362] illustrates how PM assesses the molecular characteristics of a malignant tumor and thus enables a targeted treatment.[363]

2.3 Elimination of unnecessary treatments

Most common drugs demonstrate low efficacies, but the real statistics are ignored by health practitioners. This can be explained by KAHNEMANN's "false clarity" that

---

357 SAMS (2012), p. 14.

358 E.g., FACKLER & MCGUIRE (2010), p. 6; FAULKNER ET AL. (2012), p. 1163; and SAMS (2012), p. 14.

359 Cf. BÜRKI (2015), p. 12, for the risk-age curves for BRCA1 and 2 mutation carriers.

360 ANSARI (2013), p. 405.

361 KIEVITS ET AL. (2012), p. 4.

362 Cf. for the example of lung cancer, cf. p. 63 and *note* 339.

363 FAULKNER ET AL. (2012), p. 1163; or SAMS (2012), p. 15-16, provide several examples.

doctors have about drug efficacy.[364] It is undisputed that today's "one-size-fits-all" approach leads to unnecessary treatments – only the estimates about their size vary.

The PERSONALIZED MEDICINE COALITION (2014) cites estimates of 38-75% of the patient population for which particular drugs are ineffective.[365] Other estimates for the share of ineffective drugs range from 75-96% or a little more conservative 20-50%.[366] The estimate ranges indicate that half or more of the people receive unnecessary treatments. Even, when considering the lowest estimate of 20% ineffective treatments, this means that - at least - every fifth person receives unnecessary treatments.

TRUSHEIM & BERNDT (2015)b make the following illustrative example with statins: *"The number needed to treat to avoid a single heart attack with statins is approximately 39. This means, for every 39 patients with known heart disease treated continuously with a statin for five years, one non-fatal heart attack is avoided. If we knew which single person out of the 39 would avoid the event, the other 38 would not need to take their medicine, eliminating the drug costs and side effects in those 38. Unfortunately currently we cannot predict which individual would avoid an event if s/he lowered their cholesterol, so we encourage all to take their medicine".*[367]

A similar example is *Esomeprazol* against hearth burn. It has to be given to 25 persons in order to relieve suffering for one person. Other examples are *Glatirameracetat* against multiple sclerosis with an NNT of 16, and the NNT of *Ada-*

364 KAHNEMANN (2011) cited in LEUCHT, HELFER, GARTLEHNER, & DAVIS (2015), p. 4.

365 SPEAR, HEATH-CHIOZZI & HUFF (2001) cited in PERSONALIZED MEDICINE COALITION (2014), p. 9: 38% of depression patients, 50% of arthritis patients, 40% of asthma patients, and 43% of diabetic patients are estimated to have ineffective treatments.

366 AKHMETOV ET AL. (2015), p. 214, estimated that 90% of all conventional medicines are not efficacious in 50–70% of the cases. In the areas of oncology and neuroscience, 25–62% of patients fail to respond to standard therapeutics.
HANDSCHIN & MEYER (2012), p. 425, have an estimate of 40-75% for ineffective treatments.
MUSHIRODA (2012) cited in ANSARI (2013), p. 406, estimates the drugs ineffectiveness for cancer ca. 75%, for alzheimer 68%, arthritis 49%, diabetes 42%, asthma 40%, antidepressants 38% and analgesics 19%.
REY ET AL. (2014), p. 2, with cited estimates between 33-50% of ineffective treatments.
SZUCS (2015)a, p. 5, estimates a lack of therapeutic use in 20-50% of all cases.
The ECONOMIST, "A digital revolution in health care is speeding up" (2017), estimates that *"in rich countries about one- fifth of spending on health care goes to waste, for example on wrong or unnecessary treatments".*
DAVID PETTITT ET AL. (2016), p. 323, cite the estimation for the US. It is estimated that the 10 highest grossing drugs are only effective in between 4-25 the patients who are prescribed them.

367 TRUSHEIM & BERNDT (2015)b, p. 4.

limumab against rheumatic arthritis NNT of 4 meaning that 3 persons take the medicine for nothing else than placebo.[368]

PM aims to choose the most efficacious drug for a patient, to eliminate unnecessary treatments and thereby reducing the overall therapy cost.[369] The above numbers should illustrate the potential to reduce costs. In addition, several other examples demonstrate how PM reduces the overall therapy costs.[370]

The illustrations also show that the bias "PM is only for new therapies" which some people may have is wrong. PM has the potential to add value to already existing treatments by identifying the patients for whom the treatments are effective.

2.4 Reduction of adverse drug reactions

A goal of PM is to improve drug safety by reducing adverse drug reactions (ADRs). The traditional "one-size-fits-all" clinical decisions frequently cause adverse drug reactions (ADRs). Most therapeutics provide benefit to a fraction of those who take them.[371] ADRs are estimated be responsible for ca. 7% of all hospital admissions in a number of developed European countries, and for ca. 6% in the US.[372] In the US, ADRs are the fourth leading cause of death.[373] Roughly 40 drugs have been withdrawn from the market during the past 20 years, either due to unrecognized risk for ADRs or because of inadequate evaluation of the "at risk" population.[374]

PM plays a critical role in predicting ADRs. By identifying medicines that are effective only in certain sub-groups of patients, trial and error can be avoided and

---

368 Cited in NIEDERER (2015), p. 56.

369 E.g., ROHR ET AL. (2016), p. 1.

370 E.g., it is estimated that Germany can save 4'612 EUR per patient by using a KRAS-test, cf. FORSTER & KOPACEK in "Personalisierte Medizin" (2013), p. XIII; PERSONALIZED MEDICINE COALITION (2014), p. 15, with several examples; or the EUROPEAN COMMISSION (2013), p. 13, 24-26, mentions the FRENCH CANCER INSTITUTE which showed that investing in molecular testing for the use of stratified and targeted medicines can in fact savings of ca 37%.

371 TRUSHEIM & BERNDT (2015)b, p. 3, citing several examples.

372 AKHMETOV ET AL. (2015), p. 214, cite an estimate of 7-13%; TURNER ET AL. in GRECH, SCERRI, ET AL. (2015), *chapter* 6, p. 110 ff. estimate the number of ADR in the UK to 6.5% of hospital admissions for patients were related to an ADR (peoble above 16 years), with a median inpatient stay of eight days. The EUROPEAN COMMISSION (2011), p. 8, estimates 5-7% of all hospital admissions are caused by ADRs.
A Canadian ADR study found that 23% of serious adverse related to medical management caused by drug therapy, cf. BAKER, NORTON, FLINTOFT ET AL. cited in JOHAL & AMLANI (2016), p. 2. SCHELLEKENS ET AL. (2017), p. 1, estimate 6% of hospitalizations are due to ADRs.

373 PASIC ET AL. (2013), p. 162.

374 PRASAD & BRECKENRIDGE (2011), p. 869.

ADRs can be reduced.[375] With the cited numbers above, the largely unexploited potential of PM to decrease adverse drug reactions becomes visible.

2.5 Improved dosing

PM Dx enable the selection of the correct drug dose for patients. An example is pharmacogenetic testing of the cytochrome P450 2D6 (CYP2D6). CYP2D6 genotyping can be valuable in identifying individuals likely to have altered reactions to various pharmaceuticals and for predicting patient response. The protein product encoded by the CYP2D6 gene is classified as a monooxygenase and is responsible for metabolizing roughly 25% of all commonly prescribed drugs. People can be sub-grouped in poor, intermediate and ultrafast metabolizers – and depending on their subtypes, doses should be chosen.[376] SIMOONS, MULDER, SCHOEVERS, RUHE, & VAN RON (2017) found that in the Netherlands CYP2D6 genotyping results were available for 3% of general practitioners. They found that there was no differentiating between the different metabolizer groups for the use of psychiatric pharmacoterapies and thus *"valuable information for individualizing psychiatric pharmacotherapy is lost on a large scale".*[377]

Another example of genotyping of the CYP2D9 to target dosing of the blood thinner drug warfarin.[378] PGx testing has resulted in 31% fewer hospitalizations overall for patients and up to 48% fewer hospitalizations for bleeding or thromboembolism.[379]

2.6 Improved monitoring

Further, serial biomarker tests allow to better monitor a disease status (e.g., the recurrence of a disease) or to monitor the tumor evolution in response to treatment.[380]

2.7 Targeted development

PM opens the possibility to approve medicines for sub-populations with a certain biomarker. PM-based stratification of clinical trials participants may lead to more complex clinical trials, but also to higher effect sizes.[381]

---

375 E.g., FACKLER & MCGUIRE (2010), p. 6; GARAU ET AL. (2012), p. 6-9; FAULKNER ET AL. (2012), p. 1163; THE ACADEMY OF MEDICAL SCIENCES (2013), p. 60; TURNER ET AL. in GRECH, SCERRI, ET AL. (2015), *chapter* 6; JOHAL & AMLANI (2016), p. 1; and PAOLO ET AL. (2017), p. 5.

376 E.g., SAMER (2015), p. 60-61.

377 SIMOONS ET AL. (2017), p. 1.

378 Warfarin is not approved in Switzerland.

379 PERSONALIZED MEDICINE COALITION (2014), p. 15.

380 MOORE ET AL. (2012), p. 486; PASIC ET AL. (2013), p. 159 ; and HAYES (2014), p. 960.

The relatively high numbers of ineffective treatments[382] give some indication of the hypothetical number of treatments that have been stopped in clinical trials due to low degree of average efficacy, but may have been effective for certain sub-populations.

2.8 Additional goals of personalized medicine

Various studies mention the same and additional goals of PM, such as an improved length or quality of life, increased patient adherence to treatment, the reduction of medical errors and freed-up time for clinicians.[383] Also economic goals are prominently mentioned. Several papers cite PM's potential to reduce overall healthcare costs.[384] This thesis dedicates a separate chapter to the economic value of PM.[385]

381 E.g., SAMS (2012), p. 17, or cf. literature Part III, Chapter 4.2 Incompatibility of clinical trials with personalized pharmaceuticals, p. 159 ff.

382 Cf. Part II, Chapter 2.3 Elimination of unnecessary treatments, p. 67 and *note* 366.

383 E.g., FAULKNER ET AL. (2012), p. 1163; GARAU ET AL. (2012), extensively on the different goals of PM on p. 6-9 and an overview on p. 10; SAMS (2012), p. 14 ff.; THE ACADEMY OF MEDICAL SCIENCES (2013), p. 60; JAKKA & ROSSBACH (2013), p. 1; Potential benefits of PM, ABPI (2014), p. 5 ff.; ECKHARDT ET AL. (2014), p. 4 ff., 75 ff.; KIEVITS ET AL. (2014), p. 12; PERSONALIZED MEDICINE COALITION (2014), p. 8 ff.; ARONSON & REHM (2015), p. 336; BOMBARD (2015), p.2; DAVID PETTITT ET AL. (2016), p. 320; PLUN-FAVREAU ET AL. (2016), p. 145; PAOLO ET AL. (2017), p. 5; and TRUSHEIM & BERNDT (2015)a, p. 10.

384 Cf. *note* 387.

385 Cf. next Chapter 3 Economic value of personalized medicine, p. 72 ff.

3 Economic value of personalized medicine

Globally, healthcare expenditure has been increasing faster than the gross domestic product over the past twenty years. In high income countries, the share rose from 9.2 to 12.7%, in Switzerland from 9.3 to 11.7%.[386] Maintaining this trend will become increasingly unsustainable.

Personalized medicine is praised for its potential to more effectively use healthcare resources and to reduce healthcare costs[387] – by enabling better prevention, providing more accurate diagnoses, eliminating unnecessary treatments, reducing ADRs, improving dosing and monitoring.[388]

Some authors claim that *"global figures in healthcare expenditure cry for preventive measures and personalised treatments"*[389]; whereas others are more cautious with their assessment: *"It is too early to judge the possible extent of personalized medicine and how far this concept will reach. Likewise, currently the question of the costs cannot be answered in a definite way; right now nobody can tell whether personalized medicine will lower or increase the cost of the public health system. But the huge advantage of personalized medicine for the patients is beyond any doubt".*[390]

The economic literature is not conclusive in which cases PM leads to savings or cost increases in healthcare budgets.[391] The field of genetics has historically not been a focus of health economists. Understanding the technologies used in PM requires an interdisciplinary understanding across basic, clinical, and social scientists'

---

386 For details on percentage healthcare expenditure per country per GDP cf. http://data.worldbank.org/indicator/SH.XPD.TOTL.ZS (last visited 7.7.2017).

387 ISSA (2008), p. 192; E. D. BLAIR (2010), p. 143; FACKLER & MCGUIRE (2010), p. 6; THE ACADEMY OF MEDICAL SCIENCES (2013), p. 10; JAKKA & ROSSBACH (2013), p. 1; SCHLEIDGEN & MARCKMANN (2013), p. 224; ABPI (2014), p. 5 ff.; BOMBARD (2015), p.2; TRUSHEIM & BERNDT (2015)b, p. 11; PLUN-FAVREAU ET AL. (2016), p. 145; and ROEDIGER (2016), p. 2.
SZUCS & BLANK (2016), p. 125: *„The question if PM is economically efficient is certainly to be answered with an unambiguous 'yes'", translated by the author.*

388 Cf. Part II, Chapter 2 Goals of personalized medicine, p. 67 ff.

389 GRECH, SCERRI, ET AL. (2015), p. V. A discussion about cost saving potential through PM follows in Chapter 3 Economic value of personalized medicine, p. 72 ff.

390 DIETER SCHNEIDER & BUBLAK (2015), p. 419.

391 Cf. *Annex 2:* Literature review on economic evaluations in the context of personalized medicine; and exemplary A. J. THOMPSON ET AL. (2014), p. 22 or ANTONANZAS, JUAREZ-CASTELLO, & RODRIGUEZ-IBEAZ (2015), p. 456.

knowledge.[392] There are several research gaps and unsolved questions which pose challenges to the application of economic evaluation to PM.[393]

There are two main drivers behind research gaps and limited quantity and quality of economic evaluations for PM: One problem is the *comparability* of the existing health economic studies, another is the *lack of sufficiently robust economic data* in the context of PM.[394] Economic evaluations studies have been conducted on a fraction of the available genomic tests and on a limited number of health topics.[395]

Multiple studies on the economic evaluation of a specific treatment or tests in a specific country are available. An example is the evaluation of the *Oncotype DX Breast Cancer Assay*[396] in Ireland which reduces the costs by roughly 20% compared with a non-assay guided practice.[397] Another example is the use of a KRAS[398] PM Dx to select metastatic colorectal cancer patients suitable for EGFR inhibitor therapy. In the US, it is estimated that USD 7'500–12'400 per patient could be saved; in Germany EUR 3'900–9'600 with equivalent clinical outcomes. The use of a KRAS using a KRAS Dx is estimated to save over EUR 115 million per year in Germany.[399] Another example with a different approach provide DZAU, GINSBURG, VAN NUYS, AGUS, & GOLDMAN (2015) who calculate the value of health from hypothetical personalized prevention at two levels of incidence reduction in six diseases in the USA. They find cumulative values of additional quality-adjusted life years (QALYs) generated from 2012–2060 of up to USD 600 billion for the higher incidence level.[400]

The examples illustrate the problem of comparability of the different studies. Up to date, there is *no consolidated database of economic evaluations for personalized*

392 K. PHILLIPS ET AL. (2013), p. 60.

393 TERKOLA ET AL. (2017), p. 2, identified the main elements that require further research and consensus.

394 *Discussing a lack of systematic health economic studies of PM:* PTOLEMY (2011), p. 286; FAULKNER ET AL. (2012), p. 1162 ff.; HARVEY ET AL. (2012), p. 629; ANNEMANS, REDEKOP, & PAYNE (2013), p. 20; K. PHILLIPS ET AL. (2013), p. 63; TRUSHEIM (2013), p. 325; JAIN (2015), p. 682; ROGOWSKI ET AL. (2015), p. 2; T. A. MANOLIO ET AL. (2016), p. 1; PATRINOS & MITROPOULOU (2017), p. 1ff. about the lack studies measuring the value of PGx; and TERKOLA ET AL. (2017), p. 2.

395 K. PHILLIPS ET AL. (2013), p. 63, mentioning hepatitis C and breast cancer as examples.

396 The Oncotype DX is a 21-gene molecular diagnostic test which is used in early-stage breast cancer to inform chemotherapy decisions following surgery.

397 Example cited in PLUN-FAVREAU ET AL. (2016), p. 148. A comparable example which saves 34% in chemotherapy use in the US cite WURCEL ET AL. (2016), p. 141.

398 The KRAS gene provides instructions for making a protein called K-Ras that is involved primarily in regulating cell division.

399 WURCEL ET AL. (2016), p. 141.

400 DZAU ET AL. (2015), p. 2119.

medicine.[401] Several efforts over the past few years have attempted to apply principles of evidence-based medicine to emerging PM applications.[402] How to adapt and apply economic evaluation frameworks and evidentiary standards for PM is a matter of ongoing debates.

An *overview in the appendix* summarizes the results of selected existing meta-studies on the economic evaluation of PM interventions.[403] Despite the lack of straightforward means by which to search for these studies, despite the challenge that the evaluation of PM includes a range of evaluation methods and despite the lack of a consolidated source of information for the economic value of PM, the appendix attempts to provide a compact overview. The overview illustrates the fragmented landscape of economic evaluations employing different methods and reaching different conclusions. There are some areas where the combination of tests and personalized pharmaceuticals do generate savings and others in which the application of PM increases costs – although simultaneously contributing to health improvements. Further, the overview demonstrates the difficulty to compare the studies and their conclusions because of the heterogeneous set of methodologies, models, definitions and data sources employed. Because of the scattered evidence in the published literature, it is difficult to draw conclusions about the economic value of PM.[404]

The two main drivers for the existing inconsistencies and limitations related to the economic evaluation of PM applications shall be illustrated in the following sections. The two sections demonstrate that the inconsistent results in economic valuations root first, in methodological differences of the performed studies (*Chapter 3.1*), and second, in a lack of reliable data in order to perform economic evaluations (*Chapter 3.2*).

---

401 K. PHILLIPS ET AL. (2013), p. 63 and 76. They mention efforts to aggregate evidence, such as the National Institutes of Health Genetic Test Registry, the Genomic Applications in Practice and Prevention Network (GAPPNet), and the Pharmacogenomics Knowledgebase (PharmGKB). However, these consolidated resources focus rather on the clinical and analytic characteristics of a genetic test than on economic information.
ANTONANZAS ET AL. (2015), p. 456, mention that research in the area of the economic evaluation for personalized medicine is currently a central topic of discussion in the International SOCIETIY FOR PHARMACOECONOMICS AND OUTCOMES RESEARCH (ISPOR) panels.

402 E.g., the Evaluation of Genomic Applications in Practice and Prevention Initiative (EGAPP), cf. KHOURY ET AL. (2012), p. 642.

403 Cf. *Annex 2:* Literature review on economic evaluations in the context of personalized medicine.

404 K. PHILLIPS ET AL. (2013), p. 63 and 76. They mention efforts to aggregate evidence, such as the NATIONAL INSTITUTES OF HEALTH GENETIC TEST REGISTRY, the GENOMIC APPLICATIONS IN PRACTICE AND PREVENTION NETWORK (GAPPNet), and the PHARMACOGENOMICS KNOWLEDGEBASE (PHARMGKB). However, these consolidated resources focus rather on the clinical and analytic characteristics of a genetic test than on economic information.

3.1 Existence of multiple evaluation methodologies

Even if sufficient real-world data were available, measuring the value of PM is inherently challenging *there is still no commonly accepted definition of value.*[405] The term "value" as such is ambiguous as its meaning differs both inside and outside economics. In economics, the term is broadly used to describe a market-oriented concept that includes the willingness to pay by a society for a product.

PORTER (2010) states that value in healthcare is defined as "outcomes relative to costs".[406] He further continues: *"Yet, value in health care remains largely unmeasured and misunderstood [...] The current organizational structure and information systems of health care delivery make it challenging to measure (and deliver) value".*[407] Also PORTER indicates that assessing the evidence base for "value" in PM applications as a whole is challenging. The landscape of economic evaluations is fragmented and conclusions are difficult to compare. Existing studies employ a heterogeneous set of methodologies, models, research topics, definitions and data sources.[408]

Literature stresses the need for methodological scrutiny in the economic assessments of PM. Currently there are divergent views on which evidentiary framework(s) should be applied for assessments in the context of PM.[409] The use of different frameworks may lead to inconsistent findings even when evaluating the same test. It is hypothesized that if agreement could be reached on the most appropriate methods of economic assessment in this context, health economists would be better placed to contribute to translational research in PM.[410] There are claims for defining national and international standards for evaluation studies.[411]

---

405 TERKOLA ET AL. (2017), p. 2.

406 PORTER (2010), p. 2477.

407 *Ibidem.*

408 K. PHILLIPS ET AL. (2013), p. 63.
GARAU ET AL. (2012), p. 13-15, illustrate four basic options for aggregating elements of "value": 1. Converting all value into monetary terms; 2. Creating an own unit of measurement; 3. Using a principle measure (e.g., QALY) and then up- or downrate this on other (weighted) factors; or 4. Using a *"deliberative process"* in which relative weights given to the elements of value may remain implicit.

409 MORRISON & BOUDREAU (2012) aim to identify the main evaluation frameworks for genetic tests that are used internationally and outline some of the most commonly used criteria.

410 *Criticizing the existence of multiple evaluation methodologies for PM:* STALLINGS ET AL. (2004), p. 5; PACI (2009), p. 289-290; PTOLEMY (2011), p. 286; FAULKNER ET AL. (2012), p. 1167; GARAU ET AL. (2012), p. 13; MORRISON & BOUDREAU (2012), p. 1; ANNEMANS ET AL. (2013), p. 20 ff; BUCHANAN ET AL. (2013), p. 2; SHABARUDDIN ET AL. (2015), p. 120.
According to FAULKNER ET AL. (2012), p. 1167, fundamental questions in the context of personalized medicine remain to be answered. For example as how to handle inclusion of the Dx in models;

Evaluation approaches in healthcare encompass a broad range of methodologies. Some are more narrowly considered as economic analyses based on standard welfare economic theory, but also other approaches deriving from fields such as decision analysis or operations research.[412] Moreover, there are approaches incorporating behavioral economics into value assessments in the context of PM.[413]

The extra-welfarist *(i) cost-effectiveness analysis (CEA)* is the most commonly used form of economic evaluation also for PM applications.[414] However, it is debated whether current extra-welfarist evaluation frameworks are directly applicable to inform the design and conduct of economic evaluations of PM. Challenges arise if the economic evaluation is understood as an evaluation of the benefits, harms, and cost-effectiveness at the individual patient level.[415] An alternative evaluation approach which takes this challenge into account represents the welfarist *(ii) cost-benefit analysis (CBA)*. Besides classic economic evaluations, there are also non-economic approaches to evaluate PM like the *(iii) ACCE framework* which takes also social/ethical evaluation criteria into consideration or *(iv) "value based" approaches*, including economic and non-economic criteria too. These four methodologies are illustrated in the following.[416]

---

standards for establishing links between test use, patient management, and outcomes; the impact of uncertainty on model outcomes; and whether the QALY is the best metric for diagnostics and PGx. Model structure, data used as model inputs, and model validation approaches are the three areas in which best practices must be established.
However, there are also voices that claim that *no new concepts are needed* for the economic evaluation of PM. PM has to be evidence-based like any other treatment thus "evidence-based techniques" should be applied, cf. for example WINDELER & LANGE (2013). But, they do not discuss in depth the methodological challenges arising. For example, ANNEMANS ET AL. (2013) identify ten specific issues that pose specific methodological challenges when designing and conducting robust model-based economic evaluations in the context of PM.

411 PLÖTHNER ET AL. (2016), p. 1-2.

412 Cf. K. PHILLIPS ET AL. (2013), p. 58; or FLORIAN GUTZWILLER ET AL. (2012), p. 8-50, with a detailed overview on methods to measure value in healthcare.

413 About the incorporation of *behavioral economics* into value assessments, cf. K. PHILLIPS ET AL. (2013), p. 81 ff. There have been studies of the behavioral impact of genetic testing (e.g., BLOSS ET AL (2011) cited in K. PHILLIPS ET AL. (2013), p. 81), however - to the knowledge of the author - behavioral economics has not been directly applied to the analysis of decision-making or value assessment for PM.

414 PACI (2009), p. 285; BUCHANAN ET AL. (2013), p. 2; K. PHILLIPS ET AL. (2013), p. 58; and P. MARSHALL & FLESSA (2015), p. 305.

415 For example ROGOWSKI ET AL. (2015), p. 2, with further references.

416 Besides the illustrated methodologies, related approaches are available including for example cost minimization analyses, decision analyses, stated choice methods, conjoint analyses, discrete choice experiments and willingness-to-pay, budget impact analysis, burden of illness studies, value of information analysis, and multi-criteria decision analysis.

3.1.1 *Extra-welfarist approach:* Cost-effectiveness analysis

The CEA is the predominantly used tool to assess the value of healthcare interventions.[417] It represents an *extra-welfarist approach* to evaluate health interventions. In contrast to a welfarist-approach, which is based on individual preference satisfaction, an extra-welfarist approach goes beyond the individual preference satisfaction. "Extra-welfarist" approaches are normative frameworks that do not make the restriction that welfare is a function only of individual utilities. Individual utilities are replaced by something else, in this case aiming to maximize health outcomes - therefore they are labelled as "extra-welfarist".[418] An extra-welfarist approach like the CEA intends to maximize health by choosing health interventions which are more cost-effective than a politically chosen threshold.[419] Its basic assumption is that all individuals value health similarly.[420]

A CEA in healthcare is concerned with providing evidence to compare the economic costs and the health outcomes of competing/alternative health interventions or technologies. It is common to express the cost effectiveness as a ratio of incremental costs to incremental effect (ICER):[421]

$$ICER = \frac{C_n - C_0}{E_n - E_0} \text{ with}$$

C_n = *costs of new technology/intervention expressed in monetary terms*
C_0 = *costs of old technology/intervention expressed in monetary terms*
E_n = *effectiveness of new technology/intervention (often QALY)*
E_0 = *effectiveness of old technology/intervention (often QALY)*

A basic overview on health economic evaluation techniques can be found in SZUCS (2005), p. 303-312. Also AKHMETOV & BUBNOV (2015), p. 3 ff. present some assessment frameworks (e.g., PORTER'S Value Based Healthcare model, FRYBACK AND THORNBURY'S model, as well as the ACCE model). K. PHILLIPS ET AL. (2013) provide an overview of methodologies for the economic evaluation of *personalized medicine.* PITINI ET AL. (2012) performed a systematic review of 19 tools for the evaluation of genetic tests.

417 PACI (2009), p. 285; K. PHILLIPS ET AL. (2013), p. 58 and 71; and ROGOWSKI ET AL. (2015), p. 51.

418 BROUWER ET AL. (2008), p. 326a.

419 Cf. CARRERA & IZERMAN (2016), p. 2-3; for a comparison of costs/QALY's for different countries and indications.

420 SHAFRIN (2008), p. 2. More on the distinction between welfarism and extra-welfarism in BROUWER ET AL. (2008) and ROGOWSKI ET AL. (2015). Cf. Table 4: Extra-welfarism vs welfarism, p. 81.

421 PACI (2009), p. 285. A technology/intervention is *"dominant"* if it shows the higher effectiveness while costing less than the alternative, P. MARSHALL & FLESSA (2015), p. 305.

There are relatively few PM applications that have been formally evaluated for their cost-effectiveness. It is claimed that there is a lack of CEAs for diagnostic tests for several conditions with high health burden.[422] The performance of scientifically valid CEAs is challenging for several reasons:

First, in order to perform a CEA the units of costs and effectiveness need to be clearly defined.[423] Both, *inconsistent definitions of "costs" and "effectiveness"* are drivers behind the ambiguity of the cost-effectiveness of PM treatments. The measure for "effectiveness" uses a common interpretable health outcome metric. It is frequently expressed in terms of QALYs[424], but other measures can be applied.[425] If QALYs are used, the CEA represents a *cost-utility-analysis (CUA)* – a particular type of the CEA.[426]

Second, the performance of scientifically valid CEAs is challenging due to a *lack of reliable data.* The shortage of reliable cost as well as effectiveness data is named as one of the major limitations in the quality in the existing CEA literature in the context of PM.[427]

Third, there are *methodological weaknesses* of the economic analyses performed so far which need to be addressed in order to overcome the barrier posed by inconsistent CEAs in the context of PM.[428] Probabilistic sensitivity analyses are seldom performed. Current CEAs are often exploratory.[429] Due to limited available data, basic economic models based on transparent assumptions are designed as a first step and populated with the limited available clinical and cost data supplemented if necessary

---

422 K. A. PHILLIPS ET AL. (2014), p. 254.

423 E.g., RIPPE ET AL. (2004), p. 109-110; ROEDIGER (2016), p. 2.

424 GOLD, STEVENSON, & FRYBACK (2002) with a paper providing the history, pro and cons, and calculations of health-adjusted life years (DALYs vs QALYs).

425 PACI (2009), p. 285 and 290, illustrating the challenge that the main measures used to evaluate cost-effectiveness is not uniform across studies; and P. MARSHALL & FLESSA (2015), p. 305.

426 GOLD ET AL. (1996) cited in K. PHILLIPS ET AL. (2013), p. 71.

427 For further illustration of the lack of reliable data cf. next Chapter 3.2 Lack of reliable data for measuring "value", p. 86 ff.

428 PACI (2009), p. 285, or ANNEMANS ET AL. (2013) who provide a list of ten specific issues that pose specific methodological issues specific to the challenge of conducting robust model-based CEAs of technologies designed to personalize medicine and that are more detailed than the following overview. They further discuss a. o. the importance of defining the scope of the economic evaluation, the explicit consideration of test characteristics (like sensitivity, specificity, false negatives and positives, predictive values) need to be considered explicitly and their translation into clinical utility, test combinations leading to more complex models and greater uncertainty; the need for early modeling as well as the appropriateness of QALYs.

429 PACI (2009), p. 292.

by estimated data.[430] These basic models result in preliminary, indicative conclusions on potential cost-effectiveness which help to decide whether it is worth conducting further research, such as prospective studies.[431]

Despite the practical usefulness of CEAs and CUAs, there are also a number of political barriers to using these methods. Policy-makers sometimes are reluctant to simply use CEAs because of concerns about the appearance of rationing care based on costs and discomfort with using QALYs.[432] CEAs neglect a formal assessment of the costs and benefits related to wider societal benefits, including impact on employers and careers, lost productivity, and the opportunity cost of foregone experiences.[433]

Today, there are relatively few systematic studies that prove the cost-effectiveness of pharmacogenetic testing.[434] The cost-effectiveness studies that do exist show a wide range of estimates for personalized therapeutics.[435] In general, there appears to be a *"dearth of solid supportive evidence for both drug and diagnostic clinical- and cost-effectiveness"*.[436] Considerations about the cost-effectiveness of a personal medicine intervention can significantly impact the adoption of PM innovations.[437]

430 *Ibidem.* Three examples of indicative *model-based approaches* evaluating the cost-effectiveness of PM contain A. H. WU (2010), p. 37 ff.; J. C. DAVIS ET AL. (2009), p. 282; and BRANZÉN (2013), p. 73-74.

431 PACI (2009), p. 290.

432 K. PHILLIPS ET AL. (2013), p. 71. Cf. also ANNEMANS ET AL. (2013), p.25, on the use of QALYs in the context of PM; and WHITEHEAD & ALI (2010) on limitations on the use of QALY approach. A literature review on the limitations of QALYs in general provide D. PETTITT ET AL. (2016). A critique of using QALYs in the context of PM provide CARRERA & IZERMAN (2016). TERKOLA ET AL. (2017), p. 2, also criticize the failure of QALYs to fully capture the subtleties of PM health outcomes and related well-being.

433 KIERNAN (2016), p. 2

434 RELLING & EVANS (2015), p. 347, cf. also *Annex 2:* Literature review on economic evaluations in the context of personalized medicine.

435 Cf. *Annex 2:* Literature review on economic evaluations in the context of personalized medicine; and J. COHEN (2012), p. 752.

436 J. COHEN (2011), p. 294, criticizes that even in "poster child cases" like trastumuzab (Herceptin surprisingly few CEA show conclusive evidence as to whether it represents "good value" to society.

437 *About the lack of clarity regarding PM's cost-effectiveness:* SWEN ET AL. (2007), p. 1321; PACI (2009), p. 284 with further references; YEO, BABIC, & WU (2010), p. 5; J. COHEN (2011), p. 294; HARVEY ET AL. (2012), p. 629; BRANZÉN (2013), p. 72-76; PASIC ET AL. (2013), p. 162; MOOSER (2014), p. 570; KIEVITS ET AL. (2014), p. 13; BOMBARD (2015), p. 58. GARBER & TUNIS (2009) write in the *New England Journal of Medicine* on the initial fear that cost-effectiveness research could harm the progress of PM – but conclude, that more CEAs would actually support its progress.

3.1.2 *Welfarist-approach:* Cost-benefit analysis

Health economists have begun to question whether the extra-welfarist approach is appropriate in genomics. In particular, there is uncertainty surrounding the need to capture information on nonhealth outcomes. Metrics used in a CBA, for example QALY, may be the preferred outcome measure of a number of governmental health service institutions, but they may not adequately capture nonhealth outcomes.[438]

Given the challenges associated with the frequently used outcome measures and the desire to incorporate information on personal utility, increasingly *welfarist approaches* like the cost-benefit analysis (CBA) are discussed within the context of economic evaluations of genomic tests.[439] Some authors have even argued that welfarism is the most appropriate normative framework for evaluating personalized medicine.[440] Genetic markers may provide benefits to patients who are not captured by standard measures of health outcome, for example the benefit of knowing about someone's future health prospects which may have no clinical consequences. Welfarist evaluation frameworks can account for such non clinical benefits by measuring a patient's willingness-to-pay within a cost-benefit analysis.[441]

438 BUCHANAN ET AL. (2013), p. 2.
439 *Ibidem*, p. 8 and ROGOWSKI ET AL. (2015), p. 56.
440 ROGOWSKI ET AL. (2015), p. 56.
441 *Ibidem*.

	Extra-welfarism	**Welfarism**
Focus of evaluation	Maximization of health outcomes. Outcome of medical intervention is judged against all other types of treatment.	Maximization of individual utilities. Outcome of medical intervention is judged against all other goods.
Underlying assumption	Similar individual health preferences	Differing individual health preferences
Methodological approaches	CEA	CBA
Advantage	Easier to implement compared to welfarist approach.	Including health and nonhealth outcomes.

Table 4: Extra-welfarism vs welfarism

SOURCES: Content based on BROUWER, CULYER, VAN EXEL, & RUTTEN (2008), SHAFRIN (2008), BUCHANAN, WORDSWORTH, & SCHUH (2013), and ROGOWSKI ET AL. (2015)

In contrast to the extra-welfarist CEA, the CBA is based on welfarist assumptions: Instead of aiming to maximize health outcomes, it aims to maximize patient welfare - including both health and nonhealth outcomes. "Welfare" is understood to be a function of individual utilities.[442]

From a welfarist perspective, scarce resources should be allocated in a way to maximize the satisfaction of individual preferences. CBAs express both the costs and effects of an intervention in monetary terms and evaluating whether welfare is maximized subject to social budget constraints.[443] Individuals can directly compare their benefit from a healthcare intervention with other alternative goods that they can purchase and can indicate their willingness-to-pay. In the absence of functioning markets and disregarding further distributional aspects, a CBA compares the aggre-

442 BROUWER ET AL. (2008), p. 326; and BUCHANAN ET AL. (2013), p. 2.

443 BUCHANAN ET AL. (2013), p. 8.

gated net willingness-to-pay as measure of the desirability of a healthcare intervention with its net costs.[444]

CBAs are able to evaluate the social advantages and disadvantages of an health intervention (the "outcome") in monetary units. However, the evaluation is methodologically more challenging than a CEA. Further there are concerns from an ethical perpective to measure human life in monetary units.[445]

CBAs are occasionally permitted as supplementary analyses but rarely influence HTA decisions in general.[446] To date, no full CBA for PM applications can be found in the literature. This may be the result of methodological, but also theoretical, challenges that need to be addressed. The prevailing current view of most health economists still appears to follow the extra-welfarist evaluative framework.[447]

3.1.3 ACCE framework

Besides the two presented health economic approaches for evaluating applications in the context of personalized medicine, the more comprehensive ACCE framework has been developed by the U. S. CENTERS FOR DISEASE CONTROL AND PREVENTION that has been adopted by various health evaluation entities worldwide.[448]

The criteria for evaluating genetic tests are summarized by the four components of the ACCE framework: *1. Analytic validity, 2. clinical validity, 3. clinical utility and 4. associated ethical, legal and social implications.* The first three components are the most commonly used criteria to assess the quality of a diagnostic test.[449]

Although the four criteria are imperative to genetic testing, some of their exact definitions with respect to PM are not always clear.[450] The following sections explain the four components and illustrate the associated challenges defining the terms.

---

444 ROGOWSKI ET AL. (2015), p. 55.

445 P. MARSHALL & FLESSA (2015), p. 305.

446 An exception is the evaluation of public health programs by the UK NATIONAL INSTITUTE FOR HEALTH CARE EXCELLENCE (NICE): The use of CBAs is permitted in this context if it has been judged that CEA/CUA are not suitable, BUCHANAN ET AL. (2013), p. 8.

447 ROGOWSKI ET AL. (2015), p. 55.

448 US CENTERS FOR DISEASE CONTROL AND PREVENTION (2010)b, *ACCE Model Process for Evaluating Genetic Tests.*

449 Definitions for "analytical validity", "clinical validity" and "clinical utility" can be found in SCOTT (2011), p. 6; HAYES ET AL. (2013), p. 1; HAYES (2014), p. 962; MANSFIELD (2015), p. 14 and BOMBARD (2015), p. 58.

450 SCOTT (2011), p. 6.

Analytical validity:

The analytical validity answers the question *how accurately and reliably the test measures predict the presence or absence of genes or genetic changes.*[451]

Analytic validity encompasses evaluation criteria like analytic sensitivity, specificity, predictive values, reliability and robustness of a test.[452] It is usually ensured by the testing laboratory, which undertakes a relatively straightforward, robust process to ensure accurate detection and reporting of the test results.[453] Ensuring analytical validity is the first step before any test can be de- veloped further for the market.[454]

Clinical validity:

The clinical validity answers the question *how consistently and accurately the test detects or predicts the intermediate or final outcomes of interest (e.g., presence/absence or risk of a specific disease, survival or response to therapy).*[455]

Establishing clinical validity is the bigger challenge than analytical validity. The process requires data curation and carrying out prospective randomized clinical trials.[456] As indicated previously, it is still one of the biggest scientific challenges to create evidence on how genomic variants are actually related to specific phenotypic characteristics or their associations with disease.[457]

Clinical utility:

The clinical utility answers the question *how likely the test is to significantly improve patient outcomes.*[458] The criterion measures if there is evidence that the use of

---

451 *Ibidem*, p. 6; HAYES ET AL. (2013), p. 1; HAYES (2014), p. 962; MCCARTHY ET AL. (2013), p. 8; K. PHILLIPS ET AL. (2013), p. 61 and BOMBARD (2015), p. 1.

452 KHOURY ET AL. (2008), p. 1604.

453 SCOTT (2011), p. 6; and MCCARTHY ET AL. (2013), p. 8.

454 Cf. Part III, Chapter 4.1 Inconsistencies and gaps in the regulatory framework of the approval process for personalized medicine, p. 133 ff. Analytical validity is a required approval criterion. Cf. also ELLUL (2015) p. 354, with details on the required tresholds.

455 SCOTT (2011), p. 6; HAYES ET AL. (2013), p. 1; HAYES (2014), p. 962; MCCARTHY ET AL. (2013), p. 8; and K. PHILLIPS ET AL. (2013), p. 61.

456 MCCARTHY ET AL. (2013), p. 8.

457 Cf. Part II, Chapter 1.3.1 Tapping new scientific potential, p. 62 ff; and BOMBARD (2015), p. 1 and ELLUL (2015) p. 354. Additionaly, despite known gene-disease associations, clinical validity may be much lower than expected because response to drugs is not limited only to genetic factors, because epicenetic factors (e.g., interrelationships with the environment, lifestyle, age, race, comorbidities and other drug treatments) play a role too. Moreover, gene variants can be pleiotropic – meaning that they are associated with more than one disease or drug response, cf. GRECH, SCERRI, ET AL. (2015), p. 355, for more details.

458 SCOTT (2011), p. 6; HAYES ET AL. (2013), p. 1; MCCARTHY ET AL. (2013), p. 8; K. PHILLIPS ET AL. (2013), p. 61; and BOMBARD (2015), p. 2.

the test is able to guide clinical decisions which result in improved clinical outcomes compared with those outcomes, in which the biomarker test results were not applied.[459]

To be useful in clinical practice, a test must reflect the expected health benefit attributed to the result of the test.[460] In clinical practice it is not enough to know that a biomarker separates one population into two with statistical significance, the important question is whether the marker does it in a way that is important clinically. It refers to how effectively test results alter the management of the patient and whether these changes lead to clinically important improvements in health outcomes, measured – among other measures – in terms of the choice of a more appropriate therapy, improved survival, avoided hospitalizations or fewer physician visits.[461] A healthcare provider must know whether to withhold therapy from one patient or give therapy to another patient because the results indicated the therapy or withholding it improves their outcomes.[462]

Clinical utility of a test is a widely used measure of its usefulness in the clinic and resulting changes in health outcomes. However, there is no consensus on its precise definition or on how to adequately demonstrate it, particularly with regards to PM.[463] Today, the clinical utility of PM is still under-examined.[464]

Associated ethical, legal and social implications:

Associated ethical, legal and social implications of the evaluation framework foresee a discussion about *impediments* (e.g., stigmatization, discrimination, privacy/confidentiality and personal/family social issues or legal issues regarding consent, ownership of data and/or samples, patents, licensing, proprietary testing, obligation to disclose, or reporting requirements) as well as *safeguards* of a new personalized medicine application.[465]

Additional criterion up for discussion: Personal utility

In the ACCE framework, clinical utility has been defined in medical terms. However, there are calls for incorporating measures of *"personal utility"* in assessing per-

---

459 HAYES (2014), p. 962.
460 GRECH, SCERRI, ET AL. (2015), p. 355.
461 J. COHEN (2015), p. 6.
462 HAYES ET AL. (2014), p. 2.
463 SMART (2006), p. 1; SCOTT (2011), p. 6; and FAULKNER ET AL. (2012), p. 1163; or MESSNER ET AL. (2016), p. 12.
464 Cf. discussion in Part II Chapter 3.2.2 Measuring "outcomes", p. 87 ff.
465 US CENTERS FOR DISEASE CONTROL AND PREVENTION (2010)a, *na*.

sonalized healthcare interventions. "Personal utility", encompasses benefits or harms for a patient that are primarily manifested outside medical contexts. Empirical research has shown that a patient may value the mere fact of being better informed – regardless of the actionability of the information. Or, for example, a test result may make a patient feel happier or it simply enables a more empowered involvement of a patient in health decisions.[466] Also the opposite might be the case when additional information may offer harms to a patient's wellbeing.[467]

3.1.4 Value based pricing (VBP)

PORTER belongs to the most prominent advocates for the concept of *value-based pricing (VBP)*. According to PORTER (2010) *"the failure to prioritize value improvement in health care delivery and to measure value has slowed down innovation"*.[468] He calls for the development of a consistent unit for measuring "value" in healthcare.

The basic concept behind VBP is that a healthcare procuct's price should reflect its "value" to (mainly, but not exclusively) the customer and not the costs of the product: "Value should always be defined around the customer, and in a well-functioning healthcare system, the creation of value for patients should determine the rewards for all other actors in the system".[469]

PORTER (2010) suggests to measure value as "outcomes relative to costs" with outcomes measured in a three-tiered approach.[470] However, PORTER (2010) is not explicit on what concrete units to use in the three tiers and how to weight them. The *"groups of relevant outcomes"* have to be defined for each medical condition and should cover short- and long-term health.[471]

---

466 HALVERSON, CLIFT, & MCCORMICK (2016), p. 1, for example found that patients who were genomically sequenced expressed four qualities that are separate from traditional views of clinical utility: *"Participants felt they had been empowered over their own health. They felt they had contributed altruistically to the progress of genomic technology in medicine. They felt their suffering had been legitimated. They also felt a sense of closure, having done everything they could. Patients expressed overwhelmingly positive attitudes toward sequencing"*.

467 HARVEY ET AL. (2012), p. 629; BUCHANAN ET AL. (2013), p. 7; BOMBARD (2015), p. 2; and GRECH, SCERRI, ET AL. (2015), p. 355.

468 PORTER (2010), p. 2480.

469 *Ibidem*, p. 2478.

470 *Tier 1:* Measuring the patient's health status achieved (survival & degree of health recovery); *Tier 2:* Measuring the process of recovery (time & disutility of the care process); *Tier 3:* Measuring the sustainability of health (new health problems, consequences of treatment itself). Cf. *Supplement* 2 and *figure* 1 in PORTER (2010).

471 PORTER (2010), p. 2478.

VBP differs from the standard CEA and represents a rearrangement of ICER. It contains besides economic outcome factors (e.g., QALYs) a weighting system for additional factors, for example burden of illness, innovation and societal benefit – whatever factors a country defines as appropriate for a certain condition.[472] Prior to implementation of VBP, all stakeholders have to reach a consens on the definition of outcomes.[473]

3.2 Lack of reliable data for measuring "value"

A second driver behind the inconsistent results in valuations of PM root in the *lack of reliable data* in order to perform the respective evaluations. The impact of data and evidence gaps represents a recurring theme in the literature and is a central challenge in the economic evaluation of personalized medicine.[474] Not only diagnostics and drug manufacturers, but also healthcare systems and providers are called to consider how to meet the increasing demand for evidence data in the context of personalized medicine.[475] Estimations of value will rely on the accuracy of real world data sourced from multiple locations and health practitioners. Therefore, consistent minimum standards for the capture and reporting of data need to be developed.[476]

Particular types of evidence gaps are peculiar to the concept of PM: The heterogeneity of cost data (*Chapter 3.2.1*), the challenges to measure outcomes *(Chapter 3.2.2)* and consequently and an agreement on how to measure clinical utility *(Chapter 3.2.3)*.

3.2.1 Measuring "costs"

The heterogeneity of cost data for personalized medicine applications provides a challenge for the *"cost side"* of an economic evaluation.[477] It is unclear how cost savings should be taken into account in economic analyses.[478]

---

472 KIERNAN (2016), p. 2.

473 *Ibidem*, p. 3.

474 *Studies discussing the lack of data:* ANNEMANS ET AL. (2013), p. 24; BUCHANAN ET AL. (2013); p. 5-6; HAYES ET AL. (2013), p. 3; P. MARSHALL & FLESSA (2015), p. 304 and 314; SHABARUDDIN ET AL. (2015), p. 118; TERKOLA ET AL. (2017), p. 2ff., performed a literature review and found no studies with real-world data for PM.

475 ANNEMANS ET AL. (2013), p. 24.

476 THE ACADEMY OF MEDICAL SCIENCES (2013), p. 59.

477 BUCHANAN ET AL. (2013), p. 2. For an extended discussion on measuring outcomes cf. PORTER (2010), *Supplement 1*, p. 9-12.

478 CONTI ET AL. (2010) cited in BOMBARD (2015), p. 58.

First, there are different categories of costs that can be included in an economic evaluation:[479] *Direct costs* can include patient recruitment, analysis, reporting, management of adverse drug reactions, genetic counseling, monitoring of disease progression; *indirect costs* may include morbidity and productivity or infrastructure costs; and *intangible costs* may include pain or sadness.[480]

Second, there are limited data on some cost categories.[481] For example there are unclear costs for genetic interventions due to variations between laboratories, countries or tests.[482] Additionally, the number of people responding to the biomarker has direct implications for the cost-effectiveness of treatment.[483] Another challenge leading to data is the fact that prices for genetic tests are decreasing continuously.[484] A last challenge is the existence of limited data about a testing strategy's potential to prevent adverse drug reactions and the lack of agreement on the appropriate methods to include them into economic models.[485]

3.2.2 Measuring "outcomes"

Similar challenges can be found at the "outcome side" of economic evaluations.[486] In this context, outcome measurement must take into account some specific characteristics of PM applications. A characteristic of PM applications that increases the complexity of economic analyses is that diagnostic tests produce information rather than

479 BUCHANAN ET AL. (2013), p. 5-6; P. MARSHALL & FLESSA (2015), p. 304; and SHABARUDDIN ET AL. (2015), p. 119.
AKHMETOV & BUBNOV (2015), p. 4, provide an overview, which cost categories are included in typical cost-effectiveness-studies depending on the perspectives of the whole society, a payer, an employer as well as a patient.
A report by the EUROPEAN COMMISSION (2013), p. 29, remarks that it is often recommended in the literature to use the societal viewpoint for the economic analysis, i. e. costs and outcomes for society as a whole should be valued. Also this view would include costs borne outside the healthcare sector, such as productivity losses and travel expenses and *stricto sensu* also outcomes for patients' family.

480 BUCHANAN ET AL. (2013), p. 5-6 and P. MARSHALL & FLESSA (2015), p. 305.

481 A. J. THOMPSON ET AL. (2014), p. 22 and ZARIC (2016), p. 1.

482 BUCHANAN ET AL. (2013), p. 6.

483 *"If a small number of patients respond positively to the marker for example 5%, it means that the cost of using the test on 100 persons should be divided between the five patients who receive treatment [...] If more people respond to the marker for example 50%, the total screening costs could be split between ten times more patients, making the use of the diagnostic tool much more cost-effective.In the later case, there are more people to treat and the costs of the diagnostics will be neglictible"*, EUROPEAN COMMISSION (2013), p. 27.

484 SWEN ET AL. (2007), p. 1321.

485 *Ibidem* and SHABARUDDIN ET AL. (2015), p. 118.

486 For an extended discussion on measuring outcomes cf. PORTER (2010), *Supplement* 1, p. 7-9 and *Supplement* 2.

direct value. Economic evaluations need to consider both the *test* and *therapeutic* simultaneously and to measure how that information impacts treatment decisions and outcomes.[487]

There are three fundamental mechanisms by which measuring a biomarker may impact outcomes:[488]

1. Patients' understanding: The use of a diagnostic device may help the patient understand a disease or disease risk and thereby directly improve quality of life.

2. *Patients' motivation:* It may also motivate the patient to make behavioral changes that improve health (e.g., eating a healthier diet, exercising more, or improving adherence to prescribed treatments).

3. Clinical decision making: The identification of a biomarker may help a clinician make a clinical decision that leads to improved health of the patient.

The last mechanism is the most commonly cited reason for measuring a biomarker. But outcomes measurements can also target the other two mechanisms.[489] There is a wide range of ways to measure health outcomes what challenges the *comparability of health economic studies* in personalized medicine.[490] For example, the EUROPEAN COMMISSION (2013) stresses the need for research to better measure patient outcomes in the context of personalized medicines.[491]

3.2.3 Measuring "clinical utility"

Although "clinical utility" is an increasingly used concept in healthcare, it lacks an agreed formal definition or conceptualization and it has been variably defined and

---

487 K. PHILLIPS ET AL. (2013), p. 61.

488 Three fundamental mechanisms according to PLETCHER & PIGNONE (2011), p. 1116-1117.

489 PLETCHER & PIGNONE (2011), p. 1117.

490 SHABARUDDIN ET AL. (2015), p. 119-120, criticizing the methodological issues regarding the valuation of health outcomes. For an overview of possible outcome Cf. KROUSEL-WOOD (1999). PLETCHER & PIGNONE (2011), p. 1117, mention for example the incidence or severity of disease, quality of life, risk of death, life-years, and QALY's. QALY is routinely used as a summary measure of health outcome for economic evaluation. For an explanation of the QALY approach, cf. previous Chapter 3.1.1 *Extra-welfarist approach:* Cost-effectiveness analysis, p. 77 f. Also, often *short-term endpoints* are used as surrogate for health outcomes, including patient-reported indicators (e.g., psychological, behavioral, and functional end-points) and informational indicators (e.g., knowledge, attitudes, and satisfaction), but these endpoints may not correlate with health outcomes, cf. discussion in BOMBARD (2015), p. 58.

491 EUROPEAN COMMISSION (2013), p. 25. Also T. A. MANOLIO ET AL. (2016), p. 1, mentions the lack of evidence of its impact on clinical outcomes as one of the most significant challenges to widespread implementation of PM.

measured.[492] The term is commonly used as a synonym for studies of clinical effectiveness and economic evaluations.[493] It includes elements of whether the clinical outcomes of an intervention are effective and whether its implementation offers an economically efficient solution to a healthcare problem.[494] Clinical utility can reflect the balance between benefits and harms. It can have multiple dimensions and interpretations from the traditional focus on improved health outcomes for an individual to other potential benefits (e.g., for family members).[495] The term is used to describe work that judges aspects of clinical effectiveness which can be measured using "objective" or "preference" outcome measures.[496]

There are several reasons behind the lack of evidence for clinical utility:

There is the challenge of *insufficient investigation* of the clinical utility of PM.[497] There are gaps in the current regulatory framework for CDx: In the US as well as in the EU, there is no regulatory requirement to demonstrate clinical utility of a test.[498]

Research has demonstrated that the divergent adoption of PM treatments across different clinical specialisms is less about "resistance" or "conservatism" than the perceived clinical utility of tests in specific clinical settings.[499] Intermediate steps are needed that lie between discovery and routine clinical implementation to generate the evidence base to justify implementation. The ambiguity about level of evidence for clinical utility augments other barriers to the implementation of personalized medi-

---

492 Cf. previous Chapter 3.1.3 ACCE framework, p. 82; and SMART (2006), p. 1; KHOURY ET AL. (2008), p. 1605; PERSONALIZED MEDICINE COALITION (2015), p. 7.

493 SMART (2006), p. 1.

494 *Ibidem.*

495 KHOURY ET AL. (2008), p. 1605.

496 SMART (2006), p. 2.

497 *Criticizing the lack of investigation of clinical utility in the context of PM:* PACI (2009), p. 286; RAMSEY ET AL. (2011), p. 2262; KHOURY ET AL. (2012), p. 641-642; BUCHANAN ET AL. (2013), p. 2 and 9; THE ACADEMY OF MEDICAL SCIENCES (2013), p. 52; J. COHEN, WILSON, & MANZOLILLO (2013), p. 378; HAYES ET AL. (2013), p. 3; KIEVITS ET AL. (2014), p. 13, K. PHILLIPS ET AL. (2013), p. 64; T. A MANOLIO ET AL. (2013), p. 260 and 264; MCCARTHY ET AL. (2013), p. 1; AKHMETOV ET AL. (2015), p. 223; GARATTINI, CURTO, & FREEMANTLE (2015); P. MARSHALL & FLESSA (2015), p. 314; MEADOWS ET AL. (2015), p. 8; RELLING & EVANS (2015), p. 349; ROGOWSKI ET AL. (2015), p., 2 (with further references).

498 Cf. Part III, Chapter 4.1 Inconsistencies and gaps in the regulatory framework of the approval process for personalized medicine, p. 133 ff.

499 TUTTON (2013), p. 189.

cine: a) healthcare providers refrain from applying PM,[500] and b) payers refrain from covering PM.[501]

In order to generate clear evidence for the clinical utility of genomic interventions large samples must be studied. This is described as "challenging", partly because *evaluation panels tend to work in isolation*;[502] and partly due to inherently *small sample sizes* and the rarity of some genomic markers.[503] But even with larger samples, there can be controversies about the interpretation of the evidence.[504] E.g., there is the problem of oversimplifying assumptions assuming perfect update and use in terms of prescribing practice of current economic evaluations of CDx.[505]

A further reason for the lack of evidence for clinical utility is the *ambiguity about the standards for the evaluation processes for clinical utility.* Evaluation processes for clinical utility assessments are "neither clear nor predictable". More objective and reliable standards for these evaluation processes need to become broadly accepted.[506] The promotion of evidence generation will require harmonization also to send a consistent signal to test manufacturers.[507]

Also, the generation of evidence for clinical utility in the context of personalized medicine has long *not been in the focus of academic work.*[508] Several peer-reviewed studies may suggest clinical validity, but rarely demonstrate clinical utility.[509] There is claimed to be a "paucity of randomized controlled trials" demonstrating the clinical

---

500 Cf. Part III, Chapter 5.1 Lack of healthcare providers' knowledge about personalized medicine, hp. 162 ff.

501 Cf. Part III, Chapter 6.1 Lack of reimbursement for personalized medicine diagnostics, p. 182 ff. and others stating that payers require evidence for PM in order to reimburse it: J. COHEN (2012), p. 752; PERSONALIZED MEDICINE COALITION (2015), p. 7; and MILNE & COHEN (2015)a, p. 3.

502 T. A MANOLIO ET AL. (2013), p. 260.

503 BOMBARD (2015), p. 58.

504 T. A MANOLIO ET AL. (2013), p. 264. T. A MANOLIO ET AL. (2013) cite the study by JOHNSON ET AL. (2012) discussing the data on the relationship between CYP2C19 variants and failure of antiplatelet efficacy of clopidogrel.

505 ANNEMANS ET AL. (2013), p. 24.

506 PERSONALIZED MEDICINE COALITION (2015), p. 7. There are attempts to identify the standards for the evaluation processes for clinical utility. E.g., MICHEEL ET AL. (2012), p. 79-104, explain the recommended steps for assessing a validated omics-based test for clinical utility from a US perspective.

507 PAYNE & ANNEMANS (2013), p. 33; and TOWSE & GARRISON (2013) p. 41.

508 Until 2011, only ca. 3% of the published genomics research has focused on the development of evidence-based guidelines or health services and systems research for genomics applications and their real-life health outcomes, cf. LEHOUX (2011), p. 76.

509 HAYES (2013), p. 3, with further references claiming that few researchers take *"the next step across the bright line"* into the evaluation for clinical utility. Also RAMSEY ET AL. (2011), p. 2262, identified 39 studies evaluating genomic tests for the five most common types of cancer. None of the studies contained a prospective evaluation of a test's clinical utility.

utility.[510] The ability to demonstrate clinical utility is further limited by the design requirements of randomized controlled trials which are the "gold standard for establishing clinical utility".[511] The data required are not best provided from randomized controlled trial study designs. Nevertheless, existing data gaps in clinical utility must be filled and other data sources must be used. This implies that health economists and decision makers must prepare to accept data that stem from sources other than from the current "gold standard" of the randomized controlled trial.[512]

[510] YEO ET AL. (2010), p. 5; and BUCHANAN ET AL. (2013), p. 2.

[511] BOMBARD (2015), p. 58; cf. also Part III, Chapter 4.2 Incompatibility of clinical trials with personalized pharmaceuticals, p. 159.

[512] ANNEMANS ET AL. (2013), p. 24.

4 Criticism towards personalized medicine

4.1 Personalized medicine is a "hype"

A main criticism is the argument that PM is nothing new, but an industry driven "hype". Critics argue that concept of PM has always existed.[513] The term PM is claimed to merely rebrand the claims originally attributed to the sequencing of the human genome for a new decade with the aim to *"give personalized medicine a fresh start and essentially resetting the clock".*[514] They argue that the promising term "personalized" or "individualized" is an intentional marketing construct in order to set the ideal conditions for innovation and to attract investment as a mean of "upstream product marketing". According to critics, the potential of PM is overestimated.[515]

4.2 Personalized medicine does not reduce costs in healthcare

Despite existing health economic studies[516] which show that PM can reduce healthcare costs, some critics question these findings. They argue that PM will not reduce costs and that conventional treatments are cheaper.[517] First, because personalized therapies have smaller markets with less direct competition.[518] Second, because they are more likely to be biologics (in contrast to small molecules) with higher manufacturing costs that need to be amortized. Third, PM pharmaceuticals are more efficient compared to traditional medicines and are thus able to charge higher prices. Fourth, it is argued that the R&D costs are higher and thus higher prices are charged.[519]

4.3 Personalized medicine increases costs due to orphanization

With PM sub-groups of diseases are created. Because of this stratification PM could have the "side effect" of creating "new" diseases based on an identified gene variation, and more conditions could be associated with the "orphan" definition due to

---

513 E.g., GAMMA (2013) p. 507; SCHLEIDGEN & MARCKMANN (2013), p. 224.

514 DUFFY (2015), p. 8.

515 RIPPE ET AL. (2004), p. 156; DUFFY (2015),p. 8; K. SALARI ET AL. (2012), p. 1; GAMMA (2013), p. 507; TUTTON (2013), p. 1; SCHLEIDGEN & MARCKMANN (2013), p. 224.

516 E.g., LOVGREN (2006), ROWE (2006); and RISCHER (2008) cited in FACKLER & MCGUIRE (2010), p. 2; and INTERLANDI (2016), p. 1ff.

517 Cf. next Sub-chapter 4.3 Personalized medicine increases costs due to orphanization, p. 92 ff.

518 E.g., LOVGREN (2006), ROWE (2006) and RISCHER (2008) cited in FACKLER & MCGUIRE (2010), p. 2; INTERLANDI (2016), p. 1ff.; and STERN ET AL. (2017), p. 1131 ff.

519 STERN ET AL. (2017), p. 1131-1132.

their smaller population size. This trend of emerging "new" diseases for smaller and smaller sub-groups is commonly denoted as "orphanization".

"Orphan drugs" are medicines for rare diseases. In the EU, orphan disease is defined as a disease with less than 1 patients per 2'000 inhabitants.[520] Orphan drugs commonly enjoy a comparably favorable regulatory treatment as market authorization is facilitated which in turn cuts down the cost of drug development.[521] Patient subpopulations become smaller and may be too small to be profitable. To balance smaller population sizes and growing development costs, pharmaceutical companies increase pricing for personalized therapies.[522] There is the danger that the trend towards orphanization leads to "extensively high costs".[523]

There is the tendency to use drug development strategies for orphan conditions more often. Already today, there is an observable tendency for developing orphan drugs.[524] SEILER (2016) noted that *"to exaggerate, no cancer is not 'orphan' anymore".*[525] It is estimated that, in Switzerland 7.2% of the population suffer from one of the currently ca. 6000 orphan diseases.[526] With PM, this numbers could increase.

Experts expect policy makers to be overstrained with the trend of "crumbling" diseases.[527] Critics warn that the topic of pricing has to be reevaluated with the move into a new classification system of diseases,[528] since current pricing tactics for orphan drugs would not be sustainable.[529].

4.4 Personalized medicine leads to a pathologization of society

Critics argue that PM leads to a "pathologization" or "medicalization" of society.[530] In the context of PM the term "disease mongering" has been mentioned. It stands for

---

520 FOUNDATION FOR PEOPLE WITH RARE DISEASES, HENGGELER (2017, e-mail to author).

521 E.g., in Germany it would not be necessary to provide proof under the Pharmaceutical Market Restructuring Act (AMNOG) of the additional benefit in the context of the early benefit assessment, e.g., GOTTWALD & HUSTER (2016), p. 317.
Cf. also MÜLLER & SCHÄFER in WIENKE ET AL. (2013), p. 18; and DIETER SCHNEIDER & BUBLAK (2015), p. 418.
Cf. RECHER (2014) for a quick overview of the facilitated regulatory treatment of orphan drugs in Switzerland.

522 FAULKNER ET AL. (2012), p. 1164; STERN ET AL. (2017), p. 1131.

523 ANTONANZAS ET AL. (2015), p. 455.

524 RABASSEDA ET AL. (2013), p. 117 ff.

525 SEILER, interviewed 18th of July 2016.

526 RAUCH (2015), p. 24.

527 SZEKELY at the ETH LATSIS Forum on June 29th, 2016.

528 Cf. Part II, Chapter 1.3.2 New nosology through , p. 63.

529 LEYENS, RICHER, MELIEN, BALLENSIEFEN & BRAND (2015), p. 9.

530 E.g., MÜLLER & SCHÄFER in WIENKE ET AL. (2013), p. 21; and JAMES (2014), p. 386.

the *"marketing of interventions for healthy people in whom mooted disease processes may never progress to actual pathophysiological signs and symptoms if left untreated or treated less aggressively"*.[531] It is claimed that overconfidence in the new technologies and intense commercialization may produce excess diagnoses of "non-diseases" which may never progress beyond potentiality.[532] MÜLLER UND SCHÄFER (2013) see a danger of a *„pandemia of premorbides"*.[533]

4.5 Personalized medicine diverts resources away from other healthcare priorities

Critics fear that a focus on PM comes at the expense of other public health efforts. Questions are raised about the opportunity costs of PM and the priorities set in healthcare.[534]

In an article titled *"Is precision medicine the route to a healthy world?"* COOTE & JOYNER (2015) criticize that PM distracts from proven, effective and low cost population-wide interventions and policies. They argue that the genes are *"typically not clinically informative"* and that the genetic information is not useful for complex cardiovascular disorders and diabetes as large gene-environment interactions exist. Behavioral interventions (e.g., physical activity, dietary habits) have proven to be effective at lowering of patient risk of disease and in secondary prevention.[535]

Similarly argue other critics that PM is diverting resources away from other healthcare priorities and that PM risks concentrating resources to those that already have greater access to healthcare and power in society. One argument is the *"inverse care law"*, meaning that high income populations have comparably low healthcare needs but access to it, whereas low income has comparably high need for healthcare and low access to it.[536] JAMES (2014) argues that *"the extreme levels of human and material resources required by the genomic and information technologies upon which personalised medicine is based threaten to disproportionately disadvantage those with greatest healthcare needs"* and he states that resources are captured at the expense of

531 JAMES (2014), p. 386.
532 *Ibidem.*
533 MÜLLER & SCHÄFER in WIENKE ET AL. (2013), p. 21.
534 COOTE & JOYNER (2015), p. 1617. Similarly argue VOLLMANN (2013), JAMES (2014), ANTONANZAS ET AL. (2015), BAYER & GALEA (2015), p. 499 f., an opinion piece in the *New England Journal of Medicine*; ALLEN & CHRISTIE (2016), p. 1 ff.; and GRAY, LAGERBERG, & DOMBRÁDI (2017), p. 87 ff.
535 COOTE & JOYNER (2015), p. 1617.
536 The *"availability of good medical care tends to vary inversely with the need for it in the population served"*, cf. HART (1971), p. 405, cited in JAMES (2014), p. 389.

alternative behavioral and social pathways that have the potential to effect greater improvements in population health.[537]

Further, it is criticized that PM treatments target predominantly developed countries with a relatively big market in terms of potential patients and purchase capacity exists. A point of criticism is that this kind of approach is not being used to address conditions whose prevalence is higher in less developed countries.[538] Critics fear that the new PM technologies will have a negative impact on inequalities – *"unless their user base can be radically extended to include vulnerable populations".*[539]

537 JAMES (2014), p. 389.
538 ANTONANZAS ET AL. (2015), p. 455.
539 ALLEN & CHRISTIE (2016), p. 1 ff.

5 Ecosystem of personalized medicine

The following Chapter presents an overview of the relevant stakeholders in the context of PM to whom this thesis refers in the following Parts *(Chapter 5.1)*. As personalized medicine consists of a diagnostic and a pharmaceutical component, the drug-diagnostic co-development process is a peculiarity of PM and will be presented in the second sub-chapter (*Chapter 5.2*).

5.1 Framework for the personalized medicine ecosystem

The following figure represents how this thesis understands the ecosystem of PM.[540] There are several alternative attempts to provide an orientation of the different players and their interactions in the emerging field of PM.[541]

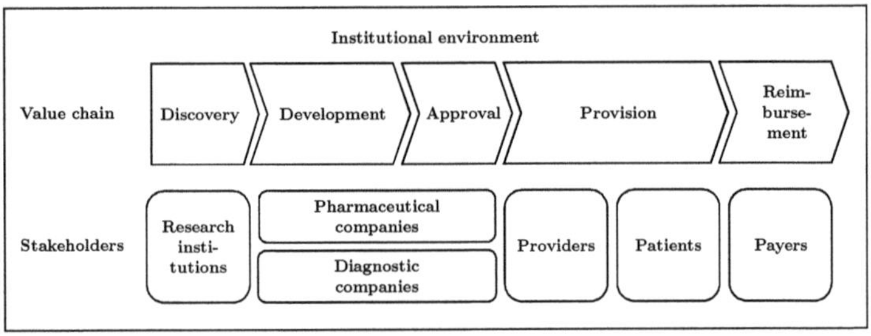

Figure 11: Ecosystem of personalized medicine

The framework provides an overview of the relevant stakeholders in the context of PM. There are five relevant stakeholders:

Research institutions are primarily involved into basic research and discovery. They can be public, like universities, or private like pharmaceutical companies' research institutes or contract research organizations.

Pharmaceutical companies are primarily involved into the development, production, approval and marketing of the pharmaceutical component of a PM application.

Diagnostics companies are primarily involved into the development, manufacturing, approval and marketing of the diagnostic component of a PM application.

[540] The term "ecosystem" stems from ARONSON & REHM (2015), p. 336. However, they use it for an own, more technically focused framework, *figure* 1.

[541] FAULKNER ET AL. (2012), p. 1163; ARONSON & REHM (2015), p. 336; E. BLAIR, STRATTON, & KAUFMANN (2012) describing the industry and value chain; JAIN (2015), p. 590, with the players in the development of PM; and JAMESON & LONGO (2015), *figure* 1.

Providers are primarily involved in diagnosing a disease, consulting and informing a patient about available treatments and preventive measures, and in providing a PM application to a patient. Providers are mainly medical doctors; in some cases they can also be other healthcare service providers like medical assistants, nurses or pharmacists.

Patients are the consumers of PM. Motives for consuming PM can differ ranging from pure curiosity to preventional motives and risk assessments, diagnostic motives, to inform and guide a treatment decision or to monitor a disease progress.

Payers are primarily involved in the reimbursement of PM. In some countries, payers are private corporations, in others they are public.

The relevant stakeholders are embedded in the institutional environment influencing the stakeholders' incentive schemes.

5.2 Rx-CDx co-development

The pharmaceutical industry has reached a certain level of maturity and PM can represent an alternative to the traditional "blockbuster strategies".[542] PM is changing the traditional approach to provide medicine. New business models are emerging.[543] With PM, the business models for diagnostics and for the pharmaceutical components come together. A pharmaceutical is tied to the availability of a diagnostic component – and vice versa – without the pharmaceutical, the diagnostic has little relevance in the healthcare system.[544]

A central element of how PM is changing the traditional business models is the Rx-CDx co-development. Essentially, there are two options to develop the Dx component of PM: Either the diagnostic component is developed together with the phar-

---

542 MILLER ET AL. (2011), p. 137; and DIETER SCHNEIDER & BUBLAK (2015), p. 417, talking about *"niche busters"*.

543 MITTRA & TAIT (2012), p. 709-710; KOELSCH, PRZEWROCKA, & KEELING (2013), p. 89 ff; BOJOVIC, SABATIER, & ROUAULT (2015), p. 81, about the transition towards user-centric business models; HALECKER, KAMPRATH & BRAUN in EPPINGER ET AL. (2015), p. 3 ff. & p. 143, with a detailed study about the pharmaceutical and diagnostic business models and their changing in the context of PM; HALECKER&HÖLZLE in EPPINGER ET AL. (2015), p. 67 ff, about business model innovation in the pharmaceutical industry; with an overview about the publications related to business models in PM, p. 156; KAMPRATH in EPPINGER ET AL. (2015), p. 241 about Dx business model typologies inclusive status quo and a list of identified PM potential; and DAVID PETTITT ET AL. (2016), p. 326.

544 E.g., MEADOWS ET AL. (2015), p. 10.

maceutical component (*Rx-CDx co-development*)[545] or the diagnostic component is developed *post hoc.*[546] The downside for pharmaceutical company with CDx being added to the drug label after a drug is on the market, the CDx decreases the potential patient population without an upside for the pharmaceutical company.[547]

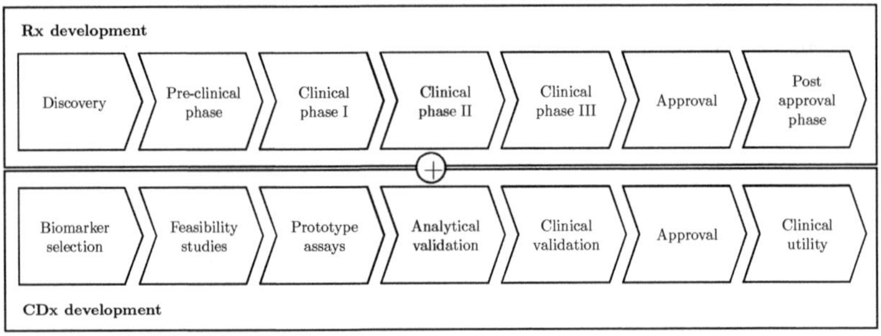

Figure 12: Rx-CDx co-development[548]

SOURCE: Illustration based on OLSEN & TRØST JØRGENSEN (2014), p. 2.

In the Rx-CDx co-development process there is an interdependency of drug and diagnostics. The CDx is developed in parallel to the drug, as illustrated in the figure above. The success of a co-development project depends mainly on the strength of the initial biomarker hypothesis, which is often deduced during the early research and preclinical phases of the drug development.[549]

Traditionally, pharmaceutical companies have limited expertise in the development of CDx.[550] Pharmaceutical companies have four basic options for obtaining diagnos-

545 One example is the breat cancer treatment trastuzumab which was co–developed with a human epidermal growth factor receptor (HER-2) immune chemistry test.

546 The tests for abacavir, irinotecan or warfarin are examples for a *post hoc* development of the CDx.

547 AGARWAL ET AL. (2015), p. 104.

548 For alternative, partially more detailed figures and descriptions of the co-development process, cf. COTTER, BABU, & MOORE (2012) p. 54 ff, *figure* 1; MOORE ET AL. (2012), *figure* 2; AKHMETOV ET AL. (2015), p. 215; and THOMAS ET AL. (2016), p. 345.

549 OLSEN & TRØST JØRGENSEN (2014), p. 2 ff., with a detailed description of the co-development process. Cf. also MITTRA & TAIT (2012), p. 714, about timing and coordination issues in the co-development; PASIC ET AL. (2013), p. 163, with a description of the multistep process of CDx development (validation, standardization, test interpretation, quality control, etc.).

550 E.g., MOORE ET AL. (2012), p. 493.

tics. 1. The internal development of CDx,[551] 2. partnering with an established Dx company, 3. acquiring a Dx company, and 4. hybrids of the first three options.[552]

In the past, there has been an increase in CDx deals.[553] However, the numbers of co-developed PM applications is still relatively low.[554] It is estimated that ca. 11% of the drugs with required CDx were approved simultaneously.[555] Several challenges are making the co-development between the industries difficult.[556]

551 This option is most applicable to drug developers that have a diagnostic division (e.g., ROCHE).

552 AGARWAL ET AL. (2015), p. 106. LANDECK ET AL. (2016), p. 25, about opportunities and challenges in strategic partnerships between diagnostic and pharmaceutical companies.

553 AGARWAL ET AL. (2015), p. 104-105, with an overview of the CDx deals from 2007-2013.

554 KIEVITS ET AL. (2014), p. 8; and AGARWAL ET AL. (2015), p. 101.

555 AGARWAL ET AL. (2015), p. 101.

556 Cf. Part III, Chapter 3.1 Strategic, operational and cultural differences between the pharmaceutical and the diagnostics industry, p. 120 ff.

Part III: Theoretical part

Identification and analysis of the institutional barriers to the translation of personalized medicine into clinical practice

The pace with which clinical applications of PM are entering clinical practice is described as slow, below expectations and dissatisfactory.[557] A growing body of literature in Translational Medicine and Public Health is dealing with the underlying reasons behind this phenomenon.

On the one hand, there are *scientific barriers*,[558] on the other hand, a number of *non-science related, institutional barriers* hold back the translation of PM into clinical practice.[559]

---

557 J. COHEN (2011), p. 293, and J. COHEN (2012), p. 751; TOWSE & GARRISON (2013); p. S39; O'DONNELL (2013); p. S1, ISSA (2008), p. 192; PRASAD & BRECKENRIDGE (2011); p. 869; VOLLMANN (2013), p. 237. This challenge is more extensively discussed in the introduction of this thesis, cf. RESEARCH CONCEPT, Chapter 1 Problem, p. 1, especially *note* 12.

558 References in Part II, Chapter 1.3.1 Tapping new scientific potential, p. 62 ff.

559 C.f. *note* 18, and RESEARCH CONCEPT, Chapter 8.1 *In scope:* Non-science related institutional barriers to the translation of personalized medicine into clinical practice, and *note* 155, p. 28.

K. Bosshard, *Law and Economics of Personalized Medicine*,
Gesundheitsmanagement und Gesundheitsökonomik,
https://doi.org/10.1007/978-3-658-22074-7_4

As illustrated in Part II[560], *scientific barriers* are prominent only in certain areas, in others PM is reality.[561] Today, there are several – although differing – guidelines with recommendations about how to use insights from PM in clinical practice.[562] Part III primarily focuses on the identification of the *non-science related, institutional barriers* hindering the uptake of PM in clinical practice.

1 Methhodological approach

First, a systematic literature analysis is conducted.[563] In a second step, the incentives set by each barrier are examined for all relevant stakeholders in the PM ecosystem: Research institutions, pharmaceutical and diagnostics companies, providers, patients and payers. Each Chapter concludes with proposing a hypothesis about the respective barrier. Concluding Part III, an overview of the resulting barriers, their induced incentives for each stakeholder and their "relevance"[564] is given.

1.1 Literature analysis

The analyzed literature covers an interdisciplinary spectrum of publications with relevance for identifying the institutional barriers behind the translation of personalized medicine into clinical practice. Publications from Public Health, Translational Medicine, law, business and economics outlets as well as reports mandated or issued by governmental or professional associations were considered. The review comprises of 170 academic publications, 18 government reports, 22 reports by professional associations, 13 articles from (science) magazines. Search terms for the literature analysis were based on terminologies used in the context of PM as described in Part I[565], combined with the search terms "regulation"/"regulatory" and "institutional" via SCIENCEDIRECT, PUBMED, EBSCOHOST, ELSEVIER, FACTIVA and the UNIVERSITY OF ST. GALLEN metasearch engine. Publications written in English or German were included

---

560 References in Part II, Chapter 1.3.1 Tapping new scientific potential, p. 62 ff.

561 Cf. *Figure 1:* Value chain of personalized medicine, p. 9.

562 Cf. Part IV, Chapter 5.3.2 Overview of existing guideline sources, p. 169 ff.
E.g., the recommendations by FLOCKHART ET AL. (2009) of which an enlarged update can be found on the homepage (medicine.iupui.edu/CLINPHARM/ddis/main-table), the guidelines from PHARMGKB (www.pharmgkb.org/search/browseAlpha.action?browseKey=allGenes), the CPIC guidelines (www.pharmgkb.org/view/dosing-guidelines.do?source=CPIC#). All links last accessed in July, 2017.

563 Cf. following Sub-chapter 1.1 Literature analysis, p. 102 f.

564 "Relevance" as defined in the RESEARCH CONCEPT, Chapter 4.3 Derivation and evaluation of policy levers, *Relevance*, p. 12.

565 Chapter 1.1 Different understandings of personalized medicine, p. 36 ff.

in the analysis. The relevance for the review of the systematically retrieved literature was assessed based on the title and abstract of the respective publication.

Some publications are focusing explicitly on the description of one and some on multiple barriers for the translation of PM into clinical practice. For the following literature analysis, both types of publications were taken into account.

Based on the identified publications, the institutional barriers for the translation of PM are 1) identified, 2) synthesized, and 3) categorized. The categorization of the identified barriers is based on the value chain of personalized medicine.[566] As indicated in the RESEARCH CONCEPT, the majority of existing studies does not contain a comprehensive picture of all potential, non-science related barriers and only a minority attempts to group the barriers into certain categories.[567] To the knowledge of the author, this thesis is the first of its kind going one step further by examining which link of the PM value chain is hampered due to an institutional barrier.

1.2 Analysis of incentives

For each of the identified barriers an incentives analysis is performed – with the aim of examining the incentives induced by the respective barrier separately for each stakeholder involved in the PM ecosystem. As set by the scope of this, the identified incentives will be negative.[568]

The analysis is based on a theoretical, qualitative, micro-economic argumentation scheme with the constitutive microeconomic assumptions and interdependencies as described in the following *Sub-chapters 1.2.1* and *1.2.2*.

---

566 Cf. *Figure 1:* Value chain of personalized medicine, p. 9.

567 Cf. RESEARCH CONCEPT, Chapter 5.1 Degree of novelty of research question, *New categorization*, p. 15.

568 Cf. RESEARCH CONCEPT, Chapter 8.1 *In scope:* Non-science related institutional barriers to the translation of personalized medicine into clinical practice, p. 28.

1.2.1 Constitutive microeconomic assumptions

The incentives analysis is based on the assumption of rationally behaving players in the PM ecosystem:

A *research institution's* primary goal is to maximize the number of its high-quality publications and discoveries.

A rational *pharmaceutical company's* goal is to maximize the profits through the selling of pharmaceuticals. The pharmaceutical company might thus want a diagnostic test with the *"highest accuracy possible, available to the greatest number of physicians at the lowest cost in the shortest period of time"*.[569]

A *diagnostic company* which has the capabilities to develop and manufacture PM Dx has an interest to offer them only in cases with positive profits, i. e. the company is able to recoup its investment costs.

A *healthcare provider's* behavior will depend on his knowledge, attitude and convictions. Following the WORLD MEDICAL ASSOCIATION's DECLARATION OF GENEVA or the SMA's professional code this thesis assumes that a healthcare provider's first consideration is the health of a patient.[570] At the same time, a healthcare provider has limited financial and personell resources to achieve this goal, and her/his behavior depends on the economic incentive structures, like for example "activity-based" billing structures.[571]

A *patient's* primary aim is the own health. The smaller the self-investment, e.g., the out-of-pocket share payment, is, the more preferred the option is. A health maximizing patient's preferences depend on his or her personal cost-value ratio and on whether the intake of the drug has any adverse event. Due to the dependent relationship, a peculiarity is the information asymmetry arising between a patient and his/her healthcare provider with expert knowledge.

A *payer's* primary aim is to minimize the payments. As its payments depend on the health costs of the insured persons, an additional goal is their health.

---

569 AGARWAL ET AL. (2015), p. 106.

570 Cf. DECLARATION OF GENEVA, p. 1 and the SMA's professional code, *preamble*.

571 Cf. Part III, Chapter ii Drivers behind the lack of reimbursement for PM Dx, *History of cost-based reimbursement*, p. 187.

1.2.2 Interdependencies between the pharmaceutical and diagnostic component

Personalized medicine is characterized by the close relationship and interdependencies between the pharmaceutical and the diagnostic component. The choice of the CDx "cut-off value"[572] impacts the drug performance. This in turn influences a pharmaceutical company's decision to personalize a pharmaceutical or not. This Chapter briefly depicts this interdependency. It will be shown that the different stakeholders' preferences for the cut-off value differ – from stakeholder to stakeholder, and also from treatment to treatment.

For some biomarkers, multiple competing test platforms are available. Despite measuring the same molecular changes they might exhibit variations in their results.[573] One explanation behind variations between test platforms is that a test developer is basically free to choose the "cut-off" value.[574] With this choice the CDx developer influences the *"clinical validity"* of a test.[575]

In some ideal cases, the cut-off of a CDx test perfectly separates the population responding to a drug from the non-responder population. If the non-responders are eliminated in a clinical trial, the observed therapeutic effect will increase.

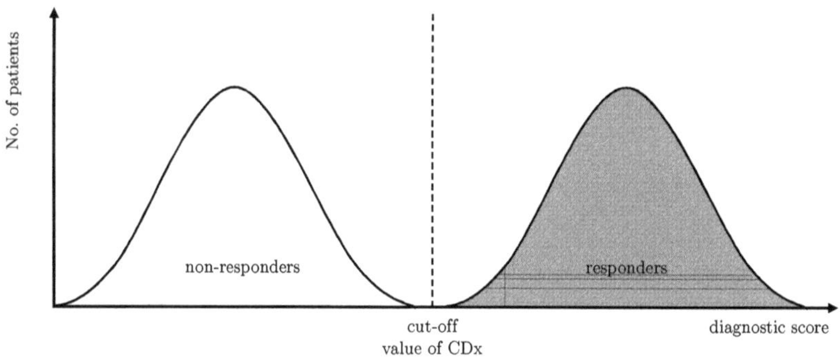

Figure 13: Perfect responder separation

SOURCE: TRUSHEIM & BERNDT (2015)b, p. 3, with adaptions by the author

[572] The biomarker-value of a CDx separating the patient population qualifying for treatment from the rest is called "cut-off value".

[573] A study of seven diseases demonstrated an agreement of 50% between the two platforms evaluated, NG, MURRAY, LEV & VENTER (2009) cited in PASIC ET AL. (2013), p. 163.

[574] Also referred to as *"diagnostic score"*.

[575] Cf. Part III, Chapter 3.1 Existence of multiple evaluation methodologies, *Clinical validity*, p. 83.

However, other patient population distributions are not dichotomous and the cut-off of a CDx test may not perfectly separate responders from non-responders as the two populations overlap. The chosen cut-off value determines the number of false positive[576] and false negative results.[577]

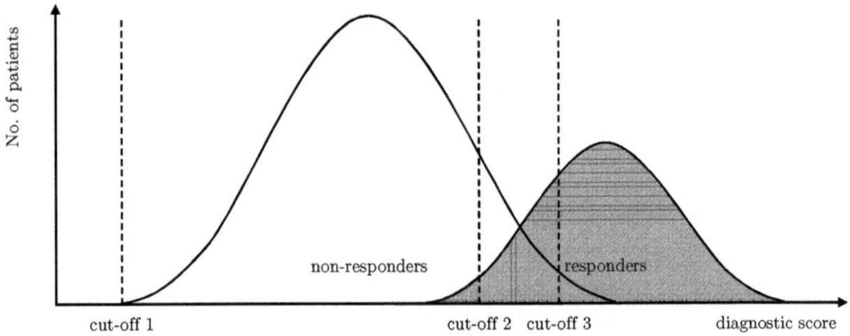

Figure 14: Imperfect responder situation

SOURCE: TRUSHEIM & BERNDT (2015)b, p. 7, with adaptions by the author.

In these cases, the choice of the cut-off impacts the performance of a drug in the treated population:

[576] *False positive* means in this case that the diagnostic score indicates that patients are responders to the treatment, but they are actually non-responders.

[577] *False negative* means in this case that the diagnostic score indicates that patients are non-responders to the treatment, but they are actually responders and would benefit from the drug.

	Cut-off 1 *"non-personalized scenario"*	**Cut-off 2** *"low cut-off scenario"*	**Cut-off 3** *"high cut-off scenario"*
Sensitivity of diagnostic[578]	100%	high	medium
Specificity of diagnostic[579]	0%	medium	high
Efficacy of drug	low	medium	high
Positive predictive value of Dx[580]	low	medium	high
Price of drug	low	medium	high
Overall market share of drug	high	medium	Low
Treated patients with drug	maximum number of false positives	several false positives	few false positives

Table 5: Overview CDx cut-off scenarios

SOURCE: TRUSHEIM & BERNDT (2015)b, p. 7, with adaptions by the author.

TRUSHEIM & BERNDT (2012) as well as TRUSHEIM & BERNDT (2015)b and to some extent RUBIN, ALLEN, NOWAK, & BATES (2014) illustrate the underlying economic incentives for different stakeholders for choosing a CDx cut-off value.

As the choice of the cut-off impacts the performance of a drug in the treated population, it also influences the incentives of *patients* and *providers* to use the drug, the incentives of *regulators* to approve the therapeutic as well as the incentives of *payers*

578 Probability of detection measuring the proportion of positives which are correctly identified as positives.

579 Measuring the proportion of negatives which are correctly identified as negatives.

580 The positive predictive value measures the number of true positives as a portion of all those who test positive, e.g., TRUSHEIM & BERNDT (2015)b, p. 8.

to reimburse the therapy. And finally, it influences the incentives of *innovators* and *investors* to develop a pharmaceutical in the first place.[581]

There is no straightforward answer to the question which stakeholder prefers which cut-off scenario. Rather multiple factors – like the drug prices (personalized and non-personalized), the size of the patient population, provider and patient expectations, etc. – influence the stakeholders' economic incentives if a drug will be personalized or not:[582]

Cut-off 1 "non-personalized scenario"

Cut-off 1 in the above figure represents the traditional "non-personalized" approach. All patients are treated with a drug and there is no CDx test separating responders from non-responders. Despite no use of a CDx, a "non-personalized" trial has 100% sensitivity as it selects all patients who might respond. But it has 0% specificity because no non-responder is excluded.

From a *drug manufacturers'* perspective, the whole patient base with the condition is eligible for treatment – thus this approach allows non-targeted marketing to the biggest possible patient base.[583] Further, in the non-personalized approach, the drug manufacturer does not depend on the use of a CDx. However with a lower positive predictive value (PPV), efficacy and price compared to personalized approaches will be lower. Thus, a drug manufacturer will only choose to develop a personalized drug in cases, in which the profit gains through higher price for the personalized drug offsets the loss due to the comparably smaller patient base.

In contrast to a *pharmaceutical company*, the *diagnostics company* will prefer a personalized approach with the use of a CDx - but only in cases, in which the institutional setting allows the Dx manufacturer to recoup the investment costs.

From a *payer's perspective,* the "non-personalized" approach has the advantage of not having to account for the reimbursement of a CDx. However, compared to a personalized approach, there might be ineffective costs due to significant number of patients that receive the drug despite it is of no benefit for them.

Cut-off 2 "low cut-off scenario"

Setting a low cut-off value (i.e., cut-off 2 in the figure above) leads to a low clinical specificity with several false positives and with a relatively low positive predictive

581 TRUSHEIM & BERNDT (2015)b, p. 1.

582 TRUSHEIM & BERNDT (2012) as well as TRUSHEIM & BERNDT (2015)b – both articles contain the same arguments. In the following the newer paper is cited.

583 TRUSHEIM & BERNDT (2015)b, p. 8.

value.[584] The number of non-responders classified as test positive and thus receiving ineffective treatment is relatively high. Instead the CDx test has a relatively high clinical sensitivity as nearly all responders are included.[585]

TRUSHEIM & BERNDT (2015)b hypothesize that such a drug would lead to more modest revenues as improvements in adoption speed, price, and market share are as well modest compared with a high cut-off scenario.[586] But the number of treated patients is potentially larger than in a high cut-off scenario. Depending on that number, the financial performance is possibly greater than in the non-personalized and high cut-off scenario.[587]

From a *patient's* and *provider's perspective*, the use of a CDx test might result in a higher *"willingness to seek, initiate, and adhere to the treatment regimen"*.[588] If a CDx exists to recommend a therapy, patients are encouraged to seek and adhere to a treatment and providers are more inclined to recommend the therapy. This effect could potentially expand the absolute number of patients and increase the overall market size.

However, such a comparably high number of *patients* might not occur in the low cut-off scenario. From a patient's perspective, the low cut-off could fail to inspire patients' interest and use compared to the high cut-off scenario, because the comparably larger number of false positive patients could lower an individual patient's expectation of response. The patients' behavior could thus trigger that, paradoxically, a low cut-off results in fewer patients pursuing the treatment than a high cut-off scenario.[589]

From a *payer's perspective*, who is solely focused on net total outlay regardless of net population clinical benefit, the low cut-off scenario could thus be preferred to a high cut-off scenario, in case fewer patients pursue the treatment. However, in case of

584 TRUSHEIM & BERNDT (2015)b, p. 8; and similarly arguing RUBIN ET AL. (2014), p. 1425.

585 *Ibidem*, p. 5.

586 *Ibidem*, p. 5 and 7.

587 *Ibidem*, p. 5. The MIT Center for Biomedical Innovation developed the "MIT Stratified Medicine Model" with which such simulations can be modeled (led by MARK TRUSHEIM and ERNST BERNDT). The model can be retrieved from http://cbi.mit.edu/research-overview/other-research-programs/strat_med/ (last visited January 26, 2106). A description is provided in TRUSHEIM ET AL. (2011).

588 TRUSHEIM & BERNDT (2015)b, p. 5.

589 TRUSHEIM & BERNDT (2015)b, p. 5. On the other hand, RUBIN ET AL. (2014) argue that from a *patient's perspective*, a low cut-off might preferred to a high cut-off value because this "would increase the likelihood that the patient would be able to receive the new treatment, even if the chances of response were low (assuming that the treatment was associated with an acceptable safety profile)", cf. RUBIN ET AL. (2014), p. 1425.

more people pursuing the treatment in the low cut-off scenario, a payer will prefer the high cut-off scenario.[590]

In this scenario, exposing patients to a treatment and risking adverse effects and delays in using other treatments might be non-desirable for *providers*. Especially for a drug with irreversible adverse effects this might be unacceptable, but it might be acceptable for a treatment with few adverse effects or treatment alternatives.[591]

For *Dx companies* a low cut-off value might result in revenues above what they might be with a higher cut-off value due to the larger number of test qualified patients. But due to the lower adoption speed than in the high cut-off scenario, peak revenues might grow higher but are reached with a lower speed. Thus a Dx manufacturer might fail to meet original revenue projections, especially if the remaining patent life of a test is short. With a lower cut-off value, a manufacturer risks demonstrating insufficient benefit to regulatory approval – especially if a competitor demonstrates a higher efficacy by choosing a high cut-off value.[592]

Cut-off 3 "high cut-off scenario"

Setting a high cut-off value (i.e., cut-off 3 in the figure above) leads to a high clinical specificity with fewer false positives setting. This will favor a positive predictive value at the expense of a negative predictive value.[593] A high cut-off value excludes almost all non-responders and ensures that almost all of the selected patients will respond to the drug. Few non-responders will be exposed to potential adverse effects of the treatment or the opportunity cost of pursuing an ineffective treatment. Setting a high cut-off also maximizes clinical trial efficacy results. TRUSHEIM & BERNDT (2015)b show that such a therapeutic could achieve a relatively high adoption speed, price as well as market share in the selected subpopulation.[594]

From a *provider's* perspective, a high cut-off might be unacceptable as it denies treatment to the false negatives, especially for severe conditions with few treatment alternatives.[595]

For *pharmaceutical company* a high cut-off value might reduce revenues below what they might be with a lower cut-off value due to the lower number of patients

590 TRUSHEIM & BERNDT (2015)b, p. 5.
591 *Ibidem.*
592 *Ibidem.*
593 TRUSHEIM & BERNDT (2015)b, p. 5; and similarly RUBIN ET AL. (2014), p. 1425.
594 *Ibidem*, p. 4.
595 *Ibidem*, p. 5.

selected in a high-cut off scenario. The higher price or greater market penetration might not offset the effects of the smaller treated patient population.[596]

From a *payer's perspective*, a high cut-off might be favored because this would restrict the use of a new therapeutic to a patient population that would have a large clinical benefit.[597] Most regulatory frameworks do classify the use of a treatment for responder patients below the cut-off value of the CDx as "off-label" use. "Off-label" use bear the risk of not being reimbursed.[598]

Prisoner's dilemma can lower the value of the personalized treatment

In cases, in which there are competing companies developing and selling a personalized drug and the corresponding CDx, each one has the choice of selecting the appropriate cut-off value. The companies might face a *prisoner's dilemma*.[599] The patients', providers' and Dx companies' preferences could be to select a low CDx cut-off value (i. e., cut-off 2), but the advantages of a potentially differentiating "high efficacy claim" might incentivize the companies to select a high cut-off value (i. e., cut-off 3). If the companies choose the high cut-off approaches, the overall value of a PM application might be reduced as several patients are excluded from treatment and those patients who receive treatment have to pay comparably high prices.[600] A regulator could theoretically solve this dilemma by requesting studies with comparable cut-off values in order to reduce the threat of competing "high efficacy claims".

Dx comp. 2 / **Dx company 1**	*Low cut-off 2*	*High cut-off 3*
Low cut-off 2	10, 10	0, 15
High cut-off 3	15, 0	5, 5

Figure 15: Prisoner's dilemma for Dx companies choosing the cut-off values

NOTE: Returns are illustrative.
The underlined numbers represent the returns chosen by a rationally acting Dx company.

596 *Ibidem*, p. 5.
597 RUBIN ET AL. (2014), p. 1425.
598 TRUSHEIM & BERNDT (2015)b, p. 5.
599 A basic introduction into this game theoretical concept provide COOTER & ULEN (2008), p. 38-41.
600 TRUSHEIM & BERNDT (2015)b, p. 7.

Multiple factors influence stakeholders' scenario preferences

The three discussed cut-off value scenarios exemplify three different strategic approaches for marketing a drug with a non-dichotomous biomarker.[601] In all three cases, the marketed drug is in fact identical and demonstrates the same efficacy in patients who are responders, but are differently marketed. The above exemplary scenarios demonstrate that the stakeholders' incentives to personalize a pharmaceutical depend on multiple factors that are different from treatment to treatment. Each stakeholder might prefer a different cut-off value. General rules of thumb for a high or low cut-offs cannot be inferred from the above illustrations.[602]

The described constitutive microeconomic assumptions and interdependencies between the pharmaceutical and the diagnostic component have to be kept in mind in the incentives analysis in the following sub-chapters.

[601] Cf. *Figure 14*: Imperfect responder situation, p. 106.
[602] *Ibidem*, p. 1.

2 Barriers in the discovery phase

The *discovery phase* describes the steps needed for detecting the underlying scientific modes of action for a PM application (i.e., a gene-phenotype/gene-disease relationships or a PGx interaction). In this phase, not only scientific barriers[603], but also non-science related, institutional barriers impede the progress of PM. The following chapters present the two institutional barriers identified for the discovery phase.

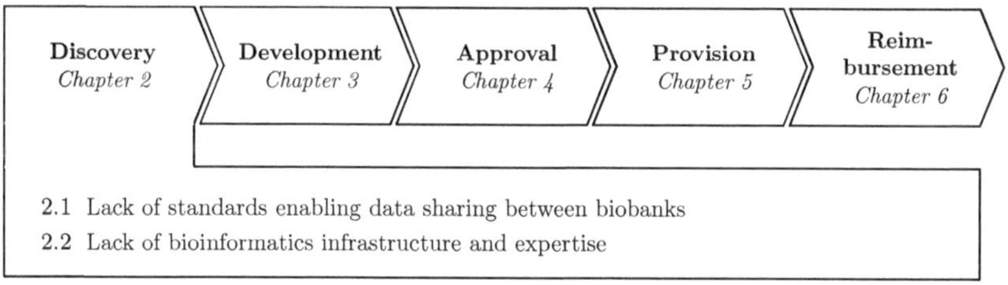

Figure 16: Barriers in the discovery phase

2.1 Lack of standards enabling data sharing between biobanks

2.1.1 Literature analysis

Personalized medicine presumes an infrastructure allowing scientists to access health data[604] for conducting basic research. The repositories for these data collections are referred to as *biobanks.*[605] Several studies highlight the existence of comprehensive knowledge bases to collect, store and manage health data as indispensable for scientific progress in personalized medicine.[606] Policy aspects to establish and manage a biobank are multifaceted: Policy has to ensure the accuracy of stored information and to provide access to the data. This involves legal aspects around patient privacy – including informed consent – and the confidentiality of health information.[607] Biobanks

603 Cf. Part II, Chapter 1.3.1 Tapping new scientific potential, p. 62.

604 E.g., predominantly genetic information, phenotypic associations as well as other "OMICs" profiles, clinical, or epigenetic (environmental or lifestyle) data.

605 For a definition, cf. Part I, Chapter 3.1.3 Biobanks, p. 51.

606 BRANZÉN (2013), p. 63 ff.; SZUCS (2014)b, p. 38; ARONSON & REHM (2015), p. 336. About the complications around the *"comprehensiveness"* of biobanks in T. A MANOLIO ET AL. (2013). They mention the general lack of phenotypic information of the existing reference databases hampering the data interpretation, p. 263.

607 E.g., SOINI (2012), p. 143 ff.; WINKLER, OSE, GLIMM, TANNER, & VON KALLE (2013), p. 195 ff, T. A MANOLIO ET AL. (2013), p. 263; MACHEINER, HUPPERTZ, & SARGSYAN (2013), p. 382. Further

have been set up in several countries and represent a central resource in advancing the understanding of the biology that underlies PM.[608]

A problem identified by the literature analysis is that research groups appear to be doing their projects in isolation. They capture and review the collected information internally and are constrained to share the data outside of their institutions.[609] The *ability to draw on data from multiple biobanks* is an important prerequisite in order to advance discoveries in personalized medicine efficiently.[610] In order to strive for a high degree of comprehensiveness and scientific relevance, biobanks must be openly accessible to clinical groups attempting to interpret the genetic data. Pooling data maximizes the utility of biobanks.[611]

Additionally, studies identify *a lack of interoperability between biobanks* as a decisive driver behind the low degree of data sharing.[612] The interoperability between biobanks is hampered due to incomparable information and heterogeneous data types.[613] With artificial intelligence approaches entering the stage in the next years, there is a need to connect and integrate the data to automated work-flows and data analysis pipelines from different sources. This depends on state-of-the-art data sharing standards.[614]

Several studies point out that different national frameworks increase the complexity of merging datasets and that *harmonization* is crucial to link the databases nationally and internationally. The EUROPEAN SCIENCE FOUNDATION (2012) saw data standardization, integration and harmonization as "key factors" for fostering the sharing of genetic data.[615] The EUROPEAN COMMISSION (2011) emphasized as well the

aspects around patient privacy are discussed in Part III, Chapter 5.5 Privacy concerns regarding the use of personalized medicine, p. 178 ff.

608 Cf. Part I Chapter 3.2 Biobanks, p. 51 ff.

609 E.g., HARVEY ET AL. (2012), p. 628; THE ACADEMY OF MEDICAL SCIENCES (2013), p. 22; and HORGAN ET AL. (2014), p. 292 ff.; EPPINGER ET AL. (2015), p. 146. The FDA is talking about a „walled garden", cf. SHERMAN & CALIFF (2016), p. 1; MESSNER ET AL. (2016), p. 11-12; DANIEL SCHNEIDER ET AL. (2016), p. 167-168; and THOMAS ET AL. (2016), p. 348.

610 HARVEY ET AL. (2012), p. 628; and THOMAS ET AL. (2016), P. 348.

611 *Ibidem.*

612 E.g., HORGAN ET AL. (2014), p. 292 ff.; HARVEY ET AL. (2012), p. 625 ff.; and WOMAK cited in DANIEL SCHNEIDER ET AL. (2016), p. 164.

613 HORGAN ET AL. (2014), p. 296; BOMBARD (2015), p. 1; and DUFFY (2015), p. 6.

614 DANIEL SCHNEIDER ET AL. (2016), p. 163-164.

615 According to the EUROPEAN SCIENCE FOUNDATION, instruments and processes for data collection and analysis across research sites must be *standardized* across research institutions. Research activity of different research institutions must be *integrated* to maximize synergies; additionally, scientific research must be integrated with healthcare to ensure effective translation. The ESF also calls for a harmonization *"between scientific practices in different research sites, between science and healthcare and between science, healthcare and wider society"*. The ESF has the aim to *"analyse in*

need for standardization with the emergence of new possibilities enabled through personalized medicine. This applies to tissue collection as well as to the maintenance of and access to national and international biobanks.[616] Similarly, the THE ACADEMY OF MEDICAL SCIENCES (2013) identified data harmonization as "key themes of progress" for personalized medicine.[617] Compliance with multiple or "poorly" defined legal frameworks that surround data gathering, testing and data storage[618] is noted as a "logistical challenge" for research institutions or companies working across several countries.[619]

2.1.2 Analysis of incentives

In the first place, the lack of data sharing standards negatively incentivizes *research institutions* to perform research concerning PM. Due to a lack of standards for data sharing, transaction costs of data sharing are prohibitively high for research institutions. Thus the value of the collected data is not fully exploited for research related to PM. The lack of data sharing standards makes data expensive. Data silos are emerging with the effect that due to a comparably small amount of genetic data, the data is less meaningfully aggregated and interpreted. Thus less scientific knowledge is generated.

In the second place, pharmaceutical and diagnostics companies are negatively affected, as their R&D activities depend on the existence of accessible and reliable genomic data.

The lack of standards enabling the sharing of genetic data make the ability to share genetic data a valuable good for companies – especially private biobanks or laboratories. It creates the commercial incentive for those companies with high-quality information resources not to share them and to use *"data as a barrier against competitors"*.[620] EVANGELATOS, REUMANN, LEHRACH, & BRAND (2016) argue that pharmaceutical companies do not want to *„share the risk to free riding"*. They compare the

---

a systematic way the complex and constantly moving field of personalised medicine to provide timely policy advice that will help prepare Europe for the likely changes in how society deals with health and disease", HARVEY ET AL. (2012), p. 625.

616 EUROPEAN COMMISSION (2011), p. 2

617 THE ACADEMY OF MEDICAL SCIENCES (2013), p. 22.

618 E.g., how participants are enrolled in biobanks or how their personal information may be stored and used.

619 HOPKINS ET AL. (2006), p. 405; and HARVEY ET AL. (2012), p. 631; WOMAK cited in DANIEL SCHNEIDER ET AL. (2016), p. 163 ff., presents a more detailed overview of the biobank-related challenges which inhibit the progress of PM. He describes the process leading to heterogeneity and existing ISO standards and standardization initiatives for the pre-examination process.

620 Also EKSTROM ET AL. (2013), p. 33; and B. J. EVANS (2014), p. 56.

governance of knowledge with governance of natural pool-resources.[621] Firms are reluctant to provide open access to their data – or analogously to contribute to a common data standard that enables data sharing – as this would render them vulnerable to competitors' free riding on their R&D investments.[622]

2.1.3 Resulting hypothesis

The overview below summarizes the argumentation of this chapter and shows the resulting incentives through the lack of standards enabling data sharing between biobanks:

Research institutions	*Pharmaceutical companies*	*Diagnostic companies*	*Providers*	*Patients*	*Payers*
negative	negative	negative	–	–	–

negative = institutional setting incentivizes a player not to foster the translation of PM
– = neutral/no conclusive statement possible on a player's incentive to foster the translation of PM

Based on the arguments presented, this chapter concludes with the following hypothesis:

Hypothesis: The lack of standards enabling data sharing between biobanks acts as a barrier to the translation of personalized medicine into clinical practice.

2.2 Lack of bioinformatics infrastructure and expertise

2.2.1 Literature analysis

Personalized medicine depends upon bioinformatics technology capable of aggregating, mining, integrating health data and finally producing models that are predictive and actionable.[623] The call for effective management and interpretation of *"big*

621 Cf. EVANGELATOS ET AL. (2016), p. 3. They refer to HARDIN'S (1968) *"Tragedy of the commons"*: Individuals, who act independently and rationally according to each one's self-interest, may behave contrary to the whole group's long-term best interests by depleting common resources.

622 Cf. EVANGELATOS ET AL. (2016), p. 3; and MESSNER ET AL. (2016), p. 11.

623 E.g., HOOD & AUFFRAY (2013), p. 2.

data'[624] and the extraction of actionable findings has a prominent claim in the literature. Studies point out the current *lack of bioinformatics infrastructure*[625] and the related *lack of bioinformatics expertise* as obstacles to the progress of PM.[626] The scale of emerging information is outpacing human cognitive capacity, requiring new tools enabling the analysis and interpretation of the information.[627] Multiple predictors of disease risks have to be modeled and understood and several sources of health data need to be integrated and analyzed.[628] PM research is moving away from the linear analysis of gene-disease interactions towards the analysis of more complex interactions[629] or towards dynamic, non-linear systems.[630] The standardization of biological data is only one challenge,[631] but if wider types of data – the phenome[632] – are to be included in analyses, then further challenges are likely to arise which are described as "far from trivial"[633] or as "computational bottleneck".[634]

Several studies emphasize the need for *interdisciplinary collaboration* in order to solve this "bottleneck".[635] Multidisciplinary teams of clinicians, laboratory scientists and bioinformatics specialists with the ability to extract meaningful information from

---

624 *"Big data"* is describing the increasing availability, volume, complexity, diversity, and timeliness of data and data sources for knowledge production, cf. for example GROVES, KAYYALI, KNOTT, & KUIKEN (2013) and ALEMAYEHU & BERGER (2016) on *"the 'big data' revolution"* in healthcare.

625 Bioinformatics is considered to be an integral part of PM and describes *"the development of methods and software tools for understanding biological data"*, DUFFY (2015), p. 4.

626 HARVEY ET AL. (2012), p. 630 ff.; HARVEY ET AL. (2012), p. 629; PRITCHARD interviewed by EASTMAN (2012), p. 25; THE ACADEMY OF MEDICAL SCIENCES (2013), p. 29 ff.; JAKKA & ROSSBACH (2013), p. 2; HOOD & AUFFRAY (2013), p. 1 ff.; PASIC ET AL. (2013), p. 162; ABPI (2014), p. 7 ff; CRAWFORD ET AL. (2014), p. 957; BOMBARD (2015), p. 58; DUFFY (2015), p. 4 ff.; ESTAPE ET AL. (2016), p. 10; DANIEL SCHNEIDER ET AL. (2016), p. 160; and TENENBAUM ET AL. (2016), p. 1 ff.

627 DUFFY (2015), p. 2. DUFFY (2015) mentions several hindering factors in the bioinformatics space, such as the dependence on "coding knowledge" instead of graphical interface or data visualization tools for "omics analysis", p. 6.

628 HORGAN ET AL. (2014), p. 289, with further references.

629 E.g., gene-environment interactions.

630 E.g., in vivo, longitudinal interactions. For an illustration and further details, cf. HARVEY ET AL. (2012), p. 628.

631 Cf. Part III, Chapter 2.1 Lack of standards enabling data sharing between biobanks, p. 113 ff.

632 The *phenome* describes the clinical phenotype including all its complexities such as environmental factors, family and economic circumstances of an individual.

633 HARVEY ET AL. (2012), p. 628.

634 BOMBARD (2015), p. 58, describes the currently limited capacity, limited number of experts and bioinformatics tools to interpret the genomic data as *"computational bottleneck"*.

635 *Mentioning the lack of interdisciplinary collaboration:* PRASAD & BRECKENRIDGE (2011), p. 869; THE ACADEMY OF MEDICAL SCIENCES (2013), p. 7; T. A MANOLIO ET AL. (2013), p. 263; PASIC ET AL. (2013), p. 163; KIEVITS ET AL. (2014), p. 16; EPPINGER ET AL. (2015), p. 122; PERMED (2015), p. 22; ESTAPE ET AL. (2016), p. 11; MESSNER ET AL. (2016), p. 8; DANIEL SCHNEIDER ET AL. (2016), p. 162.

molecular data are needed.[636] Literature criticizes the lack of funding programs and support projects targeting the interdisciplinary collaboration of research institutions across countries.[637] Further, a low degree of networking among scientists[638] and limited integration between science, academia as well as the industry are seen as drivers behind the missing expertise and low degree of collaboration.[639] *"The different branches of science in areas impacting on personalised medicine need to learn each other's languages, not fluently, but enough to work together on a common problem".*[640] With their claim of *"organizational integration"* some authors go one step beyond the mere organizational coordination and claim a *common research infrastructure* promoting synergistic working.[641] Also, the *claim for public-private partnerships* is prominent in literature.[642]

2.2.2 Analysis of incentives

On the one hand, the lack of bioinformatics infrastructure and the related expertise lowers innovation capabilities of *research institutions*, as they are lacking the input factors needed in order to produce discoveries in PM.

On the other hand, the lack of bioinformatics infrastructure and the related expertise is also a challenge for *pharmaceutical and diagnostics companies.* They are described to have limited knowledge of appropriate platforms and bioinformatics know-how, and face the difficulties of sample collection and storage strategy, as well as the complexity of data management. The relatively high staff and equipment costs needed for sampling, testing, data management and analysis makes PM a relatively expensive field of research in the view of the industry. It is hypothesized to be a major challenge to the advancement of PM, because the costs of analysis for genetic data are not falling as rapidly as the cost of generating them.[643]

---

636 PASIC ET AL. (2013), p. 163; and ESTAPE ET AL. (2016), p. 11 f.

637 EPPINGER ET AL. (2015), p. 123; and WURCEL ET AL. (2016), p. 141.

638 ECKHARDT ET AL. (2014), p. 245.

639 HARVEY ET AL. (2012), p. 630-631.

640 *Ibidem*, p. 631.

641 I. e. an environment where different research groups work on different aspects of the same problem and then pool their endeavors, cf. HARVEY ET AL. (2012), p. 630. They claim a lack of an *"integrated framework for doing science, within and across countries in the EU and beyond, making it possible for scientists in different research sites to work together on the same problems".*
In 2015, the FDA took one step into this direction by launching the cloud-based platform *"PrecisionFDA"* where the genomics research community can access and share datasets, analysis pipelines, and bioinformatics tools, in order to benchmark their approaches and advance regulatory science. Cf. FDA (2016)a, *"About PrecisionFDA".*

642 ABPI (2014), p. 7 ff.; and KIEVITS ET AL. (2014), p. 7.

643 E.g., HOPKINS ET AL. (2006), p. 405; and DUFFY (2015), p. 4.

2.2.3 Resulting hypothesis

The overview below summarizes the findings of this chapter and shows the resulting incentives through a lack of bioinformatics infrastructure and expertise in the discovery phase.

Research institutions	*Pharmaceutical companies*	*Diagnostic companies*	*Providers*	*Patients*	*Payers*
negative	negative	negative	–	–	–

negative = institutional setting incentivizes a player not to foster the translation of PM
– = neutral/no conclusive statement possible on a player's incentive to foster the translation of PM

Based on the arguments presented in the previous sub-chapters, this chapter concludes with the following hypothesis:

Hypothesis: The lack of bioinformatics infrastructure and bioinformatics expertise acts as a barrier to the translation of personalized medicine into clinical practice.

3 Barriers in the development phase

After the discovery phase, clinical applications need to be developed based on the discovered insights. The *development phase* describes the phase after a scientific discovery is made to the stage in which an application is clinically ready, but has not yet received regulatory approval. It includes the clinical phases I-III for pharmaceuticals, and analytical and clinical validation for diagnostics.[644]

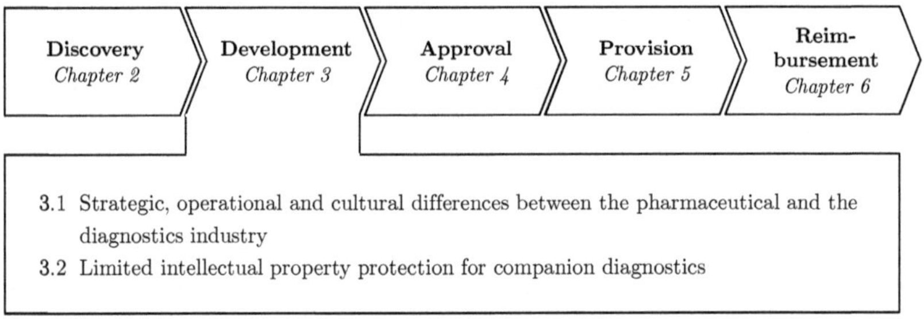

Figure 17: Barriers in the development phase

3.1 Strategic, operational and cultural differences between the pharmaceutical and the diagnostics industry

3.1.1 Literature analysis

The pharmaceutical and the diagnostics industry are two separate industries with their own industry characteristics.[645] The two industries are described as *"parallel universes"* as they have different development timelines, product lifecycles, returns on investment, customers as well as regulations.[646]

[644] For a detailed description of the phases cf. OLSEN & TRØST JØRGENSEN (2014), p. 2.

[645] Cf. Part II, Chapter 5.2 Rx-CDx co-development, p. 97 ff. LUO ET AL. (2015) show the economic independence of the two markets quantitatively. They assess the relationship between factors affecting the market for CDx and the corresponding pharmaceuticals. These factors include: CDx price, CDx sensitivity, price of Rx (standardized), duration of Rx treatment, years on the market of Rx, Rx efficacy, population of patients, subpopulation of patient population, response rate of patient subpopulation to Rx after selection with CDx, LUO ET AL. (2015), p. 6. They reveal that the regulatory co-dependence of CDx-Rx pairs is not reflected in their economic landscape. The CDx market is governed by a different set of drivers than the pharmaceutical market because they found no significant relationship between factors for the two industries, cf. LUO ET AL. (2015), p. 7.

[646] KIEVITS ET AL. (2012), p. 2; and MOORE ET AL. (2012) about strategic, logistical, regulatory and financial challenges in working together between the two industries.

The efficient introduction of a personalized pharmaceutical to the market typically requires collaboration between the two independent industries: The co-development of the drug and its companion diagnostic.[647] This collaboration presents challenges in aligning microeconomic incentives between the two industries.

Until now, there has been little co-development of therapies and diagnostics.[648] The majority of tests have been developed post-hoc.[649] The following sub-chapters present three co-development challenges inherent to the current industry structure: *Strategic*, *operational*, and *cultural challenges.*

i. Strategic challenges to the co-development process

First, there are *strategic challenges* between diagnostic and pharmaceutical companies. EPPINGER ET AL. (2015) are describing the problems of a low strategic interest of collaborations between the pharmaceutical and diagnostic industry with the metaphor of a *"low appreciation of a partner in a marriage of convenience".*[650]

Diagnostic company's strategic interests:

A diagnostic developer faces in general lower revenue prospects than drug developers.[651] One basic difference between the pharmaceutical and the diagnostic industry is the following fact: Companion diagnostic manufacturers have a one-off income stream, as a CDx acts only as a *"gatekeeper"*[652] and determines which patients will benefit. Unlike the drug developer, CDx have a selecting and not a monitoring role and are thus only used once and not multiple times, as this is the case for pharmaceuticals. Consequentially, a CDx producer earns revenues on a per test basis only.[653]

Especially if the test targets a limited number of patients, a diagnostic developer may not have an interest in developing a CDx test. Further, a diagnostic company

---

647 J. COHEN (2012), p. 753; KIEVITS ET AL. (2012), p. 2; MOORE ET AL. (2012), p. 487; and cf. Part II Chapter 5.2 Rx-CDx co-development, p. 97 ff.

648 Cf. Part II Chapter 5.2 Rx-CDx co-development, p. 97 ff.

649 J. COHEN (2012), p. 752, mentioning the tests for Abacavir, Irinotecan and Warfarin as examples.

650 *„Geringe Wertschätzung der Partner in ‚Zweckehen'"* (translated by the author), EPPINGER ET AL. (2015), p. 165.

651 TRUSHEIM & BERNDT (2015)b, p. 9, estimate that a CDx developer likely receives 1% or less of the revenue flowing to the therapeutic. They make a fictive example in which a CDx reaches a market size of USD 20 million whereas the corresponding drug may reach several billions. If a CDx company uses a standard technology (e.g., immunoassay) prices range around USD 25 per test kit. Even if a manufacturer is able to price its test with USD 2000 per patient as a monopolist, the CDx developer makes "only" USD 200 million per year with a patient base of 100'000 patients.

652 OLSEN & TRØST JØRGENSEN (2014), p. 1.

653 Cf. also Chapter 7.2, Resulting incentives, *Incentives for diagnostics companies*, p. 211 about a resulting "undervaluation" of CDx and *note* 1153.

usually has its own product lines and thus may try to direct the diagnostics development towards maximizing internal synergies and efficiency. This may not be the choice that enables the development of new companion diagnostics.[654] In addition to that, few diagnostics companies have a sales force with the capability to educate healthcare providers on ordering the appropriate diagnostic test.[655]

Pharmaceutical company's strategic interests:

In contrast to the diagnostic company, the drug developer can count on a longer – for chronic diseases potentially lifetime – stream of revenue from the treatment of a patient.[656] Pharmaceutical companies have in general higher revenue prospects than diagnostics companies.[657]

Anti-stratification strategy: A prominently mentioned thesis in the literature is that pharmaceutical companies are incentivized to pursue an *"anti-stratification strategy"*. The market entry of a targeted treatment constitutes a potential threat to the revenues through traditional "non-personalized" blockbusters for the same indication. Hence, it can be argued that the producers of the "non-personalized" blockbusters are reluctant to abandon their blockbuster model and have no incentives to promote the progress of PM. There is one strand of literature arguing that this is a decisive reason behind the slow translation of PM into practice. It is claimed that producers of non-personalized pharmaceuticals have minimal interest to awaken the patients' interests for personalized pharmaceuticals. They do not want to drive the application of pharmacogenetics to older products and to stratify generic or "soon-to-be" generic drugs, as there is the risk that this could fragment the treatable patient population into sub-segments and could decrease the market share of their "blockbusters" in some cases.[658] This incentive is enhanced if the price of the companion diagnostic of a "cheap" drug is comparably high as the price of the combined drug-diagnostic package would be higher than the price of the drug only.[659]

654 MOORE ET AL. (2012), p. 490, with real examples illustrating the strategic business challenge.

655 AGARWAL ET AL. (2015), p. 106.

656 *Ibidem.*

657 Cf. *note* 651.

658 *Claiming that pharmaceutical companies have no incentive to personalize drugs:* ASPINALL & HAMERMESH (2008), p. 5; J. C. DAVIS ET AL. (2009), p. 281; PACI (2009), p. 285; PRASAD & BRECKENRIDGE (2011), p. 267-268; J. COHEN (2012), p. 755; NOWESKI, WALENDZIK, HESSEL, JAHN, & WASEM (2013), p. 279; EPPINGER ET AL. (2015), p. 165; TRUSHEIM & BERNDT (2015)b, p. 11; WEBSTER cited in GARRISON (2016), p. 217; JOHAL & AMLANI (2016), p. 2; SCHELLEKENS ET AL. (2017), p. 2, talking about *"little economic impetus"* for pharmaceutical companies.

659 EPPINGER ET AL. (2015), p. 163.

In addition, it is argued that the producers of non-personalized pharmaceuticals refrain from personalized strategies as the diagnostic component could complicate marketing to physicians and slow down the identification of treatment-worthy patients because another step is added to the diagnostic process.[660] Further, phase II/III trials often have to be larger when CDx are used. Since it is unclear which markers will be predictive, trials need to be designed with several potential biomarkers in phase II/III.[661]

Some authors take this argument one step further by arguing that the producers of non-personalized pharmaceuticals have an incentive to influence the degree of personalization by acquiring of or collaborating with producers of CDx. This form of strategic acquisitions does not aim at the expansion of the portfolio, but at the protection of revenue streams.[662]

The above mentioned strategic interests could act as decisive driver behind the *lack of funding for personalized medicine* – another hindering factor that is sometimes mentioned behind the slow translation of PM.[663]

Stratification strategy: However, literature also mentions arguments that contradict the above illustrated "anti-stratification strategy" thesis. In theory, pursuing a strategy that includes PM applications in the portfolio can pay off financially for a pharmaceutical company. The use of CDx can improve R&D productivity by decreasing trial size. Recruiting patients who are expected to be positive responders yields in smaller clinical trials with a higher likelihood of success. This can reduce development time as well as the costs of drug development. At the same time, the use of CDx and biomarkers can enhance a drug's clinical- and cost-effectiveness for the targeted population, reduce attrition rates and thus increase the speed to market.[664] By increasing

660 ASPINALL & HAMERMESH (2008), p. 5-6; J. COHEN (2012) argues that the *"traditional blockbuster model"* will not be as viable as it once was, because it is based on selling drugs to patients of whom a significant part will be non-responders, p. 755.

661 J. C. DAVIS ET AL. (2009), p. 281.

662 Similar tendencies have been observed with the acquisitions of generics producers, cf. NOWESKI ET AL. (2013), p. 279.

663 E.g., J. COHEN (2012), p. 755; HARVEY ET AL. (2012), p. 631; MISCHAK ET AL. (2012), p. 1028; TRUSHEIM & BERNDT (2012), p. 417; HAYES ET AL. (2013), p. 6; SZUCS (2014)b, p. 41; and KONSKI (2015), p. 2.

664 J. COHEN (2012), p. 755; SAMS (2012), p. 17; AGARWAL ET AL. (2015), p. 104; TRUSHEIM & BERNDT (2015)b, p. 8; DEVERKA & MCLEOD cited in ROEDIGER (2016), p. 2; THOMAS ET AL. (2016), P. 347. However, there are also authors who argue the opposite way. For example MOORE ET AL. (2012) claim that the use of CDx tests in drug clinical trials can increase the complexity and cost of the drug-development process. A co-development agreement can also be strategically *non-desirable*, because the risk of late-stage compound failures is relatively high, cf. MOORE ET AL. (2012), p. 491 and TRUSHEIM & BERNDT (2015)b, p. 8. Additionally TRUSHEIM & BERNDT (2015)b

market share and/or supporting higher drug prices, profits can be improved.[665] Thus, the move away from non-personalized approaches into PM can be a rational strategic option for a drug developer to overcome the "patent cliff".[666]

The report of the OECD (2017) differentiates between the timing of a drugs personalization: If a drug is already marketed, pharmaceutical companies do not have an incentive to stratify the drug; this being in contrast to a new drug where personalization could lower development costs compared to a non-personalized pharmaceutical.[667]

ii. Operational challenges to the co-development process

Second, there are *operational challenges* to the co-development process. One main operational challenge is the *lack of clarity of how to include biomarkers in the pharmaceutical company's development program.* It is described to be challenging to find clinically useful biomarkers early on in a drug development program. It is easier to establish them once the patients have responded differently to the drug, which is usually in the latest stages of clinical trials.[668]

The *different development timescales* of drugs and diagnostics further lowers the incentive for diagnostic manufacturers to co-develop a diagnostic test when a drug begins its pre-clinical or clinical phase. On average it takes nine to twelve years to develop a drug whereas the development of a diagnostic takes three to five years.[669]

While some pharmaceutical companies have built biomarker programs that are incorporated in the larger R&D strategy, most pharmaceutical companies are at the beginning to establish biomarker programs in their R&D processes.[670]

iii. Cultural challenges to the co-development process

Third, *cultural barriers* between diagnostic and pharmaceutical companies are mentioned to challenge successful partnerships. These cultural barriers may be ex-

point out, that a PM approach demonstrates possibly *"no savings in trial size because of the potential need to examine patients with negative test results and the continuing need to develop an acceptably large patient safety database"*, p. 8.

665 J. C. DAVIS ET AL. (2009), p. 281.

666 *"Patent cliff"* meaning that a significant portion of financially successful drugs are going off- patent and become generics between 2014 and 2020, cf. e.g., RABASSEDA ET AL. (2013), p. 118.

667 OECD (2017), p. 164.

668 KIEVITS ET AL. (2012), p. 2.

669 THE ACADEMY OF MEDICAL SCIENCES (2013), p. 41.

670 FAULKNER ET AL. (2012), p. 1164; and M. EVERS, KULKARNI, MA, MOLLER, & OSTOJIC (2013), p. 11.

plained by the industries' different historical contexts such as a comparably more cost-based and less regulated diagnostic environment.[671]

3.1.2 Analysis of incentives

The above arguments pre-empt the incentive analysis: They have demonstrated that there are *strategic, operational and cultural differences* between the pharmaceutical and the diagnostic industry which tend to act as disincentives for the two players to foster the translation of personalized medicine. The differences lower the incentives of pharmaceutical and diagnostics companies to invest a substantial amount of time and resources needed to co-develop a PM application.

Category	*Summary of disincentives to foster PM*
Strategic difference	– Comparably low revenue prospects for diagnostics companies – Limited interest to personalize blockbusters (*anti-stratification strategy*) for pharmaceutical companies
Operational differences	– Lack of clarity of how to include biomarkers in drug development – Different timescales in Dx and Rx
Cultural differences	– Cultural mismatch complicates Rx-CDx co-development

Table 6: Incentives through strategic, operational and cultural differences between the pharmaceutical and the diagnostics industry

[671] MOORE ET AL. (2012), p. 485; and HORGAN ET AL. (2014), p. 289, for further illustrations of the cultural differences between pharmaceutical and diagnostics companies.

3.1.3 Resulting hypothesis

The overview below summarizes the previous arguments and resulting incentives that come along with the described strategic, operational and cultural differences between the pharmaceutical and the diagnostics industry:

Research institutions	*Pharmaceutical companies*	*Diagnostic companies*	*Providers*	*Patients*	*Payers*
–	negative	negative	–	–	–

negative = institutional setting incentivizes a player not to foster the translation of PM
– = neutral/no conclusive statement possible on a player's incentive to foster the translation of PM

Based on the arguments presented in the previous sub-chapters, this chapter concludes with the following hypothesis:

Hypothesis:	*Strategic, operational and cultural differences between the pharmaceutical and the diagnostics industry act as barriers to the translation of personalized medicine into clinical practice.*

3.2 Limited intellectual property protection for companion diagnostics

3.2.1 Literature analysis

"Who owns the genes?" This question is an ongoing debate in the scientific community.[672] Personalized medicine is based on the underlying assumption that a targeted pharmaceutical is selected based on a genetic biomarker. The identification of biomarkers and the corresponding development of a CDx measuring the prevalence of the biomarker is indispensable for the progress of PM.[673]

The intellectual property (IP) protection of biomarkers or molecular diagnostics sets incentives for the development of PM. The development of a molecular diagnostic requires substantial development time and costs. IP influences the data consolidation and analysis processes, and grants Dx manufacturers a time-limited monopoly in order to recover their R&D costs.[674]

A *lack of sufficient intellectual property protection* – especially for PM Dx – is a further, profoundly discussed obstacle to the progress of PM.[675] It is claimed that PM Dx face weaker intellectual property protection compared with pharmaceuticals – lowering incentives to develop the diagnostics.[676]

Prominent cases decided by the US SUPREME COURT about the non-patentability of "natural laws" concerning CDx patents have strengthened the argument that intellectual property is too weak in order to set sufficient incentives to develop molecular diagnostic tests.[677] Although patent regulations vary from country to country, the US cases – briefly outlined in the following – had a global effect, as the US is one of the biggest medical markets of interest for most non-US companies.[678]

In *Mayo Collaborative Services vs Prometheus Laboratories* (Mayo Case), the *Alice Corporation vs CLS Bank International* (Alice Case), and the *Association for Molecular Pathology (AMP) vs Myriad Genetics* (Myriad Case), the US SUPREME COURT has ruled that some molecular diagnostics are ineligible for patent protection because the molecular phenomena underlying them are *"laws of nature"* rather than

---

672 E.g., PASIC ET AL. (2013), p. 165.

673 Cf. Part I, Chapter 1 Definition of personalized medicine, p. 36.

674 E.g., NICHOLSON PRICE (2015), p. 29.

675 *Stating a lack of IP protection for CDx:* PACI (2009), p. 285; BRANZÉN (2013), p. 78-79; EKSTROM ET AL. (2013), p. 33; THE ACADEMY OF MEDICAL SCIENCES (2013), p. 41; TRUSHEIM (2013), p. 325 ff; ABPI (2014), p. 10; HOLMAN (2014), p. 639 ff.; PERSONALIZED MEDICINE COALITION (2014), p. 40; NICHOLSON PRICE (2015), p. 27 ff.; and GARRISON (2016), p. 226-227.

676 THE ACADEMY OF MEDICAL SCIENCES (2013), p. 7, 41 and 55 ff. with further references.

677 ELLIS (2016), p. 87 ff.

678 BRANZÉN (2013), p. 79 or KIEVITS ET AL. (2014), p. 9.

inventions.[679] After the decisions, the US PATENT AND TRADEMARK OFFICE (USPTO) is nearly four times more likely to deem subjects of applications in the space of PM unpatentable and patent applicants are less than half as likely to overcome those rejections.[680]

Mayo Collaborative Services vs Prometheus Laboratories[681]

Prior to this US SUPREME COURT decision, a diagnostic method was patentable as long as it was either linked to a machine or resulted in a transformation of matter (the "machine or transformation test"). Intellectual property incentives were available for diagnostic algorithms.[682]

However, patent protection for algorithms and diagnostic methods changed with the Supreme Court's decision *Mayo Collaborative Services vs Prometheus Laboratories* holding diagnostic methods claims as unpatentable.

Prometheus Laboratories was the sole and exclusive licensee of the two patents, which concern the use of thiopurine drugs to treat autoimmune diseases. The patents concerned processes to help doctors to assess the effectiveness of the drug dosage. Mayo bought and used diagnostic tests based on Prometheus' patents. In 2004, the company announced that it intended to sell and market its own, slightly different, diagnostic test. Prometheus brought an infringement action against Mayo. The US Supreme Court found that Prometheus' process is not patent eligible.

The SUPREME COURT held that the patent merely provides a natural law and *"simply tells doctors to engage in well-understood, routine, conventional activity"*[683], in this case measuring metabolite levels to inform treatment decisions. The patent in-

679 Other, less prominent patent cases are discussed by GHOSH (2015), p. 4 ff.
A tendency towards these decisions already became evident in 2010. The US DEPARTMENT OF HEALTH AND HUMAN SERVICES studied the impact of gene patents and their licensing on genetic testing over a period of almost 10 years. The 392-page report *"Gene Patents and Licensing Practices and Their Impact on Patient Access to Genetic Tests"* found that *"patents on genetic discoveries do not appear to be necessary for either basic genetic research or the development of available genetic tests"*, and that *"patents have been used to narrow or clear the market of existing tests, thereby limiting, rather than promoting availability of testing"*. Further, the Department found that patients have not been able to access genetic testing under certain circumstances. It was concluded that *"the substantial number of existing patents on genes and methods of diagnosis also pose a threat to the development of multiplex testing, parallel sequencing, and whole - genome sequencing, the areas of genetic testing with the greatest potential future benefits"*, cf. FDA (2010), cover letter of report.

680 CHAO cited in LEDFORD (2016), p. 382.

681 Supreme Court of the United States, ruling no. 10-1150.

682 NICHOLSON PRICE (2015), p. 29.

683 Supreme Court of the United States, ruling no. 10-1150, p. 2.

ventors did not invent the correlation, but the detected metabolites are the result of a natural metabolization of the thiopurine drug. The inventors have only observed that there is a relation between the naturally produced metabolites and a therapeutic effect of the drug – an observation that cannot be patented. This decision means that diagnostics developers cannot identify a useful natural law like a set of correlations (i.c., the correlations between thiopurine metabolite levels and the toxicity and efficacy of thiopurine drugs) and patent a general method for its use.[684] The majority of biological diagnostic tests involves steps measuring levels of biological molecules (including genes and their expression levels), relate this measurement to a natural connection and provide information about an individual's biological characteristics. After the decision, these steps cannot make a claim patentable if they are primarily directed to a law of nature. Consequentially, in the US, combining diagnostic methods with standard practice procedures are not patentable anymore.[685]

Association for Molecular Pathology (AMP) vs Myriad Genetics[686]

Mutations of the BRCA1 and BRCA 2 genes can significantly increase the risk of breast and ovarian cancer. Myriad obtained several patents after discovering the precise location and sequence of the BRCA1/2 genes. This knowledge allowed Myriad to determine the genes' typical nucleotide sequence. This, in turn, enabled the development of diagnostic tests useful for detecting mutations in these genes in a particular patient to assess the patient's cancer risk. The patents were found to be invalid because they covered products of nature. If valid, Myriad would have had the exclusive right to isolate an individual's BRCA1/2 genes as well as the exclusive right to synthetically create BRCA complementary DNA.[687] After the US SUPREME COURT invalidated Myriad' patents protecting the BRCA1/2 test, competitor laboratories entered the market with their own tests. The result was a reduction in price for the test.[688]

Alice Corporation vs CLS Bank International[689]

In 2014, the US SUPREME COURT reaffirmed its decision from the *Prometheus Case* in the less prominent *Alice Corporation vs CLS Bank International.* The SUPREME COURT clarified that abstract inventions, such as an algorithm, were not made patentable merely by implementation on a computer.

684 NICHOLSON PRICE (2015), p. 31.
685 *Ibidem.*
686 Supreme Court of the United States, ruling no. 12-398.
687 *Ibidem*, p. 1 ff.
688 KONSKI (2015), p. 3
689 Supreme Court of the United States, ruling no. 13–298.

Rapid Litigation Management vs Cellz Direct[690]

A recent decision by the US COURT OF APPEALS FOR THE FEDERAL CIRCUIT brought some clarity for distinguishing between something that happens in nature and the "inventive application" of it and made it harder to invalidate certain patents by claiming they simply cover laws of nature. The court explicitly held that patents can be obtained for processes relating to laws of nature if they go at least one step further.[691]

3.2.2 Analysis of incentives

IP is a legally enforceable power to exclude other users from a certain resource. Limited IP protection for CDx undermines the incentives to invest in diagnostic development and the associated evidence generation as there is no time-limited monopoly to recoup the investment made. Without the ability to protect CDx through patent protection, CDx developers either have no incentive to develop them at all or depend on other means to recoup their R&D costs. Further, IP can lower the costs of subsequent innovations as details of an innovation must be disclosed.[692]

Biomarkers and the development of the respective diagnostics are often considered as pre-competitive activities by the pharmaceutical companies.[693] Low IP protection leads to the situation that single laboratories, test aggregators or academic medical centers mostly use non-proprietary markers, for which no royalties or other compensation are paid to the discoverers of the biomarker or the developer of the clinical insight.[694] Those laboratory developed tests (LDTs)[695] are widely available in a non-exclusive fashion. Usually, a patent does not exist or is not enforced by the holders of the intellectual property in these cases. The reason behind this could be that the patent holders are simply not aware that their patent information is used, since LDTs are by definition only used in a single health institution.[696]

690 United States Court of Appeals for the Federal Circuit, ruling no. 2015-1570.

691 United States Court of Appeals for the Federal Circuit, ruling no. 2015-1570, p. 15-17; and DECKER & BLOOMFIELD (2016), p. 1.

692 LANDES & POSNER (2003), p. 11 ff., about the general benefits of IP; more specific for diagnostics FAULKNER ET AL. (2012), p. 1169; THE ACADEMY OF MEDICAL SCIENCES (2013), p. 7 and 55; TRUSHEIM & BERNDT (2015)a, p. 18 ff. and TRUSHEIM & BERNDT (2015)b, p. 10 ff.

693 TRUSHEIM & BERNDT (2015)a, p. 18-19.

694 TRUSHEIM & BERNDT (2015)b, p. 10.

695 Cf. Part III, Chapter 4.1.3 Undermining of the current approval system through LDTs, p. 148 ff. for a detailed description of LDTs and their regulatory framework.

696 CRAWFORD & ASPINALL (2012), p. 269.

As a consequence of the limited IP protection, diagnostics companies shift their product focuses towards diagnostics that are still patentable which might not necessarily be the diagnostic tools needed to foster the progress of PM.[697]

There remain, however, some strategies for Dx companies in order to stay in the field of CDx despite the limited IP protection:

A first potential response to the inability to patent CDx based on simple "natural laws" is instead of patenting the relationship itself, *shifting towards paired Dx* and patenting a combination of the relationship and some other physical machine or process.[698] Developers link their discovered "natural laws" to machines or to specific treatments which then pair the diagnostic with a drug. With this, IP is setting incentives for the industry to focus on PM applications pairing CDx with Rx, rather than broadening the R&D efforts to broader algorithms or models.[699]

A second potential response to the inability to patent CDx based on simple "natural laws" is to simply *rely on trade secrecy.*[700] A solution in order to avoid competitors using an innovation is to keep it as a secret. Trade secrecy is described as the *"strongest method available to keep competitors from accessing the data and algorithms"* and lies *"at the heart of personalized medicine".*[701] Several companies have chosen to rely on proprietary data and trade secrecy to maintain a competitive advantage, and trade secrecy is recommended as strategy for Dx companies.[702] The most prominent example of keeping the information secret is MYRIAD. After the SUPREME COURT decision, MYRIAD has turned towards this stragegy. The company has chosen to offer free testing to family members of patients. With this, MYRIAD posesses a greater set of data on BRCA1/2 variants than its competitors. It is estimated that only 3% of its samples have variants of unknown significance, whereas for competitors this number lies between 20% to 30%.[703] Trade secrecy slows down cumulative innovation and promotes duplicative investments and represents an additional factor that hampers the overall development of PM.[704]

A third solution is to *establish strong brand names* as a competitive advantage to target providers and patients.[705] In this regard, the trademark protection is slightly

697 NICHOLSON PRICE (2015), p. 33-34.
698 For details and examples, cf. *ibidem*, p. 34-35.
699 *Ibidem*, p. 34.
700 For details and examples, cf. *ibidem*, p. 35-37.
701 *Ibidem*, p. 35.
702 E.g., EKSTROM ET AL. (2013), p. 33.
703 NICHOLSON PRICE (2015), p. 36, with further examples.
704 NICHOLSON PRICE (2015), p. 37.
705 EKSTROM ET AL. (2013), p. 34.

stronger in the US than in Europe, as the EMA does usually not name a specific patented test when approving a drug.[706] This in contrast to the FDA, which names specific trademarked CDx in its list of cleared or approved CDx.[707]

Despite these three residual strategies, the above presented prominent decisions by the US SUPREME COURT had immediate global effects on the PM industry. It is claimed that the decisions have led to decreased venture capital investments and pessimistic outlooks in the diagnostic industry.[708]

3.2.3 Resulting hypothesis

The overview below summarizes the argumentation of the previous chapter and shows the resulting negative incentives through limited intellectual property protection for CDx to foster the translation of personalized medicine.

Research institutions	*Pharmaceutical companies*	*Diagnostic companies*	*Providers*	*Patients*	*Payers*
–	–	negative	–	–	–

negative = institutional setting incentivizes a player not to foster the translation of PM
– = neutral/no conclusive statement possible on a player's incentive to foster the translation of PM

Based on the arguments presented in the previous sub-chapters, this chapter concludes with the following hypothesis:

Hypothesis: Limited IP protection for CDx acts as a barrier to the translation of personalized medicine into clinical practice.

706 THE ACADEMY OF MEDICAL SCIENCES (2013), p.55 or PIGNATTI ET AL. (2014), p. 1466.

707 The FDA's list can be retrieved from http://www.fda.gov/MedicalDevices/ProductsandMedicalProcedures/InVitroDiagnostics/ucm301431.htm (last visited January 28, 2016).

708 NICHOLSON PRICE (2015), p. 33-34.

4 Barriers in the approval phase

Approval represents an indispensable link in the value chain of personalized medicine applications. The *approval phase* follows once a pharmaceutical or/and a corresponding diagnostic has been developed.

For the approval phase, literature identifies two reasons explaining why the translation of PM into clinical practice is behind its originally expected progress: First, there are several inconsistencies and gaps in the regulatory framework for approving PM. Second, the incompatibility of clinical trials with personalized medicine applications is criticized. The two institutional barriers in the approval phase shall be discussed in the following chapters.

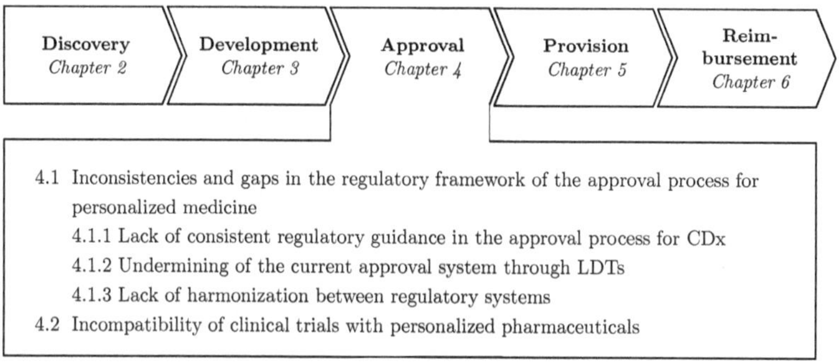

Figure 18: Barriers in the approval phase

4.1 Inconsistencies and gaps in the regulatory framework of the approval process for personalized medicine

4.1.1 Literature analysis

Gaps and inconsistencies in the approval framework of personalized medicine applications belong to the most prominently discussed obstacles behind the progress of personalized medicine. The gaps include the lack of consistent regulatory guidance in the approval process for CDx (*Chapter 4.1.2*), the undermining of the current approval system through laboratory developed tests (LDTs) (*Chapter 4.1.3*) as well as a lack of harmonization between regulatory systems (*Chapter 4.1.4*).

4.1.2 Lack of consistent regulatory guidance in the approval process for CDx

There appears to be a general lack of understanding of personalized medicine's underlying concept and the fact that personalized drugs work together with a diagnostic.[709] Studies stress the inconsistency of the regulatory environment for CDx which *"has confused people as to how they should develop new tests"*[710], others mention that the current framework places *"in jeopardy [...] the aspirations of personalized medicine"*[711] or that it deters the required investment away from CDx.[712] There is a general claim for *"smarter regulatory environments to facilitate co-development of a therapy and diagnostic"*.[713] The current regulatory paradigm *"needs to more closely match personalized medicine"*.[714]

The concept of CDx means that regulatory authorities approve a product combination, or "one package", composed of a diagnostic and a pharmaceutical.[715] The efficient introduction of a personalized pharmaceutical to the market ideally requires the co-development of the drug and its CDx and thus a collaboration between the two independent industries.[716] So far, the co-development is not always happening and most PM applications are personalized "post-hoc", meaning that a CDx is developed separately and approved after the pharmaceutical component.[717] Guidance documents from multiple regulatory agencies have attempted to outline the steps in the creation of CDx, and the complexity of the Rx-CDx co-development process, but they are still described as "rudimentary".[718]

There are established regulatory frameworks for the approval process of pharmaceuticals.[719] However, there appears to be *lack of a corresponding framework for*

---

709 Cf. Part I Chapter 1.2 PM's underlying mechanism, p. 43.
710 HAYES ET AL. (2014), p. 3.
711 TRUSHEIM (2013), p. 324.
712 MILLER ET AL. (2011), p. 1.
713 MITTRA & TAIT (2012), p. 711.
714 HOLCOMBE cited in EASTMAN (2012), p. 25.
715 Cf. Part I Chapter 2.2 Companion diagnostics, p. 45.
716 Cf. Part II, Chapter 5.2 Rx-CDx co-development, p. 97 ff.; and Part III, Chapter 3.1 Strategic, operational and cultural differences between the pharmaceutical and the diagnostics industry, p. 120 ff.
717 J. COHEN (2012), p. 751.
718 MOORE ET AL. (2012), p. 487, as well SHIMAZAWA & IKEDA (2016) criticize that regulatory guidance is insufficient, especially if contemporaneous development is not possible, thereby leaving room for improvement with respect to pharmacovigilance and retrospective validation of the CDx, p. 1.
719 E.g., BRANZÉN (2013), p. 68; K. PHILLIPS ET AL. (2013), p. 60; and HORGAN ET AL. (2014), p. 292.

CDx.[720] Even though being part of "one package", drugs and diagnostics fall under different legislations around the globe.[721]

A second point of criticism is the *different quality requirements for pharmaceuticals and CDx* being subject to different regulatory pathways. Pharmaceuticals' required measures for clinical utility and the number and scope of economic analyses are different from the requirements for diagnostics. Diagnostics have typically been low-cost, low-risk interventions and thus the level of scrutiny has been lower.[722] Thus, in most countries, the quality demands for diagnostic products are below the ones of pharmaceuticals.[723]

The following sub-chapters provide a brief overview of the regulatory framework for CDx for the US and the EU in order to illustrate the described challenges.[724] The two sub-chapters will show two different, if not opposed, systems to approach the regulatory approval process – neither of the two without being criticized for hindering the progress of PM.

i. IVD approval process in the EU

In the European Union, there are separate approval processes for pharmaceuticals and CDx. Pharmaceuticals require pre-market approval by regulators while CDx are self-certified by the manufacturer:

---

720 *A lack of regulatory guidance in the CDx approval process is mentioned in:* NAYLOR & COLE (2010) a, p. 68; MILLER ET AL. (2011), p. 1; J. COHEN (2012), p. 751-752; MOORE ET AL. (2012), p. 485; TRUSHEIM & BERNDT (2012), p. 425; MCCARTHY ET AL. (2013), p.7; TRUSHEIM (2013), p. 325 ff.; HAYES ET AL. (2014), p. 3; HORGAN ET AL. (2014), p. 289-292.; PERSONALIZED MEDICINE COALITION (2014), p. 21-25 and p. 40; MILNE & COHEN (2015)a, p. 3; NOLTING (2015), p. 22; TRUSHEIM ET AL. (2015), p. 328; JOHNSON (2016), p. 4; and DAVID PETTITT ET AL. (2016), p. 319 ff.

721 BRANZÉN (2013), p. 69.

722 K. PHILLIPS ET AL. (2013), p. 60.

723 BRANZÉN (2013), p. 68.

724 This thesis focuses on the US and the EU as these are the main markets for PM. A comparison between the US and the EU provide MEADOWS ET AL. (2015), p. 9 ff.; and DAVID PETTITT ET AL. (2016), p. 321 ff.
A broader overview on changing regulatory landscape for CDx in the US, Canada, Japan, EU and rest of the world provides ANSARI (2013) and THE ACADEMY OF MEDICAL SCIENCES (2013), p. 42 - 43; and OLSEN & TRØST JØRGENSEN (2014) for the US, EU, Japan and China. An old overview on the US, EU and Japan – but with an increased focus on PGx labeling – can be found in BARTON (2008), p. 106 ff. Brief overviews with a special focus on *Germany* can be found in KAHNERT (2015), p. 36 ff., HERMANN & SEITZ (2015), p. 5; and *Japan* in TAZAWA (2016). The analysis for Switzerland follows in Part IV Chapter 4.1.1 Institutional setting, p. 230 ff.

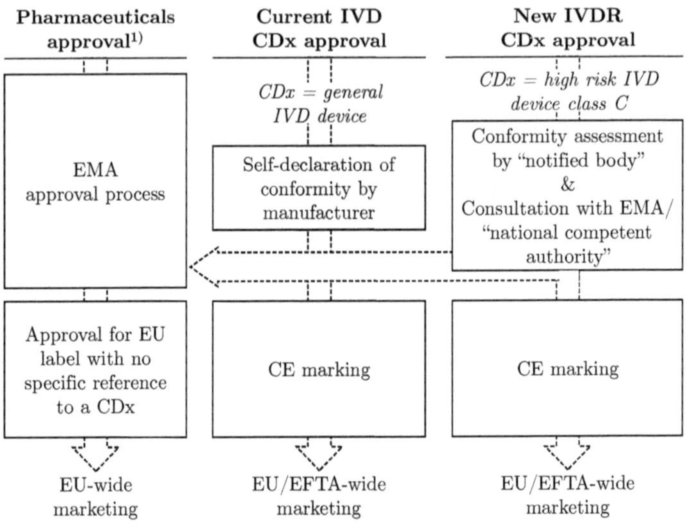

1) The option of the decentralized national approval process is not illustrated in this overview.

Figure 19: Overview of separate EU approval processes for pharmaceuticals and companion diagnostics

Pharmaceuticals

For a pharmaceutical company there are two ways of receiving marketing authorization for pharmaceuticals in the EU. The *decentralized* procedure is limited to a single Member State. It requires a manufacturer to submit its approval applications to the national competent authorities. The *centralized* procedure for the approval of pharmaceuticals seeking the EU-wide marketing authorization is conducted by the EUROPEAN MEDICINES AGENCY (EMA). After the EMA's assessment the EUROPEAN COMMISSION approves or rejects it, leading to a single EU-wide approval allowing marketing in the entire EU.[725] The centralized approval process enables a relatively high degree of harmonization with regard to identical approved indications and conditions of use within the EU and supports the concept of a European single market.[726]

In both procedures, the regulatory authorities do not specify which particular diagnostic device should be used as a CDx in the respective labels of the targeted drug.[727] For targeted approved pharmaceuticals, the label mandates the need for a

725 AKHMETOV ET AL. (2015), p. 217-218.

726 MÜLLER-GRAFF (2014), p. 17 ; and PIGNATTI ET AL. (2014), p. 1458.

727 PRASAD & BRECKENRIDGE (2011), p. 871; and PIGNATTI ET AL. (2014), p. 1458.

validated test or it describes the specific diagnostic kit or other method that have been used in the clinical studies.[728] This leads to a lack of a consistent approach of how to refer to a CDx in the label of the pharmaceutical.[729] Further, it grants permission to any validated test, which complies with the IVD Directive.[730] Since different CDx can vary in methodology, validation criteria and targeted mutations,[731] they consequentially demonstrate diverse effects on the stratified patient populations. This can cause *"significant deviations in health outcomes and benefit/risk ratios of the patients"*.[732]

Companion diagnostics

The framework for the regulation of companion diagnostics is different from the framework for the regulation of pharmaceuticals. CDx are regulated within the medical devices legal framework. CDx for genomic biomarkers fall into the classification of in vitro diagnostic medical devices (IVD)[733] and are governed by the EU DIRECTIVE ON IN VITRO DIAGNOSTIC MEDICAL DEVICES (IVD Directive).[734] The national legislations of the Member States then translate the Directive into national law.[735]

If a manufacturer of a medical device wants to market it in the EU under the IVD Directive, a relevant risk category defined in the Directive must be assigned for the device.[736] So far, CDx to assay genomic biomarkers were classified as general *low risk* IVDs.[737] If the device mets the essential requirements ensuring that the product does

728 A number of EMA approved products currently contain relevant pharmacogenomics information for patient selection. However, the format of the contained information in the label ("Summary of Product Characteristics") ranges widely from no information to detailed information specifying the trademark, the manufacturer, and the CE-marked number, cf. PIGNATTI ET AL. (2014), p. 1463 and 1465 with a table comparing oncology drugs.

729 PIGNATTI ET AL. (2014), p. 1466; and EPPING & BERCHTOLD (2014), p. 50-51.

730 DIRECTIVE 98/79/EC.

731 Cf. also explanations by TRUSHEIM & BERNDT (2015)b, illustrated in Part III, Chapter 1.2.2 Interdependencies between the pharmaceutical and diagnostic component, p. 105 ff.

732 AKHMETOV ET AL. (2015), p. 217. More details on the approval process of personalized therapeutics in Europe (incl. conditional approvals) can be found in LEYENS ET AL. (2015).

733 For a definition of IVD, cf. Art. 2 b DIRECTIVE 98/79/EC.

734 DIRECTIVE 98/79/EC.

735 E.g., in Germany the "Medizinproduktegesetz" (MPG), cf. KAHNERT (2015), p. 36. Switzerland as well adapts its legislation to the EU Directive via the "Heilmittelgesetz" (HMG) or the respective "Medizinalprodukteverordnung" (MepV), cf. SFOPH (2015), p. 1.

736 *Annex* VI, *Section* 3, DIRECTIVE 98/79/EC.

737 For IVDs with a *higher-risk* classification, additional requirements apply. Their approval involves a "notified body". A "notified body" is a third-party certification organization carrying out conformity assessment procedures. The "notified body" is designated and monitored by the national competent authority of a Member State, cf. PIGNATTI ET AL. (2014), p. 1459; VAN HEERTUM ET AL. (2015), p. 5221; OLSEN & TRØST JØRGENSEN (2014), p. 4 ff.

not compromise the health and safety of patients and users, and if the device is designed and manufactured to achieve the specified performance, the manufacturer self-certifies conformity.[738] With the self-assessed certification, the medical device gained the CE marking[739] which allowed free circulation in the EU/EFTA countries[740] and Turkey.[741] Once the medical device was on the market, manufacturers must maintain systematic procedures to monitor post-production experiences. They were obliged to notify the national competent authorities of any incidents or recalls that risked serious injury.[742]

Revision of EU legislation on in-vitro diagnostics

The described EU legislation on medical devices including CDx was under revision in a heavily debated process from 2012 until end of 2016.[743] The revised IVD Directive (IVDR) of April 2017 will take effect after a transitional period in 2022. It is described as *"an evolution of the current regime"*, but keeping the same legal approach.[744]

The most important change concerning CDx is that they will no longer be considered as "low risk" devices. The new Directive stipulates that CDx will be classified as *high individual risk* or *moderate public health risk* (Class C)[745] and that they will require a *conformity assessment by a "notified body"*.[746]

The systematic involvement of a "notified body" in the conformity assessment procedure of CDx represents a departure from the current self-certification system. The "notified body" will check the quality management system and the technical documentation of representative samples.[747] Further, CDx will have to demonstrate compliance with general safety and performance requirements, including *analytical* and

738 In practice, this means that the respective documents are provided and the marketing is indicated to the „notified body", cf. EPPINGER ET AL. (2015), p. 134.

739 CE standing for "Conformité Européene", *Annex* III, DIRECTIVE 98/79/EC.

740 I. c., Iceland, Liechtenstein, Norway, and Switzerland and Turkey.

741 PIGNATTI ET AL. (2014), p. 1459.

742 Art. 11 DIRECTIVE 98/79/EC.

743 EUROPEAN COMMISSION (2016)c, *Ongoing revision: Regulation proposals of the European Commission.*

744 PIGNATTI ET AL. (2014), p. 1458.

745 The IVDR classes range from class A (lowest risk) to class D (highest risk), cf. IVDR, *Annex* VIII, *Section* 2. Class C devices present a moderate public health risk, or a high individual risk, where an erroneous result would put the patient in an imminent life-threatening situation or would have a major negative impact on outcome.

746 IVDR, p. 186; Art. 48 (4) IVDR.

747 Art. 10 *para* 8 IVDR, Art. 41 IVDR.

clinical performance.[748] For this, the IVDR stipulates a consultation between the EMA or the respective national competent authority and the notified body.[749]

After initial certification, notified bodies shall regularly conduct audits in the post-market phase.[750] During the whole life-cycle of a device, a manufacturer has to continuously update the documentation of the clinical evidence. A manufacturer has to assess all relevant scientific validity, analytical and clinical performance data.[751]

Co-development guidance by the EU

The concept of PM is not used as frequently in official EU documents as for example compared to the official documents in the US.[752] However, the EMA has recognized and emphasized the importance of the co-development of Rx-CDx. Although the development of companion diagnostics has not been the focus of the EMA's guidance, the agency has provided several reflection papers on the co-development of biomarkers.[753] The most important is the *„Guideline on the Use of Pharmacogenetic Methodologies in the Pharmacokinetic Evaluation of Medicinal Products“* issued by the EMA's COMMITTEE FOR HUMAN MEDICINAL PRODUCTS.[754] The guideline describes study designs and how to present results from the trial, but does not contain any guideline on how to organizationally integrate Rx and CDx. Official guidelines for the coordination of the co-development and approval process did not exist[755] until mid2017, when the EMA has released a concept paper on Rx-CDx-codevelopment proposing to develop guidelines.[756]

748 Art. 56 (1) IVDR.

749 Section 5.2, *Annex IX* IVDR.

750 Art. 48 *para* 13 IVDR; *Annex* IX *section* 2.3 IVDR.

751 *Annex* VIII *part* A (1.3) IVDR.

752 BRANZÉN (2013), p. 70.

753 E.g., the EMA Committee for Human Medicinal Products published a *"Reflection paper on pharmacogenomic samples, testing and data handling"*, a *"Reflection Paper on the Use of Pharmacogenetics in the Pharmacokinetic Evaluation of Medicinal Products"* (2007), a *"Reflection paper on pharmacogenomics in oncology"* (2007), a *"Reflection paper on co-development of pharmacogenomic biomarkers and assays in the context of drug development"* (2008), a *"Reflection paper on methodological issues with pharmacogenomic biomarkers in relation to clinical development and patient selection"* (2011), etc. A list is provided in PIGNATTI ET AL. (2014), p. 1467, *references* 2-5. PIGNATTI ET AL. (2014), p. 1462-1463, further illustrate the elements of the reflection papers with examples.

754 EMA (2012), *na.*

755 NOWESKI ET AL. (2013), p. 281; and EPPING & BERCHTOLD (2014), p. 51. An older paper by PRASAD & BRECKENRIDGE (2011) provides an overview of the working groups involved and the relevant regulatory questions being discussed in the development for a EU co-development approach, p. 870 ff.

756 EUROPEAN MEDICINES AGENCY (2017), *note* 87.

Criticism of the EU approval process

Criticism of the approval process for PM treatments in Europe range from being described as *"uncoordinated"*[757] to being *"unsafe"*[758].

A lack of coordination and integration of the Rx and CDx approval process is the first point of criticism of the EU approval process. The *"work duplication"* needed for the double application of Rx and CDx is criticized to be inefficient.[759] For example, NEGROUK ET AL. (2015) find that *"having such a cumbersome legal framework, without sufficient consideration of how all its bits and pieces come together within one single pan-European project, makes all efforts at efficiency useless"*.[760] WURCEL ET AL. (2016) find that *"approval for an innovative medicine is not linked to the availability of an upstream companion diagnostic test, thus emphasising this disconnection between the regulatory and reimbursement pathways for innovative medicines and IVDs"*.[761] AKHMETOV, RAMASWAMY, AKHMETOV, & THIMMARAJU (2015) sound similar describing the approval guidelines as *"cumbersome and dissonant"*. According to them there is *"no coordinated mechanism to assess drug-diagnostic companion products in Europe, because of tremendous differences in regulatory guidelines for medicines and tests, which lead to inconsistent decision making at the EU level, hence hindering market access"*.[762] It is argued that the approval process via EMA works for pharmaceuticals, but not for CDx. *"Europe's clinical research ship seems more and more unfit to weather this storm"*.[763] The two separate approval systems mean that neither regulator sees the *"full picture of the regulatory requirements of stratified medicine products"*. Little early cross-fertilization happens unless a pharmaceutical company identifies the need for a diagnostic or a CDx company identifies the need for access to clinical data and drives the coordinated development process.[764]

The second point of criticism is that the current framework does not sufficiently ensure the security, quality, reliability or efficacy of CDx. It is criticized that many *CE marked IVDs are insufficiently reviewed*, because the manufacturer self-certifies conformity.[765] It is argued that the lack of an independent assessment could foster the

757 E.g., NEGROUK ET AL. (2015), p. 8. Similarly EUROPEAN ALLIANCE FOR PERSONALISED MEDICINE (2013), p. 4.

758 E.g., NOWESKI ET AL. (2013), p. 281.

759 KIEVITS ET AL. (2014), p. 9.

760 NEGROUK ET AL. (2015), p. 8.

761 WURCEL ET AL. (2016), p. 137 ff.

762 AKHMETOV ET AL. (2015), p. 214.

763 NEGROUK ET AL. (2015), p. 2.

764 THE ACADEMY OF MEDICAL SCIENCES (2013), p. 44.

765 NOWESKI ET AL. (2013), p. 281; and EPPINGER ET AL. (2015), p. 129.

avoidance of using CDx in clinical practice.[766] Further, the lack of an independent evaluation leads to inherent uncertainties and information asymmetries which are seen as significant driver behind the lack of reimbursement.[767]

However, there is one important positive aspect of the current self-certification system for CDx in Europe: It can be viewed as a competitive advantage for manufacturers seeking to market their diagnostics, since the system is comparably fast and simple.[768]

The *revised IVD Directive* needed to find the balance between greater co-ordination among the medicine and diagnostic regulators without the loss of flexibility in the current EU regulatory framework. There were hopes, that the new IVD Regulation would *"enhance Europe's leadership with regard to the development and early marketing of novel diagnostics"* and that *"the design of a regulatory framework for medical devices supports rather than hinders the ability of innovative companies of discovering biomarkers and further develop companion diagnostic tests"*.[769] However, the revisions of the IVD Directive are viewed with skepticism:

On the one hand, the increased regulatory requirements for the marketing of CDx may rule out any above discussed precautions or reservations against the use of CDx. The IVDR's move from a list-based to a risk-based classification system, the inclusion of CDx into a class being subject to review by a notified body, and the introduction of new requirements for clinical evidence for CDx was generally welcomed.[770] The planned requirements for demonstrating clinical validity are expected to increase security, quality or reliability of the products.[771]

On the other hand, the planned higher regulatory requirements are feared to result in higher costs. The new regime will inevitably require greater efforts of IVD manufacturers, which can have a negative effect on innovation as larger investments are needed potentially discouraging small innovative companies to develop CDx.[772] The separation between the approval process for Rx and CDx will continue to exist with the IVDR, and a "double application" will still be needed.[773] This separation is criticized to create a *"silo mentality of legislators in the EU that makes the overall new*

766 EPPINGER ET AL. (2015), p. 134.
767 ANTONANZAS ET AL. (2015), p. 456; and Part III, Chapter 6.1 Lack of reimbursement for personalized medicine diagnostics, p. 182 ff.
768 EPPINGER ET AL. (2015), p. 129 and 134.
769 KIEVITS ET AL. (2014), p. 17.
770 THE ACADEMY OF MEDICAL SCIENCES (2013), p. 71.
771 KIEVITS ET AL. (2012), p. 2; and EPPINGER ET AL. (2015), p. 134.
772 KIEVITS ET AL. (2012), p. 2.
773 NEGROUK ET AL. (2015), p. 2.

framework inconsistent and potentially highly damaging to the EU's capacity to make rapid progress in the field of personalised medicine". The planned centralization of the approval process is worrying the IVD industry as it is feared to create unnecessary delays and inefficiencies.[774] Also, the concerns about a lack of coordination remain with the IVDR. There is a call for clarity on the specifics of how the proposed consultation between EMA and the national "notified bodies" will work in practice. *"Without such clarity, there is potential for significant delays in approvals of diagnostics and associated therapeutics. Any inflexible requirement by the regulators for co-submission of a companion diagnostic for approval of a stratified medicine is likely to act as a disincentive for manufacturers in this field"*.[775]

774 E.g., SUDE in MILMO (2015), p. 2.
775 THE ACADEMY OF MEDICAL SCIENCES (2013), p. 44.

ii. IVD approval process in the US

In the Unites States, applications for pharmaceuticals and CDx can be made simultaneously to the FDA:

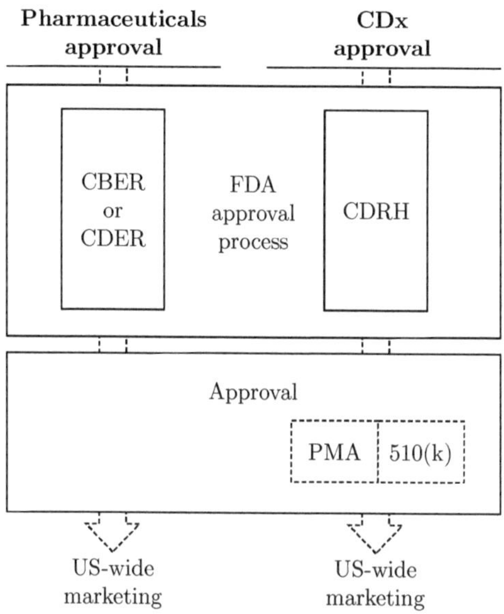

Figure 20: Overview of the US' approval process for pharmaceuticals and companion diagnostics

The CENTER FOR DRUG EVALUATION AND RESEARCH (CDER) or the CENTER FOR BIOLOGICS EVALUATION AND RESEARCH (CBER), which review the applications for pharmaceuticals, and the CENTER FOR DEVICES AND RADIOLOGICAL HEALTH (CDRH), which reviews diagnostics, are co-located within the FDA.[776] The FDA reviews a CDx submission within the context of its corresponding pharmaceutical in a collaborative consulting effort among the relevant FDA offices.[777] The drug and its companion diagnostic are jointly approved by the FDA following appropriate labeling.[778]

776 THE ACADEMY OF MEDICAL SCIENCES (2013), p. 41, with an overview on p. 42. Cf. also LEE & SHEN (2015), p. 69.

777 FDA (2014)a, p. 8. Cf. also LEE & SHEN (2015), p. 69 for details.

778 THE ACADEMY OF MEDICAL SCIENCES (2013), p. 42.

For obtaining market approval for *pharmaceuticals* in the US, a new drug application or biological license application must be submitted to the CBER or CDER. This requires testing in Phase III randomized trials, and frequently post-launch risk evaluation and mitigation strategies, both contributing data informing clinical utility.[779]

In order to determine the regulatory pathway for *IVD companion diagnostics*, the FDA applies a "risk-based approach".[780] It depends on the intended use and risk of the test, whether a premarket approval application (PMA)[781] or a premarket notification 510(k)[782], demonstrating *"substantial equivalence"*, needs to be submitted.[783] There are three medical device classifications (Class, I, II and III). With increasing risk, the classification and the regulatory controls increase.[784] Gaining marketing approval for CDx does not require the completion of clinical trials in all cases: Completely new diagnostics may need to follow the PMA path including the submission of supporting clinical trial data analogous to pharmaceutical new drug applications. If, however, a later market entrant can establish *"substantial equivalence"* to a predicate diagnostic which is already legally marketed, the 510(k) application process can be used, which requires brief bridging studies to the predicate device instead of large-scale clinical testing as in the case of a PMA path. The 510 (k) application process reduces entry barriers due to comparably lower costs, but also generates less information concerning diagnostic validation and clinical utility.[785]

Hitherto, the majority of CDx are considered high-risk devices (Class III)[786] requiring a PMA[787] in order to obtain marketing approval under section 515 of the Federal Food, Drug and Cosmetic Act. Scientific evidence supporting the safety and effectiveness of a CDx is required too in order to receive approval of a CDx for the US

---

779 TRUSHEIM ET AL. (2015), p. 327-28.

780 FDA (2014)a, p. 10.

781 PMA requiring randomized controlled trials for demonstrating analytical validity, clinical validity, clinical utility, cf. NOWESKI ET AL. (2013), p. 279.

782 The 510 (k) clearance compares a new product to approved products. However, in the case of CDx, there is often a lack of reference products, cf. NOWESKI ET AL. (2013), p. 279.

783 FDA (2014)a, p. 10.

784 For *Class I devices* general controls, like establishment registration and device listing apply. For *Class II devices* general controls and a premarket clearance 510 (k) is needed. *Class III devices* require the most stringent approval for medical devices by the FDA, the PMA, cf. OLSEN & TRØST JØRGENSEN (2014), p. 5.

785 TRUSHEIM ET AL. (2015), p. 328.

786 VAN HEERTUM ET AL. (2015), p. 5221; LEE & SHEN (2015), p. 69; and KAUFMANN ET AL. (2015), p. 390.

787 Either a *traditional PMA* (all information is submitted at the same time) or a *modular PMA* (information is submitted in modules, analytical performance and manufacturing information can be submitted while a clinical trial is ongoing, the clinical trial information is then reviewed later), cf. LEE & SHEN (2015), p. 70-71.

market.[788] This includes – amongst others –the demonstration of analytical[789] and clinical validity[790] of a CDx, but not the demonstration of clinical utility.[791]

Co-development guidance by the FDA

Since 2005, the US FDA has been at the forefront developing regulatory strategies for CDx and the Rx-CDx co-development, and has published several guidance documents.[792] In 2014, the FDA released a final guidance document called *"In Vitro Companion Diagnostic Devices: Guidance for Industry and Food and Drug Administration Staff"*. The document indicates regulatory pathways and requirements for CDx and Rx. It does not represent a legally binding document, but the FDA's current thinking.[793] The document reinforces the idea that the simultaneous development and review of a drug and its companion test is favored by the agency whenever possible: *"Ideally, a therapeutic product and its corresponding IVD companion diagnostic device should be developed contemporaneously, with the clinical performance and clinical significance of the IVD companion diagnostic device established using data from the clinical development program of the corresponding therapeutic product".*[794]

If the FDA determines that an IVD CDx is "*essential to the safe and effective use of a novel therapeutic product or indication*", FDA generally will "*not approve the therapeutic product or new therapeutic product indication if the IVD companion diagnostic device is not approved or cleared for that indication. Approval or clearance of the IVD companion diagnostic device will ensure that the device has been adequately evaluated and has adequate performance characteristics in the intended population*"[795]

Furthermore, the guidance document contains *clarifications for the labels* of a therapeutic product and the IVD device. The label of each co-developed product should specify that the product is indicated for use with the corresponding product.

---

788 FD&C Act, *part* 814.

789 LEE & SHEN (2015), p. 71, on *analytical validity* of CDx in the US.

790 *Ibidem*, p. 72, on *clinical validity* of CDx in the US.

791 HAYES ET AL. (2013), p. 3; D. K. THOMPSON (2016), p. 1.
More details on the CDx approval process in the US provide e.g., BARTON (2008); ANSARI (2013); BRANZÉN (2013); MCCARTHY ET AL. (2013); OLSEN & TRØST JØRGENSEN (2014); RUBIN ET AL. (2014) or XU (2014) and KAINZ (2016), p. 12.

792 J. COHEN (2012), p. 751, OLSEN & TRØST JØRGENSEN (2014), p. 4 ff.; and KAUFMANN ET AL. (2015), p. 390. An overview of the published policy and guidance documents from the FDA provides PERSONALIZED MEDICINE COALITION (2014), p. 22.

793 FDA (2014)a, p. 4 -5.

794 FDA (2014)a, p. 7.

795 *Ibidem*, p. 8.

The drug will be named in the label of the device and reference is made to the type of device in the package insert for the drug.[796]

With their guidance document, the FDA acknowledges different scenarios for developing PM applications. In some, the simultaneous co-development of a drug and a CDx may not possible. The guidance document contains two exceptions with regard to the co-approval of a CDx and its companion therapeutic drug: The FDA underlines that it will not hold up approval for a drug for a serious or life-threatening condition where no alternative therapy exists due to the lack of an approved companion test.[797] The second exeption concerns the revision of an existing's drug label in order to include the use of an unapproved CDx to deal with a serious safety issue.[798]

Mid 2016, the FDA released new and more detailed draft guidelines intended to be a practical, non-binding guide with principles to assist drug and CDx manufacturers in developing these two products simultaneously.[799]

Criticism of the US approval process

The FDA was an "early mover" in recognizing the developments in the field of personalized medicine.[800] The agency receives positive comments for the early familiarization with the topic. For example, the *"FDA has been very creative and swift in regulating diagnostics being developed alongside therapeutics that have earned a breakthrough designation by the agency"*[801] or the FDA has been *"fantastic"* and *"unbelievably open"*.[802]

Although the US' integrated Rx-CDx approval process appears to be more adapted to PM applications, in practice, diagnostics companies are referred to prefer the *lighter touch of the EU's approach*, because the EU approach enables a faster market introduction.[803] In exploratory interviews even harsher statements like the *"FDA is hindering innovation in an irresponsible way"* have picked up the author's attention.[804]

[796] *Ibidem*, p. 10.
[797] FDA (2014)a, p. 9; and XU (2014), p. 3.
[798] *Ibidem*.
[799] FDA (2016)b.
[800] J. COHEN (2012), p. 751, OLSEN & TRØST JØRGENSEN (2014), p. 4 ff.; and KAUFMANN ET AL. (2015), p. 390.
[801] MILLER cited in RAY (2016), p. 3.
[802] KLAUSNER in EASTMAN (2012), p. 24.
[803] THE ACADEMY OF MEDICAL SCIENCES (2013), p. 42.
[804] Statement by a *Head of Regulatory Affairs* of a top-3 (measured by revenue, 2015) pharmaceutical company (anonymized), October 14, 2015. Identity known to the author.

The recent initiatives by the FDA sparked the debate about the potential effects which such a regulation may have on discovery and innovation.[805] One question is if the FDA can regulate genomic testing – another one whether the FDA can regulate it well. *"There is no pressing emergency that demands a rushed effort to cram genomic technology into the 40-year-old medical device regulations of the FDA".*[806] For example, B. J. EVANS, BURKE, & JARVIK (2015) doubt if the PMA is the right tool for CDx approval and criticize the *"product-by-product"* regulatory focus of the FDA. Rather the FDA should focus on the *"whole forest"* – in this case all competing tests with similar intended uses – instead of ensuring the safety and effectiveness of each *"tree"* – in this case the single tests.[807] According to them, establishing the clinical validity of genomic tests is largely a post-marketing pursuit: *"It requires the accrual and review of evidence throughout the entire commercial life of a test and, indeed, requires access to post-marketing data not just from that test but from all other tests that are trolling the same region or regions of the human genome".*[808] They conclude that the current direction the FDA has chosen towards genomic testing could bring *"counterproductive regulatory burdens that may – ironically – diminish consumer safety and chill innovation".*[809]

Additionally, the US model is being criticized for *not taking into account of the different ways in which a diagnostic comes to market* due to the FDA's strong focus on the simultaneous co-development: A new CDx may be developed for an approved drug in order to target it better or for a new indication. In other cases, an existing diagnostic device may be paired with a new or marketed drug after a biomarker is discovered and validated.[810]

Despite the FDA's published last guidelines in 2016, questions remain about the *coordination of the co-development process* as such.[811] The main question is who coordinates the activities of co-development reviews –the FDA, the pharmaceutical company, or the diagnostics company?[812]

---

805 B. J. EVANS ET AL. (2015), p. 2258, with additional references.

806 *Ibidem*, p. 2262.

807 *Ibidem* further elaborate that *"statutory reforms should focus on granting the FDA a correct package of legal powers, seed funding, and legal pathways to encourage public-private partnerships to develop and sustain data resources for the right regulation of genomic testing"*, p. 2262.

808 B. J. EVANS ET AL. (2015), p. 2262.

809 *Ibidem*, p. 2258.

810 THE ACADEMY OF MEDICAL SCIENCES (2013), p. 42; and NOWESKI ET AL. (2013), p. 279, about the need for easily being able to add biomarkers to already approved markers.

811 D. K. THOMPSON (2016), p. 1; and RAY (2016), p. 4.

812 RAY (2016), p. 4.

Another criticism is, that until now, the FDA has used its regulatory discretion to not remove competing non-approved diagnostics from the market. The resulting product variety is described to create challenges for pharmaceutical companies: They hesitate to promote the diagnostic market for fear of indirectly promoting unapproved diagnostics which would be the promotion of an "off-label" drug use.[813]

Further skepticism emerged concerning *the ability of the FDA to keep up with the speed of innovation in the future.*[814] The co-development model will be challenged because of the trend towards assays based on high-throughput, "multi-target" techniques which guide treatment decisions to a range of different therapies by determining the multiple biomarkers in a single panel test.[815] So far, the focus has been on bringing one diagnostic and one therapeutic to market. Most of the FDA-approved CDx are "single-target tests".[816] The regulatory framework for CDx will likely need to be further developed in order to accommodate the upcoming challenges.[817] In the coming years, the FDA is expected to issue guidance concerning the clinical evidence required for "multi-target" tests. Hence, currently there is still uncertainty regarding future FDA data requirements for new diagnostics and whether these regulatory changes will improve the flow of high-quality diagnostics in development.[818]

4.1.3 Undermining of the current approval system through LDTs

The previously described barrier is further heightened by the threat of laboratory developed tests (LDTs). LDTs can be described "generic" tests.[819] Regulatory exemptions in several countries allow single health institutions[820] the development of tests

---

813 TRUSHEIM & BERNDT (2015)b, p. 10. "Off-label" describing the use of a drug other than for the indications mentioned its approved label, cf. WIDMER (2013), p. 17, for more about off-label use.

814 E.g., *"The challenge here is a speed of innovation - one that the FDA cannot quite handle"*, KLAUSNER cited in EASTMAN (2012), p. 24.

815 Cf. Part II, Chapter 1.3 Future developments, p. 62 ff.

816 *"Single-target"* refers to an individual biomarker. With improvements in technology (e.g., NGS) it is possible to identify multiple biomarkers using a single panel test – these tests are called *"multi-target"* tests, sometimes also *"multiplex"f* or *"multigene"* tests.

817 THE ACADEMY OF MEDICAL SCIENCES (2013), p. 41-42; LEE & SHEN (2015), p. 73; KAUFMANN ET AL. (2015), p. 391.

818 TRUSHEIM ET AL. (2015), p. 328.

819 THE ACADEMY OF MEDICAL SCIENCES (2013), p. 55. Sometimes LDTs are referred to as "in-house" tests (IHTs), e.g., THE ACADEMY OF MEDICAL SCIENCES (2013), p. 48. A detailed definition of LDTs provides the FDA (2014)c, p. 5, in their draft guidance on a Framework for Regulatory Oversight of Laboratory Developed Tests.

820 E.g., laboratories, hospitals, academic medical centers.

for use within that institution *without* being obliged to invest in the evidence generation required for an equivalent commercial test.[821]

Licensed clinical laboratories are allowed to "home brew" LDTs specific to their clinical interests and offer such testing for patient care.[822] The "home brew tests" are not placed on the market. The reasons behind the in-house development is either the absence of a commercially available equivalent (for instance in the case of rare diseases), or existing tests may be customized with the goal to identify a subset of certain diseases,[823] or in other cases economic considerations may lead to the internal development in order to avoid purchasing tests at the prices set by commercial test manufacturers.[824]

As indicated, LDTs do usually not require a full development and regulatory review. Also, for LDTs no royalties or other compensations are paid to those who discovered the biomarker or developed clinical insight.[825] The following sub-chapters briefly illustrate the regulatory exemptions in a succinct overview on the regulatory frameworks for LTDs in the EU (i) and the US (ii).

i. LDT regulation in the EU

In the European Union, medical devices manufactured and used only within the same health institution without having them transferred to another legal entity are outside the scope of the IVD Directive ("in-house derogation").[826]

That means that in practice, IVD manufacturers compete with hospital laboratories, which can "home brew" their own diagnostic tests. Consequentially, the assessment of the quality of LDTs is subject to uncertainties what further fragments the regulatory pathways for CDx in the European Union.[827]

In the revisions of the IVD it was suggested to extend the scope for certain LDTs.[828] However, the extension was controversially debated: On the one hand, the diagnostic industry welcomed this extension, because of the unequal treatment of

---

821 THE ACADEMY OF MEDICAL SCIENCES (2013), p. 55

822 LDTs are also referred to as *"home brew tests"*.

823 KULKARNI ET AL. (2013), p. 8; and THE ACADEMY OF MEDICAL SCIENCES (2013), p. 48.

824 *Ibidem.*

825 CRAWFORD & ASPINALL (2012), p. 269; and MEADOWS ET AL. (2015), p. 10.

826 Art. 1 (5) IVD Directive.

827 KIEVITS ET AL. (2012), p. 10; and ANTONANZAS ET AL. (2015), p. 456.

828 Art. 4 (4) and (5) and p. 4 IVD Proposal. In-house devices classified as class A, B and C have to be subject to the health institutions quality management system and the health institution is compliant with standard EN ISO 15189 (or equivalent), Article 4 (5) IVD Proposal.

commercial tests and LDTs regarding the level of clinical evidence and quality.[829] On the other hand, it was argued that the current exemption is intended to encourage innovation and the development of more cost-effective approaches to healthcare. The suggested inclusion of in-house Class D devises was expected to increase costs substantially. It was argued that this would delay or prohibit access to some tests, given that there are currently no CE marked tests available for several genetic conditions and rare diseases.[830]

The IVDR has found a compromise on LDTs: LDTs are exempted from the requirements (with some specific provisions for class D devices), but LDTs do not benefit from exemptions when their tests are manufactured on an "industrial scale". Furthermore, to benefit from the exemption, health institutions will now have to justify that the specific needs of target patient group cannot be met, or cannot be met at the appropriate level of performance by an equivalent device already available on the market.[831]

ii. LDT regulation in the US

LDTs are governed by Clinical Laboratory Improvement Amendments (CLIA), which are administered by the CENTERS FOR MEDICARE AND MEDICAID SERVICES (CMS).[832] In contrast to the IVD approval by the FDA, the CLIA certification focuses on technical performance and thus only addresses the analytical but not the clinical validity or clinical utility of a test.[833]

The FDA has historically used discretionary oversight in the regulation of LDTs. So far, the FDA has not enforced PMA and other applicable FDA requirements to LDTs because they were relatively simple lab tests. Since LDTs have evolved and proliferated significantly due to advances in technology and business models, the FDA plans to make a change from its policy of exercising enforcement discretion only with respect to commercial IVDs and to pursue its right to regulate LDTs.[834] In 2014, the FDA advanced two draft guidances proposing an oversight framework for LDTs.[835] The drafts proposals are based on risk to patients, rather than whether the

829 Cf. THE ACADEMY OF MEDICAL SCIENCES (2013), p. 71, and the position of the EUROPEAN DIAGNOSTICS MANUFACTURERS ASSOCIATION (2014), p. 6.

830 Cf. the position of the MEDICINES AND HEALTHCARE PRODUCTS AGENCY (2012), p. 13.

831 Preamble (29) IVDR.

832 CENTERS FOR MEDICARE & MEDICAID SERVICES (2013), p. 1.

833 *Ibidem*; and TRUSHEIM ET AL. (2015), p. 328.

834 FDA (2015)a.

835 FDA (2014)c; and FDA (2014)b.

diagnostic tests are made by a commercial manufacturer or a single health institution.[836]

Under the proposed LDT regulatory framework, LTDs acting as CDx will be required to go through all regulatory considerations outlined in the FDA's CDx guidance. That means that clinical laboratories have to submit evidence data required for the PMA or 510(k) review proofing clinical validity and utility of their LDTs classified as a test with high or medium risks. As outlined in both the LDT[837] and CDx guidances[838], unapproved LDTs could still be used to support therapeutic product approval in cases falling under the two exceptions to concurrent approval.[839] The FDA is mainly concerned that CLIA does not require labs to verify the clinical validity of LDTs. The draft guidance for LDTs is also citing gaps regarding the analytical validity in CLIA oversight.[840] The FDA recognizes that analytical validity does not only depend on devices but also on the laboratory processes and workflows for using the device.[841] End 2015, the FDA published 20 case studies on *"The Public Health Evidence for FDA Oversight of Laboratory Developed Tests"* contending that additional FDA oversight is needed as CLIA has several gaps.[842] There are concerns about the *"safety" of LDTs*. As illustrated, CLIA does neither address the clinical validity nor the clinical utility of LDT, but the tests can influence health decisions. Consequences of misinterpretation can include an ineffective therapy, an unnecessary preventive surgery or other suboptimal medical decisions.[843] The FDA is citing several examples in which faulty tests have resulted in harm to patients. In a congressional hearing on the draft guidance, the director of the FDA's CDRH referred to instances in which predictions of risks for heart disease or ovarian cancer diagnoses were inadequately supported.[844] The FDA recognizes a *"potential increased risk for patients in the absence of appropriate oversight"*.[845] The WALL STREET JOURNAL described the FDA's

---

836 The comment period for draft proposal has started and the FDA is currently collecting additional input, FDA (2015)a; and KAUFMANN ET AL. (2015), p. 390.

837 FDA (2014)c, p. 28.

838 FDA (2014)a, p. 9.

839 The exceptions are described in the previous Chapter 4.1.2, ii) Lack of consistent regulatory guidance in the approval process for CDx, p. 143 ff.

840 FDA (2014)c, p. 9.

841 *Ibidem*, p. 10.

842 FDA (2015)b.

843 PERSONALIZED MEDICINE COALITION (2014), p. 23.

844 BAYEFSKY & BERKMAN (2015), p. 3.

845 FDA (2014)c, p. 8.

findings in the case studies as the *"wild west of medicine"*.[846] Media is talking about a *"modern day gold rush"* in which profit is placed about proof.[847]

The FDA's challenge is to develop an accepted definition of technical metrics for data quality and to define appropriate validation strategies for the multiple technical options at each step in the genomic test workflow.[848] The unanswered question is *"how the standards-based approach proposed by the FDA would improve on the oversight that CMS already provides under CLIA"*.[849] The FDA argues that the tests today are characterized by such a high level of complexity requiring a level of proficiencies that CLIA high-complexity laboratories may not possess. However, there are doubts about the ability of the FDA to master the complexity in an effective manner.[850] The publication of the draft guidelines and the case studies on LTDs have attracted much controversy. Several stakeholders have been vocal in supporting and opposing the draft guidance.[851] With the political changes beginning 2017, the FDA paused its plans to regulate LDTs.[852]

4.1.4 Lack of harmonization between regulatory systems

The brief analyses in the previous Chapters 4.1.2 and 4.1.3 illustrate the fragmentation of the approval process for CDx. The approval pathway is not only fragmented within countries due to the distinction between commercial and in-house tests, but als between countries. This results in *"incomprehensible differences"* in the regulatory pathway to the market between the USA and the EU.[853] The following table summarizes the major differences:

---

[846] BURTON (2015), p. 1.
[847] CBS (2016), p. 1.
[848] B. J. EVANS ET AL. (2015), p. 2261.
[849] *Ibidem.*
[850] Cf. some select detailed concerns in B. J. EVANS ET AL. (2015), p. 2262.
[851] BAYEFSKY & BERKMAN (2015) analyze the supporting and opposing arguments in detail. Cf. also B. M. THOMPSON & BOIANI (2015) on developments in the US or criticism by TRIBE (law professor at Harvard University), CLEMENT (US solicitor), and other critical voices cited in BURTON (2015), p. 2.
[852] BRENNAN (2017), p. 1.
[853] OLSEN & TRØST JØRGENSEN (2014), p. 5.

	EU	US
Approval processes Rx and CDx	*Separate* applications for drugs and diagnostics are made to different regulatory bodies	*Joint* application to the FDA
Ensuring CDx quality	Self-certified conformity assessment	PMA or 510 (k)
	No requirement of analytical and clinical validity	Requirement of analytical and clinical validity
Rx label	No reference for specific CDx required	Reference for specific CDx required
LDTs	Not regulated (with some exceptions for class D devices in IVDR)	CLIA oversight, no FDA regulation (draft guidance on FDA oversight pending)

Table 7: Comparison CDx approval in the EU and US

The problem of internationally inconsistent approval standards has been widely cited as a barrier hindering the uptake of PM.[854]

4.1.5 Analysis of incentives

i. Approval processes avoid "market for lemons"

The need for an adequate and consistent approval framework for personalized and traditional medicines roots in the basic underlying assumption that a *"market for lemons" problem* requires institutional approval mechanisms for enabling a functional personalized medicine market:

[854] *Criticizing the lack of harmonization between regulatory systems:* HARVEY ET AL. (2012), p. 631; ANSARI (2013), p. 405 ff.; BRANZÉN (2013), p. 61; THE ACADEMY OF MEDICAL SCIENCES (2013), p. 42-43; HAYES ET AL. (2014), p. HORGAN ET AL. (2014), p. 292; OLSEN & TRØST JØRGENSEN (2014), p. 5; AKHMETOV ET AL. (2015), p. 214; EPPINGER ET AL. (2015), p. 164; MEADOWS ET AL. (2015), p. 8; TRUSHEIM & BERNDT (2015)b, p. 10; BRALL & SCHRÖDER-BÄCK (2016), p. 179; SHIMAZAWA & IKEDA (2016); DAVID PETTITT ET AL. (2016), p. 324 ff.; and WURCEL ET AL. (2016), p. 138.
Cf. also JAIN, MOLLET, & SZUCS (2017), p. 1-2, with international comparison of budgets, product approvals, timelines and fees of various regulatory authorities for new pharmaceutical products.

"The difficulty of distinguishing good quality from bad is inherent in the business world".[855]

AKERLOF (1970) has demonstrated in his seminal paper *"The Market for 'Lemons': Quality Uncertainty and the Market Mechanism"* that the quality of products in a market can degrade because of information asymmetries between buyers and sellers about the actual quality, leaving only the bad quality products – the *"lemons"* – left in the market. If a seller is better informed about product attributes than the buyer, the market may fail to arise because the buyers would be wary about contracting with a seller who has superior information.[856]

To solve AKERLOF'S problem of market failure, sellers of good quality products need to be able to reduce the information asymmetries and to make credible statements about product quality so that buyers are able to identify the level of quality they seek. AKERLOF (1970) mentions several institutional mechanisms that can counteract the effects of quality uncertainty: Guarantees, brand names or licensing practices.[857]

Without appropriate institutional mechanisms for approval, the market for personalized medicine would face the *problem of asymmetric information.* For example, it would be difficult for a buyer of a personalized pharmaceutical or companion diagnostic to judge the respective quality without trying it on a patient.

Additionally, CDx may suffer not only from the problem of asymmetric information but also from the *problem of uncertainty.*[858] As illustrated in Chapter 1.2.2,[859] the cut-off value of a CDx test significantly influences its positive predictive value. Only the developer of a CDx might know the underlying statistical distributions of the population across the measured diagnostic score that provides the basis for predicting responsiveness to a drug. If the population distributions are not clearly separated, a certain number of false positives/negatives cannot be avoided.[860] Thus, there

855 AKERLOF (1970), p. 500.

856 *Ibidem*, p. 491.

857 *Ibidem*, p. 499-500. With *"licensing"* AKERLOF means licenses issued by a state institution, and mentions the examples of doctors, lawyers, barbers and other certificates that show a certain degree of professionalism.

858 Also GHOSH (2015), p. 12 ff., is discussing the problem of uncertainty in PM. However, in his paper he fails to clearly distinguish between DTC approaches and clinical Rx-CDx applications. Further, this thesis' author does not agree with his conclusion to increase patent protection in order to solve a problem of asymmetric information.

859 Cf. Part III, Chapter 1.2.2 Interdependencies between the pharmaceutical and diagnostic component, p. 105 ff.

860 Cf. Figure 13: Perfect responder separation, p. 105.

is not a clear cut between "bad quality" and "good quality" CDx complicating the appropriate institutional mechanism regulating the transactions needed for a functional CDx market.

In the following, AKERLOF'S proposed institutional mechanisms for reducing information asymmetries and allowing a functional market shall be applied to the market of personalized medicine:

His first solution is the issuance of a *guarantee.* Guarantees can create contractual and tort liability for the seller who fails to meet the promised product quality.[861] The problem with PM is that the quality is difficult to measure due to the described problem of uncertainty. Further, there are ethical obstacles involved. A patient could receive an ineffective treatment and thus miss alternative effective treatment options. In the worst case, he could die because of a wrong choice. AKERLOF's second solution is *branding.* As touched upon in the previous chapter,[862] this is a strategy used by CDx companies to a certain degree. The third solution AKERLOF (1970) calls *"licensing practices".*[863] In medicine this happens usually through the regulatory approval of a pharmaceutical or a diagnostic. The previously illustrated lack of adequate regulation might be prohibitive that the "lemons" are picked out of the market.[864]

ii. Inconsistencies and gaps in the regulatory framework of the approval process for personalized medicine applications disincentivize pharmaceutical and diagnostics companies to develop PM treatments

The previous three chapters have illustrated the regulatory inconsistencies and gaps characterizing the current approval processes of applications for personalized medicine.[865]

The separate regulatory process for diagnostics coupled with a lack of clear regulatory guidance regarding co-development disincentivizes the co-development of Rx and CDx and leads to inefficiencies.[866]

---

861 E.g., SCHÄFER & OTT (2005), p. 473 ff.

862 Cf. Chapter 3.2.2 Analysis of incentives, p. 130 ff.

863 AKERLOF (1970), p. 500.

864 Cf. previous Chapters 4.1.2 Lack of consistent regulatory guidance in the approval process for CDx; 4.1.3 Undermining of the current approval system through LDTs; and 4.1.4 Lack of harmonization between regulatory systems.

865 Previous Chapters 4.1.2 Lack of consistent regulatory guidance in the approval process for CDx; 4.1.3 Undermining of the current approval system through LDTs; and 4.1.4 Lack of harmonization between regulatory systems.

866 J. COHEN (2012), p. 751; MITTRA & TAIT (2012), p. 711; MOORE ET AL. (2012), p. 493; EUROPEAN ALLIANCE FOR PERSONALISED MEDICINE (2013), p. 4; HORGAN ET AL. (2014), p. 289; RUBIN ET AL. (2014), p. 1419; MILNE & COHEN (2015)a, p. 3; and NEGROUK ET AL. (2015), p. 2.

Further, due to the international diversity of approval processes innovators face a range of possible regulatory paths. The inconsistent regulatory environments creates hurdles for both pharmaceutical as well as diagnostics developers, as it increases administrative burdens and costs to their approval processes:[867] Navigating these convoluted regulatory pathways and the different levels of required evidence make development and global distribution of products more expensive.[868]

iii. Lack of LDT regulation sets low incentives for Dx companies to develop commercial PM Dx

As illustrated with the two examples EU and US, the regulation of diagnostic tests is a moving target. The regulatory exemptions for LDTs create a controversial divide in the market for PM testing between LDTs versus commercial diagnostics reviewed and licensed by the respective supervisory authority.[869]

The potential substitution with LDTs undermines the commercial exclusivity of regulated IVDs and lowers the incentives for their development. MEADOWS, MORRISON, BRINDLEY, SCHUH, & BARKER (2015) and DAVID PETTITT ET AL. (2016) illustrate this with the Vectibix (panitumumab) case study: Qiagen is offering a KRAS oncogene identifying therascreen kit which is able to identify non-responders of Vectibix.[870] Soon, KRAS confirming "home brew" LDTs were available and competed for market share with QIAGEN's therascreen kit.[871] The same situation was mentioned in an exploratory interview for this thesis with ROCHE. The fact that the test for the biomarker BRAF V600 can be developed as "home brew" LDT in the EU makes it unattractive for ROCHE to develop and or provide it.[872] The two illustrative cases show how a manufacturer of a commercially regulated IVD faces direct competition from unregulated LDTs that have no development costs and simply "copy" the test.[873] Manufacturers can spend significant amounts of R&D resources on clinically validating a diagnostic which can then be replicated as an LDT. This acts as further disincentives for manufacturers to develop and generate evidence for innovative diagnostics.[874]

---

867 EUROPEAN ALLIANCE FOR PERSONALISED MEDICINE (2013), p. 4; and HAYES ET AL. (2014), p. 8.

868 MEADOWS ET AL. (2015), p. 8; and DAVID PETTITT ET AL. (2016), p. 319 ff.

869 E. g., FDA/EMA CRAWFORD & ASPINALL (2012), p. 269 ff.

870 A monoclonal antibody for the treatment of refractory EGFR-expressing metastatic colorectal cancer in patients with non-mutated KRAS.

871 DAVID PETTITT ET AL. (2016), p. 324

872 BORRMANN (2015) interviewed on October 15th, 2015.

873 KIEVITS ET AL. (2014), p. 9.

874 Similar arguments in KULKARNI ET AL. (2013), p. 8; THE ACADEMY OF MEDICAL SCIENCES (2013), p. 7 and 48; MEADOWS ET AL. (2015), p. 10; and DAVID PETTITT ET AL. (2016), p. 319 ff.

The existing LDT exemptions fragment the regulatory pathway for CDx and undermine the commercial exclusivity of regulated diagnostic tests. Unregulated LDTs act as direct "generic" competitors to commercially available, more evidence-based tests and disincentivize manufacturers to develop and generate evidence for innovative PM diagnostics.[875]

iv. Unregulated LDT's may spur innovation in research institutions

On the one hand, the lack of LDT regulation sets low incentives for Dx companies to develop PM Dx (iii) and thus comparably fewer devices can be used in research institutions. On the other hand, there are also arguments that the lack of LDT regulation may spur innovation as providers and research institutions may use LDTs without additional costs and administrative burdens. Some industry participants argue that a regulation of LDT's would *"stifle innovation"* and that it would *"slow innovation or create unnecessary regulatory hurdles"* by new requirements and costs for clinical laboratories, hospitals or some doctors.[876] Thus no conclusive statement is possible on the *research institution's* incentive to foster the translation of PM.

v. Spill-over effects into the provision phase

Inconsistencies and gaps in the regulatory framework of the approval process have indirect spill-over effects into the provision phase. If a PM pharmaceutical or diagnostic component does not receive approval, the value chain is interrupted after the approval phase.

Thus, the barrier does indirectly negatively affect the *providers*' prescription behavior as a rational provider will tend to refrain from using a non-approved treatment or test, as this could potentially increase his personal liability. Also, rationally acting patients will generally refrain from using unapproved pharmaceuticals or tests as they lack a guarantee of the safety and efficacy. For the same reasons, also payers refrain from paying unapproved pharmaceuticals or diagnostics.

As these are indirect effects due to the interruption of the PM value chain in the approval phase, the indirect negative incentives are not considered in the below summary.

---

[875] Also THE ACADEMY OF MEDICAL SCIENCES (2013), p. 7; TRUSHEIM & BERNDT (2015)b, p. 10; JOHNSON (2016), p. 4; and DAVID PETTITT ET AL. (2016), p. 321.

[876] BRENNAN (2017), p. 1.

4.1.6 Resulting hypothesis

The overview below summarizes the argumentation of the previous chapter and shows the resulting incentives through the inconsistencies and gaps in the regulatory framework of the approval process for personalized medicine.

Research institutions	*Pharmaceutical companies*	*Diagnostic companies*	*Providers*	*Patients*	*Payers*
–	negative	negative	–	–	–

negative = institutional setting incentivizes a player not to foster the translation of PM
– = neutral/no conclusive statement possible on a player's incentive to foster the translation of PM

Based on the arguments presented in the previous sub-chapters, this chapter concludes with the following hypothesis:

Hypothesis: Inconsistencies and gaps in the regulatory framework of the approval process for PM Dx and Rx act as a barrier to the translation of personalized medicine into clinical practice.

4.2 Incompatibility of clinical trials with personalized pharmaceuticals

4.2.1 Literature analysis

The "traditional" regulatory pathways for drugs with long-term clinical trial outcome requirements are criticized to be incompatible with the smaller and more targeted patient population used in PM. Finding a trial design that suits the purpose of personalized pharmaceuticals is one of the areas that has contributed to slower progress in the adoption of personalized medicine in clinical practice. Regulators are lagging behind in adapting clinical trials for subsets of patients.[877]

A "traditional" clinical trial process is *"one of the costliest and most time-consuming parts of R&D in the healthcare industry"*.[878] A pharmaceutical requires on average ca. USD 1.5 billion investment and roughly ten years of trials to gain approval in the US.[879] The "traditional model" of drug development is to give the drug to an unselected population even though it may only be effective in small percentages of the population. These traditional population-based trials expose large numbers of patients to drugs from which they may not benefit – so to say the *"antithesis of personalized medicine"*.[880]

Personalized medicine is – by definition – aiming at smaller trials. The need to stratify trial patients by molecular sub-types may not lead to the randomization which a traditional randomized control trial requires. Common pitfalls observed in personalized trials are for example the poor quality of employed analytics, lack of appropriate patient selection, lack of appropriate phenotype identification, lack of power in relation to the frequency of the genetic variation studied, irrelevant endpoints having been selected for the basis of the study, and failure to take into account the pharmacology of the drug in the design of the study.[881] Additionally, it might not be justifiable to perform a trial with the knowledge that certain patients will not/slower/faster respond to the treatment.[882] For these reasons available trials investigating genomic biomarkers might fall short of the evidence burden needed to fulfill regulatory demands.[883]

---

[877] E.g., ASPINALL & HAMERMESH (2008), p. 6-7; PRASAD & BRECKENRIDGE (2011), p. 869; BRANZÉN (2013), p. 60; HARVARD BUSINESS SCHOOL (2016), p. 1; DAVID PETTITT ET AL. (2016), p. 320; LAWLER & SULLIVAN (2015), p. 329; and PERMED (2015), p. 24.

[878] HARVARD BUSINESS SCHOOL (2016), p. 1.

[879] *Ibidem.*

[880] BRANZÉN (2013), p. 60.

[881] EMA (2016), p. 5.

[882] BOMBARD (2015), p. 58.

[883] PRASAD & BRECKENRIDGE (2011), p. 869.

Also, "traditional" clinical trials test for safety first and efficacy later. This approach fails to take advantage of continuing advances in pharmacogenomics. The development of PM should allow for this early identification of efficacy. New models may shift the focus from patient groups to the development of diagnostic tools along with new drugs.[884]

In the European Union, the revision of the CLINICAL TRIALS DIRECTIVE is expected to simplify the conduct of clinical trials. Consequently, this should also facilitate research in therapies using personalized medicine.[885] However, the revision is criticized to *"fail to take into account the changing clinical research landscape"*.[886]

4.2.2 Analysis of incentives

The incompatibility of traditional population-based clinical trials with the concept of personalized medicine disinzentivices *pharmaceutical companies* to develop personalized pharmaceuticals. The uncertainty about how to adequately design and perform the trials in order to reach the required evidence increases approval costs for pharmaceutical companies. Combined with the expected smaller market of a personalized pharmaceutical, pharmaceutical companies are disincentivized to foster PM.

884 PERMED (2015), p. 24. They suggest, e.g., early clinical trials including an ongoing analysis of patients' tissue and blood samples. In case of a failing drug, scientists can determine if the reason behind is whether the target is inappropriate, or because genetic differences prevent the drug from hitting the target in some individuals.

885 The CLINICAL TRIALS DIRECTIVE was published in the official journal of the EU in May 2014 and became applicable in 2016. EUROPEAN COMMISSION (2016)a. The Directive renders the clinical trial framework *"more efficient and better adapted to international trials"*. Further, it aims to reduce bureaucracy and costs, it consolidates patient safety and it has been praised for having addressed the demand for increased transparency in clinical research. The new regulation allows public scrutiny of results and offers the possibility for independent researchers to re-analyse data generated by the pharmaceutical industry. Cf. NEGROUK ET AL. (2015), p. 4.

886 NEGROUK ET AL. (2015), p. 2.

Research institutions	*Pharmaceutical companies*	*Diagnostic companies*	*Providers*	*Patients*	*Payers*
–	negative	–	–	–	–

negative = institutional setting incentivizes a player not to foster the translation of PM
– = neutral/no conclusive statement possible on a player's incentive to foster the translation of PM

Other *stakeholders* are not directly incentivized through the identified barrier.

4.2.3 Resulting hypothesis

The overview below summarizes the argumentation above and explicitly formulates this Chapter's hypothesis.

Hypothesis:	*The incompatibility of clinical trials with personalized pharmaceuticals acts as a barrier to the translation of personalized medicine into clinical practice.*

5 Barriers in the provision phase

After receiving approval, personalized medicine applications are ready to be provided to patients. The *provision phase* in the value chain of PM covers all aspects and conditions needed in order to provide a treatment to the patient. The payment of the treatment is not considered as provision, but as a consequential link in the value chain and is thus examined in a separate chapter (*Chapter 6*). The institutional barriers concerning the provision of PM cover a diverse spectrum, presented in the following chapters.

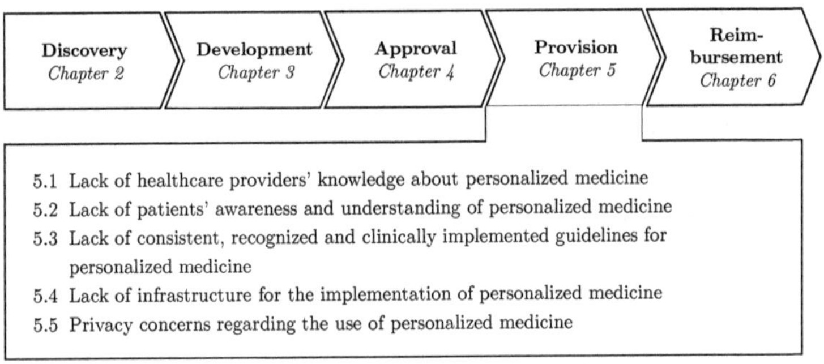

Figure 21: Barriers in the provision phase

5.1 Lack of healthcare providers' knowledge about personalized medicine

5.1.1 Literature analysis

Once a personalized pharmaceutical and the corresponding diagnostic component have passed all phases from discovery to approval, they arrive at the point of care. For the translation of PM, it is critical that a healthcare provider is aware and knowledgeable of available treatment options. Adoption by healthcare providers is indispensable to realize the potential of PM.[887]

Several studies identify the point of care as the "broken link" in the PM value chain. Healthcare providers' lack of awareness, their unfamiliarity and limited under-

[887] E.g., THE ACADEMY OF MEDICAL SCIENCES (2013), p. 7.

standing regarding available diagnostic tests are seen as barriers to the clinical adoption of PM.[888]

Physicians are described to lack the genetic literacy to be able to interpret and communicate the results of genetic tests and to translate the results into clinical decisions.[889] Or they may simply not be aware of the existence of Rx-CDx combinations.[890] For example, some healthcare providers believe that the benefits of Rx-CDx pairings are limited to oncology, without realizing the evidence existing for applications in immunology, cardiovascular, CNS and other therapeutic areas.[891] Ninety percent of the interviewees in a study of the TUFTS CENTER FOR THE STUDY OF DRUG DEVELOPMENT declared the familiarity among US physicians to be inadequate.[892] Another US study by UNERTL, FIELD, PRICE, & PETERSON (2015) describes the knowledge and attitudes of clinicians participating in a pharmacogenomics implementation program as insufficient. They found that the providers expressed an *"inability to keep up with the rapid pace of evidence generation"*, and that they need more *"clinical decision support to assist with genotype-tailored therapies"*. Concerns raised by clinicians included the effective communication of results, long-term responsibility for actionable results and the handover to other providers. Another study found that describing a test as "genetic" (vs. non-genetic) significantly decreased a physician's likelihood of offering the test.[893] In a different study by HORGAN ET AL. (2014), two-thirds of the respondents were not aware of any best practice guidelines in the field of PM.[894] Generally, healthcare providers seem to have a certain *"skepticcism"*[895] or even *"resistance"*[896] towards PM.[897]

---

888 *Studies identifying a lack of healthcare providers' knowledge about PM:* HOPKINS ET AL. (2006), p. 410; ASPINALL & HAMERMESH (2008), p. 6 f.; YEO ET AL. (2010), p. 11 ff.; SCOTT (2011), p. 7 ff.; LAM (2012) p. 279; BRANZÉN (2013), p. 77; T. A MANOLIO ET AL. (2013), p. 260-261; MCCARTHY ET AL. (2013), p. 11; HORGAN ET AL. (2014), p. 290 ff.; KIEVITS ET AL. (2014), p. 13-15; PERSONALIZED MEDICINE COALITION (2014), p. 40; BAYEFSKY & BERKMAN (2015), p. 2; EPPINGER ET AL. (2015), p. 163 and 176; GRECH, VAN SCHAIK, & BORG (2015), p. 334-335; MILNE & COHEN (2015)a, p. 1; PERMED (2015), p. 11; PERSONALIZED MEDICINE COALITION (2015), p. 7; and PRITCHARD ET AL. (2017), p. 145 ff.

889 E.g., KINGSMORE, PETRIKIN, WILLIG, & GUEST (2015), p. 1.

890 E.g., AKHMETOV ET AL. (2015), p. 223; and DUFFY (2015), p. 7.

891 AKHMETOV ET AL. (2015), p. 223, cite the example of HER2 Dx testing in breast cancer. Produders had to spend several years to educate healthcare providers for using the CDx.

892 MILNE & COHEN (2015)a, p. 3. An older study with similar findings in SCOTT (2011), p. 7.

893 SCHNOLL AND SCHIELDS (2011) cited in MCCARTHY ET AL. (2013), p. 11.

894 These findings stand in contrast to oncology. In oncology most healthcare professionals were aware of best practice guidelines. HORGAN ET AL. (2014), p. 293.
A further study from UNITEDHEALTH (2012) cited in BRANZÉN (2013), p. 77, reports that only 13% of physicians are able to *"fully understand"* the results from a genetic test.

Several factors lead to the healthcare providers' low degree of awareness and limited knowledge about PM:

When integrating PM testing into everyday clinical practice, "micro-politics" and cultures become as important as the "macro-politics" like regulation and funding.[898] One reason behind the institutional barrier is the *high degree of complexity* that PM implies.[899] Physicians' behavior is still *"deeply rooted in trial-and-error medicine"*.[900] PM is seen as too *"disruptive"*, as it leads to changes in current clinical practice.[901] In contrast to the "one-size-fits-all" approach, PM opens a whole new variety of treatments per patient. Healthcare providers often do not find the time and resources to gain orientation in the complex topic. Physician organizations are reported to be historically *"reluctant to take strong, proactive stands in recommending new standards of care"*, because they already have a large number of standards to comply with.[902] There are concerns about unnecessarily adding to physicians' burdens and overly constraining their freedom to decide what's best for their patients. More standards also increase the physicians' vulnerability to malpractice suits.[903]

An additional factor behind the healthcare providers' limited knowledge about PM is the *novelty of the concept.* Due to the current knowledge gaps in molecular biology and genetics, physicians are not committed to apply PM in their decisions.[904]

There is a growing sentiment that the slow uptake of PM[905] is due to a *lack of adequate training* in genomics. A majority of today's physicians received their medical education before the "genomics revolution". It is a challenge to educate a critical mass

---

ELLUL (2015) is citing studies showing that clinicians worry that they do not have adequate guidelines how to use tests. Canadian physicians identified a lack of clinical guidelines, a lack of personal knowledge, no evidence based clinical information and expense as obstacles to use pharmamcogenetic tests. 37% recognized that they did not have the resources to educate patients. Further, US primary care physicians also reported being uncomfortable with the level of knowledge expected to interpret the genomic tests, p. 356.

895 HERMANN & SEITZ (2015), p. 18.

896 SZUCS (2014)a, p. 38.

897 Older studies also talk about *"excessive demands"* of healthcare providers, e.g., RIPPE ET AL. (2004), p. 62.

898 TUTTON (2013), p. 190.

899 EPPINGER ET AL. (2015), p. 163.

900 ASPINALL & HAMERMESH (2008), p. 2.

901 PLUN-FAVREAU ET AL. (2016), p. 145.

902 ASPINALL & HAMERMESH (2008), p. 7.

903 *Ibidem.*

904 AKHMETOV ET AL. (2015), p. 223, citing the example of HER2 Dx testing in breast cancer. Producers had to spend several years to educate healthcare providers for using the CDx.

905 References in RESEARCH CONCEPT, Chapter 1 Problem, *note* 12.

of physicians in the new paradigm.[906] Several studies have documented the deficits in genetics education for healthcare providers, and the barriers this presents to the integration of PM into clinical practice.[907] Medical sciences education is often separated from other natural sciences, leading to a lack of knowledge in the field of medical genetics.[908] It has been suggested that the training for physicians should shift away from the current discipline-specific model towards more holistic integration of additional topics (e.g., biology, informatics).[909]

A *"silo-mentality" within single disease areas* is seen as a further hindering factor. There are suggestions to reclassify diseases in order to reflect new knowledge about the human biology.[910]

Further, the general perception of high prices associated with use of molecular diagnostics leads to *uncertainty of physicians about the cost-benefit ratio of PM applications.*[911]

5.1.2 Analysis of incentives

In the first place, a lack of *healthcare providers*' knowledge about PM incentivizes them not to offer PM as they do not have the required capabilities to do so.

Also, a lack of healthcare providers' knowledge about PM is reflected in the *patients*' knowledge and behavior. The information gap of the healthcare experts is directly transferred to the patients. The asymmetric information is enforced as patients are commonly less aware of available treatments and rely on the expertise of their providers.

---

906 ASPINALL & HAMERMESH (2008), p. 7.

907 *Claiming a lack of healthcare providers' education:* ASPINALL & HAMERMESH (2008), p. 6 and 8; N. COHEN & FRANGIOSA (2008), p. 17; PACI (2009), p. 285; FACKLER & MCGUIRE (2010), p. 8; YEO ET AL. (2010), p. 5; EUROPEAN COMMISSION (2011), p. 2; EASTMAN (2012), p. 25; THE ACADEMY OF MEDICAL SCIENCES (2013), p. 36-39; BRANZÉN (2013), p. 77; T. A MANOLIO ET AL. (2013), p. 262; PASIC ET AL. (2013), p. 162; ABPI (2014), p. 10; KIEVITS ET AL. (2014), p. 13-15; PERSONALIZED MEDICINE COALITION (2014), p. 37 ff.; DUFFY (2015), p. 7; ELLUL (2015), p. 356; EPPINGER ET AL. (2015), p. 150 and 176; RELLING & EVANS (2015), p. 347; PERSONALIZED MEDICINE COALITION (2015), p. 7; STUDNEVA ET AL. (2015), p. 1 ff.; and ESTAPE ET AL. (2016), p. 12.

908 STUDNEVA ET AL. (2015), they suggest a revision of the current medical curricula and closer collaboration between the two disciplines to alleviate the problem.

909 ESTAPE ET AL. (2016), p. 12.

910 Currently, clinical entities are described as single diseases which may in fact be more than one disease, requiring different treatment approaches, cf. EUROPEAN COMMISSION (2011), p. 2. Cf. also Part II, Chapter 1.3.2 New nosology through , p. 63 ff.

911 Cf. Part II, Chapter 3 Economic value of personalized medicine, p. 72.

Additionally, the lack of healthcare providers' knowledge about PM increases costs for *pharmaceutical and diagnostics companies* to sell their products, as they have to invest time and resources to educate healthcare providers for using PM.[912] This in turn constitutes a disincentive for pharmaceutical and diagnostics companies to foster PM due to increased marketing costs compared to traditional pharmaceuticals.

Payers are not directly confronted with the effects of the lack of *healthcare providers*' knowledge about PM. However, if personalized treatments are less frequently chosen than traditional approaches, it could be argued that payers are only confronted with payment decision in single cases and are thus not forced to develop some general payment policies for PM.

5.1.3 Resulting hypothesis

The overview below shows the resulting incentives through a lack of *healthcare providers*' knowledge about personalized medicine.

Research institutions	*Pharmaceutical companies*	*Diagnostic companies*	*Providers*	*Patients*	*Payers*
–	negative	negative	negative	negative	–

negative = institutional setting incentivizes a player not to foster the translation of PM
– = neutral/no conclusive statement possible on a player's incentive to foster the translation of PM

Based on the arguments presented in the previous sub-chapters, this chapter concludes with the following hypothesis:

Hypothesis: The lack of healthcare providers' knowledge about personalized medicine acts as a barrier to the translation of personalized medicine into clinical practice.

[912] Cf. PLUN-FAVREAU ET AL. (2016), p. 145.

5.2 Lack of patients' awareness and understanding of personalized medicine

5.2.1 Literature analysis

The patients' insufficient awareness and understanding of PM are cited as an additional barrier to the translation of personalized medicine.[913]

The uptake of PM by society depends on the perception of individuals. PM's acceptance requires a level of comfort on the part of the patients.[914] Patients may not be aware of the options in PM, they may be concerned about privacy and discrimination[915] or they may be confused about the implications of a particular genetic test result.[916] Studies find that the "genetic literacy" of the general public is insufficient for being able to deal with this unprecedented access to genomic information.[917]

5.2.2 Analysis of incentives

The lack of patients' awareness and understanding of PM is the main factor influencing the demand for PM as there is not enough "pull factor for personalized medicine".[918] Due to patient education, marketing costs for pharmaceutical and diagnostics companies are higher compared to traditional approaches. Additionally, with the patient being in a dependent relationship with the healthcare provider, possibilities for direct marketing to patients are limited. These factors impede the emergence of a functioning market.

---

913 *Claiming the lack of patients' awareness and understanding of PM:* LEHOUX (2011), p. 76; HARVEY ET AL. (2012), p. 625 ff.; BRANZÉN (2013), p. 61; T. A MANOLIO ET AL. (2013), p. 262; MCCARTHY ET AL. (2013), p. 10-11; THE ACADEMY OF MEDICAL SCIENCES (2013), p. 38 ff.; HITZ & PREVEL KATSANIS (2014), p. 371 ff.; ARONSON & REHM (2015), p. 336; ELLUL (2015), p. 354; NEGROUK ET AL. (2015), p. 8; PERMED (2015), p. 11; BUDIN-LJØSNE & HARRIS (2016), p. 4; THOMAS ET AL. (2016), p. 349; and PRITCHARD ET AL. (2017), p. 145 ff.

914 E.g., TAG (2012), p. 829; THE ACADEMY OF MEDICAL SCIENCES (2013), p. 38; ELLUL (2015), p. 354; and TURNER ET AL. in GRECH, SCERRI, ET AL. (2015), p. 138.

915 Cf. the subsequent Chapter 5.5 Privacy concerns regarding the use of personalized medicine, p. 178 ff.

916 MCCARTHY ET AL. (2013), p. 11.

917 PASIC ET AL. (2013), p. 162, with further references. For example, HITZ & PREVEL KATSANIS (2014) conducted a study sending a questionnaire to 300 potential "consumers" of PM. They found a general acceptance of PM – however a lack of clear understanding why it should be "better" than current therapies associated with fewer side effects.

918 E.g., KIEVITS ET AL. (2014), p. 15.

Correspondingly, other stakeholders are negatively incentivized: *Healthcare providers* – suffering as well from a lack of knowledge in PM[919] – do not offer PM as long as there is no demand for it. *Payers* do not reimburse PM as long as they are not obliged to, or as long as they are not confronted with a sufficient number of PM treatments in order to invest into developing general reimbursement rules for PM.

5.2.3 Resulting hypothesis

The overview below summarizes the argumentation of this chapter and shows the resulting incentives through a lack of patients' awareness and understanding of PM.

Research institutions	*Pharmaceutical companies*	*Diagnostic companies*	*Providers*	*Patients*	*Payers*
–	negative	negative	negative	negative	negative

negative = institutional setting incentivizes a player not to foster the translation of PM
– = neutral/no conclusive statement possible on a player's incentive to foster the translation of PM

Based on the arguments presented in the previous sub-chapters, this chapter concludes with the following hypothesis:

> *Hypothesis: The lack of patients' awareness and understanding of personalized medicine acts as a barrier to the translation of personalized medicine into clinical practice.*

919 Cf. previous Chapter 5.1 Lack of healthcare providers' knowledge about personalized medicine, p. 162 ff.

5.3 Lack of consistent, recognized and clinically implemented guidelines for personalized medicine

5.3.1 Literature analysis

A further barrier to the clinical uptake of personalized medicine is the lack of officially recognized guidelines for translating genetic variations into actionable recommendations encouraging the coupling of diagnostics and medicines.[920]

It is hypothesized that there are not enough trained genetic counselors available to meet the growing demands of PM. It will therefore become the responsibility of primary care physicians to ensure that genetic information is interpreted correctly and utilized appropriately.[921] Especially as soon as inexpensive "multi-target" tests[922] become available, the question will be *how* test results should be used to influence medical decisions.[923]

Thus, reliable clinical practice guidelines are needed determining when and how to utilize pharmacogenetic information and how to interpret the test results.[924]

5.3.2 Overview of existing guideline sources

Some years ago, research institutions started to publish the first overviews on drug-gene interactions.[925] Today, several initiatives aim to create clinical practice guidelines for PM. The following overview but depicts three relevant selected sources out of similar databases containing drug-gene interactions.[926]

---

920 *Mentioning a lack of consistent, recognized and clinically implemented guidelines:* FACKLER & MCGUIRE (2010), p. 8; PASIC ET AL. (2013), p. 162; PERSONALIZED MEDICINE COALITION (2014), p. 5; SZUCS (2014)b, p. 38; RELLING & EVANS (2015), p. 347; and PAOLO ET AL. (2017), p. 3.

921 E.g., FACKLER & MCGUIRE (2010), p. 8.

922 Cf. *note* 816.

923 RELLING & EVANS (2015), p. 347.

924 E.g., FACKLER & MCGUIRE (2010), p. 8.

925 Two relevant papers were published by FLOCKHART ET AL. (2009) and SWEN ET AL (2011) and the ROYAL DUTCH ASSOCIATION FOR THE ADVANCEMENT OF PHARMACY. The work of FLOCKHART ET AL. (2009) focusing on cytochrome P450 drug interactions is continued and accessible on http://medicine.iupui.edu/CLINPHARM/ddis/main-table (last accessed July 2017).

926 E.g., an overview on available databases provides DRUGBANK (http://www.drugbank.ca/w/databases). Also MCCARTHY ET AL. (2013), p. 8-9, provide an overview; they mention PharmGKB, CPIC, ClinVar, EGAPP, HuGE evidence navigator, etc. Other sources containing gene-drug pairs are CANCERCOMMONS (http://www.cancercommons.org/); DRUGBANK (http://www.drugbank.ca/); GUIDETOPHARMACOLOGY (http://www.guidetopharmacology.org/); TTP (http://bidd.nus.edu.sg/group/cjttd/); ICR CANCER GENE INDEX (https://wiki.nci.nih.gov/display/cageneindex/Cancer+Gene+Index+End+User+Documentation); Stitch 4.0 http://stitch.embl.de/); SUPERTARGET (http://bioinf-apache.charite.de/supertarget_v2/), HUMAN GENE

Database	Description
PharmGKB[927]	The PGx database provides open access, peer-reviewed, updated, evidence-based pharmacogenetic clinical practice guidelines. It encompasses clinical information including dosing guidelines and drug labels, potentially clinically actionable gene-drug associations and genotype-phenotype relationships from various sources: The *dosing guidelines* take into consideration patient genotype and have been published by the CPIC, the ROYAL DUTCH ASSOCIATION FOR THE ADVANCEMENT OF PHARMACY - Pharmacogenetics Working Group, or other professional societies. The collected information on *drug labels* contains pharmacogenetic information approved by the FDA, EMA, the PHARMACEUTICALS AND MEDICAL DEVICES AGENCY, Japan (PMDA), and HEALTH CANADA (HCSC).
CPIC[928]	Under the governance of the PHARMACOGENOMICS RESEARCH NETWORK[929] and the PHARMACOGENOMICS KNOWLEDGE BASE,[930] the CLINICAL PHARMACOGENETICS IMPLEMENTATION CONSORTIUM (CPIC) provide open access, peer-reviewed, updated, evidence-based pharmacogenetic clinical practice guidelines for all actionable germline pharmacogenes developed by CPIC. The recommendations consider a level of evidence and clinical utility defined by CPIC.[931] The guidelines focus on how genetic-test results should be translated into specific prescribing decisions.

MUTATION DATABASE (http://www.hgmd.cf.ac.uk/ac/index.php), etc. There are also commercial databases for which fees have to be paid, e.g., the CLINICAL GENOMICS TOOLKIT from REUTERS (http://lsresearch.thomsonreuters.com/pages/solutions/21/clinical-genomics-toolkit). Links all last accessed August 2017.

927 Cf. https://www.pharmgkb.org/ (last accessed August 2017).

928 Cf. https://www.pharmgkb.org/cpic/pairs (last accessed August 2017).

929 Cf. http://www.pgrn.org (last accessed August 2017).

930 Cf. http://www.pharmgk.org (last accessed August 2017).

931 CPIC levels A-D, cf. https://www.pharmgkb.org/page/cpicStatusLegend (last accessed August 2017).

DGIdb 2.0[932]	Comprehensive meta-database and web interface for identifying known and potential drug-gene relationships with drug-gene interactions from multiple sources including PharmGKB, DrugBank, TTD, and others.

Table 8: Examples of existing personalized medicine guideline sources

SOURCE: Selection and description by the author with inputs from the respective webpages.

5.3.3 Criticism of existing guidelines

The guidelines existing today are praised as *"early attempts at supporting diffusion of innovation"* and as a *"laudable first step",*[933] but they are criticized for a lack of consistency, recognition and clinical implementation:

Consistency

The professional societies and other guideline-generating groups are not always in agreement on whether and how to recommend PM testing.[934] The existing guidelines are criticized for being inconsistent.[935] Steps should be taken to coordinate guidelines for drugs and associated tests that might be used by different medical specialists.[936]

Recognition

Further, most guidelines[937] are not officially recognized by either a state or a medical professional society – often due to a lack of evidence.[938] Medical professional societies' guidelines have an immediate effect on the institutionalization of PM.[939] The lack of recognition or at least promotion from either governmental agencies or medical so-

932 THE DRUG GENE INTERACTION DATABASE, link under http://dgidb.genome.wustl.edu/ (last accessed July 2017).
933 MCCARTHY ET AL. (2013) p. 9.
934 RELLING & EVANS (2015), p. 347.
935 YEO ET AL. (2010), p. 5.
936 HOPKINS ET AL. (2006), p. 410.
937 Except for the guidelines based on pharmacogenetic information in the drug lables.
938 Cf. Part II, Chapter 3 Economic value of personalized medicine, p. 72 ff.
939 One example is HLA-B*5701 screening. In 2008, the HIV treatment guidelines were revised to incorporate HLA-B*5701 screening into routine care for patients before initiating abacavir treatment. HLA-B*5701 biomarker tests are regularly implemented in clinical practice today, cf. COHEN (2012), p. 755.

cieties may lead the clinicians' impression that adequate guidelines on how to use PM Dx do not exist – despite their actual existence today.[940]

Implementation in clinical support systems

Finally, the guidelines are of limited use, if they are not used in clinical decision making. Recent literature calls for the implementation of the guidelines into clinical decision support (CDS) systems ensuring a consistent interpretation of diagnostic tests results. [941]

5.3.4 Analysis of incentives

The lack of guidelines affects primarily *providers*. First, providers have no support in providing PM. Second, without guidelines, providers face the risk of higher liability in case of a suit due to an ineffective personalized pharmaceutical as PM is not yet considered general state-of-the-art of medical practice (*"lege artis"*[942]).

However, the opposed argument – that the existence of guidelines do promote the translation of PM – is not valid. Considering behavioral effects through guidelines, the existence of a guideline does not necessarily mean that the personalized treatments are more often prescribed compared to traditional ones. Hong Kong, for example, introduced a policy for HLA-screening before prescribing an antiepileptic drug carbamazepine.[943] The policy led clinicians to forego prescribing carbamazepine at all. Instead they began to prescribe another drug[944] that could also cause severe adverse events, but the risk factors are not as well defined as for carbamazepine. With this behavior, the overall incidence of severe skin reactions remained unchanged.[945]

Besides providers, also *patients* do not have any guidelines to which they could refer in asking for a personalized treatment. And last, *payers* are inclined to decline the payment of personalized treatments as long as they are not "lege artis" standard of care.

Research institutions, *pharmaceutical* and *diagnostics* companies are not significantly affected by the lack of guidelines.

---

940 RELLING & KLEIN (2011) cited in ELLUL (2015), p. 356.

941 Cf. the following Chapter 5.3.3 Criticism of existing guidelines, *Implementation in clinical* support systems, p. 172.

942 Cf. Part IV 5.1.1 Institutional setting, *ii. Liability rules for medical doctors in Switzerland*, p. 238 ff.

943 Patients with the allele are at risk of developing severe skin reactions to the drug carbamazepine.

944 Phenytoin – which can also cause severe skin reactions.

945 Example described in RELLING & EVANS (2015), p. 344.

5.3.5 Resulting hypothesis

The overview below summarizes the argumentation of the previous chapter.

Research institutions	*Pharmaceutical companies*	*Diagnostic companies*	*Providers*	*Patients*	*Payers*
–	–	–	negative	negative	negative

negative = institutional setting incentivizes a player not to foster the translation of PM
– = neutral/no conclusive statement possible on a player's incentive to foster the translation of PM

Based on the arguments presented in the previous sub-chapters, this chapter concludes with the following hypothesis:

Hypothesis: The lack of consistent, recognized and clinically implemented guidelines for PM acts as a barrier to the translation of personalized medicine into clinical practice.

5.4 Lack of infrastructure for the implementation of personalized medicine

5.4.1 Literature analysis

In order to provide personalized medicine, the available infrastructure – including biobanks, CDS systems and the related IT systems and processes – needs to cope with innovative technologies, especially the increasing amount of health data. A lack of adequate infrastructure capable of managing, analyzing and displaying "omics" data - is a further barrier to the translation of PM.[946]

Physicians are confronted with an *"explosion of information"* and need to adapt to this development.[947] Increasingly, the use of information technology assists physicians in decision making.[948] PM is dependent on the availability of a patient's health information including genetic information. The computational approaches required to identify, catalogue, prioritize and interpret genetic variants influencing prescribing decisions are generally characterized by a *"high degree of complexity"*.[949]

Existing *CDS systems* do often not sufficiently support the use of genetic information in decision making.[950] Further, there is a lack of standards for genomic applications in CDS.[951] Infrastructure supporting PM includes a comprehensive knowledge base capturing sequence variants and their phenotypic associations which is integrated into CDS systems.[952] With the increased use of personalized approaches, physicians are ideally assisted with informatics – not for replacing judgment but for providing facts. There are claims for developing easy-to-use interfaces enabling the management of the underlying complexity of the data and their use in clinical routine.[953]

---

946 *Mentioning the lack of infrastructure for the implementation of PM:* TAG (2012), p. 829; HOOD & AUFFRAY (2013), p. 3; T. A MANOLIO ET AL. (2013), p. 263; PASIC ET AL. (2013), p. 161; THE ACADEMY OF MEDICAL SCIENCES (2013), p. 29 ff.; ABPI (2014), p. 4; B. J. EVANS (2014), p. 54; HORGAN ET AL. (2014), p. 290; SZUCS (2014)b, p. 38; ARONSON & REHM (2015), p. 338; JAMESON & LONGO (2015), p. 2232; KINGSMORE ET AL. (2015), p. 1; OXFORD ECONOMICS (2016), p. 9 ff.; BUDIN-LJØSNE & HARRIS (2016), p. 4-5; PRITCHARD ET AL. (2017), p. 145 ff.; and SCHELLEKENS ET AL. (2017), p. 2.

947 JAMESON & LONGO (2015), p. 2232.

948 *Ibidem.*

949 RELLING & EVANS (2015), p. 347.

950 T. A MANOLIO ET AL. (2013), p. 263.

951 *Ibidem.*

952 Cf. previous Chapter 5.3.3 Criticism of existing guidelines, p. 171 ff.

953 Cf. *ibidem*; T. A MANOLIO ET AL. (2013), p. 263; HORGAN ET AL. (2014), p. 290; GRECH, SCERRI, ET AL. (2015), p. 137; JAMESON & LONGO (2015), p. 2231; PERMED (2015), p. 17; ESTAPE ET AL. (2016), p. 9 ff, stressing the importance of the availability of *"clinical warehouses"* or *"big data re-*

Electronic health records (EHR)[954] and their associated systems are the main means of providing such CDS to clinicians.[955] They are an adequate tool to provide genetic information technology support to providers. They are expected to become *"data clouds"* and are seen as *"pivotal to implementing the precision medicine revolution"*.[956] EHR systems enable information to be organized and displayed in a way which integrates with the clinicians' workflows and facilitates diagnostic and treatment decisions. Also, extra information about a genetic test result can be provided through external links to electronic resources such as websites or databases. If genomic data is integrated into EHR systems with appropriate CDS tools, patient-specific alerts can be triggered and can guide providers to use genetic information when prescribing pharmaceuticals or issue pharmacogenomic warnings that highlight potentially adverse interactions between a pharmaceutical and specific genetic variants.[957] Therefore, consistent and reliable guideline databases will be essential for providing the computational CDS in EHR systems with trusted, up-to-date recommendations.[958]

However, the establishment of an adequate infrastructure for the implementation of PM faces several challenges:

The main challenge is the identification of the proper vehicle to communicate genomic information within the healthcare system.[959] The current heterogeneity across healthcare systems is expected to slow down the creation and uptake of CDS aiming to facilitate the use of pharmacogenetic information.[960] Standardized collection protocols and formats must be in place in order to ensure that datasets can be stored and

positories"; and HOFFMAN ET AL. (2016), p. 44, who outline the key features of such knowledge bases.

954 Sometimes also referred to as *electronic medical records*. ESTAPE ET AL. (2016), p. 12-13, with a historical background on EHRs.

955 T. A MANOLIO ET AL. (2013), p. 263; and ARONSON & REHM (2015), p. 338.

956 DUFFY (2015), p. 2.

957 MCCARTHY ET AL. (2013) p. 9; ABPI (2014), p. 4; RELLING & EVANS (2015), p. 347; and ARONSON & REHM (2015), p. 338, with more details on CDS/EHR options and processes.

958 HOOD & AUFFRAY (2013), p. 3; and RELLING & EVANS (2015), p. 347.
Having recognized the limitations of the current EHRs, STANFORD MEDICINE and GOOGLE entered a collaboration in order to facilitate the basic infrastructure necessary for genomic data use in real-time. They are building cloud based applications capable of storing, processing, analyzing and sharing the genomic data sets, cf. STANFORD MEDICINE (2016), na.

959 GRECH, VAN SCHAIK, ET AL. (2015), p. 342.

960 RELLING & EVANS (2015), p. 347; EPPINGER ET AL. (2015), p. 176.

meaningfully compared or combined.[961] Policy makers are called to promote comprehensive and consistent EHRs.[962]

Second, clinicians need to have access to support. Health informatics specialists are critical partners and can assist clinicians' interpretation of data and the development of personalized therapy recommendations.[963]

Third, a governance framework for data access, quality, resources and protection must exist in order to ensure adequate patient privacy.[964]

5.4.2 Analysis of incentives

First, the lack of infrastructure in the provision phase of PM does negatively incentivize *research institutions.* A lack of infrastructure leads comparably less genetic data as input being used in order to generate scientific insight. The same argument is valid for *pharmaceutical and diagnostics companies* as they have less real-world data in order to depelop new or evaluate existing products.

Healthcare *providers* are less likely to provide personalized treatments if they do not have the resources, knowledge and time needed to filter, aggregate and analyze the increased amount of information. Their transaction costs through information acquisition are prohibitive if supportive CDSs are either not available or not suited for information allowing a personalized treatment.

Also *patients* are less likely to demand PM. Either because they are not offered the option by their healthcare provider or because information acquisition costs are prohibitively high as they would have to make up the lack of infrastructure by themselves (e.g., keeping their own EHRs, having their genomes deciphered by private services, interpreting the genomic data on their own).

---

961 Cf. Chapter 2.1 Lack of standards enabling data sharing between biobanks, p. 113 ff.; YEO ET AL. (2010), p. 5; THE ACADEMY OF MEDICAL SCIENCES (2013), p. 32; GROVES ET AL. (2013), p. 6 ff.; and DUFFY (2015), p. 5.

962 GRECH, VAN SCHAIK, ET AL. (2015), p. 342.

963 ESTAPE ET AL. (2016), p. 11.

964 Cf. Chapter 5.5 Privacy concerns regarding the use of personalized medicine, p. 178 ff.; and THE ACADEMY OF MEDICAL SCIENCES (2013), p. 32; B. J. EVANS (2014), p. 54; and DUFFY (2015), p. 5.

5.4.3 Resulting hypothesis

The overview below summarizes the argumentation above and shows the resulting incentives through the lack of infrastructure for the implementation of PM.

Research institutions	*Pharmaceutical companies*	*Diagnostic companies*	*Providers*	*Patients*	*Payers*
negative	negative	negative	negative	negative	–

negative = institutional setting incentivizes a player not to foster the translation of PM
– = neutral/no conclusive statement possible on a player's incentive to foster the translation of PM

Based on the arguments presented in the previous sub-chapters, this chapter concludes with the following hypothesis:

Hypothesis: The lack of infrastructure for the implementation of personalized medicine acts as a barrier to the translation of personalized medicine into clinical practice.

5.5 Privacy concerns regarding the use of personalized medicine

5.5.1 Literature analysis

Ensuring data protection and privacy as regards to the genetic information of people are frequently mentioned aspects in the translation of personalized medicine.

On the one hand, literature highlights *concerns of the public on privacy, confidentiality of results and genetic discrimination.* The literature analysis has demonstrated that not a lack of data protection as such is identified as a barrier to the translation of PM, but explicitly the concerns of the public about a potential lack of data protection. Although patients are interested in minimizing side effects of drugs, they are skeptical about whether their genetic data is securely stored. Regulation on privacy has to address questions about the possibility to re-identify individuals or about the ownership of genetic data.[965] Further concerns include the accessibility of test results (e.g., for prospective employers, insurance companies, legal authorities or family members who might be at risk for the same disease).[966] Especially the question of discrimination features prominently in social scientific publications.[967]

On the other hand, scientists complain about *"unnecessarily complex data protection rules"* impeding scientific progress.[968] There are cultural as well as regulatory barriers to data circulation. Some barriers are simply the consequence of insufficient technical methods for obtaining consent, or the absence of appropriate legal frameworks for obtaining, safeguarding and disclosing data.[969] One prominent topic identi-

965 KIEVITS ET AL. (2014), p. 15.

966 *Discussing privacy concerns regarding the use of PM:* J. COHEN (2012), p. 752; HARVEY ET AL. (2012) p. 631; EASTMAN (2012), p. 25; EUROPEAN ALLIANCE FOR PERSONALISED MEDICINE (2013), p. 9; PASIC ET AL. (2013), p. 165; TUTTON (2013), p. 185; ABPI (2014), p. 7; HORGAN ET AL. (2014), p. 291; PERSONALIZED MEDICINE COALITION (2014), p. 33 ff.; EPPINGER ET AL. (2015), p. 140, 150 and 176; BLOBEL ET AL. (2016), p. 1 ff.; and KICHKO ET AL. (2016), p. 16 ff.

967 HARVEY ET AL. (2012) p. 631; KOCH cited in EASTMAN (2012), p. 25; TUTTON (2013), p. 185, with further references; and KIEVITS ET AL. (2014), p. 15.

KNOPPERS ET AL. (2010), p. 225-226, arguing that *"current consent and privacy mechanisms, when applied to population genomic studies and accompanying databases, may limit their use for public health research". "One should remember that publicly funded research is a public good and ensuring that research data is easily accessible is 'primarily a matter of sound stewardship of public resources'".*

PERSONALIZED MEDICINE COALITION (2014), p. 34 ff.; and GREEN, LAUTENBACH, & MCGUIREOLIVER (2015) for an overview on the current US GENETIC NON DISCRIMINATION ACT.

968 EUROPEAN ALLIANCE FOR PERSONALISED MEDICINE (2013), p. 10.

969 *Ibidem*, and ABPI (2014), p. 4.

In 2012, the EU initiated several legislative reforms which are expected to modify the way clinical research is conducted in Europe. There are concerns about the unintentional outcomes of the *"phraseology"* of the EU draft regulation on data protection. The EUROPEAN ALLIANCE FOR PER-

fied by literature is the need for a more uniform consenting process.[970] In 2014, the GLOBAL ALLIANCE FOR GENOMICS AND HEALTH (2014) published a framework for the responsible sharing of genomic and health-related data addressing these issues. It contains *"foundational principles and core elements for responsible data sharing"*, and is *"guided by human rights, including privacy, non-discrimination, and procedural fairness"*.[971]

The two contrasting opinions illustrate the *innate trade-off between the circulation of data and data privacy*: A society conscious of the importance of personal rights as well as of the importance of personal health legitimately needs to find a balance between fostering innovation and respecting individuals' rights to data privacy - otherwise the benefits of PM suffer delays.[972]

5.5.2 Analysis of incentives

As illustrated, the institutional setting on data protection is a double-edged sword. If data protection rules are too strict – innovation may be hampered through complex, long and costly data sharing processes between research institutions and patients. If data protection rules are too loose, patients do not share their data because they fear discrimination. Thus, privacy concerns primarily disincentivize *research institutions* as well as *patients* to foster the translation of PM.

Additionally, the other stakeholders are impacted by the direct effects of the patient's privacy concerns: *Pharmaceutical* and *diagnostics companies* have difficulties to find patients for the development of personalized pharmaceuticals and face a lower demand. Also *providers* are less likely to offer PM if their patients are concerned by privacy issues. Only *payers* are not directly concerned by patient's privacy concerns.

SONALISED MEDICINE believes that the suggestions would cause serious constraints on scientific research and prevent or significantly hinder health research and innovation to such an extent that Europe would no longer be able to guarantee the quality of the healthcare to which its citizens are entitled.
Cf. KAUFMANN ET AL. (2015), p. 391; NEGROUK ET AL. (2015), p. 3; and FRIZZO-BARKER, CHOW-WHITE, CHARTERS, & HA (2016), p. 1 ff. for more criticism on existing data protection frameworks.

970 EUROPEAN ALLIANCE FOR PERSONALISED MEDICINE (2013), p. 10; T. A MANOLIO ET AL. (2013), p. 265; ABPI (2014), p. 4; ARONSON & REHM (2015), p. 337, describing the two major forms of consent that are relevant for protecting patients' privacy: consent for receiving medical as well as consent for releasing data for research; and BOMBARD (2015), p. 58.

971 GLOBAL ALLIANCE FOR GENOMICS AND HEALTH (2014), *front page*.

972 EUROPEAN ALLIANCE FOR PERSONALISED MEDICINE (2013), p. 10.

5.5.3 Resulting hypothesis

The overview below depicts the argumentation above showing the resulting incentives through privacy concerns regarding the use of PM.

Research institutions	*Pharmaceutical companies*	*Diagnostic companies*	*Providers*	*Patients*	*Payers*
negative	negative	negative	negative	negative	–

negative = institutional setting incentivizes a player not to foster the translation of PM
– = neutral/no conclusive statement possible on a player's incentive to foster the translation of PM

Based on the arguments presented in the previous sub-chapters, this chapter concludes with the following hypothesis:

Hypothesis:	*Privacy concerns regarding the use of PM act as a barrier to the translation of personalized medicine into clinical practice.*

6 Barriers in the reimbursement phase

The benefits of personalized medicine can only be realized if the financing of healthcare costs is not undermined.[973] While *"research into human genomics gives opportunity for the greatest leap forward in knowledge of human disease in the history of mankind"*, the practical use of this knowledge is predicted not to occur *"unless there are valid economic models in place for doing so"*.[974] Economic considerations are important in determining the diffusion of a new technology in any scientific field, and particularly in health related sectors.[975]

The last link of the value chain contains the reimbursement of PM. It covers all aspects around the evaluation, market access, and reimbursement of PM. In this link of the value chain, two barriers are claimed to impede the translation of PM into clinical practice – both are closely-related to the inconclusive findings for the economic value of PM as illustrated in the CONTEXT of this thesis:[976] First, *the lack of reimbursement* for PM diagnostics (*Chapter 6.1*). Second, *gaps and inconsistencies in health technology assessments* (*Chapter 6.2*). The following chapters analyze the two barriers identified for the reimbursement phase of PM.

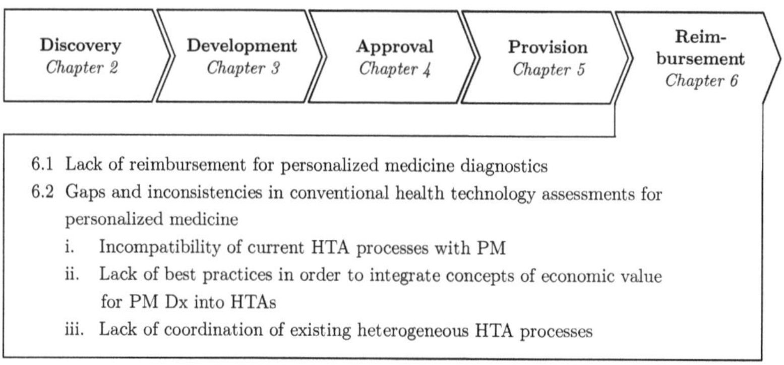

Figure 22: Barriers in the reimbursement phase

---

973 Cf. also BÜTLER (2016), p. 101, mentioning financing as the basic assumption behind the progress of PM.

974 CRAWFORD ET AL. (2014), p. 266.

975 PACI (2009), p. 284.

976 Cf. Part II, Chapter 3 Economic value of personalized medicine, p. 72 ff.

6.1 Lack of reimbursement for personalized medicine diagnostics

6.1.1 Literature analysis

When examining the institutional barriers to the uptake of personalized medicine, one barrier seems to receive the highest prominence in literature: Healthcare systems do not (sufficiently) provide reimbursement for personalized medicine diagnostics. It is argued that reimbursement systems in healthcare are still designed for a payment model in the traditional "one-size-fits-all" approach and are primarily cost-based instead of value-based.[977] They do not reflect the benefits arising from the use of PM products, and thus loom large among the most immediate challenges affecting the development of personalized medicine products, especially the diagnostic components.[978]

The literature analysis is structured into two parts: A first *sub-chapter (i)* illustrates the status quo of reimbursement systems for PM diagnostics with a brief focus on the systems in the US and the EU. It finds heterogeneous reimbursement landscapes and a general lack of reimbursement for PM Dx. A second *sub-chapter (ii)* then examines the drivers behind the identified lack of reimbursement.

---

977 For an explanation of value-based pricing (VBP), cf. Part II Chapter 3.1.4 Value based pricing (VBP), p. 85 ff.

978 *The lack of reimbursement for personalized medicines Dx is a widely cited barrier in literature*: ASPINALL & HAMERMESH (2008), p. 2; BARTON (2008), p. 126; J. C. DAVIS ET AL. (2009), p. 279; MECKLEY & NEUMANN (2010), p. 91 ff.; NAYLOR & COLE (2010) a, p. 68; A. H. WU (2010), p. 44; YEO ET AL. (2010), p. 5; J. COHEN (2011), p. 293; GARFIELD (2011), p. 1 ff.; MARCHANT (2011), p. 13; MILLER ET AL. (2011), p. 137 ff.; CRAWFORD & ASPINALL (2012), p. 274; J. COHEN (2012), p. 752; EASTMAN (2012), p. 25; GARAU ET AL. (2012), p. 4 ff.; ALBRECHT, MENU, SZLEZAK, & RUDOLPH (2013), p. 7; ANSARI (2013), p. 412; BUCHANAN ET AL. (2013), p. 2 ff.; J. COHEN ET AL. (2013), p. 378 ff.; EUROPEAN ALLIANCE FOR PERSONALISED MEDICINE (2013), p. 23; FRUEH (2013), p. S30-31; JAKKA & ROSSBACH (2013), p. 3; HAYES ET AL. (2013), p. 3-4; KULKARNI ET AL. (2013), p. 10; T. A MANOLIO ET AL. (2013), p. 262 f.; PAYNE & ANNEMANS (2013), p. 38; TOWSE & GARRISON (2013), p. 40; TRUSHEIM (2013), p. 325 ff.; THE ACADEMY OF MEDICAL SCIENCES (2013), p. 53 ff.; MCCARTHY ET AL. (2013), p. 10 ff; K. PHILLIPS ET AL. (2013), p. 59; VFA (2013), p. 6 ff.; HITZ & PREVEL KATSANIS (2014), p.371 ff.; HORGAN ET AL. (2014), p. 291; EPPING & BERCHTOLD (2014), p. 51; PERSONALIZED MEDICINE COALITION (2014), p. 5 and 40; SZUCS (2014)b, p. 58; AKHMETOV ET AL. (2015), p. 223 ff.; EPPINGER ET AL. (2015), p. 130, 150, 163; JOSEPH (2015), p. 1; HERMANN & SEITZ (2015), p. 18; RELLING & EVANS (2015), p. 347; KAUFMANN ET AL. (2015), p. 391-399; KINGSMORE ET AL. (2015), p. 1; LUO ET AL. (2015), p. 10 ff, MILNE & COHEN (2015)b, p. 1; PERSONALIZED MEDICINE COALITION (2015), p. 6; TRUSHEIM & BERNDT (2015)b, p. 10; BUGULISKIS (2016), p. 4-6; GARRISON (2016), p. 224; JOHNSON (2016), p. 3 ff.; KICHKO ET AL. (2016), p. 15 ff; MESSNER ET AL. (2016), p. 8.; DAVID PETTITT ET AL. (2016), p. 326; PLUN-FAVREAU ET AL. (2016), p. 144-145; and WURCEL ET AL. (2016), p. 141.

i. Heterogeneous reimbursement systems for PM diagnostics

The pricing and reimbursement landscape for PM Dx differs significantly from region to region. This heterogeneity in the reimbursement landscape negatively influences the adoption of PM.[979] For securing reimbursement, manufacturers need strategies and tactics to deal with the complexity, administrative work and uncertainty due to the heterogeneous reimbursement landscapes.

Reimbursement for PM Dx ranges from a total lack of reimbursement - preliminary in emerging countries such as China, India, or Brazil – to partial reimbursement in developed regions such as the US, the EU or Japan.[980]

Below follows a brief illustration of the pricing and reimbursement systems for the US and the EU in order to understand the status quo and the most prominent differences between the systems. It will be demonstrated, that barriers to the adoption of PM exist in both regions, whereas additional barriers and complexity are faced in the EU context.

Reimbursement for PM Dx in the US:

In the US, reimbursement for diagnostic tests is typically determined according to a clinical laboratory fee schedule which does not distinguish between traditional diagnostics and molecular CDx – which might have similar production costs but a different clinical value.[981] Unlike pharmaceutical companies which have a greater ability to set the prices of new drugs, Dx players have to rely on a process known as *CPT code stacking* handled by the CENTERS FOR MEDICARE & MEDICAID SERVICES (CMS)' MEDICARE program[982] as well as on *private health plan policies* to obtain premiums for their innovations:[983]

CENTERS FOR MEDICARE & MEDICAID SERVICES (CMS): In the *Current Procedure Terminology (CPT)* system for laboratory diagnostic tests – which is handled primarily by the CENTERS FOR MEDICARE & MEDICAID SERVICES (CMS)' MEDICARE program – PM Dx are typically reimbursed by payers in one of two ways:

First, diagnostic laboratories can file claims using stacked CPT codes. CPT codes describe generic laboratory procedures. This system is able to accommodate various technical approaches applied to measure molecular analytes at a time when technolo-

979 KULKARNI ET AL. (2013), p. 10.
980 ANSARI (2013), p. 412, provides a global perspective on the reimbursement of CDx.
981 DZAU ET AL. (2015), p. 2119.
982 PERSONALIZED MEDICINE COALITION (2015), p. 6.
983 MILLER ET AL. (2011), p. 137-138; MOORE ET AL. (2012), p. 492; KULKARNI ET AL. (2013), p. 10; RUBIN ET AL. (2014), p. 1425; and LUO ET AL. (2015), p. 10.

gy is rapidly evolving. Thus, payment is based on a technical cost-derived fee schedule, rather than the time-consuming analytical process that goes into interpreting the results.[984] CPT code stacking does not reward the value a PM Dx test may offer.[985] The basic challenge in the system is that code stacking combinations are not unique to biomarkers or tests and consequently the used diagnostic tests cannot be identified. The system rather allows "representing" a test procedure in several diffrent code stacking combinations. Payers criticized the lack of transparency of those codes and the need to report multiple codes for single procedures.[986] This lack of transparency represents a hurdle to identify a value-based reimbursement price for the used personalized medicine Dx.[987] The US procedural coding system is considered to be *"archaic"* and *"complex"*, and it is criticized that no CPT codes specific to PM Dx exist.[988]

Between 2012 and 2014, there have been administrative changes in the coding and pricing approaches for genomic tests[989] resulting in a *"nearly complete cessation of federal payments for genomic tests in the first quarter of 2013".*[990] Currently, CMS are establishing new rules for pricing of multiple medical technologies. With these expected new rules it is hoped to increase incentives for PM Dx manufacturers again.[991]

Second, also the CPT system contains value-based approaches, but only for the reimbursement of selected PM Dx. It relies on the use of *"not otherwise listed codes"*, or *"catch all miscellaneous CPT codes"* resulting in a payment that is unique to the value of the specific test performed.[992]

---

984 MILLER cited in EASTMAN (2012), p. 25.

985 MILLER ET AL. (2011), p. 137-138.

986 YEO ET AL. (2010), p. 5; and RUBIN ET AL. (2014), p. 1425-1426.
CRAWFORD & ASPINALL (2012), p. 274, call for a substantive revision in the payment schemes for genomic medicine: *"There is desperate need for payment revision, so that payers can know what they are paying for, gaps in coverage for molecular diagnostic services between inpatient and outpatient settings can be addressed, and the coding system for genetic- and genomic-testing can be simplified"*, p. 281.

987 ANSARI (2013), p. 412.

988 BARTON (2008), p. 13.

989 PERSONALIZED MEDICINE COALITION (2015), p. 6 ; MCCARTHY ET AL. (2013), p. 10 ; RUBIN ET AL. (2014), p. 1425-1426; PERSONALIZED MEDICINE COALITION (2014), p. 27 ff. for details on amendments and AMERICAN MEDICAL ASSOCIATION'S development of a new set of analyte-specific pathological codes.

990 PERSONALIZED MEDICINE COALITION (2015), p. 6. *"Payments began to be distributed erratically, and some tests were not paid for at all – they were rejected for payment"*, PERSONALIZED MEDICINE COALITION (2015), p. 6. Cf. also ANSARI (2013), p. 412.

991 PERSONALIZED MEDICINE COALITION (2015), p. 6.

992 E.g., the reimbursement of Oncotype DX in the US is based on this system. Cf. MILLER ET AL. (2011), p. 137-138.

US private health plans: In private health plans, coverage and reimbursement for PM Dx is decided on a case by case basis on health plan level.[993] Nonetheless, private insurers often mimic the coverage decisions by MEDICARE whichs decisions are made by CMS.[994] However, commercial payers increasingly enter agreements with PM manufacturers.[995]

As illustrated, the current US system lacks standardization. The existence of different private health insurance plans along with a national payer system leads to a wide range for the price of PM Dx and a fragmentation of access to PM.[996] There is a lack of comprehensive reimbursement, even in cases where the diagnostic is on the label and recommended by the FDA.[997]

Reimbursement for PM Dx in the EU:

Across Europe, pricing and reimbursement processes for PM Dx are variable and idiosyncratic.[998] The rate of adoption of PM is significantly influenced by the existing

993 MCCARTHY ET AL. (2013), p. 10; and LUO ET AL. (2015), p. 10.

994 MCCARTHY ET AL. (2013), p. 10.

995 For example, AETNA has placed several personalized therapeutics under a "pre-certification list" to ensure that diagnostic tests are done before the use of the pharmaceutical. Additionally, they have several programs in place to accelerate the adoption of PM (e.g., active messaging of members to talk to their physicians or genetic counselors), cf. BRINO (2013). A second example: UNITEDHEALTH GROUP has announced to cover FOUNDATION MEDICINE'S test for certain lung cancers. The decision by the country's largest private health insurer represents a milestone, cf. JOSEPH (2015). Cf. also the PM initiatives by KAISER PERMANENTE (e.g., EHR system containing pharmacogenetic information) cited in HALVORSON (2016).

996 LUO ET AL. (2015), p. 10.

997 J. COHEN ET AL. (2013), p. 378 ff.

998 MILLER ET AL. (2011), p. 138; EUROPEAN COMMISSION (2013), p. 28; PAYNE & ANNEMANS (2013), p. 32; or TOWSE & GARRISON (2013) p. 41; LEOPOLD (2014) with a whole chapter 2 on price regulation systems across Europe; EPPINGER ET AL. (2015), p. 130; and KAUFMANN ET AL. (2015), p. 391.
For country analyses cf. GARFIELD (2011) with an overview of the reimbursement systems in *Germany, France, Italy,* and the *UK*, p. 5-11; MILLER ET AL. (2011) for an overview of the reimbursement systems in *Germany, France, Italy, Spain* and the *Nordic countries* and on the market access challenges in the EU.
More details on the *UK reimbursement system*, cf. GARAU ET AL. (2012), p. 5, and THE ACADEMY OF MEDICAL SCIENCES (2013), p. 54 and 60-61, about efforts of NICE towards VBP; BYRON ET AL. (2014) describing reimbursement and evaluation challenges with CDx.
More details on the *German reimbursement system*, cf. HUSTER & GOTTWALD cited in p. 54-55 in BIERMANN, WASEM, & MOSTARDT (2013); MÖLL cited in WIENKE ET AL. (2013), p. 31; NOWESKI ET AL. (2013), p. 282; PLANTÖR cited in "Personalisierte Medizin" (2013); and EPPINGER ET AL. (2015), p. 137.

reimbursement regimes which differ from country to country.[999] Member States apply different procedures to determine, on the one hand, the reimbursement status of medicinal therapeutics, and, on the other hand, the inclusion of medical devices and IVDs in the health insurance system.[1000] The heterogeneity can impact the speed of adoption of PM tests and provides uncertainty to tailor clinical and economic evidence.[1001]

The differences across Member States are confounded by the problem of centralized versus decentralized systems within individual states, including the tendency of most EU nations to review tests at the national level. This presents a barrier to a consistent market access for Rx-CDx combinations in the whole EU.[1002] The substantial diversity across reimbursement systems is referred to be conflicting with the idea of a system of undistorted competition.[1003]

Further, lacking or not clearly defined reimbursement pathways limit the access to and the use of PM Dx across Europe. The reimbursement processes for innovative diagnostics are described to be *"difficult, unclear, time consuming, and, in some countries, not able to be initiated by manufacturers"*.[1004] The length of these processes represents a further challenge. The reimbursement of a PM Dx may depend on whether it is applied in the hospital or ambulatory setting. Also, the presence of "silo budgets" is claimed to hinder the uptake of PM.[1005]

There is the claim for European reimbursement systems to *"reassess their evaluation and payment systems to accommodate the growing number of personalized medicine technologies that are being brought to market". "Currently, all European countries' reimbursement infrastructures are limited in their ability to adequately evaluate and rapidly provide access to personalized medicine diagnostics or combined drug and diagnostic products"*.[1006]

---

999 For example, stack coding in *Germany*, limitation of the total number of reimbursed tests per disease in the *UK*, or no reimbursement for *CDx* existing in Spain. Cf. ANSARI (2013), p 412; and KAUFMANN ET AL. (2015), p. 391.

1000 EUROPEAN COMMISSION (2013), p. 28. On the reimbursement of personalized therapies and diagnostics in Germany: HUSTER & GOTTWALD (2012); WIENKE ET AL. (2013), p. 44 ff. and KEIL (2015), p. 94 ff; and PLUN-FAVREAU ET AL. (2016), p. 146.

1001 WURCEL ET AL. (2016), p. 141.

1002 MILLER ET AL. (2011), p. 146; and KAUFMANN ET AL. (2015), p. 391.

1003 MÜLLER-GRAFF (2014), p. 14.

1004 WURCEL ET AL. (2016), p. 141; and PLUN-FAVREAU ET AL. (2016), p. 146, mentioning Germany, where the reimbursement process is *"not clearly defined"* and France, where the existing reimbursement process is described to be *"complex"* and *"time-consuming"*.

1005 WURCEL ET AL. (2016), p. 141.

1006 GARFIELD (2011), p. 1.

ii. Drivers behind the lack of reimbursement for PM Dx

The main drivers behind the insufficient reimbursement for PM Dx are manifold: The lack of reimbursement for PM Dx is a consequence of the lack of evidence for the economic value for PM Dx combined with inadequate and diverse HTA processes. Additionally, the history of cost-based reimbursement approaches for diagnostics and the absence of payers' longitudinal accounting for outcomes augment the problem as illustrated in the following.

Lack of evidence for the economic value of personalized medicine diagnostics

Limited compelling evidence for the health economic impact of PM Dx represents a first main reason for payers remaining conservative in their reimbursement decisions for PM applications.[1007]

In the current regulatory environment, the majority of PM Dx enter the market with analytical and clinical validity but insufficient information on clinical utility.[1008] The proof of clinical utility[1009] remains a reimbursement challenge.[1010] Consequently, the tests are not included in evidence-based guidelines by professional societies, leaving providers or payers unsure of whether and how to use the tests, or how much to pay for them, respectively.[1011]

Inadequate and diverse HTAs

A second driver behind the lack of and reimbursement for PM Dx is the fact that conventional HTAs lack the ability to consistently evaluate PM Dx. A separate chapter is devoted to this driver, illustrating the details behind.[1012]

History of cost-based reimbursement

A third factor leading to insufficient reimbursement for PM Dx is historically rooted: Diagnostics have a history of relatively low reimbursement.[1013]

1007 Cf. Part II, Chapter 3 Economic value of personalized medicine, p. 72 ff.

1008 Cf. Chapter 4.1 Inconsistencies and gaps in the regulatory framework of the approval process, p. 133 ff.; similar argumentation in MILLER ET AL. (2011), p. 146; and KAUFMANN ET AL. (2015), p. 399.

1009 Cf. Part II, Definition of Clinical utility, p. 83.

1010 MILNE & COHEN (2015)a, p. 1-2.

1011 HAYES ET AL. (2013), p. 3; and MECKLEY & NEUMANN (2010), p. 94, who show that professional society guidelines seem to strongly influence reimbursement. For many of their case studies, reimbursement seemed associated with a positive recommendation from professional society guidelines. An example of this occurred in 2008 when HIV treatment guidelines were revised to incorporate HLA-B*5701 screening into routine care for patients before initiating abacavir treatment, cf. J. COHEN (2011), p. 294.

1012 Cf. Chapter 6.2 Gaps and inconsistencies in conventional health technology assessments, p. 197 ff.

While a PM test creates the value in combination with its respective therapeutic, in general, the financial value is captured by therapeutic developers.[1014] Pricing decisions for the drug and the diagnostic component are carried out separately. For traditional drugs, pricing and reimbursement decisions are currently made largely at the time of launch on the basis of evidence from randomized clinical trials.[1015] Pharmaceuticals are generally reimbursed in a value-based[1016] manner based on clinical outcome – with a price supporting the attrition that occurs during development.[1017]

Most healthcare systems exist on a *fee-for-service reimbursement model (FFS).* They are grounded in the paradigm of "activity-based" [1018] billing. They reimburse based on the number of procedures instead of the outcome for patients.[1019] In contrast to the pharmaceutical components, healthcare systems value diagnostics on a cost-plus basis covering expected production costs and administrative activities. They do not reflect the actual value provided by the diagnostic component, and cover the costs of large-scale evidence generation.[1020] The lack of a consistent definition for value also prompts decision makers to prioritize cost-based over value-based reimbursement.[1021]

The cost-based payment systems in combination with the virtual absence of precedents for value-based reimbursement for PM Dx are described as the two core shortcomings of general reimbursement process inefficiencies, especially in Europe.[1022] The US system exhibits first attempts towards value-based pricing of PM Dx. Legislation towards a value-based approach was introduced in the US House of Representatives

1013 HAYES ET AL. (2013), p. 2; KIEVITS ET AL. (2014), p. 13; AKHMETOV ET AL. (2015), p. 223 ff. *"The high priced tests are relatively inexpensive at a few thousand dollars compared to the associated surgeon fees, hospital bed day costs or branded specialty medicines"*, cf. TRUSHEIM & BERNDT (2015)b, p. 10, illustrating some exceptions.

1014 HAYES ET AL. (2013), p. 2; TRUSHEIM & BERNDT (2015)b, p. 10; and WURCEL ET AL. (2016), p. 141.

1015 "Traditional" clinical trials evaluate the average effect of a therapeutic and set a price for each dose prescribed – neglecting the effect on individual patients. Cf. Part III Chapter 4.2 Incompatibility of clinical trials with personalized pharmaceuticals, p. 159 ff.

1016 For an explanation of value-based pricing (VBP), cf. Chapter 3.1.4 Value based pricing (VBP), p. 85 ff.

1017 MEADOWS ET AL. (2015), p. 9; AKHMETOV ET AL. (2015), p. 223 ff.

1018 JAKKA & ROSSBACH (2013), p. 3, call it a *"procedure-based"* reimbursement system.

1019 JOHNSON (2016), p. 4; and PRITCHARD ET AL. (2017), p. 146.

1020 *About the cost-based pricing of Dx:* GARAU ET AL. (2012), p. 18; ANSARI (2013), p. 412; THE ACADEMY OF MEDICAL SCIENCES (2013), p. 55; TRUSHEIM (2013), p. 325 ff.; EKSTROM ET AL. (2013), p. 33; KULKARNI ET AL. (2013), p. 10; KIEVITS ET AL. (2014), p. 13; AKHMETOV ET AL. (2015), p. 223 ff.; MEADOWS ET AL. (2015), p. 9; TRUSHEIM ET AL. (2015), p. 332; BUGULISKIS (2016), p. 5; and PLUN-FAVREAU ET AL. (2016), p. 147.

1021 AKHMETOV ET AL. (2015), p. 223 ff.

1022 MILLER ET AL. (2011), p. 146.

in 2013, however, it was not enacted.[1023] In January 2015, the ENERGY AND COMMERCE COMMITTEE issued draft legislation for 21st Century Cures which, among other goals, seeks to streamline diagnostic regulation including value-based reimbursement of PM Dx.[1024]

Value-based payment arrangements are less common in the EU compared to the US.[1025] The integration of clinical value and real-world evidence demonstration with the process of incorporating medical innovation in patient care in a timely manner is *"only in its infancy"*.[1026] Though several models exist which could theoretically increase the reimbursement rates for PM Dx (e.g., DRG-based[1027] or FFS approaches), EKSTROM ET AL. (2013) find that none of them are primarily value-based for innovative diagnostics.[1028] In the EU, differences in pricing decisions are also observed between private and public healthcare sectors. Value-based pricing for pharmaceuticals has been practiced for long in the European private sector, but the public sector is known for negligently developed value-based pricing.[1029] Moreover, there are no pricing guidelines for innovative diagnostics in any of the EU member states.[1030]

The reviewed studies agree that reimbursement models will need change to keep up with the developments through PM technologies, and that the existing cost-plus mindset for reimbursement of PM Dx is hindering innovation.[1031]

Lack of longitudinal accounting

A last reason behind the lack of reimbursement for PM Dx is the lack of longitudinal accounting for outcomes at payers.[1032]

Generally, there is a certain suspicion of innovation in healthcare, as people tend to believe that new technologies and treatments are inherently expensive and are one

1023 TRUSHEIM & BERNDT (2015)b, p. 10.
1024 US ENERGY AND COMMERCE COMMITTEE (2015).
1025 GARFIELD (2011), p. 13; MILLER ET AL. (2011), p. 146; EKSTROM ET AL. (2013), p. 33; and EUROPEAN COMMISSION (2013), p. 28.
1026 MILLER ET AL. (2011), p. 137-138, with a review of UK, Germany and France, Italy and the Nordics.
1027 *"Diagnosis-related-group" (DRG)* is a system to classify hospital cases into groups and standard practice to establish reimbursement.
1028 EKSTROM ET AL. (2013), p. 33.
1029 AKHMETOV ET AL. (2015), p. 223 ff.
1030 *Ibidem.*
1031 OLMSTED TEISBERG (2007), p. 27 ff; GARAU ET AL. (2012), p. 18; ANSARI (2013), p. 412; THE ACADEMY OF MEDICAL SCIENCES (2013), p. 55; TRUSHEIM (2013), p. 325 ff.; EKSTROM ET AL. (2013), p. 33; KULKARNI ET AL. (2013), p. 10; KIEVITS ET AL. (2014), p. 13; MEADOWS ET AL. (2015), p. 9; TRUSHEIM ET AL. (2015), p. 332; and BUGULISKIS (2016), p. 5.
1032 DAVIS ET AL. (2009), p. 279; DAVIS ET AL. (2010), p. 2; and JAKKA & ROSSBACH (2013), p. 3.

of the main drivers of escalating healthcare costs.[1033] However, whether new technologies or treatments cost sould be reimbursed depends on their medical outcomes *over the full cycle of care*. If more expensive care in one part of the care cycle reduces costs later in the cycle, it may be cost-effective. Neglecting outcome measurement and costs over the full cycle carries the danger of increasing the costs of care by shifting spending to less effective or less efficient approaches.[1034]

This problem is inherent in several reimbursement systems. Payers usually have a certain turnover of insurees leading to a lack of longitudinal accounting. Longitudinal accounting would enable payers to capture long-term cost savings from near-term testing. A high turnover of insurees makes it less economically attractive for payers to reimburse tests that minimize the likelihood of conditions that will occur at a later stage in life (e.g., due to predictive tests like for BRCA1 or the avoidance of certain long-term adverse events).[1035]

Payer systems with a relatively low patient turnover, such as integrated systems like KAISER PERMANENTE in the United States or single-payer systems in Europe, are less exposed to this incentive challenge.[1036] They may represent the best partners for diagnostics companies seeking direct collaboration with payers as the identification and implementation of policies to promote cost-saving PM Dx can offer a source of competitive advantage for them.[1037]

6.1.2 Analysis of incentives

A lack of reimbursement incentivizes the relevant stakeholders in the PM ecosystem in different ways. The resulting incentives are analysed in the following subsections:

Pharmaceutical companies

Due to nonexistent or insufficient reimbursement for the diagnostic component of PM, a pharmaceutical company has generally an incentive to offer a non-personalized drug compared to a personalized drug, as the diagnostic component acts as the "gatekeeper" for the pharmaceutical.[1038] If the reimbursement of the diagnostic component is not guaranteed, providers and patients are less likely to use the pharmaceutical. This incentive is strengthened by additional factors: With the non-personalized prod-

[1033] OLMSTED TEISBERG (2007), p. 48.
[1034] *Ibidem.*
[1035] Cf. *note* 1032.
[1036] DAVIS ET AL (2010), p. 3.
[1037] DAVIS ET AL (2009), p. 280.
[1038] Expression used in OLSEN & TRØST JØRGENSEN (2014), p. 1.

uct traditional clinical trials can be performed, the pharmaceutical does not depend on the use of a test component, a broader population can be targeted and reimbursement is usually guaranteed.[1039] Thus, the lack of sufficient reimbursement of the Dx component – amongst other factors – incentivizes pharmaceutical companies to follow a non-personalized approach.

In cases in which a pharmaceutical company sells personalized drugs, the company has an incentive to subsidize or sponsor reimbursement for the diagnostic component in order to be able to sell the personalized pharmaceutical.[1040] In this case, the prices of the test as well as the pharmaceutical component do not reflect their real value. If a subsidy or sponsorship is financially not possible, the personalized treatment is less likely to be offered.

Diagnostics companies

The nonexistent or insufficient reimbursement generally disincentivizes diagnostics companies to foster the use of PM due to the following reasons:

a) Lack of reimbursement sets negative incentives for Dx companies to offer PM Dx

Current diagnostic reimbursement policies do not support the development of PM Dx.[1041] By not recognizing the value of combining PM Dx with targeted pharmaceuticals, regulators and payers are failing to create incentives for diagnostics companies to take on the risks associated with the development.[1042] Industry experts agree that reimbursement is a necessity, since a test may not be developed or used if it is not reimbursed. Although lower prices can reflect more efficient and more widespread technologies, reimbursement levels need not only to ensure access to high quality PM tests but also to allow for their development.[1043] If reimbursement is not sufficient, there are no incentives for investments in the development and improvement of existing PM Dx and for generating evidence to demonstrate the clinical and economic value of these tests.[1044]

1039 Cf. Chapter 3.1.1 Literature analysis, *i) Strategic challenges to the co-development process, Pharmaceutical companies' strategic interests*, p. 122 f.

1040 MILLER ET AL. (2011), p. 146, with examples.

1041 Amongst others MOORE ET AL. (2012), p. 493; KAUFMANN ET AL. (2015), p. 399; and PERSONALIZED MEDICINE COALITION (2015), p. 6.

1042 KAUFMANN ET AL. (2015), p. 399.

1043 PERSONALIZED MEDICINE COALITION (2015), p. 6.

1044 ASPINALL & HAMERMESH (2008), p. 2; BARTON (2008), p. 126; MILLER ET AL. (2011), p. 137; PERSONALIZED MEDICINE COALITION (2015), p. 6; and PLUN-FAVREAU ET AL. (2016), p. 147.

b) Lack of value-based reimbursement schemes lead Dx companies to target private sector patients

Suboptimal cost-based payment systems in combination with the virtual absence of precedents for the value-based diagnostic reimbursement incentivize manufacturers of PM Dx to use a workaround: It entails the temporary targeting of private sector patients. In the case of Europe, such a workaround would deprive approximately 90% of the population of access to PM.[1045]

c) Upfront costs for demonstrating clinical utility and cost-effectiveness disinsentivize Dx companies to offer PM Dx

Reimbursement authorities or insurance companies are asking Dx companies for health economic evidence, which requires additional evidence beyond what is currently being required by the regulatory authorities.[1046] Payers might not have in place internal processes and resources to assess the cost-effectiveness of tests even when the evidence of the clinical utility and of the relative test performance is available.[1047] Consequently, diagnostics companies have to demonstrate cost-effectiveness in addition to clinical utility. However, in contrast to large pharmaceutical companies, diagnostics companies often have neither the incentives nor the resources to invest in the required evidence development.[1048]

EKSTROM ET AL. (2013) argue that even when payers are willing to consider value-based reimbursement for innovative PM diagnostics, manufacturers have to bear the upfront cost for demonstrating both clinical utility and cost-effectiveness, although they have no guarantee of the later sufficient reimbursement for achieving a premium.[1049]

d) Dx companies are incentivized to offer LDTs due to better chance for reimbursement and limited regulatory oversight

Due to the uncertainty about the reimbursement of PM tests, some diagnostics companies started to look for alternative ways to establish the evidence needed for approval as well as for reimbursement decisions. It is stated that there appears to be a trend towards LDTs. LDTs do not only enjoy less strict regulatory approval pro-

1045 MILLER ET AL. (2011), p. 146.
1046 BUGULISKIS (2016), p. 5.
1047 DAVIS ET AL. (2009), p. 279; DAVIS ET AL. (2010), p. 4; JAKKA & ROSSBACH (2013), p. 3; and TOWSE & GARRISON (2013), p. 41.
1048 TRUSHEIM & BERNDT (2015)b, p. 11.
1049 EKSTROM ET AL. (2013), p. 33, mentioning GENOMIC HEALTH'S Oncotype Dx as an example.

cesses,[1050] but also their reimbursement might be more favorable, because there is sometimes the possibility to directly negotiate and manage the reimbursement process with payers.[1051]

Providers

The nonexistent or insufficient reimbursement generally disincentivizes providers to foster the use of PM due to the following reasons:

a) Providers avoid self-payment

Providers will not make use of PM treatments in case of nonexistent or insufficient reimbursement since they will avoid self-payment by either their patients or themselves.

b) FFS models incentivize providers to select PM tests which increase the number of medical procedures performed

As mentioned in the previous *Chapter ii*, many reimbursement schemes are based on a "fee-for-service" (FFS) paradigm. Physicians bill based on the performed activities and receive fees for the services they provide to patients. A FFS model creates incentives for providers to perform as many procedures as medically justifiable, since their compensation is directly related to the volume of services rendered.[1052]

FFS reimbursement systems pose a challenge to the adoption of PM. In these systems, provider economics will create incentives for the use of some PM tests, but might discourage the use of others. Physicians could be more likely to embrace tests that increase the number of procedures performed. Basically, there is a lack of incentives for providers to conduct tests or implement procedures that prevent adverse events.[1053] This can be due to a lack of reimbursement or also due to a lack of other financial incentives for a healthcare provider.[1054] Driven by their financial interests, providers could be more likely to perform tests that increase the number of procedures performed than tests reducing the number of procedures.[1055]

1050 Cf. previous Chapter 4.1.3 Undermining of the current approval system through LDTs, p. 148 ff.

1051 FRUEH (2013), p. 30-31.

1052 JOHNSON (2016), p. 4.

1053 ASPINALL & HAMERMESH (2008), p. 6; EPPINGER ET AL. (2015), p. 163; and RELLING & EVANS (2015), p. 347.

1054 ASPINALL & HAMERMESH (2008), p. 6; and DAVIS ET AL. (2009), p. 280.

1055 JAKKA & ROSSBACH (2013), p. 3; and DAVIS ET AL. (2009), p. 285. DAVIS ET AL. (2009) show that there might be little to no financial incentive for physicians to perform tests that might prevent downstream activities. They note that a test which reduces cancer treatments may reduce physi-

c) DRGs limit innovations in stationary in-patient settings

Healthcare systems with hospital tariffs based on diagnosis-related groups (DRGs) are described to limit the integration of new PM Dx into clinical practice. Certain DRG based systems[1056] expect hospitals to fund new diagnostic tests out of existing DRGs. These DRGs will then be increased after a period of time. So, in order to fund innovative PM Dx, providers have to cut-back existing DRG income streams. This system does not incentivize providers to introduce innovative Dx into clinical practice. DRG induced "budget silos" can create perverse incentives by not reimbursing obviously cost-effective new treatments.[1057] The overall effect of these limitations to the reimbursement system is that patients have limited and unequal access to those new tests.[1058]

Patients

In case of inconsistent or a total lack of reimbursement, the patient bears the risk of missing reimbursement of the diagnostic component. Additionally, a patient often depends on the expert knowledge of the provider. Consequentially, a patient does not have an incentive to ask for PM, unless he is knowledgeable and financially potent enough to do so.

Payers

Payers are generally incentivized to uphold the current reimbursement approaches and thus do not foster the translation of PM due to the following reasons:

---

cians'revenues, a test that increases the number of patients using treatments may increase physician revenues. DAVIS ET A. (2009) take the screening for colon cancer risk and breast cancer risk as hypothetical examples. In the case of colon cancer, a patient with a positive test will receive colonscopy more frequently – increasing the physicians financial incentives to perform a test. In contrast, if the breast cancer test predicts a low recurrence of breast cancer, fewer patients will receive follow-on chemotherapy, reducing a physicians' financial incentive to perform the genetic test, cf. *figure* S2 in DAVIS ET A. (2009).

1056 PLUN-FAVREAU ET AL. (2016), p. 147, mentioning Germany and the UK as examples.

1057 PLUN-FAVREAU ET AL. (2016), p. 147, mention one example in which a DRG system may lead to counterincentives for providers: Oncotype DX, a predictive molecular test for early-stage breast cancer. This test has the potential to pay-off by reducing chemotherapy use and costs. Because the total chemotherapy cost is borne by different parties or budget sources, no party has an incentive to fund the test to recoup the savings. With chemotherapy attached to specific DRGs, hospitals *"may lose revenue by receiving fewer chemotherapy tariffs and be penalized from a financial perspective"*.

1058 PLUN-FAVREAU ET AL. (2016), p. 147.

a) Inconsistent evidence for the health economic impact of PM Dx incentivizes payers to uphold current lack of reimbursement

Payers are viewed as the *"linchpin for market access"*.[1059] They act as bridge between the development and the clinical adoption as they mediate the market through their reimbursement policies.[1060]

Compared to non-personalized approaches, PM targets narrower populations of patients who are more likely to respond to the treatment. Payers would therefore actually have an incentive to support the reimbursement of PM, which allows them to pay only for the treatment of responders.[1061] In this context, PM is referred to as *"Holy Grail of Payers"* because no money is spent on ineffective treatments.[1062]

Payers require evidence that PM is clinically useful and cost-effective relative to existing treatments.[1063] Especially in a context of healthcare budget restrictions, payers are concerned about negative budget impacts that new technologies may have. They fear that new personalized therapies may ultimately become more expensive as a consequence of testing many individuals to identify relatively few responders for a particular therapy.[1064]

However, at present there is limited compelling evidence for the health economic impact of PM Dx and uncertainty about how to measure the value of PM. Limits on reimbursement occur because certain PM Dx lack clinical utility, or their health economic evidence is inconsistent.[1065]

The inconsistent evidence for the value for PM Dx incentivizes payers to remain conservative in their reimbursement decisions for PM, and has been mentioned as a common reason for PM Dx failing to obtain appropriate coverage.[1066]

1059 J. COHEN (2011), p. 294.

1060 *Ibidem.*

1061 FAULKNER ET AL. (2012), p. 1163; EUROPEAN ALLIANCE FOR PERSONALISED MEDICINE (2013), p. 23-24; PAYNE & ANNEMANS (2013), p. S33; and AKHMETOV ET AL. (2015), p. 223 ff.

1062 PAYNE & ANNEMANS (2013), p. S33.

1063 J. COHEN (2011), p. 294; J. COHEN (2012), p. 751- 754; and PLUN-FAVREAU ET AL. (2016), p. 145. J. COHEN ET AL. (2013), p. 378 ff., show for the US, that the majority of payers claim to have concerns about the accuracy of tests for personalized medicines. Even though these medicines were successfully personalized, payers have doubts about the efficacy of the tests in stratifying subpopulations. Across the majority of personalized medicines, payers questioned the link between diagnostic tests and health outcomes.

1064 J. COHEN (2015), p. 6; and PLUN-FAVREAU ET AL. (2016), p. 145.

1065 Cf. Part II, Chapter 3 Economic value of personalized medicine, p. 72 ff.

1066 SWEN ET AL. (2007), p. 1321; BARTON (2008), p. 126; DAVIS ET AL. (2009), p. 279; DAVIS ET AL.(2010), p. 4; MECKLEY & NEUMANN (2010), p. 92; A. H. WU (2010), p. 44; YEO ET AL. (2010), p. 5; ANSARI (2013), p. 412; EUROPEAN ALLIANCE FOR PERSONALISED MEDICINE (2013), p. 23-24;

Even for cases in which evidence of clinical utility and of relative test performance is available, payers themselves might not have in place internal processes and resources to assess the cost-effectiveness of tests.[1067]

Further, there is the fear by payers that although individual diagnostic tests or systems may not be expensive, the overall costs could be unjustifiably high because it is difficult to track the use of PM tests.[1068] As the ultimate cost effects may not be known until the test has been on the market for some time, it will remain in a payer's best interest to delay the adoption of PM Dx.[1069]

b) Lack of longitudinal accounting incentivizes payers to uphold current lack of reimbursement for personalized medicine applications that are only cost-efficient over the long-term

Reimbursement systems without longitudinal accounting for payers - meaning that patients may switch between payers – do not enable payers to capture long-term cost savings from near-term testing.[1070] This lowers the incentives for a payer to reimburse personalized tests and treatments which are only cost-efficient over the long-term.

6.1.3 Resulting hypothesis

The overview below summarizes the argumentation of the previous chapter and shows the resulting incentives through a lack of sufficient reimbursement.

Research institutions	*Pharmaceutical companies*	*Diagnostic companies*	*Providers*	*Patients*	*Payers*
–	negative	negative	negative	negative	negative

negative = institutional setting incentivizes a player not to foster the translation of PM
– = neutral/no conclusive statement possible on a player's incentive to foster the translation of PM

TOWSE & GARRISON (2013), p. 40; JAKKA & ROSSBACH (2013), p. 3; HORGAN ET AL. (2014), p. 291; T. A MANOLIO ET AL. (2013), p. 260; AKHMETOV ET AL. (2015), p. 223 ff.; J. COHEN (2015), p. 6; OOSTERHOFF, VAN DER MAAS, & STEUTEN (2015), p. 1-2; and JOHNSON (2016), p. 3.

1067 DAVIS ET AL. (2009), p. 279; DAVIS ET AL., p. 4; JAKKA & ROSSBACH (2013), p. 3; and TOWSE & GARRISON (2013), p. 41.

1068 DAVIS ET AL. (2009), p. 279; DAVIS ET AL. (2010), p. 4; and JAKKA & ROSSBACH (2013), p. 3.

1069 DAVIS ET AL. (2009), p. 280.

1070 DAVIS ET AL. (2010), p. 4.

Based on the arguments presented in the previous sub-chapters, this chapter concludes with the following hypothesis:

Hypothesis: The lack of reimbursement for personalized medicine diagnostics acts as a barrier to the translation of personalized medicine into clinical practice.

6.2 Gaps and inconsistencies in conventional health technology assessments for personalized medicine

6.2.1 Literature analysis

Besides unclear or non-existent reimbursement pathways, a second barrier, related to reimbursement is discussed to hinder the translation of PM into clinical practice: The lack adequate HTA processes with clear evidence requirements is claimed to lead to delays in the translation of PM Dx.[1071]

The term HTA is defined in various ways.[1072] A HTA builds the bridge between science and political decision-making.[1073] It is a form of policy research with the aim to identify policy issues and social consequences, to ensure quality, and in the long-term to guarantee cost-effectiveness of healthcare interventions.[1074] HTAs can be used to inform clinical guidelines, pricing or reimbursement decisions.[1075] They are considered being essential in any solidarity-based healthcare system for supporting funding decisions. BRÜGGER ET AL. (2015) argue that the rising gap between unlimited health requests and limited resources requires transparent assessment of the allocation of financial means.[1076] From the public health systems' and private insurers' perspective, a HTA is a mechanism to check whether an evaluated product adds value, and whether it is as effective in terms of costs and clinical benefit as comparable existing treatments.[1077] Generally, a HTA is commonly viewed as a tool to assist evidence-based

[1071] PLUN-FAVREAU ET AL. (2016), p. 144.

[1072] This thesis does not offer a comprehensive discussion on how to define HTAs. For a comprehensive overview on definitions, application area, structure and types of HTAs, cf. WIDRIG (2015), *chapter* 3.

[1073] WIDRIG (2015), p. 45.

[1074] FACKLER & MCGUIRE (2010), p. 7; and WIDRIG (2015), p. 45.

[1075] STEPHENS, HANKE, & DOSHI (2012), p. 29; and WIDRIG (2015), p. 45-46.

[1076] BRÜGGER ET AL. (2015), p. 1.

[1077] AKHMETOV ET AL. (2015), p. 220 ff.

healthcare decisions.[1078] Simply stated, a HTA asks four fundamental questions: *"Does the technology work?", "For whom?", "At what cost?"*, and *"How does it compare with alternatives?"*[1079]

A HTA represents a method of evidence synthesis that considers evidence regarding clinical effectiveness, safety, and cost-effectiveness. When applied more broadly, they can include social, ethical, and legal aspects of the use of health technologies.[1080] The purpose of each individual HTA determines the precise balance of these inputs.[1081]

Research concerning economic evaluations is receiving increased attention in HTAs, as payers seek to optimize the "value for money" spent on treatments.[1082] Payers in countries with formal HTA programs increasingly deny or restrict reimbursement of therapies when the clinical or economic value proposition is unfavorable or unclear.[1083]

For this thesis, a HTA is *"the systematic evaluation of a medical or health technology for evidence of its safety, efficacy, effectiveness, cost, cost-effectiveness, and ethical and legal implications, both in absolute terms and in comparison with other competing technologies"*.[1084]

A HTA can separate useful from ambiguous diagnostics used for PM and thus support the translation of PM into clinical practice by reaching patients in an equitable and transparent fashion.[1085] However, the translation of PM requires HTA bodies

---

1078 BRÜGGER ET AL. (2015), p. 1.

1079 FACKLER & MCGUIRE (2010), p. 7.

1080 AKHMETOV & BUBNOV (2015) assessed how miscellaneous assessment frameworks define value in PM. They call for a value-based assessment that accounts for social and ethical parameters of value. They find that the role of a societal perspective in the evaluation process is evolving resulting in the fact that today, some countries start considering costs and benefits outside the health sector as additional criteria for assessing value. Also ALI-KHAN, BLACK, PALMOUR, HALLETT, & AVARD (2015) perform a systematic review of HTAs and find multiple calls for explicit integration of ethical, legal, and social issues (ELSI) in HTAs. Addressing ELSI has been highlighted as key in optimizing benefits in the field of personalized medicine.

1081 LUCE ET AL. (2010), p. 271; and EUROPEAN COMMISSION (2013), p. 26.

1082 FACKLER & MCGUIRE (2010), p. 7.

1083 FAULKNER ET AL. (2012), p. 1163.

1084 Definition by STEPHENS ET AL. (2012), p. 29. Similar definitions for example in LUCE ET AL. (2010), p. 258, a HTA is method of evidence synthesis that receives inputs from comparative effectiveness research, economic evaluation, and the consideration of social, ethical, and legal aspects. It is *"a multidisciplinary field of policy analysis, studying the medical, economic, social and ethical implications of development, diffusion and use of health technology"*, p. 269. Other definitions in PAYNE & ANNEMANS (2013), p. 32.

1085 HORGAN ET AL. (2014), p. 291; and more details in the following Chapter i) Incompatibility of current HTA processes with PM, p. 199 ff.

to develop and apply novel concepts of HTA for measuring the effectiveness of PM pharmaceuticals and tests.[1086] Current gaps and inconsistencies in conventional health technology assessments impede the market access of PM.

The lack of adequate HTAs is closely related to the challenge to consistently measure the economic value of PM. Thus, reference is made to Part II, Chapter 3,[1087] illustrating the inconsistent findings about the economic value of PM due to a lack of systematic and comparable health economic evaluations and sufficiently robust economic evidence for PM.

The existing gaps and inconsistencies in conventional HTAs are discussed in the following sections: First, it is shown why the concept of PM faces challenges in fitting into current HTA processes (*Sub-chapter i*). Two hurdles – first, a lack of best practices in order to integrate concepts of economic value for PM diagnostics into HTAs (*Sub-chapter ii*) and second, a lack of coordination of existing heterogeneous HTA processes (*Sub-chapter iii*) – complicate that problem.

i. Incompatibility of current HTA processes with PM

A successful HTA evaluation of PM requires the HTA process to take into account the specificities of the technologies involved. However, currently PM technologies face the challenge to fit into health systems that are configured for broad populations and "average" patients.[1088] Studies claim that the new technologies do *"not neatly fit into existing health technology assessment and reimbursement processes"*[1089] and that *"conventional HTA impedes market access of personalised medicine"*.[1090]

A common challenge in HTA processes is separate evaluation of the therapeutic and the diagnostic component which does not capture the benefits of using the Rx and Dx in combination.[1091] This challenge is further accentuated by the fact that diagnostic tests generally have a more limited evidence base than pharmaceuticals making their evaluation methodologically complex.[1092] Additionally, experience with the evaluation of CDx technologies is limited compared to the evaluation of pharmaceuti-

---

[1086] *Criticizing a lack of adequate HTAs for PM:* PACI (2009), p. 284; FACKLER & MCGUIRE (2010), p. 7; BECLA ET AL. (2011), p. 118 ff.; EUROPEAN COMMISSION (2013), p. 29; PASIC ET AL. (2013), p. 162; HORGAN ET AL. (2014), p. 291; KIEVITS ET AL. (2014), p. 10-18; BOMBARD (2015), p. 1; and AKHMETOV & BUBNOV (2015), p. 5.

[1087] Cf. Part II, Chapter 3 Economic value of personalized medicine, p. 72 ff.

[1088] KIEVITS ET AL. (2014), p. 11.

[1089] FAULKNER ET AL. (2012), p. 1162; WURCEL ET AL. (2016), p. 141 and also *note* 1086.

[1090] KIEVITS ET AL. (2014), p. 10.

[1091] BYRON ET AL. (2014), p. 1475.

[1092] BYRON ET AL. (2014), p. 1475.

cals.[1093] It is criticized that HTA bodies currently lack the capacity to address the new complexity through PM.[1094] Rarely do HTAs inform reimbursement, funding or uptake decisions for CDx.[1095] There are calls for the establishment of mechanisms through which HTA bodies can separate, and therefore reward, the value of personalization between the Rx and Dx component.[1096]

Whereas study designs for the Rx component are generally well agreed upon in terms of acceptability for HTA and reimbursement decision processes, this is not the case with Dx components.[1097] Reasons behind this incompatibility of PM Dx with HTAs are illustrated in the following sub-sections:

Inconclusive findings from economic evaluations for the value of PM

One reason why the conventional HTA approach complicates the testing of PM has already been discussed in the context of this thesis: There are inconclusive findings from evaluations for the economic value of PM applications due to the existence of multiple evaluation methodologies and due to a lack of reliable data for measuring the value of PM.[1098] The lack of sufficient evidence linking PM Dx use to patient management and correlated health outcomes remains a fundamental challenge for reimbursement decisions.[1099]

Lack of comparators

In HTAs, the relative effectiveness of a given treatment is an important element. In order to evaluate if a new technology adds value, a HTA often compares the new technology with an existing standard-of-care alternative from the reimbursement list.

The challenge in case of a Rx-CDx combination is the lack of existing benchmark products – for the pharmaceutical component as well as for the test[1100]: Relevant comparator data may not be generated in the same clinical trial, and will thus usually not be available for the specific target population in question.[1101] The provided clinical trial evidence for personalized pharmaceuticals is limited to a defined group of patients who are expected to deliver the most positive risk-benefit ratio. This data cannot be compared with data on "unselected" patients from traditional non-

1093 *Ibidem.*
1094 PLUN-FAVREAU ET AL. (2016), p. 145.
1095 WURCEL ET AL. (2016), p. 141.
1096 E.g., in THE ACADEMY OF MEDICAL SCIENCES (2013), p. 61.
1097 FAULKNER ET AL. (2012), p. 1162.
1098 Cf. Part II, Chapter 3 Economic value of personalized medicine, p. 72 ff.
1099 FAULKNER ET AL. (2012), p. 1167, *with further references.*
1100 AKHMETOV ET AL. (2015), p. 220.
1101 EUROPEAN COMMISSION (2013), p. 27.

personalized clinical trials. The targeted sub-group's response in the existing trial might not be reflected by the overall results. As a consequence, the relative benefit of the personalized pharmaceutical in its specific patient sub-group may not be quantifiable with current methods.[1102] Moreover, evidence from European HTA agencies demonstrates that only few HTAs have been performed for CDx which could potentially act as comparators for the test component of PM.[1103] Therefore, in spite of the fact that many tests displayed a favorite utility in stratification of populations, there is a gap in evidence of their health outcomes impact.[1104]

Additionally, patients are selected by a CDx in a PM trial, and are hence more likely to respond to the treatment compared to a traditional trial. Thus, it is more likely that therapeutic benefit becomes evident in an early stage of the trial. This effect is intensified in the case of life threatening diseases in which patients from the control group are usually moved to the treatment group as soon as their health deteriorates. As a result, PM therapies are approved on the basis of more limited, but compelling, early clinical trial data with a more positive risk-benefit-ratio than traditional medicines. This fact complicates conventional HTA approaches as well.[1105]

Due to this challenge, there is a call for a certain "portion of pragmatism" by HTA bodies. According to a white paper of EUROPABIO HTA bodies should be *"pragmatic in using the available evidence to assess the relative benefit of a new personalised medicine, and understand that there will be potential to misrepresent the benefit of medicines when making indirect comparisons with older trial data"*.[1106]

Existence of multiple CDx for one pharmaceutical treatment

A potential HTA may target two types of tests with each different preconditions for the performance of successful HTA:

1. *Existence of one specific CDx:* The test used in clinical practice is the same as the test used in the clinical trials for the Rx ("Rx-CDx-package"). This is most often the case for *commercially available CDx*.[1107] In these cases, a HTA of a Rx requiring a

1102 KIEVITS ET AL. (2014), p. 10-11.

1103 AKHMETOV ET AL. (2015), p. 220. E.g., the UK NICE has published 134 appraisals of health technologies since 2006, only five of these involved CDx, cf. EUROPEAN COMMISSION (2013), p. 26. PLANTÖR in "Personalisierte Medizin" (2013) about AMNOG (ACT ON THE REFORM OF THE MARKET FOR MEDICAL PRODUCTS, December 2010) and the problem of missing comparators in Germany.

1104 AKHMETOV & BUBNOV (2015), p. 219.

1105 KIEVITS ET AL. (2014), p. 10-11.

1106 KIEVITS ET AL. (2014), p. 11.

1107 In contrast to LTDs, cf. Chapter 4.1.3 Undermining of the current approval system through LDTs, p. 148.

CDx adds little additional complexity compared to non-personalized Rx. Health outcomes from the Rx, informed by the CDx, are used as the basis for the evaluation.[1108]

2. *Existence of multiple CDx:* The test used in clinical practice is *not* the same as the test used in the clinical trials for the Rx. This is particularly the case for *laboratory developed tests (LDTs).*[1109] In these cases, studies following patients through diagnosis and treatment to outcomes are rarely available. In the absence of such pivotal trials, a linked evidence approach and complex modeling are typically required to estimate patient outcome benefits. Follow-on versions of LDTs may have different technical characteristics compared to the first-in-class test, including diagnostic accuracy, leading to different patient sub-populations being selected for treatment with an impact on the clinical- and cost-effectiveness. This has an impact on the overall health gains of Dx-Rx-combinations, and flaws the generation of evidence across tests.[1110] Having a range of alternative CDx used in routine clinical practice for the same purpose presents challenges to payers. If an evidence-based approach to reimbursement is taken, an HTA of *all* available CDx in addition to the assessment of the corresponding pharmaceutical needs to be undertaken, increasing the complexity of an HTA and accentuating the lack of available data for generating evidence.[1111]

The existence of multiple CDx has also consequences for the corresponding Rx: Every time a new CDx is developed, the effectiveness of the associated pharmaceutical should in principle be re-assessed, as a sub-optimal test may lead to incorrect estimation of the effectiveness of the pharmaceutical, which in turn may give rise to a wrong recommendation on its use.[1112]

Negligence of wider societal benefits and risks of PM

It is further criticized that current HTA processes neglect the wider societal benefits and risks of PM. Without developing an understanding of citizens' concerns and expectations, HTA bodies and policy makers may miss drivers and barriers to the successful translation of PM into clinical practice. PLUN-FAVREAU ET AL. (2016) state that HTAs are rarely concerned with assessing the wider societal benefits and risks of health technologies and services. They criticize that *"without recognising these wider aspects of the proposition of a societal value of personalised medicine, suboptimal in-*

[1108] BYRON ET AL. (2014), p. 1470.
[1109] Cf. Chapter 4.1.3 Undermining of the current approval system through LDTs, p. 148.
[1110] GARAU ET AL. (2012), p. 17; and BYRON ET AL. (2014), p. 1471.
[1111] *Ibidem.* They mention the example of an assessment of the CDx EGFR–TK mutation testing for the treatment of non–small cell lung cancer in which the NICE had to include ten different tests in the HTA.
[1112] EUROPEAN COMMISSION (2013), p. 27.

centivisation of corresponding innovation activity is a likely consequence".[1113] Also other authors call for the integration of a broader definition of value into HTAs, which includes the wider benefits from PM.[1114]

ii. Lack of best practices in order to integrate concepts of economic value for PM Dx into HTAs

Literature stresses the need for *identifying best practices* for economic modeling[1115] and corresponding HTAs[1116] in the field of PM – for co-development situations and as well as for the development of Dx as stand-alone PM Dx.

Existing HTA guidelines do not explicitly address the special aspects of PM. There is no transparently established and commonly agreed HTA standard for assessing PM Dx and Rx-CDx combinations.[1117] Existing guidelines related to HTA methodology usually do not account for the specificities of the diagnostic component. They contain methods related to the ones used to assess pharmaceuticals, posing *"unrealistic"* and *"non-fit-for-purpose evidence"* requirements which impede value demonstration and patient access.[1118]

Several alternative evaluation frameworks for diagnostics have been proposed, however, no single approach has emerged as standard.[1119] Without any "best practice

---

1113 PLUN-FAVREAU ET AL. (2016), p. 146.

1114 Cf. Part II, Chapters 3.1.3 ACCE framework and 3.1.4 Value based pricing (VBP), p. 82 ff.

1115 Cf. *note* 410.

1116 *Mentioning the lack of HTA best practices:* FAULKNER ET AL. (2012), p. 1167; EUROPEAN ALLIANCE FOR PERSONALISED MEDICINE (2013), p. 21; and PERSONALIZED MEDICINE COALITION (2014), p. 40; PERSONALIZED MEDICINE COALITION (2015), p. 6. Cf. also references in *note* 1086. The EUROPEAN ALLIANCE FOR PERSONALISED MEDICINE (2013), p. 21, concretely calls for a *"better understanding among HTA bodies of the specificities of the -omics technologies"; the "adaption of assessment methodologies to take account of new ways of developing evidence"*; the *"integration of the concepts of overall economic value and equity into HTA", "wider input from stakeholders into HTA bodies' methodologies, and clarity over the patient role within the HTA structure"; "an EU-wide HTA standard method to support developments in personalised medicine"*, for *"greater cross-border sharing of expertise among HTA bodies"; "closer alignment of the assessment of therapies and companion diagnostics"; "advice and support on how to prepare for HTA requirements"*; and for *"early engagement in terms of dialogue and advice with the HTA agencies"*.

1117 FAULKNER ET AL. (2012), p. 1167-1168, citing several organizations working to explore evidentiary criteria for diagnostics and PGx applications (e.g., the EUROPEAN PERSONALIZED MEDICINE DIAGNOSTICS ASSOCIATION, the EU Framework VII program, the Evaluation of Genomic Applications in Practice and Prevention of the US CENTERS FOR DISEASE CONTROL AND PREVENTION, and the UK NICE).

1118 WURCEL ET AL. (2016), p. 141.

1119 FAULKNER ET AL. (2012), p. 1167.

standards", both industry and HTA agencies face difficulties to sufficiently demonstrate the accuracy and effectiveness of the tests.[1120]

Strengthening the evidence base in PM will require investments in the areas of HTA and health outcomes research.[1121] This shortcoming must be addressed if PM is to be implemented in clinical practice.[1122] Research activities in this field need to take into account aspects specific to PM.[1123]

iii. Lack of coordination of existing heterogeneous HTA processes

The existence of multiple evaluation methodologies for the value of PM[1124] is reflected in the diversity of methodologies for HTA that are used across the globe. There is substantial variation in the process of funding and producing HTAs, the technical details used in the evaluative methods, and the intended use of the HTA differs across countries:[1125]

For example, in *England*, there are national HTA processes in place led by NICE.[1126] *England, Canada, Australia*, or the *Netherlands* base reimbursement decisions of healthcare interventions on CUAs, with health outcomes measured using a metric, such as QALYs.[1127] *France* or *Germany* account for clinical added value, followed by value-based pricing debates.[1128] Belgium follows a dual track for Dx. In one track, Dx for which reimbursement is claimed by the manufacturer undergo a process and a judgment by a technical commission within the NATIONAL INSTITUTE FOR HEALTH AND DISABILITY INSURANCE on the basis of unclear criteria; and in a second track, the Belgian HTA body KCE can select specific diagnostic tests to perform a full HTA.[1129] In other countries, such as *Greece*, there are no dedicated HTA organi-

[1120] EUROPEAN COMMISSION (2013), p. 27.

[1121] FACKLER & MCGUIRE (2010), p. 7; and KIEVITS ET AL. (2014), p. 11.

[1122] FACKLER & MCGUIRE (2010), p. 7.

[1123] KIEVITS ET AL. (2014), p. 11, mention e.g., the fact that there is only provisional evidence available at the time of launch; the need for a new diagnostic step in HTA processes which may not have large quantities of clinical data to demonstrate its value; the need to fit into health systems that are still configured for broad populations and 'average' patients.

[1124] Cf. II, Chapter 3.1 Existence of multiple evaluation methodologies, p. 75 ff.

[1125] Cf. also MILLER ET AL. (2011), p. 138; FLORIAN GUTZWILLER ET AL. (2012), p. 51; PAYNE & ANNEMANS (2013), p. 33 or AKHMETOV & BUBNOV (2015), p. 220; WURCEL ET AL. (2016), p. 141. KANAVOS (2016), p. 16 ff. compares HTA decisions from NICE England, SMC Scotland, TLV Sweden and HAS France and finds only a match of 39% of the HTA recommendations.

[1126] PAYNE & ANNEMANS (2013), p. 33,

[1127] BUCHANAN ET AL. (2013), p. 8; BYRON ET AL. (2014), p. 1475; and AKHMETOV ET AL. (2015), p. 221.

[1128] AKHMETOV ET AL. (2015), p. 221.

[1129] PAYNE & ANNEMANS (2013), p. 33.

zations and no economic evidence is used to inform reimbursement decisions or guideline development.[1130]

In the European Union, the diversity of HTA systems is further complicated by centralized versus decentralized HTA and reimbursement processes.[1131]

There are also differences in the progress between countries in adapting their methods to accommodate the growing number of therapeutics associated with a companion diagnostic entering the market.[1132] For example, *Australia* has created the "HTA Access Point" to coordinate, manage, and monitor CDx through governmental HTA processes; in Germany, the HTA body of the INSTITUT FÜR QUALITÄT UND WIRTSCHAFTLICHKEIT IM GESUNDHEITSWESEN is aiming to simplify the process of evaluating CDx; and also the UK is extending HTA arrangements to Dx.[1133]

As the previous examples illustrate how countries employ miscellaneous analytical frameworks to guide their evaluations. Each national HTA body imposes diverse restrictions and has different conclusions on the acceptability of a drug.[1134] Consequently, also coverage for many CDx tests varies across Europe.[1135]

The diversity of HTAs creates market access hurdles for innovative Dx tests. Therefore, joined efforts among various stakeholders are required to shape the way assessment is carried out in different healthcare systems. Several studies call for a common language and terminology, uniform HTA assessment frameworks, more cross-border sharing of expertise, systematic collaboration among HTA bodies, a clear

[1130] *Ibidem.*

[1131] AKHMETOV ET AL. (2015), p. 221.

[1132] BYRON ET AL. (2014), p. 1475.

[1133] GARAU ET AL. (2012), p. 18; BYRON ET AL. (2014), p. 1475.

[1134] The diversity of HTA approaches is illustrated in more detail by AKHMETOV & BUBNOV (2015), p. 5, with an overview table of the Austrian, Belgian, Swiss, German, Finnish, French, Dutch, Norway, Sweedish and English HTA approach from the EUROPEAN OBSERVATORY ON HEALTH SYSTEMS AND POLICIES.
They also mention EGFR testing before Iressa (gefitinib) an example reflecting the consequences of the high variability of approaches to assess molecular Dx: While the diagnostics manufacturer's submission estimated cost-effectiveness of the test at GBP 23'615 per QALY, the assessment conducted by NICE demonstrated GBP 35'700 per QALY and the study by SCOTTISH MEDICINES CONSORTIUM (SMC) measured cost-effectiveness as GBP 154'022 per QALY.
Alternatively, MARTINALBO ET AL. (2016) who discuss the differences in pricing and reimbursement decisions and approval times at the national level.

[1135] E.g., while the oncology drug trastuzumab is widely reimbursed across the EU, reimbursement for its HER-2 companion diagnostic test varies across Europe. In the UK, France, Germany, Italy and Switzerland, HER-2 testing is publicly funded, but in Spain, the pharmaceutical manufacturer funds the majority of testing, not assuring the continuation of this funding stream in the future. Cf. LEOPOLD (2014), *chapter 4*, and WURCEL ET AL. (2016), p. 141; and *Annex* 1 KLV for Switzerland.

stating of appropriate methods concerning comparators, and a more transparent and comprehensive reporting of the findings – especially for European countries.[1136]

So far, evaluation bodies have typically relied on expert panels and local committees to evaluate available evidence and form recommendations. Such groups have tended to work in isolation from each other, assessing the same evidence sometimes with duplication work.[1137] It is estimated that 10-12% of the performed evaluations across Europe are identical and that ca. 30% have similar contents.[1138] The systematic international exchange of information can foster decision making on reimbursement across borders and ensure timely access for patients to effective PM.[1139] Explicit requirements for health outcomes and economic evidence to support the evaluation of molecular Dx are beginning to evolve.[1140]

So far, the role and use of HTAs have varied considerably between the EU Member States.[1141] In 2013, the EUROPEAN UNION has established a permanent, HTA network at European level with the aim to strengthen further the cooperation between national HTA bodies. The network allows work models for joint assessments of new health technologies. The information generated can be reused at national level, thereby reducing duplication of work between Member States.[1142] The EU cooperation focuses on clinical issues – economic, organizational, legal, and ethical considerations are more addressed at national/regional level.[1143]

6.2.2 Analysis of incentives

Pharmaceutical companies

The lack of clear evidence requirements for CDx and the diversity in HTA processes negatively incentivizes pharmaceutical companies to pursue PM strategies. As

---

[1136] *Criticizing inconsistency in HTA assessments concerning PM:* MILLER ET AL. (2011), p. 138; FAULKNER ET AL. (2012), p. 1168; PAYNE & ANNEMANS (2013), p. 33; TOWSE & GARRISON (2013), p. 41; HORGAN ET AL. (2014), p. 292; AKHMETOV & BUBNOV (2015), p. 5; and WURCEL ET AL. (2016), p. 141.

[1137] T. A MANOLIO ET AL. (2013), p. 260; and LEYENS & BRAND (2016), p. 190.

[1138] EUnetHTA cited in WIDRIG (2015), p. 408.

[1139] EUROPEAN COMMISSION (2013), p. 29; T. A MANOLIO ET AL. (2013), p. 260; HORGAN ET AL. (2014), p. 292; KIEVITS ET AL. (2014), p. 11; AKHMETOV & BUBNOV (2015), p. 5; and references in *note* 1086.

[1140] Cf. FAULKNER ET AL. (2012), p. 1168.

[1141] EUROPEAN COMMISSION (2013), p. 27.

[1142] EUROPEAN COMMISSION IMPLEMENTING DECISION of 26 June 2013 providing the rules for the establishment, management and transparent functioning of the network of national authorities or bodies responsible for health technology assessment.

[1143] EUROPEAN COMMISSION (2013), p. 27.

HTA bodies are more experienced with the assessment of pharmaceuticals, the evidence requirements for non-personalized pharmaceutical components are more established compared to PM. The insecurity, ambiguity and complexity a pharmaceutical company faces with the approval of personalized drugs deter a rational pharmaceutical company to pursue personalized approaches.[1144]

Diagnostics companies

The same argumentation counts for diagnostics companies. Unclear or non-existent reimbursement pathways, together with the lack of clear evidence requirements in HTA processes, lead to delays and gaps in the assessment of PM Dx in certain countries.[1145] Dx manufacturers have no predictability and clarity regarding necessary steps for value demonstration, and how this will lead to effective funding of the diagnostic test. Thus, they have no incentives to invest, neither in tests, nor in PM Dx evidence development.[1146]

Providers

HTAs are not only used to inform pricing and reimbursement decisions, but in certain cases also to inform clinical guidelines.[1147] Non-existent or inadequate HTA processes for PM treatments generally disincentivize providers to foster the use of PM.

First, if there are no official recommendations for a PM, a provider will tend to be hesitant to prescribe it, because his interest is to follow the standard of care.

Second, the information contained in a HTA report has the potential to reduce the information asymmetry between providers and patients. A HTA report is based on the latest scientific knowledge and points out, why and under which conditions a certain health technology should be applied or not. With the existence of an adequate HTA report, a patient can be informed in more detail and the physician reduces his or her liability risk of not having sufficiently informed the patient.[1148]

Thirdly, inexistent or inadequate HTAs lead to non-existent or inadequate reimbursement decisions generally deterring a providers from prescribing a treatment.[1149]

1144 Cf. also Chapter 3.1.1 Literature analysis, *i) Strategic challenges to the co-development process, Pharmaceutical companies' strategic interests*, p. 122 f.

1145 PLUN-FAVREAU ET AL. (2016), p. 144.

1146 WURCEL ET AL. (2016), p. 141.

1147 STEPHENS ET AL. (2012), p. 29; WIDRIG (2015), p. 45-46.

1148 WIDRIG & TAG (2015), p. 592.

1149 Cf. arguments for provider incentives, p. 193 ff.

Patients

Due to the dependent relationship of a patient from a provider, and due to the asymmetric information between both, a patient has no incentive to ask for a PM, especially if a treatment is not reimbursed due to gaps in the HTA process.

Payers

HTAs are essential tools for informing reimbursement decisions. They help to inform payers whether an assessed treatment adds value, and whether it is as effective in terms of costs and clinical benefit as comparable existing treatments. In-existent, unclear or inadequate HTA mechanisms for PM treatments incentivize payers not to reimburse PM and to remain conservative in their reimbursement decisions.

6.2.3 Resulting hypothesis

The overview below summarizes the argumentation of the previous chapter and shows the resulting incentives through the gaps and inconsistencies in conventional HTAs for personalized treatments.

Research institutions	*Pharmaceutical companies*	*Diagnostic companies*	*Providers*	*Patients*	*Payers*
–	negative	negative	negative	negative	negative

negative = institutional setting incentivizes a player not to foster the translation of PM
– = neutral/no conclusive statement possible on a player's incentive to foster the translation of PM

Based on the arguments presented in the previous sub-chapters, this chapter concludes with the following hypothesis:

> *Hypothesis: Gaps and inconsistencies in conventional health technology assessments for personalized medicine act as a barrier to the translation of personalized medicine into clinical practice.*

7 Results

7.1 Categorized barriers to the translation of personalized medicine

The literature analysis in Part III 1) identifies, 2) synthesizes, and 3) categorizes the institutional barriers hindering the uptake of PM in clinical practice.

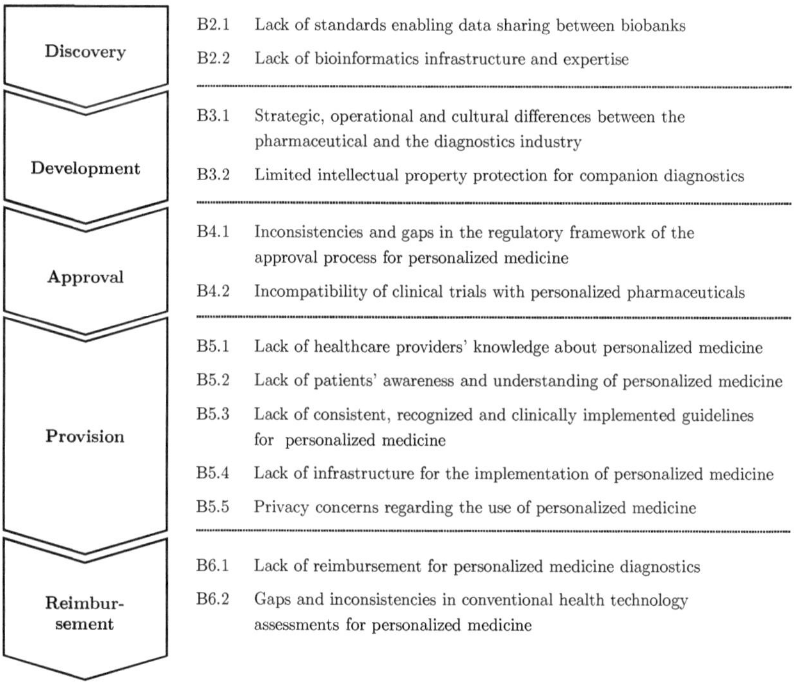

Figure 23: Overview of barriers to the translation of personalized medicine

The resulting overview provides a comprehensive picture of non-science related factors hindering the translation of PM into clinical practice. It demonstrates that barriers persist along every link of the value chain of PM applications.

7.2 Resulting incentives

The following overview presents the incentives for each stakeholder set through the identified institutional barriers:

Value chain phase	*Barrier*	*Research institutions*	*Pharmaceutical companies*	*Diagnostic companies*	*Providers*	*Patients*	*Payers*
Discovery	2.1 Lack of standards enabling data sharing between biobanks	neg.	neg.	neg.	–	–	–
	2.2 Lack of bioinformatics infrastructure and expertise	neg.	neg.	neg.	–	–	–
Development	3.1 Strategic, operational and cultural differences between Rx and Dx industry	–	neg.	neg.	–	–	–
	3.2 Limited intellectual property protection for CDx	–	–	neg.	–	–	–
Approval	4.1 Inconsistencies and gaps in the regulatory framework of the approval process for PM	–	neg.	neg.	–	–	–
	4.2 Incompatibility of clinical trials with personalized pharmaceuticals	–	neg.	–	–	–	–
Provision	5.1 Lack of healthcare providers' knowledge about PM	–	neg.	neg.	neg.	neg.	–
	5.2 Lack of patients' awareness and understanding of PM	–	neg.	neg.	neg.	neg.	neg.
	5.3 Lack of consistent, recognized and clinically implemented guidelines on PM approaches	–	–	–	neg.	neg.	neg.
	5.4 Lack of infrastructure for the implementation of PM	neg.	neg.	neg.	neg.	neg.	–
	5.5 Privacy concerns regarding the use of PM	neg.	neg.	neg.	neg.	neg.	–
Reimbursement	6.1 Lack of reimbursement for personalized medicine diagnostics	–	neg.	neg.	neg.	neg.	neg.
	6.2 Gaps and inconsistencies in conventional HTAs for PM	–	neg.	neg.	neg.	neg.	neg.

Table 9: Overview of incentives for each stakeholder and each institutional barrier

The two players at the beginning and end of the value chain – *research institutions* and *payers* – are affected by the lowest number of barriers, whereas *pharmaceutical* and *diagnostics companies* are affected by the highest number of barriers. The following sub-chapters summarize and discuss the resulting incentives for each stakeholder.

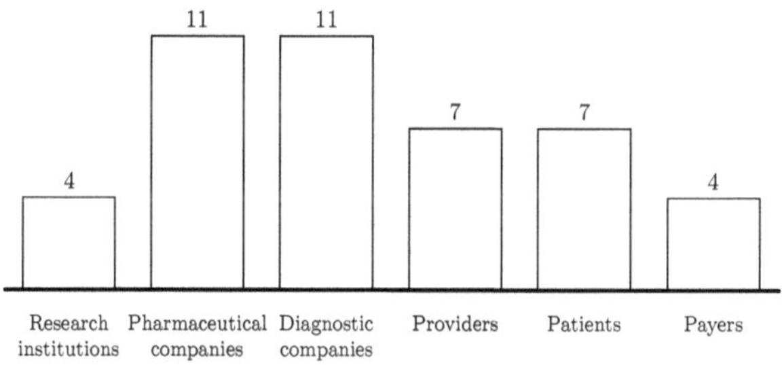

Figure 24: Resulting incentives by number of barriers negatively incentivizing stakeholders

Incentives for research institutions

The barriers for research institutions are found in the first link of the value chain concerning the discovery of PM applications. There are additional negative incentives through institutional barriers in the provision phase lowering the amount of data available for research (*B5.4 & B5.5*).

Incentives for diagnostics companies

The largest number of barriers concern diagnostic and pharmaceutical companies. Both players are involved from discovery until reimbursement and are thus confronted with several barriers along the value chain.

Diagnostics companies will only make investments to develop clinically useful PM diagnostics tests if there is a chance of amortizing the investment costs with future revenues.[1150] The analysis of incentives reveales several barriers hindering diagnostics companies in capturing the full share of value they generate for the healthcare system.

[1150] Cf. Chapter 1.2.1 Constitutive microeconomic assumptions, p. 104 f.

As long as providers and patients are not aware of PM (*B5.1, B5,2*), and as long as there are no guidelines consistently recommending PM (*B5.3*), PM Dx face a comparably low demand. The lack of reimbursement for PM Dx (*B6.1*) and the lack of HTAs for PM (*B6.2*) further add to the undervaluation of PM Dx.

The barriers contribute to a negative vicious cycle.[1151] The lower the incentives for Dx companies to develop PM Dx, the lower is the data availability and thus the evidence generation for PM –which in turn enforces the low incentives for Dx companies to develop PM Dx. This cycle can be positively or negatively influenced through the institutional setting governing the barriers.

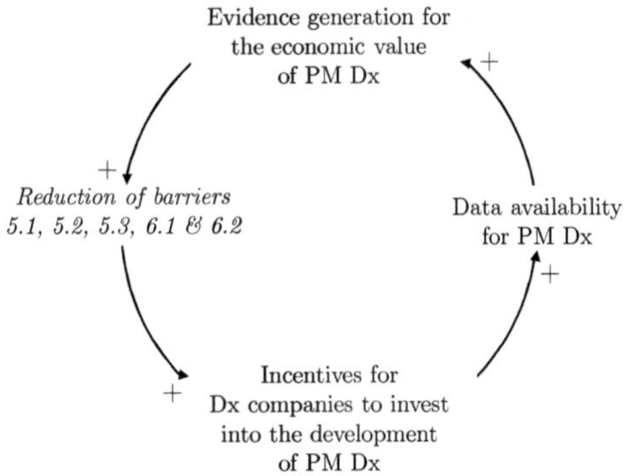

\+ = positive causal relationship amplifying the behavior of the target variable

Figure 25: Vicious cycle leading to the undervaluation of personalized medicine diagnostics

The identified barriers lead to *"uneconomic economics"*[1152] for diagnostics companies. The undervaluation of diagnostic tests compared to pharmaceuticals is an economic discrepancy that is seen as one decisive reason behind the slow or insufficient translation of PM.[1153] The relative value of diagnostic tests compared to the value of the pharmaceuticals is empirically observable. It is described as *"highly skewed"* and *"inconsistent"* with the importance of diagnostics to healthcare decision making.[1154] Empirical studies by EKSTROM ET AL. (2013) and ROHR ET AL. (2016) confirm this:

1151 HAYES ET AL. (2014), p. 3; and ROHR ET AL. (2016), p. 12, argue similarly with a negatively perpetuating vicious cycle leading to the undervaluation of PM Dx.

1152 Expression used in TRUSHEIM & BERNDT (2012), p. 413. In this publication they use a DCF model (incl. transparent assumptions) to illustrate the economic challenges facing an PM developer.

1153 *Discussing the undervaluation of the diagnostic component:* J. DAVIS ET AL. (2010), p. 7-8; EKSTROM ET AL. (2013), p. 1; HAYES ET AL. (2013), p. 1 ff.; TRUSHEIM & BERNDT (2015)b, p. 10 and p. 21; DANIEL SCHNEIDER ET AL. (2016), p. 160; and WURCEL ET AL. (2016), p. 137 ff.

1154 HAYES ET AL. (2013), p. 2.

Although diagnostics tests are estimated to influence ca. 70%[1155] of the decisions made by physicians, only ca. 2% of healthcare spending flows to diagnostics providers.[1156] ROHR ET AL. (2016) assessed the perceived value of IVDs on clinical decision-making and found a *"poor awareness of actual healthcare expenditure on IVDs"*, but a *"high attributable value of diagnostic procedures for patient management"*.[1157] Pricing for CDx indicates that diagnostic tests are valued as utility - comparable to e.g. a needle for injections – instead of an integral part of the Rx-CDx-combination. However, unlike the needle, a diagnostic test can direct a physician towards a specific course of treatment and is thus as important to a treatment as the drug itself.[1158]

As long as the institutional setting governing PM Dx does not recognize the inherent value of information for patients and decision makers which the diagnostics bring to the "joint product" Rx-CDx combination, Dx companies do not have the opportunity to profitably offer PM Dx products.

Incentives for pharmaceutical companies

Pharmaceutical companies face basically the same challenges as diagnostics companies. They will only make investments to develop clinically useful PM applications if there is a chance of positive profits.[1159]

For an *existing generic or soon-to-be generic drug,* however, personalization is not profitable for pharmaceutical companies, because market sizes as well as prices would decrease. For these cases, pharmaceutical companies are unlikely to personalize drugs.[1160]

For the development and offering of *personalized first-in-class drugs*, pharmaceutical companies have a several disincentives compared to the development and first-in-class offering of a traditional, non-personalized treatment. First, a pharmaceutical company is disincentivized through the identified barriers. Thus, personalization of a

---

1155 EKSTROM ET AL. (2013), p. 1; ROHR ET AL. (2016), p. 2 found that 66% of decision-making was based on IVD.

1156 EKSTROM ET AL. (2013), p. 1, with estimates for the U. S. only; ROHR ET AL. (2016) found that IVD costs account for 2,3% (US) and 1,4% (Germany) of total healthcare expenditure. Similarly J. C. DAVIS ET AL. (2009), p. 282, who estimate that tests influence 60–70% of all treatment decisions, yet account for only 5% of hospital costs and 2% of Medicare expenditures in the US.

1157 Most physicians (81%) believed that the actual expenditure on IVDs was >5%; 19% rated the spending correctly. When informed of the actual amount, a majority of providers rated this as appropriate. Cf. ROHR ET AL. (2016), p. 1 ff.

1158 LUO ET AL. (2015), p. 7.

1159 Cf. Chapter 1.2.1 Constitutive microeconomic assumptions, p. 104 f.

1160 Cf. Chapter 3.1 Strategic, operational and cultural differences between the pharmaceutical and the diagnostics industry, *Pharmaceutical company's strategic interests:*, p. 122 ff.

drug may require an increased investment – especially due to the development of the diagnostic component, which faces undervaluation problems.[1161] Second, a personalized approach may result in a smaller market size. If the profit decrease due to the smaller market size is not offset by increased prices, a personalized strategy is not attractive for a pharmaceutical company.

In certain situations there are sufficient economic incentives for pharmaceutical companies to develop *new personalized pharmaceuticals.* One example would be diseases where multiple drugs are already on the market. Personalization could differentiate the drug from its competitors by representing improved efficacy in the responder population and thus achieving higher price levels.[1162]

Today's environment favors the latter two cases. Both cases are likely to increase overall public health but unlikely to reduce a healthcare's system costs.

Incentives for providers

Providers represent the link between science and clinical practice. This thesis agrees with others identifying the point of care as a *"broken link"* [1163] in the value chain of personalized medicine, as the barriers negatively incentivizing healthcare providers involve all identified barriers in the last two links of the PM value chain.

Incentives for patients

Like providers, also patients are affected by all the identified barriers in the last two links of the PM value chain. Additionally, patients are in a dependent relationship to their providers,[1164] thus all barriers negatively incentivizing providers are reflected in the patients' incentive structures.

Incentives for payers

PM can lower healthcare costs without lowering the level of health. This is reached by avoiding ineffective treatments and their adverse side effects.[1165] Consequentially, in theory, a payer would have the incentive to foster the translation of PM.[1166]

[1161] Cf. explanations in previous chapter.

[1162] Cf. Chapter 1.2.2, Interdependencies between the pharmaceutical and diagnostic component, p. 105 ff.

[1163] Cf. *note* 888.

[1164] Cf. Chapter 1.2.1 Constitutive microeconomic assumptions, p. 104 f.

[1165] Cf. Part II, Chapter 2 Goals of personalized medicine, page 67 ff. and Chapter 3 Economic value of personalized medicine, p. 72 ff.

[1166] Cf. Part III Chapter 6.1.2 Analysis of incentives, *Payers,* a) Inconsistent evidence for the health economic impact of PM Dx incentivizes payers to uphold current lack of reimbursement, p. 195, *note* 1061.

However, current HTA processes do not adequately assess PM. Multiple evaluation methodologies and a lack of reliable data for measuring the economic value of PM further complicates the assessment process.[1167] Today's reimbursement systems are often cost-based instead of value-based.[1168] They favor the reimbursement of traditional, non-personalized pharmaceuticals and exhibit gaps in the reimbursement of PM Dx. A lack of consistent and recognized guidelines on PM approaches and patients' low awareness about PM further adds to the low incentives of payers to foster the translation of PM.[1169]

7.3 Relevance assessment

A reader may hypothesize that some barriers are more relevant than others. There is not one definite answer to the question of what is the most relevant barrier to the translation of personalized medicine. Relevance is a subjective term. For a patient it might be concerns about data protection, for a diagnostics company it might be the lack of reimbursement, whereas for a researcher it might be obstacles in data sharing. Also, the institutional barriers might be differently weighted according to a normative measure.

Following an objective attempt[1170] that simply counts and equally weights the number of negatively influenced stakeholders leads to the conclusion that the most relevant barriers tend to be towards the end of the value chain. The most relevant barriers are *B5.2, B5.4, B5.5, B6.1* and *B6.2*.

[1167] Cf. Part II, Chapter 3 Economic value of personalized medicine, p. 72 ff.

[1168] Cf. Part III, Chapter 6.1.1 Literature analysis, *History of cost-based reimbursement*, p. 187.

[1169] Cf. Part III, Chapter 5.3 Lack of consistent, recognized and clinically implemented guidelines for personalized medicine, p. 169 ff.

[1170] Cf. RESEARCH CONCEPT, Chapter 4.3 Derivation and evaluation of policy levers, *Relevance*, p. 12.

		Number of negatively incentivized stakeholders[1]
Discovery	2.1 Lack of standards enabling data sharing between biobanks	3
	2.2 Lack of bioinformatics infrastructure and expertise	3
Develop-ment	3.1 Strategic, operational and cultural differences between Rx and Dx industry	2
	3.2 Limited intellectual property protection for CDx	1
Approval	4.1 Inconsistencies and gaps in the regulatory framework of the approval process for PM	2
	4.2 Incompatibility of clinical trials with personalized pharmaceuticals	1
Provision	5.1 Lack of healthcare providers' knowledge about PM	4
	5.2 Lack of patients' awareness and understanding of PM	5
	5.3 Lack of consistent, recognized and clinically implemented guidelines	3
	5.4 Lack of infrastructure for the implementation of PM	5
	5.5 Privacy concerns regarding the use of PM	5
Reimbur-sement	6.1 Lack of reimbursement for PM diagnostics	5
	6.2 Gaps and inconsistencies in conventional HTAs for PM	5

Figure 26: Barriers' incentives by number of negatively incentivized stakeholders

7.4 Conclusion

The results of Part III underline the complexity behind the translation of PM. The translation does not face one single barrier that could be removed. Instead this thesis results demonstrate how multifaceted and intertwined the non-science related, institutional barriers behind the translation of PM are.

Therefore, any strategy to foster the translation of PM requires a multi-targeted approach with an interdisciplinary, broad perspective. Part III has identified the barriers that must be reduced in order to increase the translation of PM into clinical practice. Policy levers aiming to lower barriers towards the end of the PM value chain tend to positively incentivize more stakeholders in the PM ecosystem to foster the translation of PM and is therefore be more effective than policy levers lowering barriers at the beginning of the PM value chain.

Part IV: Applied part

Analysis of institutional barriers to the translation of personalized medicine in Switzerland

Part III provided a comprehensive, theoretical picture of the institutional barriers which are suggested to hinder the translation of personalized medicine into clinical practice. The identification of the barriers was based on a literature analysis, and the identification of the incentives for the stakeholders in the PM ecosystem was based on a theoretical microeconomic analysis. Part III is of general, theoretical value and can be tested in the context of other countries.

Part IV's primary goal is to test the hypotheses proposed in the previous Part III for the case of Switzerland.

1 Methodological approach

In a first step, the institutional setting concerning each of respective barriers is examined. Based on this, the incentives analysis tests the hypotheses proposed in Part III and assesses to what extend the incentives for the stakeholders in the Swiss PM ecosystem differ from the theoretical analysis in Part III.

Concluding Part IV, an overview of the resulting institutional barriers for Switzerland, their induced incentives for each stakeholder and their relevance is given and compared to the findings in the theoretical Part III.

The Law and Economic analysis in Part IV forms the basis for the derivation of potential policy levers to foster the translation of PM in Switzerland in Part V.

K. Bosshard, *Law and Economics of Personalized Medicine*,
Gesundheitsmanagement und Gesundheitsökonomik,
https://doi.org/10.1007/978-3-658-22074-7_5

1.1 Analysis of the institutional setting concerning each barrier in Switzerland

In a first step, the current institutional setting governing the barriers to PM in Switzerland is examined. The main sources for the identification of the relevant institutions concerning the respective barriers range from non-legal institutional mechanisms to formal hard law requirements.

1.2 Incentives analysis

The methodology of the incentives analysis is the same as applied in Part III – with the same constitutive assumptions.[1171] Where possible and available, the incentives analysis is supplemented with empirical findings like e.g. statements from experts.

The hypotheses proposed in Part III are tested by examining the incentives induced by the institutional setting. It is examined, whether evidence in the Swiss institutional environment indicates that the barrier does not exist in Switzerland.

[1171] Cf. Part III, Chapter 1.2 Analysis of incentives, p. 103 ff.

2 Barriers in the discovery phase

2.1 Lack of standards enabling data sharing between biobanks

2.1.1 Institutional setting

This chapter identifies the relevant institutions governing data sharing between biobanks in Switzerland.

National institutions:

There is no dedicated regulation concerning biobanks in Switzerland.[1172] However, there are several legal acts and soft law guidelines aiming for the privacy protection with regards to genetic data. This thesis dedicates a separate chapter for the analysis of the institutional setting governing the *privacy protection* of genetic data in Switzerland.[1173]

The HUMAN RESEARCH ACT (HFG) and the corresponding ORDINANCE (HFV)[1174] regulate the authorization and notification procedures for human research, for example the authorization of research projects by the ethics committee.[1175]

Further, relevant for the storing of genetic data in biobanks is the requirement of an „informed consent" stated in the LAW ON GENETIC TESTS ON HUMANS (GUMG).[1176] Every further use of genetic data – beyond the original use for which a patient has given his or her consent – requires either another specific consent of the patient or a legal basis, except for anonymized data.[1177] This requirement complicates the sharing of data between biobanks, as sometimes the donators of the genetic data in the biobank are not traceable or alive anymore. So far, a harmonized consent form did not exist in Switzerland. In 2017, the SAMS has developed a "general consent" in collaboration with SWISSETHICS allowing people to permit the use of their health data for fu-

[1172] Cf. SWISS NATIONAL ADVISORY COMMISSION ON BIOMEDICAL ETHICS (2015) *note* 204. The report examines the legal and ethical framework for biobanks in Switzerland.

[1173] Cf. following Chapter 5.5 Privacy concerns regarding the use of personalized medicine, p. 250 ff.

[1174] In German "Humanforschungsgesetz" (HFG) and "Humanforschungsverordning" (HFV). This thesis does not use English abbreviations for any official Swiss legal materials as they are usually only available in German, French and Italian. Instead, this thesis uses the German abbreviations.

[1175] Art. 14 ff HFV.

[1176] Art. 5 GUMG, Art. 8 *para.* 2 HFG or Art. 5 CONVENTION ON HUMAN RIGHTS AND BIOMEDICINE.

[1177] Art. 4 *para.* 3 DSG; and cf. Sub-chapter 4. The requirement of an "informed consent", p. 254 f.

ture research projects.[1178] With the definitive use of the general consent, a hurdle for the data sharing between biobanks will be taken.

Additionally, the NATIONAL ADVISORY COMMISSION ON BIOMEDICAL ETHICS (NCE) provides standards and templates for the establishment and running of biobanks. A biobank must have an own regulation written and reviewed by an expert. The NCE provides templates to *"ensure compliance with national legislation and promote the harmonization of biobanks in Switzerland"*.[1179] The templates stipulate, if stored data or samples are used for other research projects, or are transferred to other biobanks, it must be governed by a material transfer agreement and must be appropriately documented.[1180]

However, all the above mentioned acts do have rather the protection than the sharing of data as a focus of interest. Neither the legal nor the standards by the NCE contain harmonized standards for data sharing between biobanks.

A statement from a health expert two years ago was: *"Switzerland has too many different norms in the health data management. The SWISS MEDICAL ASSOCIATION leaves the issue to the industry which in turn does not move on without public pressure for a harmonization. And the doctors do not care as long they do not have more work and costs"*.[1181] The key to success is the establishment of an infrastructure enabling the data exchange of multiple clinics. However, this is a major project which could be compared to the *"construction of the Gotthard tunnel"*.[1182]

Having recognized this gap, the SWISS STATE SECRETARIAT FOR EDUCATION, RESEARCH AND INNOVATION has initiated a research initiative SWISS PERSONALIZED HEALTH NETWORK (SPHN). The FEDERAL COUNCIL granted CHF 70 million over four years for the network. SPHN will establish *"nationwide interoperability of clinical, 'omics' and other health-related data, allowing researchers in Switzerland to share information and collaborate efficiently"*. The SPHN started in 2017, and brings together university hospitals, schools of higher education, research institutes, organizations working in the area of personalized health, as well as other health-related research activities across Switzerland.[1183] The initiative is being coordinated by the SWISS ACADEMY OF MEDICAL SCIENCES in the initial phase from 2017-2020.[1184] In ad-

[1178] SAMS (2017)b, *Vorlage Generalkonsent.*
[1179] SWISSETHICS (2014), p. 1.
[1180] SWISSETHICS (2017), *paras.* 6 and 7.
[1181] Anonymized statement of a Swiss health expert in summer 2015 (identity known to the author).
[1182] MOCH at the ETH LATSIS Forum on June 29th, 2016.
[1183] Cf. FISCH (2016), SAMS (2017)a, and SWISS INSTITUTE FOR BIOINFORMATICS (2017).
[1184] Cf. MEIER-ABT (2016), p. 1.

dition, the SWISS NATIONAL SCIENCE FOUNDATION provides grants for the networking of biobanks.[1185]

International institutions:

There is a diversity of legal requirements for biobanking activities across the globe,[1186] but no uniformly applied standard for the data sharing between biobanks.

One international initiative is the GLOBAL ALLIANCE FOR GENOMIC HEALTH. Amongst others, the organization aims to standardize data creation, access and retrieval in an effort to realize the full potential of genetic and clinical data in research. To achieve this objective, the alliance established an international framework for data sharing promoting effective and ethically responsible approaches.[1187] Switzerland is represented with seven participating organizations.[1188]

In the last years, the European Union took steps towards a framework for standardization of biobanks data within Europe. In late 2013 the BBMRI-ERIC was founded and awarded the Community legal framework for a EUROPEAN RESEARCH INFRASTRUCTURE CONSORTIUM (ERIC).[1189] The legal status as ERIC allows pooling biobanks and biomolecular resources into a pan-European facility. It aims to provide access to collections of partner biobanks and biomolecular resources, their expertise and services on a non-economic basis.[1190] Amongst others, the BBMRI-ERIC aims to support certain standard operating procedures and minimum standards.[1191] The BBMRI-ERIC does not only provide standards increasing the technical interoperability between biobanks, it does also provide support on ethical, legal and societal issues related to biobanking activities.[1192] Switzerland represented by SWISS BIOBANKING is not a member, but an observer of the project.[1193] Following the BBMRI-ERIC, the SWISS NATIONAL SCIENCE FOUNDATION has initiated a corresponding SWISS BIOBANKING PLATFORM (BBMRI.ch) in 2015. The platform coordinates and harmonizes bi-

[1185] Cf. SWISS NATIONAL SCIENCE FOUNDATION (2017) with the infrastructure program "BioLink".

[1186] An overview in EUROPEAN COMMISSION (2012), *chapter* 6.

[1187] Cf. https://genomicsandhealth.org/about-the-global-alliance/mission-founding-principles (last visited June 7, 2017)

[1188] Three companies, and four research institutions, cf. https://genomicsandhealth.org/members (last visited July 7, 2017).

[1189] The ERIC is a specific legal form designed to facilitate the joint establishment and operation of research infrastructures of European interest, BBMRI-ERIC (2015), *"The History"*.

[1190] Art. 3 EU BBMRI-ERIC decision, OJ L 320/63. A simplified, streamlined, and coordinated EU legal framework to stimulate international secondary use of biospecimen research projects. Similarly to what DANIEL SCHNEIDER ET AL. (2016), p. 167-168, suggested.

[1191] E.g., MIABIS 2.0, c. f. www.bbmri-eric.eu/services/standardisation/ (last visited June 4, 2017).

[1192] Cf. http://www.bbmri-eric.eu/services/elsihelpdesk/ (last visited June 4, 2017).

[1193] Cf. www.bbmri-eric.eu/national-nodes/switzerland (last visited June 4, 2017).

obanking activities in Switzerland. It is planned to establish harmonized procedures by 2017 which will be implemented in a pilot feasibility study in 2018. Further, the BBMRI will create a central web-based catalogue of existing and de novo biobanks with data and samples' access policies.[1194]

2.1.2 Analysis of incentives

With the projects described in the previous chapter, Switzerland has initiated the establishment of standards enabling data sharing between biobanks in line with the newest international developments in this field.

Against the backdrop of the analysis in Part III, research institutions, pharmaceutical and diagnostics companies are more likely to share data between biobanks. Switzerland has relevant standards or is in the process of creating such. Thus, the negative incentives identified in Part III are less likely to be valid for Switzerland.

Research institutions	*Pharmaceutical companies*	*Diagnostic companies*	*Providers*	*Patients*	*Payers*
–	–	–	–	–	–

negative = institutional setting incentivizes a player not to foster the translation of PM
– = neutral/no conclusive statement possible on a player's incentive to foster the translation of PM

2.1.3 Result

This chapter finds that Switzerland's institutional setting supports standards enabling the data sharing between biobanks. With these findings, the hypothesis from Part III must be rejected.

2.2 Lack of bioinformatics infrastructure and expertise

2.2.1 Institutional setting

Switzerland has made efforts in order to increase its bioinformatics infrastructure and the corresponding expertise related to PM: New bioinformatics roles are being

[1194] Cf. BBMRI.CH (2017), *na.*

created at medical institutes in Switzerland.[1195] A mentionable public initiative was SystemX.ch from 2008-2016. It was the largest ever public research initiative in Switzerland and focused specifically on a broad topical area of basic research in the field of systems biology.[1196]

Also at the COMPETENCE CENTER FOR PERSONALIZED MEDICINE at the UNIVERSITY OF ZURICH and ETH, it has been recognized that *"doctors and bio-informatics specialists today often speak different languages". "We need to strengthen their respective understanding for one another".* The universities plan new programs for bachelor and masters in Molecular and Translational Biomedicine.[1197]

In 2017, a joint venture by the ETH Lausanne and ETH Zürich opened the SWISS DATA SCIENCE CENTER (SDSC) with the aim to accelerate data science through education and research, and the provision of infrastructure for data science users across disciplines, with a particular focus a. o. on applications in PM. Together with the SDSC, a new master in data science was introduced.[1198]

Further, the SWISS INSTITUTE FOR BIOINFORMATICS plays a leading role in the above described SPHN initiative and the PERSONALIZED HEALTH INFORMATICS GROUP (PHI) ensuring that expertise in bioinformatics is provided in the initiative. The institute is responsible for the SPHN's data coordination center. A dedicated "Data Expert Group" consisting of IT-experts of the institute, universities and the university hospitals defines appropriate standard processes and will initiate the needed measures ensuring data-interoperability.[1199]

2.2.2 Analysis of incentives

Similarly to the first barrier, Switzerland has taken action in order to strengthen its bioinformatics infrastructure and expertise. Against the backdrop of the analysis in Part III, Switzerland's institutional environment regulating the bioinformatics infrastructure and expertise tends not to impose any negative incentives for the involved stakeholders.

1195 For example, a professorship for bioinformatics is being created at the INSTITUTE OF PATHOLOGY AND MOLECULAR PATHOLOGY, MOCH at the ETH LATSIS Forum on June 29th, 2016.

1196 SYSTEMSX (2017). Its sub-project SyBIT helped the initiative's research projects to cope with the *"flood of data".*

1197 MOCH cited in CC-PM (2017), *PhD MTB Program.*

1198 ETH (2017)b, *Bringing experts together.*

1199 MEIER-ABT & EGLI (2016), p. 3.

Research institutions	*Pharmaceutical companies*	*Diagnostic companies*	*Providers*	*Patients*	*Payers*
–	–	–	–	–	–

negative = institutional setting incentivizes a player not to foster the translation of PM
– = neutral/no conclusive statement possible on a player's incentive to foster the translation of PM

2.2.3 Result

This chapter finds that Switzerland's institutional setting promotes bioinformatics infrastructure and expertise in Switzerland. With these findings, the hypothesis from Part III must be rejected.

3 Barriers in the development phase

3.1 Strategic, operational and cultural differences between the pharmaceutical and the diagnostics industry

3.1.1 Institutional setting

In Switzerland, strategic, operational and cultural differences between pharmaceutical and diagnostics companies are not governed by hard law, but mainly by company internal policies and decisions, which do rather differ from company to company than being specific to Swiss companies. The institutional setting in a country may only indirectly influence these internal policies and decisions.

3.1.2 Analysis of incentives

This thesis has found no evidence in Switzerland's institutional setting influencing the strategic, operational and cultural differences between the pharmaceutical and the diagnostic industry indicating that the differences would differ from the ones described in the theoretical Part III.[1200]

Research institutions	*Pharmaceutical companies*	*Diagnostic companies*	*Providers*	*Patients*	*Payers*
–	negative	negative	–	–	–

negative = institutional setting incentivizes a player not to foster the translation of PM
– = neutral/no conclusive statement possible on a player's incentive to foster the translation of PM

3.1.3 Result

Thus, the hypothesis cannot be rejected for Switzerland: *Strategic, operational and cultural differences between pharmaceutical and diagnostics industry act as barriers to the translation of personalized medicine into Swiss clinical practice.*

1200 Cf. Part III, Chapter 3.1.2 Analysis of incentives, p. 125.

3.2 Limited intellectual property protection for companion diagnostics

3.2.1 Institutional setting

This chapter analyses the intellectual property (IP) protection for CDx in Switzerland. Legal grounds for intellectual property protection in Switzerland are based on international and national law.

International law

The international legal basis for IP in Switzerland consists of several international treaties.[1201] With Switzerland being a member of the EUROPEAN PATENT ORGANISATION, the EUROPEAN PATENT CONVENTION (EPC) is essential for the IP protection of CDx. With regards to the protection for biotechnological inventions, the national PATG is adapted to the level of IP protection given by the EPC.[1202]

In the EPC, methods of treatment by surgery, therapy and diagnostic methods practiced on human or animal body are barred from patentability. Nevertheless, the EPC has carved out certain exceptions allowing for use-limited product claims as well as for claims to second medical uses.[1203] Pharmaceuticals and diagnostics are eligible for patent protection at the EUROPEAN PATENT OFFICE. In contrast to the US, the focus in Europe lies not in asking whether a claim is for a natural law or natural product. In order to be patentable, an invention has to be "new" – amongst other things – no matter if the substance already exists in nature or not.[1204]

Now the question is if it is a patentable "new" invention, if the pharmaceutical targets only a sub-group of patients with a specific biomarker – when the biomarker was previously not yet identified but present, and when some patients with the marker already received the respective treatment? Or is a biomarker patentable, which was known to exist, but its significance was not yet known? The TECHNICAL BOARD OF APPEALS at the EPO has established case law that sheds light on these questions: Patent claims relating to sub-groups overlapping with those treated in the past are valid in the eyes of the TECHNICAL BOARD OF APPEALS. However, for the claimed

1201 International law governing IP in Switzerland: EPC, PARIS CONVENTION FOR THE PROTECTION OF INDUSTRIAL PROPERTY, PATENT LAW TREATY (PLT), the PATENT COOPERATION TREATY (PCT), and the AGREEMENT ON TRADE RELATED ASPECTS OF INTELLECTUAL PROPERTY RIGHTS (TRIPS).

1202 SWISS FEDERAL INSTITUTE OF INTELLECTUAL PROPERTY (2016), *Patent law reform - biotechnological inventions;* and RENTSCH (2016), p. 63 ff. Except for Art. 8 *litera* c PATG, cf. *note* 1213.

1203 Art. 53 *lit.* c EPC.

1204 DIETER SCHNEIDER & BUBLAK (2015), p. 415 ff.; ENSTHALER in EPPINGER ET AL. (2015), p. 323 ff.; and THOMAS ET AL. (2016), p. 349, with more details.

sub-group to be considered "new", it remains a requirement that the biomarker recited in the claim must be capable of distinguishing the claimed sub-group over those patients already known. Sufficient supporting data must be provided establishing that the identified sub-group was not arbitrary, but rather the result of a functional relationship between the claimed biomarker and an improved effect of the claimed treatment.[1205]

So far, the patent practice in Europe has been unchanged by the US Myriad decision.[1206] The consequence of the decision is that Europe has a stricter IP protection for gene-related technologies. The BIOTECH DIRECTIVE and the EPC allow patents for genetic sequences as long as the industrial applicability is explicitly stated in the patent application but not necessarily in the claims themselves.[1207]

National law

The FEDERAL LAW ON PATENTS FOR INVENTIONS (PATG) and its corresponding Ordinance (PatV) build the national legal foundations for the IP protection of CDx.[1208] According to the basic principle patents are granted for "new" inventions applicable in industry.[1209] Excluded from patentability are a. o. diagnostic methods practiced *on* the human body.[1210] *E contrario*, diagnostic methods *outside* the human body are patentable.

A naturally occurring sequence or partial sequence of a gene is not patentable as such. Sequences which are derived from a naturally occurring sequence or partial sequence of a gene may, however, be patented as an invention if they are *produced by means of a technical process* and if their *function is specifically indicated*.[1211] Addi-

1205 Cf. HEARE (2015), p. 1-8, provides an overview regarding the case law at the TECHNICAL BOARD OF APPEALS at the EPO. LUNZE & EPPING (2015), p. 38, about the "unproblematic" patentability of biomarkers in Europe.
However, the case law does not provide a uniform picture. In recent times, the EPO has taken a stricter view of the patentability of biomarkers – what would curtail patent protection for PM, cf. DANNER (2013), p. 3. Also COMAN (2015), p. 5, states that PGx inventions in which a new patient sub-group is defined by a biomarker are not eligible for patent as they lack novelty.

1206 Cf. Part III, Chapter 3.2 Limited intellectual property protection for companion diagnostics, *Mayo Collaborative Services vs Prometheus Laboratories*, p. 128 f.

1207 Cf. WAECHTER (2013), COMAN (2015), JANZE ET AL. in EPPINGER ET AL. (2015), p. 328 ff.; LAI (2015) for analyses of the differences between the IP protection in the US and Europe.

1208 In German "Bundesgesetz über die Erfindungspatente" (PATG) and "Verordnung über die Erfindungspatente" (PatV).

1209 Art. 1 *para.* 1 PATG.

1210 Art. 2 *lit.* a PATG.

1211 Art. 1 *lit.* b PATG or 29 EPA, discussed in detail by WILDHABER (2012), p. 687 ff.; and STAUDER (2014), p. 260 ff.

tionally, there are some exceptions for the protection of "purpose-limited compounds": Any substance which forms part of the state of the art as such, but not in relation to a specific use in a surgical, therapeutic or diagnostic method, and which is distinct from the first medical use, is deemed to be "new" provided it is intended for use in the manufacture of a means to a surgical, therapeutic or diagnostic end.[1212] The protection conferred by a claim to a nucleotide sequence being derived from a naturally occurring sequence or partial sequence of a gene is limited to the sequence segments which perform the function specifically described in the patent.[1213]

With these national legal foundations, the Swiss law provides no obstacle which would prohibit the patentability of CDx in Switzerland – as long as the patent claim does not concern purely isolated gene sequences. Its scope of protection is even slightly higher compared to the EU.[1214] However, so far, the Swiss case law does not contain any decision on the scope of protection for CDx.[1215]

3.2.2 Analysis of incentives

In summary, it must be noted, that the European approach towards IP protection of CDx is less strict than in the US. A limited IP protection of CDx in Europe is not a barrier to the translation of PM. Rather in contrast, the existing EPO case law is *"encouraging for research and development in the precision medicine field"* and *"Europe continues to provide a favorable forum for patenting precision medicine invention"*.[1216]

For the analysis, this thesis assumes that any potential future cases on patent claims for CDx, the Swiss courts would consider the existing case law by the TECHNICAL BOARD OF APPEALS at the EUROPEAN PATENT ORGANISATION and thus follow a similar interpretation of the level of protections for CDx.

Thus, the analysis finds no negative incentives to the translation of PM through a claimed lack of IP protection for CDx.

1212 Art. 7 *lit.* d PATG, *"purpose-limited compound protection"*, cf. WILDHABER (2012), p. 698.

1213 Art. 8 *lit.* c PATG, commonly understood as "absolute protection" and not "compound-limited protection", cf. WILDHABER (2012), p. 695. Discussion about "absolute" and "compound-limited" protection in ADDOR cited in LÜTHI & MENN (2014), p. 189; and STAUDER (2014), p. 261 ff. STAUDER (2014) is describing the conflict that Art. 8 *lit.* c PATG provides a higher level of protection compared to Art. 69 EPC, p. 261 ff.

1214 Cf. *note* 1213.

1215 In this respect, the SWISS FEDERAL INSTITUTE OF INTELLECTUAL PROPERTY (2008), p. 39 explicitly points out the importance of the court decisions.

1216 HEARE (2015) p. 2 and 5-6; similarly DIETER SCHNEIDER & BUBLAK (2015), p. 415 ff.

Research institutions	*Pharmaceutical companies*	*Diagnostic companies*	*Providers*	*Patients*	*Payers*
–	–	–	–	–	–

negative = institutional setting incentivizes a player not to foster the translation of PM
– = neutral/no conclusive statement possible on a player's incentive to foster the translation of PM

3.2.3 Result

With these findings, Switzerland's institutional environment regulating the intellectual property protection for CDx does not impose any negative incentives for the involved stakeholders. The hypothesis proposed in Part III must be rejected.

4 Barriers in the approval phase

4.1 Inconsistencies and gaps in the regulatory framework of the approval process for personalized medicine

4.1.1 Institutional setting

i. Approval process in Switzerland

Pharmaceutical and medical devices[1217] – incl. CDx – are both regulated in the LAW ON THERAPEUTIC PRODUCTS ("Heilmittelgesetz", HMG) but have a completely separate approval process in Switzerland:[1218]

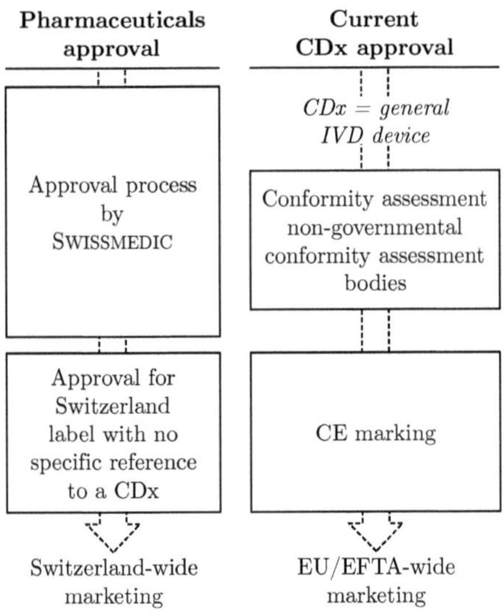

Figure 27: Overview of approval process for pharmaceuticals and companion diagnostics in Switzerland

[1217] Cf. WILDHABER (2013) about the term *"medical devices"* in the Swiss and European law.
[1218] Definitions for pharmaceuticals and medical products in Art. 4 *litera* a and b HMG.

Pharmaceuticals

For the marketing in Switzerland, pharmaceuticals have to be approved by the Swiss agency for the authorization and supervision of therapeutic products, SWISSMEDIC.[1219] A pharmaceutical has to be of high quality, safe and effective in order to obtain approval. The applicant has to proof that a pharmaceutical fulfills these criteria.[1220] For orphan drugs the Swiss law contains a simplified approval process.[1221] In order to accelerate the approval process, the Swiss law allows taking into account the results of examinations in other countries with a comparable approval authority.[1222]

Companion diagnostics

The Swiss law governing the approval process of medical devices – the MEDICAL DEVICES ORDINANCE (MepV) – is harmonized with the EU regulation based on bilateral agreements. The aim of the harmonization of the Swiss law with the EU regulation is to enable the free movement of goods and the mutual recognitions of controls and registrations.[1223]

Also medical devices need to be safe and effective.[1224] However, in contrast to pharmaceuticals, medical devices do not undergo a governmental approval process and can be marketed without, as long as they comply to valid norms confirmed by conformity assessment bodies.[1225] With this, Switzerland has taken over the EU's system of compliance assessment and certification, and follows the *"new and global approach"*.[1226]

1219 Art. 9 HMG. Art. 10 HMG mentioning the approval criteria and Art. 11 HMG details the application. STÖCKLI EGGENBERGER (2015), *recital* 15.55 ff. about the detailed approval process for pharmaceuticals.

1220 Art. 10 *para.* 1 HMG; Art. 2 AMZV.

1221 Art. 14 *para.* 1 *litera* f HMG.

1222 Art. 13 HMG.

1223 AGREEMENT BETWEEN THE SWISS CONFEDERATION AND THE EUROPEAN COMMUNITY ON MUTUAL RECOGNITION IN RELATION TO CONFORMITY ASSESSMENT („Abkommen zwischen der Schweizerischen Eidgenossenschaft und der Europäischen Gemeinschaft über die gegenseitige Anerkennung von Konformitätsbewertungen", AGA); GÄCHTER & BURCH (2013), p. 96 ff; and WILDHABER (2013), p. 31-32.

1224 Art. 45 *para.* 1 HMG.

1225 Art. 47 HMG; POLEDNA & VOKINGER (2013), p. 158; SPRECHER (2015), p. 116; and SWISSMEDIC (2016), *basic information on medical devices.*

1226 SPRECHER (2015), p. 116; STÖCKLI EGGENBERGER (2015), *recital* 15.125 ff.; and SWISSMEDIC (2016), *basic information on medical devices.*
The *"new and global approach"* describes the principle of a high degree of the manufacturers' self-responsibility and the internationally connected market supervision. Cf. e. g., GÄCHTER & BURCH (2013), p. 101; WILDHABER (2013), p. 10; and STÖCKLI EGGENBERGER (2015), *recital* 15.125.

Medical devices are accredited by non-governmental conformity assessment bodies.[1227] The assessment bodies are recognized by the SWISS ACCREDITATION AGENCY (SAS) and are designated and supervised by SWISSMEDIC. The assessment bodies evaluate compliance with the norms designated by SWISSMEDIC.[1228] For the relevant norms concerning CDx, the Swiss law refers to the EU Directives.[1229] The market placement of IVDs has to be reported to SWISSMEDIC.[1230] The result of a conformity assessment is the CE label.[1231]

ii. Regulation of LDTs in Switzerland

LDTs as well have to fulfill the requirements of the HMG and MepV. However, LDTs do not require a conformity assessment by a notified body, and they do not require reporting to SWISSMEDIC.[1232] The institution manufacturing the LDT has to self-assess the IVDs performance parameters.[1233] LDTs may not be offered for sale.[1234] SWISSMEDIC (2010) has published a dedicated information document on LDTs.

With its approach towards LDTs, Switzerland basically follows the IVD Directive's "in-house derogation" for LDTs.[1235]

iii. Impact of the revised EU legislation on Switzerland

The revision of the EU IVD Directive will require an adaption of the Swiss law. The most important change of the revision in the context of PM is the stricter regulation for CDx. For Switzerland, the revised IVD Directive does not automatically enter into force. The Swiss law has to be adapted accordingly.[1236] Due to the more precise approval requirements for high-risk products, the time and costs needed in or-

---

1227 Art. 46 HMG. In exemptions, for example in the case of an increased health hazard, the FEDERAL COUNCIL has the competence to make IVDs – of which CDx are a sub-category –subject to a special approval process. Art. 11 *para.* 1 *litera* a MepV.

1228 Art. 45 *para* 4 HMG.

1229 Art. 4 MepV and IVD Directive.

1230 Art. 6 *para.* 2 MepV.

1231 More details about the process in GÄCHTER & BURCH (2013), p. 126-127; SPRECHER (2015), p. 115-116; STÖCKLI EGGENBERGER (2015), *recital* 15.132 ff.

1232 Art. 6 *para.* 2bis MepV and Art. 8 *para.* 3 MepV, excluding the exemptions listed in *Annex* II of the IVD Directive.

1233 SWISSMEDIC (2010), p. 1 ff.

1234 Art. 17 *para.* 4 MepV.

1235 Art. 1 (5) IVD Directive.

1236 The needed revision of the Swiss law on medical devices will be elaborated by the SFOPH together with SWISSMEDIC, SECO and the FEDERAL DEPARTMENT FOR FOREIGN AFFAIRS, cf. SPRECHER (2015), p. 120; FASMED (2016)a, SFOPH, *Swissmedic und Seco arbeiten an Anpassung des Schweizer Rechts.*

der to receive a CE mark is estimated to double – representing a challenge for Swiss small and medium enterprises.[1237]

4.1.2 Analysis of incentives

The above analysis of the institutional setting governing the approval process of personalized pharmaceuticals and diagnostic components has shown, that the Swiss law is essentially harmonized with the EU regulation.

Thus, the same criticism[1238] and conclusion count for Switzerland: There is a separated, largely uncoordinated approval process for pharmaceuticals on the one hand, and diagnostic components on the other. Further, the existence of the regulatory derogation for LDTs undermines the current process and allows for regulatory exemptions for "home brew" tests. The incentives for the different stakeholders do not differ from the analysis made in the theoretical Part III.[1239]

Research institutions	*Pharmaceutical companies*	*Diagnostic companies*	*Providers*	*Patients*	*Payers*
–	negative	negative	–	–	–

negative = institutional setting incentivizes a player not to foster the translation of PM
– = neutral/no conclusive statement possible on a player's incentive to foster the translation of PM

4.1.3 Result

Consequentially, the hypothesis cannot be rejected for Switzerland:[1240] *Inconsistencies and gaps in the Swiss regulatory framework of the approval process for PM applications act as a barrier to the translation of personalized medicine into clinical practice.*

1237 Time in order to receive a CE mark is estimated to double from 1.5-3 to 6-8 years; costs from CHF 0.5-1 million to CHF 3 million, cf. FASMED (2017), *conference summary*.

1238 Cf. Part III, Chapter 4.1.2 i) IVD approval process in the EU, p. 135 ff. and 4.1.3 i) LDT regulation in the EU, p. 149 ff.

1239 Cf. Part III, Chapter 4.2.2 Analysis of incentives, p. 160 ff.

1240 Cf. Part III, Chapter 4.1.5 Analysis of incentives, p. 153 ff.

4.2 Incompatibility of clinical trials with personalized pharmaceuticals

4.2.1 Institutional setting

Clinical trials in Switzerland are governed by the LAW ON MEDICAL PRODUCTS (HMG) and the ORDINANCE ON CLINICAL TRIALS ON HUMAN RESEARCH (KlinV).[1241] The HMG sets the ground rules for protecting the patients involved in clinical trials.[1242] The ordinance details the rules for the requirements for clinical trials, the authorization and reporting process, the tasks of the competent ethics committee as well as the registration of clinical trials.[1243] Amongst other criteria, clinical trials have to be of scientific integrity[1244] and scientific quality.[1245]

Besides the mentioned rules, the Swiss institutional setting neither sets any regulations nor guidelines on trials in the context of PM. SWISSMEDIC (2012) published an information sheet concerning genetic tests –the document, however, does not contain any specific guidelines on the design of PM clinical trials.

Thus, the illustrated challenges in Part III[1246] to design and perform clinical trials for PM applications in the current trials setting do not stop at the Swiss border.

4.2.2 Analysis of incentives

With the above insights, the analysis of incentives does not differ from the analysis made in the theoretical in Part III.[1247]

1241 In German "Verordnung über klinische Versuche in der Humanforschung" (KLINV).

1242 Art. 53-56 HMG.

1243 Art. 3 HFG and Art. 1 KlinV. For details cf. e.g., STÖCKLI EGGENBERGER (2015), *recital* 15. p. 143 ff.

1244 Art. 3 KLINV.

1245 Art. 4 KLINV.

1246 Cf. Part III, Chapter 4.2 Incompatibility of clinical trials with personalized pharmaceuticals, p. 159 ff.

1247 Cf. Part III, Chapter 4.2.2 Analysis of incentives, p. 161.

Research institutions	*Pharmaceutical companies*	*Diagnostic companies*	*Providers*	*Patients*	*Payers*
–	negative	–	–	–	–

negative = institutional setting incentivizes a player not to foster the translation of PM
– = neutral/no conclusive statement possible on a player's incentive to foster the translation of PM

4.2.3 Result

The stated hypothesis[1248] must be upheld in the Swiss context: *The incompatibility of clinical trials with personalized medicine applications acts as a barrier to the translation of personalized medicine into Swiss clinical practice.*

[1248] Cf. Part III, Chapter 4.2.3 Resulting hypothesis, p. 161.

5 Barriers in the provision phase

5.1 Lack of healthcare providers' knowledge about personalized medicine

5.1.1 Institutional setting

i. Education of medical doctors in Switzerland

The main institutional mechanism influencing the lack of healthcare providers' knowledge about personalized medicine is education. The FEDERAL LAW ON MEDICAL PROFESSIONS sets the quality the quality standards for the university education, postgraduate training and the professional practice of medical doctors in Switzerland.[1249] Objectives of the education and further training are a. o. *"to provide comprehensive, individual and high-quality care for patients"*.[1250] The COMMISSION FOR MEDICAL PROFESSIONS of the FEDERAL OFFICE OF PUBLIC HEALTH consults the FEDERAL COUNCIL in its decisions regarding the medical education.[1251]

a) University education

The FEDERAL LAW ON MEDICAL PROFESSIONS states general objectives for the university education. For example one objective is the goal that graduates in human medicine are able to *"learn in the interdisciplinary collaboration with other professions"*, and to *"assess the effectiveness, appropriateness and effectiveness of the medical services they provide"*.[1252] The FEDERAL COUNCIL determines the content of the final federal exam needed to practice as doctor.[1253]

A SWISS CATALOGUE OF LEARNING OBJECTIVES (SCLO) for undergraduate medical training has been developed for all medical professions and represents the basis for the final federal exam.[1254] The SCLO contains two objectives directly related to PM. The catalogue states, that in case of a *"request for genetic counceling"* a physician must be able to assess a patient presenting approaching him/her in a well-structured way and must be able to propose appropriate diagnostic, therapeutic, social, preven-

[1249] Art. 1 *para* 1 and 3a Medizinalberufegesetz (MEDBG).
[1250] Art. 4 MEDBG.
[1251] Art. 50 MEDBG.
[1252] Art. 6 MEDBG.
[1253] Art. 13 MEDBG.
[1254] The legal basis is the ORDINANCE ON THE EXAM FOR MEDICAL PROFESSIONS. The Catalogue is accessible under http://sclo.smifk.ch/ (last visited April 16, 2017).

tive and other measures.[1255] Additionally, physicians must have some knowledge on an "overview level" in "genetics" in the pediatric context, meaning that he/she can roughly define the concepts behind and is able to recognize its possible relevance in a clinical situation.[1256] In the SCLO, there is no objective of e.g. a general awareness of existing drug-gene interactions, basic knowledge of medical genetics or medical statistics.

The universities have recognized the need for a *"new generation of clinicians"* who know *"how to handle biomedical data"*.[1257] The ETH has introduced a bachelor in medicine with a special focus on biomolecular and medical-technical aspects.[1258] The COMPETENCE CENTER FOR PERSONALIZED MEDICINE at the UNIVERSITY OF ZURICH and the ETH (CC-PM) offer an international PhD program for Molecular and Translational Biomedicine and plan to offer programs for bachelor and master students.[1259]

b) Further postgraduate training

After university education, graduates may choose a specialization to pursue. A medical title is a condition for a private practice. Currently, there are 44 different, accredited medical titles. Out of the 21'633 medical doctors in Switzerland, 21 have the medical title of "Medical genetics", representing less than one percent of the total physician population.[1260] With this comparably low number, it is questionable, if there are sufficient experts for medical genetics and thus PM in Switzerland.[1261]

[1255] P. 176 SCLO.
[1256] C PE 217-220 SCLO.
[1257] BEERENWINKEL cited in CC-PM (2017), *PhD MTB Program.*
[1258] ETH (2017)a.
[1259] CC-PM (2017), *PhD MTB Program.*
[1260] Data based on SFOPH (2016)d, *Rohdaten Eidg. Weiterbildungstitel MED 2016.*
[1261] E.g., MATYAS and HENGGELER interviewed 3rd of September, 2015.

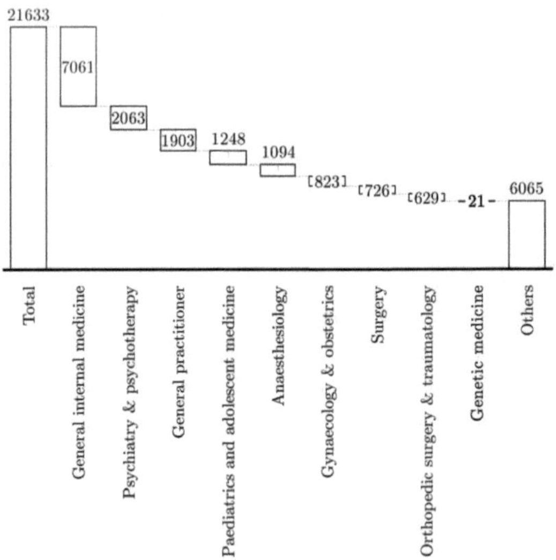

Figure 28: Distribution of medical titles of Swiss physicians

SOURCE: Data based on SFOPH (2016)d,
Rohdaten Eidg. Weiterbildungstitel MED 2016.

ii. Liability rules for medical doctors in Switzerland

It can be argued, that the liability rules for medical doctors act as a second institutional mechanism influencing the level of healthcare providers' knowledge about PM. An increasing liability risk for doctors with the use or non-use of PM,[1262] may correspondingly increase their level of knowledge in risk-averse doctors.

A medical doctor has to meet a certain standard of care – the professional duties are listed in the MEDBG.[1263] Swiss doctors have to *"practice their profession carefully and conscientiously"*, and adhere to the limits of the competencies they have acquired in the context of their education and postgraduate training. A doctor bears civil liability, if there is a causal link between the damage for the patient and a behavior in breach of a doctor's duty. A breach of duty is given, if the doctor's treatment or approach does not comply with the general state-of-the-art of medical practice (*"lege ar-*

1262 For Switzerland: GÄCHTER & VOKINGER (2012), p. 968; and ECKHARDT ET AL. (2014), p. 199-200. For Germany: HUSTER & GOTTWALD (2012), and MÜLLER & SCHÄFER in WIENKE ET AL. (2013). For the US: WONG ET AL. (2010), p. 47 ff.; and EHMANN ET AL. (2015), p. 8.

1263 Art. 40 MEDBG.

tis"). A breach of duty can be, if a doctor refrained from an indicated treatment or if a doctor treated a patient incorrectly.[1264]

The legal questions are: Who is responsible for choosing a personalized treatment and for performing the corresponding genetic test? Is it the medical doctor, a pharmacologist, or an expert in medical genetics? As demonstrated in the previous *paragraph i)*, the availability of trained medical genetic counselors is limited in Switzerland. Therefore, the responsibility of primary care physicians to ensure that genetic information is interpreted correctly and utilized appropriately is likely to increase, and the challenges through the option of a personalized treatment bring additional responsibilities to a physician. If the methods of PM will scientifically prevail in clinical practice and will become "general state of the art of medical practice", a doctor in Switzerland is obliged to perform a genetic test with a given indication, to interpret the results and to choose adequate medical measures.[1265] Outside Switzerland, the legal debate already exists over whether genomic interpretation should be deemed the practice of medicine.[1266]

In Switzerland several drug labels contain pharmacogenetic information.[1267] Is a doctor now liable in a case of adverse events without having screened for individual suitability of the drug? In Switzerland, this question remains – to the knowledge of the author – unresolved.

1264 Art. 398, 97 and 41 OR. More about the liability of doctors e.g., in BÜCHLER & MICHEL (2014), p. 181 ff.

1265 GÄCHTER & VOKINGER (2012), p. 968; and ECKHARDT ET AL. (2014), p. 199-200.

1266 Cf. EHMANN ET AL. (2015); and MESSNER ET AL. (2016).

1267 Cf. www.pharmgkb.org/view/drug-labels.do with a list of drugs for which genetic testing is required/recommended for the e US FOOD AND DRUG ADMINISTRATION, EUROPEAN MEDICINES AGENCY, PHARMACEUTICALS AND MEDICAL DEVICES AGENCY OF JAPAN and HEALTH CANADA (SANTÉ CANADA). The corresponding Swiss labels can be retrieved from compendium.ch of the labels of the corresponding Swiss (last visited June 17, 2017).

5.1.2 Analysis of incentives

The two identified institutional mechanisms do not positively influence the knowledge of healthcare providers in Switzerland:

Medical education in Switzerland shows gaps and potential for improvement in order to foster the translation of PM. The SAMS found *„striking knowledge gaps in simple about simple statistical and epidemiological principles"* among physicians in Switzerland.[1268]

Liability rules in Switzerland follow the "lege artis" approach. As long as PM cannot be counted as "general state-of-the-art of medical practice", doctors are not liable despite not choosing a personalized approach in cases where a patient would benefit from a personalized treatment.

The overview below shows the resulting incentives through a lack of *healthcare providers'* knowledge about personalized medicine in Switzerland.

Research institutions	*Pharmaceutical companies*	*Diagnostic companies*	*Providers*	*Patients*	*Payers*
–	negative	negative	negative	negative	–

negative = institutional setting incentivizes a player not to foster the translation of PM
– = neutral/no conclusive statement possible on a player's incentive to foster the translation of PM

5.1.3 Result

With the presented institutional setting, this thesis follows the argumentation in Part III[1269] and upholds the initial hypothesis for Switzerland: *The lack of healthcare providers' knowledge about personalized medicine acts as a barrier to the translation of personalized medicine into Swiss clinical practice.*

1268 SAMS (2012), p. 19.

1269 Cf. Part III, Chapter 5.1.2 Analysis of incentives, p. 164 and 5.1.3 Resulting hypothesis, p. 166.

5.2 Lack of patients' awareness and understanding of personalized medicine

5.2.1 Institutional setting

In Switzerland, there are several institutional mechanisms influencing the patients' awareness and understanding of personalized medicine. Examples are information through the patients' healthcare providers, public health campaigns, public panel discussions and conferences, media or reimbursement incentives for patients – all separately presented in the following.

Information by healthcare providers

As illustrated in the last Chapter 5.1, the healthcare providers' knowledge about personalized medicine in Switzerland may be limited itself. This is correspondingly transferred to the patients, as healthcare providers act as primary information channel for patients.

Public health campaigns

An additional source of information for patients is the SWISS FOUNDATION FOR THE PROMOTION OF HEALTH. The foundation has the legal mandate to identify, support and evaluate measures to support health and avoid disease.[1270] Despite the foundation's strategic goal of health promotion and prevention, no reference is made of PM.[1271]

Open debates

Also, Swiss universities do provide a range of public *panel discussions and conferences* through which citizens and journalists can learn from experts and participate in the current discussions.[1272]

[1270] Art. 19 KVG.

[1271] For example in Zürich only: The public discussion rounds of the interdisciplinary lecture series by the University and ETH Zürich about *"Personalized Medicine: Hope or empty promise?"*, December 19th, 2013, the ETH mind set Event avout the *"Upcoming revolution in digital health"*, June 18, 2015, or the ETH LATSIS Forum on June 29th, 2016. Others to come: http://www.cc-pm.uzh.ch/de/news/ss.html.

[1272] A screening of the foundation's homepage (gesundheitsfoerderung.ch) and annual reports from the past five years for "personalized" or "genetic" medicine led to no results. Last update on April 23, 2017.

Media

Probably the most effective institution reaching the broad public in Switzerland is media. The SWISS CONSTITUTION holds that publicly funded radio and television a. o. *"shall contribute to education"* and are obliged to produce programs of educational value.[1273] A systematic search through the contents of the SWISS BROADCASTING CORPORATION (SRG SSR) found that PM is a covered and discussed topic in Swiss public media, but has recently been lost attentetion.[1274]

Private media exhibit a similar trend: The topic of personalized medicine has started to gain attention after 2006, but has recently experienced a decline of media coverage:

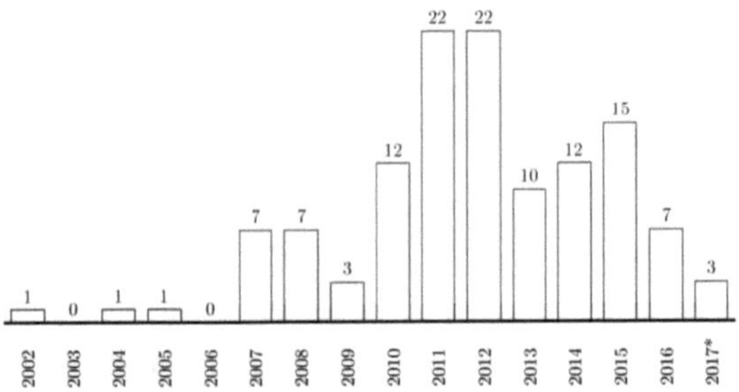

Figure 29: Media coverage of personalized medicine in Switzerland

SOURCE: FACTIVA (2017)

Search based on representative German magazines NEUE ZÜRCHER ZEITUNG, NZZ AM SONNTAG, TAGESANZEIGER and SONNTAGSZEITUNG with keywords „personalisierte Medizin" or „genetische Medizin" or „stratifizierte Medizin".

* updated April 30, 2017

Reimbursement schemes

In the context of PM, academic literature discusses, if patients should be incentivized through reimbursement rules to demand more PM.[1275]

The results of a presymptomatic test may identify certain disease risks for a person. Should solidarity still pay for that individual in case of a disease, in which a pa-

1273 Art. 93 CONSTITUTION, Art. 24 RTVG.

1274 A search on www.srf.ch with the key words "personalisierte Medizin", "genetische Medizin", "stratifizierte Medizin" (German only) found 19 entries directly related to PM in the last five years, only two of them published in 2016/2017 (until April 23, 2017, last visit of page).

1275 Cf. *note* 978.

tient did not allow to test a disease risk at all, or in which patients did not undertake the respective preventive measures in order to avoid the disease?[1276] If a payer was not obliged to reimburse the costs due to the disease in both of the above cases, patients would be incentivized to choose the respective tests and preventive measures.

In Switzerland, the SWISS FEDERAL LAW ON THE GENERAL PART OF THE SOCIAL SECURITY LAW (ATSG) knows the duty to minimize damages – which is also valid for patients requesting reimbursement under the SWISS FEDERAL LAW ON BASIC SICKNESS INSURANCE (KVG).[1277] The duty to minimize damages reflects self-responsibility and obliges a person to choose adequate and reasonable measures in order to avoid an incurred or threatening damage.[1278] A genetic test could help to avoid costs incurred through a disease.[1279] Further, information asymmetries between the insurer and the insuree are limited: The ATSG contains the duty to provide information needed for the assessment or sizing of the claim in order to receive any payment from a Swiss social insurance.[1280]

However, there is a field of tension between the interests for reducing information asymmetries in an insurance relationship and a person's privacy interests. Article 18 of the LAW ON GENETIC TESTS ON HUMANS (GUMG) states the non-mandatory character of genetic tests which has to be upheld in any case. The law contains an explicit prohibition: Insurance institutions are not allowed to request any presymptomatic or prenatal genetic tests as a prerequisite of an insurance contract.[1281] Further, such an obligation would infringe the "right not to know".[1282]

Thus, under the current law in Switzerland, a de-facto obligation for genetic tests through reimbursement incentives in the mandatory health insurance would be unlawful.[1283]

1276 E.g., WIENKE ET AL. (2013), p. 88, in this context, are talking about "paternalistic nudges" to choose genetic testing.

1277 Art. 21 ATSG, NOVENTA (2014), *note* 121.

1278 NOVENTA (2014), *note* 121.

1279 Art. 6 and 18 GUMG, and cf. the following Chapter 5.5.1 Institutional setting, *3. The „right not to know"*, p. 253.

1280 Art. 28 ATSG.

1281 Art. 26 GUMG.

1282 Cf. Chapter 5.5.1 Institutional setting, *3. The „right not to know"*, p. 253.

1283 However, the same argumentation does not count for the non-mandatory health insurance in Switzerland. Cf. discussion in Chapter 6.1.1 Institutional setting, *Reimbursement for PM Dx by the Swiss supplementary health insurance*, p. 271.

5.2.2 Analysis of incentives

The above illustrations have analyzed institutional mechanisms influencing the patients' awareness and understanding of PM. However, information through healthcare providers, public initiatives, and media seem to be limited. Further, no reimbursement incentives confront patients with the decision to choose or not to choose PM.[1284] Currently, PM is a topic mainly discussed in academic circles. It is debatable whether these limited initiatives reach the broad public. The analysis in Part IV did not find any evidence in Switzerland's institutional setting indicating that the incentives differ from the analysis in the theoretical Part III.

Research institutions	*Pharmaceutical companies*	*Diagnostic companies*	*Providers*	*Patients*	*Payers*
–	negative	negative	negative	negative	negative

negative = institutional setting incentivizes a player not to foster the translation of PM
– = neutral/no conclusive statement possible on a player's incentive to foster the translation of PM

5.2.3 Result

The hypothesis proposed in Part III must be upheld: *The lack of patients' awareness and understanding of personalized medicine acts as a barrier to the translation of personalized medicine into Swiss clinical practice.*

5.3 Lack of consistent, recognized and clinically implemented guidelines for personalized medicine

5.3.1 Institutional setting

"Genetics in everyday clinical practice" published by the SWISS ACADEMY FOR MEDICAL SCIENCES are central guidelines concerning genetic applications in Switzerland. The guidelines introduce a practitioner into genetics, describe some genetic diseases, provide an overview on how to perform genetic analyses, and list legal and ethical foundations when performing genetic analyses. The guidelines recommend the use of genotyping only for therapies with a limited therapeutic potential or a risk for se-

[1284] Cf. Chapter 6.1 Lack of reimbursement for personalized medicine diagnostics, p. 182 ff.

vere, genetically determined adverse events.[1285] The guidelines are rather critical towards the use of pharmacogenetics due to a *"lack of prospective studies"*. However, they underline the future importance of pharmacogenetics.[1286] The guidelines stem from 2011. In the meantime costs of a full-genome-sequencing have fallen below USD 1000[1287] and it is questionable if the guidelines are still up to date.

In addition, the SWISS SOCIETY FOR MEDICAL GENETICS refers to some links on genetic reporting, informed consent and the reimbursement of genetic analyses, but the society does not refer to guidelines for the application of PM.[1288] Besides, Swiss literature in the field of PM refers to existing guidelines like PHARMGKB or CPIC.[1289]

In Switzerland, the application of genetic knowledge and PM is rather *discipline driven* – meaning that specialists use the relevant genetic tests if they are reimbursed[1290] – and *research driven* via the centers for medical genetics at the universities.[1291]

5.3.2 Analysis of incentives

Besides the existing initiatives presented in Part III,[1292] Switzerland knows no additional, dedicated guidelines for personalized treatments incentivizing practitioners to apply PM in everyday clinical practice. Thus, the argumentation as presented in the theoretical Part III, Chapter 5.3.4 stays valid.[1293]

1285 ANTONARAKIS ET AL. (2011), p. 51.

1286 *Ibidem.*

1287 Cf. *note* 269.

1288 Cf. http://sgmg.ch/?page_id=7329 (last visited April 12, 2017).

1289 E.g., TAEGTMEYER (2012), p. 811; and SZUCS (2015)a, p. 11.

1290 For example, a specialist of HIV tests the HLA composition of a patient before using Abacavir. Or a gynecologist performs genetic analyses in certain cases of breast or ovarian cancer, e.g., BÜRKI (2015). For reimbursement of PM Dx in Switzerland, cf. Chapter 6.1.1 Institutional setting, p. 261 ff.

1291 Cf. for example *Zürich*: www.medgen.uzh.ch, *Basel:* www.unispital-basel.ch/das-universitaets spital/bereiche/medizinische-querschnittsfunktionen/kliniken-institute-abteilungen/medizinische-genetik/, *Bern:* www.dkf.unibe.ch/forschung/forschungsgruppen/humangenetik/index_ger.html, *CHUV:* www.chuv.ch/laboratoires/dl-laboratoires-genetique.htm, *Lausannee*: https://applications pub.unil.ch/interpub/noauth/php/Un/UnUnite.php?UnId=136&LanCode=37, *Geneva:* www.med gen.unige.ch/ (last visited August 20, 2017).

1292 Cf. Part III, Chapter 5.3.2 Overview of existing guideline sources, p. 169 ff.

1293 Cf. Part III, Chapter 5.3.4 Analysis of incentives, p. 172 and Chapter 5.3.5 Resulting hypothesis, p. 173.

Research institutions	*Pharmaceutical companies*	*Diagnostic companies*	*Providers*	*Patients*	*Payers*
–	–	negative	negative	negative	negative

negative = institutional setting incentivizes a player not to foster the translation of PM
– = neutral/no conclusive statement possible on a player's incentive to foster the translation of PM

5.3.3 Result

With this finding, the hypothesis must be upheld for Switzerland: *The lack of consistent, recognized and clinically implemented guidelines for PM acts as a barrier to the translation of personalized medicine into Swiss clinical practice.*

5.4 Lack of infrastructure for the implementation of personalized medicine

5.4.1 Institutional setting

Healthcare system based on federalism

The SWISS CONSTITUTION contains the *principle of subsidiarity.* According to this principle, the higher political instance may only overtake a certain task in case the lower is not able to. The federal government is only responsible in the areas stated in the CONSTITUTION. Cantons are given a maximum degree of sovereignty and healthcare is one of the responsibilities left to the Cantons.

In line with the principle of subsidiarity, the health system in Switzerland is based on federalism with the federal government simply providing the conditions for it. Within these conditions, Cantons may build their health system autonomously.[1294]

The federalistic structure has the effect, that the Swiss healthcare landscape is characterized by a relatively high degree of diversity and complexity with each Canton having an own healthcare strategy and structure.[1295] Another effect is that each hospital has its own infrastructure and IT systems. Switzerland does not know a countrywide, harmonized approach of saving and transferring patient information. The Swiss federalism in healthcare negatively affects the exchange of data and in-

1294 Art. 5a SWISS CONSTITUTION; and ACHTERMANN & BERSET (2006), *chapter 2.2.*
1295 A comprehensive overview provide ACHTERMANN & BERSET (2006).

creases the administrative work. There are different IT-systems, EHRs, CDSs and processes increase the time needed for acquiring a patient's health history.[1296] Swiss doctors are increasingly faced with administrative tasks – capturing ca. two thirds of their time. They spend only one third of their time with patients – a share being expected to further decrease.[1297]

Strategy e-health Switzerland

In 2007, the FEDERAL COUNCIL adopted the *"Strategy 'e-health' Switzerland"*.[1298] The strategy paper admitted Switzerland's backlog concerning electronic health systems and services.[1299] Five years later, an evaluation showed mixed results in the target achievement with roughly half of the targets not being reached.[1300] The elaboration of a e-health strategy 2.0 started in spring 2017.[1301]

Core piece of the strategy was the introduction of an electronic patient file ("elektronisches Patientendossier, EPD) until 2015.[1302] The introduction original plan was delayed by three years. In 2015 the LAW FOR THE ELECTRONIC PATIENT FILE (EPDG) was passed, and the introduction of the EPD is planned to happen in mid2018.[1303] The EPD is a *"virtual file with data that was decentrally stored from a patient's medical history or submitted by the patient himself and that is accessible in case of a concrete treatment"*.[1304] For a patient the participation in the EPD is optional. Stationary healthcare providers (hospitals etc.) have to participate in the EPD system, but for ambulatory healthcare providers (doctors, pharmacies, etc.) the offering of the EPD is not mandatory.[1305]

The introduction of the EPD bears criticism. Besides the voluntary nature of the EPD, there remain questions about the interoperability of IT-systems in hospitals, pharmacies and medical practices or ambiguities about the financing of the project.[1306] However, the main criticism relevant for this thesis is its format: The EPD, so far,

---

1296 Statement stemming from several conversations with Swiss doctors by the author and BLASER and STUPP at the Latsis Symposium ETH Zurich on Personalized Medicine, June 29, 2016.

1297 Cf. B. MEYER, ROHNER, GOLDER, & LONGCHAMP (2016), p. 6, 35% fully educated doctors, 29% assistant doctors; with similar results WENGER ET AL. (2017).

1298 SFOPH (2007); SCHMID (2015), p. 68-69.

1299 EHEALTH SUISSE (2012). Also other sources criticized the shortcoming of Switzerland concerning patient data, e.g., BRACHER (2013), *na*.

1300 SFOPH (2007), p. 27 ff.

1301 EHEALTH SUISSE (2017)b, *na*.

1302 SFOPH (2007), p. 27 ff.

1303 EHEALTH SUISSE (2017)a, *na*.

1304 Art. 2 *lit.* a EPDG, *translated by the author*.

1305 Art. 25 EPDG.

1306 E.g., HEHLI (2017), *na*.

does not offer the possibility to save a patient's genetic data and to directly connect it to a patient's prescribed medicines. The EPD can be compared to a simple PDF-folder, that can be accessed from different parties. However, the EPD does not support the representation of genomic data in a comprehensible and clinically actionable format.[1307] Also, it is criticized that there is no directive on the EPD's interoperability.[1308] Thus, from a translational perspective for PM, the EPD is no progress in its currently planned format.

Swiss Personalized Health Network

The SWISS PERSONALIZED HEALTH NETWORK (SPHN) is the most central initiative concerning Switzerland's infrastructure for personalized medicine. The initiative is not only relevant in the discovery phase with the goal of making clinical data to become accessible for research,[1309] it also aims to apply bioinformatics methodologies to the point of care, and to provide support in the provision phase (i.e., the support with diagnoses, the anticipation of risks, the adaption of therapies, or the monitoring of patients).[1310]

In an initial phase the initiative targets universities and university hospitals with patient data, but in the longer term, other hospitals, disease registries, patients and healthy citizens may be involved. The initiative shall build the conditions for Switzerland being able to establish itself nationally and internationally in the field of personalized health.[1311] The initiative aims to bundle competences (e.g., bioinformatics), methods (e.g., omics-technologies) with infrastructure (e.g., existing biobanks). This process has already started bottom-up.[1312]

Other initiatives creating infrastructure

Besides the two publicly supported initiatives SPHN and the EPD, other initiatives strengthen the infrastructure for PM in Switzerland.

1307 HAFEN at the ETH mindset *"Upcoming Revolution Digital Health"*, 18th of June, 2015. Cf. for potential solutions PETERSON ET AL. (2013).

1308 BARBIÉ (2016), p. 9.

1309 Cf. description of the SPHN in Chapter 2.1.1 Institutional setting, *National institutions*, p. 219 ff.

1310 Cf. BARBIÉ (2016), p. 2 and 19.

1311 Cf. MEIER-ABT in MEIER-ABT & EGLI (2016), p. 2.

1312 The LAC LEMAN CENTER FOR PERSONALIZED HEALTH has formed itself among the CENTRE HOSPITALIER UNIVERSITAIRE VADOIS, the GENEVA UNIVERSITY HOSPITALS, the EPFL and the UNIVERSITIES OF GENEVA, LAUSANNE and BERN. Zürich has a COMPETENCE CENTER FOR PERSONALIZED MEDICINE consisting of the collaboration between the ETH, UNIVERSITY OF ZÜRICH, and the UNIVERSITY HOSPITAL. The PERSONALIZED HEALTH PLATFORM BASEL will be associated to Zürich. Cf. MEIER-ABT & EGLI (2016), p. 2-3.

One of them is MIDATA.GOV, an open innovation platform allowing people to *"store, manage and control access to their personal data by helping them to establish and own national/regional not-for-profit MIDATA cooperatives".*[1313] Members can contribute to medical research and clinical trials by providing access to sets of their personal data via the cooperative.

Another one is the PRACTICE FOR PERSONALISED MEDICINE at KLINIK HIRSLANDEN, where patients can book a pharmacogenetic analysis that helps them to provide an individually tailored drug regime.[1314]

Also locally at hospitals and universities, infrastructure is being created.[1315] The BBMRI will create a central web-based catalogue of existing and de novo biobanks with data and samples' access policies.[1316]

Besides, several foreign DTC companies are collecting data from Swiss citizens.[1317] These data, however, collections do not contribute to Switzerland's infrastructure.

5.4.2 Analysis of incentives

Switzerland's federalistic healthcare system complicates the establishment of common, country-wide infrastructure. Currently, Switzerland is lacking an infrastructure supporting the implementation of PM. With these findings, the argumentation of the theoretical analysis in Part III, Chapter 5.4.2 holds true for this chapter.[1318]

Research institutions	*Pharmaceutical companies*	*Diagnostic companies*	*Providers*	*Patients*	*Payers*
negative	negative	negative	negative	negative	–

negative = institutional setting incentivizes a player not to foster the translation of PM
– = neutral/no conclusive statement possible on a player's incentive to foster the translation of PM

[1313] Cf. https://midata.coop/ (last visited June 17, 2017).

[1314] E.g., at the UNIVERSITY HOSPITAL ZÜRICH infrastructure is being created – the data is kept locally and not in a cloud solution, according to MOCH at the ETH LATSIS Forum on June 29th, 2016.

[1315] Cf. https://www.hirslanden.ch/global/en/home/hospitals_and_centres/centers_and_institutes/zuerich/praxis_fuer_personalisiertemedizin.html (last visited June 17, 2017).

[1316] Cf. BBMRI.CH (2017).

[1317] For more about DTCs, cf. RESEARCH CONCEPT, Chapter 8.3 *Out of scope:* Direct-to-consumer tests (DTCs), p. 29 ff.

[1318] Cf. Part III, Chapter 5.4.2 Analysis of incentives, p. 176 ff.

However, with the SWISSBIOBANKING platform, the SWISS PERSONALIZED HEALTH NETWORK and the developments of the EPD, this barrier is expected to be lowered in the future.

5.4.3 Results

The hypothesis proposed in Part III must be upheld:[1319] *The lack of infrastructure for the implementation of personalized medicine acts as a barrier to the translation of personalized medicine into Swiss clinical practice.*

5.5 Privacy concerns regarding the use of personalized medicine

5.5.1 Institutional setting

This chapter analyses the institutional setting governing privacy protection of genetic data in Switzerland. It influences the privacy concerns regarding the use of PM.

The LAW ON HUMAN RESEARCH (HFG) as well as the LAW ON GENETIC TESTS ON HUMANS (GUMG)[1320] lay out the ground rules for the protection of genetic data in Switzerland. Additionally, all regulations relevant in the healthcare context generally apply, like for example the SWISS LAW ON DATA PROTECTION (DSG), the SWISS CRIMINAL CODE (StGB) or the CONVENTION ON HUMAN RIGHTS AND BIOMEDICINE.[1321] Also international medical soft law like the INTERNATIONAL DECLARATION ON HUMAN GENETIC DATA or the WORLD MEDICAL ASSOCIATION'S DECLARATION OF TAIPEI ON ETHICAL CONSIDERATIONS REGARDING HEALTH DATABASES AND BIOBANKS influences the Swiss legislation.[1322]

In Switzerland, genetic data are seen as *"particularly sensitive"*[1323] and therefore enjoy a special level of protection. The societal practice of treating genetic data as dif-

[1319] Cf. Part III, Chapter 5.4.3 Results, p. 177 ff.

[1320] In German "HUMANFORSCHUNGSGESETZ" (HFG) and „BUNDESGESETZ ÜBER GENETISCHE UNTERSUCHUNGEN BEIM MENSCHEN" (GUMG).

[1321] CONVENTION FOR THE PROTECTION OF HUMAN RIGHTS AND DIGNITY OF THE HUMAM BEING WITH REGARD TO THE APPLICATION OF BIOLOGY AND MEDICINE.

[1322] Cf. MOLNÁR-GÁBOR (2012), p. 696 ff., on *international medical soft law* on genetic sequencing. One of their finding is that the international soft law faces the *„impossibility of keeping up promptly with the human genetic developments"* and does not have *„satisfactory answers in the context of new possibilities for genetic examinations"* (translated by the author).

[1323] Art. 3 *para.* 2c DSG.

ferent from other types of health data for the purposes of assessing privacy and security protection is also known as *"genetic exceptionalism"*.[1324]

The GUMG increases the level of protection of human genetic information compared to the general privacy and data protection. The GUMG intends to protect human dignity and the personality. It aims to prevent the abuse of genetic testing and the misuse of genetic data; and it aims to ensure the quality of the genetic testing and the interpretation of its results.[1325] It contains the non-discrimination principle, rules about informed consent and self-determination, the "right not to know", the protection of genetic data and rules for the performance of genetic tests.[1326] The GUMG only covers germline DNA; currently not covered by the GUMG are somatic mutations.[1327] Additionally, the GUMG is not applicable for research purposes.[1328]

The following points illustrate the ground rules of the Swiss law concerning privacy issues related to PM:

1. The principle of non-discrimination

In Switzerland, any form of discrimination on grounds of the genetic heritage is prohibited.[1329] The non-discrimination principle between private persons concerns discrimination due to genetic material. However, it does not concern health risks in general.[1330] The principle is valid in state-private as well as in private relationships.[1331] It does also count for the establishment of employment, insurance contracts or for the calculations of damages in the liability insurance.

1324 SOINI (2012), p. 143 ff., gives an overview on how major transnational and national legislations (EU, Austria, France, Germany, Norway, Portugal, Spain, Sweden and Switzerland) treat genetic data. BRÄM & SZUCS (2016), p. 4, are discussing *"genetic exceptionalism"* in the Swiss context.

1325 Art. 2 GUMG.

1326 GÄCHTER & VOKINGER (2012), p. 966 ff.; and BÜCHLER & MICHEL (2014), p. 303 ff. ECKHARDT ET AL. (2014), p. 126-127, provide a tabular overview on GUMG.

1327 However, the D-GUMG is likely to change this and will also address somatic biomarkers, cf., Subchapter "The current revision of the LAW ON GENETIC TESTS ON HUMANS (GUMG)", p. 256 f.

1328 Art. 1 *para.* 3 GUMG. Genetic examinations for research purposes are governed by the HMG, cf. Chapter 4.2.1, Institutional setting, p. 234 ff.

1329 Art. 8 para. 2 SWISS CONSTITUTION and Art. 4 GUMG and Art. 11 CONVENTION ON HUMAN RIGHTS AND BIOMEDICINE; cf. also ECKHARDT ET AL. (2014), p. 120 ff.

1330 ECKHARDT ET AL. (2014), p. 123.

1331 BÜCHLER & MICHEL (2014), p. 303; and ECKHARDT ET AL. (2014), p. 1223.

An *employer* in Switzerland is not allowed to request any presymptomatic genetic information. Neither may an employer request existing information nor is an employer allowed to perform a genetic test. [1332]

Neither does the Swiss law allow *insurance companies* to request presymptomatic or pre-natal genetic examinations in order to conclude the insurance contract.[1333] But if there are already some results from earlier presymptomatic testing available, a private health insurer may ask for disclosure of those previous genetic tests. These genetic testing results need to be reliable from a technical and clinical perspective, and the scientific value of the test needs to be guaranteed for the calculation of the insurance rate. Additionally, doctors are restricted from disclosing the results of specific disorders. They can only inform the insurer that the policy taker falls into a particular risk group.[1334] However, the Swiss health insurers do currently have a "gentleman's agreement" stating that the question regarding previously conducted genetic tests is not asked. Practically, every Swiss citizen would have to indicate that he or she has already done at least one genetic test: the test for the own blood group.[1335]

Last, the GUMG contains a general prohibition of presymptomatic genetic examinations for the purpose of calculations of risks in the liability insurance.[1336]

With its regulation, Switzerland follows article 12 of the BIOMEDICINE CONVENTION. The convention allows genetic tests *"only for health purposes or for scientific research linked to health purposes"*, and not for the evaluation of risk.[1337]

Legal scholars hypothesize that – due to the non-discrimination principle – a contract may be void, if it ex- or includes a person with a specific genetic variation from access to service.[1338] Following this interpretation, not only insurance or employment contracts, but *any other contract* would be void if it discriminates somebody based on the person's genetic information.

[1332] Art. 21 ff. GUMG with some exemptions for healthcare providers facing the risk of an occupational disease.

[1333] Art. 26 GUMG, followed by Art. 27 GUMG containing some financial limits for *life insurance* sums, above which presymptomatic tests results may be requested.

[1334] Art. 27 with exemptions and Art. 28 GUMG with some limitations and precautionary measures in order not to infringe a person's *"right not to know"*. Cf. also BRÄM & SZUCS (2016), p. 2, with more details on the discussion, if previous DTCs have to be disclosed to an insurance company.

[1335] SZUCS at the Latsis Symposium ETH Zurich on PM, June 29, 2016; and BRÄM & SZUCS (2016), p. 7.

[1336] Art. 29 and 30 GUMG.

[1337] Art. 12 CONVENTION ON HUMAN RIGHTS AND BIOMEDICINE and BRÄM & SZUCS (2016), p. 3.

[1338] GÄCHTER & VOKINGER (2012), p. 967.

2. The right of self-determination

Genetic examinations of humans may only be performed for a medical reason and under full reserve to the right of self-determination.[1339] The right of self-determination is codified in national as well as international law.[1340] It allows people to lead their own lives based on their own values and according to their own personality. For example, it has to be tolerated if a person takes a decision that may lead to a worse health condition or a shorter life.[1341]

The right of self-determination in the context of PM does not only concern a patient's consent for genetic examinations, but also the protection of the genetic data as such:

According to the SWISS CONSTITUTION *"every person has the right to privacy in their private and family life and in their home, and in relation to their mail and telecommunications"*. Further, *"every person has the right to be protected against the misuse of their personal data"*.[1342] In its current wording, the CONSTITUTION only protects against the *"misuse"* of personal data meaning that a person has the burden of proof in case of a misuse.[1343] Legal experts agree that the formulation of the second passage is unfortunate.[1344] The passage should protect a person from any disadvantage through the use of personal data. However, the Swiss courts follow a broader interpretation of the passage going beyond the protection against "misuse". In its case law, the FEDERAL COURT OF JUSTICE has developed the right for *"informational self-determination"*.[1345] VISCHER (2014) has submitted – the currently still pending – parliamentary initiative aiming to explicitly formulate the right of "informational self-determination" in the CONSTITUTION.

3. The „right not to know“

National[1346] as well as international law[1347] contain the *"right not to know"*. It represents an informational defense right and is part of the *right of self-determination*. It states that every person has the right to decide freely if he or she wants to know or

[1339] Art. 10 GUMG.
[1340] Art. 10 *para.* 2 and Art. 13 SWISS CONSTITUTION; Art. 8 EUROPEAN CONVENTION.
[1341] ECKHARDT ET AL. (2014), p. 92-93.
[1342] Art. 13 SWISS CONSTITUTION.
[1343] HOFMANN (2014), p. 2.
[1344] SCHWEIZER and SCHEFER cited in HOFMANN (2014), p. 2.
[1345] HOFMANN (2014), p. 2.
[1346] Art. 6 GUMG.
[1347] Art. 5 CONVENTION ON HUMAN RIGHTS AND BIOMEDICINE; Art. 5 CONVENTION ON HUMAN RIGHTS AND BIOMEDICINE or Art. 8 EUROPEAN CONVENTION ON HUMAN RIGHTS.

not to know about the results of a genetic test and to determine the use of the collected data. The genetic constitution of a person represents an inviolable sphere of the protection of a person's personality.[1348]

However, there are limitations to the "right not to know". If there is immediate physical avertable danger for a person, the person has to be informed about the finding.[1349] This is also the case, if a genetic examination leads incidentally to a positive finding for which was not explicitly screened for – a so-called "incidentalome".[1350] Moreover, there are exemptions from the "right not to know", if a genetic examination was ordered by a court or an authority.[1351]

Also consanguineous relatives have the "right not to know".[1352] However, if the healthcare provider considers the information of cognates as indispensable – e.g., in the case of an avertable danger for the cognates – and if the patient does not give his permission to tell them, release from professional confidentiality has to be requested by the treating medical doctor at the respective cantonal authority.[1353] The question is, how this right can be fully enforced in practice.[1354] Especially, if related persons share their genetic data in the internet or other media, cognates currently have no legal possibility to object.[1355]

4. The requirement of an "informed consent"

The concept of „informed consent“ is a central element in healthcare law.[1356] Examinations and treatments are only allowed after a patient has been informed sufficiently and has given his or her consent.[1357] A patient's consent can be withdrawn anytime in any form.[1358]

[1348] GÄCHTER & VOKINGER (2012), p. 966; TAG (2012), p. 835, BÜCHLER & MICHEL (2014), p. 303; ECKHARDT ET AL. (2014), p. 99; and HOLLENSTEIN (2014), *note* 1 ff.

[1349] Art. 18 *para.* 2 GUMG.

[1350] Cf. *note* 179.

[1351] Art. 32 and 33 GUMG, also BÜCHLER & MICHEL (2014), p. 304.

[1352] Cf. BÜCHLER & MICHEL (2014), p. 304.

[1353] Cf. Art. 19 *para.* 3 and 321 *para.* 2 StGB; BÜCHLER & MICHEL (2014), p. 307; and ECKHARDT ET AL. (2014), p. 99-101. ECKHARDT ET AL. (2014) identify the need for discussion, to what extent cognates should be protected from genetic data published in the internet by their relatives.

[1354] Cf. BÜCHLER & MICHEL (2014), p. 304.

[1355] ECKHARDT ET AL. (2014), p. 272. There are scholars pleading for a ban on publication of own genetic data.

[1356] Art. 5 GUMG, Art. 8 *para.* 2 HFG and Art. 5 CONVENTION ON HUMAN RIGHTS AND BIOMEDICINE.

[1357] GÄCHTER & VOKINGER (2012), p. 966, on the elements of the duty to inform and the criminal consequences if neglected.

[1358] Art. 3 GUMG. More on the informed consent in GUMG in BÜCHLER & MICHEL (2014), p. 303-304.

Already the *storage of genetic data* requires a person's explicit consent as genetic data is treated as "particularly sensitive" data by Swiss law.[1359] The technical and organizational details for the storage of data in clinical trials is regulated in the LAW ON THERAPEUTIC PRODUCTS (HMG) and detailed out in ORDINANCE ON CLINICAL TRIALS ON HUMAN RESEARCH (KlinV).[1360]

Genetic data is usually systematically stored in registers or biobanks. Besides the registration of clinical trials[1361] and the provisions in the HMG and KlinV, biobanks do not have a particular institutional regulation in Switzerland.[1362]

Every *further use of genetic data* beyond the original use for which a patient has given his or her consent requires either another specific consent of the patient or a legal basis.[1363] If the data is further used for *medical reasons*, an additional consent including the genetic counseling regarding the further use is required.[1364] If the data is further used for *research purposes*, the Swiss law contains a balancing of research interests and the principle of self-determination. Depending on the extent the further use of the data endangers the protection of a patient's personality, a specific consent, a general consent or only a right to object is required.[1365] For certain cases there is also no requirement of other exempts.[1366]

The Swiss law generally allows the use of data *without the consent* of the respective patient only if the data is anonymized.[1367] However, for the anonymization as such the patient's consent is required.[1368] The question is only if today's anonymization techniques are sufficient in order to guarantee a full anonymization of genetic data without the possibility to draw conclusions on the identity of the data providing patient.[1369] For the treatment of patients, the anonymization is only a "pseudo-

1359 Art. 3 *para.* 2c and e and Art. 4 *para.* 5 DSG.
1360 Art. 18 KlinV.
1361 Cf. Chapter 4.2.1, Institutional setting, p. 234 ff.
1362 ECKHARDT ET AL. (2014), p. 113-114.
1363 Art. 4 *para.* 3 DSG; ECKHARDT ET AL. (2014), p. 108 ff.
1364 Art. 14 and 20 GUMG.
1365 Art. 32 ff. HMG; or ECKHARDT ET AL. (2014), p. 109-110.
1366 Conditions in Art. 34 HMG; and additionally the approval of the SWISS ETHICS COMMITTEE is required, cf. Art. 45 *para.* 2 HFG.
1367 Art. 2 *para.* 2c HFG.
1368 Art. 32 *para.* 3 HFG.
1369 ECKHARDT ET AL. (2014), p. 274, being critical about this question. However, data encryption expert BEERENWINKEL at the ETH LATSIS Forum on June 29th, 2016, was positive that the technology is able to guarantee anonymization. It is standard procedure in Switzerland that genetic data is anonymized.

anonymization" – as it is required that patients can be re-identified in case of an incidentalome.[1370]

So far, a harmonized consent form did not exist in Switzerland. In 2017, the SAMS has developed a "general consent" in collaboration with SWISSETHICS allowing people to permit the use of their health data for future research projects.[1371] With the general consent, a person gives up a significant portion of his/her sovereignity over his/her health data. On the other hand, a general consent contributes to more efficient research - from which the public can profit.

5. The requirement of professional confidentiality

The processing of genetic data in Switzerland is subject to professional confidentiality.[1372] A healthcare provider may only tell the results of a genetic examination to the respective person and only with explicit consent to related persons.[1373]

6. The assurance of scientific quality and the requirement of genetic counseling

Ensuring the scientific quality of genetic examinations is a central element of the GUMG. Genetic examinations require an authorization, and only medical doctors are allowed to initiate them ensuring adequate genetic counselling.[1374]

In contrast to pharmacogenetic tests and genetic tests to diagnose an existing illness, presymptomatic and prenatal genetic tests face stricter rules. They may only be initiated by medical doctors with adequate training and if genetic counceling is provided.[1375]

The current revision of the LAW ON GENETIC TESTS ON HUMANS (GUMG)

The LAW ON GENETIC TESTS ON HUMANS (GUMG) is currently under revision. The new draft (D-GUMG) extends the current scope to *all genetic examinations* – also genetic examinations without medical purposes[1376] and non-hereditary/somatic biomarkers.[1377] The D-GUMG introduces some general rules for genetic examinations.

1370 MOCH at the ETH LATSIS FORUM, 2016.
1371 SAMS (2017)b, *Vorlage Generalkonsent.*
1372 Art. 7 GUMG and Art. 321/321bis StGB.
1373 Art. 19 and 24 GUMG.
1374 Art. 8 and 13 GUMG.
1375 Art. 13 *para.* 2 GUMG.
1376 Cf. dispatch for the D-GUMG, p. 21.
1377 Cf. dispatch for the D-GUMG, p. 24 ff.

In *any case*, the D-GUMG stipulates that a person has to give an "informed consent", and the "right not to know" has to be respected.[1378]

For the different kinds of genetic tests, the D-GUMG introduces a graduated level of protection: The level of protection is highest for *tests with a medical purpose.* It stays at the same level as in the current GUMG.[1379] Additionally, the D-GUMG explicitly addresses the cases of an "incidentalome". A patient has to decide, which kind of incidental findings he or she would like to know and which ones not.[1380]

The D-GUMG categorizes genetic tests *beyond medical purposes* into two categories: Tests for properties which are *"particularly worth protecting"*[1381] and tests testing *"other"*[1382] properties which are not explicitly regulated by the D-GUMG. The first ones have to be conducted by a specialist and by laboratories approved by the SFOPH.[1383] The latter enjoy are lower level of regulation. They may be distributed over the internet and the laboratories need no special approval.

Additionally, the D- GUMG stipulates new measures against the misuse of online genetic tests (DTCs). The current, comparably solid and broad institutional setting in Switzerland can be undermined by foreign providers of genetic tests. So far, neither the quality of the tests nor the adequate information of the consumer/patients can be guaranteed.[1384] The D-GUMG attempts to address this problem. The marketing of genetic examinations in Switzerland has to meet the requirements of the D-GUMG.[1385] This offers the possibility to Swiss authorities to interfere, if tests offered by non-Swiss providers infringe the GUMG.[1386]

5.5.2 Analysis of incentives

The illustrations in the previous chapter demonstrate that Switzerland has a dense and multi-layered institutional setting governing privacy protection in the context of genetic data in Switzerland.

1378 Art. 5-6 and 8 D-GUMG.

1379 Cf. dispatch for the D-GUMG, p. 3.

1380 Art. 27 and 33 D-GUMG.

1381 Testing examining physiological (e.g., nutritional information), personal characteristics (eg., intelligence, skills, character, behavior), the genealogy, or ethnic information, cf. Art. 31 D-GUMG or dispatch for the D-GUMG, p. 21.

1382 E.g., size, hair or eye color, cf. dispatch for the D-GUMG, p. 22.

1383 Art. 34 D-GUMG.

1384 GÄCHTER & VOKINGER (2012), p. 967; and dispatch fot the D-GUMP, p. 28.

1385 Art. 14 D-GUMG.

1386 Cf. dispatch fot the D-GUMG, p. 28 and 78.

Patients in Switzerland incline to share their genetic data

The existence of privacy concerns regarding personalized medicine depends on the risk-awareness and preferences of Swiss citizens. Data protection and privacy issues are a central topic in the context of PM. Also in Switzerland, the topic is on top of minds and is the most prominently discussed issue during public debates about PM.[1387]

The extent to which the existing institutional setting actually affects the privacy concerns of the public in Switzerland is empirically not extensively examined. However, there is one study by VAYENA, GOURNAA, STREULIA, HAFEN, & PRAINSACK (2012) that explored the attitudes, motivations and self-reported impact in connection with DTC genomic testing amongst students in Switzerland. The study found that besides the motivator *"receiving actionable health information"*, other motivators like *"curiosity"* as well as the *"will to contribute to research"* or *"fun"* ranked high as motive for testing.[1388]

In fact, also Swiss practitioners mention their experience that the *patients' willingness to share their data* is perceived as high. They see the hindering factor behind the progress of PM rather in an information overload of the patients induced by the required data protection procedures. When asked about the biggest barrier behind the progress of PM into clinical practice, a majority mentioned the high data protection standards or even called it *"overregulation"*.[1389]

1387 E.g., the public discussion rounds of the interdisciplinary lecture series by the University and ETH Zürich about *"Personalized Medicine: Hope or empty promise?"*, December 19th, 2013 or at the ETH LATSIS Forum on June 29th, 2016.

1388 VAYENA ET AL. (2012), p. 352 ff. A limitation of the study is, however, that students are a comparably young test group, potentially being more open towards data sharing compared to the Swiss average.
Similarly, a survey designed to measure public attitudes about the US PRESICION MEDICINE INITIATIVE COHORT PROGRAM, a majority (79%) of respondents expressed support for the nationwide research effort, cf. KAUFMAN ET AL. (2016).

1389 STUPP, MOCH and BEERENWINKEL at the ETH LATSIS Forum on June 29th, 2016, when explicitly asked this question. HAFEN identified the *"empowerment of citizens"* as most critical factor to the progress of PM. SZEKELY saw the biggest barrier in the overburdening of the regulator due to orphanization.

Providers and researchers have to deal with additional work due to privacy protection regulation

If providers deliver professional and individual information to the patient required for an "informed consent", significantly more knowledge is needed with a personalized approach than with traditional approaches.[1390]

Additionally, experts criticize the double work arising through the required data protection procedures. Several examinations are repeated because of the impossibility to share a patient's data. In general, experts feel that the legislation significantly lags behind reality. The Swiss policy maker is trying to protect the patient but at the same time inhibits medical progress.[1391]

Payers are generally not allowed to discriminate on a genetic basis

As illustrated, Swiss payers are generally not allowed to request *new* genetic tests in order to discriminate on a genetic basis. Further, the compulsory health insurance is based on solidarity: A patient can always change the insurance company and has to be accepted – regardless of his or her genetic profile.[1392] However, there is an obligation to disclose the results of *previous* genetic tests under certain conditions. Despite Swiss insurance companies to not make use of this obligation, it might deter people to undergo genetic testing due to the fear of high insurance rates.[1393]

[1390] GÄCHTER & VOKINGER (2012), p. 966.

[1391] STUPP, MOCH or HAFEN at the ETH LATSIS Forum on June 29th, 2016. STUPP *"There is the danger of suffocating patients with data protection procedures"* or *"administrators and the ethics commission want to protect the patients from the 'evil doctor'"*. HAFEN mentioned the informed consent form of ZÜRICH'S UNIVERSITY HOSPITAL comprises several pages and is difficult to understand – even for an expert.

[1392] Cf. Chapter 6.1.1 Institutional setting, *1. Compulsory health insurance*, p. 261.

[1393] BRÄM & SZUCS (2016), p. 5.

5.5.3 Result

The analysis has shown that there is a field of tension between privacy protection and data sharing:

On the one hand, it has been demonstrated, that Switzerland has a dense and multi-layered institutional setting governing privacy protection of genetic data appropriate to build trust among the public, and adequate to address the the public's privacy concerns regarding the use of PM. First empirical evidence seems to confirm this hypothesis and indicates that patients in Switzerland incline to share their genetic data.[1394]

On the other hand, it has been demonstrated that the comprehensiveness of the Swiss privacy and data protection regulation may be a barrier to the translation of PM. It is criticized to slow down medical progress by impeding data sharing.[1395]

This thesis does not examine which of the above two tendencies prevail in practice. With these opposing findings for Switzerland, no conclusive statement concerning the incentives of the relevant stakeholders was made – this in contrast to the theoretical analysis in Part III.[1396]

Research institutions	*Pharmaceutical companies*	*Diagnostic companies*	*Providers*	*Patients*	*Payers*
–	–	–	–	–	–

negative = institutional setting incentivizes a player not to foster the translation of PM
– = neutral/no conclusive statement possible on a player's incentive to foster the translation of PM

1394 Cf. Part IV, Chapter 5.5.2 Analysis of incentives, *Patients in Switzerland incline to share their genetic data*, p. 258.

1395 Cf. Part IV, Chapter 5.5.2 Analysis of incentives, *Providers and researchers have to deal with additional work due to privacy* protection regulation, p. 259.

1396 Cf. Part III, Chapter 5.5.2 Analysis of incentives, p. 179 ff.

6 Barriers in the reimbursement phase

6.1 Lack of reimbursement for personalized medicine diagnostics

6.1.1 Institutional setting

This chapter analyses the institutional setting for the reimbursement of PM in Switzerland. The chapter starts with an overview of the Swiss health insurance system (i) and its basic governing principles (ii). Then it illustrates, how the Swiss health insurance system deals with new or disputed technologies for which effectiveness, appropriateness and efficiency is not conclusively evaluated yet – as this is the case for many emerging diagnostics and therapeutics of personalized medicine (iii). Based on these three sub-chapters, it is subsequently examined how PM pharmaceuticals and PM diagnostics are reimbursed by the Swiss compulsory health insurance (iv). A last paragraph illustrates the reimbursement for PM Dx by the Swiss supplemental health insurance (v).

i. Overview of health insurance system in Switzerland

The Swiss healthcare system offers three options to finance a medical service:

1. Compulsory health insurance

The SWISS FEDERAL LAW ON BASIC SICKNESS INSURANCE (KVG)[1397] obliges every resident in the country to buy a basic health insurance package of one of the competing health insurance companies.[1398] The basic health insurance system is based on the *principle of solidarity*: Insurees have the free choice amongst health insurance companies, and every person has to be accepted by a basic health insurance company. Individual risk-based calculations are not allowed.[1399]

2. Supplementary health insurance

Additionally, a Swiss resident might also choose to buy supplementary health insurance, governed by the SWISS FEDERAL LAW ON INSURANCE CONTRACTS (VVG).[1400] The law is based on the principle of freedom of contracts.[1401]

[1397] Art. 3 KVG. KVG stands for "Bundesgesetz über die Krankenversicherung".
[1398] There are ca. 60–70 competing health insurance companies in Switzerland, cf. BRÜGGER ET AL. (2015), p. 2.
[1399] Art. 4 KVG. Cf. also NOVENTA (2014), *recital* 127.
[1400] VVG stands for "Versicherungsvertragsgesetz".

3. Self-payment

Finally, medical services can also be paid for out-of-the pocket by the consumers/patients themselves.

ii. Governing principles in the Swiss compulsory health insurance

The Swiss compulsory health insurance is characterized by four basic principles guiding reimbursement decisions:

1. Principles of "effectiveness", "appropriateness" and "economic efficiency" of medical services (EAE-criteria) in the Swiss compulsory health insurance

The Swiss compulsory insurance covers the costs incurred through diagnosing or treating a disease.[1402] The KGV stipulates the principle that medical services have to be covered when they are "effective", "appropriate" and "economically efficient" (*EAE-criteria*).[1403] The EAE-criteria of a medical service shall be periodically reassessed.[1404] The three criteria are preconditions for coverage by the Swiss compulsory health insurance scheme, and are a central element in the Swiss health insurance legislation.

The primary and most important criterion *"effectiveness"* is given, if a cause (i.c., medical service/intervention) leads to the desired effect (i.c., outcome) *in general.* Effectiveness has to be proven based on scientific methods.[1405]

The second criterion *"appropriateness"* is given, if the medical service leads to the desired effect *in a specific case.* A medical service may be "effective" and "efficient" in general, but has also to be "appropriate" from a medical and economic perspective for the concrete case at hand. Thus, the criterion contains an "effectiveness" and an "efficiency" component for the specific case[1406] and has a comparative character.[1407]

1401 Cf. BRÄM & SZUCS (2016), p. 2. With the exceptions of Art. 99 VVG.

1402 Art. 25 KVG.

1403 Art. 21 KVG. „EAE-criteria" in German „WZW-criteria" standing for „Wirksamkeit",, „Zweckmässigkeit" and „Wirtschaftlichkeit".

1404 Art. 32 *para.* 2 KVG.

1405 Art. 32 KVG. More on the criterion in WIDRIG ET AL. (2012), *recital* 56, and ECKHARDT ET AL. (2014), p. 195. ZOLLIKOFER (2009), *chapter* 15, is using the term *„Evidence Based Health Care"* in order to describe the criterion "effectiveness". He further distinguishes between *"efficacy"* – the effectiveness under controlled conditions like clinical trials – and *"effectiveness"* in reality.

1406 ZOLLIKOFER (2009), *chapter* 15.

1407 WIDRIG ET AL. (2012), *recital* 57.

The third criterion *"economic efficiency"* is given if a medical treatment causes the intended medical outcome at the lowest possible costs.[1408] The criterion stipulates that in the case of multiple alternative medical measures with the same effectiveness, the cheapest one will be covered for.[1409] Further, the cost-effectiveness-ratio has to follow the principle of proportionality.[1410] In the *"Myozime-decision"* the SWISS FEDERAL COURT OF JUSTICE has set the limit of *"max. ca. CHF 100'000 per saved human life year"* as a proportionate cost-effectiveness ratio.[1411] Several methods are being discussed in order to evaluate the cost-effectiveness-ratio. The SWISS FEDERAL COURT OF JUSTICE mentions the QALY-concept as most prominent method,[1412] however there do not (yet) exist any commonly agreed methods or ICER thresholds.[1413]

2. Principle of "positive" and "negative" lists

Technically, the *Swiss Healthcare Benefits Ordinance (KLV)*[1414] and its corresponding annexes –containing "positive"[1415] and "negative"[1416] lists – contain the the medical measures being reimbursed.[1417] Also the details for price setting of pharmaceuticals are stipulated by the ordinances.[1418]

Specialty list: Pharmaceuticals fulfilling the EAE-criteria and being approved by SWISSMEDIC are listed in the *specialty list*[1419] published by the SWISS FEDERAL OFFICE OF PUBLIC HEALTH (SFOPH). The list contains maximum prices for the listed pharmaceuticals.[1420]

1408 Art. 62b KVV. More on the criterion in ZOLLIKOFER (2009), *chapter* 15; WIDRIG ET AL. (2012), *recital* 58; WIDMER (2013), p. 16.

1409 WIDRIG ET AL. (2012), *recital* 58.

1410 Art. 5 para. 2 SWISS CONSTITUTION; more in WIDRIG ET AL. (2012), *recital* 58; WIDMER (2013), p. 16.

1411 BGE 136 V 395, E. 7.6.3.

1412 *Ibidem.*

1413 E.g., SFOPH (2011), p. 6; FLORIAN GUTZWILLER ET AL. (2012), p. 80; WIDRIG (2015), p. 99. WIDRIG ET AL. (2012), *recital* 61-74 about common criticism and the discussion of further concretization of the EAE-criteria. Cf. also Chapter 6.2.1 Institutional setting, *Criticism of current evaluation process in Switzerland*, p. 282.

1414 KLV stands for "Krankenpflege-Leistungsverordnung".

1415 Containing medical services that must be reimbursed by the mandatory health insurance. E.g., the specialty list (SL) or the list of analyses (AL)

1416 Containing medical services that are not – or just under certain conditions – reimbursed by the mandatory health insurance. Cf. Annex 1 KLV.

1417 WIDRIG ET AL. (2012), *recitals* 46-47 with more about the Swiss "list principle".

1418 Art. 64-75 KVV; and Art. 30-38a KLV.

1419 Art. 30 KLV.

1420 Cf. SL ("specialty list").

List of analyses: Annex 3 of the KLV contains the *list of analyses* representing a "positive" list. The compulsory health insurance is not allowed to reimburse others than the listed medical analyses.[1421] Analyses not listed have to be paid out-of-pocket or are covered by a supplementary insurance. Basically anyone is eligible to file an application for reimbursement for an analysis.[1422]

3. Principle of trust in the Swiss compulsory health insurance

The reimbursement of medical services provided by Swiss physicians is handled in a *"pragmatic"* way[1423] as it is governed by the so-called *principle of trust.*[1424] All Swiss physicians enjoy the "principle of trust". The principle assumes that medical services provided to patients fulfill the EAE-criteria. Thus the principle stipulates that these medical services[1425] have to be reimbursed unless they are listed on a negative list.[1426] With this principle the reimbursement decisions for medical services provided by medical doctors are left directly to the providers and payers. Just in case of doubt, anyone with a legitimate interest (e.g., a health insurance company) can challenge the medical service and a formalized assessment process is triggered. Its outcomes are then published in the appendix of the relevant procedures ordinance.[1427]

In contrast to medical services by medical doctors, pharmaceuticals, analyses and medical objects are just reimbursed and listed on a positive list in case they meet the EAE-criteria.[1428] In this sense, the lists complement the principle of trust.[1429]

4. Principle of territoriality

For reimbursing medical services, Swiss compulsory health insurers are bound to the *principle of territoriality.* The place of provided medical treatments being reim-

---

1421 Art. 34 para 1 KVG.

1422 WIDRIG ET AL. (2012), p. 85; and WIDRIG (2015), p. 86.

1423 WIDRIG ET AL. (2012), p. 4. FASMED (2012), p. 3, stresses that the principle of trust enables a fast introduction of innovative therapies in Switzerland.

1424 Art. 33 para 1 KVG. More about the principle of trust in WIDRIG ET AL. (2012), *recital* 48; and GÄCHTER & MEIENBERGER (2013), p. 21.
Note: The English term *"principle of trust"* is not a fully accurate translation. The German "Pflichtleistungsvermutung" would actually be translated more accurately with *"compulsory reimbursement presumption"*.

1425 Including in vivo diagnostics and devises, but *not* drugs and *not* in vitro diagnostics like PM Dx, cf. BRÜGGER ET AL. (2015), p. 2. The prices for these services are negotiated directly between the providers and the health insurance companies (ambulatory TARMED/stationary DRG system), WIDRIG ET AL. (2012), p. 85.

1426 WIDRIG ET AL. (2012), p. 4; and ECKHARDT ET AL. (2014), p. 195.

1427 WIDRIG ET AL. (2012), *recital* 48; and BRÜGGER ET AL. (2015), p. 2.

1428 BRÜGGER ET AL. (2015), p. 2; and WIDRIG (2015), p. 4.

1429 GÄCHTER & MEIENBERGER (2013), p. 21.

bursed by the compulsory health insurance is limited to Switzerland.[1430] The purpose of this principle is to guarantee a controlled healthcare of qualitatively high standard.[1431]

There are some exceptions from the principle of territoriality. These exceptions concern mainly emergencies, services that cannot be provided in Switzerland, and approved pilot-projects in the border area.[1432]

iii. Coverage with evidence in the Swiss compulsory health insurance scheme

"Coverage with Evidence" (CED) is defined as a type of *"managed entry agreement between manufacturers or service providers and the paying healthcare system".*[1433] It is a tool to evaluate evolving technologies before sufficient evidence for a final reimbursement decision has been generated.

In the case of novel medical services, funding decisions are required before sufficient evidence has been generated. In these cases a policy maker needs to find the balance between the desire not to commit to a technology that may prove to be ineffective and/or unsafe and the wish to provide patient access to innovative approaches early in their life cycle. CED is an approach that aims to address this balance, and to allow for early adoption of pharmaceuticals, medical procedures and devices for a limited period of time and under explicit restricting conditions. Reimbursement can be linked with the requirement of further evidence development.[1434] BRÜGGER, RUCKSTUHL, HORISBERGER, & GRATWOHL (2014) describe as the most interesting aspects of CED *"that it integrates HTA into decision making, allowing direct 'implementation' of HTA results into the technology appraisal process".*[1435] The term CED stems from the US CENTERS FOR MEDICARE AND MEDICAID SERVICES (CMS) in 2005. However, the concept as such existed before and its concrete terminology varies from country to country.[1436]

[1430] Art. 34 *para.* 2 KVG.

[1431] FELIX GUTZWILLER & BLANK (2013), p. 631.

[1432] Art. 34 *para.* 2 KVG; and Art. 36 *lit.* f KVV.

[1433] BRÜGGER ET AL. (2015), p. 1.

[1434] BRÜGGER ET AL. (2014), p. 253; and BRÜGGER ET AL. (2015), p. 1.

[1435] BRÜGGER ET AL. (2014), p. 253.

[1436] *Ibidem.*

Today, Switzerland has over 20 years of experience with CED. The SFOPH has adopted CED in early 1996 and represents *"a particularly remarkable example of CED in the area of non-drug technologies"*.[1437]

The SWISS FEDERAL COUNCIL determines to what extent the compulsory health insurance reimburses the costs of a new or disputed medical service, for which the fulfillment of the EAE-criteria is still pending.[1438] The medical services (including diagnostics and devices) and the corresponding reimbursement conditions are listed in Annex 1 KLV. A potentially controversial medical service has to be reported to the SFOPH. After an assessment process, the decision for reimbursement can be "Yes", "No" or "Yes, in evaluation".

With this regulation, the Swiss system of CED enables patients' access to some new technologies early in their life cycle. CED could specifically apply to the emerging diagnostic and therapeutic services of PM, where traditional phase III trials do no longer suffice.[1439]

However, the current CED system is being criticized for a lack of criteria and the lack of a structured process enabling consistent reimbursement decisions.[1440] BRÜGGER ET AL. (2015) claim that the Swiss CED system should follow internationally agreed principles, and that it should be integrated into a clear and structured process and consistent decision making.[1441]

iv. Reimbursement for personalized medicine diagnostics by the Swiss compulsory health insurance

The *Swiss Federal Law on Basic Sickness Insurance* (KVG) insures health – meaning that compulsory health insurance only reimburses incurred costs due to ill-

1437 BRÜGGER ET AL. (2014), p. 253-254. WIDRIG (2015), p. 60, is describing the Swiss solution as *„pioneering work"* gaining attention in the international HTA-community.

1438 Art. 33 para. 3 KGV and Art. 33 *lit.* c KVV.

1439 BRÜGGER ET AL. (2015), p. 8.

1440 According to BRÜGGER ET AL. (2015), p. 7-8. They found *"an absence of clear criteria for a CED decision and a definition of the decision pathway, the arbitrariness in decision-making, and the lack of scientific evaluation of what was performed"*. Their interviewees were concerned *"about the erratic structure of the evaluation process"* and had concerns *"about the lack of scientific and administrative criteria"* and the absence of evaluation of the evaluation process itself. They criticized the absence of academia from the HTA appraisal process, p. 8.

1441 BRÜGGER ET AL. (2015), p. 1.

ness.[1442] The clear distinction between health and illness represents a first basic challenge with the emergence of PM. With PM the boundaries between health and illness become increasingly blurred and the focus of medicine is expected to become more preventive than reactive.[1443]

Diagnostic tests

The above distinction between health and illness means, that diagnostic treatments for diagnosing symptoms of an illness or checking the effectiveness of a therapy are part of the Swiss compulsory health insurance system. As far as genetic testing is used as part of a medical examination or treatment in the case of *illness* – as this is the case with diagnostic tests like companion diagnostics/pharmacogenetic tests – the principle of trust applies.[1444] If the costs for the test are not excluded from the obligation to pay, they have to be reimbursed as listed on the list of analyses.[1445] Additionally, the EAE-criteria have to be fulfilled on a case-by-case basis.[1446]

The list of analyses[1447] is only valid for the ambulatory setting. In case of stationary settings, the prices for analyses are included in the DRG's.[1448]

So, diagnostic tests are reimbursed if they are included in the positive list of analyses. There are certain PM Dx explicitly on the list.[1449] There is also one position included for Dx testing for orphan diseases.[1450] If there are two test alternatives available, the health insurer has to pay only the listed test – although other tests with potentially lower prices would be available.

Some diagnostic tests may also only be reimbursed under certain conditions. Besides the direct inclusion on the list of analyses, diagnostic tests are potential candidates for a CED process and reimbursement with conditions with the status "yes, in

1442 Art. 25 KVG states that *"the compulsory health insurance reimburses costs incurred due to the diagnosis or treatment of an illness or its consequences"* (translated by the author). There are exceptions to this in case, e.g., motherhood (Art. 29 KVG) or prevention (Art. 26 KVG). More about the distinction between *"health"* and *"illness"* in the Swiss social insurance system, cf. ECKHARDT ET AL. (2014), p. 26-27.

1443 Cf. Part II, Chapter 1.3.4 Shift from reaction to prevention, p. 65.

1444 ECKHARDT ET AL. (2014), p. 279.

1445 GÄCHTER & VOKINGER (2012), p. 967-968. E.g., chromosomal micro-array analyses, sequencing, or NGS, cf. SFOPH (2016)c, p. 1. For the explanation of the list of analyses, cf. p. 263.

1446 ECKHARDT ET AL. (2014), p. 195, and SFOPH (2016)c, p. 2.

1447 For the explanation of the list of analyses, cf. p. 263.

1448 Pricing and reimbursement of listed analyses are based on a federal regulated tariff system with tax points and a tax point values. More in K. MÜLLER (2012).

1449 AL *chapter* 2.2.1 and 2.2.2.

1450 AL *position* 2160.00, p. 103-104, listing the criteria which have to be fulfilled for reimbursement or an Orphan disease.

evaluation" in Annex 1 of the KLV. The FOPH has published a checklist for CED reimbursement of diagnostic tests.[1451] Currently the annex mentions one diagnostic test.[1452]

Presymptomatic tests

In contrast to diagnostic tests, presymtomatic tests are in principle not subject to the Swiss compulsory health insurance system, as they serve a preventive purpose and not the treatment of an "illness". Presymptomatic tests uncover only genetic predispositions or risks for certain diseases. At the point of testing symptoms of a disease did not appear and may never appear.

The SWISS FEDERAL LAW ON BASIC SICKNESS INSURANCE (KVG) contains an exemption: According to Art. 26 KVG, *"the compulsory sickness insurance covers the costs for certain preventive examinations for the early detection of diseases and precautionary measures for insures who are at particular risk".*[1453] The FEDERAL COUNCIL has to designate the covered preventive measures.[1454]

Presymtomatic tests have to be reimbursed if they are listed as a measure of prevention in Art. 12 ff. KLV and in the corresponding list of analyses.[1455] The KLV contains explicitly genetic consultations and the respective genetic tests for certain hereditary cancers.[1456] Genetic examinations in order to detect a predisposition in healthy persons in regards to their offspring are not reimbursed.[1457]

The list of analysis published beginning 2016 takes into account the new diagnostic possibilities available. For the first time, its chapter "Genetics" contains the possibility to have NGS-tests reimbursed. RAUCH (2015) indicates that NGS-tests may proof to become important differential diagnostic tools, however, in many cases the "classic" single-gene-tests performed by an expert may stay more economically efficient in many cases.[1458]

1451 Checklist published by SFOPH (2014).
1452 This is the multi-gen test for the breast cancer assay listed in Annex 1 of the KVG as *"yes, in evaluation".*
1453 Translated by the author.
1454 Art. 33 *para.* 2 KVG.
1455 Art. Art. 12 *lit.* a-e KLV.
1456 Art. 12d *lit.* f KLV.
1457 AL, *introduction into chapter "Genetics"*, p. 84.
1458 RAUCH (2015), p. 24-25.

Requirement of a therapeutic consequence for reimbursement

Even if a diagnostic test is explicitly listed for compulsory reimbursement, a health insurance company can refuse reimbursement of the test on a case-by-case base claiming that the test does not meet the EAE-criteria.

The SWISS FEDERAL COURT OF JUSTICE held that the result of a reimbursed diagnostic has to have *"to an acceptable probability"* a consequence for 1) a decision about the necessity and kind of a medical treatment, 2) a change in the current medical treatment, 3) a change in the needed medical examinations or 4) the decision to abandon any further medical examinations.[1459] Other court decisions have followed the SWISS FEDERAL COURT OF JUSTICE opinion[1460] and the requirement of a "therapeutic consequence" is also restated in the list of analysis[1461] and explained in a letter to the Swiss payers by the FOPH.[1462]

Consequentially, it is not sufficient if a PM Dx is listed for reimbursement. Reimbursement can be refused by a payer if the use of the diagnostic does not lead to a therapeutic consequence with an "acceptable probability" in a specific case.

Off-label use of personalized pharmaceuticals and tests

The Swiss law contains a peculiarity for the off-label use of pharmaceuticals. A pharmaceutical is used "off-label", if it is not used for the officially approved indication. This is the case if a pharmaceutical is used beyond the intended indication stated in the label approved by SWISSMEDIC.[1463]

Art. 71 *lit.* a and b KVV prescribe the compulsory reimbursement of an off-label use of a pharmaceutical under certain conditions. Also in the cases of an off-label use the EAE-criteria must be fulfilled, however, the "list principle" does not apply.[1464]

1459 BGE 137V295 E6.1, E6.2 and E6.3.1; p. 303 ff., *translated by the author.*

1460 FEDERAL INSURANCE COURT, decision 9C_748/2014.

1461 AL, p. 5.

1462 SFOPH (2016)c, p. 3 ff.

1463 WIDMER (2013), *recital* 55, RÜEGSEGGER & SZUCS (2014), p. 11. WIDMER (2013), *recital* 55-56, further distinguishes between *off-limitation use* (pharmaceuticals used beyond the limitations stated in the SL, Art. 71 *lit.* a KVV), *hors-liste pharmaceuticals* (pharmaceuticals that are not on the SL, Art. 71 *lit.* b *para.* 1 KVV) and *unlicensed use* (pharmaceuticals which may be imported, but are not approved by SWISSMEDIC, Art. 71 *lit.* b *para.* 2 KVV).

1464 The pharmaceutical has to bring a *"major therapeutic benefit"*, has to be approved by the insurer after consultation of an independent medical examiner, Art. 71 a and b KVV. For more details on the conditions for reimbursement of off-label use, cf. WIDMER (2013) and WIDRIG (2015), p. 320-321.

However, Art. 71 *lit.* a and b KVV do explicitly apply for pharmaceuticals and in the case of "illness". Off-label use of PM Dx could be understood as using a PM Dx in cases where the EAE-criteria are fulfilled - despite the label of the pharmaceutical not explicitly prescribing such a test before administration. In this sense, off-label use is not reimbursed for PM Dx – neither in the case of diagnostic nor in the case of pre-symtomatic tests.

Principle of territoriality in the context of personalized medicine diagnostics

Due to the principle of territoriality stipulated by the Swiss compulsory health insurance, diagnostic tests have to be conducted in Switzerland. Vice versa, mandatory reimbursement is not stipulated for tests conducted outside of the country.

There are currently some exemptions to the principle of territoriality in the context of PM and orphan diseases.[1465]

SwissDRG reimbursement in case of stationary in-patient settings

In contrast to the ambulatory treatment of patients, the reimbursement of stationary medical services by the mandatory health insurance is based on a system called SwissDRG.[1466] DRG's are co-financed by the Cantons and health insurers.[1467] In the SwissDRG each hospitalization is assigned to a "diagnosis-related group" based on certain criteria and given a DRG price.[1468]

It takes five years from application to admission of a medical service into the DRG catalogue.[1469] In order to "bridge" this time, the DRG system stipulates a direct negotiation between hospitals and payers for the admission of medical innovations into the DRG catalogue.[1470] The medical innovation has to meet certain criteria, amongst others the EAE-criteria do apply.[1471]

1465 E.g., AL, p. 103-104, *limitations.*

1466 Art. 49 KVG.

1467 Art. 49a KVG, the canton's part is min. 55%, the insurers' part max. 45%.

1468 The compensation for a DRG is calculated on the equation DRG=cost weight x base rate. "Base rates" are negotiated by the providers and health insurers. "Cost weights" are empirically calculated based on the actual costs of Swiss hospitals and are recalculated and published every year. Cf. SWISSDRG (2015), p. 4.

1469 FASMED (2016)b, p. 1.

1470 SWISSDRG (2011) cited in FASMED (2016)b, p. 2.

1471 SWISSDRG (2014), *Anforderungen zur Verhandlung von Innovationsentgelten.*

v. Reimbursement for PM Dx by the Swiss supplementary health insurance

In contrast to the principle of solidarity in the compulsory health insurance system, the supplementary health insurance is based on the principle of freedom of contracts. This means, that the reimbursement of PM depends on the content of the contract between the insuree and the insurance company.

However, in Switzerland there are currently certain limitations to the principle of freedom of contracts in the context of PM: An insurance company is not allowed to request genetic information in order to conclude an insurance contract.[1472]

6.1.2 Analysis of incentives

The previous analysis of Switzerland's institutional setting has shown, that there is no straight-forward answer to the question, if PM Dx are reimbursed. Reimbursement depends primarily on a patient's chosen insurance scheme. For *reimbursement by the compulsory health insurance* further factors are involved. Reimbursement depends on a PM Dx' listing for compulsory reimbursement on a "positive" or "negative" list, on the country in which a test has been conducted, and finally on the factor if a test is considered to have a concrete therapeutic consequence.

This chapter analyses the resulting incentives set by the institutional setting governing the reimbursement of PM Dx in Switzerland. If not explicitly stated otherwise, the argumentation is based on the current regulation for reimbursement by the *compulsory health insurance.*

Pharmaceutical companies

The analysis of the institutional environment in the previous chapter has primarily examined the reimbursement of the diagnostic component. It has shown that the reimbursement of the diagnostic component depends on several factors that differ for each individual case. This leads to legal uncertainty about the reimbursed of PM Dx by the compulsory health insurance in Switzerland.

The risk of lacking reimbursement for the diagnostic component generally incentivizes a pharmaceutical company to sell a non-personalized drug as no diagnostic component is needed. Thus, the argumentation of Part III stays valid for Switzerland.[1473]

[1472] Cf. Chapter 5.5.1 Institutional setting, *1. The principle of non-discrimination*, p. 251.
[1473] Cf. Part III, Chapter 6.1.2 Analysis of incentives, *Pharmaceutical companies*, p. 190.

Diagnostics companies

The legal uncertainty about the reimbursement of the diagnostic component lowers a diagnostic company's incentive to offer PM Dx. Thus, the argumentation in Part III is valid for Switzerland too.[1474]

Test providers for the diagnosis of orphan diseases face a special situation: Under certain conditions their tests are reimbursed.[1475] This increases the incentive for Dx companies towards orphanization instead of developing tests for measuring polymorphisms targeting the broader population.[1476]

Besides the list of analysis, an alternative to get reimbursement for a PM Dx is the "principle of trust". If the PM Dx is considered to be an element of a "medical service", the test will be reimbursed via DRG or TARMED. Just in cases in which the total costs are paid via DRG/TARMED, a provider is incentivized to consider the use of the diagnostic test. However, if the costs of a diagnostic test result in additional costs not being payed via DRG/TARMED, a provider will not use the test due to economic restrictions.

Besides reimbursement through the compulsory insurance, PM Dx have the option of being reimbursement via the *supplementary health insurance*. Thus, Dx companies may approach payers in order to directly negotiate reimbursement with the result of some tests being reimbursed, others not. Insurance companies often do not have the capacity to internally assess the tests requested for reimbursement by the supplementary health insurance.[1477]

Nevertheless, through direct negotiations between providers and payers new forms of collaboration emerge beyond governmental regulations. The new forms of collaboration have the potential to lead to "faster" voluntary business than within the existing regulatory framework.[1478]

1474 Cf. Part III, Chapter 6.1.2 Analysis of incentives, *Diagnostics companies*, p. 191.

1475 AL position 2160.00, p. 103-104, listing the criteria which have to be fulfilled for reimbursement in case of diagnosing an orphan disease.

1476 Cf. Part II, Chapter 4.3 Personalized medicine increases costs due to orphanization, p. 92.

1477 *„Every two weeks a new ‚magic test' appears whose provider claims it to be cost-efficient, but the test is not yet on a reimbursement list"*, SCHÄFER on November 17, 2015.

1478 SZUCS interviewed December 5, 2013.

Providers

a) Providers bear administrative costs for the confirmation of coverage lowers the incentive to use PM

De facto, the current regulation has the effect that the reimbursement of genetic tests requires a confirmation of coverage by the payer before the actual test can be performed.[1479] The obtainment of a cost confirmation implies administrative costs for a provider. Additionally, it can delay the beginning of the test by several months.[1480]

b) Inconsistencies between drug labels and reimbursement rules leads to ambiguous situations for providers

In cases in which a drug's label explicitly mentions the pharmacogenetic limitations, but the corresponding test is not listed for reimbursement, a provider is in an ambiguous situation. The provider may decide not to perform the pharmacogenetic test. First, because the test is not reimbursed, and second, the provider might decide not wanting to bear the administrative burden to obtain a prior cost confirmation by a payer.[1481]

c) Fee-for-service model in ambulatory settings incentivize providers to select PM tests that increase the number of medical procedures performed

Physicians working in an ambulatory setting are paid on a FFS model. Thus, for the ambulatory setting, the argumentation in Part III is valid for Switzerland too.[1482]

d) DRGs limit innovations in stationary in-patient settings

With five years from submission to admission of medical innovations to the DRG catalogue, the SwissDRG system is criticized for being too slow.[1483] Providers are incentivized not to use medical innovations until they are reimbursed via DRGs. The existing solution for limiting the admission time foresees direct DRG negotiations between providers and payers. However, this solution is expected to lead to regional differences in the reimbursement of medical innovations, because the providers' dedication – if any – to initiate such negotiations varies. Combined with the payers' reser-

---

1479 KULLAK-UBLICK (2013), p. 8; BÜRKI (2015), p. 6, and the INSTITUT FÜR MEDIZINISCHE GENETIK (2016) recommends obtaining a cost confirmation before conducting a genetic test.

1480 INSTITUT FÜR MEDIZINISCHE GENETIK (2016), *na.*

1481 SZUCS (2014)b, p. 58, asks the question if a provider might be found liable in case in which no test was performed despite the label's content, and the patient suffers from adverse events due to the treatment.

1482 Cf. Part III, Chapter 6.1.2 Analysis of incentives, *Payers*, p. 194.

1483 SWISSDRG (2011) cited in FASMED (2016)b, p. 2.

vation against the reimbursement of new services, the solution is described as ineffective. So far, the option of the direct negotiation has not led to any new reimbursement of a medical innovation.[1484]

Patients

In Switzerland, the patient bears the risk of the lacking reimbursement for certain PM Dx. Unless a specific supplementary health insurance reimburses the costs, a patient has to pay the costs out of pocket. Part III's argumentation is valid for Switzerland too,[1485] and a patient will tend not have an incentive to demand PM.

Payers

a) Inconsistent evidence for the health economic impact of PM Dx incentivizes payers to uphold current lack of reimbursement

The evidence for the health economic impact of using PM Dx is often unclear and consistent data for the proof of clinical utility or the cost-effectiveness of a PM Dx is not available.[1486] Thus, Part III's argumentation is valid for Switzerland.[1487] This incentive is closely related to the lack of an appropriate HTA process in Switzerland, discussed in the next Chapter 6.2.[1488]

b) Different interpretation of EAE-criteria leads to inconsistent reimbursement or refusal of payment for PM Dx

Despite explicit listing for reimbursement of a diagnostic or presymtomatic tests, reimbursement can be refused by a payer if the use of the diagnostic does not fulfill the EAE-criteria, and if it does not lead to a therapeutic consequence with an "acceptable probability" in a specific case.[1489]

The requirements leads to the fact that payers do not consistently handle the reimbursement of PM Dx. In fact, tests are more often reimbursed in the French speaking part than in the German speaking part of Switzerland.[1490] 60-70% of the genetic

[1484] FASMED (2016)b, p. 2.

[1485] Cf. Part III, Chapter 6.1.2 Analysis of incentives, *Patients*, p. 194.

[1486] Cf. next Chapter 3 Economic value of personalized medicine, p. 72 ff.

[1487] Cf. Part III, Chapter 6.2.2 Analysis of incentives, *Payers*, p. 194.

[1488] Cf. Chapter 6.2 Gaps and inconsistencies in conventional health technology assessments for personalized medicine, p. 279 ff.

[1489] Cf. Chapter 6.1.1 Institutional setting, *iv) Reimbursement for personalized medicine diagnostics by the Swiss compulsory health insurance*, p. 266 ff.

[1490] FELIX GUTZWILLER & BLANK (2013), p. 631.

analyses are reimbursed.[1491] Experts criticize the reimbursement to be arbitrary and inconsistent.[1492]

The current regulation leads to the fact that some payers *refuse* – despite explicit listing – *the reimbursement* of genetic tests with the argument that a test has no therapeutic consequence in a specific case.[1493] Others refuse reimbursement as they do not regard the tests as cost-efficient in a specific case.[1494]

c) Not updated list of analysis leads to paradox situations for payers

Despite its regular updates, the list of analysis is criticized for lagging behind reality. In some cases, there are paradox situations forcing payers to reimburse the more expensive test alternative that is listed on the AL, not allowing a payer to reimburse for a less expensive alternative.[1495]

Several pharmacogenetic tests – especially tests testing polymorphisms – are not listed in the AL for reimbursement, despite their potential to reduce the consumption of ineffective treatments.[1496]

An additional example are drugs that require pharmacogenetic testing on their label approved by SWISSMEDIC, but the respective tests are not contained in the list of analyses.[1497] This is a legal inconsistency.

1491 GALLATI cited in NOVOTNY (2016), *na*.

1492 BREITINGER (2014), p. 44-45; FELIX GUTZWILLER & BLANK (2013), p. 631; ECKHARDT ET AL. (2014), p. 196-197; and MATYAS & HENGGELER interviewed 3rd of September, 2015.

1493 GALATTI cited in HIRSTEIN (2012); GALATTI cited in ROOS (2013); FELIX GUTZWILLER & BLANK (2013), p. 631; and GUMEK (2016), p. 2.

1494 RAUCH (2015), p. 24.

1495 SEILER interviewed 18th of July 2016.

1496 *Ibidem.* E.g., already TAEGTMEYER (2012), p. 808, criticized that since the revision of the list of analyses in 2009 most pharmacogenetic tests were excluded from reimbursement through the compulsory health insurance. Only HLA-B*5701-genotyping for Abacavir and HLA-A*3101-Genotypisierung for Carbamazepin are still reimbursed.

1497 E.g., the label of Lapatinib states that the drug has an increased risk of liver toxicity in case a patient is carrier of the HLA-allele DQA1*02:01 and DRB1*07:01 b (http://compendium.ch/mpro/mnr/15775/html/de, retrieved June 16, 2016). Cf. previous Sub-chapter Providers, *b) Inconsistencies between drug labels and reimbursement rules leads to ambiguous situations for providers,* p. 275.

d) Principle of territoriality leads to high testing costs, decreasing the Swiss payer's incentive to foster the translation of PM

Assuming the compulsory health insurance system prescribes reimbursement for a PM Dx, the principle of territoriality obliges a Swiss compulsory health insurer to pay the test only if it has been conducted in Switzerland. If the test has not been conducted in Switzerland, a payer does not have to pay.[1498]

In many cases Swiss testing laboratories require higher fees per test compared to other test providing laboratories. Compared to Swiss laboratories, foreign test providers have higher economies of scale due to a higher throughput of samples. Additionally, the higher the number of tests is, the better the reliability of the test results are.[1499] Further, the tests performed by foreign providers are described to deliver the results faster.[1500] This leads to the paradox of the Swiss insurer having to pay for a more expensive test of potentially lower quality, speed and reliability.[1501]

e) Prohibition of risk-based customer selection in the VVG leads to danger of adverse selection:

In connection with PM and the supplementary health insurance companies (VVG) the topic of *risk-based customer selection* is central. Two cases can be distinguished:

1. Risk-based customer selection is allowed: In contrast to the compulsory insurance, classic insurance principles apply and individual risk-based customer selection and grouping is generally allowed for supplementary health insurance.[1502] A private insurance company may request transparency about all relevant risk factors before signing the insurance contract. This would not only violate the "right not to know" of an applicant, but it would also endanger the functioning of an insurance system as a whole: PM leads to an increasingly bigger stratification of patients with certain risks. Risk groups are shrinking and the "law of large numbers" – upon which the business of insurance is based – cannot apply anymore, and thus the idea of an insurance could not work anymore.[1503] In cases, in which the payer is allowed to ask for full genetic transparency, the payer will not be willing to provide insurance for persons with "high risks". These patients would all be left in the compulsory health insurance gov-

---

[1498] Cf. Principle of territoriality in Chapter 6.1.1 Institutional setting, *ii) Governing principles in the Swiss compulsory health insurance*, 4. Principle of territoriality, p. 264.

[1499] FELIX GUTZWILLER & BLANK (2013), p. 631, FELIX GUTZWILLER (2013); and HOFFMANN, interviewed 16th of November 2015.

[1500] FELIX GUTZWILLER & BLANK (2013), p. 631.

[1501] HOFFMANN interviewed 16th November 2015.

[1502] BAUMANN in ECKHARDT ET AL. (2014), p. 198.

[1503] *Ibidem*, p. 198.

erned by the principle of solidarity. In this context, BÜTLER (2016) is talking of the *"insurance destruction effect".*[1504] For solving these cases in the context of PM, BÜTLER (2016) suggests two solutions: Either a *compulsory insurance* is forcing all patients – also the patients with low risks – to buy health insurance in order to uphold the functioning balance of risks and to lower the risk selection by payers. Second, she suggests a direct *cost compensation* to persons with high risks for illness.[1505] Both solutions would mean the end of the supplementary health insurance in Switzerland.

2. Risk-based customer selection is not allowed: If a payer is not allowed to require the genetic information before concluding an insurance contract, but the applicant knows his or her genetic risks, the information asymmetry between the insurance provider and applicant would lead to adverse selection with all "high risk" persons choosing supplementary insurance.[1506] Also this development would endanger the insurance principle as only "high risk" patients would be pooled in the supplementary insurance scheme. This would increase premiums for the supplementary insurance contracts.

The Swiss law currently does not clearly choose between the two extremes. It holds that risk-based customer selection is not allowed. However, if there are some results from earlier presymptomatic testing available, a private health insurer is allowed to request those.[1507] The question is if patients will provide them to the insurance company or only use the results for their own information.

f) Lack of longitudinal accounting lowers the incentive to reimburse tests that are cost-efficient in the long term:

In the Swiss health insurance system, citizens have the free choice amongst health insurance companies. Every person has to be accepted by a basic compulsory health insurance company.[1508] This lowers the incentive for a payer to reimburse personalized tests and treatments, which may only be cost-efficient over the long-term.

1504 BÜTLER (2016), p. 108.

1505 *Ibidem*, p. 114.

1506 *Ibidem*, p. 108; RIPPE ET AL. (2004), p. 108; MÜLLER and SCHÄFER in WIENKE ET AL. (2013), p. 20; and BRÄM & SZUCS (2016), p. 6.

1507 Cf. previous Chapter 5.5.1 Institutional setting, *1. The principle of non-discrimination*, p. 251 ff.

1508 Cf. Chapter 6.1.1 Institutional setting, *i) Overview of health insurance system in* Switzerland, p. 261 ff.

6.1.3 Result

The overview below summarizes the argumentation of the previous chapter and shows the resulting incentives through the institutional setting in Switzerland concerning the reimbursement for PM Dx in Switzerland.

Research institutions	*Pharmaceutical companies*	*Diagnostic companies*	*Providers*	*Patients*	*Payers*
–	negative	negative	negative	negative	negative

negative = institutional setting incentivizes a player not to foster the translation of PM
– = neutral/no conclusive statement possible on a player's incentive to foster the translation of PM

With these findings, the hypothesis of Part III must be upheld: *The lack of reimbursement for personalized medicine diagnostics acts as a barrier to the translation of personalized medicine into Swiss clinical practice.*

6.2 Gaps and inconsistencies in conventional health technology assessments for personalized medicine

6.2.1 Institutional setting

This chapter describes the institutional setting of the current HTA process in Switzerland. It presents the existing "HTA" process in Switzerland (i), its criticism (ii) and ends with a description of the current HTA developments in Switzerland (iii).

i. "HTA" process in Switzerland

Switzerland does not have an official HTA body.[1509] The evaluation process of medical services is led by the FOPH supported by dedicated commissions. The main differences to other systems are the pragmatism of the approach, the non-systematic (re-)evaluation of medical services and the lower degree of transparency during the evaluation process.[1510] Experts dispute if the Swiss approach can be called "HTA".[1511]

The EAE-criteria[1512] are the central principle in the Swiss compulsory health insurance. Medical services not meeting the EAE-criteria have to be paid out-of-pocket or by a patient's supplementary health insurance.[1513] For receiving reimbursement by the compulsory health insurance, pharmaceuticals, analyses and medical objects have to undergo an evaluation. In case they meet the EAE-criteria, they are listed on a list for reimbursement.[1514] In the evaluation manual, the SFOPH (2009) calls this evaluation an "HTA".[1515]

However, the SFOPH (2009) indicates that the Swiss "HTA" has its limitations. Due to their sheer number, it would be an illusion to evaluate all medical services. The evaluation has to focus on services for which the EAE-criteria are contested and have to be (re-)evaluated. Additionally, there are not sufficient financial means for the responsible authorities to perform a more comprehensive HTA.[1516]

1509 E.g., the NICE in the UK, the HAS in France, the IQWiG in Germany or the INESS in Canada, cf. or WIDRIG (2015) p. 347-398, for detailed descriptions on HTA processes of other countries.

1510 FLORIAN GUTZWILLER ET AL. (2012), p. 80-85; and WIDRIG & TAG (2015), p. 590.

1511 WIDRIG (2015), p. 4 and 399.

1512 Cf. previous Chapter 6.1.1 Institutional setting, *ii) Governing principles in the Swiss compulsory health insurance*, 1. Principles of "effectiveness", "appropriateness" and "economic efficiency" of medical services (EAE-criteria) in the Swiss compulsory health insurance, p. 262 ff.

1513 Art. 32 *para.* 1 KVG and previous *note* 1512.

1514 Cf. previous Chapter 6.1.1 Institutional setting, *ii) Governing principles in the Swiss compulsory health insurance*, 2. Principle of "positive" and "negative" lists, p. 263 ff.

1515 SFOPH (2009), p. 3.

1516 *Ibidem.*

As illustrated in the last chapter, in contrast to medical services provided by medical doctors, pharmaceuticals, analyses and medical objects are just reimbursed and listed on a positive list in case they meet the EAE-criteria.[1517] Every new pharmaceutical intervention is typically evaluated after approval as well as re-evaluated every three years.[1518] Analyses and medical objects follow a less stringent process. An evaluation is made only upon request, and there is no mechanism for re-evaluation.[1519]

Limitations in the Swiss process are the following: First, it is decided if a closer evaluation and assessment is appropriate[1520] and if yes, the responsibility of the commission is asigned.[1521] The lack of a systematic evaluation is a major difference compared to other HTA processes.[1522] Second, not the authorities but the interested party is responsible for pulling together the needed information. The applicant – which can be any interested party – is responsible for producing the scientific evidence on effectiveness, appropriateness and cost-effectiveness by filling out the official application form.[1523]

[1517] BRÜGGER ET AL. (2015), p. 2; and WIDRIG (2015), p. 4.

[1518] Art. 34d KLV. An exemption is the lack of an HTA in the case of off-label use, cf. Chapter 6.1.1 iv, "Off-label use of personalized pharmaceuticals and tests", p. 269. In the case of reimbursement based on Art. 71a and b KVV, the payer determines the reimbursed amount without in-depth evaluation/HTA process, cf. WIDMER (2013), p. 21.

[1519] HEIMGARTNER (2015), p. 11; RENGGLI (2016) with critical documentation on Swiss TV.

[1520] For this, the FOPH consults the SWISS HEALTH INSURER'S ASSOCIATION and the SWISS MEDICAL ASSOCIATION. If this first rough assessment of a medical service by the FOPH judges it to be undisputed, it is reimbursed, BRÜGGER ET AL. (2014), p. 254

[1521] There are three commissions: The FEDERAL COMMISSION FOR GENERAL SERVICES AND FUNDAMENTAL QUESTIONS (Eidgenössische Kommission für allgemeine Leistungen und Grundsatzfragen, ELGK); the FEDERAL COMMISSION FOR ANALYSES, EQUIPMENT AND OBJECTS with an committee on analyses (Eidgenössische Kommission für Analysen, Mittel und Gegenstände; Ausschuss für Analysen, EAK) and with a committee for equipment and objects (Eidgenössische Kommission für Analysen, Mittel und Gegenstände; Ausschuss für Mittel- und Gegenstände, EAMGK). The commissions consist on the basis of parity of representatives of the medical profession, insurance companies, patient organizations, hospitals, industry, ethics and sometimes some additional experts. They are appointed by the FEDERAL COUNCIL. More details in SFOPH (2009), p. 5, and BRÜGGER ET AL. (2014), p. 254.

[1522] WIDRIG & TAG (2015), p. 587.

[1523] SFOPH (2009), p. 5; and BRÜGGER ET AL. (2014), p. 254.

The Swiss evaluation process consists of the following stages:

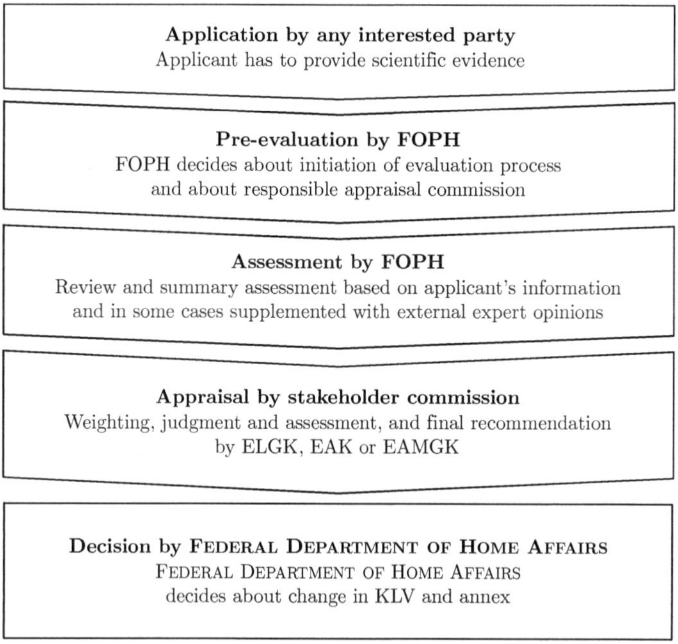

Figure 30: HTA in Switzerland

Source: Illustrated by the author, mainly based on SFOPH (2009).

Assessment: Based on the information in the application – sometimes supplemented with own research by the FOPH – the FOPH creates a summary assessment with the following points:[1524]

- Quantitative illustration of the burden of disease
- Legal, ethical and societal aspects
- Effectiveness: "Effectiveness" under controlled conditions like clinical trials – and "efficacy" in reality.
- Appropriateness: Security, risks, questions of implementation
- Efficiency: Costs of the service, quantity structure, cost consequences, cost-effectiveness based on literature, and in exceptional cases cost-effectiveness-studies requested by the FOPH from the applicant.

[1524] SFOPH (2009), p. 7.

All information about the case is assembled in a dossier which is then handed over to the commission for appraisal.[1525]

Appraisal: There are three commissions for the appraisal – the ELGK, EAK and EMGK. The commissions consist on the basis of parity of representatives of the medical profession, insurance companies, patient organizations, hospitals, industry, ethics and sometimes some additional experts. They are appointed by the FEDERAL COUNCIL.[1526]

The responsible commission has to weight, judge and assess the different, sometimes contradicting facts and to come up with a recommendation to the final decision maker - the FEDERAL DEPARTMENT OF HOME AFFAIRS. Neither the discussions within the appraisal commission, nor the recommendation are made public.[1527]

Decision: Based on the recommendation, the FEDERAL DEPARTMENT OF HOME AFFAIRS will then decide about any changes in the KLV or its annex.[1528]

ii. Criticism of current evaluation process in Switzerland

The Swiss HTA approach has some major advantages compared to alternative HTA approaches. It is being described as *"pragmatic, liberal and integrative"*, because everyone is allowed to initiate the reimbursement decision process. Especially the evaluation process for pharmaceuticals is described to *"work well"* and to be a *"relatively slim process"*.[1529] The Swiss approach is also claimed to be less expensive compared to alternative approaches, because the applicant must provide the scientific evidence.[1530]

However, the Swiss HTA approach is also being criticized for not meeting international HTA standards.[1531] The evaluation process faces the following common criticism:

Danger of biased appraisals with lack of objectivity: The requirement of the applicant providing the scientific evidence bears the risk of conflicts of interest, a biased

[1525] BRÜGGER ET AL. (2014), p. 254.
[1526] Cf. *note* 1521, for details, cf. the commissions' standing orders EAK (2012); EAMGK (2012) and ELGK (2014).
[1527] SFOPH (2009), p. 7; BRÜGGER ET AL. (2014), p. 254; Art. 10 EAK (2012); Art. 13 EAMGK (2012) and Art. 10 ELGK (2014).
[1528] SFOPH (2009), p. 7.
[1529] HEIMGARTNER (2015), p. 22.
[1530] WIDRIG & TAG (2015), p. 589-590.
[1531] *Ibidem*, p. 590.

assessment and appraisal.[1532] Further, it is feared that the appraisals are influenced by particular interests of the different stakeholders in the committees and are thus not consistent or not fair.[1533]

Lack of transparency: The assessment and appraisal are claimed to lack transparency and clear responsibilities. Especially the fact that the consultations in the appraisal phase are not made public decreases the transparency of the Swiss process significantly.[1534]

Lack of concretization of EAE-criteria leading to inconsistencies: Additionally, the EAE-criteria in their current form are being criticized for lacking concretization.[1535] Further, it is claimed that health economic facts are not considered sufficiently.[1536]

Lack of systematic or prioritized choice of HTA (re-)evaluations: The Swiss HTA process is usually triggered by an applicant. No HTA institution or other governmental body initiates the process in a systematic way. The application-based limitation for triggering the evaluation lacks the opportunity to prioritize HTA topics and systematic controls and correction mechanisms in order to systematically (re-)evaluate medical services.[1537]

iii. HTA developments in Switzerland

Since Switzerland does not have a public HTA agency, there have evolved several private companies, foundations and academic institutes that are specialized on HTA consulting.[1538] The promotion of a more systematic HTA approach as an evaluation tool for reimbursement in the Swiss compulsory health insurance has been discussed for several years.[1539]

In the past, there have been several, fragmented groups and attempts to institutionalize a HTA in Switzerland:[1540]

1532 *Ibidem.*
1533 *Ibidem;* and WIDRIG (2015), p. 171.
1534 SEITZ (2011), p. 64; HEIMGARTNER (2015), p. 11-12 and 23; and WIDRIG (2015), p. 171.
1535 FLORIAN GUTZWILLER ET AL. (2012), p. 58, and WIDRIG ET AL. (2012), *recital* 61-63.
1536 FLORIAN GUTZWILLER ET AL. (2012), p. 53 and 58, claiming that the focus lies too much on effectiveness and appropriateness and not economic efficiency.
1537 RIPPE ET AL. (2004), p. 260; FLORIAN GUTZWILLER ET AL. (2012), p. VIII and 57-58; and WIDRIG (2015), p. 171.
1538 KOCH cited in WIDRIG (2015), p. 61-62.
1539 WIDRIG (2015), p. 3.
1540 EDI (2014), p. 25-26, with an overview.

TA-Swiss

The institution TA-Swiss, founded in 1992, evaluates and assesses new technologies in an interdisciplinary team of experts. The goal is to produce a solid, easy to understand report for enabling decision making on a political level.[1541] In the context of PM, TA-Swiss has produced two reports: The first one, published in 2004, focusing on *"Pharmacogenetics and pharmacogenomics"*;[1542] the second one, published in 2014, focusing on *"Personalized medicine"*.[1543] The reports provide a broad overview and solid scientific basis to understand a new topic, however, they do not focus on the evaluation of a specific treatment or technology.

SNHTA

In 1998, the FEDERAL COUNCIL has initiated the foundation of a national network, in order to better coordinate and promote HTA activities in Switzerland. The initiative resulted 1999 in foundation of the SWISS NETWORK OF TECHNOLOGY ASSESSMENT (SNHTA). Today, the network still exists with the main goal of *"the scientific evaluation of medical technologies regarding their effectiveness, appropriateness, efficiency as well as social and ethical aspects and implications"*.[1544]

Swiss Medical Board

In 2008, the Canton of Zürich initiated the pilote project MEDICAL BOARD in order to establish an independent HTA body in Switzerland. The MEDICAL BOARD assesses the EAE-criteria of existing medical services in Switzerland. The pilot project was expanded to a national level in 2011 to the SWISS MEDICAL BOARD (SMB).[1545] The SMB produces on average two HTA-reports annually, however they do not directly affect the reimbursement process.[1546]

1541 WIDRIG (2015), p. 60.

1542 RIPPE ET AL. (2004).

1543 ECKHARDT ET AL. (2014).

1544 Sub-goals are *"To promote HTA-projects, to gather, exchange and disseminate information, expertise and reports, to avoid double track work through cooperation in order to make optimal use of limited resources available for HTA, to cooperate in international HTA-networks and projects and at a later stage, to pool the Swiss HTA-expertise of all members in order to realize joint Swiss HTA-projects"*, cf. SNHTA (2016), *about us*.

1545 SMB (2016), *Vorgeschichte*.

1546 SMB (2016), *abgeschlossene Berichte*. More about SMB in FLORIAN GUTZWILLER ET AL. (2012), p. 54; and WIDRIG (2015), p. 62 ff.

SwissHTA

Not all stakeholders supported the idea of the SMB and another initiative, the SWISSHTA, was launched. SWISSHTA elaborated a consensus papers for the future of HTA in Switzerland, published in 2012 and 2013 by SANTÉSUISSE, INTERPHARMA as well as the SAMS and the SMA.[1547]

SMB as the union between old SMB and SwissHTA

Beginning 2014, the SMB and SWISSHTA initiated a „convergence process“, in order to unify the two approaches. In January 2015, the two initiative merged under the roof of SMB with a broader member spectrum.[1548] The HTA institution has the goal of establishing a scientifically based assessment of medical services.[1549]

HTA pilot program 2015-2017 by FOPH

The introduction of a more systematic HTA process reached the political discussions as well. In 2010 a motion to found a national HTA body was accepted and the responsibility was handed over to the FEDERAL COUNCIL beginning 2011.[1550]

In 2013, the FEDERAL COUNCIL published a strategic report with an overview of the priorities which have been set in the field of health policy in Switzerland until 2020. One priority area is to *"safeguard and increase the quality of healthcare provision"*. Among other measures, it is mentioned that HTAs should play a stronger role in the future, in order to *"reduce ineffective and inefficient services, medicines and processes in order to increase quality and lower costs"*.[1551]

In May 2014, the FEDERAL COUNCIL proposed a draft bill with the aim to create a NATIONAL CENTER FOR QUALITY with two departments: One department focused on quality improvement, the other one focused on HTA.[1552] The center was supposed to work together with the existing players in the healthcare system.[1553] However, the draft was abandoned due to resistance by several stakeholders. Due to the responses in the consultation process, the FEDERAL COUNCIL decided to address the topics

---

1547 FLORIAN GUTZWILLER ET AL. (2012), p. 56; and WIDRIG (2015), p. 63.

1548 Members are the CONFERENCE OF THE CANTONAL HEALTH DIRECTORS, the SAMS, the PRINCIPALITY OF LIECHTENSTEIN, INTERPHARMA und SANTÉSUISSE. The SMA left the SMB. The FOPH is not a member. Cf. SMB (2016), *Vorgeschichte.*

1549 SMB (2016), *Vorgeschichte.*

1550 WIDRIG (2015), p. 64.

1551 EDI (2013), p. 11.

1552 EDI (2014), p. 41-42.

1553 *Ibidem*, p. 3-4.

"quality improvement" and "HTA" separately and not to pursue the solution with a NATIONAL CENTER FOR QUALITY.[1554]

For addressing the topic "quality improvements", a "network solution" was proposed end 2015.[1555] The draft proposal for a change in the KVG aims at the strengthening of the quality and efficiency of the compulsory health insurance. According to the draft, the FEDERAL COUNCIL is supposed to establish, lead and evaluate programs for quality improvement or to transfer this task to third parties. A non-parlamentiary commission shall consult the FEDERAL COUNCIL.[1556]

In order to gradually strengthen the HTA in Switzerland, a dedicated department within the FOPH will be created. The department will outsource the re-evaluation mandates to external institutions. Its task is to systematically and periodically re-evaluate medical services that are reimbursed by the compulsory health insurance. Its main focus will be the re-evaluation of existing services on a prioritized basis in order to identify potential *"disinvestments"* from the compulsory health insurance.[1557] Also the evaluation of new treatments or prophylactic measures are in the scope of a potential assessment.[1558] The new department will also be responsible for a "horizon scanning" for early recognition of new services or indication expansions.[1559] A first pilot program 2015-2017 has started on three prioritized medical services – however none of them in the field of personalized medicine.[1560]

Besides the HTA department within the FOPH, the new process does not involve the establishment of any additional new bodies. The existing commissions will keep their roles and the evaluation process stays the same – except for the selected evaluations. The final reimbursement decision-making power after an evaluation lies at the FEDERAL DEPARTMENT OF HOME AFFAIRS.[1561] Further, the planned approach towards HTAs does neither change the fact of evaluationg just some prioritized, selected med-

[1554] Report draft KVG, p. 281.

[1555] *Ibidem.*

[1556] Art. 58 and 58a D-KVG, BBl 2016 257.

[1557] SFOPH (2016)b, *Zielsetzung.* Details about the prioritization process under *Prozess zur Re-Evaluation bestehender Leistungen der OKP.*

[1558] SFOPH (2016)a, p. 2. As an example for a prophylactic measure the SFOPH (2016)a mentions explicitly prophylactic measures for patients with BRCA1/2 mutations (breast/ovarian cancer risk).

[1559] SFOPH (2016)a, p. 2.

[1560] SFOPH (2016)e, *na.*

[1561] STRAUMANN (2015), p. 2; SFOPH (2016)e, *na.*

ical interventions. The claim by the SMB for a more comprehensive, national HTA strategy is being upheld.[1562]

6.2.2 Analysis of incentives

The previous analysis of the institutional setting governing the HTA process has illustrated its process and limitations. The main differences to other systems is the pragmatism of the Swiss approach, the non-systematic (re-)evaluation of medical services, and the lower degree of transparency during the evaluation process.

The establishment of an improved HTA process in Switzerland has been a disputed topic for several years, and has gained additional momentum with the FEDERAL COUNCIL'S health 2020 priorities.[1563] With the current pilot HTA program within the new HTA agency by the FOPH, the first steps towards a more systematic approach have been made.

In all the current discussions, there seems to be no room for debate around the incompatibility of current HTA process with PM; and respective needs for adaptation of the HTA process in the context of PM. The evaluation of personalized pharmaceuticals and Dx follows the existing HTA approach – including its current limitations.

This chapter analyses the resulting incentives set by the existing institutional setting governing the HTA process in Switzerland.

Pharmaceutical companies

The Swiss evaluation process for pharmaceuticals is perceived to be relatively well-established, slim and efficient.[1564] In contrast to pharmaceuticals, analyses and medical objects follow a less stringent process. An evaluation is only made upon request and there is no mechanism for re-evaluation.[1565] Further, the evaluation process is criticized for lacking transparency and objectivity.

The relatively well-established evaluation process for pharmaceuticals combined with the lack of clear evidence requirements and transparency in the evaluation process for CDx does not incentivize pharmaceutical companies to deviate from the traditional approach. The argumentation in Part III is valid for the Swiss case too.[1566]

1562 STRAUMANN (2015), p. 2.
1563 EDI (2013), p. 11.
1564 HEIMGARTNER (2015), p. 22-23.
1565 HEIMGARTNER (2015), p. 11; RENGGLI (2016) with a critical documentation on Swiss TV.
1566 Cf. Part III, Chapter 6.2.2 Analysis of incentives, *Pharmaceutical companies*, p. 206.

Diagnostics companies

A diagnostic company aiming for reimbursement of a PM Dx has to apply for reimbursement and to provide scientific evidence for its product. However, the applicant has no predictability or clarity regarding the necessary steps for value demonstration. The Swiss situation means arbitrariness for the applicant, because it is not transparent which argumentation and which degree of scientific evidence will lead to a positive reimbursement decision.[1567] Neither the internal reports of the commissions nor the final report for the FEDERAL DEPARTMENT OF HOME AFFAIRS are made public. Thus, a PM Dx company has no incentives to invest neither in tests nor in PM Dx evidence development.[1568]

Providers & patients

Gaps and inconsistencies in the Swiss HTA processes for PM treatments generally disincentivizes providers and patients to foster the use of PM. The argumentation in Part III is valid for the Swiss case too.[1569]

Payers

In-existent, unclear or inadequate HTA mechanisms for PM treatments incentivize payers not to reimburse them and to remain conservative in their reimbursement decisions for personalized medicine applications. The argumentation in Part III is valid in the Swiss case too.[1570]

1567 Cf. also FLORIAN GUTZWILLER ET AL. (2012), p. 57.
1568 WURCEL ET AL. (2016), p. 141.
1569 Cf. Part III, Chapter 6.2.2 Analysis of incentives, *Providers & Patients*, p. 207-208.
1570 Cf. Part III, Chapter 6.2.2 Analysis of incentives, *Payers*, p. 208.

6.2.3 Result

The overview below summarizes the argumentation of the previous chapter and shows the resulting incentives through institutional setting in Switzerland concerning the regulation of the HTA process in Switzerland.

Research institutions	*Pharmaceutical companies*	*Diagnostic companies*	*Providers*	*Patients*	*Payers*
–	negative	negative	negative	negative	negative

negative = institutional setting incentivizes a player not to foster the translation of PM
– = neutral/no conclusive statement possible on a player's incentive to foster the translation of PM

The resulting incentives for Switzerland demonstrate that the hypothesis cannot be rejected for Switzerland: *Gaps and inconsistencies in the current Swiss health technology assessments for personalized medicine act as a barrier to the translation of personalized medicine into clinical practice.*

7 Results

7.1 Resulting incentives in the Swiss institutional setting

Part IV analyses the institutional setting governing the barriers to the translation of PM in Switzerland. It demonstrates that the Swiss institutional setting tends to lower certain barriers identified in the theoretical Part III:

Value chain phase	*Barrier*	*Research institutions*	*Pharma. companies*	*Diagnostic companies*	*Providers*	*Patients*	*Payers*
Discovery	2.1 Lack of standards enabling data sharing between biobanks	–*	–*	–*	–	–	–
	2.2 Lack of bioinformatics infrastructure and expertise	–*	–*	–*	–	–	–
Development	3.1 Strategic, operational and cultural differences between Rx and Dx industry	–	neg.	neg.	–	–	–
	3.2 Limited intellectual property protection for CDx	–	–	–*	–	–	–
Approval	4.1 Inconsistencies and gaps in the regulatory framework of the approval process for PM	–	neg.	neg.	–	–	–
	4.2 Incompatibility of clinical trials with personalized pharmaceuticals	–	neg.	–	–	–	–
Provision	5.1 Lack of healthcare providers' knowledge about PM	–	neg.	neg.	neg.	neg.	–
	5.2 Lack of patients' awareness and understanding of PM	–	neg.	neg.	neg.	neg.	neg.
	5.3 Lack of consistent, recognized and clinically implemented guidelines on PM approaches	–	–	–	neg.	neg.	neg.
	5.4 Lack of infrastructure for the implementation of PM	neg.	neg.	neg.	neg.	neg.	–
	5.5 Privacy concerns regarding the use of PM	–*	–*	–*	–*	–*	–
Reimbursement	6.1 Lack of reimbursement for PM diagnostics	–	neg.	neg.	neg.	neg.	neg.
	6.2 Gaps and inconsistencies in conventional HTAs for PM	–	neg.	neg.	neg.	neg.	neg.

** incentives structure deviating from the theoretical findings in Part III.*

Table 10: Overview of incentives for each stakeholder and each institutional barrier in Switzerland

Against the backdrop of the theoretical findings in Part III, the analysis demonstrates that Switzerland's institutional environment governing the barriers behind the translation of PM into clinical practice imposes less negative incentives during the discovery and development phases of PM, wheareas the barriers in the second half of the value chain remain similar.

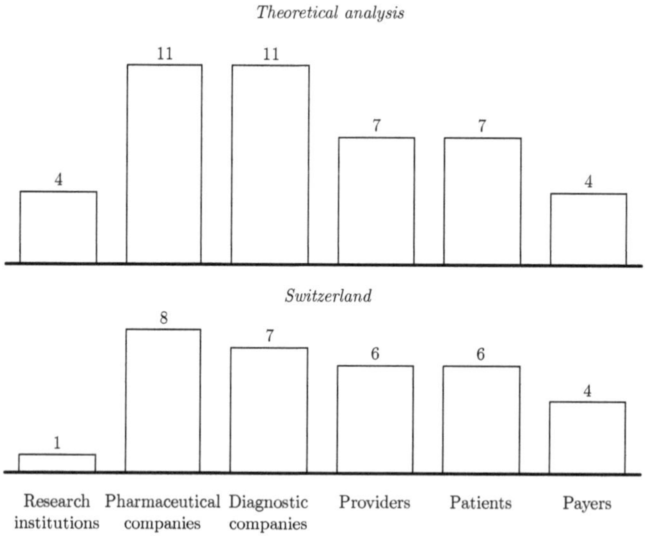

Figure 31: Switzerland vs theoretical case of resulting incentives by number of barriers negatively incentivizing stakeholders

Fewer barriers are hindering the translation of PM in Switzerland.[1571] Particularly, the institutional environment for *research institutions* in the discovery phase imposes fewer barriers to the translation of PM compared to the barriers identified in Part III. With the lack of infrastructure for the implementation of PM, one barrier still remains. *Payers* are the only stakeholders facing the same number of barriers as identified in Part III. The relatively high number of barriers affecting *pharmaceutical and Dx companies* is also found in the Swiss case.

[1571] This is attributable to the differences discussed in the following Sub-chapter 7.2 Relevance assessment, p. 292 ff.

7.2 Relevance assessment

		Number of negatively incentivized stakeholders[1]	
		Theoretical analysis	Switzerland
Discovery	2.1 Lack of standards enabling data sharing between biobanks	3	0
	2.2 Lack of bioinformatics infrastructure and expertise	3	0
Development	3.1 Strategic, operational and cultural differences between Rx and Dx industry	2	2
	3.2 Limited intellectual property protection for CDx	1	0
Approval	4.1 Inconsistencies and gaps in the regulatory framework of the approval process for PM	2	2
	4.2 Incompatibility of clinical trials with personalized pharmaceuticals	1	1
Provision	5.1 Lack of healthcare providers' knowledge about PM	4	4
	5.2 Lack of patients' awareness and understanding of PM	5	5
	5.3 Lack of consistent, recognized and clinically implemented guidelines	3	3
	5.4 Lack of infrastructure for the implementation of PM	5	5
	5.5 Privacy concerns regarding the use of PM	5	0
Reimbursement	6.1 Lack of reimbursement for PM diagnostics	5	5
	6.2 Gaps and inconsistencies in conventional HTAs for PM	5	5

1 Stakeholders' incentives all equally weighed

Figure 32: Comparison of barriers' incentives by number of negatively incentivized stakeholders

Compared to Part III, the relevance[1572] of the barriers in Switzerland differs in the following three points:

1. The analysis finds that Switzerland's institutional environment in the discovery phase does not impose any negative incentives to the stakeholders involved in this phase. Switzerland has initiated several projects aiming at the sharing of data between biobanks in line with the newest international developments in this field.[1573] Also, Switzerland has taken action in order to strengthen its bioinformatics infrastructure and expertise.[1574]

2. A second difference is a more favourable intellectual property environment in Switzerland. The Swiss approach towards IP protection of CDx is less strict compared to the US and limited IP protection of CDx is not a barrier to the translation of PM.[1575]

[1572] Cf. RESEARCH CONCEPT, Chapter 4.3 Derivation and evaluation of policy levers, *Relevance*, p. 12.
[1573] Cf. Chapter 2.1 Lack of standards enabling data sharing between biobanks, p. 219 ff.
[1574] Cf. Chapter 2.2 Lack of bioinformatics infrastructure and expertise, p. 222 ff.
[1575] Cf. Chapter 3.2 Limited intellectual property protection for companion diagnostics, p. 226 ff.

3. A last difference is related to the privacy concerns regarding the use of PM. This thesis finds a field of tension between privacy protection and data sharing. On the one hand, it is demonstrated, that Switzerland has a dense and multi-layered institutional setting governing privacy protection of genetic data appropriate to address the the public's privacy concerns regarding the use of PM.[1576] On the other hand, it is demonstrated that the comprehensiveness of the Swiss regulation may be an barrier to the translation of PM as it is criticized to slow down medical progress by impeding data sharing.[1577] With these opposing findings for Switzerland, no conclusive statement concerning the incentives of the relevant stakeholders is made.

7.3 Conclusion

The results of Part IV demonstrate that Switzerland's institutional environment imposes several barriers to the translation of PM into clinical practice. These barriers predominantly concern the second half of the PM value chain, namely the approval, provision, and reimbursement phase. In the discovery and development phase, Switzerland's institutional setting imposes fewer barriers to the translation of PM compared to the number of barriers identified in the theoretical Part III.

Therefore, any strategy to foster the translation of PM in Switzerland should primarily target the latter links of the PM value chain. Policy levers in order to reduce the existing barriers to the translation of PM in Switzerland are presented in the next part of this thesis (*Part V*).

[1576] Cf. Part IV, Chapter 5.5.2 Analysis of incentives, *Patients in Switzerland incline to share their genetic data*, p. 258.

[1577] Cf. Part IV, Chapter 5.5.2 Analysis of incentives, *Providers and researchers have to deal with additional work due to privacy* protection regulation, p. 259.

Part V: Policy implications

Institutional levers to foster the translation of personalized medicine into Swiss clinical practice

The previous *Part IV* found that the institutional setting in Switzerland imposes several barriers to the translation of personalized medicine into clinical practice - primarily in the second half of the PM value chain. One central research question has not been addressed so far: What levers has the Swiss policy maker in its incentives armamentarium in order to foster the translation of personalized medicine into clinical practice?

Grounded on the findings of previous *Parts III* and *IV*, *Part V* addresses this question by identifying and evaluating available policy levers to change the institutional setting of the identified barriers in order to increase the incentives for the provision of personalized medicine.

K. Bosshard, *Law and Economics of Personalized Medicine*,
Gesundheitsmanagement und Gesundheitsökonomik,
https://doi.org/10.1007/978-3-658-22074-7_6

1 Methodological approach

1.1 Identification of policy levers

The main source of the identification of policy levers for each barrier provides the analysis of the institutional setting governing each respective barrier in Switzerland. Based on the Law and Economic analysis in Part IV, available policy levers are derived.

1.2 Categorization of policy levers

At the end of Part V[1578] the identified policy measures to foster the translation of PM are assessed for their binding character and are categorized into three categories:

- Levers that do require *no legal changes* in the current institutional setting
- Levers that do require *soft law changes* in the current institutional setting
- Levers that do require *hard law changes* in the current institutional setting

The categories represent the *"ability to change"* an institutional barrier to the translation of PM for the Swiss policy maker.[1579]

1.3 Evaluation of policy levers

Combined with the identified incentives for each stakeholder in the previous Part IV, the relevance of this part's policy levers can be derived. The more disincentives to foster the translation of PM a policy lever alleviates, the more relevant the policy lever is.[1580]

[1578] Cf. Chapter 7.1 Categorization, p. 328 ff.
[1579] Cf. Figure 2: Evaluation matrix, p. 11.
[1580] Cf. RESEARCH CONCEPT, Chapter 4.3 Derivation and evaluation of policy levers, *Relevance*, p. 12.

2 Discovery policy levers

2.1 Lack of standards enabling data sharing between biobanks

The analysis in Part IV found that Switzerland has initiated the establishment of standards allowing the sharing of data between biobanks in line with the newest international developments in this field.[1581] Thus, this thesis did not identify additional policy levers concerning this barrier.

2.2 Lack of bioinformatics infrastructure and bioinformatics expertise

The analysis in Part IV has found that the Swiss government, in collaboration with academia, the SAMS and the industry, has initiated projects in order to provide the bioinformatics infrastructure and corresponding expertise.[1582] Similarly to the previous chapter thesis did not identify additional policy levers concerning this barrier. The Swiss policy maker should continue to fund collaborative, cross-/interdisciplinary research projects via the SWISS NATIONAL SCIENCE FOUNDATION in order to avoid silos in academic research.[1583]

1581 Cf. Part IV, Chapter 2.1 Lack of standards enabling data sharing between biobanks, p. 219 ff.

1582 Cf. Part IV, Chapter 2.2 Lack of bioinformatics infrastructure and expertise, p. 222 ff.

1583 Similarly suggested for the EU/US by EUROPEAN ALLIANCE FOR PERSONALISED MEDICINE (2013), p. 4; KIEVITS ET AL. (2014), p. 5; EPPINGER ET AL. (2015), p. 146; PERMED (2015), p. 3 and 33, (via "open innovation"); and TRUSHEIM & BERNDT (2015)b, p. 10.

3 Development policy levers

3.1 Strategic, operational and cultural differences between pharmaceutical and diagnostics industry

This thesis argues that the Swiss policy maker has limited means to reduce company-internal strategic, operational or cultural differences and increase the incentives for PM strategies by pharmaceutical and diagnostics companies. However, one policy lever should be considered:

Support the creation of co-development guidelines & best practice sharing platforms

The Swiss policy maker should initiate the creation of soft law co-development guidelines or best practice sharing platforms – as this is e.g. done by the FDA.[1584]

3.2 Limited intellectual property protection for companion diagnostics

The analysis in Part IV Chapter 3.2 has resulted in no negative incentives to the translation of PM through a claimed lack of IP protection for CDx in Switzerland. Thus, this thesis did not identify any additional policy levers in the field if CDx related IP protection.

1584 Cf. Part III, Chapter 4.1.2 Lack of consistent regulatory guidance in the approval process for CDx, *ii) IVD approval process in the US, Co-development* guidance by the FDA, p. 143; and e.g., FDA (2016)b.

4 Approval policy levers

4.1 Inconsistencies and gaps in the regulatory framework of the approval process for personalized medicine

The following chapter lists and discusses available policy levers in order to reduce the inconsistencies and gaps in the regulatory framework of the approval process for PM in Switzerland. Based on the Law and Economic analysis for Switzerland in Part IV, the following policy implications are derived.[1585]

Synchronize approval processes of PM Rx and PM Dx

The Swiss approval system for pharmaceuticals does currently follow a separate approval path than the conformity assessment process of CDx – with limited coordination between the two processes. In order to foster the translation of PM, Switzerland should treat personalized pharmaceuticals and diagnostic components equitable and synchronize the two currently separated processes including timelines and approval criteria.[1586]

Additionally, the required data inputs should be aligned as far as possible with the data required for the HTA process in order to create synergies between the approval and reimbursement application process.[1587] This would allow pharmaceutical and diagnostics companies to reduce unnecessary costs and administrative burdens.

Regulate laboratory developed tests (LDTs)

A regulator needs to strike a balance between leaving freedom to develop and offer tests and ensuring adequate patient safety. In order to justify new regulation in the area of genetic testing, a regulator must demonstrate *"a state interest that outweighs the risks posed by increased oversight to innovation, investment, and access to genetic tests needed for clinical care in the era of personalized medicine".*[1588]

[1585] Cf. Part IV Chapter 4.1 Inconsistencies and gaps in the regulatory framework of the approval process for personalized medicine, p. 230 ff.

[1586] BRÜGGER in the interview on August 10, 2016. Cf. also THOMAS ET AL. (2016), p. 347, who discuss the topic and policy levers for Germany, facing similar challenges like Switzerland.

[1587] BRÜGGER in the interview on August 10, 2016; and cf. policy lever in following Chapter 6.2 Gaps and inconsistencies in conventional health technology assessments for personalized medicine, "Align requirements for approval process with HTA process", p. 325.

[1588] BAYEFSKY & BERKMAN (2015), p. 1 ff. with several pro and con arguments for regulating LDTs.

There is one major argument *speaking against a stricter oversight of LDTs:* LDTs enable the broadest and least expensive public availability of molecular testing.[1589] Today, the majority of medical genetics tests are developed and offered by individual laboratories as LDTs.[1590] It is estimated, that over 90% of the high complexity clinical laboratory testing done today occurs in a LDT setting.[1591] LDTs have lower direct costs and thus hospitals tend to perform these "in house" tests in place of commercially available tests.[1592]

Two major arguments *speak in favor of a stricter regulation of LDTs* as this is currently planned in the EU and the US: First, reduced incentives for manufacturers to develop diagnostics, and second, safety concerns due to variation in standards between sites and countries.

First, the regulation of LDTs brings more consistency in the legal approval framework for CDx by creating *equal treatment* with commercially available diagnostic tests. So far, laboratories or hospitals could provide substitutes to approved diagnostic tests, undercutting the value captured by commercial diagnostic manufacturers.[1593]

Second, the regulation of LDTs helps to "pick out the lemons in the market". The sale of an officially approved test can act as a commercial incentive for development[1594] of PM tests and underpin the financial success of the PM market.

The Swiss policy maker needs to find a balance between the two streams of arguments. However – there is limited room for choice as the Swiss law must be adapted to the EU Directive.[1595]

1589 E.g., CRAWFORD & ASPINALL (2012), p. 269.

1590 MCCARTHY ET AL. (2013), p. 10; PERSONALIZED MEDICINE COALITION (2014), p. 22; BAYEFSKY & BERKMAN (2015), p. 2. Also tests used in the DTC field are often LDTs, e.g., 23ANDME or diverse non-invasive prenatal tests, e.g., NATERA, cf. "Genetica Now Offering PanoramaTM NIPT in Switzerland via Natera's Constellation™ Software Platform" (2016).

1591 CRAWFORD & ASPINALL (2012), p. 69.

1592 MEADOWS ET AL. (2015), p. 10.

1593 In fact, in the US there have been commercial players urging the FDA to take LDTs into their regulatory scope as well. For example, in 2008 GENENTECH filed a citizen petition urging the FDA to regulate all in vitro diagnostic tests aimed for use in therapeutic decision making. GENENTECH argued that the regulatory inconsistency between commercial IVDs and LDTs poses a serious threat to patients' health because *"the future of personalized medicine depends on the development of pharmacogenomic tests"* and *"it is critical that they are accurate, reliable, and clinically valid (i.e., effective)"*, GENENTECH (2008) cited in CONSTANCE (2010), p. 35.

1594 CRAWFORD & ASPINALL (2012), p. 269 ff.

1595 According to the IVDR LDTs – with some specific provisions for class D devices – will be exempted from the requirements. Further, LDTs do not benefit from exemptions when their tests are manufactured on an "industrial scale". Cf. Part III, Chapter 4.1.3 Undermining of the current approval system through LDTs, *i) LDT regulation in the EU*, p. 149.

Introduce risk categories for CDx

The Swiss law should adapt its respective regulations and the requirements in the approval process to the new risk-based product classification system for IVDs as foreseen in the IVDR.[1596]

As stipulated in the IVDR, CDx in Switzerland do not only undergo a self-confirmation process, but are accredited by non-governmental conformity assessment bodies. With the current institutional set-up, the Swiss law is prepared to ingest the required changes. The Swiss law explicitly contains an exemption for the case of an increased health hazard. In these cases the FEDERAL COUNCIL has the competence to make IVDs – of which CDx are a sub-category – subject to a special approval process.[1597]

Keep reference to EU regulation

In both of the last two recommendations, Switzerland has limited room for regulatory choices as the Swiss law generally refers to the EU Directives.

Literature emphasizes the need for harmonization in order to address the existing inconsistencies in the approval processes.[1598] A more comprehensive standardized roadmap is needed at the regional and global level and an increased dialogue on the differences between regulatory authorities, academia and industry to facilitate access to PM.[1599]

By directly referring to the EU regulation, Switzerland addresses this call for harmonization in the approval process in case of CDx.[1600]

[1596] Cf. Part IV, Chapter 4.1.1 Institutional setting, iii) Impact of the revised EU legislation on Switzerland, p. 232.

[1597] Art. 11 *para.* 1 *lit.* a MepV.

[1598] Cf. Part III, Chapter 4.1.4 Lack of harmonization between regulatory systems, p. 152 ff.

[1599] E.g., BRANZÉN (2013), p. 61; EUROPEAN ALLIANCE FOR PERSONALISED MEDICINE (2013), p. 4; THE ACADEMY OF MEDICAL SCIENCES (2013), p. 52; MEADOWS ET AL. (2015), p. 8; SHIMAZAWA & IKEDA (2015), p. 157 ff.; DAVID PETTITT ET AL. (2016), p. 326-627. An attempt into the direction of regulatory harmonization represents the INTERNATIONAL MEDICAL DEVICE REGULATORS FORUM (IMDRF). Conceived in 2011, the forum is a voluntary group of medical device regulators from around the world with the aim to build on the foundational work of a previous group, the GLOBAL HARMONIZATION TASK FORCE ON MEDICAL DEVICES (GHTF), and to accelerate international medical device regulatory harmonization and convergence, cf. IMDRF (2016). Another attempt represents the GLOBAL COALITION FOR REGULATORY SCIENCE RESEARCH, which aims to foster regulatory consensus amongst international partners and integrate novel technologies into regulatory decision-making, cf. DAVID PETTITT ET AL. (2016), p. 324.

[1600] Cf. Part IV, Chapter 4.1.1 Institutional setting, *iii) Impact of the revised EU legislation on Switzerland*, p. 232.

Create exclusivities for new indications using existing pharmaceuticals

Though not related to the diagnostic but to the pharmaceutical approval process, an idea is to create exclusivities for new indications using existing compounds. Currently, there are no incentives for any player in the PM ecosystem to invest into the identification of new indications for patient sub-groups using already existing pharmaceuticals (original compounds or generics).

4.2 Incompatibility of clinical trials with personalized pharmaceuticals

The following Chapter lists and discusses available policy levers to ensure the compatibility of clinical trials in Switzerland with PM in order to increase the incentives – primarily for pharmaceutical companies – to develop personalized pharmaceuticals.[1601]

Discuss and allow for new forms of clinical trials for personalized applications

The institutional framework governing clinical trials needs to adapt in order to permit access to smaller groups of subjects and to recognize the validity of results from trials with groups smaller than the "traditional" randomized approach.[1602] The current challenge is to find a trial design best supporting the investigation of personalized new drugs while suiting the established drugs. The same trial design might not serve the "traditional" as well as the "personalized" purpose equally well.[1603]

In order to find innovative solutions to this barrier, HARVARD BUSINESS SCHOOL (2016) launched the "Precision Trials Challenge". Several ideas have been submitted and discussed.[1604] The winning idea was the introduction of an open computational platform for matching patient-specific genomic profiles to personalized cancer medicine clinical trials.[1605]

There are already some new forms of trials emerging,[1606] e.g., there are new study designs to adapt randomized controlled trials for rare diseases. However, less rigorous

[1601] Insights are based on the Law and Economic analysis in Part IV, Chapter 4.2, Incompatibility of clinical trials with personalized pharmaceuticals, p. 234.

[1602] Also EUROPEAN ALLIANCE FOR PERSONALISED MEDICINE (2013), p. 19; and KIEVITS ET AL. (2014), p. 18.

[1603] LE TOURNEAU (2013); KAMAL (2013); HOLLINGSWORTH (2015); MTSUI, BUYSE, & SIMON (2015) and RUBERG & SHEN (2015) provide overviews of the main challenges and proposed diverse solutions associated with PM trials. PERMED (2015), p. 24.

[1604] Ideas can be read on https://openforum.hbs.org/challenge/precision-medicine/submit-ideas (last visited July 17, 2017).

[1605] More info about the winning project on https://openforum.hbs.org/challenge/precision-medicine/announce/matchminer (last visited July 17, 2017).

[1606] BOMBARD (2015), p. 58, for further references for new trial designs for rare diseases.

study designs can yield lower quality clinical utility data.[1607] Other examples are patient-centric approaches like *umbrella*[1608] or *basket*[1609] studies.[1610]

SCHELLEKENS, ALDOSARI, TALSMA, & MASTROBATTISTA (2017) go one step further and suggest to omit the *"outmoded regulatory approach"*.[1611] They discuss the idea to *"retool the development and production of drugs so that they are as close as possible to the patient"*. They suggest a "magistral model" in which a treatment occurs in the same legal entity as the production of a drug. Thus, they argue, no restrictive, expensive and time-consuming approval processes would be necessary. Such a scheme would combine healthcare provider and drug manufacturer into the same entity, increasing the incentive for drug pricing to be cost-effective.[1612]

Current thought leadership also moves towards *"n=1" trials*.[1613] The terminology stemming from GUYATT (1986) with "n" standing for the statistical population, which is in the case of "n=1" trials just one person.[1614] Especially with regard to the developments of PM the call for "n=1" trials become louder again.[1615] However, in Switzerland "n=1" trials are not done so far.[1616]

The Swiss policy maker should discuss these new emerging forms of clinical trials in the approval process and allow for their timely implementation into today's institutional setting.[1617]

Introduce adaptive licensing for personalized pharmaceuticals

A prominent suggestion is the introduction of *"adaptive licensing"* (AL) in which the regulator works early in the development process with drug sponsors in approving

---

1607 BOGAERTS ET AL. (2015) cited in BOMBARD (2015), p. 2.

1608 Studies *within tumor types*, selected by *different markers* for single or multiple candidate drugs, cf. HOLLINGSWORTH (2015), p. 2.

1609 Studies *across tumor types*, often selected by *single marker* or for a single candidate drug, cf. HOLLINGSWORTH (2015), p. 2.

1610 *Ibidem*, p. 1; and KANAVOS (2016), p. 9 ff. with more "new" study design options.

1611 SCHELLEKENS, ALDOSARI, TALSMA, & MASTROBATTISTA (2017), p. 3.

1612 *Ibidem*, p. 1 and 4.

1613 EUROPEAN SCIENCE FOUNDATION (2012), p. 44; NIEDERER (2015), p. 56; and SCHORK (2015).

1614 GUYATT ET AL. (1986), p. 889 ff.

1615 MEIER-ABT and SCHORK cited in NIEDERER (2015), p. 56.

1616 ROSEMAN cited in NIEDERER (2015), p. 56.

1617 Similarly ECKHARDT ET AL. (2014), p. XVII.

trial designs, and then accepting data in sequential partial submission.[1618] AL will require the cooperation between the industry and the regulator.[1619]

The Swiss policy maker should consider introducing AL for personalized pharmaceuticals. AL is also known as "staggered approval". It consists of iterative phases of information gathering before regulatory evaluation and differs from the prevailing binary regulatory approval decision. Compared to "traditional trials", the approach allows approval to align more closely with patient needs for timely access to new technologies and for data to inform medical decisions.[1620] From 2014-2016, the EMA has conducted a pilot project to explore the practical implications of the AL concept and has published its take aways in a report from which Switzerland could profit.[1621]

Create guidelines with principles for PM clinical trials

Until 2016, there was no guideline on "good pharmacogenomic practice" in Europe. Mid2016 the EMA has published a respective document sketching out certain principles for personalized clinical trials in order to generate reliable evidence for decision making and patient treatment.[1622] The document reviews past issues which have been encountered in studies, and contains suggestions for improvement.

The Swiss policy maker – or *in concreto* SWISSMEDIC – should consider providing explicit guidelines for PM trials. With the issuance of guidelines, SWISSMEDIC could signal its support of the use of biomarkers to streamline the drug approval process and facilitate clinical trials in the context of PM.

Pursue innovative biobank approaches for clinical trials

The Swiss policy maker should continue to support innovative biobank approaches which can be used by the industry for clinical trials. For example, EVANGELATOS ET AL. (2016) propose the construction of a web-based platform for the exchange of

---

1618 *"Adaptive licensing"* is also *called "adaptive pathways"* or *"roling approvals"*. E.g., TRUSHEIM & BERNDT (2012), p. 424; AKHMETOV ET AL. (2015), p. 222; and PERMED (2015), p. 29. SCHULLER (2011) describing several options for conducting adaptive clinical trials.

1619 MEADOWS ET AL. (2015), p. 9, mentioning the NEW DRUG DEVELOPMENT PARADIGMS (NEWDIGS) initiative that has begun to pilot programs to explore frameworks to facilitate public–private partnerships with adaptive licensing.

1620 Cf. TUNIS ET AL. (2012), p. 3; KIEVITS ET AL. (2014), p. 18; EUROPEAN MEDICINES AGENCY (2016), p. 1-2. MEADOWS ET AL. (2015), p. 9, for a description of the INNOVATIVE MEDICINES INITIATIVE and the MASSACHUSETTS INSTITUTE OF TECHNOLOGY pilot program to explore frameworks to facilitate public–private partnerships with adaptive licensing. Also suggested by EUROPEAN ALLIANCE FOR PERSONALISED MEDICINE (2013), p. 4, MORGON (2015), p. 81 ff.; PERMED (2015), p. 24; and BUDIN-LJØSNE & HARRIS (2016), p. 5.

1621 Cf. EUROPEAN MEDICINES AGENCY (2016), *na*.

1622 EMA (2016), p. 3.

health data from clinical trials. A platform working as a *"Virtual Knowledge Bank"* on which clinical trial data in electronic format is stored as information resources. Depositors would be private for-profit biopharmaceutical companies. They would be entitled to deposit and also withdraw information resources from the platform. Transactions would be regulated by applying only one excludability criterion: companies would be allowed to download the same amount of data, quantitatively and qualitatively, which they would upload. Data from clinical trials would be used as a currency for carrying out transactions.[1623]

1623 EVANGELATOS ET AL. (2016), p. 4.

5 Provision policy levers

5.1 Lack of healthcare providers' knowledge about personalized medicine

Update the SWISS CATALOGUE OF LEARNING OBJECTIVES (SCLO) and further medical education with learning goals for medical genetics, medical statistics, pharmacogenetics and epidemiology

The current gaps in the medical education should be closed.[1624] University graduates should have a solid knowledge of medical genetics, medical statistics pharmacogenomics and epidemiology. Thus, the SCLO should be updated.[1625] Postgraduate and further education should ensure to cover the newest scientific findings related to drug-gene interactions in the respective field (e.g., presentation of successful case examples, demonstration efforts of early adopters). The SWISS INSTITUTE FOR POSTGRADUATE AND FURTHER EDUCATION IN MEDICINE could think of offering regularly updated distance-learning formats in the respective disciplines.

Additionally, the educational update should not be limited to medical doctors. The training should include nurses and pharmacist and other participants in the healthcare workforce.

Further integrate medical sciences with other natural sciences

As illustrated, new university programs start to address the required integration of medical sciences with other natural sciences (e.g., the bachelor at the ETH focusing on biomolecular and medical-technical aspects or bachelors and masters in molecular and translational biomedicine).[1626] Further integrative measures in this direction should be pursued (e.g., elective subjects of the respective complementary topics should be offered, cross-internships, etc.).

1624 Also recommended by SAMS (2012), p. 6 and 24, and similarly THE ACADEMY OF MEDICAL SCIENCES (2013), p. 70; EUROPEAN ALLIANCE FOR PERSONALISED MEDICINE (2013), p. 6; T. A MANOLIO ET AL. (2013), p. 261; HORGAN ET AL. (2014), p. 293, ECKHARDT ET AL. (2014), p. 271; KIEVITS ET AL. (2014), p.13; EPPINGER ET AL. (2015), p. 150; EUROPABIO (2015), p. 14; and PLUN-FAVREAU ET AL. (2016), p. 145.

1625 E.g., an update with the objectives "A physician must be able to show knowledge of common drug-gene interaction" or "A physician must demonstrate a solid knowledge of medical genetics and statistics" or "A physician shows basic genetic counseling skills and is able to recommend appropriate genetic tests".

1626 Cf. Part IV, Chapter 5.1.1 Institutional setting, *a) University education*, p. 236.

Create new medical titles bridging medical and bioinformatics knowledge

New types of healthcare roles should be created bridging bioinformatics and medical knowledge and which are able to manage, interpret and translate patient data to patients and other participants of the healthcare workforce.[1627] The "embedded bioinformatics specialist" has to understand a disease and the data.[1628]

Raise awareness of PM among healthcare professionals

Not only healthcare providers in a narrow sense are claimed to lack sufficient knowledge about PM, also other healthcare professions are described to have a knowledge gap in this regard influencing the healthcare providers awareness and knowledge. This thesis argues that informed health professionals are a supporting condition to increase the public awareness of PM. There are claims for expanding the current educational scope to include more stakeholders in the healthcare industry, rather than narrowly focusing on educating current and future health practitioners.[1629] Policy makers, investors, regulators, lawyers, and payers should have a basic level of understanding in genomics in order to be able to work together and to accept a paradigm change in their current approaches.[1630]

Some authors go as far as to call for curricula revisions beyond the one's of medical schools. For example, WONG ET AL. (2010) recognize that law schools do not offer similar curricula updates analog to medical schools and thus endanger the acceptance of PM innovations by the legal profession. They stress the importance to educate judges, lawyers, and legal academics about the concept and welfare potential PM.[1631]

There is an additional policy lever which helps to raise the knowledge and awareness of PM which is discussed the following Chapter 5.3: Guidelines implemented in CDS may help to raise the awareness of PM among healthcare providers.[1632]

1627 BEERENWINKEL at the LATSIS SYMPOSIUM ETH ZURICH ON PERSONALIZED MEDICINE, June 29, 2016. Also DUFFY (2015), p. 7.

1628 STUPP at the LATSIS SYMPOSIUM ETH ZURICH ON PERSONALIZED MEDICINE, June 29, 2016.

1629 LAM (2012) p. 277.

1630 Similarly EASTMAN (2012), p. 25; LAM (2012) p. 277; HOOD & AUFFRAY (2013), p. 1; MCCARTHY ET AL. (2013), p. 11; KIEVITS ET AL. (2014), p. 13; PERMED (2015), p. 34, and ESTAPE ET AL. (2016), p. 12.

1631 Similarly WONG ET AL. (2010), p. 47-49.

1632 Cf. Part V, Chapter 5.3, Implement guidelines in CDS, p. 310.

5.2 Lack of patients' awareness and understanding of personalized medicine

This chapter lists and discusses available policy levers in order to accelerate the increase in patients' awareness and understanding of PM. Adequately informing and educating patients is a process that should ideally be adapted to each patient's health literacy. In an exploratory interview AEBERSOLD expressed his fears that without adequate and transparent information processes of the public PM will *"suffer the same fate as gene technology"* despite its promising potential.[1633]

Inform patients about available treatment options through healthcare providers

The increase of healthcare providers' knowledge and understanding of PM (*previous Chapter 5.1*) is a first step towards a higher level of awareness among patients. Thus, all the policy levers in the previous chapter are indirectly valid for this chapter too. A healthcare provider is obliged to inform a patient about alternative treatment options[1634] – thus, about traditional as well as personalized approaches.

When a patient chooses a personalized approach, a healthcare provider should be aware of potential patient biases when communicating genetic information.[1635]

Raise awareness about PM through public health campaigns

The SWISS FOUNDATION FOR THE PROMOTION OF HEALTH should consider bringing PM on its agenda. A public health initiative should communicate PM in an understandable way to patients and the broader public, address fears and doubts with the aim to increase patients' health literacy and to raise patients' awareness about PM. Additionally, available options to participate in collaborative partnerships between health professionals and patients as well as PM initiatives should be promoted in order to create a certain "pull factor" for PM.

Demonstrate successful case examples and stories

The SWISS FOUNDATION FOR THE PROMOTION OF HEALTH and publicly financed media should provide relevant and accurate information in combination with successful case examples and stories. Real stories may appeal to peoples' emotions and make

---

1633 Exploratory interview with RUDOLPH AEBERSOLD on May 10, 2015. In Switzerland, the use of genetically modified organisms in agriculture is currently prohibited by a strict moratorium.

1634 Art. 10 SWISS MEDICAL ASSOCIATION'S PROFESSIONAL CODE.

1635 E.g., BLUMENTHAL-BARBY ET AL. (2015) about behavioral biases when handing over genetic information to patients (information seeking bias, affect bias, impact bias) and corresponding solutions.

the general public understand the value of testing relative to their medical outcomes.[1636]

Educate patients about the value of genetic data

The WORLD ECONOMIC FORUM calls personal data a *"new asset class"*.[1637] Experts argue that people are not aware about the value of their own data.[1638] They fear a dependence of Swiss patients from (foreign) private firms collecting genetic data.[1639]

The SWISS FOUNDATION FOR THE PROMOTION OF HEALTH, the FOPH, and publicly financed media could educate people about the value of their "asset". Research has shown that patients are actually willing to share their data if they know that they can contribute to better medical outcomes.[1640] However, patients should be motivated to take individual responsibility and ownership of their personal health data. Therefore, appropriate data storing and sharing models could be promoted (e.g., citizen-owned and citizen-controlled health data cooperatives like the Swiss MIDATA.COOP). Available educational tools are manifold, e.g., information campaigns, public debates, magazine articles or TV documentaries, information sheets for the waiting rooms at healthcare providers.

Besides the mentioned levers, it is hypothesized that patients' awareness will automatically increase with more consistent reimbursement of PM technologies.[1641]

5.3 Lack of consistent, recognized and clinically implemented guidelines for personalized medicine

This chapter lists and discusses available policy levers to create and implement consistent guidelines for the application of PM.

1636 E.g., VAYENA ET AL. (2012).

1637 Cited in HAFEN & BRAUCHBAR (2014), p. 1.

1638 *"We are willing to pay for a coffee, but do expect free digital storage space for our pictures."* cf. discussion about data as "a new asset class" in HAFEN & BRAUCHBAR (2014), p. 2.

1639 E.g., HAFEN, at the ETH LATSIS Forum on June 29th, 2016, warned from the dependence of American firms collecting genetic data. Also COOK-DEEGAN, CONLEY, EVANS, & VORHAUS (2013), p. 1-2, criticize for example that MYRIAD GENETICS keeps the collected clinical BRCA1/2 data private database. Keeping the data private provides MYRIAD GENETICS a competitive advantage in data interpretation.

1640 E.g., A. H. B. WU (2016), p. 233, promotes the power of stories in the context of PM translation.

1641 E.g., HITZ & PREVEL KATSANIS (2014), p. 371 ff. Cf. Part V, Chapter 6 Reimbursement policy levers, p. 315 ff.

Agree on guidelines valid for Switzerland

Professional societies, like the SAMS, the SMA, or the SFOPH should discuss and agree which drug-gene interactions they recommend to test for and officially recognize or adapt guidelines for Switzerland.

One first step is to update the SAMS guidelines (or comparable ones) with the newest knowledge. A table with the recommended and most important drug-gene interactions to test for used in everyday clinical care should be included together with some illustrative case studies. This would raise the awareness for available genetic tests and promote PM.

Implement guidelines in CDS

Guidelines are of limited use, if they are not used in clinical decision making. One way to support the use of guidelines in everyday clinical practice could the automated linking the guidelines with a CDS system or with the Swiss electronic health record (EPD). When the healthcare provider enters a certain drug into the system, the drug-gene interactions would automatically pop up.

5.4 Lack of infrastructure for the implementation of personalized medicine

With the SWISSBIOBANKING platform, the SWISS PERSONALIZED HEALTH NETWORK and the developments of the EPD, this thesis argues that the Swiss policy maker has started to establish the infrastructure needed for the implementation of PM. This thesis adds two policy levers:

Coordinate between existing infrastructure initiatives

The Swiss policy maker should consider setting incentives (e.g., regular coordination workshops, research projects connecting the initiatives) in order to guarantee the needed coordination between existing initiatives that strengthen the infrastructure for the development of PM (e.g., between SWISS BIOBANKING, the SWISS PERSONALIZED HEALTH NETWORK and the establishment of the EPD, etc.). Silo budget structures that focus only on the individual projects have to be avoided.[1642]

[1642] About the danger of silo budget structures: PERMED (2015), p. 25; PLUN-FAVREAU ET AL. (2016), p. 144; and WURCEL ET AL. (2016), p. 142.

Guarantee interfaces to electronic patient dossier (EPD) allowing clinical decision making based on genomic information

Due to its federalistic healthcare system,[1643] there is the danger that the EPD misses the chance to integrate genomic data in a comprehensible and clinically actionable format. Today, it is possible to apply an algorithm to identify patients with disease risk factors or to apply pharmacogenomic guidelines to assist with drug selection and administration.[1644] With the costs of genetic testing further decreasing, EHRs can be prepopulated with relevant genetic or pharmacogenomic data, providing healthcare providers with actionable information. Medical practice will become increasingly dependent on automated CDSs. For MOOSER it is "imaginable" that a genetic sequencing will become part of the standard health check-up in Switzerland.[1645]

In the US there are examples for EHR-based treatment decisions and EHR-based research, e.g., the MAYO CLINIC uses IT applications transmitting results from genetic tests to the EHR environment for clinical decision making. The MAYO CLINIC also conducts EHR-based genetic studies.[1646]

5.5 Privacy concerns regarding the use of personalized medicine

This chapter lists and discusses available policy levers to alleviate potential privacy concerns in the context of PM. One way to reduce and to address privacy concerns is to increase privacy protection regulations. However, stricter privacy protection regulation increases the administrative burden for healthcare providers and lowers their incentives to foster PM as the sharing of genetic data is one driver behind the progress of PM.

Global genetic data sharing was identified as the most critical contributor to the progress of PM at the ETH LATSIS FORUM in June 2016.[1647] However, *"where there is light, there is also shadow"*[1648] and genetic data can be misused. For example, there is

[1643] Cf. Part IV, Chapter 5.4.1 Institutional setting, *Healthcare system based on federalism*, p. 246.

[1644] Examples in JAMESON & LONGO (2015), p. 2231.

[1645] MOOSER (2014), Head Lab Department CHUV and vice-dean Clinical Research UNIVERSITY OF LAUSANNE, p. 568-69. Similarly argue RELLING & EVANS (2015), p. 344: *"As the cost of sequencing continues to fall, many have predicted that every individual will in the not-too-distant future have their germline genome sequenced early in life and the results will be available for clinical use throughout their lifetime"*.

[1646] Cf. http://mayoresearch.mayo.edu/center-for-individualized-medicine/information-technology-program.asp or http://www.mayo.edu/research/labs/cardiovascular-biomarkers/research-projects/ehr-based-genomic-medicine-implementation (last visited June 17, 2017).

[1647] According to MOCH at the ETH LATSIS Forum on June 29th, 2016.

[1648] SZUCS at the ETH LATSIS Forum on June 29th, 2016.

the danger of the anonymization code being hacked and traced back to an individual. Experts agree that today, the potential damage through the public availability of one's own genom is difficult and hypothetical to assess.[1649]

The tension between an individual's data and privacy protection and data sharing contributing to research is reinforced through the near impossibility to fully annonymize a genome.[1650] The Swiss policy maker needs to find and discuss an adequate *balance between privacy protection and data sharing regulation.* In the following subchapters both aspects are discussed.

5.5.1 Policy levers to increase privacy protection regulation in the context of personalized medicine

Implement the planned changes suggested by the D-GUMG

Several policy levers in order to increase the privacy protection regulation in the context of PM are already addressed by the D-GUMG: The D-GUMG extends its scope to tests for somatic biomarkers and tests with no medical purposes[1651] and addresses the regulatory gap of foreign tests marketed in Switzerland.[1652] Beyond the envisaged changes in the D-GUMG, the following levers should be discussed.

Extend the scope of the GUMG to research purposes

The current as well as the D-GUMG exclude genetic tests for research purposes from their scopes.[1653] It could be criticized that the data protection standards are less strict in the context of research projects (governed by the HMG) compared to tests used for medical purposes. The protection level should be the same, no matter if a test is performed in the context of a research project or not.[1654]

1649 SZUCS, BEERENWINKEL and MOCH at the ETH LATSIS Forum on June 29th, 2016. STUPP with the following comparison: *"Should we prohibit airplanes because one can fly into skyscrapers with them?"*

1650 Cf. Part IV, Chapter 5.5 Privacy concerns regarding the use of personalized medicine, p. 254 ff. and *note* 1369.

1651 This is similarly suggested by ECKHARDT ET AL. (2014), p. 103-106 and 272. They especially criticize that the data protection standards are less strict in the context of research projects (governed by the HMG) compared to tests used for medical purposes. The protection level should be the same, no matter if a test is performed in the context of a research project or not, p. 106.

1652 Cf. Part IV, Chapter 5.5 The current revision of the LAW ON GENETIC TESTS ON HUMANS (GUMG), p. 256 ff.

1653 Art. 1 *para.* 3 GUMG; Art. 2 *para.* 4 D-GUMG.

1654 Cf. ECKHARDT ET AL. (2014), p. 106.

Introduce the explicit prohibition of discrimination due to health risks

Although the Swiss law knows the non-discrimination principle and stipulates the explicit prohibition of any form of discrimination on grounds of the genetic heritage, it does not concern the discrimination due to health risks in general.[1655] The prohibition of discrimination due to health risks can only be inferred from the general right of equality.[1656] Thus, the introduction of the explicit prohibition of discrimination due to health risks of should be discussed.[1657]

Introduce a criminal norm penalizing the discrimination due to genetic data

The SWISS CRIMINAL CODE (StGB) does not contain any norm on which basis a potential discrimination due to genetic data could be prosecuted. It is doubted, if the existing non-discrimination principle could be effectively enforced. In order to strengthen the efficacy of the non-discrimination principle, the introduction of such a norm should be discussed.[1658]

Introduce the possibility to object the sharing of genetic data for cognates

The Swiss policy maker should discuss and choose the level of privacy protection for cognates of persons who choose to undergo presymptomatic genetic examinations. If related persons share their genetic data in the internet or other media, cognates currently have no legal possibility to object.[1659] The introduction of a right to object should be discussed; however, the question remains how such a right could be fully enforced in practice.[1660]

5.5.2 Policy levers to increase incentives for genetic data sharing

At the same time the Swiss policy maker should ensure that policies incentivize data sharing. People should be empowered to control and share their own genetic data: In order to lower the privacy concerns regarding genetic data, people have become aware about the available options to control of their own genetic data.[1661] Besides the

[1655] Cf. Part IV, Chapter 5.5.1 Institutional setting, *1. The principle of non-discrimination,* p. 251.
[1656] Art. 8 *para.* 1 SWISS CONSTITUTION.
[1657] Suggested by ECKHARDT ET AL. (2014), p. 14 and 123.
[1658] *Ibidem,* p. 123.
[1659] *Ibidem,* p. 272.
[1660] Cf. also BÜCHLER & MICHEL (2014), p. 304; and ECKHARDT ET AL. (2014), p. 272.
[1661] HAFEN, at the LATSIS SYMPOSIUM ETH ZURICH ON PERSONALIZED MEDICINE, June 29, 2016.

policy levers presented in Chapter 5.2,[1662] the following policy levers should be discussed:

Ensure a standardized, simple informed consent process

Currently the informed consent process in Switzerland is complex and sometimes difficult to understand – even for experts.[1663] This process should be simplified, standardization should be discussed, and best practices should be shared. For example, it should be sufficient to obtain a broad informed consent at the point of data collection – as later additional consents are an administrative burden for providers and researchers and sometimes not possible anymore.[1664] The "general consent" initiative by the SAMS and SWISSETHICS is a step into this direction.[1665]

Identify privacy concerns and solutions in pilot projects

Similar like the US government supports the national PMI COHORT PROGRAM,[1666] the Swiss government could support personalized pilot programs in order to understand the privacy concerns of the participants and identify solutions to address these concerns.

Raise awareness for consumer-driven data commons

Literature contains calls for e.g., consumer-driven data commons and bottom-up approaches for developing new regulatory standards.[1667] One approach initiated in Switzerland is MIDATA.COOP. – a consumer-driven data base that enables citizens to store, manage and control access to their personal health data. [1668] The Swiss policy should raise awareness about available options.

[1662] Cf. Part V, Chapter 5.2 Lack of patients' awareness and understanding of personalized medicine, p. 308 ff.

[1663] Cf. Part IV, Chapter 5.5.1 Institutional setting, *2. The right of self-determination*, p. 253 ff.

[1664] Suggestion by GUMEK cited in ECKHARDT ET AL. (2014), p. 111. Similarly CHOW-WHITE, MACAULAY, CHARTERS, & CHOW (2015) who provide six recommendations for designing a proactive informed consent process that addresses risks and benefits of digital genomic information.

[1665] SAMS (2017)b, *Vorlage Generalkonsent.*

[1666] In the PMI COHORT PROGRAM a review of the current US regulatory landscape is prepared to support the data privacy protection of cohort participants. Furthermore, it is intended to work closely together with patients, bioethicists and IT specialists, as well as to create jointly the base for the improved privacy regulations for PM. Cf. KICHKO ET AL. (2016), p. 18.

[1667] Consumer-driven data commons offer a *"laboratory in which groups of consenting individuals can discover the common purposes that they share and can enunciate ethical and privacy standards that [...] will be of the people, by the people, and for the people"*, cf. B. J. EVANS (2016).

[1668] Cf. www.MIDATA.coop (last visited August 8, 2016).

6 Reimbursement policy levers

6.1 Lack of reimbursement for personalized medicine diagnostics

The following chapter lists and discusses available policy levers in order to increase the incentives for the relevant stakeholders to foster the translation of PM and to reduce the legal uncertainty regarding the reimbursement of PM Dx in Switzerland. The following policy levers are derived based on the Law and Economic analysis of incentives in Part IV, Chapter 6.1.[1669]

Introduce reimbursement criteria for PM Dx

In order to reduce the inconsistent reimbursement of PM Dx, reimbursement criteria have to be introduced. The criteria have to detail the EAE-criteria in the case of PM diagnostics and describe under which conditions they are reimbursed by a compulsory health insurance.[1670]

Allow exemptions from the principle of territoriality

Exemptions should be made from the principle of territoriality, in cases in which a foreign provider of PM Dx has higher economies of scale and is therefore able to ensure more reliable test results of higher quality and lower costs than a Swiss provider.

There is a current discussion about more exemptions to the principle of territoriality in the context of OM.[1671] Already in 2013, FELIX GUTZWILLER (2013) made an interpellation requiring that foreign genetic tests are not bound to the principle of territoriality. However, the FEDERAL COUNCIL did not see any need for action with the argument that the FOPH has no control over the quality of foreign laboratories.[1672]

Despite opposition from the Swiss laboratories,[1673] the current draft revision on the LAW ON GENETIC TESTS ON HUMANS (D-GUMG) on genetic examination on humans contains an exemption of the principle of territoriality. Doctors or laboratories in

1669 Cf. IV, Chapter 6.1 Lack of reimbursement for personalized medicine diagnostics, p. 261 ff.

1670 Similarly FELIX GUTZWILLER & BLANK (2013), p. 631. This was also mentioned by BRÜGGER in the interview on August 16, 2016.

1671 Cf. ECKHARDT ET AL. (2014), p. 195.

1672 FELIX GUTZWILLER (2013), Antwort des Bundesrates vom 28.8.2013.

1673 The FAMH (2015) argues that the exemptions from the principle of territoriality endanger quality and data security of genetic tests, cf. FAMH (2015), p. 1-2.

Switzerland may – under certain conditions – delegate the performance of a genetic test to a foreign laboratory.[1674]

Ensure an up-to-date reimbursement list and avoid of legal incongruences

In order to foster the translation of PM, it is important to ensure that the reimbursement lists are up-to-date and contain all relevant diagnostic tests.[1675] The newly created HTA department in the SFOPH[1676] should establish a "horizon scanning" mechanism in order to detect cost-efficient tests and treatments early, for which no other player has an incentive to apply for reimbursement. An option to "feed" this horizon scanning mechanism could be based on the inputs from independent medical examiners.[1677]

The existing legal incongruences of a label stating pharmacogenetic limitations for a drug combined with the lack of the reimbursement for the corresponding test should be avoided.[1678]

The reimbursement for pharmacogenomic tests testing for polymorphisms should be considered, since they have the potential to reduce the burden of ineffective treatments in the population.

Also the inclusion of further presymptomatic tests in the list of analyses should be considered and politically discussed. The exclusion of presymptomatic tests due to the narrow definition of "illness" in the Swiss compulsory health insurance scheme should be reconsidered – especially in cases with an existing therapy for avoiding the outbreak of an "illness". The Swiss policy maker should decide in which cases between the clear borderlines "health" and "illness" the compulsory health insurance will bear the costs for a presymptomatic test – regardless of a person's "particular risk".[1679]

1674 Doctors initiating genetic tests as well as laboratories are allowed to delegate the entire or partial conducting of the genetic investigation to a foreign laboratory, if the foreign laboratory is able to guarantee state-of-the-art testing according to scientific and technical standards and an appropriate quality management system and if the lab has the permission to perform such an investigation in its country, cf. Art. 29 D-GUMG.

1675 Similarly the OECD (2017), p. 15, emphasizes in its recommendations the need for updating payment policies regularly.

1676 Cf. Part IV, Chapter 6.2.1 Institutional setting, *iii) HTA developments in Switzerland*, p. 283 ff.

1677 Suggestion from SEILER, interviewed 18th of July 2016.

1678 Cf. Part IV, Chapter 6.1.2 Analysis of incentives, *Providers b) Inconsistencies between drug labels and reimbursement rules leads to* ambiguous situations for providers, p. 273.

1679 Cf. also recommendation of TA-Swiss already in RIPPE ET AL. (2004), p. 260, and ECKHARDT ET AL. (2014), p. 27-28, 196 and 279.

In this context, an additional question will gain importance in the future: Should the Swiss compulsory health insurance also reimburse treatments which potentially cannot be effective from a pharmacogenetic point of view, but a patient refuses testing for the relevant biomarker?[1680] *"The principle of solidarity does not forsee to pay for something of which we know it does not work".*[1681]

Make use of CED and introduce clear criteria for CED process

Innovative reimbursement models, like CED or other managed entry agreements (MEAs)[1682], are considered to be effective and cohesive approaches that take into consideration the specificities of PM evaluation. They offer opportunities for earlier patient access to innovative molecular diagnostic tests.[1683]

With the existing possibility of CED in the Swiss healthcare system, the application of this legal tool might be used more often for PM applications. Thus, it is important that clear and transparent criteria are introduced for conditional reimbursement, also for Rx-CDx combinations.[1684]

Expand the "off-label" article to diagnostics

The Swiss policy maker should consider expanding the scope of the "off-label" regulation for pharmaceuticals[1685] also to diagnostics. Off-label use of PM Dx could be understood as using a PM Dx in cases where the EAE-criteria are fulfilled despite the label of the pharmaceutical not explicitly prescribing such a test before administration.

1680 RIPPE ET AL. (2004), p. 124; ECKHARDT ET AL. (2014), p. 194, stressing that this question touches the "right not to know" and the "right of self-determination".

1681 SZUCS on Latsis Symposium ETH Zurich on PM, June 29, 2016.

1682 Managed entry agreements, also "risk sharing agreements", represent *"formal arrangements between payers and manufacturers, aimed at sharing financial risks due to uncertainty related to the introduction of new technologies (e.g., price-volume agreements, outcome guarantee, coverage with evidence development and disease management programs)"*, AKHMETOV ET AL. (2015), p. 222. MOREL ET AL. (2013) with an overview and classification of MEA's used in Europe for orphan diseases.

1683 KIEVITS ET AL. (2014), p. 18; PLUN-FAVREAU ET AL. (2016), p. 150; PERMED (2015), p. 29; and PLUN-FAVREAU ET AL. (2016), p. 150.
In this context, J. COHEN (2015), p. 7, is talking about *"informed coverage decisions"* of payers. For example, in the US, payers are implementing CED. They have begun asking drug and diagnostic manufacturers to engage with them at Phases II and III, in which they can have an impact on clinical trial design end points.

1684 Cf. BRÜGGER & GRATWOHL (2015), p. 18; BRÜGGER ET AL. (2015), p. 8; and BRÜGGER in an interview on August 10, 2016.

1685 Art. 71 *lit.* a and b KVV.

Increase longitudinal accounting for payers

On the one hand, the existing free choice of patients between several compulsory health insurance companies secures competition among Swiss health insurers. On the other hand, it lowers the incentive for a payer to reimburse personalized tests and treatments, which may only be cost-efficient over the long-term.

Ten years ago, a report has initiated the discussion to increase the value-based competition in the Swiss healthcare system.[1686] The report is claiming that health plans should compete on value and measure the health and healthcare outcomes of their membership: *"Switzerland's multi-payer system can add value if health plans are not just payers, but measure their success by the health of their member populations. Health plans offering multi-year contracts and measuring health outcomes of subscribers will have incentives to encourage effective, timely treatment rather than delaying care to shift costs. Health plans can compete in driving innovation that improves public health as well as the results of healthcare in Switzerland".*[1687]

Strengthen value-based reimbursement in Swiss compulsory healthcare system

As illustrated in Part III and IV, diagnostics have a history of relatively low reimbursement and are reimbursed on cost-based principles.[1688] Due to the previously illustrated challenges, industry participants and academics highlight the need to address the "cost-value dilemma" in PCM and to move towards value-based[1689] rather than cost-based pricing and reimbursement structures for PM Dx. Instead of "activity-based" billing and reimbursement, incentives are needed for personalized clinical decision-making based on its "value to care" rewarding patient outcomes.[1690]

1686 Cf. report by OLMSTED TEISBERG (2007) published by ECONOMIESUISSE, INTERPHARMA, HIRSLANDEN, SIA & SWISSCOM. The principles formulated in the report are based on PORTER & OLMSTED TEISBERG (2006).

1687 Detailed suggestions in OLMSTED TEISBERG (2007), p. 9 and 63 ff.

1688 Cf. Part III, Chapter ii) Drivers behind the lack of reimbursement for PM Dx, *History of cost-based reimbursement,* p. 187 ff., and Part IV, Chapter 6.1.1 Reimbursement for personalized medicine diagnostics by the Swiss compulsory health insurance, p. 266 ff.

1689 For an explanation on VBP cf. Part II Chapter 3.1.4 Value based pricing (VBP), p. 85 ff.

1690 *Calling for value-based reimbursement approaches:* OLMSTED TEISBERG (2007), p. 27 ff; PORTER (2010), p. 2480; EASTMAN (2012), p. 25; GARAU ET AL. (2012), p. 17-18; ANSARI (2013), p. 412; EKSTROM ET AL. (2013), p. 33; EUROPEAN ALLIANCE FOR PERSONALISED MEDICINE (2013), p. 23; AKHMETOV ET AL. (2015), p. 1; EUROPABIO (2015), p. 15; LAWLER & SULLIVAN (2015), p. 329; PERMED (2015), p. 29; TRUSHEIM ET AL. (2015), p. 330; TRUSHEIM & BERNDT (2015)b, p. 10 and 19; JOHNSON (2016), p. 4; PLUN-FAVREAU ET AL. (2016), p. 149, or FELDER (2016), p. 132, calling for a price differentiation for pharmaceuticals in different indications. Value-based pricing for diagnostics as an important policy lever was also mentioned by BRÜGGER in the interview on August 16, 2016.

Reimbursement systems must consider the costs of evidence generation and not simply the costs of production in determining the reward for a new PM Dx.[1691]

According to PORTER (2010) – one of VBP's most prominent advocates – the identified "unit of value" for a healthcare intervention should be aligned with the unit of reimbursement: *"Reimbursement must shift from fees for individual services or capitation for any service needed to bundled reimbursement for the care of medical conditions, including all physician fees, services, facilities, and drugs required over the care cycle".*[1692] *"Aligning reimbursement with value in this way* [with a bundled reimbursement approach][1693] *rewards providers for efficiency in achieving good outcomes while creating accountability for substandard care".*[1694]

There are several approaches to strengthen value-based reimbursement in a healthcare system.[1695] One method is *CED.*[1696] Another method to support value-based approaches is the introduction of *flexible pricing and reimbursement systems* which reward PM technologies that demonstrate evidence of value. PM varies according to the type of intervention and target. Several studies therefore recommend the development of a reimbursement system that enables prices to be adjusted over time to reflect increases or decreases in value. Allowing *value-based flexible pricing* for both Dx and Rx could strengthen the economic incentives for the development of PM.[1697]

Payment levels for new drugs are generally not flexible after the initial price negotiation at launch – except for a potential decrease. This provides a disincentive to personalized pharmaceuticals as the patient population might be narrowed.[1698] With this, the benefits of personalization can not be accurately rewarded.[1699]

Reimbursement schemes with flexible pricing are a form of risk-sharing agreements, which allow reimbursement depending on the availability of further evidence.

1691 THE ACADEMY OF MEDICAL SCIENCES (2013), p 72.

1692 PORTER (2010), *Supplement* 1, p. 12.

1693 *Inserted by the author.*

1694 PORTER (2010), *Supplement 1*, p. 12.

1695 Cf. KIERNAN (2016) who discusses how to develop a value-based pricing policy as part of a national drug policy.

1696 Cf. Policy lever "Make use of CED and introduce clear criteria for CED process", p. 317.

1697 *Calling for flexible pricing approaches (in non-Swiss contexts):* MECKLEY & NEUMANN (2010), p. 97; FAULKNER ET AL. (2012), p. 1169 ff.; THE ACADEMY OF MEDICAL SCIENCES (2013), p. 7; TOWSE & GARRISON (2013), p. 42; KIEVITS ET AL. (2014), p. 18; PERMED (2015), p. 29; and LEYENS & BRAND (2016), p. 187.

1698 THE ACADEMY OF MEDICAL SCIENCES (2013), p. 58; TOWSE & GARRISON (2013), p. 42. Cf. also Part III, Chapter 3.1.1 Literature analysis, *i) Strategic challenges to the co-development process, Pharmaceutical companies' strategic interests*, p. 122 f.

1699 THE ACADEMY OF MEDICAL SCIENCES (2013), p. 58; and TOWSE & GARRISON (2013), p. 42.

The concept of risk-sharing agreements does already exist in pharmaceutical negotiations.[1700] Pricing flexibility would be introduced through a formula, or renegotiation-based mechanism, using clinical performance data collected post-launch.[1701]

However, the introduction and operationalization of value-based approaches applied to PM applications also poses some challenges: PM implies that a drug and a diagnostic component are used in combination and create the value as a *"joint product"*. The total value created depends on the combination and the attribution of some portion of the value to one or the other part can be seen as "essentially arbitrary".[1702] Two basic scenarios describe the emergence of a personalized medicine combination:

1st scenario: If the diagnostic and the therapeutic component are *launched in combination* - providing that the overall value of the combination is identified, assessed and rewarded by payers - Rx and Dx companies may negotiate appropriate commercial arrangements to maximize their joint opportunity for creating value.[1703] However, relatively few if any models exist for evaluating Rx-CDx combinations.[1704]

2nd scenario: Value-based pricing is more complex when a *diagnostic test alone* is being considered. This may be the case when a new test comes to market for targeting an existing treatment or a better test may become available that is able to increase the overall joint value of an existing Rx-CDx combination. This situation presents a challenge to the concept and operationalization of value-based pricing for both the diagnostic as well as the pharmaceutical component.[1705] In this second scenario, an additional challenge will evolve in the near future: The current model of one drug paired with one companion diagnostic is likely to change with *platform diagnostics* that will direct the use of multiple drugs for multiple indications. A pricing and reimbursement system will need to be able to evaluate not only the value of CDx of one

---

1700 E.g., conditional coverage or performance-linked coverage, cf. KIERNAN (2016), p. 4.
The EUROPEAN COMMISSION (2013), p. 28, observes a trend towards an increased uptake of so-called "managed entry" agreements whereby continued reimbursement is made conditional upon proven real-life effectiveness. The EUROPEAN COMMISSION (2013) hypothesized that enhanced data collection in the frame of such schemes could further advance the evidence base underpinning PM.

1701 THE ACADEMY OF MEDICAL SCIENCES (2013), p. 58.

1702 GARAU ET AL. (2012), p. 16, with an example.

1703 Suggested by GARAU ET AL. (2012), p. 17.

1704 KIEVITS ET AL. (2014), p. 13. Cf. also Part II, Chapter 3 Economic value of personalized medicine, p. 72 ff.

1705 GARAU ET AL. (2012), p. 17.

biomarker but also the value of large platform tests for multiple biomarkers of these platform diagnostics.[1706]

For both scenarios a value-based pricing and reimbursement mechanism need to be able to separate, and therefore reward, the overall value between the drug and diagnostic component necessary for the personalization.[1707] There are two basic value-based approaches for such a separation of the overall value generated by Rx-CDx-combinations:[1708]

1. Manufacturers negotiate separate values

For processes with CDx introduced at the launch of the drug (*1st scenario*), the value of the combination could be assessed through new drug assessment processes considering a broad range of value elements and a balanced analysis of the diagnostic impacts. This value would then be subject to private negotiation between the diagnostic and the pharmaceutical manufacturer.[1709]

However, there are challenges associated with this model. First, the challenge to quantify separate values for drug and diagnostic still exists – it is simply a "private assessment" instead of an assessment performed by a HTA body or alike. Second, this approach would imply that only one specific CDx is required to be used to inform prescription of a given drug potentially conflicting with anti-trust legislation and stifling innovation by acting as a disincentive for ongoing improvements of diagnostics.[1710]

2. HTA calculate separate values

Option 1 does not exist for the *2nd scenario* in which a diagnostic test is launched separately from the corresponding pharmaceutical. In this case a dedicated HTA committee using value-based principles could quantify the separate values of therapeutics and diagnostics.[1711] PM Dx manufacturers would have to be transparent and deliver data for evidence collection.[1712] However, the main challenges with an HTA

1706 THE ACADEMY OF MEDICAL SCIENCES (2013), p. 59; and KAUFMANN ET AL. (2015), p. 389 ff., call this trend *"the evolution of 'ensemble' relationships" (e.g., multiplex and multiparameter diagnostics) which needs to be recognized by value-based reimbursement of the Rx-CDx bundle".*

1707 THE ACADEMY OF MEDICAL SCIENCES (2013), p. 60-61.

1708 GARAU ET AL. (2012), p. 4; and THE ACADEMY OF MEDICAL SCIENCES (2013), p. 60-61.

1709 GARAU ET AL. (2012), p. 4.

1710 THE ACADEMY OF MEDICAL SCIENCES (2013), p. 60.

1711 GARAU ET AL. (2012), p. 4; and THE ACADEMY OF MEDICAL SCIENCES (2013), p. 61.

1712 JOHNSON (2016), p. 4-5.

approach for PM Dx has already been illustrated in Part III, Chapter 6.2.[1713] Policy levers illustrating on how to approach these challenges in Switzerland are illustrated in the next Chapter 6.2.[1714]

Create consistent economic evidence for the value of PM Dx

As illustrated in Part IV, inconsistent evidence for the value for PM Dx incentivizes Swiss payers to remain conservative in their reimbursement decisions for PM. The lack of consistent evidence has been mentioned as a common reason for PM Dx failing to obtain appropriate coverage.[1715]

A tool to support the creation and the consistent comparison of empirical evidence is an appropriately designed HTA mechanism. Policy levers to improve the HTA process in Switzerland – especially in the context of PM – is explicitly discussed in the next Chapter.[1716]

Foster the political dialogue about increasing information asymmetries through PM in an insurance system

As illustrated in Part IV, PM may lead to bigger information asymmetries between insurance buyers and sellers and therefore endanger a functioning insurance approach in the supplementary health insurance.[1717]

The question rises to what extend the principle of solidarity in the compulsory health insurance should be upheld with the growth of personalized medicine in the long term. Are the non-risk-based premiums still adequate for the compulsory health insurance system? To what extent has the society to compensate for the "social lottery"? If health risks can be detected and treated early, some authors see the health insurance's principle of solidarity endangered.[1718]

1713 The current problem is that the concept of PM does not fit into existing HTA processes, that there is a lack of best practices in order to integrate concepts of economic value for CDx and PGx applications into HTAs, and that existing HTA processes lack of coordination, cf. in Part III, Chapter 6.2 Gaps and inconsistencies in conventional health technology assessments, p. 197.

1714 Cf. Part V, Chapter I6.2 Gaps and inconsistencies in conventional health technology assessments for personalized medicine, p. 323 ff.

1715 Cf. Part IV, Chapter 6.1.2 Analysis of incentives, *Payers, a) Inconsistent evidence for the health economic impact of PM Dx incentivizes payers to uphold current lack of reimbursement*, p. 274 f.

1716 Cf. Part V, I6.2 Gaps and inconsistencies in conventional health technology assessments for personalized medicine, p. . 323 ff.

1717 Cf. Part IV, Chapter 6.1.2 Analysis of incentives, *e) Prohibition of risk-based customer selection in the VVG leads to danger of adverse selection:*, p. 276.

1718 Cf. ECKHARDT ET AL. (2014), p. XVII.

Experts see the Swiss principle of solidarity in compulsory health insurance as a major advantage compared to other insurance systems. Currently Swiss compulsory health insurance could not discriminate a patient due to genetic information, because they are obliged to take every applicant.[1719]

It is essential to foster the political dialogue needed for tackling the potential consequences of the emerging information asymmetries through PM on the Swiss supplementary health insurance scheme. During the political discussions, it is important to point out the differences and to distinguish between the compulsory system based on solidarity and the supplementary system based on the principle of contractual freedom.

6.2 Gaps and inconsistencies in conventional health technology assessments for personalized medicine

The following chapter lists and discusses available policy levers concerning the HTA approach in Switzerland in order to increase the incentives for the relevant stakeholders to foster the translation of PM. The below policy implications are derived based on the Law and Economic analysis in Part IV.[1720]

Establish a transparent, systematic and methodologically sound HTA framework for Switzerland

A first policy lever is not particularly related to PM, but is rather a claim that is valid for the HTA approach in Switzerland as a whole: The criticism of the current approach has to be addressed. As previously illustrated, the Swiss approach has potential for conflicts of interest, biased assessments and stakeholder influenced appraisals.[1721] WIDRIG & TAG (2015) stress that the success of an HTA depends on the applicable domestic law. If the process of a reimbursement decision is not in accordance with the theory of HTA – which includes multidisciplinarity, independency, scientific methods, and transparency – the legally prescribed process may lead to biased reimbursement decisions. The legal framework must be aligned in such a way that the results of unbiased HTA reports can impact the health system in a legally binding way.[1722]

[1719] Cf. Part IV, Chapter 6.1.1 Institutional setting, *i) Overview of health insurance system in* Switzerland, *1. Compulsory health insurance*, p. 261.

[1720] Cf. Part IV, Chapter 6.2.2 Analysis of incentives, p. 287 ff.

[1721] Cf. Part IV, Chapter 6.2.1 Institutional setting, *ii) Criticism of current evaluation process in Switzerland*, p. 282 ff.

[1722] WIDRIG & TAG (2015), p. 587 and 590; and PLUN-FAVREAU ET AL. (2016), p. 150.

A first step towards a more systematic and prioritized choice of HTA-topics has been introduced in 2016 with the established HTA department by the FOPH. With this novelty, the HTA evaluation process is not solely applicant triggered anymore and thus objectivity is increased. Another promising aspect of the new HTA process is the fact that not only individual products but full disease patterns are assessed as a whole.[1723]

The remaining criticism[1724], however, should be addressed too. An important step into this direction would be an increase of the transparency and the methodological soundness of the assessment and appraisal process in order to let applicants know on what criteria a decision is based upon. The relevant criteria and methods have to be formulated in guidelines.[1725]

Consider specificities of PM applications in HTA process

At the same time, the Swiss policy maker should avoid creating new barriers, such as "non-fit-for-purpose" HTAs, which can limit access to valuable PM applications.

In the *context of PM*, the use of HTA for the reimbursement of PM Dx has to be aligned with existing practices for pharmaceuticals. Timelines have to be synchronized, and the collaboration between the pharmaceutical and the medical device process have to be strengthened, e.g., with a delegate being part of both assessment bodies.

Further, the HTA department should agree on an approach to separate the value between the drug and diagnostic components.[1726]

Additionally, an applicant for either a personalized pharmaceutical or diagnostic should have clarity about the required evidence as well as the criteria for reimbursement.[1727] In order to increase this clarity, the EAE-criteria have to be concretized in the context of PM. Challenges, like the lack of adequate comparators, inconclusive findings from economic evaluations as well as the existence of multiple tests for one personalized drug[1728] have to be addressed and transparently discussed. Healthcare

1723 Also BRÜGGER in the interview on August 10, 2016.

1724 Cf. Part IV, Chapter 6.2.1 ii) Criticism of current evaluation process in Switzerland, p. 282 ff.

1725 Similarly FLORIAN GUTZWILLER ET AL. (2012), p. 8085 and WIDRIG (2015), p. 425 ff. with further recommendations on how to improve the HTA process in Switzerland. Also mentioned by BRÜGGER in the interview on August 10, 2016.

1726 THE ACADEMY OF MEDICAL SCIENCES (2013), p. 71, with a suggestion.

1727 Cf. also Policy Lever in Chapter 6.1 "Introduce reimbursement criteria for PM Dx", p. 315.

1728 Cf. Part III, Chapter 6.2.1 Literature analysis, i) Incompatibility of current HTA processes with PM, p. 199.

providers, payers, and regulators should agree on the evidentiary standards required for implementation of a PM intervention.[1729]

In order to bring forward the full value of PM Dx, the HTA process would benefit from being tailored specifically to the ways in which PM Dx are developed and tested. Currently, the market for PM is still mainly dependent on pharmaceutical companies to demonstrate the value of Rx-CDx-combinations. Pragmatic methodologies for the assessment of PM Dx have to be developed, being different from the ones applied for pharmaceuticals and other therapeutic technologies. The required evidence should take into account the broad spectrum of medical devices and diagnostics and to adapt to the potential risk of a device and diagnostic to a patient. For example, dressing materials require another level of assessment than a molecular in-vitro CDx.[1730] The requested evidence level should be made specific to the development of diagnostics as they are developed using different methodologies and have shorter cycles of development. Besides traditional cost-effectiveness analyses[1731], the requested evidence level needs to be adjusted to take into account other dimensions of value that are specific to the PM Dx, such as increased certainty in treatment decision-making[1732] and clinical and economic value in the long-term.[1733]

Align requirements for approval process with HTA process

Currently, there are separate processes and data inputs required for the approval, HTA and sometimes also for post-market surveillance studies.[1734] In order to limit regulatory and reimbursement efforts for pharmaceutical and diagnostic companies and to increase their incentives to develop and offer PM treatments, the evidence requirements for the approval process have to be harmonized and aligned with the requirements in the HTA process.[1735] E.g., the EMA is considering the possibility to include more HTA-relevant information in their assessment report for approval in order to facilitate the work for the HTA and reimbursement evaluation processes.[1736]

1729 Similarly for other countries TOWSE & GARRISON (2013), p. 40; HORGAN ET AL. (2014), p. 291; KIEVITS ET AL. (2014), p. 18; T. A. MANOLIO ET AL. (2016), p. 2 ff; PLUN-FAVREAU ET AL. (2016), p. 146-147; and WURCEL ET AL. (2016), p. 143.

1730 Cf. claim by FASMED (2012), p. 6.

1731 Cf. Part II Chapter 3.1.1 *Extra-welfarist approach:* Cost-effectiveness analysis, p. 77.

1732 The so-called *"value of knowing"*, cf. PLUN-FAVREAU ET AL. (2016), p. 146-147.

1733 Cf. Part II, Chapter 3 Economic value of personalized medicine, p. 72 ff.

1734 BRÜGGER in the interview on August 10, 2016.

1735 Cf. similarly J. C. DAVIS ET AL. (2009), p. 283; PACI (2009), p. 287; and EUROPEAN ALLIANCE FOR PERSONALISED MEDICINE (2013), p. 23. Also BRÜGGER in the interview on August 10, 2016.

1736 LEYENS & BRAND (2016), p. 190.

Use the HTA process for evidence generation for PM applications

The translation of PM into clinical practice faces a "chicken and egg" problem: On the one hand, there is insufficient reimbursement for PM Dx due to the lack of evidence.[1737] On the other hand, current HTA processes lack a clear approach to consistently generate the required evidence.[1738]

An appropriately designed HTA mechanism with clear evidence criteria can be a direct way to actually generate the desired empirical evidence in a consistent way and can thus solve the "chicken and egg" problem. A HTA can generate an evidence base for decision making such that healthcare resources are used for the maximum benefit as "useful" PM Dx are separated from "ambiguous" PM Dx.[1739]

If reimbursement criteria are given for PM, consistency and comparability of the collected evidence is increased enabling more objective reimbursement decisions for PM. The creation of health economics evidence would represent a starting point contributing to the decreasing of several other barriers.[1740]

Collaborate and use synergies with other HTA bodies

The need for a dedicated HTA framework in the context of PM is not only present in Switzerland, but also in other healthcare systems.[1741] However, HTA processes across countries vary, lack coordination and ask for heterogeneous evidence requirements. HTA agencies regularly re-analyze the same information which other agencies have already studied in detail.[1742]

Switzerland has allocated limited resources for the evaluation of medical services. Consequently, the evaluation of all medical services is not feasible and a prioritization has to be made.[1743] Thus, it is legitimate and reasonable to use and combine HTA elements from other HTA systems. Such an approach avoids the duplication of work and saves resources. Closer collaboration and the use of foreign HTA elements do not mean that a HTA in Switzerland has to come up with the same final decision like a

---

1737 Cf. Part III, Chapter 6.1.1 ii) Drivers behind the lack of reimbursement for PM Dx, *Lack of evidence for the economic value of personalized medicine* diagnostics, p. 187.

1738 Cf. Part II, Chapter 3 Economic value of personalized medicine, p. 72 ff. and previous Policy Lever in Chapter 6.1 "Create consistent economic evidence for the value of PM Dx", p. 322.

1739 Similarly PAYNE & ANNEMANS (2013), p. 38; HORGAN ET AL. (2014), p. 291; and OOSTERHOFF ET AL. (2015), p. 2.

1740 Cf. *Figure 25:* Vicious cycle leading to the undervaluation of personalized medicine diagnostics, p. 212.

1741 PLUN-FAVREAU ET AL. (2016), p. 146.

1742 Cf. Part III, 6.2.1 iii) Lack of coordination of existing heterogeneous HTA processes, p. 204 ff.

1743 SFOPH (2009), p. 3.

foreign one does. The Swiss conclusion will stay object of a political discussion. Switzerland has to find a political consensus on which criteria this decision is based upon. The scientific evidence base, however, can be used for decision making in Switzerland. The existing HTA process foresees the option to request external expert opinions; this includes the consideration of (foreign) HTA-reports and other studies.[1744]

There are several ideas and efforts to increase collaboration and leverage synergies between HTA agencies: For example, there are suggestions to *harmonize data requirements for HTA processes.* Integrated data collection systems and analytical tool sharing among countries are mentioned as suggestions to overcome the scarcity of current economic evidence and the limited number of cost-effectiveness studies for PM.[1745] Relative effectiveness of PM applications could be evaluated centrally with a common conclusion. The produced insights could then be used by each country according to its own applicable priorities and regulations.[1746]

Additionally, several *collaboration alliances* aim to facilitate the efficient use of resources available for HTAs and promote best practices. Despite their lack of a legally binding nature, international collaborations in HTAs are considered to be effective.[1747] In order to keep pace with the international developments, to observe or actively contribute to the development of best practices standards of HTA for PM Dx, it is important for Switzerland to stay involved in these alliances. Switzerland is generally broadly represented – either through representatives of the government or of academic institutions – in several international HTA networks and projects, e.g., EUR-ASSESS; EUROMET; HARMET; EURO-SCAN; HTA Europe; BIOMED; EUnetHTA or INAHTA.[1748]

1744 WIDRIG (2015), p. 297.

1745 PACI (2009), p. 287; and EUROPEAN ALLIANCE FOR PERSONALISED MEDICINE (2013), p. 23.

1746 E.g., LEYENS & BRAND (2016), p. 190.

1747 EUROPEAN ALLIANCE FOR PERSONALISED MEDICINE (2013), p. 23; and WIDRIG & TAG (2015), p. 590.

1748 WIDRIG (2015), p. 59-60 and 409 ff.; EUNETHTA (2016); and INAHTA (2016).

7 Results

In this concluding Chapter, the identified policy levers are assessed for their binding character and evaluated for their relevance on the basis of findings in the previous Part IV.

7.1 Categorization

The overview below summarizes the presented policy levers in order to foster the translation of PM in Switzerland. The binding character of a lever is categorized into three categories:

- Levers that do require *no legal changes* in the current institutional setting (green)
- Levers that do require *soft law changes* in the current institutional setting (blue)
- Levers that do require *hard law changes* in the current institutional setting (red)

Value chain	**No.**	**Policy lever**
Development	B3.1 L1	Support the creation of co-development guidelines & best practice sharing platforms
Approval	B4.1 L2	Synchronize approval processes of PM Rx and PM Dx
	B4.1 L3	Regulate high-risk LDTs
	B4.1 L4	Introduce risk categories for CDx
	B4.1 L5	Keep reference to the EU regulation
	B4.1 L6	Create exclusivities for new indications using existing pharmaceuticals
	B4.2 L7	Discuss and allow for new forms of clinical trials for personalized applications
	B4.2 L8	Introduce adaptive licensing for personalized pharmaceuticals
	B4.2 L9	Create guidelines with principles for PM clinical trials
	B4.2 L10	Pursue innovative biobank approaches for clinical trials
Provision	B5.1 L11	Update the SCLO and further medical education with learning goals for medical genetics, medical statistics, pharmacogenetics and epidemiology
	B5.1 L12	Further integrate medical sciences with other natural sciences
	B5.1 L13	Create new medical titles bridging medical and bioinformatics knowledge
	B5.1 L14	Raise awareness of PM among healthcare professionals
	B5.2 L15	Inform patients about available treatment options through healthcare providers

	B5. L162	Raise awareness about PM through public health campaigns
	B5.2 L17	Demonstrate successful case examples and stories
	B5.2 L18	Educate patients about the value of their genetic data
	B5.3 L19	Agree on guidelines valid for Switzerland
	B5.3 L20	Implement guidelines in CDS
	B5.4 L21	Coordinate between existing infrastructure initiatives
	B5.4 L22	Guarantee interfaces to EPD allowing clinical decision making based on genetic information
	B5. L235	*Increase data protection:* Implement the planned changes suggested by the D-GUMG
	B5.5 L24	*Increase data protection:* Extend the scope of the GUMG to research purposes
	B5.5 L25	*Increase data protection:* Introduce the explicit prohibition of discrimination due to health risks
	B5.5 L26	*Increase data protection:* Introduce a criminal norm penalizing the discrimination due to genetic data
	B5.5 L27	*Increase data protection:* Introduce the possibility to object the sharing of genetic data for cognates
	B5.5 L28	*Foster data sharing:* Ensure a standardized, simple informed consent process
	B5.5 L29	*Foster data sharing:* Identify privacy concerns and solutions in pilot projects
	B5.5 L30	*Foster data sharing:* Raise awareness for consumer-driven data commons
Reimbursement	B6.1 L31	Introduce reimbursement criteria for PM Dx
	B6.1 L32	Allow exemptions from principle of territoriality
	B6.1 L33	Ensure an up-to-date reimbursement list and avoid legal incongruences
	B6.1 L34	Make use of CED and introduce clear criteria for CED process
	B6.1 L35	Expand the "off-label" article to diagnostics
	B6.1 L36	Increase longitudinal accounting for payers
	B6.1 L37	Strengthen value-based reimbursement in Swiss compulsory healthcare system
	B6.1 L38	Create consistent economic evidence for the value of PM Dx
	B6.1 L39	Foster the political dialogue about increasing information asymmetries through PM in an insurance system
	B6.2 L4	Establish a transparent, systematic and methodologically sound HTA framework for Switzerland
	B6.2 L41	Consider specificities of PM applications in HTA process
	B6.2 L42	Align requirements for approval process with HTA process

B6.2 L43	Use the HTA process for evidence generation for PM applications
B6.2 L44	Collaborate and use synergies with other HTA bodies

Table 11: Overview of policy levers

Color code: green=no law, blue=soft law, red =hard law;
the darker the color, the more relevant, cf. Figure 33, p. 332.

Policy levers requiring no change of law

The majority of policy levers requiring no change of law were found in the provision phase of PM. The category covers levers concerning processes and decisions by political commissions and professional associations,[1749] collaboration between government, academia and industry,[1750] the promotion of PM,[1751] or technical implementation work.[1752]

Amongst others, this category includes *nudges*. A nudge is *"an aspect of choice architecture that alters people's behavior in a predictable way without forbidding any options or significantly changing their economic incentives"*.[1753] VAN AAKEN (2015) distinguishes between three means of nudging: i) invisible choice manipulation, ii) prohibition of choice and mandatory choice and iii) instruments supporting choice (isolated or communicative).[1754]

In the context of this thesis, the latter category of nudges is most relevant and mainly needed in the provision phase in order to raise the awareness of PM. *Isolated instruments* supporting an individual's choice appeal to the "slow system" of thinking like reason or logical thinking of an individual targeting the isolated decision-making of that respective individual without using the instrument of communication.[1755] This thesis identified several policy levers representing isolated instruments supporting choice. They include levers that raise the awareness of PM among health professionals and patients in a isolated information processes, like the information of patients about available treatment options through their healthcare providers, public health

1749 Policy levers *L11-13, 38, 43.*
1750 Policy levers *L21, 29, 30, 39.*
1751 Policy levers *L14-18* and Policy levers *L29, 30, 39*, cf. *notes* 1756 and 1758.
1752 Policy levers *L10, 20, 22.*
1753 Cf. THALER & SUNSTEIN, CAAS (2009) p. 6.
1754 VAN AAKEN (2015), p. 9-17.
1755 Cf. KAHNEMANN & TVERSKY cited in VAN AAKEN (2015), p. 6; and VAN AAKEN (2015), p. 13-15.

campaigns aiming at increasing the awareness of PM, the presentation of stories and successful case examples, as well as patient education.[1756]

Communicative instruments support choice by appealing to the "slow system" of thinking in a consultative, deliberative process.[1757] This thesis also identified policy levers representing communicative instruments supporting choice. They include levers that raise the awareness of PM among health professionals and patients in deliberative processes. For example, the identification of privacy concerns and solutions in pilot projects or the public support of consumer-driven data commons or the political discussion about increasing information asymmetries through PM in an insurance system. Also the required collaboration and synchronization between HTA bodies can be seen as nudges for the respective HTA decisions.[1758]

Policy levers requiring changes in soft law

Policy levers requiring changes – including additions – in soft law concern three main aspects: First, the *coordination of the pharmaceutical and the diagnostic component* in the development and approval phase. Second, *guidelines* helping to guide health providers in their decisions during the provision phase. Third, a standardized *informed consent* process in Switzerland.

Policy levers requiring changes in hard law

The majority[1759] of policy levers identified for Switzerland do require a change in hard law. This finding underlines the importance of law in the translation of PM into clinical practice.

7.2 Evaluation

As stated in the introduction, the primary aim of this thesis is to identify policy levers that foster the translation of PM in Switzerland. Nevertheless, this thesis makes an attempt to conclude on most relevant[1760] levers.

[1756] Policy levers *L14-18.*

[1757] Cf. KAHNEMANN & TVERSKY cited in VAN AAKEN (2015), p. 6; and VAN AAKEN (2015), p. 15-16.

[1758] Policy levers *L29, 30, 39.*

[1759] In total, 44 policy levers were identified – 18 requiring no change of law, 5 requiring a change/addition on soft law, 21 requiring a change in hard law.

[1760] Cf. RESEARCH CONCEPT, Chapter 4.3 Derivation and evaluation of policy levers, *Relevance*, p. 12.

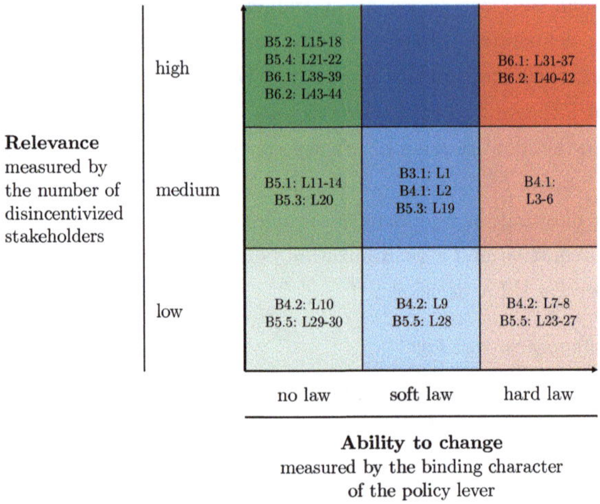

Figure 33: Evaluation of the policy levers

Three main conclusions are drawn from the above illustration:

First, congruent with the findings of Part III,[1761] the most relevant policy levers are found in the later phases of the PM value chain – in the provision and reimbursement phase.

Second, there are several policy levers in the provision phase that *do no require any change of the law* and that incentivize all stakeholders. This category of levers represents relatively easy to implement and effective measures for a policy maker.

Third, the other category with the most relevant policy levers is during the reimbursement phase and they *do require changes of Swiss law.* The suggested changes primarily concern the reimbursement for PM Dx and the current HTA process. The Swiss policy maker should consider putting the suggested policy levers on the law making agenda.

[1761] Cf. Part III, Chapter 7.3 Relevance assessment, p. 215.

7.3 Conclusion

Based on the Law and Economic analysis in Part IV, Part V identified a set of policy levers in order to foster the translation of PM in Switzerland.

Despite this thesis' aim to stay methodologically a non-normative level, an evaluation of the policy levers based on their relevance[1762] has been performed. The evaluation found that the most relevant levers are in the provision and reimbursement phase of the PM value chain. During the provision phase, the most relevant levers do not require any change of law. Amongst others, the policy maker should consider nudges to foster the translation of PM. This in contrast to the reimbursement phase, for which several suggestions to change the Swiss law are made.

[1762] Cf. RESEARCH CONCEPT, Chapter 4.3 Derivation and evaluation of policy levers, *Relevance*, p. 12.

Final conclusion

1 Summary of the findings

This thesis states that there are not only science-related, but also non-science-related, institutional barriers to the translation of personalized medicine (PM) into clinical practice. Its *primary research subject* is to identify and evaluate policy levers to reduce existing institutional barriers in order to foster the translation of personalized medicine into clinical practice – applied to the Swiss healthcare system.

Part I defines personalized medicine as a medical model using individuals' pheno- and genotypes for tailoring the right therapeutic strategy for the right person at the right time, for determining the predisposition to a disease or for delivering targeted prevention. It illustrates that PM involves two components: A diagnostic test and a targeted treatment or prevention plan.

Part II demonstrates that PM represents an ongoing paradigm shift away from the traditional "one-size-fits-all" approach to medicine. Applications of PM more than doubled in the last few years. PM is praised for its potential to more effectively use healthcare resources and to reduce healthcare costs – by enabling better prevention, providing more accurate diagnoses, eliminating unnecessary treatments, reducing adverse drug reactions, improving dosing and monitoring. However, health economic literature is not conclusive about the economic value of PM. The two main challenges to the health economic evaluation of PM are the existence of multiple evaluation methodologies and the lack of reliable, comparable data. *Part II* also addresses the main points of criticism towards PM. It is criticized that PM is a "hype" which increases costs in the healthcare system, that PM leads to a pathologization of the society and that it diverts resources away from other priorities in healthcare. *Part II* ends with presenting the ecosystem for PM with research institutions, diagnostic and pharmaceutical companies, providers, patients, and payers as its most relevant stakeholders.

K. Bosshard, *Law and Economics of Personalized Medicine*,
Gesundheitsmanagement und Gesundheitsökonomik,
https://doi.org/10.1007/978-3-658-22074-7_7

Part III provides a comprehensive overview of the institutional barriers to the translation of personalized medicine into clinical practice. It demonstrates that non-science related barriers exist along every link of the PM value chain. The translation of PM does not face one single barrier that could be removed; instead, the results underline the complexity behind the translation of PM.

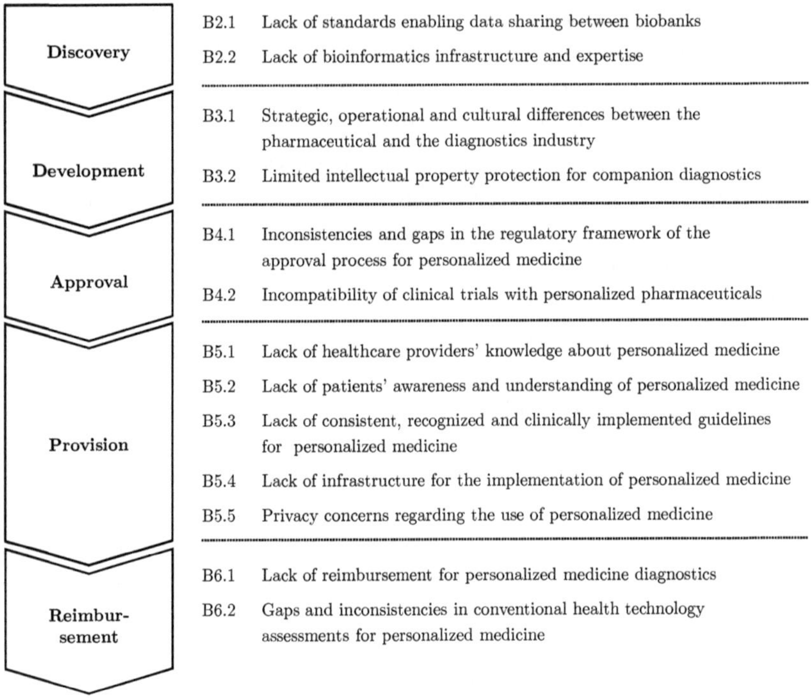

Figure 23: Overview of barriers to the translation of personalized medicine

All stakeholders in the PM ecosystem are confronted with multiple barriers which negatively incentivize them to foster the translation of PM into clinical practice. According to this thesis' definition of relevance,[1763] the most relevant barriers were found in the second half of the PM value chain in the provision and reimbursement phase as they negatively incentivize most stakeholders.

[1763] Cf. RESEARCH CONCEPT, Chapter 4.3 Derivation and evaluation of policy levers, *Relevance*, p. 12.

The results of *Part IV* demonstrate that Switzerland's institutional environment imposes several barriers to the translation of PM into clinical practice.[1764] These barriers predominantly concern the latter three links of the PM value chain, namely the approval, provision, and reimbursement phase.

The relevance of the barriers in Switzerland differs in three points from the theoretical Part III:

First, the analysis finds that Switzerland's institutional environment does not impose any negative incentives to the stakeholders involved in the discovery phase for PM. Switzerland has initiated several projects aiming at the sharing of data between biobanks in line with the newest international developments in this field.[1765] Also, Switzerland has taken action in order to strengthen its bioinformatics infrastructure and expertise.[1766]

Second, Switzerland has a favourable intellectual property environment for PM. The Swiss approach towards IP protection of CDx is less strict compared to for example the US. Limited IP protection of CDx is not a barrier to the translation of personalized medicine in Switzerland.[1767]

Third, this thesis finds a field of tension between privacy protection and data sharing. On the one hand, it is demonstrated, that Switzerland has a dense and multilayered institutional setting governing privacy protection of genetic data appropriate to address the the public's privacy concerns regarding the use of PM.[1768] On the other hand, it is demonstrated that the comprehensiveness of the Swiss regulation may be an barrier to the translation of PM as it is criticized to slow down medical progress by impeding data sharing.[1769] With these opposing findings for Switzerland, no conclusive statement concerning the incentives of the relevant stakeholders is made.

Based on the Law and Economic analysis in *Part IV*, the policy levers in order to reduce the remaining barriers in Switzerland are suggested and evaluated in *Part V*.[1770]

[1764] Cf. Part IV, Chapter 7.1 Resulting incentives , p. 290 ff.

[1765] Cf. Part IV, Chapter 2.1 Lack of standards enabling data sharing between biobanks, p. 219 ff.

[1766] Cf. Part IV, Chapter 2.2 Lack of bioinformatics infrastructure and expertise, p. 222 ff.

[1767] Cf. Part IV, Chapter 3.2 Limited intellectual property protection for companion diagnostics, p. 226 ff.

[1768] Cf. Part IV, Chapter 5.5.2 Analysis of incentives, *Patients in Switzerland incline to share their genetic data*, p. 258.

[1769] Cf. Part IV, Chapter 5.5.2 Analysis of incentives, *Providers and researchers have to deal with additional work due to privacy* protection regulation, p. 259.

[1770] Cf. Part V, Chapter 7 Results, p. 328.

Value chain	No.	Policy lever
Develop-ment	B3.1 L1	Support the creation of co-development guidelines & best practice sharing platforms
Approval	B4.1 L2	Synchronize approval processes of PM Rx and PM Dx
	B4.1 L3	Regulate high-risk LDTs
	B4.1 L4	Introduce risk categories for CDx
	B4.1 L5	Keep reference to the EU regulation
	B4.1 L6	Create exclusivities for new indications using existing pharmaceuticals
	B4.2 L7	Discuss and allow for new forms of clinical trials for personalized applications
	B4.2 L8	Introduce adaptive licensing for personalized pharmaceuticals
	B4.2 L9	Create guidelines with principles for PM clinical trials
	B4.2 L10	Pursue innovative biobank approaches for clinical trials
Provision	B5.1 L11	Update the SCLO and further medical education with learning goals for medical genetics, medical statistics, pharmacogenetics and epidemiology
	B5.1 L12	Further integrate medical sciences with other natural sciences
	B5.1 L13	Create new medical titles bridging medical and bioinformatics knowledge
	B5.1 L14	Raise awareness of PM among healthcare professionals
	B5.2 L15	Inform patients about available treatment options through healthcare providers
	B5. L162	Raise awareness about PM through public health campaigns
	B5.2 L17	Demonstrate successful case examples and stories
	B5.2 L18	Educate patients about the value of their genetic data
	B5.3 L19	Agree on guidelines valid for Switzerland
	B5.3 L20	Implement guidelines in CDS
	B5.4 L21	Coordinate between existing infrastructure initiatives
	B5.4 L22	Guarantee interfaces to EPD allowing clinical decision making based on genetic information
	B5. L235	*Increase data protection:* Implement the planned changes suggested by the D-GUMG
	B5.5 L24	*Increase data protection:* Extend the scope of the GUMG to research purposes
	B5.5 L25	*Increase data protection:* Introduce the explicit prohibition of discrimination due to health risks
	B5.5 L26	*Increase data protection:* Introduce a criminal norm penalizing the discrimination due to genetic data
	B5.5 L27	*Increase data protection:* Introduce the possibility to object the

		sharing of genetic data for cognates
	B5.5 L28	*Foster data sharing:* Ensure a standardized, simple informed consent process
	B5.5 L29	*Foster data sharing:* Identify privacy concerns and solutions in pilot projects
	B5.5 L30	*Foster data sharing:* Raise awareness for consumer-driven data commons
Reimbursement	B6.1 L31	Introduce reimbursement criteria for PM Dx
	B6.1 L32	Allow exemptions from principle of territoriality
	B6.1 L33	Ensure an up-to-date reimbursement list and avoid legal incongruences
	B6.1 L34	Make use of CED and introduce clear criteria for CED process
	B6.1 L35	Expand the "off-label" article to diagnostics
	B6.1 L36	Increase longitudinal accounting for payers
	B6.1 L37	Strengthen value-based reimbursement in Swiss compulsory healthcare system
	B6.1 L38	Create consistent economic evidence for the value of PM Dx
	B6.1 L39	Foster the political dialogue about increasing information asymmetries through PM in an insurance system
	B6.2 L4	Establish a transparent, systematic and methodologically sound HTA framework for Switzerland
	B6.2 L41	Consider specificities of PM applications in HTA process
	B6.2 L42	Align requirements for approval process with HTA process
	B6.2 L43	Use the HTA process for evidence generation for PM applications
	B6.2 L44	Collaborate and use synergies with other HTA bodies

Table 11: Overview of policy levers

Color code: green=no law, blue=soft law, red =hard law;
the darker the color, the more relevant, cf. Figure below.

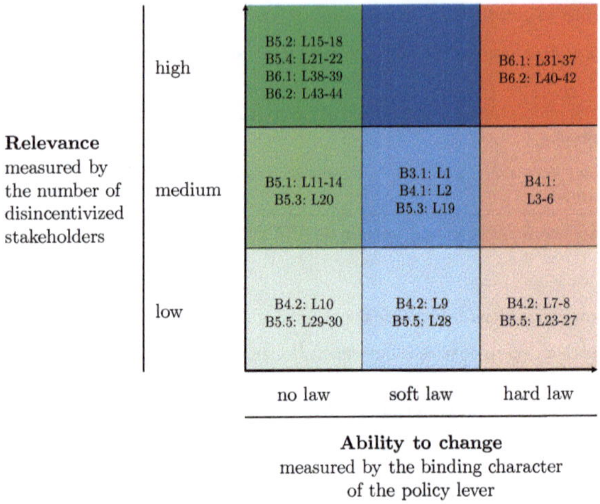

Figure 33: Evaluation of the policy levers

As Switzerland has become active in addressing the barriers in the first half of the PM value chain, any strategy to foster the translation of PM in Switzerland should primarily target the subsequent links of the Personalized Medicine value chain. The most relevant levers target the barriers in the provision and reimbursement phase. During the provision phase, the most relevant levers do not require any change of law. The identified policy levers predominantly concern the raising of the healthcare providers', patients', and health professionals' awareness of PM. For the reimbursement phase several suggestions to change the Swiss law concerning the reimbursement scheme and the health technology assessment for personalized medicine diagnostics are made. The Swiss policy maker should consider putting them on the law making agenda.

2 Theoretical contributions

From a research theoretical perspective, the results of this thesis shed light from a *social science perspective* on the translation of personalized medicine into clinical practice.

Traditionally, Translational Medicine has primarily focused on science related barriers, primarily in the translational phases T1 and T2.[1771] However, existing literature calls for more interdisciplinary approaches in the context of the translation of PM into clinical practice.[1772] In recent times, Translational Medicine experienced an opening towards new disciplines. The spectrum of targeted research subjects has broadened and has expanded to include also social scientific aspects.[1773] A New Institutional Economics or Law and Economics perspective to the translation of personalized medicine has been neglected so far.

This thesis contributes to this broadening by adding a Law and Economics perspective to the translation of PM. Some TM scholars observe this broadening of TM with skepticism as it blurs the traditional focus of TM and makes TM a less clearly defined research stream.[1774] However, the need for a broadening is reflected in the findings of this thesis as more and more relevant institutional barriers were found in the latter links of the PM value chain than in the links of the value chain primarily related to scientific discoveries and product development.[1775] Further, the majority[1776] of policy levers identified for Switzerland do require a change in hard law. This finding underlines the importance of law in the translation of PM into clinical practice.

[1771] Cf. RESEARCH CONCEPT, Chapter 6.3 Translational Medicine, p. 24 ff.

[1772] As this is called for in the current literature, cf. *note* 24.

[1773] Cf. RESEARCH CONCEPT, Chapter 6.3 Translational Medicine, p. 24 ff.

[1774] E.g., SOLOMON (2015), p. 6, *"Some of the wider usages of the term [Translational Medicine] are, in my view, more opportunistic than substantive and I see no reason to develop them"*, MITTRA (2013), p. 111, with an interviewee stating *"I think in many ways translational medicine is a very murky term [...] I think that a narrower definition gives some clear goals and directives and ways of unifying the academic and industrial community in partnership"*.

[1775] Cf. Part III, Chapter 7 Results, p. 209 ff.

[1776] In total, 44 policy levers were identified – 18 requiring no change of law, 5 requiring a change/addition in soft law, 21 requiring a change in hard law.

3 Practical contributions

This thesis makes not only a contribution to a reader interested in personalized medicine in the *Swiss context*, but it may also make a useful contribution for readers who are specifically interested in the translation of PM and who are not related to the Swiss context.

General contribution

First, this thesis adds to the discussion about strategic approaches towards the translation of personalized medicine into clinical practice, and it aims to increase the general knowledge about personalized medicine. Its results stress the importance of non-science related barriers to the progress of personalized medicine by providing a structured overview of the institutional barriers to the translation of personalized medicine.

Second, the value chain based categorization shall enable the targeting of each of the institutional barriers at its root and shall contribute to a clear separation of the different institutional barriers behind the translation of PM, not only in the academic, but also in the practical dialogue.

Third, the Law and Economic analysis of incentives of Part III represents a methodological approach to better understand the institutional barriers behind the translation of PM that can be tested in the context of additional countries.

Contribution in the Swiss context

Besides the contributions of general value, this thesis' main addressee is the Swiss policy maker. This thesis shall help to fulfill the Swiss *constitutional objective* of every person having *"access to the healthcare that they require"*.[1777]

The results of this thesis identify the available scope of action for Swiss policy makers to foster the translation of PM into clinical practice.[1778] This thesis makes an attempt to conclude on most relevant levers. The evaluation of the identified policy levers represents a supporting tool for decision making, strategically choosing and prioritizing the levers.[1779]

[1777] Art. 41(1)b SWISS CONSTITUTION: *"The Confederation and the Cantons shall, as a complement to personal responsibility and private initiative, endeavor to ensure that [...] b) every person has access to the healthcare that they require".*

[1778] Cf. Part V, Chapter 7 Results, p. 328.

[1779] Cf. RESEARCH CONCEPT, Chapter 4.3 Derivation and evaluation of policy levers, p. 12.

The evaluation distinguishes between three categories describing the legally binding degree of the levers: Levers that do require *1) no legal changes, 2) soft law or 3) hard law changes* in the current institutional setting.[1780]

[1780] Cf. Part V Chapter 7 Results, p. 328 ff.

4 Limitations & future research directions

4.1 Underlying assumption

This thesis is based on a central underlying assumption: It assumes that *the translation of PM into clinical practice is a normative goal.* As illustrated, there is skepticism and criticism towards the concept of Personalized Medicine.[1781] For a reader who is convinced that PM's costs outweigh its benefits, the findings of this thesis are of limited value.

The criticism represents a starting point for future research directions: As illustrated,[1782] there are research gaps on the economic value of the different applications in PM. Future research is needed concerning the *comparison* and the *measurement* of the value of the different treatment possibilities in PM.[1783]

4.2 Scope

This thesis intends to provide an overview of *all* non-science related institutional barriers to the translation of PM, the incentives they evoke for the involved stakeholders, and the respective levers for their reduction. The scope has the effect that this thesis has a relatively high breadth-depth ratio.

The broad scope of this thesis has the advantage of providing an exhaustive overview representing the complexity of the translation of PM into clinical practice. The theoretical framework can be useful for other geographies: A potential future research direction is the testing of the theoretical part's hypotheses in the context of additional countries.

This thesis as a whole can act as future research agenda. Each barrier can represent a starting point for a more detailed "deep dive"-study. For example, each of Part IV's results could be empirically tested for in the context of Switzerland and could be compared to the findings in additional countries.

1781 Cf. Part II, Chapter 4 Criticism towards personalized medicine, p. 92 ff.

1782 Cf. Part II, Chapter 3 Economic value of personalized medicine, p. 72 ff.

1783 Cf. *notes* 393 and 394.

4.3 Methodology

Literature analysis

The literature analysis in Part III provides the grounds for the identification of institutional barriers for the translation of PM into practice. The relevance for the review of the systematically retrieved literature was assessed based on the title and abstract of the respective publication.[1784] Although this thesis aims to provide a mutually exclusive, collectively exhaustive collection of the non-science related barriers to the translation of PM, there might be additional barriers or sub-barriers that have not been identified as the literature analysis was based on a limited selection of literature. Additionally, the barriers might be phrased in different ways than in this thesis. Alternative ways for the identification of the barriers do exist, for example an empirical approach by surveying the involved stakeholders.

Further, the identified barriers are categorized based on the value chain[1785] of personalized medicine based on the author's own judgement. Such a categorization is not unambiguous as a barrier may concern multiple links in the value chain. Alternative ways for categorizing the identified barriers are valid too.

Law and Economic analysis of incentives

The Law and Economic analysis of incentives which is performed for identifying the incentives for the stakeholders in the context of PM was predominantly based on a theoretical, qualitative argumentation scheme following classic economic theory with the assumption of rationally behaving actors.

This assumption of rationality does not necessarily reflect reality. The term *bounded rationality* coined by SIMON (1979) describes the idea of behavioral theories that do not assume perfect rationality.[1786] Subsequent scholars, e.g., KAHNEMAN and TVERSKY further explored SIMON's idea and identified several heuristics that contradict the rationality assumption.[1787] This thesis lacks the discussion of behavioral as-

[1784] Cf. Part III, Chapter 1.1 Literature analysis, p. 102 f.

[1785] Cf. *Figure 1:* Value chain of personalized medicine, p. 9 ff.

[1786] SIMON (1979), p. 496.

[1787] Cf. KAHNEMAN (2003), p. 697 ff., mapping bounded rationality; JOLLS, THALER, & SUNSTEIN (1998), p. 1 ff, with *"a behavioral approach to law and economics"*; KOROBKIN & ULEN (2000); VAN AAKEN (2003), p. 29, about criticism of the rational choice theory in L&E. An overview of the behavioral heuristics that contradict the rationality assumption present SCHÄFER & OTT (2005), p. 65-71; and ZUZAK (2008), p. 42-61.

pects related to the translation of personalized medicine.[1788] Research in this field is currently limited and represents a further future research direction.

A major point of criticism of the Law and Economic analysis of incentives is its *theoretical approach*. The analysis examined the incentives induced by the institutional setting concerning a barrier to the translation of PM on the basis of a theoretical argumentation scheme – but did not empirically test for their validity in reality. Despite the analysis looking at real institutions concerning each identified barrier, this thesis did not undertake an empirical testing of the existence of every barrier. Only in Part IV, the findings were anecdotally supplemented with empirical findings. The empirical examination of Part IV's findings represents a broad basis for future research.

Derivation and evaluation of the policy levers

This thesis suggested a set of policy levers in order to foster the translation of personalized medicine into clinical practice. Despite this thesis' aim to be comprehensive, additional policy levers might exist.

The suggested policy levers were evaluated based on the two evaluation criteria *"relevance"*[1789] and *"ability to change"*[1790]. Both evaluation criteria can be defined in alternative ways. This thesis measured a *barrier's relevance* by the number of stakeholders who are disincentivized to foster the translation of PM by the respective barrier. In this definition of "relevance", all stakeholders were weighted equally – despite the critique that the stakeholders' influence might vary. The definition is based on a simplified view of reality. Similarly the *"ability to change"* can be alternatively defined. Furthermore, this thesis does not suggest that the categories chosen for the *"ability to change"* represent a certain ease or speed to implement the suggested levers. The category "no law" might be the easiest or fastest category for some of the suggested levers, whereas it might be the category "hard law" for others.

The evaluation presents an attempt to prioritize the suggested policy levers. This thesis does not take any further normative position on the prioritization of the policy levers. Neither does it make a statement, if a policy lever should be triggered at all. This political decision is left to the Swiss policy maker.

1788 E.g., BLUMENTHAL-BARBY ET AL. (2015) focusing on how behavioral economics can help to foster the translation of PM.

1789 Cf. RESEARCH CONCEPT, Chapter 4.3 Derivation and evaluation of policy levers, *Relevance*, p. 12.

1790 Cf. RESEARCH CONCEPT, Chapter 4.3 Derivation and evaluation of policy levers, *Ability to change*, p. 12.

Future research could explore alternative approaches for prioritizing the suggested policy levers and testing them for feasibility in Switzerland. For example, a study could rate the identified policy levers on the basis of additional expert interviews, focus groups, an expert survey or a Delphi study.[1791]

[1791] Cf. MESSNER ET AL. (2016) performed a Delphi study in the US context on the importance of 28 barriers in the context of IP, reimbursement and FDA regulation.

5 Concluding remarks

Personalized medicine presents a promising opportunity to revolutionize the healthcare landscape. Hopefully this thesis helps to strengthen and increase our generation's and future generations' health in keeping with HIPPOCRATES' ethos *"it's far more important to know what person the disease has than what disease the person has"*.[1792]

[1792] HIPPOCRATES cited in DAVID PETTITT ET AL. (2016), p. 326.

Bibliography

A digital revolution in health care is speeding up. (2017). *The Economist.* Retrieved from http://www.economist.com/news/business/21717990-telemedicine-predictive-diagnostics-wearable-sensors-and-host-new-apps-will-transform-how (April 2, 2017)

ABE, H. (2016). New era in personalized medicine. *Personalized Medicine Universe, forthcoming,* Editorial. Retrieved from http://linkinghub.elsevier.com/retrieve/pii/S2186495016300025 (May 6, 2017)

ABPI. (2014). *The stratification of disease for personalised medicines: Research driven recommendations to strengthen a unified UK strategy through a stakeholder alliance.* Retrieved from http://www.abpi.org.uk/our-work/library/medical-disease/Documents/strat_med.pdf (October 23, 2015)

ACHTERMANN, W., & BERSET, C. (2006). *Gesundheitspolitiken in der Schweiz - Potential für eine nationale Gesundheitspolitik. Band 1. Analyse und Perspektiven.* Bern: SWISS FEDERAL OFFICE OF PUBLIC HEALTH [SFOPH]. Retrieved from http://www.fasmed.ch/fileadmin/pdf/polit_dossiers/Band_1_d.pdf (April 2, 2017)

AGARWAL, A., SNYDER, G., & RESSLER, D. (2015). The current and future state of companion diagnostics. *Pharmacogenomics and Personalized Medicine, 8,* 99–110.

AKERLOF, G. A. (1970). The Market for "Lemons": Quality Uncertainty and the Market Mechanism. *The Quarterly Journal of Economics, 84*(3), 488–500.

AKHMETOV, I., & BUBNOV, R. V. (2015). Assessing value of innovative molecular diagnostic tests in the concept of predictive, preventive, and personalized medicine. *EPMA Journal,* (December), 1–9.

AKHMETOV, I., RAMASWAMY, R., AKHMETOV, I., & THIMMARAJU, P. (2015). Market Access Advancements and Challenges in "Drug-Companion Diagnostic Test" Co-Development in Europe. *Journal of Personalized Medicine, 5*(2), 213–228.

ALANAZI, A. (2017). Incorporating Pharmacogenomics into Health Information Technology, Electronic Health Record and Decision Support System: An Overview. *Journal of Medical Systems, 41*(2), 19.

ALBRECHT, B., MENU, P., SZLEZAK, N., & RUDOLPH, T. (2013). Market insights in cancer: Trends in personalized medicine. McKinsey & Company. Retrieved from http://www.mckinsey.com/industries/pharmaceuticals-and-medical-products/our-insights (July 17, 2014)

ALEMAYEHU, D., & BERGER, M. L. (2016). Big Data: transforming drug development and health policy decision making. *Health Services and Outcomes Research Methodology,* 1–11.

K. Bosshard, *Law and Economics of Personalized Medicine*,
Gesundheitsmanagement und Gesundheitsökonomik,
https://doi.org/10.1007/978-3-658-22074-7

ALI-KHAN, S. E., BLACK, L., PALMOUR, N., HALLETT, M. T., & AVARD, D. (2015). Socio-Ethical Issues in Personalized Medicine: a Systematic Review of English Language Health Technology Assessments of Gene Expression Profiling Tests for Breast Cancer Prognosis. *International Journal of Technology Assessment in Health Care*, *2*, 1–15.

ALLEN, L. N., & CHRISTIE, G. P. (2016). The Emergence of Personalized Health Technology. *Journal of Medical Internet Research*, *18*(5), 1–8.

ANNEMANS, L., REDEKOP, K., & PAYNE, K. (2013). Current methodological issues in the economic assessment of personalized medicine. *Value in Health*, *16*, 20–26.

ANSARI, M. (2013). The Regulation of Companion Diagnostics: A Global Perspective. *Therapeutic Innovation & Regulatory Science*, *47*(4), 405–415.

ANTONANZAS, F., JUAREZ-CASTELLO, C. A., & RODRIGUEZ-IBEAZ, R. (2015). Is personalized medicine a panacea for health management? Some thoughts on its desirability. *European Journal of Health Economics*, *16*, 455–457.

ANTONARAKIS, S. E., BARTHOLDI, D., FILGES, I., GALLATI, S., IMHASLY, P., MINY, P., ... WENZEL, F. (2011). *Genetik im medizinischen Alltag - ein Leitfaden für die Praxis.* (Schweizerische Akademie der Medizinischen Wissenschaften SAMW, Ed.) (2nd ed.). Basel: Schwabe.

ARONSON, S. J., & REHM, H. L. (2015). Building the foundation for genomics in precision medicine. *Nature*, *526*(7573), 336–342.

ASPINALL, M. G., & HAMERMESH, R. G. (2008). Realizing the promise of personalized medicine. *Harvard Business Review*, *86*(3), 128.

AUFFRAY, C., CAULFIELD, T., GRIFFIN, J. L., KHOURY, M. J., LUPSKI, J. R., & SCHWAB, M. (2016). From genomic medicine to precision medicine: highlights of 2015. *Genome Medicine*, *8*(1), 12.

BARBIÉ, V. (2016). Bioinformatics challenges for Personalized Health in Switzerland. Tools and technologies: enabling genome-based personalized medicine. *Presentation at the LATSIS Symposium ETH Zurich on personalized medicine.* Zürich: SIB Swiss Institute of Bioinformatics.

BARTON, C. L. (2008). *Impact of Pharmacogenomics on Public Healthcare - Educating patients, payors and healthcare providers. Pharmacogenomics.* London: Business Insights.

BAYEFSKY, M., & BERKMAN, B. E. (2015). Should Regulators Balance the Risks and Promise of Innovation. *FDLIs Food Drug Policy Forum*, *5*(2).

BAYER, R., & GALEA, S. (2015). Public Health in the Precision-Medicine Era. *New England Journal of Medicine*, *373*(6), 499–501.

BBMRI-ERIC. (2015). The History. Retrieved from http://bbmri-eric.eu/history (December 22, 2015)

BBMRI.CH. (2017). Production of harmonized process. Retrieved from http://bbmri.ch/#visionmisson (March 12, 2017)

BECLA, L., LUNSHOF, J. E., GURWITZ, D., SCHULTE IN DEN BÄUMEN, T., WESTERHOFF, H. V, LANGE, B. M. H., & BRAND, A. (2011). Health technology assessment in the era of personalized health care. *International Journal of Technology Assessment in Health Care, 27*(2), 118–126.

BEERENWINKEL, N. (2015). Implementing research in personalized medicine. ZHAW - Zürcher Hochschule für angewandte Wissenschaften. Retrieved from https://www.zhaw.ch/storage/lsfm/weiterbildung/icbt/chemietag/2015-speech-beerenwinkel.pdf (October 5, 2015)

BIERMANN, J., WASEM, J., & MOSTARDT, S. (2013). Notwendiges Evidenzlevel und verfügbare Verfahrenswege der Erstattungsfähigkeit von prognostischen und prädiktiven diagnostischen Tests: Probleme und Lösungsvorschläge. Universität Duisburg Essen. Retrieved from https://www.wiwi.uni-due.de/fileadmin/fileupload/WIWI/pdf/IBES_2013_nr201.pdf (August 3, 2015)

BLAIR, E. D. (2010). Molecular diagnostics and personalized medicine: value-assessed opportunities for multiple stakeholders. *Journal of Personalized Medicine, 7*(2), 143–161.

BLAIR, E., STRATTON, E., & KAUFMANN, M. (2012). Aligning the Economic Value of Companion Diagnostics and Stratified Medicines. *Journal of Personalized Medicine, 2*(4), 257–266.

BLOBEL, B., LOPEZ, D. M., & GONZALEZ, C. (2016). Patient privacy and security concerns on big data for personalized medicine. *Health and Technology*, 1–7.

BLUMENTHAL-BARBY, J. S., MCGUIRE, A. L., GREEN, R. C., & UBEL, P. A. (2015). How behavioral economics can help to avoid "The last mile problem" in whole genome sequencing. *Genome Medicine, 7*(1), 8–10.

BMBF. (2013). Aktionsplan Individualisierte Medizin - Ein neuer Weg in Forschung und Gesundheitsversorgung. Deutsches Bundesministerium für Bildung und Forschung. Retrieved from https://www.bmbf.de/pub/Aktionsplan_Individualisierte_Medizin.pdf (July 7, 2017)

BOJOVIC, N., SABATIER, V., & ROUAULT, S. (2015). What innovative business models can be triggered by precision medicine? Analogical reasoning from the magazine industry. *Innovation and Entrepreneurship in Health*, (October), 81-94.

BOMBARD, Y. (2015). Translating personalized genomic medicine into clinical practice: evidence, values, and health policy. *Genome, 7*, 1–7.

BRACHER, K. (2013). Forscher greifen nach Patientendaten. *NZZ Am Sonntag.* Retrieved from https://www.nzz.ch/schweiz/forscher-greifen-nach-patientendaten-1.18150651 (April 3, 2016)

BRALL, C., & SCHRÖDER-BÄCK, P. (2016). Personalised Medicine and Scarce Resources: A Discussion of Ethical Chances and Challenges from the Perspective of the Capability Approach. *Public Health Genomics, 19*, 178–186.

BRÄM, C., & SZUCS, T. (2016). Is It Desirable that I Must Disclose My Genetic Data to Swiss Private Medical Insurances? *Public Health Genomics.* Retrieved from http://www.karger.com/?doi=10.1159/000448276 (April 11, 2017)

BRANZÉN, K. (2013). *Personalized Medicine: a new era for healthcare and industry.* (Life Science Foresight Institute, Ed.). Lund: Media Tryck Lunds.

BRAUN, M., RIED, J., & DABROCK, P. (2013). Riding New Waves. Sozialethische Metabeobachtungen zur Individualisierten Medizin. *Ethik in der Medizin, 25*(3), 251–258.

BREITINGER, E. (2014). Seltene Krankheiten: Patienten der Willkür der Kassen ausgesetzt. *Saldo*, (4), 44-45.

BRENNAN, Z. (2017). FDA Further Explains Delay on LDT Guidance. *GenomeWeb.* Retrieved from http://raps.org/Regulatory-Focus/News/2017/01/13/26608/FDA-Further-Explains-Delay-on-LDT-Guidance/ (February 23, 2017)

BRINO, A. (2013). How Aetna approaches personalized medicine. Retrieved from http://www.healthcarepayernews.com/content/qa-how-aetna-approaches-personalized-medicine#.Vv6dN9J97IU (April 1, 2016)

BRONWYN, H. H., & ROSENBERG, N. (EDS.). (2010). *Handbook of the Economics of Innovation.* Amsterdam: North-Holland.

BROUWER, W. B. F., CULYER, A. J., VAN EXEL, N. J. A., & RUTTEN, F. F. H. (2008). Welfarism vs. extra-welfarism. *Journal of Health Economics, 27*(2), 325–338.

BRÜGGER, U., & GRATWOHL, A. (2015, October 24). Wenn die Evidenz fehlt. *Neue Zürcher Zeitung*, 18.

BRÜGGER, U., HORISBERGER, B., RUCKSTUHL, A., PLESSOW, R., EICHLER, K., & GRATWOHL, A. (2015). Health technology assessment in Switzerland: a descriptive analysis of "Coverage with Evidence Development" decisions from 1996 to 2013. *BMJ Open, 5*(3). Retrieved from http://www.scopus.com/inward/record.url?eid=2-s2.0-84926429993&partnerID=tZOtx3y1 (March 27, 2016)

BRÜGGER, U., RUCKSTUHL, A., HORISBERGER, B., & GRATWOHL, A. (2014). Development of Coverage With Evidence Development for Medical Technologies in Switzerland From 1996 To 2012. *International Journal of Technology Assessment in Health Care, 30*(3), 253–259.

BUCHANAN, J., WORDSWORTH, S., & SCHUH, A. (2013). Issues surrounding the health economic evaluation of genomic technologies. *Pharmacogenomics, 14*(15), 1833–47.

BÜCHLER, A., & MICHEL, M. (2014). *Medizin - Mensch - Recht: Eine Einführung in das Medizinrecht der Schweiz.* Bern: Schulthess Juristische Medien AG.

BUDIN-LJØSNE, I., & HARRIS, J. R. (2016). Patient and interest organizations' views on personalized medicine: a qualitative study. *BMC Medical Ethics*, *17*(1), 28.

BUGULISKIS, J. S. (2016, April 4). The Potential of Precision Medicine Rests in Bringing Molecular Diagnostics to Market. *Clinical Omics*, 4–6. Retrieved from http://www.genengnews.com/insight-and-intelligence/the-potential-of-precision-medicine-rests-in-bringing-molecular-diagnostics-tomarket/77900632/ (April 6, 2016)

BÜRKI, N. (2015). Genetische Beratung, gesetzliche Grundlagen und Konsequenzen am Beispiel Familiäres Mamma- und Ovarialkarzinom. Basel: Universitätsspital Basel.

BURTON, B. T. M. (2015, December 11). The "Wild West" Of Medicine – Largely unregulated industry of lab testing comes under scrutiny. *The Wall Street Journal*, 1–4.

BÜTLER, M. (2016). Versicherungen, Informationen und personalisierte Medizin. In I. KLUSMAN & E. VAYENA (Eds.), *Personalisierte Medizin - Hoffnung oder leeres Versprechen?* (101–117). Zürich: vdf Hochschulverlag AG an der ETH Zürich.

BYRON, S. K., CRABB, N., GEORGE, E., MARLOW, M., & NEWLAND, A. (2014). The Health Technology Assessment of Companion Diagnostics: Experience of NICE. *Clinical Cancer Research: An Official Journal of the American Association for Cancer Research*, *20*(6), 1469–1476.

CARRERA, P., & IZERMAN, M. J. (2016). Are current ICER thresholds outdated? Valuing medicines in the era of personalized healthcare. *Expert Review oj Pharmacoeconomics & Outcomes Research*, *7167*(May), p. na. Retrieved from http://www.tandfonline.com/doi/full/10.1080/14737167.2016.1180980 (September 22, 2016)

CARRIGAN, P., & KRAHN, T. (2015). Impact of Biomarkers on Personalized Medicine. In W. Rosenthal (Ed.), *Handbook of Experimental Pharmacology*. Springer International Publishing.

CBS. (2016). In modern day gold rush of genetic testing, profit placed above proof. *CBS News*, 1–2. Retrieved from http://omnifeed.com/article/www.cbsnews.com/news/cbs-news-investigation-genetic-tests-pathway-genomics-profit-over-evidence/ (February 11, 2016)

CC-PM. (2017). PhD MTB Programm. Retrieved from http://www.ccpm.uzh.ch/en/teaching.html (May 8, 2017)

CENTERS FOR MEDICARE & MEDICAID SERVICES. (2013). Laboratory Developed Tests (LDTs) FAQs Document. Retrieved from https://www.cms.gov/Regulations-and-Guidance/Legislation/CLIA/Downloads/LDT-and-CLIA_FAQs.pdf (February 9, 2016)

CHADWICK, R. (2014). The ethics of personalized medicine. *Personalized Medicine*, *11*(1), 5–6.

CHANG, H. J. (2011). Institutions and economic development: theory, policy and history. *Journal of Institutional Economics, 7*(4), 473–498.

CHATAWAY, J., FRY, C., MARJANOVIC, S., & YAQUB, O. (2012). Public–private collaborations and partnerships in stratified medicine: making sense of new interactions. *New Biotechnology, 29*(6), 732–740.

CHOW-WHITE, P. A., MACAULAY, M., CHARTERS, A., & CHOW, P. (2015). From the bench to the bedside in the big data age: ethics and practices of consent and privacy for clinical genomics and personalized medicine. *Ethics and Information Technology*, p. n.a. Retrieved from http://link.springer.com/10.1007/s10676-015-9373-x (April 28, 2017)

COASE, R. H. (1937). The Nature of the Firm. *Economica, 4*(16), 386–405.

COHEN, J. (2011). Personalized medicine: are payers the weak link? *Personalized Medicine, 8*(3), 293–296.

COHEN, J. (2012). Overcoming regulatory and economic challenges facing pharmacogenomics. *New Biotechnology, 29*(6), 751–756.

COHEN, J. (2015). Roadblocks preventing personalized medicine from reaching its potential. *Biomarkers in Medicine, 9*, 5–8.

COHEN, J., & FELIX, A. (2014). Personalized Medicine's Bottleneck: Diagnostic Test Evidence and Reimbursement. *Journal of Personalized Medicine, 4*(2), 163–175.

COHEN, J., WILSON, A., & MANZOLILLO, K. (2013). Clinical and economic challenges facing pharmacogenomics. *The Pharmacogenomics Journal, 13*(4), 378–388.

COHEN, N., & FRANGIOSA, T. (2008). Pharmacogenomics and Personalized Medicine. In N. Cohen (Ed.), *Pharmacogenomics and Personalized Medicine* (1–27). Louisville: Humana Press.

COLLINS, F. S., & VARMUS, H. (2015). A New Initiative on Precision Medicine. *New England Journal of Medicine, 372*(9), 794–795

COMAN, G. I. (2015). Procuring Personalized Medicine Patents In US vs. Europe. *Law 360*. Retrieved from http://www.law360.com/articles/677723/procuring-personalized-medicine-patents-in-us-vs-europe (August 29, 2016)

CONSTANCE, J. A. (2010). *The Future of Molecular Diagnostics - Innovative technologies driving market opportunities in personalized medicine*. London: Business Insights.

COOK-DEEGAN, R., CONLEY, J. M., EVANS, J. P., & VORHAUS, D. (2013). The next controversy in genetic testing: clinical data as trade secrets? *European Journal of Human Genetics, 21*(6), 585–8.

COOTE, J. H., & JOYNER, M. J. (2015). Is precision medicine the route to a healthy world? *The Lancet, 385*(9978), 1617.

COOTER, R., & ULEN, T. (2008). *Law & Economics*. Boston: Pearson.

COTTER, P. D., BABU, D., & MOORE, M. W. (2012). A new paradigm for personalized medicine and companion diagnostics: the contract diagnostics organization. *The Open Conference Proceedings Journal*, *3*, 52–58.

COUNCIL OF THE EUROPEAN UNION. (2015). Council conclusions on personalised medicine for patients. *Official Journal of the European Union.* Retrieved from http://eur-lex.europa.eu/legal-content/EN/TXT/?uri=CELEX%3A52015XG1 217(01) (June 28, 2017)

CRAWFORD, J. M., & ASPINALL, M. G. (2012). The business value and cost – effectiveness of genomic medicine. *Personalized Medicine*, *9*(3), 265–286.

CRAWFORD, J. M., BRY, L., PFEIFER, J., CAUGHRON, S. K., BLACK-SCHAFFER, S., KANT, J. A., & KAUFMAN, J. H. (2014). The business of genomic testing: a survey of early adopters. *Genetics in Medicine*, *16*(12), 954–961.

CREWS, K. R., HICKS, J. K., PUI, C. H., RELLING, M. V., & EVANS, W. E. (2012). Pharmacogenomics and individualized medicine: Translating science into practice. *Clinical Pharmacology and Therapeutics*, *4*, 467–475.

CYRANOSKI, D. (2016). China embraces precision medicine on a massive scale. *Nature*, 9–10. Retrieved from http://www.nature.com/news/china-embraces-precision-medicine-on-a-massive-scale-1.19108 (January 8, 2016)

D'ANDREA, E., MARZUILLO, C., PELONE, F., DE VITO, C., & VILLARI, P. (2015). Genetic testing and economic evaluations: a systematic review of the literature. *Epidemiologia E Prevenzione*, *39*(4), 45–50.

DACIN, M. T., OLIVER, C., & ROY, J.-P. (2007). The Legitimacy of Strategic Alliances: An Institutional Perspective. *Strategic Management Journal*, *28*, 169–187.

DANNER, S. (2013). Patentability of diagnostics under the EPC - general guidance for claim drafting. VOVO, Patent- und Rechtsanwaltskanzlei. Retrieved from http://www.patents4life.com/wp-content/uploads/2013/04/03-13-Diagnostic-claims.pdf (August 29, 2016)

DAVIS, J. C., FURSTENTHAL, L., DESAI, A. A, NORRIS, T., SUTARIA, S., FLEMING, E., & MA, P. (2009). The microeconomics of personalized medicine: today's challenge and tomorrow's promise. *Nature Reviews. Drug Discovery*, *8*(4), 279–286.

DAVIS, J., MA, P., & SUTARIA, S. (2010). The microeconomics of personalized medicine. *McKinsey Quarterly*, (Feb 2010), 1–12.

DECKER, S., & BLOOMFIELD, D. (2016). Personalized Medicine Gets Boost From Court Ruling on Patents. *Bloomberg.* Retrieved from http://www.bloomberg.com/news/articles/2016-07-05/personalized-medicine-gets-boost-from-court-ruling-on-patents (July 17, 2016)

DIETEL, M. (2016). Personalized Medicine Challenges the Health Care System. In H. Albach (Ed.), *Boundaryless Hospital* (143–155). Berlin: Springer.

DIMAGGIO, P. J., & POWELL, W. W. (1983). The Iron Cage Revised: Institutional Isomorphism and Collective Rationality in Organizational Fields. *American Sociological Review, 48*(2), 147–160.

DORSCHNER, M. O., AMENDOLA, L. M., TURNER, E. H., ROBERTSON, P. D., SHIRTS, B. H., GALLEGO, C. J., ... JARVIK, G. P. (2013). Actionable, Pathogenic Incidental Findings in 1,000 Participants' Exomes. *The American Journal of Human Genetics, 93*(4), 631–640.

DORWALD, A., KYDD, J., MORRISON, C., POULTON, C., & SMITH, L. (2000). New Institutional Economics: insights on innovation dissemination and uptake. In S. HAINSWORTH & EDEN-GREEN S. (Eds.), *Sustaining change: Proceedings of a workshop on the factors affecting uptake and adaption of research outputs* (97–105). Kent: UK Departement for International Development. Retrieved from http://www.envirobase.info/PDF/CPP Sustaining_Change.pdf#page=104 (June 21, 2017)

DOWNING, G. J. (2009). Key aspects of health system change on the path to personalized medicine. *Translational Research, 154*(6), 272–276.

DROBAK, J. N. (2008). Introduction: Law & The New Institutional Economics Washington University. *Washington University Journal of Law & Policy, 26*, na. Retrieved from http://openscholarship.wustl.edu/law_journal_law_policy/vol26/iss1/2 (June 6, 3016)

DUFFY, D. J. (2015). Problems, challenges and promises: perspectives on precision medicine. *Briefings in Bioinformatics*, 1–11.

DUSTER, T. (2015). A post-genomic surprise. The molecular reinscription of race in science, law and medicine. *The British Journal of Sociology, 66*(1), 1–27.

DZAU, V. J., GINSBURG, G. S., VAN NUYS, K., AGUS, D., & GOLDMAN, D. (2015). Aligning incentives to fulfil the promise of personalised medicine. *The Lancet, 385*, 2118–2119.

EAK. (2012). Geschäftsordnung Eidgenössische Arzneimittelkommission. Bern: Swiss Federal Office of Public Health [SFOPH]. Retrieved from http://www.bag.admin.ch/themen/krankenversicherung/00263/00264/04013/index.html?lang=de (July 1, 2016)

EAMGK. (2012). Geschäftsordnung Eidgenössische Kommission für Analysen, Mittel und Gegenstände. Bern: Swiss Federal Office of Public Health [SFOPH]. Retrieved from http://www.bag.admin.ch/themen/krankenversicherung/00263/00264/04013/index.html?lang=de (July 1, 2016)

EASTMAN, P. (2012, November 25). Summit Explores Best Ways to Integrate Personalized Medicine into Health Care. *Oncology Times*, 24–25.

EBERBACH, W. H. (2014). Personalisierte Prävention: Wirkungen und Aus-wirkungen. *Medizinrecht, 32*(7), 449–464.

ECKHARDT, A., NAVARINI, A. A., RECHER, A., RIPPE, K. P., RÜTSCHE, B., TELSER, H., & MARTI, M. (2014). *Personalisierte Medizin.* (TA-Swiss - Zentrum für Technologiefolgen-Abschätzung, Ed.). Zürich: vdf Hochschulverlag AG an der ETH Zürich. Retrieved from http://www.vdf.ethz.ch/service/3591/3592_Personalisierte-Medizin_OA.pdf (June 14, 2014)

EDI. (2013). *The Federal Council's health-policy priorities.* Bern. Retrieved from http://www.bag.admin.ch/gesundheit2020/index.html?lang=en (Oct-ober 10, 2015)

EDI. (2014). *Erläuternder Bericht zum Bundesgesetz über das Zentrum für Qualität in der obligatorischen Krankenpflegeversicherung (Stärkung von Qualität und Wirtschaftlichkeit).* Bern. Retrieved from https://www.admin.ch/ch/d/gg/pc/documents/2425/BG-Zentrum-fuer-Qualitaet_Erl.-Bericht_de.pdf (July 4, 2016)

EHEALTH SUISSE. (2012). Zwischenbilanz der Ziele „ Strategie eHealth Schweiz “. Retrieved from https://www.e-health-suisse.ch/fileadmin/user_upload/Dokumente/2012/D/120419_Zwischenbilanz_Ziele_Strategie_eHealth_Schweiz_D.pdf (July 14, 2017)

EHEALTH SUISSE. (2017)a. Einführungsplan EPD. Retrieved from https://www.e-health-suisse.ch/fileadmin/user_upload/Dokumente/2017/D/170320_Einfuehrungsplan_EPD_Big-Picture_v09_D.pdf (April 2, 2017)

EHEALTH SUISSE. (2017)b. Strategie eHealth Schweiz 2007. Retrieved from https://www.e-health-suisse.ch/politik-recht/strategische-grundlagen/strategie-ehealth-schweiz.html (April 2, 2017)

EHMANN, F., CANEVA, L., PRASAD, K., PAULMICHL, M., MALIEPAARD, M., LLERENA, A., ... PAPALUCA-AMATI, M. (2015). Pharmacogenomic information in drug labels: European Medicines Agency perspective. *The Pharmacogenomics Journal*, 1–10.

EKSTROM, L., FLAHERTY, D., HENRY, J., KULKARNI, S., PATTABIRAMAN, K., & RUDOLPH, T. (2013). Capturing value for Dx in personalized medicine – is there a path? In: *Personalized Medicine - The Path Forward.* Edited by McKinsey & Company, 31–37. Retrieved from http://www.mckinsey.com/~/media/mckinsey/dotcom/client_service/pharma%20and%20medical%20products/pmp%20new/pdfs/mckinsey%20on%20personalized%20medicine%20march%202013.ashx (June 8, 2014)

EL SHANTI, H., CHOUCHANE, L., BADII, R., GALLOUZI, I. E., & GASPARINI, P. (2015). Genetic testing and genomic analysis: a debate on ethical, social and legal issues in the Arab world with a focus on Qatar. *Journal of Translational Medicine, 13*(358), 1–22.

ELGK. (2014). Geschäftsordnung Eidgenössische Kommission für allgemeine Leistungen und Grundsatzfragen. Bern: Swiss Federal Office of Public Health [SFOPH]. Retrieved from http://www.bag.admin.ch/themen/krankenversicherung/00263/00264/04013/index.html?lang=de (July 1, 2016)

ELLIS, J. (2016). Does patent protection for personalized medicine still exist in the USA? *Pharmaceutical Patent Analyst*, *5*(2), 87–90.

ELLUL, B. (2015). Ethical Considerations in the Genomic Era. In G. Grech & I. Grossman (Eds.), *Preventive and Predictive Genetics: Towards Personalised Medicine* (349–375). Heidelberg: Springer.

EMA. (2012). Guideline on the use of pharmacogenetic methodologies in the pharmacokinetic evaluation of medicinal products, *44*, 1–23. Retrieved from http://www.ema.europa.eu/docs/en_GB/document_library/Scientific_guideline/2012/02/WC500121954.pdf (December 15, 2015)

EMA. (2016). Guideline on good pharmacogenomic practice. Retrieved from http://www.ema.europa.eu/docs/en_GB/document_library/Scientific_guideline/2016/05/WC500205758.pdf (May 27, 2016)

EPPING, M., & BERCHTOLD, C. (2014). Companion Diagnostics und „personalisierte" Arzneimittel Herausforderungen des Zulassungs- und Erstattungsrechts. *GoingPublic Life Sciences*, 50-52.

EPPINGER, E., HALECKER, B., HÖLZLE, K., & KAMPRATH, M. (EDS.). (2015). *Dienstleistungspotentiale und Geschäftsmodelle in der Personalisierten Medizin - Konzepte, Analysen, Potentiale.* Wiesbaden: Springer Gabler.

ESCHER CLAUSS, S. (2016). Krankenversicherer und Ärzte sind in der Pflicht. *Schweizer Versicherung*, (May), 8–12.

ESTAPE, E. A., MAYS, M. H., & STERNKE, E. A. (2016). Translation in Data Mining to Advance Personalized Medicine for Health Equity. *Intelligent Information Management*, *8*, 9–16.

ETH. (2017)a. Bachelor in Humanmedizin. Retrieved from https://www.ethz.ch/de/studium/bachelor/studienangebot/systemorientierte-naturwissenschaften/medizin.html (April 16, 2017)

ETH. (2017)b. Bridge the divide. Retrieved from https://www.ethz.ch/en/news-and-events/eth-news/news/2017/02/bridge-the-divide.html (March 10, 2017)

ETH. (2017)c. Systems Medicine. Retrieved from https://www.biol.ethz.ch/en/studies/master/master-degree-majors/systems-biology.html and http://www.systemsbiology-phd.ethz.ch/ (June 29, 2017)

EUNETHTA. (2016). EUnetHTA. Retrieved from http://www.eunethta.eu/ (June 6, 2016)

EUROPABIO. (2015). EuropaBio calls for the removal of access barriers to personalised medicine for European patients. EuropaBio. Retrieved from http://www.europabio.org/sites/default/files/press/europabio_calls_for_the_removal_of_access_barriers_to_personalised_medicines_for_european_patients.pdf (retrieved August, 28, 2015)

European Alliance for Personalised Medicine. (2013). Innovation and patient access to personalised medicine. European Alliance for Personalized Medicine. Retrieved from http://euapm.eu/pdf/EAPM_REPORT_on_Innovation_and_Patient_Access_to_Personalised_Medicine.pdf (July 15, 2015)

European Commission. (2011). *European Perspectives in Personalised Medicine, 12-13 May 2011.* Brussels. Retrieved from http://ec.europa.eu/research/health/pdf/personalised-medicine-conference-report_en.pdf (July 6, 2015)

European Commission. (2012). *Biobanks for Europe - a challenge for governance.* Brussels: European Commission. Retrieved from http://www.coe.int/t/dg3/healthbioethic/Activities/10_Biobanks/biobanks_for_Europe.pdf (September 19, 2015)

European Commission. (2013). Use of "-omics" technologies in the development of personalised medicine. European Commission. Retrieved from http://ec.europa.eu/health/files/latest_news/2013-10_personalised_medicine_en.pdf (July 5, 2015)

European Commission. (2016)a. Personalised Medicine. Retrieved from http://ec.europa.eu/health/human-use/personalised-medicine/index_en.htm (February 13, 2016)

European Commission. (2016)b. Personalised Medicine Conference 2016: Conference report. European Commission. Retrieved from https://ec.europa.eu/research/conferences/2016/permed2016/pdf/permed-2016_report.pdf (June 28, 2016)

European Commission. (2016)c. Revisions of Medical Device Directives. Retrieved from http://ec.europa.eu/growth/sectors/medical-devices/regulatory-framework/revision/index_en.htm (February 3, 2016)

European Diagnostics Manufacturers Association. (2014). EDMA Position Paper regarding the Revision of Directive 98/79/EC on In Vitro Diagnostic Medical Devices. Retrieved from http://www.medtecheurope.org/sites/default/files/2014_01_24_EDMA_IVDD_revision_PP_PUB%5B1%5D.pdf (February 9, 2016)

European Medicines Agency. (2016). Final report on the adaptive pathways pilot, 1–23. Retrieved from http://www.ema.europa.eu/docs/en_GB/document_library/Report/2016/08/WC500211526.pdf (March 3, 3017)

European Medicines Agency (2017). Concept paper on predictive biomarker-based assay development in the context of drug development and lifecycle. Retrieved from http://www.ema.europa.eu/docs/en_GB/document_library/Scientific_guideline/2017/07/WC500232420.pdf (July 29, 2017)

European Patent Institute. (2015). Translational Medicine. Retrieved from https://www.eupati.eu/non-clinical-studies/translational-medicine/ (retreived June 25, 2017)

EUROPEAN SCIENCE FOUNDATION. (2012). *Personalised medicine for the European citizen: Towards more precise medicine for the diagnosis, treatment and prevention of disease (iPM).* Retrieved from http://www.esf.org/fileadmin/Public_documents/Publications/Personalised_Medicine.pdf (June 8, 2016)

EVANGELATOS, N., REUMANN, M., LEHRACH, H., & BRAND, A. (2016). Clinical Trial Data as Public Goods: Fair Trade and the Virtual Knowledge Bank as a Solution to the Free Rider Problem - A Framework for the Promotion of Innovation by Facilitation of Clinical Trial Data Sharing among Biopharmaceutical Companies in the Era of Omics and Big Data. *Public Health Genomics.* Retrieved from http://www.karger.com/?doi=10.1159/000446101 (June 6, 2016)

EVANS, B. J. (2014). Economic Regulation of Next-Generation Sequencing. *Journal of Law, Medicine & Ethics, Fall*, 51–66.

EVANS, B. J. (2016). Big Data and Individual Autonomy in a Crowd. *2016 Annual Conference: Big Data, Health Law, and Bioethics; Petrie-Flom Center for Health Law Policy, Biotechnology, and Bioethics at Harvard Law School, in Collaboration with Berkman Center for Internet and Society at Harvard University and the Health Ethics and Policy Lab, University of Zurich*, [unpublished conference draft].

EVANS, B. J., BURKE, W., & JARVIK, G. P. (2015). The FDA and Genomic Tests - Getting Regulation Right. *New England Journal of Medicine, 372*(23), 2258–2264.

EVANS, J. P., & GREEN, R. C. (2009). Direct to consumer genetic testing: Avoiding a culture war. *Genetics in Medicine: Official Journal of the American College of Medical Genetics, 11*(8), 568–569.

EVERS, A., ROVERS, A., KREMER, J., VELTMAN, J., SCHALKEN, J., BLOEM, B., & VAN GOOL, A. (2012). An integrated framework of personalized medicine: From individual genomes to participatory health care. *Croatian Medical Journal, 53*, 301–304.

EVERS, M., KULKARNI, S., MA, P., MOLLER, M., & OSTOJIC, I. (2013). Managing for success in biomarker R&D: Challenges and opportunities. In: *Personalized Medicine - The Path Forward.* Edited by McKinsey & Company, p. 31--37. Retrieved from http://www.mckinsey.com/~/media/mckinsey/dotcom/client_service/pharma%20and%20medical%20products/pmp%20new/pdfs/mckinsey%20on%20personalized%20medicine%20march%202013.ashx (June 8, 2014)

FACKLER, J. L., & MCGUIRE, A. L. (2010). Paving the Way to Personalized Genomic Medicine: Steps to Successful Implementation. *Pharmacogenomics and Personalized Medicine, 7*(2), 1–12.

FAMH. (2015). Gefährdete Datensicherheit bei genetischen Analysen. FAMH. Retrieved from http://www.famh.ch/assets/Dokumente/FAMHMMStellungnahme-GUMG.pdf (October 7, 2015)

FASMED. (2012). Wie sind Kosten und Nutzen von Medizinprodukten zu bewerten ?Retrieved from http://www.implantate-schweiz.ch/fileadmin/media/pdf/positionspapiere/Position_des_FASMED_zum_Thema-Wie_sind_Kosten_und_Nutzen_von_Medizinprodukten_zu_bewerten.pdf (25. May 2016)

FASMED. (2016)a. Neuregulierung von Medizinprodukten: Bundesrat setzt sich für freien Warenverkehr mit der EU ein. Retrieved from http://www.fasmed.ch/de/info-center/news/news-detail/article////title/neuregulieru-2.html?no_cache=1&cHash=92d80ca0ec (July 21, 2016)

FASMED. (2016)b. Zeitnaher Zugang zur Vergütung von Innovationen unter SwissDRG nicht gewährleistet Einführung. Retrieved from http://www.fasmed.ch/fileadmin/pdf/fasmed/2016%20FASMED%20Innovationsabbildung%20DRG.pdf (June 19, 2016)

FASMED. (2017). "Monsterwelle erfasst die Branche": Stimmen zu MDR/IVDR aus der Schweiz. Retrieved from http://www.fasmed.ch/de/info-center/news/news-detail/article/2017/04/24/title/monsterwell.html?no_cache=1&cHash=7f7831c125 (May 28, 2017)

FAULKNER, E., ANNEMANS, L., GARRISON, L., HELFAND, M., HOLTORF, A.-P., HORNBERGER, J., ... WATKINS, J. (2012). Challenges in the development and reimbursement of personalized medicine-payer and manufacturer perspectives and implications for health economics and outcomes research: a report of the ISPOR personalized medicine special interest group. *Value in Health: The Journal of the International Society for Pharmacoeconomics and Outcomes Research*, *15*(8), 1162–71.

FDA. (2010). *Gene Patents and Licensing Practices and Their Impact on Patient Access to Genetic Tests.* Washington. Retrieved from http://osp.od.nih.gov/sites/default/files/SACGHS_patents_report_2010.pdf (September 15, 2015)

FDA. (2013). *Paving the Way for Personalized Medicine - FDA's Role in a New Era of Medical Product Development.* Retrieved from http://www.fda.gov/downloads/ScienceResearch/SpecialTopics/PersonalizedMedicine/UCM372421.pdf (retrieved July 2, 2015)

FDA. (2014)a. Draft Guidance for Industry and Food and Drug Administration Staff: In Vitro Companion Diagnostic Devices. U. S. Food and Drug Administration [FDA]. Retrieved from http://www.fda.gov/downloads/medicaldevices/deviceregulationandguidance/guidancedocuments/ucm262327.pdf (July 5, 2015)

FDA. (2014)b. FDA Notification and Medical Device Reporting for Laboratory Developed Tests (LDTs). Retrieved from http://www.fda.gov/downloads/medicaldevices/deviceregulationandguidance/guidancedocuments/ucm416684.pdf (February 9, 2016)

FDA. (2014)c. Framework for Regulatory Oversight of Laboratory Developed Tests (LDTs). Retrieved from https://www.fda.gov/downloads/medicaldevices/deviceregulationandguidance/guidancedocuments/ucm416685.pdf (July 19, 2016)

FDA. (2015)a. Laboratory Developed Tests. Retrieved from http://www.fda.gov/MedicalDevices/ProductsandMedicalProcedures/InVitroDiagnostics/ucm407296.htm (February 9, 2016)

FDA. (2015)b. The Public Health Evidence for FDA Oversight of Laboratory Developed Tests : 20 Case Studies. Retrieved from http://www.fda.gov/downloads/AboutFDA/ReportsManualsForms/Reports/UCM472777.pdf (May 5, 2016)

FDA. (2016)a. About PrecisionFDA. Retrieved from https://precision.fda.gov/about/what (March 7, 2016)

FDA. (2016)b. Principles for Codevelopment of an In Vitro Companion Diagnostic Device with a Therapeutic Product - Draft Guidance for Industry and Administration Staff. U. S. Food and Drug Administration [FDA]. Retrieved from http://www.fda.gov/downloads/MedicalDevices/DeviceRegulationandGuidance/GuidanceDocuments/UCM510824.pdf?source=govdelivery&utm_medium=email&utm_source=govdelivery (July 16, 2016)

FDA. (2016)c. Use of Standards in FDA Regulatory Oversight of Next Generation Sequencing (NGS) - Based In Vitro Diagnostics (IVDs) Used for Diagnosing Germline Diseases (Draft). Retrieved from https://www.fda.gov/ucm/groups/fdagov-public/@fdagov-meddev-gen/documents/document/ucm509838.pdf (July 1, 2017)

FDA. (2017). FDA allows marketing of first direct-to-consumer tests that provide genetic risk information for certain conditions. Retrieved from https://www.fda.gov/NewsEvents/Newsroom/PressAnnouncements/ucm551185.htm (April 28, 2017)

FELDER, S. (2016). Was braucht es, damit sich die personalisierte Medizin für die pharmazeutischen Unternehmen und die Gesellschaft rechnet? In I. KLUSMAN & E. VAYENA (Eds.), *Personalisierte Medizin - Hoffnung oder leeres Versprechen?* Zurich: vdf Hochschulverlag AG an der ETH Zürich.

FERRARA, J. (2007). Personalized medicine: Challenging pharmaceutical and diagnostic company business models. *McGill Journal of Medicine, 10*(1), 59–61.

FISCH, F. (2016). Data improves therapy. *Horizons, June.* Retrieved from http://www.snf.ch/en/researchinFocus/newsroom/Pages/news-160610-horizons-data-improves-therapy.aspx (April 1, 2017)

FLECK, L. M. (2012). Pharmacogenomics and personalized medicine: Wicked problems, ragged edges and ethical precipices. *New Biotechnology, 29*(6), 757–768.

FLOCKHART, D. A., SKAAR, T., BERLIN, D. S., KLEIN, T. E., & NGUYEN, A. T. (2009). Clinically Available Pharmacogenomics Tests. *Clinical Pharmacology & Therapeutics, 86*(1), 109–113.

FLORES, M., GLUSMAN, G., BROGAARD, K., & HOOD, L. (2013). P4 medicine: how systems medicine will transform the healthcare sector and society Perspective. *Personalized Medicine, 10*(6), 565–576.

FRIZZO-BARKER, J., CHOW-WHITE, P. A., CHARTERS, A., & HA, D. (2016). Genomic Big Data and Privacy: Challenges and Opportunities for Precision Medicine. *Computer Supported Cooperative Work, 2-3*, 115-136.

FRUEH, F. W. (2013). Regulation, reimbursement, and the long road of implementation of personalized medicine - A perspective from the United States. *Value in Health, 16*(6th supplement), S27–S31.

FURUBOTN, E., & RICHTER, R. (2005). *Institutions and Economic Theory - The Contribution of the New Institutional Economics* (2nd ed.). Ann Arbor: The University of Michigan Press.

GÄCHTER, T., & BURCH, S. (2013). Inverkehrbringen von Medizinprodukten in der Schweiz und in der EU. In B. Rütsche (Ed.), *Medizinprodukte: Regulierung und Haftung*. Stämpfli Verlag AG.

GÄCHTER, T., & MEIENBERGER, A. (2013). *Evaluation der Zulassung und Überprüfung von Medikamenten in der obligatorischen Kranken-pflegeversicherung*. Retrieved from https://www.parlament.ch/centers/documents/de/matx-medikamente-total -d.pdf (May 23, 2016)

GÄCHTER, T., & VOKINGER, K. N. (2012). Personalisierte Medizin aus juristischer Perspektive. *Praxis, 101*(15), 695–696. Retrieved from http://www.biham.unibe.ch/unibe/medizin/biham/content/e7950/e9805/e9806/linkliste220034/Polypharmazie_ger.pdf (May 23, 2016)

GALLI, S. J. (2016). Toward precision medicine and health: Opportunities and challenges in allergic diseases. *Journal of Allergy and Clinical Immunology, 137*(5), 1289–1300.

GAMMA, A. (2013). The role of genetic information in personalized medicine. *Perspectives in Biology and Medicine, 56*(4), 485–512.

GARATTINI, L., CURTO, A., & FREEMANTLE, N. (2015). Personalized medicine and economic evaluation in oncology: all theory and no practice? *Expert Review of Pharmacoeconomics & Outcomes Research, 15*(5), 733-738.

GARAU, M., TOWSE, A., GARRISON, L., HOUSMAN, L., & OSSA, D. (2012). Can and should value-based pricing be applied to molecular diagnostics? *University of Washington Office of Health Economics Research Paper*, Washington: University of Washington.

GARBER, A. M., & TUNIS, S. R. (2009). Does Comparative-Effectiveness Research Threaten Personalized Medicine? *New England Journal of Medicine, 360*(19), 1925–1927.

GARFIELD, S. (2011). Advancing Access to Personalized Medicine: A Comparative Assessment of European Reimbursement Systems. London: Personalized Medicine Coalition. Retrieved from http://www.personalizedmedicinecoalition.org/Userfiles/PMC-Corporate/file/pmc_bridgehead_issue_brief_european_reimbursement.pdf (May 4, 2015)

GARRISON, L. P. (2016). Health Policy and Economic Issues in Biotechnology and Personalized Medicine. In T. R. FULDA, A. LYLES, & A. I. WERTHEIMER (Eds.), *Pharmaceutical Public Policy* (209–229). Boca Raton: CRC Press, Taylor & Francis Group.

GASSER, U. (2008). How can Law foster Innovative Entrepreneurship? A Blueprint for a Research Program. *Law and Information - Archive for the "New Institutional Economics."* Retrieved from https://blogs.harvard.edu/ugasser/category/new-institutional-economics/ (June 21, 2017)

Genetica Now Offering PanoramaTM NIPT in Switzerland via Natera's Constellation™ Software Platform. (2016, February 9). *PR Newswire*, 9–12. Retrieved from http://www.prnewswire.com/news-releases/genetica-now-offering-panoramatm-nipt-in-switzerland-via-nateras-constellation-software-platform-300216831.html (February 11, 2016)

GHOSH, S. (2015). Decentering the Consuming Self: Personalized Medicine, Science, and the Market for Lemons. *Wake Forest Journal of Law and Policy*, *299*(6), 1–36.

Global 2000: Hall Of Fame CEOs. (2015). *Forbes*. Retrieved from http://www.forbes.com/pictures/gike45mk/mark-schneider-fresenius/ (June 11, 2015)

GLOBAL ALLIANCE FOR GENOMICS AND HEALTH. (2014). Framework for Responsible Sharing of Genomic and Health-Related Data. Retrieved from https://genomicsandhealth.org/files/public/Framework for Responsible Sharing of Genomic and Health-Related Data - Version 10 September 2014.pdf (September 21, 2015)

Global innovation rankings: The innovation game. (2015). *The Economist*. Retrieved from http://www.economist.com/node/21664995/print (February 11, 2016)

GoingPublic Spezialausgabe Personalisierte Medizin. (2015). *GoingPublic*. Retrieved from http://www.goingpublic.de/product/life-sciences-seriepersonalisierte-medizin-2015-2 (September 15, 2016)

GOLD, M. R., STEVENSON, D., & FRYBACK, D. G. (2002). HALYS and QALYS and DALYS, Oh My: similarities and differences in summary measures of population Health. *Annual Review of Public Health*, *23*, 115–34.

GOTTWALD, S., & HUSTER, S. (2016). Personalised Medicine as Orphan Drugs? Legal and Ethical Questions. In J. VOLLMANN, V. SANDOW, & J. SCHILDMANN (Eds.), *The Ethics of Personalised Medicine: Critical Perspectives* (p. 231 ff.). New York: Routledge.

GRAY, M., LAGERBERG, T., & DOMBRÁDI, V. (2017). Equity and Value in "Precision Medicine." *The New Bioethics*, *23*(1), 87–94.

GRECH, G., SCERRI, C., SCERRI, J., & CESUROGLU, T. (2015). *Preventive and Predictive Genetics: A Perspective.* In G. GRECH & I. GROSSMAN (Eds.), *Preventive and Predictive Genetics: Towards Personalised Medicine* (7-43). Heidelberg: Springer.

GRECH, G., VAN SCHAIK, R., & BORG, J. (2015). Implementation of Genomic Medicine: Tools and Challenges. In G. GRECH & I. GROSSMAN (Eds.), *Preventive and Predictive Genetics: Towards Personalised Medicine* (329–349). Heidelberg: Springer.

GREEN, R. C., LAUTENBACH, D. M., & MCGUIREOLIVER, A. L. (2015). GINA, Genetic Discrimination, and Genomic Medicine. *New England Journal of Medicine, 372*(5), 397–399.

GRONOWICZ, G. (2016). *Personalized Medicine - Promises and Pitfalls.* Boca Raton: CRC PRess, Taylor & Francis Group.

GROVES, P., KAYYALI, B., KNOTT, D., & KUIKEN, S. VAN. (2013). The "big data"revolution in healthcare. McKinsey & Company. Retrieved from http://www.mckinsey.com/industries/healthcare-systems-and-services/our-insights/the-big-data-revolution-in-us-health-care (September 12, 2014)

GUCHET, X. (2015). What's in a word? The person of Personalized (nano) Medicine. *Nanomedicine, 10*(20), 3167–79.

GUMEK. (2016). Tätigkeitsbericht der Expertenkommission für genetische Untersuchungen beim Menschen. Bern: SWISS FEDERAL OFFICE OF PUBLIC HEALTH [SFOPH]. Retrieved from http://www.bag.admin.ch/themen/medizin/00683/02724/04638/07052/index.html?lang=de (July 25, 2016)

GUTZWILLER, F. (2013). Zulassung von qualitativ hochstehenden Gentests im In- und Ausland. Die Bundesversammlung - Das Schweizer Parlament. Retrieved from http://www.parlament.ch/d/suche/seiten/geschaefte.aspx?gesch_id=20133654# (September 30, 2015)

GUTZWILLER, F., BILLER-ANDORNO, N., HARNACKE, C., BOLLHALDER, L., SZUCS, T., GUTZWILLER, F., & SCHWENKGLENKS, M. (2012). Methoden zur Bestimmung von Nutzen bzw. Wert medizinischer Leistungen und deren Anwendung in der Schweiz und ausgewählten europäischen Ländern. *Akademien der Wissenschaften Schweiz*, 1–131.

GUTZWILLER, F., & BLANK, P. R. (2013). Gentests in der Schweiz : Es herrscht Handlungsbedarf. *Schweizerische Ärztezeitung, 94*(16), 629–631.

GUTZWILLER, F., & BLANK, P. R. (2014). Current challenges in handling genetic data. *Swiss Medical Weekly*, (144). Retrieved from http://www.smw.ch/content/smw-2014-13998/ (May 25, 2016)

GUYATT, G., SACKETT, D., TAYLOR, W., GHONG, J., ROBERTS, R., & PUGSLEY, S. (1986). Determining Optimal Therapy — Randomized Trials in Individual Patients. *New England Journal of Medicine, 314*, 889–892.

HAFEN, E., & BRAUCHBAR, M. (2014). Befreiung aus der digitalen Leibeigenschaft. *Neue Zürcher Zeitung*. Zürich. Retrieved from http://www.nzz.ch/meinung/debatte/befreiung-aus-der-digitalen-leibeigenschaft-1.18256191#disqus_thread (April 3, 2014)

HALVERSON, C., CLIFT, K. E., & MCCORMICK, J. B. (2016). Was it worth it? Patients' perspectives on the perceived value of genomics-based individualized medicine. *Journal of Community Genetics, 1*, 1–14.

HALVORSON, G. (2016). *What Can You Attribute Kaiser Permanente's Disease Control Success to?* Kaiser Permanente. Retrieved from https://www.sharecare.com/video/healthmakers/george-halvorson/what-can-you-attribute-kaiser-permanentes-disease-control-success-to (April 2, 2016)

HAMBURG, M. A. (2013). Personalized Medicine: The Future is Now. *FDA Voice*. Retrieved from http://blogs.fda.gov/fdavoice/index.php/2013/11/personalized-medicine-the-future-is-now/ (November 11, 2015)

HANDSCHIN, C., & MEYER, U. A. (2012). Warum reagiert mein Patient anders auf dieses Medikament? Pharmakogenomik und Personalisierte Medizin in der Praxis. *Schweizer Medizin Forum, 12*(22), 425–433.

HARDIN, G. (1968). The Tragedy of the Commons. *Science, 162*(June), 1243–1248.

HARVARD BUSINESS SCHOOL. (2016). Harvard Business School Launches Precision Trials Challenge. Retrieved from http://www.hbs.edu/news/releases/Pages/hbs-launches-precision-trials-challenge.aspx (February 02, 2016)

HARVEY, A., BRAND, A., HOLGATE, S. T., KRISTIANSEN, L. V., LEHRACH, H., PALOTIE, A., & PRAINSACK, B. (2012). The future of technologies for personalised medicine. *New Biotechnology, 29*(6), 625–633.

HATZ, M. H. M., SCHREMSER, K., & ROGOWSKI, W. H. (2014). Is individualized medicine more cost-effective? A systematic review. *PharmacoEconomics, 32*(5), 443–55.

HAYES, D. F. (2013). OMICS-based personalized oncology: if it is worth doing, it is worth doing well! *BMC Medicine, 11*(221), 1–4.

HAYES, D. F. (2014). Biomarker validation and testing. *Molecular Oncology, 9*(5), 1–7.

HAYES, D. F., ALLEN, J., COMPTON, C., GUSTAVSEN, G., LEONARD, D. G. B., MCCORMACK, R., ... TUNIS, S. R. (2013). Breaking a vicious cycle. *Science Translational Medicine, 5*(196), 196cm6, 1-7.

HAYES, D. F., MARKUS, H. S., LESLIE, R. D., & TOPOL, E. J. (2014). Personalized medicine: risk prediction, targeted therapies and mobile health technology. *BMC Medicine, 12*, 37.

HEARE, T. (2015). Patenting Precision Medicines at the European Patent Office. Venner Shipley. Retrieved from https://www.vennershipley.co.uk/resources/publications/2015/12/14/patenting-precision-medicines-at-the-european-patent-office (August 31, 2016)

HENGGELER, C., & MATYAS, G. (2017). Gentests in der Medizin - ein Update. *Hausarzt Praxis*, *12*(9), 14-18.

HEHLI, S. (2017). Elektronisches Patientendossier: Der E - Patient braucht noch Pflege. *Neue Zürcher Zeitung*. Retrieved from https://www.nzz.ch/schweiz/medizin-20-stolpersteine-auf-dem-weg-zum-e-patienten-ld.142590 (April 2, 2017)

HEIMGARTNER, A. (2015). Strengthening of Health Technology Assessment (HTA) in Switzerland. Bachelorthesis at University of St. Gallen.

HERMANN, S., & SEITZ, H. (2015). Personalisierte Medizin und Diagnostika - der Stand der Dinge. *GIT Labor-Fachzeitschrift*, *18* (August), 18.

HIRSTEIN, A. (2012). Verhinderte Gentests. *Neue Zürcher Zeitung*. Retrieved from http://www.nzz.ch/verhinderte-gentests-1.15873677 (September 15, 2015)

HITZ, A., & PREVEL KATSANIS, L. (2014). A consumer adoption model for personalized medicine: an exploratory study. *International Journal oj Pharmaceutical and Healthcare Marketing*, *8*(4), 371–391.

HOFFMAN, M. J., DUNNENBERGER, H. M., KEVIN, H. J., CAUDLE, K. E., WHIRL CARRILLO, M., FREIMUTZ, R. R., & WILLIAMS, M. S. (2016). Developing knowledge resources to support precision medicine: principles from the Clinical Pharmacogenetics Implementation Consortium (CPIC). *Journal of the Amrican Medical Informatics Association*, *23*(2), 43–56.

HOFMANN, M. (2014). Symbolische Datenschutzpolitik. *Neue Zürcher Zeitung*. Retrieved from http://www.nzz.ch/schweiz/symbolische-datenschutzpolitik-1.18381178 (August 3, 2016)

HOLDER, A. M., & MERIC-BERNSTAM, F. (2016). Toward Personalized Therapy for Cancer. In R. C. BAST, M. MARKMANN, & E. HAWK (Eds.), *Targeted Therapy in Translational Cancer Research*. New Jersey: Wiley Blackwell.

HOLLENSTEIN, M. (2014). Das Recht auf Nichtwissen im Bereich genetischer Untersuchungen. *Hill Zeitschrift Für Recht Und Gesundheit*, *177*.

HOLLINGSWORTH, S. J. (2015). Precision medicine in oncology drug development: a pharma perspective. *Drug Discovery Today*, *0*(0), 1–9. Retrieved from http://www.ncbi.nlm.nih.gov/pubmed/26482740 (March 26, 2016)

HOLMAN, C. M. (2014). Mayo, Myriad, and the Future of Innovation in Molecular Diagnostics and Personalized Medicine. *North Carolina Journal of Law & Technology*, *15*(4), 639–679.

HOOD, L. (2013). Systems Biology and P4 Medicine: Past, Present, and Future. *Rambam Maimonides Medical Journal, 4*(2), e0012. Retrieved from http://www.rmmj.org.il/(S(z4ullue0adz4zg2ohtqc4p45))/Pages/Article.aspx?manuId=263 (June 23, 2016)

HOOD, L., & AUFFRAY, C. (2013). Participatory medicine: a driving force for revolutionizing healthcare. *Genome Medicine, 5*(110), 1-4.

HOPKINS, M. M., IBARRETA, D., GAISSER, S., ENZING, C. M., RYAN, J., MARTIN, P. A., ... FORDE, T. (2006). Putting pharmacogenetics into practice. *Nature Biotechnology, 24*(4), 403–410.

HORGAN, D. (2016). Access for All: A Personalised Approach. *Public Health Genomics, 19*(129) 129–131.

HORGAN, D., JANSEN, M., LEYENS, L., LAL, J. A., SUDBRAK, R., HACKENITZ, E., ... BRAND, A. (2014). An index of barriers for the implementation of personalised medicine and pharmacogenomics in Europe. *Public Health Genomics, 17*(5–6), 287–298.

HUMAN GENOME PROJECT. (2015). Major Events in the U.S. Human Genome Project and Related Projects. Human Genome Project. Retrieved from http://web.ornl.gov/sci/techresources/Human_Genome/project/timeline.shtml (July 25, 2015)

HUSTER, S., & GOTTWALD, S. (2012). Rechtliche Implikationen der personalisierten Medizin - Welche juristischen Herausforderungen und Probleme müssen bewältigt werden? *GesundheitsRecht, 8*, 449–456.

IMDRF. (2016). About International Medical Device Regulators Forum. Retrieved from http://www.imdrf.org/about/about.asp (February 22, 2016)

INAHTA. (2016). Members List. Retrieved from http://www.inahta.org/members/members_list/ (July 5, 2016)

INSTITUT FÜR MEDIZINISCHE GENETIK. (2016). Informationen zu Kosten und Kostenübernahme. University of Zürich, Institut für Medizinische Genetik. Retrieved from http://www.medgen.uzh.ch/dam/jcr:00000000-7a6a-e119-ffff-ffff94679cf2/Genetische_Sprechstunde_Merkblatt_Kosten.pdf (June 1, 2016)

INTERLANDI, J. (2016). The Paradox of Precision Medicine. *Scientific American, 314*(4), 24–25.

ISSA, A. M. (2008). Beyond Health Insurance: Public Policy to Improve Health. *Advances in Health Economics and Health Services Research, 19*, 191-206.

JAIN, A. B., MOLLET, A., & SZUCS, T. D. (2017). Regulatory watch: Structural and procedural characteristics of international regulatory authorities. *Nature Reviews Drug Discovery*, n. a. Retrieved from http://www.nature.com/nrd/journal/vaop/ncurrent/full/nrd.2017.135.html?foxtrotcallback=true (August 20, 2017)

JAIN, K. K. (2015). *Textbook of Personalized Medicine* (2nd edition). New York: Springer.

JAKKA, S., & ROSSBACH, M. (2013). An economic perspective on personalized medicine. *The HUGO Journal*, *7*(1), 1.

JAMES, J. E. (2014). Personalised medicine, disease prevention, and the inverse care law: More harm than benefit? *European Journal of Epidemiology*, *29*(6), 383–390.

JAMESON, J. L., & LONGO, D. L. (2015). Precision Medicin - Personalized, Problematic and Promising. *New England Journal of Medicine*, *372*(23), 2229–2234.

JOHAL, G., & AMLANI, A. (2016). Integrating pharmacogenomics into clinical practice. *University of Ottawa Journal of Medicine*, *6*(1), 1–3.

JOHNSON, A. (2016). An Impediment to Personalized Medicine Commercialization is the Lack of Understanding of the Value of the Testing. *Journal of Commercial Biotechnology*, *22*(1), 3–5.

JOLLS, C., THALER, R., & SUNSTEIN, C. R. (1998). A Behavioral Approach to Law and Economics. *Stanford Law Review*, *50*(55), 1471–1549.

JORDAN, B. (2015). Current and future trends in Personalised Healthcare. Conference presentation at the ZHAW - Zürcher Hochschule für angewandte Wissenschaften. Retrieved from https://www.zhaw.ch/storage/lsfm/weiterbildung/icbt/chemietag/2015-speech-jordan.pdf (October 5, 2015)

JOSEPH, A. (2015). Precision medicine faces great promise but few payers. *STAT*, 2–3. Retrieved from http://www.statnews.com/2015/12/23/precision-medicine-tests/ (December 27, 2015)

KAHNEMAN, D. (2003). A perspective on judgment and choice: Mapping bounded rationality. *American Psychologist*, *58*(9), 697–720.

KAHNERT, M. (2015). Hürden für Companion Diagnostics - Neues von der Europäischen In-Vitro-Diagnostik-Richtlinie 98/79/EG. *GoingPublic*, 36–38.

KAINZ, W. (2016). Regulatory Aspects for Personalized Medical Devices. *Presentation at the LATSIS Symposium ETH Zurich on personalized medicine.* Zürich: FDA.

KAMAL, M. (2013). Challenges for the Clinical Implementation of Precision Medicine Trials. In C. LE TOURNEAU & M. KAMAL (Eds.), *Pan-cancer Integrative Molecular Portrait Towards a New Paradigm in Precision Medicine* (133–149). Heidelberg: Springer International Publishing.

KANAVOS, P. (2016). Key trends in regulatory affairs and reimbursement policies in Europe. London: London School of Economics.

KAUFMAN, D. J., BAKER, R., MILNER, L. C., DEVANEY, S., & HUDSON, K. L. (2016). A Survey of U.S Adults' Opinions about Conduct of a Nationwide Precision Medicine Initiative Cohort Study of Genes and Environment. *Plos One*, *11*(8), e0160461. Retrieved from http://dx.plos.org/10.1371/journal.pone.0160461 (September 25, 2016)

KAUFMANN, M., KEPPENS, M., & BLAIR, E. D. (2015). A perspective analysis: companion diagnostics: an evolving paradigm in 21st century healthcare. *Personalized Medicine*, *12*(4), 389–402.

KEIL, M. (2015). Rechtsfragen der individualisierten Medizin. In C. KATZENMEIER (Ed.), *Kölner Schriften zum Medizinrecht.* Köln: Springer.

KHOURY, M. J., BERG, A., COATES, R., EVANS, J., TEUTSCH, S. M., & BRADLEY, L. A. (2008). The Evidence Dilemma In Genomic Medicine. *Health Affairs*, *27*(6), 1600–1611.

KHOURY, M. J., GWINN, M. L., GLASGOW, R. E., & KRAMER, B. S. (2012). A Population Approach to Precision Medicine. *American Journal of Preventive Medicine*, *42*(6), 639–645.

KHOZIN, S., & BLUMETHAL, G. (2015). Personalized Medicine: On the Brink of Revolutionizing Cancer Care. *American Journal of Managed Care.* Retrieved from http://www.ajmc.com/journals/evidence-based-oncology/2015/august2015/personalized-medicine-on-the-brink-of-revolutionizing-cancer-care (September 27, 2016)

KICHKO, K., MARSCHALL, P., & FLESSA, S. (2016). Personalized Medicine in the U.S. and Germany: Awareness, Acceptance, Use and Preconditions for the Wide Implementation into the Medical Standard. *Journal of Personalized Medicine*, *6*(2), 15. Retrieved from http://www.mdpi.com/2075-4426/6/2/15 (September 27, 2016)

KIERNAN, F. (2016). The future of pharmacoeconomic policy - does value-based pricing really have a role? *Journal of Pharmaceutical Health Services Research.* Retrieved from http://doi.wiley.com/10.1111/jphs.12126 (Jan-uary 11, 2017)

KIEVITS, T., LE GLEDIC, S., HEATHFIELD, A., WILMINK, M.-C., GROENEVELD, M., RUTTER, M., ... JOOS, A. (2014). Realising the potential of personalised medicine. EUROPABIO. Retrieved from http://www.europabio.org/sites/default/files/report/europabio_2014_white_paper_pm.pdf (May 6, 2015)

KIEVITS, T., NIESE, D., HANSEN, L. T., COLLINS, P., GLEDIC, S. LE, ROEDIGER, A., ... HALLERSTEN, A. (2012). Personalised medicine : status quo and challenges. EuropaBio. Retrieved from http://www.vitromics.nl/media/47473/personalised_medicine_status_quo_and_challenges.pdf (May 6, 2015)

KINGSMORE, S. F., PETRIKIN, J., WILLIG, L. K., & GUEST, E. (2015). Emergency medical genomes: a breakthrough application of precision medicine. *Genome Medicine*, *7*(1), 82, 1-7.

KIRCHNER, C. (1997). *Ökonomische Theorie des Rechts - überarbeitete und ergänzte Fassung eines Vortrages gehalten vor der juristischen Gesellschaft zu Berlin am 16. Oktober 1996.* Berlin: De Gruyter.

KLEIN, P. G. (1999). New Institutional Economics. In *Encyclopedia of Law and Economics.* Retrieved from http://reference.findlaw.com/lawandeconomics/0530-new-institutional-economics.pdf (June 22, 2017)

KLUSMAN, I., & VAYENA, E. (2016). *Personalisierte Medizin - Hoffnung oder leeres Versprechen?* Zürich: vdf Hochschulverlag AG an der ETH Zürich.

KNOPPERS, B. M., LEROUX, T., DOUCET, H., GODARD, B., LABERGE, C., STANTON-JEAN, M., ... AVARD, D. (2010). Framing genomics, public health research and policy: points to consider. *Public Health Genomics, 13*(4), 224–34.

KOELSCH, C., PRZEWROCKA, J., & KEELING, P. (2013). Towards a balanced value business model for personalized medicine: an outlook. *Pharmacogenomics, 14*, 89–102.

KONSKI, A. F. (2015). Three Pressing Challenges for Personalized Medicine. *National Law Review.* Retrieved from http://www.natlawreview.com/article/three-pressing-challenges-personalized-medicinesthash.gS7oajbD.dpuf (November 5, 2015)

KOROBKIN, R. B., & ULEN, T. S. (2000). Law and Behavioral Science: Removing the Rationality Assumption from Law and Economics. *California Law Review, 88*(4), 1051–1144.

KROUSEL-WOOD, M. A. (1999). Practical considerations in the measurement of outcomes in healthcare. *The Ochsner Journal, 1*(4), 187–194.

KULKARNI, S., MA, P., FURSTENTHAL, L., & EVERS, M. (2013). The outlook for personalized medicine. In: *Personalized Medicine - The Path Forward.* Edited by McKinsey & Company, p. 31--37. Retrieved from http://www.mckinsey.com/~/media/mckinsey/dotcom/client_service/pharma%20and%20medical%20products/pmp%20new/pdfs/mckinsey%20on%20personalized%20medicine%20march%202013.ashx (June 8, 2014)

KULLAK-UBLICK, G. A. (2013). Personalisierte Medizin: Fokus der Klinischen Pharmakologie. *Pipette - Swiss Laboratory Medicine,* (1), 8–9.

LAI, J. C. (2015). Myriad Genetics and the BRCA Patents in Europe: The Implications of the US Supreme Court Decision. *UC Irvine Law Review, 5*, 1041–1057.

LAM, F. Y. W. (2012). Rethinking pharmacogenomics education beyond health professionals: Addressing the "know-do" gap across the personalized medicine innovation ecosystem. *Current Pharmacogenomics and Personalized Medicine, 10*(4), 277–287.

LANDECK, L., LESSL, M., REISCHL, J., BUSCH, A., CARRIGAN, P., GOTTWALD, M., ... ASADULLAH, K. (2016). Collaboration for success: the value of strategic collaborations for precision medicine and biomarker discovery. *Advances in Precision Medicine*, *1*(1), 25–33.

LANDER, E. S. (2015). Cutting the Gordian Helix — Regulating Genomic Testing in the Era of Precision Medicine. *New England Journal of Medicine*, 1–2.

LANDES, W. M., & POSNER, R. A. (2003). *The Economic Structure of Intellectual Property Law.* Cambridge: Harvard University Press.

LAWLER, M., & SULLIVAN, R. (2015). Personalised and Precision Medicine in Cancer Clinical Trials: Panacea for Progress or Pandora's Box? *Public Health Genomics*, *18*, 329–337.

LE TOURNEAU, C. (2013). Introducton: Rationale for Precision Medicine Clinical Trials. In C. LE TOURNEAU & M. KAMAL (Eds.), *Pan-cancer Integrative Molecular Portrait Towards a New Paradigm in Precision Medicine* (1–9). Heidelberg: Springer International Publishing.

LEDFORD, H. (2016). Personalized medicine takes hit. *Nature*, 382.

LEE, E. Y., & SHEN, J. (2015). Regulatory Considerations for Companion Diagnostic Devices. *Biomarkers in Medicine*, *9*(1), 67–75.

LEHOUX, P. (2011). Moving Beyond Our Mutual Ignorance. Or, How would Engaging the Public Benefit the Personalized Medicine Community? *Current Pharmacogenomics and Personalized Medicine*, *9*, 76–79.

LEOPOLD, C. (2014). *Pharmaceutical Policy Analysis - A European Perspective on Pricing and Reimbursement in Challenging Times.* PhD thesis at the Utrecht University.

LEUCHT, S., HELFER, B., GARTLEHNER, G., & DAVIS, J. M. (2015). How effective are common medications: a perspective based on meta-analyses of major drugs. *BMC Medicine*, *13*(1), 253.

LEYENS, L., & BRAND, A. (2016). Early Patient Access to Medicines: Health Technology Assessment Bodies Need to Catch Up with New Marketing Authorization Methods. *Public Health Genomics*, 187–191.

LEYENS, L., RICHER, T., MELIEN, Y., BALLENSIEFEN, W., & BRAND, A. (2015). Available Tools to Facilitate Early Patient Access to Medicines in the EU and the USA: Analysis of Conditional Approvals and the Implications for Personalized Medicine. *Public Health Genomics.* Retrieved from http://www.karger.com/?doi=10.1159/000437137 (March 23, 2016)

LITAN, R. E. (ED.). (2011). *Handbook on Law, Innovation and Growth.* Cheltenham: Edward Elgar.

LUCE, B. R., DRUMMOND, M., JONSSON, B., NEUMANN, P. J., SCHWARTZ, J. S., SIEBERT, U., & SULLIVAN, S. D. (2010). EBM, HTA, and CER: Clearing the confusion. *Milbank Quarterly*, *88*(2), 256–276.

LUNZE, A., & EPPING, M. (2015). Patentschutz für Personalisierte Medizin - Herausforderungen und Chancen bei der Patentierung von Companion Diagnostics und Biomarkern. *GoingPublic*, 38–39.

LUO, D., SMITH, J. A., MEADOWS, N. A., MANESCU, K., BURE, K., HORNE, R., ... BRINDLEY, D. A. (2015). A Quantitative Assessment of Factors Affecting the Technological Development and Adoption of Companion Diagnostics. *Frontiers in Genetics, [forthcoming].*

LUTERBACHER, C., & HUNT, J. (2015, November). Wenn die Gene die Therapie bestimmen. *Swissinfo.* Retrieved from https://www.swissinfo.ch/ger/-personalized-medicine-_wenn-die-gene-die-therapie-bestimmen/41754994 (November 6, 2015)

LÜTHI, L., & MENN, A. (2014). 125-Jahr-Jubiläum IGE - Patentrecht. *Sic! Zeitschrift für Immaterialgüter-, Informations- und Wettbewerbsrecht*, 184–191.

MACHEINER, T., HUPPERTZ, B., & SARGSYAN, K. (2013). Innovative ways for information transfer in biobanking. *Campus-Wide Information Systems, 30*(5), 379–385.

MALOTTKI, K., BISWAS, M., DEEKS, J. J., RILEY, R. D., CRADDOCK, C., JOHNSON, P., & BILLINGHAM, L. (2014). Stratified medicine in European Medicines Agency licensing: a systematic review of predictive biomarkers. *BMJ Open, 4*(1), e004188. Retrieved from http://www.pubmedcentral.nih.gov/articlerender.fcgi?artid=3913033&tool=pmcentrez&rendertype=abstract (March 29, 2015)

MANOLIO, T. A., WARD, R., & GINSBURG, G. S. (2016). Clinical implementation of genomic medicine : the importance of global collaboration. *Expert Review oj Precision Medicine and Drug Development, forthcoming*, 1–12.

MANOLIO, T. A, CHISHOLM, R. L., OZENBERGER, B., RODEN, D. M., WILLIAMS, M. S., WILSON, R., ... GINSBURG, G. S. (2013). Implementing genomic medicine in the clinic: the future is here. *Genetics in Medicine, 15*(4), 258–67.

MANSFIELD, E. (2015). Complexities in Personalized Medicine: Harmonizing Companion Diagnostics Across a Class of Targeted Therapies. U.S. FOOD AND DRUG ADMINISTRATION. Retrieved from http://www.fda.gov/downloads/MedicalDevices/NewsEvents/WorkshopsConferences/UCM439878.pdf (January 8, 2016)

MARCHANT, J. (2011). *Strategies for Effective Partnerships Between Pharmaceutical and Diagnostic Companies - Realizing The Potential of Personalized Medicine.* London: SCRIP Business Insights.

MARSHALL, A. (1997). Laying the foundations for personalized medicines. *Nature Biotechnology, 15*, 954–957.

MARSHALL, P., & FLESSA, S. (2015). Gesundheitsökonomische Bewertung der Personalisierten Medizin. In E. EPPINGER, B. HALECKER, K. HÖLZLE, & M. KAMPRATH (Eds.), *Dienstleistungspotentiale und Geschäftsmodelle in der Personalisierten Medizin - Konzepte, Analysen, Potentiale* (302–315). Wiesbaden: Springer Gabler.

MARTINALBO, J., BOWEN, D., CAMARERO, J., CHAPELIN, M., DÉMOLIS, P., FOGGI, P., ... PIGNATTI, F. (2016). Early market access of cancer drugs in the EU. *Annals of Oncology, 27*(1), 96–105.

MCCARTHY, J. J., MCLEOD, H. L., & GINSBURG, G. S. (2013). Genomic Medicine: A Decade of Successes, Challenges and Opportunities. *Science Translational Medicine, 5*(189), 1–17.

MEADOWS, N. A., MORRISON, A., BRINDLEY, D., SCHUH, A., & BARKER, R. W. (2015). An evaluation of regulatory and commercial barriers to stratified medicine development and adoption. *The Pharmacogenomics Journal, 15*(1), 6–12.

MECKLEY, L. M., & NEUMANN, P. J. (2010). Personalized medicine: Factors influencing reimbursement. *Health Policy, 94*(2), 91–100.

MEDICINES AND HEALTHCARE PRODUCTS AGENCY. (2012). The Revision of European Legislation on Medical Devices. Medicines and Healthcare products Agency. Retrieved from http://www.ipem.ac.uk/Portals/0/Documents/Consultations/Revision of European Legislation on Medical Devices Nov 2012.pdf (February 9, 2016)

MEIER-ABT, P. (2016). SPHN: Setting up the Organiation. Swiss Academy of Medical Sciences. Retrieved from http://www.samw.ch/de/Projekte/Personalized-Health.html (April 3, 2017)

MEIER-ABT, P., & EGLI, F. (2016). Kräfte bündeln: "Swiss Personalized Health Network." *Bulletin SAMW*, 1–5. Retrieved from http://www.samw.ch/de/Projekte/Personalized-Health.html (April 3, 2017)

MERGES, R. P. (2014). Economics of intellectual property law. In F. PARISI (Ed.), *Oxford Handbook of Law and Economics.* Oxford: Oxford University Press. Retrieved from https://papers.ssrn.com/sol3/papers.cfm?abstract_id=2412251 (June 26, 2017)

MESSNER, D. A., AL NABER, J., KOAY, P., COO-DEEGAN, R., MAJUMDER, M., JAVITT, G., ... MAGUIRE, A. (2016). Barriers to Clinical Adoption of Next Generation Sequencing: Perspectives of a Policy Delphi Panel. *Applied & Translational Genomics, [forthcoming]*, 1–17.

MEYER, B., ROHNER, B., GOLDER, L., & LONGCHAMP, C. (2016). Administrativer Aufwand für Ärzte steigt weiter an. *Schweizerische Ärztezeitung, 97*(1), 6–8.

MEYER, J. W., & ROWAN, B. (1977). Institutionalized Organizations : Formal Structure as Myth and Ceremony. *American Journal of Sociology, 83*(2), 340–363.

MEYER, U. A. (2015). Pharmakogenomik. [Workshop materials "Genomische Medizin für Kliniker"] Basel: Biozentrum der Universität Basel.

MICHEEL, C. M., NASS, S. J., & OMENN, G. S. (EDS.). (2012). *Evolution of Translational Omics : Lessons Learned and the Path Forward IOM.* Washington: Institute of Mecicine, The National Academies Press.

MILLER, I., ASHTON-CHESS, J., SPOLDERS, H., FERT, V., FERRARA, J., KROLL, W., ... HURIEZ, A. (2011). Market access challenges in the EU for high medical value diagnostic tests. *Personalized Medicine, 8*(2), 137–148.

MILMO, S. (2015). Regulation of Medical Devices and Companion Diagnostics. *Pharmaceutical Technology, 39*(8). Retrieved from http://www.pharmtech.com/print/296204?page=full (August 21, 2015)

MILNE, C. P., & COHEN, J. (2015)a. Personalized medicine gains traction but still faces multiple challenges - Key hurdles relate to science, regulation, reimbursement, clinical adoption. *Tufts Center for the Study of Drug Development Impact Report, 17*(3), 3–6.

MILNE, C. P., & COHEN, J. (2015)b. Where is personalized medicine in industry heading ? *Nature Reviews Drug Discovery,* (October), 1–2.

MISCHAK, H., IOANNIDIS, J. P. A, ARGILES, A., ATTWOOD, T. K., BONGCAM-RUDLOFF, E., BROENSTRUP, M., ... VLAHOU, A. (2012). Implementation of proteomic biomarkers: making it work. *European Journal of Clinical Investigation, 42*(9), 1027–36.

MITTRA, J. (2013). Repairing the "Broken Middle" of the Health Innovation Pathway: Exploring Diverse Practitioner Perspectives on the Emergence and Role of "Translational Medicine." *Science and Technology Studies, 26*(3), 103–123.

MITTRA, J., & MILNE, C. P. (2013). *Translational Medicine - the future of Therapy?* Singapore: Pan Standford Publishing.

MITTRA, J., & TAIT, J. (2012). Analysing Stratified Medicine Business Models and Value Systems : Innovation - Regulation Interactions. *New Biotechnology, 29*(6), 709–719.

MODELL, S. M., KARDIA, S. L. R., & CITRIN, T. (2014). Stakeholder consultation insights on the future of genomics at the clinical-public health interface. *Translational Research, 163*(5), 466–477.

MOLNÁR-GÁBOR, F. (2012). Die Herausforderung der medizinischen Entwicklung für das internationale soft law am Beispiel der Totalsequenzierung des menschlichen Genoms, *Zeitschrift Für Ausländisches Öffentliches Recht Und Völkerrecht, 72,* 695–737.

MOORE, M. W., BABU, D., & COTTER, P. D. (2012). Challenges in the codevelopment of companion diagnostics. *Personalized Medicine, 9,* 485–496.

MOOSER, V. (2014). Genomik und personalisierte Medizin Personalisierte Medizin. *Praxis, 103*(10), 567–571.

MOREL, T., ARICKX, F., BEFRITS, G., SIVIERO, P., VAN DER MEIJDEN, C., XOXI, E., & SIMOENS, S. (2013). Reconciling uncertainty of costs and outcomes with the need for access to orphan medicinal products: a comparative study of managed entry agreements across seven European countries. *Orphanet Journal of Rare Diseases, 8*, 198. Retrieved from http://www.pubmedcentral.nih.gov/articlerender.fcgi?artid=3882782&tool=pmcentrez&rendertype=abstract (March 18, 2015)

MORGON, P. A. (ED.). (2015). *Sustainable Development for the Healthcare Industry - Reprogramming the Healthcare Value Chain.* Lausanne: Springer.

MORRISON, A., & BOUDREAU, R. (2012). *Evaluation Frameworks for Genetic Tests.* Ottawa: Canadian Agency for Drugs and Technologies in Health (CADTH).

MOSER, V. (2014). Preparing the Swiss System for Personalized Medicine. Swiss Tropical and Public Health Institute. Retrieved from http://www.swisstph.ch/news-events/symposia/autumn-2014/programme-and-presentations.html (December 28, 2014)

MTSUI, S., BUYSE, M., & SIMON, R. (EDS.). (2015). *Design and Analysis of Clinical Trials for Predictive Medicine.* CRC PRess, Taylor & Francis Group.

MÜLLER-GRAFF, J. (2014). Binnenmarkt konzept und Arzneimittelsektor. In J. DREXL (Ed.), *MSEIK - Münchner Schriften zum Europäischen und Internationalen Kartellrecht* (p. 9 ff.). Bern: Stämpfli Verlag AG.

MÜLLER, H., & SCHÄFER, C. (2013). Individualisierte Medizin: Wer antwortet auf Fragen (aus Sicht) der Gesundheitsversorgung? In A. WIENKE, C. DIERKS, & K. JANKE (Eds.), *Rechtsfragen der Personalisierten Medizin* (11–29). Heidelberg: Springer.

MÜLLER, K. (2012). Medical Devices and Diagnostics - Switzerland. International Society for Pharmacoeconomics and Outcomes (ISPOR). Retrieved from http://www.ispor.org/HTARoadMaps/SwitzerlandMDD.asp (May 31, 2016)

NAYLOR, S., & COLE, T. (2010). CDx in pharmaceutical industry - Part II: business models. *Drug Discovery World, 11*(2), 61–68.

NEGROUK, A., HORGAN, D., GORINI, A., CUTICA, I., LEYENS, L., SCHEE GENANNT HALFMANN, S., & PRAVETTONI, G. (2015). Clinical Trials, Data Protection and Patient Empowerment in the Era of the New EU Regulations. *Public Health Genomics*, 1-10. Retrieved from http://www.ncbi.nlm.nih.gov/pubmed/26565798 (February 23, 2016)

NICHOLSON PRICE, W. (2015). Intellectual Property, and Black Box Personalized Medicine. *Harvard Journal of Law and Technology, forthcomin.* Retrieved from https://www.law.berkeley.edu/files/Price_Nicholson_IPSC_paper_2014.pdf (October 12, 2015)

NICOL, D., BUBELA, T., CHALMERS, D., CHARBONNEAU, J., CRITCHLEY, C., DICKINSON, J., ... ZEPS, N. (2016). Precision Medicine: Drowning in a Regulatory Soup? *DSpace Cambridge.* Retrieved from https://www.repository.cam.ac.uk/handle/1810/254775 (April 12, 2016)

NIEDERER, A. (2015, November 20). Klinische Studien am einzelnen Patienten. *Neue Zürcher Zeitung*, p. 56.

NIH. (2016). The Cost of Sequencing a Human Genome. US National Human Genome Research Institute. Retrieved from https://www.genome.gov/sequencingcosts/ (July 7, 2017)

NOLTING, A. (2015). *Companion Diagnostics Development and Commercialization - A Case Study from the Diagnostics' Perspective.* Stockholm: Master thesis at the KTH Industrial Engineering and Management.

NORTH, D. (1990). *Institutions, institutional change and economic performance.* New York: Cambridge University Press.

NOVENTA, C. (2014). Genomisierte Prävention in der obligatorischen Krankenpflegeversicherung. *Hill Zeitschrift Für Recht Und Gesundheit, 196.*

NOVOTNY, S. (2016). Krankenkassen drücken sich vor Bezahlung genetischer Untersuche. SRF SCHWEIZER RADIO UND FERNSEHEN. Retrieved from http://www.srf.ch/play/radio/echo-der-zeit/audio/krankenkassen-druecken-sich-vor-bezahlung-genetischer-untersuche?id=3665ea60-c5fb-48f8-b34f-145971c0e876 (July 25, 2016)

NOWESKI, M., WALENDZIK, A., HESSEL, F., JAHN, R., & WASEM, J. (2013). Zulassung und Erstattung personalisierter Arzneimittel: Zwischenbilanz des Anpassungsprozesses. *Ethik in der Medizin, 25*(3), 277–284.

O'DONNELL, J. C. (2013). Personalized medicine and the role of health economics and outcomes research: issues, applications, emerging trends, and future research. *Value in Health: The Journal of the International Society for Pharmacoeconomics and Outcomes Research, 16*(6 Suppl), S1-3. Retrieved from http://www.ncbi.nlm.nih.gov/pubmed/24034305

OECD. (2017). *New Health Technologies: Managing Access, Value and Sustainability.* Paris: OECD Publishing.

OLMSTED TEISBERG, E. (2007). *Opportunities for Value-Based Competition in Swiss Health Care.* Virginia: Economiesuisse; Klinik Hirslanden AG; Interpharma; Swiss Insurance Association SIA and Swisscom IT Services AG. Retrieved from http://www.interpharma.ch/sites/default/files/teisberg-2008_nutzenorientierter-wettbewerb-im-schweizerischen-gesundheitswesen_e.pdf (February 18, 2015)

OLSEN, D., & TRØST JØRGENSEN, J. (2014). Companion Diagnostics for Targeted Cancer Drugs - Clinical and Regulatory Aspects. *Frontiers in Oncology, 4*(105), 1–8.

OOSTERHOFF, M., VAN DER MAAS, M. E., & STEUTEN, L. M. G. (2015). A Systematic Review of Health Economic Evaluations of Diagnostic Biomarkers. *Applied Health Economics and Health Policy.* Retrieved from http://link.springer.com/10.1007/s40258-015-0198-x (December 18, 2015)

OXFORD ECONOMICS. (2016). *Healthcare gets personal.* Oxford. Retrieved from https://dam.sap.com/mac/preview/a/67/UmEUnxHHnJJzOOlUwAmnyXggPmAJJzgxUPAEmOXHxcwxPEPc/open20160412042800.htm (May 7, 2016)

PACI, D. (2009). Economic and Cost-Effectiveness Considerations for Pharmacogenetics Tests: An Integral Part of Translational Research and Innovation Uptake in Personalized Medicine. *Current Pharmacogenomics and Personalized Medicine*, *7*(4), 284–296.

PAOLO, A. DI, SARKOZY, F., RYLL, B., & SIEBERT, U. (2017). Personalized medicine in Europe: not yet personal enough ? *BMC Health Services Re-search*, *17*(289), 1–9.

PARISI, F. (2004). Positive, Normative and Functional Schools in Law and Economics. *European Journal of Law and Economics*, *18*, 259–272.

PASIC, M. D., SAMAAN, S., & YOUSEF, G. M. (2013). Genomic Medicine : New Frontiers and New Challenges, *Clinical chemistry 59*(1), 158–167.

PATRINOS, G., & MITROPOULOU, C. (2017). Measuring the Value of Pharmacogenomics Evidence. *Clinical Pharmacology & Therapeutics*, *0*(0), 1–3. Retrieved from http://doi.wiley.com/10.1002/cpt.743 (June 23, 2017)

PAYNE, K., & ANNEMANS, L. (2013). Reflections on market access for personalized medicine: recommendations for Europe. *Value in Health: The Journal of the International Society for Pharmacoeconomics and Outcomes Research*, *16*(6th supplement), S32-S38.

PEIKOFF, K. (2013). I Had My DNA Picture Taken, With Varying Results. *New York Times.* Retrieved from http://www.nytimes.com/2013/12/31/science/i-had-my-dna-picture-taken-with-varying-results.html (December 15, 2015)

PERMED. (2015). *Shaping Europe's Vision for Personalised Medicine: Strategic Research and Innovation Agenda (SRIA).* Köln.

PERSONALIZED MEDICINE COALITION. (2013). Personalized Medicine regulation: Pathways for oversight of Diagnostics. Washington: Personalized Medicine Coalition. Retrieved from http://www.personalizedmedicinecoalition.org/Userfiles/PMC-Corporate/file/pmc_pathways_for_oversight_diagnostics.pdf (July 3, 2015)

PERSONALIZED MEDICINE COALITION (ED.). (2014). *The case for Personalized Medicine* (4th ed.). Washington: Personalized Medicine Coalition. Retrieved from http://www.personalizedmedicinecoalition.org/Resources/The_Case_for_Personalized_Medicine (December 12, 2014)

PERSONALIZED MEDICINE COALITION. (2015). *The future of coverage and payment for personalized medicine diagnostics.* Retrieved from https://www.personalizedmedicinebulletin.com/wp-content/uploads/sites/6/2015/11/pmc_the_future_coverage_payment_personalized_medicine_diagnostics.pdf (January 9, 2016)

PERSONALIZED MEDICINE COALITION. (2016). 2015 Progress Report Personalized Medicine at FDA. Personalized Medicine Coalition. Retrieved from http://www.personalizedmedicinecoalition.org/Userfiles/PMC-Corporate/file/2015_Progress_Report_PM_at_FDA.pdf (January 22, 2016)

PERSONALIZED MEDICINE COALITION. (2017). Personalized Medicine at FDA - 2016 Progress Report. Retrieved from https://www.personalizedmedicinebulletin.com/wp-content/uploads/sites/6/2017/02/Personalized-Medicine-at-FDA-2016-Progress-Report.pdf (July 6, 2017)

PETERSON, J. F., BOWTON, E., FIELD, J. R., BELLER, M., MITCHELL, J., SCHILDCROUT, J., ... DENNY, J. C. (2013). Electronic health record design and implementation for pharmacogenomics: a local perspective. *Genet Med*, *15*(10), 833–841.

PETTITT, D., RAZA, S., NAUGHTON, B., ROSCOE, A., RAMAKRISHNAN, A., ALI, A., ... BRINDLEY, D. A. (2016). The Limitations of QALY : A Literature Review. *Journal of Stem Cell Research & Therapy*, *6*(4), 1–7.

PETTITT, D., SMITH, J., MEADOWS, N., ARSHAD, Z., SCHUF, A., DIGUISTO, D., ... BRINDLEY, D. (2016). Regulatory Barriers to the Advancement of Precision Medicine. *Expert Review of Precision Medicine and Drug Development*, *1*(3), 319–329.

PHILLIPS, K. A., ANN SAKOWSKI, J., TROSMAN, J., DOUGLAS, M. P., LIANG, S.-Y., & NEUMANN, P. (2014). The economic value of personalized medicine tests: what we know and what we need to know. *Genetics in Medicine*, *16*(3), 251–257.

PHILLIPS, K., SAKOWSKI, J. A., LIANG, S.-Y., & PONCE, N. (2013). Economic Perspectives on Personalized Health Care and Prevention. *Forum for Health Economics and Policy*, *16*(2), 57–86.

PIGNATTI, F., EHMANN, F., HEMMINGS, R., JONSSON, B., NUEBLING, M., PAPALUCA-AMATI, M., ... RASI, G. (2014). Cancer Drug Development and the Evolving Regulatory Framework for Companion Diagnostics in the European Union. *Clinical Cancer Research*, *20*(6), 1458–1468.

PITINI, E., DE VITO, C., MARZUILLO, C., D'ANDREA, E., DAGUANNO, S., & VILLARI, P. (2012). How should genetic tests be evaluated? Preliminary results of a systematic review, *8th European Public Health Conference,* 187.

PLETCHER, M. J., & PIGNONE, M. (2011). Evaluating the clinical utility of a biomarker: A review of methods for estimating health impact. *Circulation*, *123*(10), 1116–1124.

PLÖTHNER, M., RIBBENTROP, D., HARTMAN, J.-P., & FRANK, M. (2016). Cost-Effectiveness of Pharmacogenomic and Pharmacogenetic Test-Guided Personalized Therapies: A Systematic Review of the Approved Active Substances for Personalized Medicine in Germany. *Advances in Therapy*. Retrieved from http://link.springer.com/10.1007/s12325-016-0376-8 (December 11, 2016)

PLUN-FAVREAU, J., IMMONEN-CHARALAMBOUS, K., STEUTEN, L., STROOTKER, A., ROUZIER, R., HORGAN, D., & LAWLER, M. (2016). Enabling Equal Access to Molecular Diagnostics: What Are the Implications for Policy and Health Technology Assessment. *Public Health Genomics*, 144–152.

PMC. (2015). Annual report. Washington: Personalized Medicine Coalition. Retrieved from http://www.personalizedmedicinecoalition.org/Userfiles/PMC Corporate/file/PMC_2015_annual_report.pdf (June 28, 2017)

POKORSKA-BOCCI, A., STEWART, A., SAGOO, G. S., HALL, A., KROESE, M., & BURTON, H. (2014). "Personalized medicine": what's in a name? *Personalized Medicine*, *11*(2), 197–210.

POLEDNA, T., & VOKINGER, K. N. (2013). Abgabe und Vertrieb von Medizinprodukten. In B. RÜTSCHE (Ed.), *Medizinprodukte: Regulierung und Haftung* (149–170). Stämpfli Verlag AG.

PORTER, M. E. (1990). *Competitive Advantage of Nations*. London: McMillan.

PORTER, M. E. (2010). What Is Value in Health Care? *New England Journal of Medicine*, *363*, 2477–2481.

PORTER, M. E., & OLMSTED TEISBERG, E. (2006). *Redefining health care : creating value-based competition on results*. Harvard, MA: Harvard Business School Press.

POSNER, R. A. (1993). The New Institutional Economics Meets Law and Economics. *Journal of Institutional and Theoretical Economics*, *149*(1), 73–87.

POSNER, R. A. (2014). *Economic Analysis of Law* (9th ed.). Wolters Kluver.

PRAINSACK, B. (2015). Is personalized medicine different? (Reinscription: the sequel) A response to Troy Duster. *The British Journal of Sociology*, *66*(1), 28–35.

PRASAD, K., & BRECKENRIDGE, A. (2011). Pharmacogenomics: a new clinical or regulatory paradigm? European experiences of pharmacogenomics in drug regulation and regulatory initiatives. *Drug Discovery Today*, *16*(19–20), 867–872.

PRECISION MEDICINE FORUM. (2017). National Danish strategy for Personalized Medicine. Retrieved from http://precisionmedicineforum.com/national-danish-strategy-personalized-medicine-pmf-nordic2017/ (July 7, 2017)

PRITCHARD, D., MOECKER, F., MARY, V. S., HOUSMAN, L., MCCARTY, L., & MCLEOD, H. (2017). Strategies for integrating personalized medicine into healthcare practice. *Personalized Medicine*, *14*(2), 141–152.

PTOLEMY, A. S. (2011). Biomarker diversity, validation and clinical translation: Tenets for emergent personalized medicine initiatives. *Current Pharmacogenomics and Personalized Medicine*, *9*, 286–298.

PWC, & PMI. (2015). *Roadmap for Bringing Personalized Medicine to British Columbians Summit Partners*. Retrieved from http://www.pwc.com/ca/en/healthcare/publications/pwc-personalized-medicine-summit-green-paper-2015-06-en.pdf (June 22, 2015)

RABASSEDA, X., DULSAT, C., NAVARRO, D., CRUCES, E., GRAUL, A. I., JAGO, C., & TRACY, M. (2013). Overcoming the obstacles in the pharma/biotech industry. *Drugs Today, 49*(2), 117–128.

RAMSEY, S., VEENSTRA, D., TUNIS, S., GARRISON, L., CROWLEY, J., & BAKER, L. (2011). How comparative effectiveness research can help advance "personalized medicine" in cancer treatment. *Health Affairs, 30*(12), 2259–2327.

RAUCH, A. (2015). Eine neue Ära der Gendiagnostik – nicht nur für seltene Erkrankungen. *Swiss Medical Forum, 15*(1–2), 24–26.

RAVEGNINI, G., & ANGELINI, S. (2016). Toward precision medicine: How far is the goal? *International Journal of Molecular Sciences, 17*(245), 1–5.

RAY, T. (2016). FDA Reinforces Common Key Regulatory Principles for Industry in CDx, Draft LDT Guidances. *GenomeWeb.* Retrieved from https://www.genomeweb.com/clinical-genomics/fda-reinforces-common-key-regulatory-principles-industry-cdx-draft-ldt-guidances (January 16, 2016)

RECHER, A. (2014, September 16). Seltene Krankheiten - Zu wenig Medikamente gegen seltene Krankheiten. *Neue Zürcher Zeitung*, p. 10.

REDEKOP, W. K., & MLADSI, D. (2013). The faces of personalized medicine: a framework for understanding its meaning and scope. *Value in Health : The Journal of the International Society for Pharmacoeconomics and Outcomes Research, 16*(6th Supplement), S4-9.

RELLING, M. V., & EVANS, W. E. (2015). Pharmacogenomics in the clinic. *Nature, 526*(7573), 343–350.

RENGGLI, M. (2016). Überteuerte Medizinalgeräte: Amtlich bewilligte Abzocke. SRF Schweizer Radio und Fernsehen. Retrieved from http://www.srf.ch/sendungen/kassensturz-espresso/themen/gesundheit/ueberteuerte-medizinalgeraete-amtlich-bewilligte-abzocke (July 1, 2016)

RENTSCH, R. A. (2016). *Das Europäische Patentrecht und seine Harmonisierungswirkungen in der nationalen Rechtsprechung der Schweiz.* Bern: Stämpfli.

REY, L., BAERISWYL, B., RUDIN, B., BERNHARD, M., SCHWEIZER, R. J., & KARJOTH, G. (2014). Wenn Medizin es persönlich nimmt. Nebst medizinischer Vorteile zieht personalisierte Medizin auch gesellschaftliche und ethische Fragen nach sich. *Digma - Zeitschrift Für Datenrecht Und Informationssicherheit*, 54-58.

RICHTER, R. (2008). On the New Institutional Economics of Markets. University of Bielefeld. Retrieved from http://www.uni-saarland.de/fak1/fr12/richter/institut/nie_of_markets.pdf (June 21, 2017)

RIPPE, K. P., BACHMANN, A., FAISST, K., OGGIER, W., PAULI-MAGNUS, C., PROBST-HENSCH, N., & VÖLGER, M. (2004). *Pharmakogenetik und Pharmakogenomik.* Bern: TA-Swiss Zentrum für Technologiefolgen Abschätzung.

ROEDIGER, A. (2016). Personalized Medicine : Health Economic Aspects. *GEN Genetic Engineering & Biotechnology News*, 1–5. Retrieved from http://gen.liebertpub.com/keywordsandtools/print/1/30879/ (May 12, 2016)

ROGOWSKI, W., PAYNE, K., SCHNELL-INDERST, P., MANCA, A., ROCHAU, U., JAHN, B., ... SIEBERT, U. (2015). Concepts of "Personalization" in Personalized Medicine: Implications for Economic Evaluation. *PharmacoEconomics*, *33*(1), 49–59.

ROHR, U.-P., BINDER, C., DIETERLE, T., GIUSTI, F., MESSINA, C. G. M., TOERIEN, E., ... SCHÄFER, H. H. (2016). The Value of In Vitro Diagnostic Testing in Medical Practice: A Status Report. *Plos One*, *11*(3), e0149856. Retrieved from http://dx.plos.org/10.1371/journal.pone.0149856 (December 14, 2016)

ROOS, N. (2013). Gentests: Krankenkassen bezahlen nicht immer. SRF Schweizer Radio und Fernsehen. Retrieved from http://www.srf.ch/sendungen/kassen sturz-espresso/themen/versicherungen/gentests-krankenkassen-bezahlen-nicht-immer (May 25, 2016)

ROSE, N. (2013). Personalized Medicine: Promises, Problems and Perils of a New Paradigm for Healthcare. *Procedia - Social and Behavioral Sciences*, *77*, 341–352.

RUBERG, S. J., & SHEN, L. (2015). Personalized Medicine: Four Perspectives for Clinical Drug Development. *Statistics in Biopharmaceutical Research*, 00–00. Retrieved from http://www.tandfonline.com/doi/full/10.1080/19466315.2015.1059354 (January 17, 2016)

RUBIN, E. H., ALLEN, J. D., NOWAK, J. A., & BATES, S. E. (2014). Developing Precision Medicine in a Global World. *Clinical Cancer Research*, *20*(6), 1419–1427. Retrieved from http://clincancerres.aacrjournals.org/cgi/doi/10.1158/1078-0432.CCR-14-0091 (March 25, 2015)

RÜEGSEGGER, N. E., & SZUCS, T. D. (2014). *Brennpunkt Off-label Use. Medikamente in der Grauzone: Regulierung und medizinische Realität im Widerspruch*. Bern: Schweizerische Gesellschaft für Gesundheitspolitik.

RYBAKOWSKI, J. K., & SERRETTI, A. (EDS.). (2016). *Genetic Infuences on Response to Drug Treatment for Major Psychiatric Disorders*. Heidelberg: Springer International Publishing.

SALARI, K., WATKINS, H., & ASHLEY, E. A. (2012). Personalized medicine: Hope or hype? *European Heart Journal*, *33*(13), 1564–1570.

SALARI, P., & LARIJANI, B. (2017). Ethical Issues Surrounding Personalized Medicine: A Literature Review. *Acta Medica Iranica*, *55*(3), 209–217.

SALZBERGER, E. M. (ED.). (2012). *Law and Economics of Innovation*. Cheltenham: Edward Elgar.

SAMER, C. F. (2015). Auf dem Weg zu einer personalisierten Medizin. *Schweizerisches Medizin-Forum*, *15*(3), 60–62.

SAMS. (2012). Potenzial und Grenzen von “Individualisierter Medizin.” Swiss Academy of Medical Sciences [SAMS]. Retrieved from https://www.google.ch/url?sa=t&rct=j&q=&esrc=s&source=web&cd=1&cad=rja&uact=8&ved=0ahUKEwjLhP3S4JfTAhUlDsAKHWuRC7gQFgghMAA&url=http%3A%2F%2Fwww.samw.ch%2Fdam%2Fjcr%3A7b211388-6d72-4421-b799-2a50f60f19ea%2Fpositionspapier_samw_individualisierte_medizin.pdf (May 15, 2015)

SAMS. (2017)a. Personalized Health. Swiss Academy of Medical Sciences [SAMS]. Retrieved from http://www.samw.ch/en/Projects/Personalized-Health.html (April 1, 2017)

SAMS. (2017)b. Vorlage Generalkonsent. Retrieved from http://www.samw.ch/de/Ethik/Forschungsethik/Vorlage-GK.html (May 26, 2017)

SCHÄFER, H.-B., & OTT, C. (2005). *Lehrbuch der ökonomischen Analyse des Zivilrechts* (3rd editio.). Berlin, Heidelberg: Springer.

SCHELLEKENS, H., ALDOSARI, M., TALSMA, H., & MASTROBATTISTA, E. (2017). Making individualized drugs a reality. *Nature Biotechnology*, 1–8.

SCHLEIDGEN, S., KLINGLER, C., BERTRAM, T., ROGOWSKI, W. H., & MARCKMANN, G. (2013). What is personalized medicine: sharpening a vague term based on a systematic literature review. *Medical Ethics*, *14* (55), 1-12.

SCHLEIDGEN, S., & MARCKMANN, G. (2013). Alter Wein in neuen Schläuchen? Ethische Implikationen der Individualisierten Medizin. *Ethik in der Medizin*, *25*(3), 223–231.

SCHMID, A. (2015). eHealth. In W. OGGIER (Ed.), *Gesundheitswesen Schweiz* (5th ed., 67–76). Bern: Hogrefe.

SCHNEIDER, D., & BUBLAK, W. (2015). Personalized medicine: its implications and its impact on patents. *Pharmaceutical Patent Analyst*, *4*(7), 415–425.

SCHNEIDER, D., RIEGMAN, P., CRONIN, M., NEGROUK, A., MOCH, H., BALLING, R., ... HORGAN, D. (2016). Accelerating the Development and Validation of New Value-Based Diagnostics by Leveraging Biobanks. *Public Health Genomics*, *19*, 160–169.

SCHORK, N. J. (2015). Time for one-person trials. *Nature*, 609–611. Retrieved from http://www.nature.com/polopoly_fs/1.17411!/menu/main/topColumns/topLeftColumn/pdf/520609a.pdf (July 7, 2015)

SCHULLER, J. C. (2011). Adaptive Designs in der klinischen Forschung. *Schweizerisches Medizin-Forum*, *11*, 296–299.

SCOTCHMER, S. (2004). *Innovation and Incentives*. Cambridge: MIT Press.

SCOTT, S. A. (2011). Personalizing medicine with clinical pharmacogenetics. *Genetics in Medicine*, *13*(12), 987–995.

SEITZ, S. (2011). Health Technology Assessment in der Schweiz – Heute und wie weiter? Institut für Sozial- und Präventivmedizin, University of Zürich.

SFOPH. (2007). Strategie „eHealth" Schweiz. Bern: Swiss Federal Office of Public Health [SFOPH]. Retrieved from https://www.e-health-suisse.ch/fileadmin/user_upload/Dokumente/2007_2008/D/070627_Strategie_eHealth_Schweiz_D.pdf (March 24, 2015)

SFOPH. (2009). Handbuch zur Antragstellung auf Kostenübernahme bei neuen oder umstrittenen Leistungen. Bern: Swiss Federal Office of Public Health [SFOPH]. Retrieved from http://www.bag.admin.ch/themen/krankenversicherung/00263/00264/04853/ (June 30, 2016)

SFOPH. (2011). Operationalisierung der Begriffe Wirksamkeit, Zweckmässigkeit und Wirtschaftlichkeit. Swiss Federal Office of Public Health [SFOPH]. Retrieved from http://www.bag.admin.ch/themen/krankenversicherung/00263/00264/04853/index.html?lang=de&download=NHzLpZeg7t,lnp6I0NTU042l2Z6ln1acy4Zn4Z2qZpnO2Yuq2Z6gpJCKdXt9g2ym162epYbg2c_JjKbNoKSn6A-- (June 14, 2016)

SFOPH. (2014). Leistungen in Evaluation (Coverage with Evidence Development, CED) CED-Checkliste für Diagnostische Tests. Swiss Federal Office of Public Health [SFOPH]. Retrieved from http://www.bag.admin.ch/themen/krankenversicherung/00263/00264/04853/index.html?lang=de&download=NHzLpZeg7t,lnp6I0NTU042l2Z6ln1acy4Zn4Z2qZpnO2Yuq2Z6gpJCMdH15f2ym162epYbg2c_JjKbNoKSn6A--. (March 24, 2015)

SFOPH. (2015). Projekt zur Revision der Medizinprodukteverordnung (MepV). Swiss Federal Office of Public Health [SFOPH]. Retrieved from http://www.bag.admin.ch/themen/medizin/00709/04667/14494/index.html?lang=de&print_style=yes (August 5, 2015)

SFOPH. (2016)a. Faktenblatt: Bewertung von Gesundheitstechnologien (HTA). Swiss Federal Office of Public Health [SFOPH]. Retrieved from http://www.bag.admin.ch/themen/krankenversicherung/00263/00264/15806/index.html?lang=de (May 23, 2016)

SFOPH. (2016)b. HTA-Programm des Bundes: Re-Evaluation von Leistungen der obligatorischen Krankenpflegeversicherung. Retrieved from http://www.bag.admin.ch/themen/krankenversicherung/00263/00264/15806/index.html?lang=de (July 4, 2016)

SFOPH. (2016)c. Rechtliche Grundlagen zur Vergütung genetischer Analysen durch die obligatorische Krankenpflegeversicherung (OKP). Bern: Swiss Federal Office of Public Health [SFOPH]. Retrieved from http://sgmg.ch/wordpress/wp-content/uploads/2017/03/Brief-vom-BAG-an-die-Krankenversicherer-vom-3.-Mai-2016.pdf (April 9, 2017)

SFOPH. (2016)d. *Statistiken Ärzte und Ärztinnen.* Retrieved from https://www.bag.admin.ch/bag/de/home/service/zahlen-fakten/statistiken-berufeimgesundheitswesen/statistiken-medizinalberufe1/statistiken-aerztinnen-aerzte.html (April 16, 2017)

SFOPH. (2016)e. Unwirksame und ineffiziente medizinische Leistungen sollen reduziert werden. Retrieved from http://www.bag.admin.ch/aktuell/00718/01220/index.html?lang=de&msg-id=61615 (July 5, 2016)

SHABARUDDIN, F., PAYNE, K., & FLEEMAN, N. (2015). Economic evaluations of personalized medicine: existing challenges and current developments. *Pharmacogenomics and Personalized Medicine*, *8*, 115-126.

SHAFRIN, J. (2008). Welfarists vs. extra–welfarists. *Healthcare Economist*, 1–7. Retrieved from http://healthcare-economist.com/2008/02/13/welfarists-vs-extra-welfarists/ (February 24, 2016)

SHERMAN, R. E., & CALIFF, R. (2016). What We Mean When We Talk About EvGen, Part II : Building Out a National System for Evidence Generation. *FDA Voice*, 1-4. Retrieved from http://blogs.fda.gov/fdavoice/index.php/2016/05/what-we-mean-when-we-talk-about-evgen-part-ii-building-out-a-national-system-for-evidence-generation/ (May 9, 2016)

SHIMAZAWA, R., & IKEDA, M. (2015). International differences in companion diagnostic approvals: how are we able to manage the differences? *Expert Review of Molecular Diagnostics*, *15*(2), 157–159.

SHIMAZAWA, R., & IKEDA, M. (2016). Overcoming regulatory challenges in the development of companion diagnostics for monitoring and safety. *Personalized Medicine*, pme.15.51. Retrieved from http://www.futuremedicine.com/doi/10.2217/pme.15.51 (November 11, 2016)

SIMMONS, L. A., DINAN, M. A., ROBINSON, T. J., & SNYDERMAN, R. (2012). Personalized medicine is more than genomic medicine: confusion over terminology impedes progress towards personalized healthcare. *Personalized Medicine*, *9*(1), 85–91.

SIMON, B. H. A. (1979). Rational decision-making in business organizations. *American Economic Review*, *69*(4), 493–513.

SIMOONS, M., MULDER, H., SCHOEVERS, R. A., RUHE, H. G., & VAN RON, E. N. (2017). Availability of CYP2D6 genotyping results in general practitioner and community pharmacy medical records. *Pharmacogenomics*, 1–8.

SMART, A. (2006). A multi-dimensional model of clinical utility. *International Journal for Quality in Health Care*, *18*(5), 377–382.

SMB. (2016). Swiss Medical Board. Retrieved from http://www.swissmedicalboard.ch/index.php?id=803 (August 8, 2017)

SNHTA. (2016). Swiss Network or Health Technology Assessment. Retrieved from http://www.snhta.ch/about-us (July 4, 2016)

SNYDER, M. (2016). *Genomics and Personalized Medicine: What Everyone Needs to Know*. Oxford: Oxford University Press.

SOINI, S. (2012). Genetic testing legislation in Western Europe - A fluctuating regulatory target. *Journal of Community Genetics*, *3*(2), 143–153.

SOLOMON, M. (2015). What Is Translational Medicine? In *Making Medical Knowledge* (1–28). Oxford: Oxford University Press.

SPRECHER, F. (2015). Anpassung der Medizinprodukteverordnung (MepV). *Sicherheit & Recht*, *2*, 115.

STALLINGS, S. C., WITT, W. P., CROWN, W. H., FINKELSTEIN, S. N., HILLER, A. J., & SINSKEY, A. J. (2004). *An economic framework for evaluating personalized medicine.* industry Studies Association Working Paper, Program on the Pharmaceutical Industry (POPI) & Biology Department Massachusetts Institute of Technology (MIT).

STANFORD MEDICINE. (2016). Stanford Medicine, Google team up to harness power of data science for health care. Retrieved from http://med.stanford.edu/news/all-news/2016/08/stanford-medicine-google-team-up-to-harness-power-of-data-science.html (January 8, 2017)

STAUDER, D. (2014). Embrionale Stammzellen und biotechnologische Erfindungen - Fragen der Patentierung. *Sic! Zeitschrift für Immaterialgüter-, Informations- und Wettbewerbsrecht*, 251–262.

STELZER, B., MEYER-BRÖTZ, F., SCHIEBEL, E., & BRECHT, L. (2015). Technological Forecasting & Social Change Combining the scenario technique with bibliometrics for technology foresight : The case of personalized medicine. *Technological Forecasting & Social Change*, *98*, 137–156.

STEPHENS, J., HANKE, & DOSHI, J. (2012). International survey of methods used in health technology assessment (HTA): does practice meet the principles proposed for good research? *Comparative Effectiveness Research*, 29-44.

STERN, A. D., ALEXANDER, B. M., & CHANDRA, A. (2017). How economics can shape precision medicines. *Science*, *355*(6330), 1131–1133.

STÖCKLI EGGENBERGER, U. (2015). Gesundheitsrecht - Heilmittel. In G. BIAGGINI, I. HÄNER, U. SAXER, & M. SCHOTT (Eds.), *FHB Fachbuch Verwaltungsrecht* (573–627). Zürich: Schulthess Juristische Medien AG.

STRAUMANN, F. (2015, January 12). Diese Therapien stehen auf dem Prüfstand. *Tagesanzeiger*. Retrieved from http://www.tagesanzeiger.ch/wissen/medizin-und-psychologie/Diese-Therapien-stehen-auf-dem-Pruefstand/story/30498550 (January 12, 2015)

STUDNEVA, M., MANDRIK, M., SONG, S., TRETYAK, E., KRASNYUK, I., YAMADA, Y., ... SUCHKOV, S. (2015). Strategic aspects of higher education reform to cultivate specialists in diagnostic and biopharma industry as applicable to Predictive, Preventive and Personalized Medicine as the Medicine of the Future. *EPMA Journal*, *6*(1), 18-14.

SWEN, J. J., HUIZINGA, T. W., GELDERBLOM, H., DE VRIES, E. G. E., ASSENDELFT, W. J. J., KIRCHHEINER, J., & GUCHELAAR, H.-J. (2007). Translating Pharmacogenomics: Challenges on the Road to the Clinic. *PLoS Medicine*, *4*(8), e209. Retrieved from http://www.plosmedicine.org/article/info:doi/10.1371/journal.pmed.0040209 (March 13, 2015)

SWEN, J. J., NIJENHUIS, M., DE BOER, A., GRANDIA, L., MAITLAND-VAN DER ZEE, A. H., MULDER, H., ... GUCHELAAR, H.-J. (2011). Pharmacogenetics: From Bench to Byte— An Update of Guidelines. *Clinical Pharmacology & Therapeutics*, *89*(5), 662–673.

SWISS FEDERAL INSTITUTE OF INTELLECTUAL PROPERTY. (2008). Fragen und Antworten. Retrieved from https://www.ige.ch/fileadmin/user_upload/Juristische_Infos/d/j10010d.pdf (October 25, 2016)

SWISS FEDERAL INSTITUTE OF INTELLECTUAL PROPERTY. (2016). Patent law reform - Biotechnological inventions. Swiss Federal Institute of Intellectual Property. Retrieved from https://www.ige.ch/en/legal-info/legal-areas/patents/biotechnological-inventions.html (August 31, 2016)

SWISS INSTITUTE FOR BIOINFORMATICS. (2017). Personalized Health Informatics. Retrieved from http://www.sib.swiss/personalized-health-2017/phi (April 1, 2017)

SWISS NATIONAL ADVISORY COMMISSION ON BIOMEDICAL ETHICS. (2015). Biobanken für die Forschung. Retrieved from http://www.nek-cne.ch/fileadmin/nek-cne-dateien/D_Broschure_NEK_Biobank.pdf (February 2, 2016)

SWISS NATIONAL SCIENCE FOUNDATION. (2017). BioLink. Retrieved from http://www.snf.ch/en/funding/infrastructures/biolink/Pages/default.aspx (March 12, 2017)

SWISSDRG. (2014). Finanzierung neuer Leistungen - Anforderungen zur Verhandlung von Innovationsentgelten. Retrieved from http://www.swissdrg.org/de/03_tarifdokumente/finanzierung_neuer_leistungen.asp?navid=22 (June 27, 2016)

SWISSDRG. (2015). Fallpauschalen in Schweizer Spitälern Basisinformationen für Gesundheitsfachleute. Retrieved from http://www.swissdrg.org/assets/pdf/Broschuere/150212_SwissDRG_Broschuere_D.PDF (June 27, 2016)

SWISSETHICS. (2014). Leitfaden von swissethics für die Erstellung eines Biobank Reglements im Zusammenhang mit Forschungsprojekten am Menschen. Retrieved from http://www.swissethics.ch/doc/ab2014/Biobanken_Leitfaden_d.pdf (February 4, 2017)

SWISSETHICS. (2017). Biobank regulations in connection with research projects involving human beings [Template]. Retrieved from http://www.swissethics.ch/doc/ab2014/Biobanken_Vorlage_e.pdf (February 2, 2017)

SWISSMEDIC. (2010). Merkblatt für In-house IVD. Retrieved from https://www.swissmedic.ch/medizinprodukte/02668/02671/index.html (July 20, 2016)

SWISSMEDIC. (2012). Informationsblatt zu Gentests. Swissmedic. Retrieved from https://www.swissmedic.ch/marktueberwachung/03186/03198/index.html?lang=de&download=NHzLpZeg7t,lnp6I0NTU042l2Z6ln1acy4Zn4Z2qZpnO2Yuq2Z6gpJCDdIB4hGym162epYbg2c_JjKbNoKSn6A-- (July 24, 2015)

SWISSMEDIC. (2016). Regulation of medical devices. Retrieved from https://www.swissmedic.ch/medizinprodukte/02636/index.html?lang=en (July 19, 2016)

SYSTEMSX. (2017). Systems Biology IT (SyBIT). Retrieved from http://www.systemsx.ch/index.php?id=77&L=%273 (April 1, 2017)

SZUCS, T. D. (2005). Health Economics in the Genomic Age. In H. J. SENN & R. MORANT (Eds.), *Tumor prevention and genetic tests* (299–313). Zürich: Springer.

SZUCS, T. D. (2014)a. Pharmacogenetics - Clinical Application. Swiss Tropical and Public Health Institute. Retrieved from http://www.swisstph.ch/fileadmin/user_upload/Pdfs/Symposium/Winter_2014/1.05_Sucz_Pharmacogenetics_SwissTPH-AS2014.pdf (September 29, 2015)

SZUCS, T. D. (2014)b. Pharmacogenetics - clinical applications. Swiss Tropical and Public Health Institute. Retrieved from http://www.swisstph.ch/news-events/symposia/autumn-2014/programme-and-presentations.html (December 28, 2014)

SZUCS, T. D. (2015)a. Die Pharmakogenetik lohnt sich. *Praxis Arena.* Retrieved from http://www.hirslanden.ch/content/global/de/startseite/gesundheit_medizin/mediathek_bibliothek/fachartikel/verschiedenes/die_pharmakogenetiklohntsich/_jcr_content/download/file.res/Die Pharmakogenetiklohnt sich.pdf (December 23, 2015)

SZUCS, T. D. (2015)b. Einführung in die genomische Medizin. [Workshop materials "Genomische Medizin für Kliniker"] Basel: Universität Basel & Klinik Hirslanden.

SZUCS, T. D., & BLANK, P. R. (2016). Wird sich personalisierte Medizin rechnen? Betrachtungen aus gesundheitsökonomischer Sicht. In I. KLUSMAN & E. VAYENA (Eds.), *Personalisierte Medizin - Hoffnung oder leeres Versprechen?* (117–128). vdf Hochschulverlag AG an der ETH Zürich.

TAEGTMEYER, A. B. (2012). Pharmakogenetik in der Praxis : Warum, wie, wann? *Schweizerisches Medizin-Forum, 12*(43), 824–826.

TAG, B. (2012). Rechtliche Aspekte der personalisierten Medizin. In *Liber amicorum für Andreas Donatsch* (825–849). Zürich: Schulthess Juristische Medien AG.

TAG, B., & BAUR, I. (2016). Rechtliche Aspekte der personalisierten Medizin. In I. KLUSMAN & E. VAYENA (Eds.), *Personalisierte Medizin - Hoffnung oder leeres Versprechen?* (135–152). Zürich: vdf Hochschulverlag AG an der ETH Zürich.

TAZAWA, Y. (2016). Perspective for the development of companion diagnostics and regulatory landscape to encourage personalized medicine in Japan. *Breast Cancer, 23*(1), 19–23.

TENENBAUM, J. D., AVILLACH, P., BENHAM-HUTCHINS, M., BREITENSTEIN, M. K., ZHOA, Z., FREIMUTZ, R. R., ... SUBHA MADHAVAN, J. (2016). An informatics research agenda to support precision medicine: seven key areas. *Journal of the American Medical Informatics, 10*, 93-97.

TERKOLA, R., ANTON, F., & POSTMA, M. J. (2017). Economic evaluation of personalized medicine : a call for real-world data. *European Journal of Health Economics*, 10–12.

THALER, R. H., & SUNSTEIN, CAAS, R. (2009). *Nudge - Improving Decisions about Health, Wealth and Happiness.* London: Penguin Books.

THE ACADEMY OF MEDICAL SCIENCES. (2013). *Realising the potential of stratified medicine.* Retrieved from https://www.acmedsci.ac.uk/viewFile/51e915f9f09fb.pdf (October 23, 2015)

THOMAS, M., KIERMAIER, A., & CANNARILE, M. (2016). Die Bedeutung von Biobanken für die klinische Entwicklung. *Bundesgesundheitsblatt, 59*, 344–350.

THOMPSON, A. J., NEWMAN, W. G., ELLIOTT, R. A., ROBERTS, S. A., TRICKER, K., & PAYNE, K. (2014). The Cost-Effectiveness of a Pharmacogenetic Test: A Trial-Based Evaluation of TPMT Genotyping for Azathioprine. *Value in Health, 17*(1), 22–33.

THOMPSON, B. M., & BOIANI, J. (2015). The Legal Environment for Precision Medicine. *Clinical Pharmacology & Therapeutics, [forthcoming].*

THOMPSON, D. K. (2016). From Research to Clinical Application: Challenges in Regulating Companion Biomarker Tests for " Personalized " Drugs. *Journal of Pharmaceutical Analytics and Insights, 1*(1), 1–2.

TOPOL, E. J. (2015). *The patient will see you now - the future of medicine is in your hands.* New York: Basic Books.

TOWSE, A., & GARRISON, L. P. (2013). Economic Incentives for Evidence Generation : Promoting an Efficient Path to Personalized Medicine. *Value in Health: The Journal of the International Society for Pharmacoeconomics and Outcomes Research, 16*, 39–43.

TRUSHEIM, M. R. (2013). Uncertain prognosis for high - quality diagnostics : clinical challenges, economic barriers and needed reforms. *Pharma-cogenomics, 14*(3), 325–334.

TRUSHEIM, M. R., AUSTIN, M. J. F., RAUSCH, C., & BERNDT, E. R. (2015). Uncertain prognosis for high - quality diagnostics : clinical challenges, economic barriers and needed reforms. PubMed Commons, *14*(3), 325-334.

TRUSHEIM, M. R., & BERNDT, E. R. (2012). Economic challenges and possible policy actions to advance stratified medicine. *Personalized Medicine, 9*(4), 413–427.

TRUSHEIM, M. R., & BERNDT, E. R. (2015)a. *An overview of the stratified economics of stratified medicine* (No. 212333). Cambridge. Retrieved from http://www.nber.org/papers/w21233 (July 6, 2015)

TRUSHEIM, M. R., & BERNDT, E. R. (2015)b. The clinical benefits, ethics, and economics of stratified medicine and companion diagnostics. *Drug Discovery Today, 0*(0). Retrieved from http://linkinghub.elsevier.com/retrieve/pii/S1359644615003943 (July 6, 2015)

TRUSHEIM, M. R., BERNDT, E. R., & DOUGLAS, F. L. (2007). Stratified medicine: strategic and economic implications of combining drugs and clinical biomarkers. *Nature Reviews. Drug Discovery, 6*(4), 287–293.

TRUSHEIM, M. R., BURGESS, B., HU, S. X., LONG, T., AVERBUCH, S. D., FLYNN, A. A., ... PALMER, M. C. (2011). Quantifying factors for the success of stratified medicine. *Nature Reviews Drug Discovery, 10*(11), 817–833.

TUNIS, S. R., MOHR, P., PHURROUGH, S., KRACZKOWSKY, K., DUTTA, T., & AL., E. (2012). Coverage with evidence development & adaptive licensing: Two sides of the same coin? CENTER FOR MEDICAL TECHNOLOGY POLICY (CMTP) and MASSACHUSETTS INSTITUTE OF TECHNOLOGY'S (MIT) CENTER FOR BIOMEDICAL INNOVATION (CBI). Retrieved from http://www.cmtpnet.org/docs/resources/CED-and-Adaptive-Licensing.pdf (April 1, 2017)

TUTTON, R. (2012). Personalizing medicine: Futures present and past. *Social Science and Medicine, 75*(10), 1721–1728.

TUTTON, R. (2013). Personalized Medicine in Context: Social Science Perspectives. *Drug Discovery Today, 10*(4), 183–187.

UNERTL, K. M., FIELD, J. R., PRICE, L., & PETERSON, J. F. (2015). Clinician perspectives on using pharmacogenomics in clinical practice. *Personalized Medicine, 12*(4), 339–347.

US CENTERS FOR DISEASE CONTROL AND PREVENTION. (2010)a. ACCE Model List of 44 Targeted Questions Aimed at a Comprehensive Review of Genetic Testing. Retrieved from http://www.cdc.gov/genomics/gtesting/acce/acce_proj.htm (March 10, 2016)

US CENTERS FOR DISEASE CONTROL AND PREVENTION. (2010)b. ACCE Model Process for Evaluating Genetic Tests. Retrieved from http://www.cdc.gov/genomics/gtesting/acce/index.htm (March 8, 2016)

US ENERGY AND COMMERCE COMMITTEE. (2015). Discussion draft to establish a regulatory framework for in vitro clinical tests. Retrieved from http://docs.house.gov/meetings/IF/IF14/20151029/104127/BILLS-114pihHR__ __.pdf (April 1, 2016)

VAN AAKEN, A. (2003). *"Rational Choice" in der Rechtswissenschaft. Zum Stellenwert der ökonomischen Theorie im Recht.* Baden-Baden: Nomos.

VAN AAKEN, A. (2015). *Judge the Nudge: In Search of the Legal Limits of Paternalistic Nudging in the EU* (No. 2015–1). *University of St. Gallen Law School: Law and Economics Research Paper Series.* Retrieved from http://papers.ssrn.com/abstract=2563296%5Cnhttp://papers.ssrn.com/sol3/papers.cfm?abstract_id=2563296 (January 27, 2017)

VAN HEERTUM, R., SCARIMBOLO, R., FORD, R., BERDOUGO, E., & O'NEAL, M. (2015). Companion diagnostics and molecular imaging- enhanced approaches for oncology clinical trials. *Drug Design, Development and Therapy, 9*, 5215–5223.

VAYENA, E., GOURNAA, E., STREULIA, J., HAFEN, E., & PRAINSACK, B. (2012). Experiences of Early Users of Direct-to-Consumer Genomics in Switzerland : An Exploratory Study. *Public Health Genomics, 15*, 352–362.

VEGTER, S., JANSEN, E., POSTMA, M. J., & BOERSMA, C. (2010). Economic evaluations of pharmacogenetic testing. *Drug Development Research, 71*, 492–501.

VFA. (2013). vfa-Positionspapier „Personalisierte Medizin". Verein forschender Pharmaunternehmen, Germany. Retrieved from www.vfa.de/download/pos-personalisierte-medizin (June 23, 2015)

VISCHER, D. (2014). Grundrecht auf informationelle Selbstbestimmung. Die Bundesversammlung - Das Schweizer Parlament. Retrieved from https://www.parlament.ch/de/ratsbetrieb/suche-curia-vista/geschaeft?AffairId=20140413 (August 3, 2016)

VOIGT, S. (2009). *Institutionenökonomik* (2nd edition). Stuttgard: Wilhelm Fink GmbH.

VOLLMANN, J. (2013). Persönlicher – besser – kostengünstiger? Kritische medizinethische Anfragen an die „personalisierte Medizin". *Ethik in der Medizin, 25*(3), 233–241.

WAECHTER, D. (2013). Life Sciences and IP : how emerging technologies influence the field. In *BioValley Basel Stammtisch*. Basel. Retrieved from http://www.biovalley.ch/biovalley-newsletter-container/invitation-inetbiovalley-basel-stammtisch-42013-life-sciences-and-ip-how-emerging-technologies-influence-the-field.html (January 15, 2016)

WENGER, N., MÉAN, M., CASTIONI, J., MARQUES-VIDAL, P., WAEBER, G., & GARNIER, A. (2017). Allocation of Internal Medicine Resident Time in a Swiss Hospital: A Time and Motion Study of Day and Evening Shifts. *Annals of Internal Medicine, January*. Retrieved from http://annals.org/aim/article/2599281/allocation-internal-medicine-resident-time-swiss-hospital-time-motion-study (April 3, 2017)

WERTZ, D. C., FLETCHER, J. C., & BERG, K. (2003). *Review of Ethical Issues in Medical Genetics. World Health Organization.* Retrieved from http://www.who.int/genomics/publications/en/ethical_issuesin_medgenetics report.pdf (March 14, 2016)

What happened to personalized medicine? (2012). *Nature Biotechnology, 30*(1), 1–1.

WHITEHEAD, S. J., & ALI, S. (2010). Health outcomes in economic evaluation: The QALY and utilities. *British Medical Bulletin, 96*(1), 5–21.

WIDMER, S. (2013). Off-label-use in der Schweiz: Heilmittelrechtliche Zulässigkeit und Kostenübernahme. *Hill*, (132), 1–25.

WIDRIG, D. (2015). *Health Technology Assessment.* (T. HILLENKAMP, L. KUHLEN, A. LAUFS, & E. RIEDEL, Eds.). Heidelberg: Springer.

WIDRIG, D., & TAG, B. (2015). HTA and Its Legal Issues: a Framework for Identifying Legal Issues in Health Technology Assessment. *International Journal of Technology Assessment in Health Care, 30*(6), 587–594.

WIDRIG, D., TAG, B., FRÉSARD-FELLAY, G., GÄCHTER, T., LEU, A., POLEDNA, T., ... EFFIZIENTE, A. (2012). Rechtliche Aspekte der Kosten- / Nutzenbewertung in der Medizin. *Hill Zeitschrift Für Recht Und Gesundheit, 65*, 1–26.

WIENKE, A., DIERKS, C., & JANKE, K. (Eds.). (2013). *Rechtsfragen der personalisierten Medizin. Medizinrecht.* Heidelberg: Springer.

WILDHABER, I. (2012). Aktuelle Rechtsprechung zum Patentschutz für Gene und Gensequenzen. *Sic! Zeitschrift für Immaterialgüter-, Informations- und Wettbewerbsrecht*, 687-699.

WILDHABER, I. (2013). Zum Begriff des Medizinprodukts. In B. RÜTSCHE (Ed.), *Medizinprodukte: Regulierung und Haftung.* Stämpfli Verlag AG.

WINDELER, J., & LANGE, S. (2013). Nutzenbewertung personalisierter Inter-ventionen: Methodische Herausforderungen und Lösungsansätze. *Ethik in der Medizin, 25*(3), 173–182.

WINKLER, E. C., OSE, D., GLIMM, H., TANNER, K., & VON KALLE, C. (2013). Personalisierte Medizin und Informed Consent: Klinische und ethische Erwägungen im Rahmen der Entwicklung einer Best Practice Leitlinie für die biobankbasierte Ganzgenomforschung in der Onkologie. *Ethik in der Medizin, 25*(3), 195–203.

WONG, S. H., HAPPY, C., BLINKA, D., GOCH, S., JENSEN, J. M., DONALD, J. M., ... YEO, K. T. (2010). From Personalized Medicine to Personalized Justice: The Promises of Translational Pharmacogenomics in the Justice System. In A. H. WU & K. T. YEO (Eds.), *Pharmacogenomic Testing in Current Clinical Practice.* London: Springer.

WU, A. H. (2010). Economics of Pharmacogenomic Testing in Clinical Practice. In K. YEO & A. H. WU (Eds.), *Pharmacogenomic Testing in Current Clinical Practice* (35–47). London: Springer.

WU, A. H. B. (2016). Promoting the value of precision medicine to the public: the power of story telling. *Expert Review of Precision Medicine and Drug Development, 1*(3), 233–234.

WURCEL, V., PERCHE, O., LESTEVEN, D., WILLIAMS, D.-A., SCHÄFER, B., HOPLEY, C., ... GLORIOSO, V. (2016). The Value of Companion Diagnostics: Overcoming Access Barriers to Transform Personalised Health Care into an Affordable Reality in Europe. *Public Health Genomics*, 137–143.

XU, A. S. L. (2014). Companion Diagnostics for Personalized Medicine. *AACC*, 1–7. Retrieved from https://www.aacc.org/publications/cln/articles/2014/september/companion-diagnostics (January 28, 2016)

YEO, K., BABIC, N., & WU, A. H. (2010). Issues in Translation of Pharmacogenomics into Clinical Practice. In K. YEO & A. H. WU (Eds.), *Pharmacogenomic Testing in Current Clinical Practice* (3–14). London: Springer.

ZARIC, G. S. (2016). Cost Implications of Value-Based Pricing for Companion Diagnostic Tests in Precision Medicine. *PharmacoEconomics*, *1*, 1–10.

ZETTLER, P. J., SHERKOW, J. S., & GREELY, H. T. (2014). 23andMe, the Food and Drug Administration and the Future of Genetic Testing. *JAMA Internal Medicine*, *174*(4), 409.

ZOLLIKOFER, J. (ED.). (2009). *Manual der Schweizer Vertrauens- und Versicherungsärzte: ein Handbuch der Versicherungsmedizin* (3. edition.). Vertrauensärzte.ch. Retrieved from https://www.vertrauensaerzte.ch/manual/(August 26,2015)

ZUZAK, M. (2008). *Ökonomische Analyse der Regulierung des Insiderhandels.* (H. GEIGER, B. BERNET, C. HIRSZOWICZ, A. GRÜNBICHLER, E. KILGUS, K. SPREMANN, & R. VOLKART, Eds.). Bern: Haupt.

Conference proceedings

Four conferences and academic conventions have fostered the knowledge, enabled discussions and inspired for thoughts that contributed to the content of this thesis:

"Personalized Medicine: Hope or empty promise"

Interdisciplinary lecture series by the UNIVERSITY OF ZURICH and ETH, Zürich, fall semester 2013.

"Health Economics and Policy"

PhD seminar by the SWISS SCHOOL OF PUBLIC HEALTH, Grindelwald, January 2014.

"Genomische Medizin für Kliniker"

Advanced training workshop for Swiss clinicians by Prof. Dr. THOMAS SZUCS, Prof. Dr. URS A. MEYER, AND Prof. Dr. NICOLE BÜRKI, EUROPEAN CENTER FOR PHARMACEUTICAL MEDICINE, Basel, August 2015.

"Big Data, Health Law and Bioethics"

HARVARD PETRIE-FLOM CENTER Annual Conference, Cambridge, May 2016.

"Personalized Medicine"

LATSIS Symposium ETH, Zürich, June 2016.

Any publication from these conferences that has been cited in this thesis is listed in the bibliography.

K. Bosshard, *Law and Economics of Personalized Medicine*,
Gesundheitsmanagement und Gesundheitsökonomik,
https://doi.org/10.1007/978-3-658-22074-7

Legal materials

Switzerland

SWISS CONSTITUTION	SR 101	FEDERAL CONSTITUTION OF THE SWISS CONFEDERATION of 18th of April 1999
VVG	SR 221.229.1	FEDERAL LAW ON INSURANCE CONTRACTS (in German "Bundesgesetz über den Versicherungsvertrag")
PATG	SR 232.14	FEDERAL LAW ON PATENTS FOR INVENTION (in German „Bundesgesetz über die Erfindungspatente, Patentgesetz")
PATV	SR 232.141	ORDINANCE ON PATENTS FOR INVENTION (in German „Verordnung über die Erfindungspatente, Patentverordnung")
DSG	SR 235.1	FEDERAL LAW ON DATA PROTECTION (in German "Bundesgesetz über den Datenschutz")
STGB	SR 311.0	SWISS CRIMINAL CODE (in German „Schweizerisches Strafgesetzbuch)
RTVG	SR 784.40	LAW ON RADIO AND TV (in German „Bundesgesetz über Radio und Fernsehen")
GUMG	SR 810.12	LAW ON GENETIC TESTS ON HUMANS (in German „Bundesgesetz über genetische Untersuchungen beim Menschen")
D-GUMG	AS 2017	Draft revision on the LAW ON GENETIC TESTS ON HUMANS

K. Bosshard, *Law and Economics of Personalized Medicine*,
Gesundheitsmanagement und Gesundheitsökonomik,
https://doi.org/10.1007/978-3-658-22074-7

HFG	SR 810.30	LAW ON HUMAN RESEARCH (in German „Humanforschungsgesetz")
HFV	SR 810.301	ORDINANCE ON HUMAN RESEARCH WITH THE EXCEPTION OF CLINICAL TRIALS (in German "Verordnung über die Humanforschung mit Ausnahme der klinischen Versuche")
EXAM ORDINANCE MEDBG	SR 811.113.3	ORDINANCE ON THE EXAM FOR MEDICAL PROFESSIONS, (in German „Prüfungsverordnung MedBG")
HMG	SR 812.21	FEDERAL LAW ON THERAPEUTIC PRODUCTS (in German "Heilmittelgesetz")
AMZV	SR 812.212.22	ORDINANCE OF THE SWISS INSTITUTE FOR THERAPEUTIC PRODUCTS ON THE REQUIREMENTS FOR THE MARKETING AUTHORISATION OF MEDICINAL PRODUCTS (in German "Verordnung des Schweizerischen Heilmittelinstitutes über die Anforderungen an die Zulassung von Arzneimitteln")
KLINV	SR 812.305	ORDINANCE ON CLINICAL TRIALS ON HUMAN RESEARCH (in German „Verordnung über klinische Versuche in der Humanforschung")
EPDG	SR 816.1	LAW FOR THE ELECTRONIC PATIENT FILE (in German "Bundesgesetz über das elektronische Patientendossier)
KVG	SR 832.10	FEDERAL LAW ON BASIC SICKNESS INSURANCE (in German „Bundesgesetz über die Krankenversicherung")
D-KVG	BBl 2016	Draft revision on the FEDERAL LAW ON BASIC SICKNESS INSURANCE
KLV	SR 832.112.31	HEALTHCARE BENEFITS ORDINANCE (in German „Krankenpflege-Leistungsverordnung")

KVV	SR 832.102	ORDINANCE ON BASIC SICKNESS INSURANCE (in German „Verordnung über die Krankenversicherung")

Other legal materials Switzerland

SL	Specialty list, retrieved from https://www.bag.admin.ch/bag/de/home/themen/versicherungen/krankenversicherung krankenversicherung-leistungen-tarife/Arzneimittel.html (last visited August 8, 2017)
Dispatch for the D-GUMG	Dispatch for the FEDERAL LAW ON GENETIC TESTS ON HUMANS, retrieved from https://www.bag.admin.ch/bag/de/home/themen/mensch-gesundheit/biomedizin-forschung/genetische-untersuchungen/aktuelle-rechtsetzungs-projekte1.html (last visited August 8, 2017)
AGA	Agreement between the SWISS CONFEDERATION AND THE EUROPEAN COMMUNITY ON MUTUAL RECOGNITION IN RELATION TO CONFORMITY ASSESSMENT (in German „Abkommen zwischen der Schweizerischen Eidgenossenschaft und der Europäischen Gemeinschaft über die gegenseitige Anerkennung von Konformitätsbewertungen") retrieved from https://www.admin.ch/opc/de/classified-compilation/19994644/2015041 40000/0.946.526.81.pdf (last visited August 8, 2017)

Swiss court decisions

BGE 136 V395	"Myozyme decision", retrieved from http://relevancy.bger.ch/php/clir/http/index.php?lang=de&zoom=&type=show_document &highlight_docid=atf%3A%2F%2F136-V-395%3Ade (last visited August 8, 2017)
BGE 137 V295	retrieved from http://relevancy.bger.ch/php/clir/http/index.php?highlight_docid=atf%3A%2F%2F137-V-295%3Ade&lang=de&type=show_document (last visited August 8, 2017)

9C_748/2014	FEDERAL INSURANCE COURT, decision 9C_748/2014, retrieved from http://www.servat.unibe.ch/dfr/bger/150414_9C_748-2014.html (last visited August 8, 2017)

European Union

EUROPEAN CONVENTION ON HUMAN RIGHTS.	COUNCIL OF EUROPE, European Convention for the Protection of Human Rights and Fundamental Freedoms, as amended by Protocols Nos. 11 and 14, 4th of November 1950, retrieved from http://www.echr.coe.int/Documents/Convention_ENG.pdf (last visited August 8, 2017)
EU BIOMEDICINE CONVENTION	COUNCIL OF EUROPE, Convention for the Protection of Human Rights and Dignity of the Human Being with regard to the Application of Biology and Medicine: Convention on Human Rights and Biomedicine. Retrieved from https://rm.coe.int/168007cf98 (last visited August 8, 2017)
EUROPEAN PATENT CONVENTION	16th edition, June 2016, published by the EUROPEAN PATENT OFFICE, retrieved from http://www.epo.org/law-practice/legal-texts/epc.html (last visited August 19, 2017)
PLT	PARIS CONVENTION FOR THE PROTECTION OF INDUSTRIAL PROPERTY, PATENT LAW TREATY, retrieved from http://www.wipo.int/wipolex/en/details.jsp?id=12633 (last visited August 19, 2017)
PCT	PATENT COOPERATION TREATY, retrieved from http://www.wipo.int/pct/en/ (last visited August 19, 2017)

TRIPS	AGREEMENT ON TRADE RELATED ASPECTS OF INTELLECTUAL PROPERTY RIGHTS, https://www.wto.org/english/docs_e/legal_e/27-trips_01_e.htm retrieved from (last visited August 19, 2017)
CLINICAL TRIALS DIRECTIVE	Regulation No 536/2014 of the European Parliament and the Council f 16 April 2014 on clinical trials on medicinal products for human use, and repealing Directive 2001/20/EC, retrieved from http://ec.europa.eu/health/files/eudralex/vol-1/reg_2014_536/reg_2014_536_en.pdf (last visited August 8th, 2017)
IVD DIRECTIVE	Directive 98/79/EC of the European Parliament and of the Council of 27 October 1998 on in vitro diagnostic medical devices, OJ L 331, p. 1-37. Retrieved from http://eur-lex.europa.eu/legal-content/EN/TXT/PDF/?uri=CELEX:31998L0079&from=EN (last visited August 8th, 2017)
IVD Proposal	Proposal for a REGULATION OF THE EUROPEAN PARLIAMENT AND OF THE COUNCIL on in vitro diagnostic medical device, Brussels, 26.9.2012, 2012/0267 (COD), retrieved from http://eur-lex.europa.eu/legal-content/EN/TXT/PDF/?uri=CELEX:52012PC0541&from=EN (last visited August 8th, 2017)
IVDR	Regulation (EU) 2017/746 of the European Parliament and of the Council of 5 April 2017 on in vitro diagnostic medical devices and repealing Directive 98/79/EC and Commission Decision 2010/227/EU Retrieved from http://eur-lex.europa.eu/legal-content/EN/TXT/PDF/?uri=OJ:L:2017:117:FULL&from=EN (last visited August 8th, 2017)
EU DATA PROTECTION PROPOSAL 15039/15	Proposal regarding the GENERAL DATA PROTECTION REGULATION, Interinstitutional File: 2012/0011 (COD) Brussels, 15 December 2015, 15039/15.

		Retrieved from http://www.statewatch.org/news/2015/dec/eu-council-dp-reg-draft-final-compromise-15039-15.pdf_(last visited August 8th, 2017)
EUROPEAN COMMISSION HTA IMPLEMENTING DECISION	2013/329/EU	European Commission Implementing Decision of 26 June 2013 providing the rules for the establishment, management and transparent functioning of the NETWORK OF NATIONAL AUTHORITIES OR BODIES RESPONSIBLE FOR HEALTH TECHNOLOGY ASSESSMENT, Retrieved from http://ec.europa.eu/health/technology_assessment/docs/impl_dec_hta_network_en.pdf (last visited August 8th, 2017)
BBMRI-ERIC Decision	OJ L 320/63	Official Journal of the European Union European Commission, Implemention decision of 22 November 2013 on setting up the Biobanks and Biomolecular Resources Research Infrastructure Consortium (BBMRI-ERIC) as a European Research Infrastructure Consortium (2013/701/EU). Retrieved from http://eurlex.europa.eu/LexUriServ/LexUriServ.do?uri=OJ:L:2013:320:0063:0080:EN:PDF (last visited August 8th, 2017)

United States

FD&C ACT, Title 21	FEDERAL FOOD, DRUG AND COSMETIC ACT, United States Code, Title 21. Retrieved from http://www.ecfr.gov/cgi-bin/text-idx?SID=3ee286332416f26a91d9e6d786a604ab&mc=true&tpl=/ecfrbrowse/Title21/21tab_02.tpl (last visited August 8th, 2017)

US court decisions

ALICE CORPORATION PTY. LTD. v. CLS BANK INTERNATIONAL et al.	Supreme Court of the United States. Ruling No. 13–298. Decided June 19, 2014, retrieved from http://www.supremecourt.gov/opinions/13pdf/13-298_7lh8.pdf (last visited August 8th, 2017)
ASSOCIATION FOR MOLECULAR PATHOLOGY et al. v. MYRIAD GENETICS INC.	Supreme Court of the United States. Ruling No. 12-398. Decided June 13, 2013, retrieved from http://www.supremecourt.gov/opinions/12pdf/12-398_1b7d.pdf (last visited August 8th, 2017)
MAYO MEDICAL LABORATORIES, et al. v. PROMETHEUS LABORATORIES, INC.	Supreme Court of the United States. Ruling No. 10-1150. Decided March 20, 2012, retrieved from http://www.supremecourt.gov/opinions/11pdf/10-1150.pdf (last visited August 8th, 2017)
RAPID LITICATION MANAGEMENT Ltd. formerly CELSIS HOLDINGS Inc. v. CELLZDIRECT, Inc.	United States Court of Appeals for the Federal Circuit, ruling no. 2015-1570. Retrieved from http://www.cafc.uscourts.gov/sites/default/files/opinions-orders/15-1570.Opinion.6-30-2016.1.PDF (last visited August 8th, 2017)

Professional codes

WORLD MEDICAL ASSOCIATION'S DECLARATION OF TAIPEI ON ETHICAL CONSIDERATIONS REGARDING HEALTH DATABASES AND BIOBANKS	Adopted by the 53rd WMA General Assembly, Washington, DC, USA, October 2002, retrieved from https://www.wma.net/policies-post/wma-declaration-of-taipei-on-ethical-considerations-regarding-health-databases-and-biobanks/ (last visited August 8th, 2017)
WORLD MEDICAL ASSOCIATION'S DECLARATION OF GENEVA	Retrieved from https://www.wma.net/what-we-do/medical-ethics/declaration-of-geneva/ (last visited August 8th, 2017)
SWISS MEDICAL ASSOCIATION'S PROFESSIONAL CODE	Retrieved from http://www.fmh.ch/files/pdf18/Standesordnung_August_2016_De.pdf (last visited August 8th, 2017)

Expert interviews

AEBERSOLD, RUDOLPH, PROF. DR. Institute of Molecular Systems Biology, ETH Zürich, serving on the Scientific Advisory Committees of numerous academic and private sector research organizations and is a member of several editorial boards in the fields of protein science, genomics, and proteomics. *Interviewed July 10, 2015.*

BENEDETTI, CHRISTINA, expert Swiss Federal Office of Public Health, Section Biomedicine, Member of the commission for genetic examinations in humans (GUMEK). *Interviewed August 8, 2015.*

BORRMANN, HARALD, general manager Roche Switzerland AG and member of the board of the Swiss Association of the Diagnostics Industry. *Interviewed October 15, 2015.*

BRÜGGER, URS, PROF. DR., manager of the ZHAW's institute for health economics. *Interviewed August 10, 2016.*

HAFEN, ERNST, PROF. DR., professor at the institute for molecular systems biology at the ETH Zürich, leader of the Midata.coop project, cofounder of the association data and health Switzerland. *Interviewed April 18, 2013.*

HENGGELER, CAROLINE, deputy director of the Swiss Center for Cardiovascular Genetics and Gene Diagnostics, deputy manager and foundation board member of the Foundation for People with Rare Diseases, Switzerland. *Interviewed September 3, 2015.*

MATYAS, GABOR, PROF. DR., head and founding director of the Swiss Center for Cardiovascular Genetics and Gene Diagnostics, manager and foundation board member of the Foundation for People with Rare Diseases Switzerland. *Interviewed September 3, 2015.*

K. Bosshard, *Law and Economics of Personalized Medicine*,
Gesundheitsmanagement und Gesundheitsökonomik,
https://doi.org/10.1007/978-3-658-22074-7

MÜLLER, KURT, DR., principal and managing director Pharmalevers GmbH. *Interviewed July 7, 2016.*

REICH, OLIVER, DR., director health sciences at Helsana Versicherungen AG. *Interviewed February 5, 2016.*

REUSCHLING, MONIKA, Head of Diagnostics Development & Communications at Roche Diagnostics Switzerland AG. *Interviewed August 26, 2015.*

SCHÄFER, OLAF, DR. director reimbursement management at Helsana Versicherungen AG. *Interviewed November 17, 2015.*

SEILER, BEAT, Dr., Senior Medical Director at Helsana Versicherungen AG. *Interviewed July 18, 2016.*

SZUCS, THOMAS, PROF. DR., Chairman Helsana Versicherungen AG, director, European Center for pharmaceutical medicine (ECPM), University of Basel, Member of the Institute of Social- and Preventive Medicine University of Zürich, Founder of the "Praxis für personalisierte Medizin" at Klinik Hirslanden. *Interviewed August 26, 2015.*

VAYENA, EFFY, PROF. DR., head of the Health Ethics and Policy Lab at the University of Zürich, consultant at the World Health Organization. *Interviewed July 17, 2015.*

WIDRIG, DANIEL, DR., author of PhD thesis titled "Heath Technology Assessment", strategic pricing and reimbursement manager at Novartis. *Interviewed July 26, 2016.*

Appendix

Annex 1: Share of patients in Switzerland taking a medicine for which pharmacogenetic testing is strongly recommended

The following analysis estimates the share of patients taking a medicine for which pharmacogenetic testing is strongly recommended by the CLINICAL PHARMACOGENETICS IMPLEMENTATION CONSORTIUM (CPIC), (CPIC level A).[1793]

With ca. 1,2 million health insurees in 2014, HELSANA is Switzerland's biggest health insurance company. The figure below demonstrates that 5.5% of the insurees take at least one drug, for which the CPIC recommends at least one moderate or strong action.

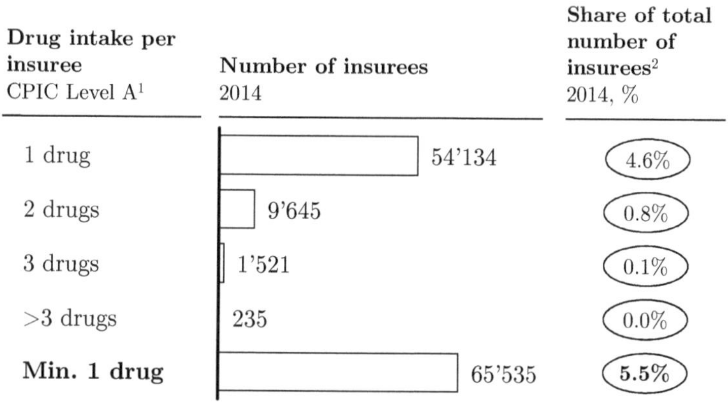

[1] 34 ingredients (exclusively ingredients which are not available in Switzerland, like Imipramin, Warfarin, Desipramin, Tegafur): Abacavir; Allopurinol; Amitriptyline; Atazanavir; Azathioprine; Boceprevir; Capecitabine; Carbamazepine; Citalopram; Clopidogrel; Codeine; Doxepin; Escitalopram; Fluorouracil; Fluvoxamine; Irinotecan; Ivacaftor; Mercaptopurine; Nortriptyline; Oxycodone; Paroxetine; Peginterferon alfa 2a & 2b; Phenytoin; Rasburicase; Ribavirin; Simvastatin; Tacrolimus; Tamoxifen; Telaprevir; Tioguanine; Tramadol; Trimipramine; Voriconazole.
[2] Total of 1'189'514 insurees of HELSANA in the compulsory health insurance in 2014

SOURCE: HELSANA, Dr. Oliver Reich, 1st of March 2016

Figure 34: Share of patients in Switzerland taking a medicine for which pharmacogenetic testing is strongly recommended by CPIC

[1793] Cf. *Table 12*: Recommendation levels by the CLINICAL PHARMACOGENETICS IMPLEMENTATION CONSORTIUM (CPIC) on the following page.

K. Bosshard, *Law and Economics of Personalized Medicine*, Gesundheitsmanagement und Gesundheitsökonomik, https://doi.org/10.1007/978-3-658-22074-7

This estimate is concervative and rather at the lower end of the real share as only drugs with CPIC Level A were taken into account. The 5,5% would increase, if additional CPIC Levels were taken into account (*cf. below*).

The CLINICAL PHARMACOGENETICS IMPLEMENTATION CONSORTIUM (CPIC) publishes guidelines in order to help healthcare providers to understand how available genetic test results should be used to optimize drug therapy. The guidelines distinguish between four levels of recommendations:

CPIC Level	Strenght of recommendation	Clinical context	Level of evidence
Level A	At least one moderate or strong action (change in prescribing) recommended	Genetic information should be used to change prescribing of affected drug	Preponderance of evidence is high or moderate in favor of changing prescribing
Level B	At least one optional action (change in prescribing) is recommended	Genetic information could be used to change prescribing of the affected drug because alternative therapies/dosing are extremely likely to be as effecttive and as safe as non-genetically based dosing	Preponderance of evidence is weak with little conflicting data
Level C	No prescribing actions are recommended.	There are published studies at varying levels of evidence, some with mechanistic rationale, but no prescribing actions are recommended[1794]	Evidence levels can vary
Level D	No prescribing actions are recommended.	There are few published studies, clinical actions are unclear, little mechanistic basis, mostly weak evidence, or substantial conflictting data. If the genes are not widely tested for clinically, evaluations are not needed	Evidence levels can vary

SOURCE: https://cpicpgx.org/prioritization/#cpicLevels (last visited July 2017)

Table 12: Recommendation levels by the CLINICAL PHARMACOGENETICS IMPLEMENTATION CONSORTIUM (CPIC)

[1794] Because (a) dosing based on genetics convincingly makes no difference or (b) alternatives are unclear, possibly less effective, more toxic, or otherwise impractical. Most important for genes that are subject of other CPIC guidelines or genes that are commonly included in clinical or DTC tests.

Annex 2: Literature review on economic evaluations in the context of personalized medicine

Authors	Focus	Findings
PLÖTHNER, RIBBENTROP, HARTMAN, & FRANK (2016)	Systematic literature review on xamination of CE of PGx test-guided personalized therapies (Germany only)	In the majority of the included studies, the PGx test-guided therapy represented a cost-effective/cost-saving treatment option. A minority of the reviewed studies lacked a clear statement of CE or cost-savings, because of uncertainty, restriction to specific patient populations, or assumptions for comparative therapy.
DZAU ET AL. (2015)	Calculation of the value of health from hypothetical personalized medicine prevention innovation at two levels of incidence reduction in six diseases (cancer, diabetes, heart disease, hypertension, lung disease, stroce; US focus only).	Dependent on the disease, a PM innovation that reduces incidence by 10%/50% generates from USD 33 bn/USD 161 bn (stroke) to USD 114 bn/USD 607 bn (heart disease) in the form of longer, healthier lives enjoyed by the US population. Of the six diseases studied, PM innova-tions aimed at reducing heart disease have the greatest eff ect on public health because heart disease is highly prevalent and has relatively large eff ect on life expectancy.
D'ANDREA, MARZUILLO, PELONE, DE VITO, & VILLARI (2015)	Review of primary economic evaluations (EEs) of predictive genetic and pharmacogenetic testing programs and an overview of previously published systematic reviews of such economic evaluations (economic reviews, ERs).	CUA was the methodology most fre-quently used followed by CEAs Only 12% of predictive genetic tests and 21% of PGx tests are cost-saving. The majority of the cost-utility ra -tios indicate that these tests provide better healthcare, but at higher cost. One identified concern is the absence of demonstrated clinical utility for a significant proportion of genetic tests. Some genetic tests may not be cost – effectivebecause of a lack of demonstrated clinical utility.
JAIN (2015)	Chapter 23 of his textbook summarizes results from four PGx testing strategies, p. 688 ff.	Identifies and describes four cost-effective PGx testing strategies: HIV genotyping, Warfarin, analysis of KRAS and BRAF screening in colorectal cancer, lowering the costs of cancer chemotherapy.
HATZ, SCHREMSER, & ROGOWSKI (2014)	Literature review on cost-effectiveness in context of personalized medicine (84 studies published since 2005)	Results ranged from dominant to dominated. Personalized medicine neither seems to display superior cost- effectiveness than other types of medical interventions nor to be economically inferior. Instead, rather than 'whether' healthcare was individualized, the question of 'how' it was individualized was of economic relevance. The median value (CUAs) was USD 22'000 per QALY gained which is equal to the rounded me-

		dian cost-effectiveness in the peer-reviewed English-language literature. Several studies reported more than one strategy of personalized medicine with varying cost-effectiveness ratios. Results differed according to test type, and tests for disease prognosis or screening appeared to be more favorable than tests to stratify patients by response or by risk of adverse effects.
J. COHEN & FELIX (2014)	Review of the Tufts cost-effectiveness registry[1795] to retrieve U. S. based peer-reviewed publications on the clinical- and cost-effectiveness of ten drug-diagnostic combinations.	In seven of ten examples the CDx test was not included in the CEA. Four examples were considered as cost-effective, two as inconclusive, two as not cost-effective. There were no clinical- or cost-effective-ness studies for four of the ten drugs in their sample.
K. A. PHILLIPS ET AL. (2014)	Review of 59 CUAs that examine personalized medicine tests (1998–2011)	A majority of the cost-utility ratios reported indicate that personalized medicine tests provide better health at higher cost, although there are relatively few studies demonstrating cost savings. 74% of the cost/quality-adjusted life year ratios indicate that testing provides better health although at higher cost, with almost half of the ratios falling below USD 50'000 per QALY gained. 20% of the results indicate that tests may save money. Many available or emerging medicine tests have not been evaluated. More evidence on value will be needed to inform decision making and assessment of genomic priorities.
K. PHILLIPS, SAKOWSKI, LIANG, & PONCE (2013)	Meta-review of seven literature reviews[1796]	The majority of the economic evaluations identified in these reviews are CEAs followed by CUAs, with fewer CBAs and cost minimization analyses. A majority of studies included in these reviews found PM interventions to have favorable CEA ratios, although fewer interventions were cost-saving.

[1795] The registry's goal is to provide a database of published cost-utility analyses, J. COHEN & FELIX (2014), p. 169.

[1796] GIACOMINI ET AL. (2003); PHILLIPS & VAN BEBBER (2004);); CARLSON ET AL. (2005); VEGTER ET AL. (2008); BEAULIEU ET AL. (2010); WONG ET AL. (2010); DJALALOV ET AL. (2011) cited in K. PHILLIPS ET AL. (2013), p. 63.

VEGTER, JANSEN, POSTMA, & BOERSMA (2010)	Review of economic evaluation of PGx testing (42 studies from 2000-2010)	Over time, more CUA were performed with longer time windows. The quality of the economic analyses improved over time – however, input variables were not always clearly described (especially in the reported costs of the PGx tests). Considerable differences in costs of screening tests for the same polymorohism were found. These often had an influence on the costs of the screening strategies. The authors argue that the economic studies seem to be conducted to increase awareness of the possibilities of genetic testing rather than to influence policy makers and reimbursement decision.
PACI (2009)	Synthesis of the past and emerging literature on CEAs that evaluate PGx tests (30 studies)	Scarcity of convincing evidence on the cost-effectiveness of genomics products creates a barrier in the uptake of pharmacogenetics in personalized medicine. 73% of studies reported favourable economic evidence with respect to the adoption of PGx technology; 17% of the studies showed no favourable evidence, while 10% of them found evidence on the cost-effectiveness of PGx testing. Significantly fragmented landscape of economic evaluations which employ different methods and reach conclusions that are difficult to assess. The main measures used to evaluate cost-effectiveness is not uniform across the stu-dies.

MIX
Papier aus verantwortungsvollen Quellen
Paper from responsible sources
FSC® C105338

If you have any concerns about our products,
you can contact us on
ProductSafety@springernature.com

In case Publisher is established outside the EU,
the EU authorized representative is:
Springer Nature Customer Service Center GmbH
Europaplatz 3, 69115 Heidelberg, Germany

Printed by Libri Plureos GmbH
in Hamburg, Germany